Lecture Notes in Computer Science 7067

Commenced Publication in 1973
Founding and Former Series Editors:
Gerhard Goos, Juris Hartmanis, and Jan va~

Halimah Badioze Zaman   Peter Robinson
Maria Petrou   Patrick Olivier
Timothy K. Shih   Sergio Velastin
Ingela Nyström (Eds.)

Visual Informatics: Sustaining Research and Innovations

Second International Visual Informatics Conference,
IVIC 2011
Selangor, Malaysia, November 9-11, 2011
Proceedings, Part II

 Springer

Volume Editors

Halimah Badioze Zaman
Universiti Kebangsaan Malaysia, Bangi, Malaysia; hbzukm@yahoo.com

Peter Robinson
University of Cambridge, UK; pr10@cam.ac.uk

Maria Petrou
Imperial College, London, UK; maria.petrou@imperial.ac.uk

Patrick Olivier
Newcastle University upon-Tyne, UK; p.l.olivier@ncl.ac.uk

Timothy K. Shih
National Central University, Jhongli City, Taiwan; timothyshih@gmail.com

Sergio Velastin
Kingston University, UK; sergio.velastin@kingston.ac.uk

Ingela Nyström
Uppsala University, Sweden; ingela.nystrom@it.uu.se

ISSN 0302-9743   e-ISSN 1611-3349
ISBN 978-3-642-25199-3   e-ISBN 978-3-642-25200-6
DOI 10.1007/978-3-642-25200-6
Springer Heidelberg Dordrecht London New York

Library of Congress Control Number: 2011940133

CR Subject Classification (1998): I.4, I.5, I.2.10, I.3.5, I.3.7, I.7.5, F.2.2

LNCS Sublibrary: SL 6 – Image Processing, Computer Vision, Pattern Recognition,
and Graphics

Typesetting: Camera-ready by author, data conversion by Scientific Publishing Services, Chennai, India

Printed on acid-free paper

Springer is part of Springer Science+Business Media (www.springer.com)

Preface

Visual informatics is currently a multidisciplinary field that is well accepted among researchers and industry in computer science, information technology and engineering. The basic areas of research, such as virtual real image processing and engineering; computer vision and simulation; visual computing and visualization and social computing, have been applied in various domains such as education, medical and health, finance, agriculture and security. We currently also see various Centres of Excellence (CoE) in the field of visual informatics being established in various institutions of higher learning (IHLs) around the world (Europe, USA and UK). Malaysia has just established a similar CoE called the Institute of Visual Informatics (IVI) at Universiti Kebangsaan Malaysia (UKM) or *The National University of Malaysia*. It is therefore important that researchers from these various CoEs, research institutes, technology centers and industry form networks and share and disseminate new knowledge in this field for the benefit of society.

It is for this reason that the Institute of Visual Informatics (IVI) at UKM decided to host the Second International Visual Informatics Conference (IVIC 2011), to bring together experts in this very important research area so that more concerted efforts can be undertaken not just locally but globally. The first IVIC held in 2009 brought together experts from Asia, the UK, Oceania and the USA. This time we also managed to bring in an expert from Sweden. Like the first IVIC, this time too the conference was conducted collaboratively by the visual informatics community from various public and private universities and industry. The second conference was co-sponsored by the Malaysian Information Technology Society (MITS), Multimedia Development Corporation (MDeC), and the Malaysian Research Education Network (MyREN). The conference was co-chaired by seven professors from four different countries (UK, Sweden, Taiwan and Malaysia).

The theme of the conference, 'Visual Informatics: Sustainable Innovations for Wealth Creation,' reflects the importance of bringing research from 'laboratories to the market.' It also portrayed the shared belief of the organizers (both locally and globally) of the importance of creating a seamless value-chain R&D ecosystem: from fundamental, applied research to 'proof of concept' and commercialization. With the slow economic trend experienced around the world today, research and innovation are more important than ever before in creating high-income jobs in order to accelerate economic growth. Thus, the relevance of the theme of the conference was apt and timely.

The conference focused on four tracks related to the basic areas of visual informatics over two days (November 9 and 10, 2011) and ended with a one-day workshop (November 11, 2011). There were four keynote speakers and 75 paper presentations based on topics covered by the four main tracks mentioned earlier. The reviewing of the papers was conducted by experts who represented a 150-member Program Committee from Asia, Europe, Oceania and North America. Each paper was reviewed by three reviewers and the rejection rate was 60%. The reviewing process was managed using an electronic conference management system (CoMS^{TM}) created by the Institute of Visual Informatics, UKM.

On behalf of the Organizing and Program Committees of IVIC 2011, we thank all authors for their submissions and camera-ready copies of papers, and all participants for their thought-provoking ideas and active participation in the conference. We also thank the Vice-Chancellor of UKM (host University), and Vice-Chancellors and Deans of all IT faculties of the IHLs for their support in organizing this conference. We also acknowledge the sponsors, members of the Organizing Committees, Program Committee members, support committees and individuals who gave their continuous help and support in making the conference a success. We fervently believe that IVIC will grow from strength to strength and we also hope that one day it will be held in different host countries in Asia, Europe, Oceania or North America. We also hope that IVIC will continue to provide a stimulating and enriching platform for research and innovations that will transcend religions, cultures, race and beliefs to contribute to better general human well-being.

November 2011

Halimah Badioze Zaman
Peter Robinson
Maria Petrou
Patrick Olivier
Timothy Shih
Sergio Velastin
Ingela Nyström

Organization

The Second International Visual Informatics Conference (IVIC 2011) was organized by the Institute of Visual Informatics and Faculty of Information Science and Technology, Universiti Kebangsaan Malaysia, in collaboration with 13 local public and private universities in Malaysia, the Malaysian Information Technology Society (MITS), Multimedia Development Corporation (MDeC), Malaysian Institute of Microelectronic Systems (MIMOS) and Malaysian Research Educational Network (MYREN).

Local Executive Committee

General Chair	Halimah Badioze Zaman (UKM)
Deputy Chair	Fatimah Dato'Ahmad (UPNM)
Secretary	Azlina Ahmad (UKM)
Assistant Secretary I	Nazlena Mohamad Ali (UKM)
Assistant Secretary II	Mohd M. Kadhum (UUM)
Treasurer	Haslina Arshad (UKM)
Assistant Treasurer I	Rabiah Abdul Kadir (UPM)
Assistant Treasurer II	Syaimak Abd Shukor (UKM)

Program Committee

Program Co-chairs

Halimah Badioze Zaman	Universiti Kebangsaan Malaysia, Malaysia
Peter Robinson	University of Cambridge, UK
Patrick Olivier	University of Newcastle Upon-Tyne, UK
Ingela Nyström	Uppsala University, Sweden
Maria Petrou	Imperial College, UK
Timothy Shih	National Central University, Taiwan
Sergio Velastin	Kingston University, UK

Members/Referees

Europe

Ahmad Khurshid	Edie Rasmussen
Alan Smeaton	Gregor Rainer
Burkhard Wuensche	Hassan Ugail
Daniel Thalmann	Ingela Nyström

Jian Jun Zheng
Jonathon Furner
Ligang He
Neil Andrew Gordon
Peter Robinson
Rainer Malaka
Sergio Velastin
Tony Pridmore
Ann Blandford
Carol Peters
Donatella Castelli
Gerald Schaefer

Harold Timbleby
Ingeborg Solvberg
Jian J. zhang
John Wilson
Keith van Rjsbergen
Maria Petrou
Patrick Olivier
Qingde Li
Roy Sterritt
Stephen McKenna
Wenyu Liu

USA

Archan Misra
Dick Simmons
Hshinchun Chen
Josep Torellas
Micheal H. Hinchey
Per-Ake (Paul) Larson
Vicky Markstein

Carl K. Chang
Eric Wong
James Hughes
Joseph Urban
Paul R. Croll
T. Kesavadas

Asia and Oceania

Abd Razak Yaakub
Abdul Razak Hamdan
Abdul Samad
   Hasan Basari
Abdul Samad
   Shibghatullah
Abdullah Gani
Aboamama Atahar
   Ahmed
Alex Orailoglu
Amirah Ismail
Ang Mei Choo
Anup Kumar
Asim Smailagic
Azizah Jaafar
Azizi Abdullah
Azlina Ahmad
Azreen Azman
Azurah Abu Samah

Bahari Belaton
Bryon Purves
Burairah Hussin
Burhanuddin Mohd
   Aboobaider
Chen Chwen Jen
Choo Wou Onn
Choo Yun Huoy
Christopher C. Yang
Chung Jen-Yao
Dayang Norhayati
   Abg Jawawi
Dayang Rohaya
   Awang Rambli
Dhanesh
   Ramachandram
Dzulkifli Mohamad
Edwin Mit
Effirul Ikhwan Ramlan

Elankovan A.
   Sundararajan
Faaizah Shahbodin
Faieza Abdul Aziz
Farid Ghani
Fatimah Dato' Ahmad
Faudziah Ahmad
Hajah Norasiken Bakar
Halimah Badioze Zaman
Hamid Abdalla Jalab
Hanspeter Pfister
Haslina Arshad
Hwee Hua Pang
Jane Labadin
Jie-Wu
Juan Antonio Carballo
Khairulmizam Samsudin
Lai Jian Ming
Li Jian Zhong

Lili Nurliyana Abdullah
Ling Teck Chaw
Li-Zhu Zhou
M. Iqbal Bin Saripan
Maizatul Hayati
   Mohamad Yatim
Maryam Nazari
Masatoshi Yoshikawa
Masnizah Mohd
Mazleena Salleh
Md. Nazrul Islam
Mohamad Ishak Desa
Mohammad
   Khatim Hasan
Mohd Faizal Abdollah
Mohd Khanapi Abdul
   Ghani
Mohd Shafry Mohd
   Rahim
Mohd. Taufik Abdullah
Mun-Kew Leong
Muriati Mukhtar
Narhum Gershon
Nazlena Mohamad Ali
Nazlia Omar
Ng Giap Weng
Ning Zhong
Nor Aniza Abdullah
Nor Azan Hj Mat Zin
Nor Faezah M. Yatim
Nor Hasbiah Ubaidullah
Norafida Ithnin
Noraidah Sahari Ashaari

Norasikin Fabil
Norrozila Sulaiman
Norshahriah Abdul
   Wahab
Nur'Aini Abdul Rashid
Nurazzah Abd Rahman
Nursuriati Jamil
Osman Ghazali
Patricia Anthony
Phillip C.-Y. Sheu
Puteh Saad
Rabiah Abd Kadir
Ramlah Mailok
Reggie Caudill
Riaza Rias
Ridzuan Hussin
Riza Sulaiman
Roselina Sallehuddin
Shahrin Sahib
Shahrul Azman
   Mohd Noah
Shahrul Azmi
   Mohd. Yusof
Sharifah Mumtazah
   Syed Ahmad
   Abdul Rahman
Sharlini R. Urs
Sim Kok Swee
Siti Mariyam
   Hj Shamsuddin
Sobihatun Nur
   Abdul Salam
Suliman Hawamdeh

Syaimak Abdul Shukor
Syamsiah Mashohor
Syed Nasir Alsagoff
Tan Tien Ping
Teddy Surya Gunawan
Tengku Siti
   Meriam Tengku Wook
Timothy Shih
Tutut Herawan
Wai Lam
Wan Abdul Rahim
   Wan Mohd Isa
Wan Azlan Wan Zainal
   Abidin
Wan Fatimah
   Wan Ahmad
Wan Mohd Nazmee
   Wan Zainon
Wee Mee Chin
Wei Zhao
Willian Hayward
Wong Kok Sheik
Yin Chai Wang
Yin-Leng Theng
Zailani Mohd Nordin
Zainab Abu Bakar
Zainul Abidin
Zaipatimah Ali
Zarinah Mohd Kasirun
Zulikha Jamaluddin
Zulkarnain Md Ali

Local Arrangements Committee

Technical Committee

Head	Halimah Badioze Zaman (UKM)
Members	Azlina Ahmad (UKM)
	Muriati Mukhtar (UKM)
	Riza Sulaiman (UKM)
	Nazlena Mohamad Ali (UKM)
	Mohd M. Kadhum (UUM)
	M. Iqbal Saripan (UPM)

Haslina Arshad (UKM)
Syaimak Abd Shukor (UKM)
Rabiah Abdul Kadir (UPM)
Elankovan A. Sundararajan (UKM)
Norazan Mat Zin (UKM)
Mohammad Khatim Hassan (UKM)
Wan Mohd Nazmee Wan Zainon (USM)
Tengku Siti Meriam Tengku Wook (UKM)
Azizah Jaafar (UKM)
Bahari Belaton (USM)
Wan Fatimah Wan Ahmad (UTP)
Fatimah Ahmad (UPNM)
Noraidah Sahari Ashaari (UKM)
Ang Mei Choo (UKM)
Nursuriati Jamil (UiTM)
Syed Nasir Alsagoff (UPNM)
Azreen Azman (UPM)
Dayang Rohaya Bt Awang Rambli (UTP)
Suziah Sulaiman (UTP)
Riaza Mohd Rias (UiTM)
Faaizah Shahbodin (UTeM)
Hajah Norasiken Bakar (UTeM)
Norshahriah Wahab (UPNM)
Nurazzah Abdul Rahman (UiTM)

Publicity
Head   Elankovan A. Sundararajan (UKM)
Members   Norazan Mat Zin (UKM)
Mohammad Khatim Hassan (UKM)
Wan Mohd Nazmee Wan Zainon (USM)
Tengku Siti Meriam Tengku Wook (UKM)
Azlina Ahmad (UKM)
Aidanismah Yahya (UKM)
Nurdiyana Mohd Yassin (UKM)

Logistic
Head   Ang Mei Choo (UKM)
Members   Nursuriati Jamil (UiTM)
Syed Nasir Alsagoff (UPNM)
Riaza Mohd Rias (UiTM)
Maslina Abdul Aziz (UiTM)
Norshahriah Wahab (UPNM)
Mohd Hanif Md Saad (UKM)

Financial
Head   Azizah Jaafar (UKM)
Members   Halimah Badioze Zaman (UKM)
                        Azlina Ahmad (UKM)
                        Wan Fatimah Wan Ahmad (UTP)
                        Fatimah Dato Ahmad (UPNM)

Workshop
Head   Riza Sulaiman (UKM)
Members   Wan Mohd Nazmee Wan Zainon (USM)
                        Faaizah Shahbodin (UTeM)
                        Choo Wou Onn (UTAR)

Secretariat   Nurul Aini Kasran (UKM)
                        Aw Kien Sin (UKM)

Conference Management System (CoMS ^{TM})

Institute of Visual Informatics, Universiti Kebangsaan Malaysia

Sponsoring Institutions

Universiti Kebangsaan Malaysia (UKM)
Universiti Putra Malaysia (UPM)
Universiti Sains Malaysia (USM)
University Teknologi PETRONAS (UTP)
Universiti Teknologi MARA (UiTM)
Universiti Pertahanan Nasional Malaysia (UPNM)
Universiti Teknologi Malaysia (UTM)
Universiti Malaysia Sarawak (UNIMAS)
University Malaya (UM)
Universiti Utara Malaysia (UUM)
Universiti Teknikal Malaysia (UTeM)
Universiti Tunku Abdul Rahman (UTAR)
Multimedia University (MMU)
Malaysian Information Technology Society (MITS)
Multimedia Corporation Malaysia (MDeC)
Malaysian Research Educational Network (MyREN)
Malaysian Institute of Microelectronics (MIMOS)

Table of Contents – Part II

Visual Computing

Visualisation and Social Computing

Table of Contents – Part I

Virtual Image Processing and Engineering

Capturing Mini Brand Using
a Parametric Shape Grammar

Mei Choo Ang[1,2], Huai Yong Chong[2], Alison McKay[3], and Kok Weng Ng[4]

[1] Institute of Visual Informatics
[2] Faculty of Information Science and Technology, Universiti Kebangsaan Malaysia,
43600 UKM Bangi, Selangor, Malaysia
[3] School of Mechanical Engineering
University of Leeds
LS2 9JT Leeds, UK
[4] Design Engineering Section, Product Design and Engineering Center,
SIRIM Berhad
Bukit Jalil, 57000 Kuala Lumpur
amc@ftsm.ukm.my, kwng@sirim.my

Abstract. Enterprises strive to survive in competitive consumer markets and seek means to meet consumer demands cost effectively. From this aspect, generative design methods such as shape grammars are being investigated and explored with the aim to support enterprises and their designers in creating new products that meet consumers' demands and aspirations. Shape grammars have been used to visually generate branded consumer products. However, existing shape grammars tend to use simple basic shapes and are not well-suited to the complex shapes that typify many branded consumer products. With the introduction of the parametric shape grammars, the applicability of shape grammars improves for branded consumer product. In this paper, an adapted parametric shape grammar is applied to capture the evolution of Mini brand automobiles. The investigation carried out was focused on the front view designs of the Mini automobiles from different time periods. The information collected from this study will provide the basis to support the implementation of a computerised generative design system.

Keywords: Shape grammars, generative design system, brand identity, Mini, shape analysis, Visual Informatics.

1 Introduction

In a competitive consumer market, many enterprises strive to survive and seek means to meet consumers demand timely and cost effectively. Enterprises brand their products and promote their brands to gain market share. Brand identity of the products is regarded as an essential strategy to increase competitiveness and also a vital factor to determine the success of brand extensions [1-5]. The tasks of designers in these enterprises have become more challenging. They have to create new designs that meet consumer demands and, at the same time, fulfil both branding and

H. Badioze Zaman et al. (Eds.): IVIC 2011, Part II, LNCS 7067, pp. 1–12, 2011.

functional requirements. This prompts the need to use computer technology to support designers in these enterprises. Generative design systems [6] that generate product structure or shape are being investigated in the literature with the aim to support designers in these kinds of task. However, generative design methods based on shape grammar are usually semi manual and computerised generative design systems that are able to support designers effectively when working with complex geometries are not common. Shape grammar is a generative design system that has been applied to visually generate branded consumer products [7-9] and their applications involved manual interactions. The existing shape grammars for branded product are typically manual type generative design systems due to the complexity of grammar computation.

Shape grammars are defined using a set of basic shapes, a set of rules and labels to guide the shape computation. The basic shapes are usually rectilinear shapes such as straight lines, squares, rectangle triangles. These basic shapes are sufficient to be applied in areas such as architectural plans and decorative art where the shapes are in two dimensions but it is more difficult to apply these methods directly in 3D product design problems. Consumer products usually involved complex curvilinear outlines and shapes. There are a number of branded product shape grammars reported in the literature that capture the outline of product forms with curved lines [7-9]. The rules of these shape grammars were applied without explicit explanations on the parameters determination and the use of semantic descriptions were not quantified, for example the usage of semantic description such as soft and hard points to represent curves [8] were ambiguous. These reported shape grammars had also been applied with necessary constraints to capture the product brand identity but there were limited information provided on how to determine these constraints [8]. These deficiencies posed difficulties for researchers to create a basis for computer implementation of such generative design system to give support to designers. Thus, the existing branded product shape grammars had to rely on designers to manually select rules and preferred parameters to generate the desired shapes.

A parametric shape grammar that can be used to define curvilinear shapes was proposed by Prats et al. [10]. The parametric shape grammar was used to define shapes for consumer products and it allowed exploration of design alternatives. In this research work, the parametric shape grammar [10] was adapted to visualise the outline of Mini models' front views. It is demonstrated that the grammar can generate the car outline by manually specifying the parameter values [10] but in this research work, the parameter grammar is adapted to provide a basis of computer-based implementation for a branded products. The generation results not only visualise the different versions of Mini models but also provide data for further shape analysis that would help to develop the constraints necessary for Mini models.

This article will first describe the evolution of Mini car front views since 1959. The most represented Mini shapes will be identified. These shapes are further generated using a parameterised shape grammar. The generation data collected from the car model will be further analysed to identify the structure and constraints of the Mini car front views. The structure and constraints will provide the basis of the Mini Shape Grammar to capture the Mini brand identity.

2   Evolution of Mini

Mini, a British icon, was produced by British Motor Corporation (BMC) in 1959. It is the first small car being built with two doors [11, 12]. During the Suez crisis and to confront the competition from other car manufacturers in 1956, Lord Leonard from BMC decided to seek the help of a car designer and engineer, Sir Alec Lssigonis to design a small car that is big enough to fit for four adults and their luggage [11, 12].

The Mini was officially launched in 27 August 1959 [11-13]. The earlier versions were known as Austin 850 or Morris 850. The name 'Mini' was used for the first time in 1961. The launching of the first Mini was not successful and Mini was considered weird by the public. It was believed that the sale of Mini was improved only after the Mini was driven by some famous figures such as the Queen Elizabeth II and a few singer and movie stars in the early 1960s. Mini became class-less where it had become a favourite car of the public and even the noble class. Table 1 lists the evolution of the Mini in a chronological order. Fig. 1 shows a Mini Cooper front view during MKII production year.

Table 1. Model-model Mini in the history

Production year	Model Name	Description
1959–1967	Mini Mark I (MK1)	Mini Mark I was launched in 1959. However, the name 'Mini' was not used, instead, Mini Mark I was known as Austin Mini or Morris Mini. The name, 'Mini' was used for the first time by BMC in 1961.
1961–2000	Mini Cooper and Cooper S	Mini Cooper is an efficient and economical car designed by John Cooper and Sir Alec Issigonis. The engine power of the Mini Cooper was increased from 848 cc, 34 bhp (it was used to be Morris Mini engine) to 997 cc and 55 bhp. It was made to suit a car racing competition. Another new Mini Cooper, Mini Cooper S was built with even bigger engine capacity. The front view is similar to Mini Mark II.
1969–1980	Mini Clubman	In 1969, the ownership was changed and the new owner was the British Leyland. Mini was redesigned by Roy Haynes and it was named Mini Clubman. The front view of the new Mini was squarer than previous Mini versions. Mini Clubman was created to replace the old Riley and Wolseley.
1967–1973	Mini Mark II (MKII)	Mini Mark II is similar with Mini Mark I but it had a new grill and a few cosmetic changes.
1969–2000	Mini Mark III - VI	Mini Mark III, IV, V and VI have modified car body and engine technology. The modifications include bigger car boot with concealed hinges, installation of winding windows and engine twin injection point. The outline of the car is not significantly changed and still maintained similar front view to the Mini Cooper.
Since 2001	BMW MINI	When the classic Mini production stopped in 2000, BMW (the new owner of the brand) announced a Mini replacement. The brand name for the new car is called the MINI or referred as "BMW MINI". The new MINI is larger than the original Mini and the front view had changed significantly.

The Mini car has gone through several versions and modifications since its first conception. Although there's some different versions of the car front views, the Mini still maintain a distinct look of the front light and the grill. Mini cars had changed mainly on the car technology such as engine capacity, car accessory and the interior design. The front view of Mini models in the history had not changed dramatically and had four distinct versions: Mini MKI (such as Austin Mini and Morris Mini), Mini MKII (such as Mini Cooper), Mini Clubman and the current BMW MINI. These car front views were collected from different resources such as books [11-13] and internet and formed the basis of the investigations in this paper. The four front views were modelled using a parametric shape grammar and were further analysed to capture the Mini brand essence in the following sections.

Fig. 1. Mini Cooper (MKII) [14]

3   A Brief Introduction to Shape Grammars

Shape grammar formalism is introduced in a seminal paper by Stiny and Gips [15] in 1972. Shape grammars have been used in many different areas, notably in the areas such as paintings, decorative art, architecture, product design and engineering. In these different areas, shape grammars were used to capture a style within certain design corpus, such as the painting style of an artist, the design style of a craftsman, or floor planning style of an architect. In a similar manner, shape grammars were used to capture the identity of some branded consumer products.

A shape grammar can be regarded as a grammar for design. In linguistic, a grammar consists of alphabets and a set of rules on how to form phrases and how to arrange words into sentences. Similarly, a shape grammar also has a set of basic shapes and rules that are applied to govern how shapes can be manipulated step by step to generate into final forms. To illustrate the application of a shape grammar, Fig. 2 shows a simple shape grammar consists of an initial shape and two rules.

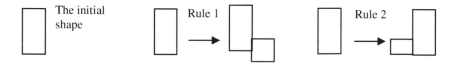

Fig. 2. A two rules shape grammar

An example application of shape computation is shown in Fig. 3. In Fig. 3, starting from the initial shape of a rectangle, rule 1 is used followed by rule 2 and then lastly by rule 1 again. This will transform the initial shape of a rectangle to a distinct final shape as shown in the Fig. 3. Note that I had selected the smaller rectangle for the application of rule 1 in the last transformation.

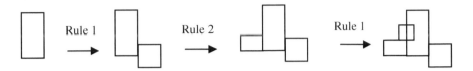

Fig. 3. Example shape computation using the two rules shape grammar

4 Parametric Shape Grammar

It is typical for shape grammars to use simple straight lines as their basic shapes and the parametric shape grammar defined by Prats et. al. [10] also used such simple shapes. However, Prats et. al. [10] used simple lines which had a length size of 1 unit. Hence, a line with the length of x can be formed by connecting x number of such line with 1 unit length. Similarly, a curve can be formed by connecting a series of 1 unit length line with a bearing angle specified for each of the line respectively. Each of such line with 1 unit length can be considered as a line unit. Hence, depending on the design requirements, these line units were used to build curves or straight line segments. These segments were then connected to generate the outline of a product. Grammar rules form the basis for building relationships between line segments. The parametric shape rule was specified [10] to connect a new line unit to the previous line unit with a certain angle. Fig. 4 shows the parameters being used where the unit line was repeated four times ($R = 4$) with a rotation angle, β. The β is a parameter that gives the fine detail for the bearing angle of a curve segment. If β was zero and R was the repetition number of unit line, then the curve in Fig. 4 would be a straight line. Consequently, R was also equivalent to the total length of the straight line.

Rule (β, R, γ)

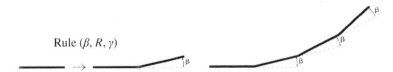

Fig. 4. A line unit is repeated four times ($R = 4$) with β angle between line unit and $\gamma = 0$ to approximate a curve (adapted from [10])

An additional parameter, γ is used to create the discontinuity point between line segments. The line segment in Fig. 4 is continuous with the same rotation angle and rate of change, and thus the γ is null. If γ is not null, then line segments with different tangent could be created. An example of two line segments that had a discontinuous point is shown in Fig. 5.

However, the manual implementation of this parametric shape grammar was time consuming and a tedious task since it involved connecting several unit lines to complete a small part of a curve segment in a complete outline. For this research work, the parametric shape grammar was applied with the β set to zero. With β set to zero, the line unit in this research work can only form curves based on the parameter γ, the angle between two tangents of the line segments at the point of discontinuity. This setting would speed up the generating process but may lead to the potential of creating jagged shape in the outline. However, as demonstrated in Section 5, the generated car front views projected a good approximation to the actual image of the Mini car front view with minimal jagged shape outline.

Fig. 5. Discontinuous line segments when $\gamma \neq 0$ (adapted from [10])

5   Generating Mini Car Models Using the Adapted Parametric Shape Grammar

Mini car front view comprises outlines for several main parts, namely, the roof, the windscreen, the fenders (left and right), the front light, the grill, the emblem, the hood and the bumper. These parts contribute to the outline of the front view and can be group into three sections: top, middle and bottom (refer Fig. 6). The top section includes the roof and the windscreen, middle section includes the fenders, the hood, the front light, the grill and the emblem, whereas the bottom section includes the car bumper. The front light is assumed to be a circle shape for most of the classic Mini.

Since this research work concerned mainly on the outline of the car front view, the details of the emblem and bumper were not considered. The front light and the grill were also not considered in this research work. Only the outline of the car front view was considered in this research work.

Fig. 6. Mini Cooper (MK II) front view outline is divided into three parts

An iconic model, Mini Cooper (MKII) was used to demonstrate the application of the adapted parametric shape grammar (β set to zero) in details. The Mini Cooper car front view was divided into three sections: top, middle and bottom as shown in Fig. 6. The adapted parametric shape grammar explained in Section 4 is applied manually to construct the line segments for the different sections (top, middle and bottom) as shown in Table 2-6. These line segments are combined together to form the final outline of the Mini front view.

Table 2. Implementation details of the parametric shape grammar to generate the top section of the Austin Mini Cooper

Segment	Parameter values for Rule $(\beta=0, \gamma, R)$	Line segments being produced with the shape rules
0	$\gamma = -1.64°$ $R = 7$	0
1	$\gamma = -4.8°$ $R = 7$	0 1
2	$\gamma = -20°$ $R = 2.2$	0 1 2
3	$\gamma = -41.6°$ $R = 5.4$	0 1 2 3
4	$\gamma = -3.3°$ $R = 6.3$	0 1 2 3 4

Table 3. The summary of the parameter values for the Austin Mini Cooper (MKI)

Section	Top		Middle		Bottom	
Outline						
Parameter values	γ	R	γ	R	γ	R
	-1.64	7	15.2	3.6	65.7	0.9
	-4.8	7	11.3	2.8	-36.5	1
	-20	2.2	-24.4	4.3	-41	1
	-41.6	5.4	-11.1	3	-51.3	1.2
	-3.3	6.3	-17.7	5.5	-38.7	8

Table 4. The summary of the parameter values for the Mini Cooper (MKII)

Section	Top		Middle		Bottom	
Outline						
Parameter values	γ	R	γ	R	γ	R
	0	3	60.2	3.1	70.3	1.8
	-2.3	5	-37.8	3.6	-56.3	
	-9	4	-26.5	4	-63.4	1.1
	-15.2	2.2	-7.1	3	-26.5	7
	-45	6.3	-7.1	4	0	8
	-7.1	5	-6.9	2	0	7

Table 5. The summary of the parameter values for the Mini Clubman

Section	Top		Middle		Bottom	
Outline						
Parameter values	γ	R	γ	R	γ	R
	0	8	19.654	5.8	36.027	3
	-18.435	3.162	0	5.8	-53.13	1
	-1.548	5.852	-16.928	2	-49.4	4
	-47.397	6.5	-14.036	2	-14.036	6
	-11.31	5	-9.462	3	4	7
					-	8

Table 6. The summary of the parameter values for the BMW MINI

Version	Top		Middle		Bottom	
BMW MINI						
Parameter Values	γ	R	γ	R	γ	R
	0	8	18.	5.6	45	2.8
	-9.5	6	-18.4	2.2	-40 9	7
	-49.5	5.8	-30 1	8	-4	8
	-4.4	6.7	-13.1	5		
			-24.3	1.4		
			-45	5		

As all cars generally have a symmetrical front view, it is sufficient to define one side of the car (half of the car front view) to model the outline of a car. Thus, the generating process began from the middle of the car roof. Table 2 shows how the line segments in top section of the Mini Cooper (MKII) are being produced using the parametric shape grammar. The implementation of the parametric shape grammar was continued with the middle and bottom section of the Mini Cooper (MKII). The value of the parameters and the section outlines are shown in Table 3. Similar implementations were conducted to generate the outlines of the other three models identified (Mini MKI, Mini Clubman and BMW MINI) in section 2 using the parametric shape rules. Table 4, Table 5 and Table 6 show the generated top, middle and bottom sections of the these three Mini car models.

The generated top, middle and bottom sections were joined together to form the right hand side half of the car front view outlines. These right hand side outlines were then used to form the respective mirror images to produce the left hand side outlines. The two right and left outlines were then joined together to form the complete front view outline. The complete outline for Mini MKI, MKII, Mini Clubman and BMW MINI are shown in Table 7.

6 Discussions

Comparing the four outlines generated in Table 7, Mini Cooper (MKII) was noticed to have rounder body than the other models. The Mini Cooper (MKII) also had a rounder fender at the middle section. Mini MKI and Mini Clubman were the most similar when compared to rest of the models. The classic Mini models i.e. models of Mini except the BMW Mini had protruding bumper and it was visible in the front view outline. The BMW MINI outline has no protruding bumper in the front view outline.

Table 7. The complete outline of the Mini MKI, MKII, Clubman and BMW MINI car front views

Version	Generated outline
MK1 [16]	
MKII [14]	
Clubman [17]	
BMW MINI [18]	

These characteristics mentioned above were also reflected in their respective parameter values. The top sections of these front views were not showing any significant differences. The middle sections were the main sections that differentiated these models. The Mini Cooper (MKII) has bigger change in tangent value at the connecting point between top section and the middle section and the value of γ at the connecting point was the largest when compared to the other models. This large change in γ value caused the middle section to look higher and thus rounder than the other models. The MKI has more evenly distributed changes in γ and R values in the middle section. Mini Clubman has null γ values along the middle section and thus it had straighter middle section than the other models. BMW MINI had larger γ values along the middle section when compared to the other Mini models and it had more angular corner than the rest of the models.

The outlines generated not only presented the existing style of the Mini car models; the details parameter values and the outline characteristics were also obtained. This outlines also provide further basis to determine the range of the parameter values to scope the Mini outlines. The characteristics and constraints obtained from further analysis would capture the design knowledge necessary to represent the style of the Mini brand. Similar work is necessary to obtain the outline of the other front view components to investigate the details of the characteristics and their constraints. This research work has reduced the controlling parameters of shape grammar for products to two parameters, namely R number of repetition of line unit and γ. When coupled with all these generated outlines, the results of this research work will substantiate the design knowledge necessary to support the basis of the future work on the computer implementation of a generative design system that supports the exploration of the Mini brand.

7 Conclusions

The adapted parametric shape grammar was demonstrated to be able to regenerate the Mini car models. The generated models resembled the outlines of the respective car front views. A few observations have been identified to characterise the classic Mini front view outlines, such as Mini MKII has the rounder fender, Mini Clubman has straighter fender, BMW MINI had angular fender than the rest of the models. Bumper outlines were visible in the front view of classic Mini than the new Mini (BMW MINI). The parameter values had also showed the fine details of the front view outlines.

This work had offer a systematic way of using a parametric shape grammar to generate and analyse the Mini front view outlines. However, these observations were only based on the generated front view outlines and there were many front view components not being considered, namely, the front light, the windscreen, the grill, the hood, the fender and the bumper. This work had only capturing the front view outlines that gave limited design knowledge for Mini brand. Further work is necessary to capture more design knowledge and the brand identity of Mini. The remaining part of the Mini front views need to be explored and further analysed to obtain more design knowledge of the Mini brand.

Acknowledgments. The authors would like to thank Universiti Kebangsaan Malaysia for sponsoring this research by using the funding of the research project UKM-GGPM-ICT-102-2010 and UKM-DIPM-041-2011.

References

1. Batra, R., Lenk, P., Wede, M.: Brand Extension Strategy Planning: Empirical Estimation of Brand Category Personality Fit and Atypicality. Journal of Marketing Research 47, 335–345 (2010)
2. Viot, C.: Can Brand Identity Predict Brand Extensions' Success or Failure? Journal of Product & Brand Management 20, 216–227 (2011)
3. Aaker, D.A., Joachimsthaler, E.: Brand Leadership. The Free Press, New York (2000)
4. Kapferer, J.-N.: Strategic Brand Management. Kogan Page, London (1997)
5. de Chernatony, L.: From Brand Vision to Brand Evaluation. Butterworth-Heinemann, Oxford (2001)
6. Eckert, C., Kelly, I., Stacey, M.: Interactive generative systems for conceptual design: An empirical perspective. Artificial Intelligence for Engineering Design, Analysis and Manufacturing 13, 303–320 (1999)
7. Chau, H.H., Chen, X., McKay, A., de Pennington, A.: Evaluation of a 3D shape grammar implementation. In: Design Computing and Cognition 2004, pp. 357–376. Kluwer, Dordrecht (2004)
8. McCormack, J.P., Cagan, J., Vogel, C.M.: Speaking the Buick language: capturing, understanding, and exploring brand identity with a shape grammar. Design Studies 25, 1–29 (2004)
9. Pugliese, M.J., Cagan, J.: Capturing a rebel: modeling the Harley-Davidson brand through a motorcycle shape grammar. Res. Eng. Design-Theory Appl. Concurrent Eng. 13, 139–156 (2002)
10. Prats, M., Jowers, I., Garner, S., Earl, C.: Improving Product Design via a Shape Grammar Tool. In: International Design Conference - Design 2004, Dubrovnik, Croatia (2004)
11. Filby, P.: Amazing MINI. Haynes Publishing Group, Somerset (1989)
12. Nahum, A.: Issigonis and the Mini. Icon Books Ltd., Cambridge (2004)
13. Slade, T.: Classic Cars: Celebrating The Legends. Igloo Books Ltd., Sywell (2006)
14. Graham Smith, http://www.seight.net
15. Stiny, G., Gips, J.: Shape grammars and the generative specification of painting and sculpture. In: Proceedings of IFIP Congress, pp. 1460–1465. North Holland, Amsterdam (1972)
16. Californiaclassix.com, http://www.californiaclassix.com/archive/64_Mini_c225.html
17. Classic-Car-Magazine, http://www.classic-car-magazine.co.uk/
18. MINI, http://www.miniusa.com/#/MINIUSA.COM-m

Development and Usability Evaluation of Virtual Environment for Early Diagnosis of Dementia

Syadiah Nor Wan Shamsuddin[1], Hassan Ugail[1], and Valerie Lesk[2]

[1] School of Computing, Informatics and Media, University of Bradford,
Bradford, BD7 1DP, UK
[2] School of Social & International Studies, University of Bradford,
Bradford, BD7 1DP, UK
{S.N.B.WanShamsuddin,h.ugail,v.lesk}@bradford.ac.uk

Abstract. Virtual Technology (VT) plays a vital role in many areas. It is a promising tool in healthcare and offers opportunities and solutions for early detection of dementia. Dementia is associated with loss of brain function from the process of ageing. This serious illness needs early diagnosis if medical treatment and healthcare services are to be deployed in time. We developed a new prototype called Virtual Reality for Early Detection of Dementia (VReDD), and have applied psychology theories in an attempt to make an early diagnosis of dementia. In this paper, we will focus on the usability of user satisfaction for young participants to see the complexity and effectiveness of the prototype as a first step prior to the implementation the experiment with elderly, those with a mild cognitive impairment and Alzheimer patients. These preliminary findings show that the prototype is reliable and suitable to be used with elderly people.

Keywords: Virtual Environment, spatial memory, topographical disorientation, dementia.

1 Introduction

One of the biggest fears in the process of ageing is associated with brain memory which leads to dementia. In the year 2010, there are currently 510,000 people living with dementia in England and this number is expected to double over the next 30 years [1]. This dementia occurs in people aged over 65 and it is slightly more common in women than in men [1].

Topographical disorientation is the inability to orient and navigate in the environment [2]. Topographical disorientation is usually the expression of defects in a variety of cognitive processes including memory, attention, spatial skills or visual perceptual skills [3]. This is a common manifestation of dementia of the Alzheimer's type that can occur in the early stages of the disease, particularly in less familiar settings [4]. The ability to find one's way involves knowing the procedural components of the route to the destination which may require topographical knowledge about the surroundings [3]. It is not unusual for Alzheimer's disease

H. Badioze Zaman et al. (Eds.): IVIC 2011, Part II, LNCS 7067, pp. 13–22, 2011.
© Springer-Verlag Berlin Heidelberg 2011

patients to get lost in unfamiliar places in the early stages of the disease and, in the later stages they may become lost or disoriented in familiar places such as their home or neighbourhood [5].

Virtual environments(VE) present a unified workspace allowing a more or less complete functionality without requiring all the functions to be located in the same physical space [6]. VE can be defined as interactive, virtual image displays enhanced by special processing and by non-visual display modalities, such as auditory and haptic, to convince users that they are immersed in a synthetic space [7]. VE can also be defined as the presence of environments simulated by a computer that can be experienced [8]. A VE can be quite effective in immersing the user within a realistic 3D world and in providing a high level of sensory richness to the user [9]. With VR technology, a VE lets the user freely explore the 3D space.VEoffers experimental research conditions that are easy to define, control, and duplicate [10].

Virtual Reality can be applied in many applications including gaming, entertainment, training, education and health. At present, this technology can be said to offer specific attributes or ingredients that are well-matched to the needs of many mental health and rehabilitation targets, and these fundamental attributes include exposure, distraction, motivation and interaction [11].Virtual Reality (VR) is rapidly becoming a popular application in healthcare. Its promising technology offers opportunities to create new products in everyday situations. Virtual Reality-based software is thought to be potentially more representative of everyday life situations than paper and pencil treatment procedures or limited software [12]. Werner et. al. developed Virtual Supermarket to examine the feasibility and the validity of the virtual action planning supermarket for the diagnosis of patients with mild cognitive impairment(MCI) [13]. Tippet et. al. designed and developed virtual city to examine the ability of MCI participants to navigate effectively through the VE [14].

2   System Design

2.1 Virtual Environment

A prototype simulation was develoedusing a 3D authoring tool called Virtools. VReDD consists of three modules: VR Practice, VR Park and VR Games (see Figure 1 and Figure 2). VR Park and VR Games both have five levels from easy to complex (see Figure 3).

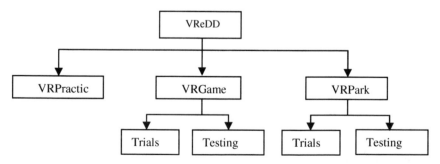

Fig. 1. Overview of VReDD

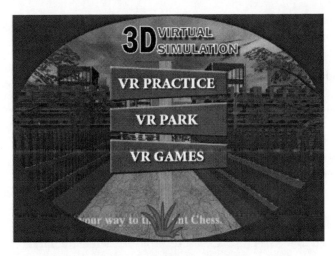

Fig. 2. Main Menu of VReDD

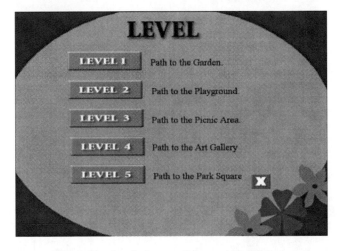

Fig. 3. Five levels in one of the module VR Park

VR Practice

The VR Practice is the training module. In this module, users have the opportunity to practise cursor keys using keyboards. This module has been developed to meet the needs of the target users who are aged over 45 and who may need some time to practice with cursor keys so they can use the application easily.

VR Park

The scenario settings for this module are in a park. There are five specific target destinations including playground, art gallery, garden, rest area and picnic area. Users experience walking through a park in the city where there are tall buildings to be seen, trees all around and various other things.

VR Games Land

In this module, the location is surrounded by tall buildings and houses. Inside the park, there are five different and specific types of giant games available, such as giant chess, giant board games, lawn bowls and mini golf.

Figure 3: Procedure in VReDD

Figure 3 represents a procedure done in VReDD. First, users' information are recorded in the system. A unique user ID is given to each user. Then, in the VR simulation, users are ableto see one of the two environments. The users are allowed to repeat the exercise of reaching the target destination three times by following the red ribbon attached to the path. Next, the user is tested on their ability to recollect given path. All data are collected and recorded during this phase. Lastly, all data were exported to the system to be analysed.

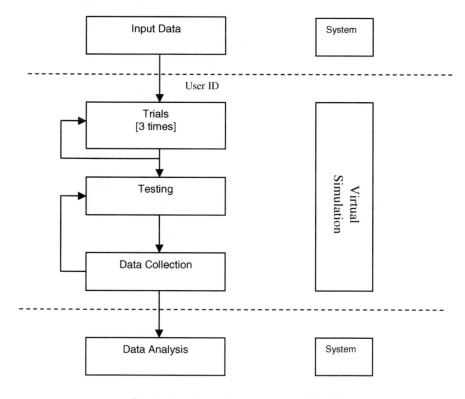

Fig. 4. Procedures of experiment in VReDD

Fig. 4. Interface with red ribbon attached to the path

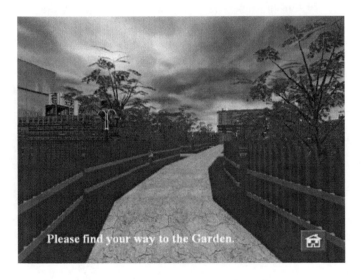

Fig. 5. Interface during the testing phase

2.2 Data Collection

Data are collected during the testing phase. There are five attributes needed to diagnose early detection of dementia: correct path, incorrect path, correct sequences, incorrect sequences, timing and scores.

Path
During testing, users are allowed to move freely to the target destination. All the movement are captured and recorded for data analysis.

Path Sequence and Path Squares
Users are required to reach the target destination in the correct path sequence. The data from path-tracking will show correct and incorrect sequences and path squares.

Timing
During testing, the amount of time taken to complete the journey from the starting point to the target destination was recorded.

Score
Scores are then calculated based on path sequences and path squares. The scores show the percentage of performance done by users.

2.3 Information System

An information system has also been developed to keep the users information and data collected. The text file produced by VReDD is then be transferred to the system to be recorded and analysed. Figure 6 and 7 shows interfaces of the system.

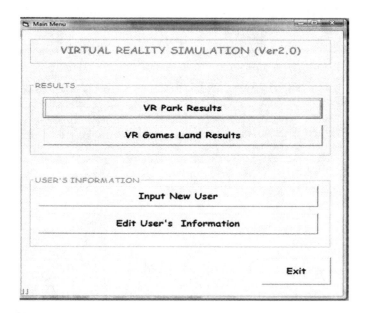

Fig. 6. Main Menu of Information System

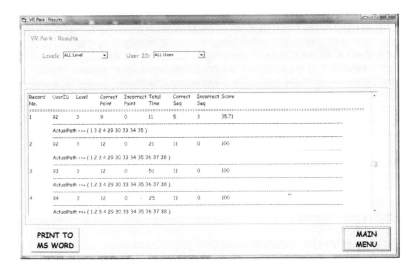

Fig. 7. Interface results of the system

3 Methods

3.1 Design

The participants were students of University of Bradford following different courses. A total of 11 participants (8 female and 3 male) from age 18 to 35 were recruited for this experiment.

3.2 Instruments

VR System

VRREDD operates on a standard PC and simulates a fully textured of two various scenes: VR Park and VR Games. The participants are allowed to repeat the exercise of reaching the target destination three times by following the red ribbon attached to the path. Then, the participants are tested on their ability to recollect the given path and they must find the destination themselves. Each level gets progressively harder, with more complex navigation required.

Feedback Questionnaire

The questionnaire features several questions, the answers to which will produce a score of between 1 and 5. The questionnaires assess the participant's; learned controls quickly, moved easily, clear instructions, system control, preferred more freedom and looking around easily.

Procedure

Each participant was trained to use the arrow keys using the module VR practice. After the training the participant will carry out the real experiment. The users will be allowed to repeat the exercise of reaching the target destination three times by following the red ribbon attached to the path. After this, the test phase begins where the participant sees the VE without the red ribbon and they have to make their own way to the destination with the cursor keys.   This terminates either when the participant completes all levels or when the participant takes longer than 5 minutes to reach the destination on the test phase at any level. When this is complete, participants will commence on word memory test where they have to try to remember 60 words in any particular order.

4   Usability Evaluation and Results

Usability evaluation of any system is essential to ensure systems meet both design specifications and user requirement criteria. Usability can be broadly defined as ease of use, usefulness including such quantifiable characteristics as learnability, speed and accuracy of user task performance, user error rate and subjective user satisfaction [15]. This section only focused on user satisfaction based on the questionnaire given.

   To evaluate the usability of our prototype system (VReDD), we undertook a user evaluation study with 11 participants. The questionnaire was based on participants' responses on five-point Likert Scale (strongly agree, agree, undecided, disagree, strongly disagree). The responses are summarised in Table 1.

Table 1. Feedback results from questionnaires

	Agree		**Disagree**	
	Number of Participants	(%)	Number of Participants	(%)
1. Learned to move quickly through application	11	100	0	0
2. Moved easily	11	100	0	0
3. Clear instructions	11	100	0	0
4. Control using arrow keys	11	100	0	0
5. Feel disoriented	0	0	11	100
6. Looking around easily	11	100	0	0
7. Preferred more freedom	6	55	5	45
8. Fast speed of movement	10	91	1	9
9. Comfortable using application	11	100	0	0
10. Overall satisfaction	11	100	0	0

In the experiment, users were learning to move through application using the cursor keys from the keyboard. In response to question 1, they do agree 100% and a possible explanation was because they were asked to use VR Practice first before going through the testing modules. The users are required to move through application without any help from researchers using control keys from the keyboard. All participants reported that they can move easily through the application. Since the general purpose of this research is for Dementia people, instructions must be simple and clear. From the results, it shows that they all agree to the clear instructions given throughout this application. From the study, it was found that all the participants were able to use the control keys for navigation and interaction without any problem. Disorientation is one main issue arises in health and safety implication for using VR. The overall response to this question was very positive as they do not feel disoriented while using the application. All participants agree that it was easy to look around in the application. Of all 11 participants, six of them responded that they would prefer to have more freedom. This may be because users are limited to walk on the path without going to the grass and other places. The reason for limited movement was not to let users feel disoriented or getting lost while using the application. Only one participant responded the speed of movement was too fast. For both questions of overall satisfaction and comfort using application, the overall response was 100% which is positive. The findings demonstrated that the application is reliable and suitable to be used by the elderly participants.

5   Conclusions

The results of this study demonstrate the usability of VReDD. The finding is important as a first step prior to the implementation to the elderly people with Alzheimer disease. To date, we have carried out the experiment with healthy elderly and young participants. In future work, experiments need to be conducted with elderly Alzheimer patients and data will be analysed to see the comparison and discriminate between elderly, those with a mild cognitive impairment and Alzheimer patients. The ability of this prototype to track and record all the movements of users will be easier to analyse. Furthermore, using VReDD will save time and reduce health and safety risks.

Acknowledgments. The authors would like to express their gratitude to School of Computing, Informatics and Media, University of Bradford and University of Sultan Zainal Abidin (UNISZA) for the support and facilities provided.

References

1. National Health Service, Dementia,
    http://www.nhs.uk/Conditions/Dementia/Pages/Introduction.aspx
2. Iaria, G., Bogod, N., Fox, C.J., Barton, J.J.: Developmental topographical disorientation: Case one. Neuropsychologia 47(1), 30–40 (2009)

3. Aguirre, G.K., D'Esposito, M.: Topographical disorientation: a synthesis and taxonomy. Brain 122(9), 1613–1628 (1999)

4. Passini, R., Rainville, C., Marchand, N., Joanette, Y.: Wayfinding in dementia of the Alzheimer type: Planning abilities. Journal of Clinical and Experimental Neuropsychology 17(6), 820–832 (1995)

5. Cherrier, M.M., Mendez, M., Perryman, K.: Route Learning performance in Alzheimer disease patients. Neuropsychiatry, Neuropsychology and Behavioral Neurology 14(3), 159–168 (2001)

6. Moline, J.: Virtual reality for health care: a survey. In: Riva, G. (ed.) Virtual Reality in Neuro-Psycho-Physiology, pp. 3–34. IOS Press, Amsterdam (1998)

7. Ellis, S.R.: What are virtual environments? IEEE Computer Graphics and Applications 14(1), 17–22 (1994)

8. Sherman, W.R., Craig, A.B.: Understanding virtual reality: Interface, applicationand design. Morgan Kaufmann, San Francisco (2003)

9. Bowman, D.A., North, C., Chen, J., Polys, N.F., Pyla, P.S., Yilmaz, U.: Information-rich virtual environments: theory, tools, and research agenda. In: VRST 2003 Proceedings of the ACM Symposium on Virtual Reality Software and Technology, Japan, pp. 81–90 (2003)

10. Riecke, B.E., Van Veen, H.A.H.C., Bulthoff, H.H.: Visual Homing is possible without Landmarks - A Path Integration Study in Virtual Reality. Presence: Teleoperators and Virtual Environments 11(5), 443–473 (2002)

11. Rizzo, A.A., Wiederhold, M., Buckwalter, J.G.: Basic issues in the use of virtual environments for mental health applications. In: Riva, G., Wiederhold, B.K., Molinari, E. (eds.) Virtual Environments in Clinical Psychology and Neuroscience: Methods and Techniques in Advanced Patient-Therapist Interaction, pp. 123–145. IOS Press, Amsterdam (1998)

12. Costa, R.M., Carvalho, L.A.V., Aragon, D.F.: AVIRC: A Virtual city for cognitive rehabilitation. In: International Conference on Disabilities, Virtual Reality, and Associated Technologies, Italy, pp. 299–304 (2000)

13. Werner, P., Rabinowitz, S., Klinger, E., Korczyn, A.S., Josman, N.: The use of the virtual action planning supermarket for the diagnosis of mild cognitive impairment. Dementia and Geriatric Cognitive Disorders 27, 301–309 (2009)

14. Tippett, W.J., Lee, J.H., Zakzanis, K.K., Black, S.E., Mraz, R., Graham, S.J.: Visually navigating a virtual world with real-world impairments: A study of visually and spatially guided performance in individuals with mild cognitive impairments. Journal of Clinical and Experimental Neuropsychology 31(4), 447–454 (2008)

15. Hix, D., Hartson, H.R.: Developing User Interfaces: Ensuring Usability through Product & Process. John Wiley and Sons, New York (1993)

Usability Study of Mobile Learning Course Content Application as a Revision Tool

Ahmad Sobri Hashim, Wan Fatimah Wan Ahmad, and Rohiza Ahmad

Department of Computer and Information Sciences, Universiti Teknologi PETRONAS
Bandar Seri Iskandar, 31750 Tronoh, Perak, Malaysia
sob_87@yahoo.com,
{fatimhd,rohiza_ahmad}@petronas.com.my

Abstract. Mobile learning (m-learning) is a learning tool in which it can be operated on mobile devices. Mobile System Analysis and Design (MOSAD) have been developed with the content of a topic from the System Analysis and Design (SAD) course conducted at Universiti Teknologi PETRONAS (UTP). This paper presents the results of usability study that has been conducted for MOSAD application. Two methods of usability test have been used; questionnaire and observation. Both methods have been chosen in order to get more reliable data of usability since both results will support each other. The usability questionnaire has been distributed to 66 students from SAD course whereas 12 of them were chosen to participate in usability observation. There are five usability factors involved in this usability test; consistency, learnability, flexibility, minimal action and minimal memory load. The usability questionnaire result shows that all tested usability factors have been given the score of 3.5 and above which is higher than Likert scale mean (2.5). Besides, the usability observation result has supported the result of usability questionnaire which indicates that the MOSAD application usability level is good and it can be a useful revision tool for the students of higher education.

Keywords: mobile learning, usability test, usability questionnaire, usability observation, Visual Informatics.

1 Introduction

Recently, the development of communication technologies in the form of mobile technology and wireless technology has further provided the opportunity to introduce a new mode of learning into the education system. Mobile learning (m-learning) is a step forward in the development of electronic learning [1]. Generally, it is very important to ensure that the developed application benefit the users. Same goes to the m-learning application in which the usable application will be very beneficial to the students in conducting the daily learning activities in much smoother. Previously, an m-learning course content application as a revision tool namely Mobile System Analysis & Design (SAD) has been developed [2]. It was developed for one topic in System Analysis & Design (SAD) course which is Project Initiation. The topic is being taught to second year students of Universiti Teknologi PETRONAS (UTP)

H. Badioze Zaman et al. (Eds.): IVIC 2011, Part II, LNCS 7067, pp. 23–32, 2011.

Business & Information System programme. Therefore, the objective of this study is to conduct a usability evaluation to assess the usability level of the developed application. The evaluation is also will only focus on the content, structure and navigation of the application. This study is limited to the case study in UTP.

The paper is organized as follows: Section 2 presents the literature studies that discussed on the usability issues on mobile human-computer interaction (HCI). In Section 3, the methodologies of the usability test for the developed m-learning application will be explained. Section 4 illustrates the results and discussions of the tests and finally, the whole contents of this paper will be concluded in section 5.

2 Literature Study

The mobile devices' user interfaces are often simple, but every developer comes out with the different interfaces. Current thinking suggests that elements of user-centered and usage context in m-learning will lead to the better usability level of m-learning applications. User-centered design means specifying the different usage contexts and the different users' requirements which include the instructors and the learners [3].

Another approach to improve the m-learning usability is to make the user interface or content adaptable to the learners. Making learning content valuable to the target users in a given context, as suggested in the MOBIlearn guideline [4], is one way of adapting to the user. The understanding of mobile user interface limitations is vital. The limitations include small screens, limited input methods and limited battery life. Because of that, the developers need to design the user interface that meet the user's requirements without putting much complexity, slow processing and large amount of power consumption [5]. All mobile phones' limitations should be considered in developing the m-learning application. The mobile usability aspects that need to be focused in designing m-learning application are including content, natural usage, navigation, consistency and flexibility.

2.1 Content

In term of the m-learning content, it is advisable for the developers to organize the content in chunks or by parts. By managing the contents in chunks, it can minimize the cognitive load of the users [6]. Usually, smaller screens will slow down the reading speed by disrupting the eye movements' normal pattern [7]. By designing the contents into parts, it can minimize the long texts to be put in one page screen and it will ease the users in reading the contents of the application. It also advised to find the best mechanisms in providing the learners the way to go through the content and move to the preferred page whenever learners click on it [7].

Besides that, it is also necessary to avoid unneeded or unnecessary information to be put in the contents [5]. Basically, the unnecessary information will make the novice users confuse in finding the important point of the contents. Furthermore, it will also slow down the experts' learning pace [8]. Hence, it is advised to the developer to implement less is more rules in ensuring the contents accurate and solid [7-9].

2.2 Natural Usage

The developed m-learning application must always be user friendly to the users. User-friendliness can be measured when the users just need few minutes to understand how the application works [9]. In other words, when users are executing the application, they should be able to understand or become familiar with the application in only few seconds and they should know what is going to happen if certain actions are done. For example, users will always know if the "Exit" command is clicked, the application will either be closed or exit to the main page of the application. Thus, it is advisable for the developers to use the usual set of commands in the application so that users or learners are already aware of what is going to happen when the commands are clicked. The user friendliness is very important for the users in ensuring the focus is more to the contents learning rather than studying how the application operated.

2.3 Navigation

Navigation is a mechanism that is developed in helping the users move from a page or section to the desired pages or sections. In term of navigation, it is advised to avoid from using the complex navigation [6]. Complex navigation will give difficulties to the users in accessing the application. Besides, navigation must always be consistent at every page of the application [6, 8]. Buchanan et al. [10] found that consistent navigation will maintain the learner's pace and retaining users' learning interest, and it can also minimize the number of keystrokes in performing a task.

Donnelly and Walsh [6] also gave the advice for navigation aspect whereby the designed application should avoid the users from scrolling frequently. Generally, by implementing scrolling mechanism into the mobile application will slow down the time for users in accessing and reading the content. Users need to scroll many times in the reading period and sometimes users need to scroll slowly to find only one key point from the contents. It will really reduce the users' learning speed. Therefore, it is advisable to find other mechanism in replacing the scrolling mechanism.

2.4 Consistency

Consistency is the most basic characteristic in usability interface design principles [11]. In ensuring the consistency of the application, similar information and action need to be inserted in the similar position. Basically, consistency of the application will enhance the user friendliness of the application. It happens when the users already know that every page provides similar sets of actions. Because of that, the users can access the application from any pages or sections easily. Users need lesser time in studying the application and the focus can be used more on studying prepared learning content.

2.5 Flexibility

Flexible actions can help the users in navigating the application. Some applications provided several actions that perform the similar tasks. It is to give the users more than one method or way in accessing the application. Donnelly and Walsh [6] defined flexibility as preparing the alternative displays to perform the same function and that additional displays can work as the shortcut functions. For example, m-learning application provides the main menu list for the users to choose the section that need to be studied. After studying that section, users need to exit to main menu list and choose another section, and then users can continue the study. By inserting the shortcut menu list in each section, it will help the users in navigating to the desired section without exiting to the main menu list. Besides, it is also can minimize keystrokes in performing one task.

In m-learning course content development, all principles that were identified above will be adopted in producing a usable application for the users.

3 Methodology

In conducting this study, there are two methods that have been used which are questionnaire and observation. Both methods are used to measure the usability level of the developed prototype, MOSAD.

3.1 Usability Questionnaire

Usability questionnaire was conducted in getting the usability data from the end users. The data will show whether the MOSAD prototype is usable to them or not. The questionnaire was adopted from Purdue Usability Test [12]. The survey questionnaire was distributed to sixty-six second year students from SAD course. In the questionnaire, there are five usability factors involved. The factors include consistency, flexibility, learnability or user friendly, minimal action and user's memory load. In each aspect, there are five questions presented. The users need to rate each question using a Likert scale from 1 to 5 (1=strongly disagree, 2=disagree, 3=neutral, 4=agree, 5=strongly agree). Once the data was gathered, it has been analyzed in order to see the MOSAD prototype usability level.

3.2 Usability Observation

Usability observation was conducted to get the data that supports the usability questionnaire result data. The observation was conducted to twelve students from second year SAD course. The chosen number of test participants is more than reliable according to [13] in which five testers are enough to conduct usability test. It is a quantitative method in which it measures the steps of actions and time taken by the users in performing the given tasks using the MOSAD prototype. All tasks performed by the students have been recorded. The parameters that have been measured include:

- Time taken to understand how the MOSAD application works.
- Time taken to complete the revision using MOSAD application.
- Number of key-presses used to move from page to other page.
- Number of key-presses used to move from section to other section.
- Number of key-presses to exit from the section.
- Frequencies of using shortcut key to move from section to other section.
- Frequencies of using main menu list to move from section to other section.

The details of all identified parameters will be explained in the next section. The value of each parameter has been measured by taking the average from twelve students. Finally, the observation and questionnaire usability data has been compared to proof that both data are match each other in terms of usability.

4 Results and Analysis

As mentioned in previous section, the usability evaluation for MOSAD application will be on the consistency, learnability, minimal action, minimal memory load and flexibility, which have been used to test the capability of the application as a revision tool for the students.

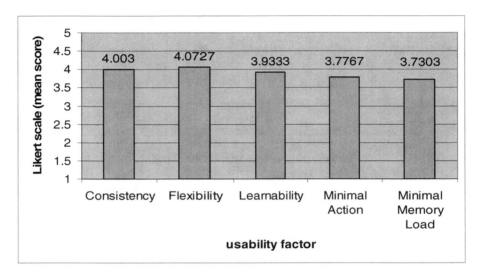

Fig. 1. Mean of Tested Usability Factors

As shown in Figure 1, the feedbacks from the usability test conducted to the users have shown that the flexibility factor has gained the highest mean score (4.0727) when compared to the other four factors. Flexibility was measured based on the use of several mechanisms in performing similar tasks. The second highest mean score is consistency whereby the mean is 4.003. This means that the students find that the developed application implemented the same displays at every page of the application. Whereas, the mean score for learnability factor is 3.933, which indicates that the application is fairly easy to operate. Besides, the mean score for the evaluation on the minimal action and minimal memory load factors are also considerably high which are 3.7667 and 3.7303 respectively. The results thus indicate that majority of the students agreed that the developed MOSAD application has met the requirement of usability elements as the revision tool.

In order to proof the reliability of usability questionnaire result, an observation method of usability study has been conducted. As stated before, there are five usability factors need to be measured which are consistency, flexibility, learnability, minimal action and minimal memory load. The observation method can only be conducted to three of the five factors which are flexibility, learnability and minimal action. Even though the consistency and minimal memory load factors cannot be measured using this method, the learnability factor is very much dependant to both factors and there are related to each other. As stated by Su et al. [14], the consistency of contents and displays of mobile application interfaces will make the mobile application users learn the operations of the application much faster. Hence, this parameter can be measured under learnability factor. Same goes to the minimal memory load factor whereby the elements include the short application, usage of short sentences, utilization of point form and different text colours and the images. All stated elements will improve the users' memory load [5-9]. In this case, learnability factor is also very much related to the minimal memory load factor in which the users will take shorter time to study the contents of the application since the application content provides all elements stated under the minimal memory load factor . Table 1 shows the results of elements covered in each factor.

Table 1. Results of Usability Observation

No	Usability Factor	Studied Element	Result
1	Flexibility	Frequencies of using shortcut key menu list to move from section to other section.	5.8333 ≈ 6 times
		Frequencies of using main menu list to move from section to other section.	3.1667 ≈ 3 times
2	Learnability	Time taken to understand how the application works.	1 minute 34 seconds
		Time taken to complete the revision using the application.	6 minutes 41 seconds
3	Minimal Action	Average number of key-presses to move from section to other section.	2.713 ≈ 3 key-presses
		Average number of key-presses to move from page to other page	1 key-press
		Average number of key-presses to exit from the section.	1 key-press

MOSAD application contains nine sections which include Objective, Introduction, System Request, Feasibility Analysis, Project Selection, Summary, Quiz, Reference and Help [2]. Figure 2 and Figure 3 illustrate the screenshot of each MOSAD application section. For flexibility factor, in average, the students used the shortcut key menu list to move from section to other section for six times as compared to the use of main menu list which only three times. This result shows that the users really use the prepared flexible function to navigate the application and it became the most preferable choice in easing them to move from section to the other section.

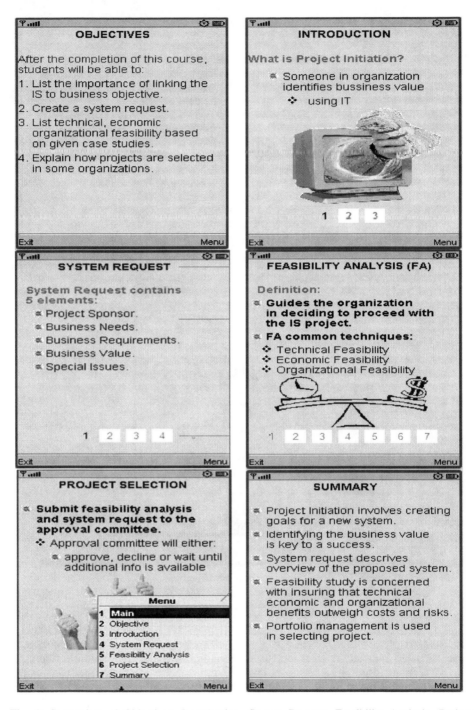

Fig. 2. Screenshot of Objectives, Introduction, System Request, Feasibility Analysis, Project Selection and Summary Sections of MOSAD Application

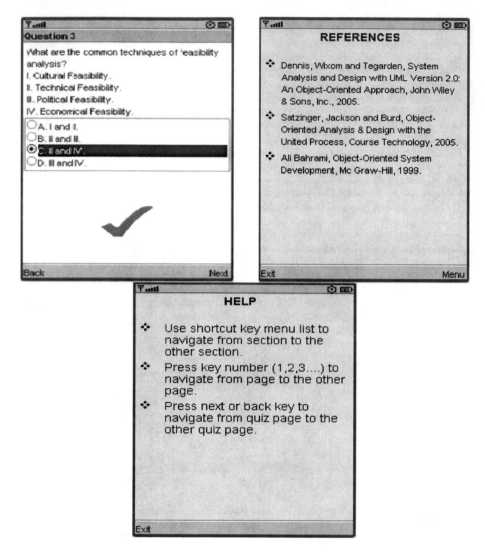

Fig. 3. Screenshot of Quiz, References and Help Sections of MOSAD Application

In terms of learnability, there are two elements that have been measured which are time taken to understand the application works and time taken to complete the revision using MOSAD application. The average time taken by the students to understand how the MOSAD application operates is 1 minute and 34 seconds, whereas the average time taken by the students to complete the revision using the application is 6 minutes and 41 seconds. Based on both times taken, it can be concluded that, the students just took few minutes to study on how the application works and to complete the revision as stated in [15-17], as compared to doing revision using other conventional methods. This scenario happened due to the utilization of the measured elements identified in the consistency and minimal memory load usability factors.

Finally, for minimal action usability factor, the average number of key-presses by the students to move from section to other section is almost three, whereas the average number of key-press to move from page to other page and to exit from the section is only one. According to Nielsen [11] and Sharp et al. [18], the usable and acceptable maximum number of keystrokes in performing one task in an application is three. Thus, the MOSAD application can be considered as usable in terms of key-presses since the average number of key-presses used by the students throughout using the application is less than three.

In conclusion, the presented results of usability observation have supported the validity of usability questionnaire results. Thus, it indicates that MOSAD application has met the requirement of mobile usability factors as a revision tool.

5 Conclusion

This paper has described the usability of the developed application namely MOSAD. The conducted usability questionnaire and observation have only limited to the case study in UTP specifically second year Business and Information students. Result of usability questionnaire shows that majority of the students agreed the developed application has met the requirement of usability elements as the revision tool. Meanwhile, it has been supported by the usability observation result. The overall results of this project proved that the m-learning course content application is usable and will be a useful tool to help students in doing revision as a preparation before facing the test or examination.

References

1. Hashim, A.S.: Study of Mobile Learning Course Content Application As A Revision Tool. In: Computer & Information Sciences Department, Universiti Teknologi PETRONAS (2011)
2. Hashim, A.S., Wan Ahmad, W.F., Ahmad, R.: Usability and Effectiveness of Mobile Learning Course Content Application as a Revision Tool. Computer Technology and Application 2(2), 149–158 (2011)
3. Pehkonen, M., Turunen, H.: Preliminary Guidelines for the Design Of The Mobile Learning Activities And Materials. In: EUROPRIX Scholars Conference. Mindtrek Association, Tampere (2003)
4. O'Malley, C., Vavoula, G., Glew, G.P., Taylor, J., Sharples, M., Lefrere, P.: Guidelines for Learning / Teaching / Tutoring in a Mobile Environment. In: Mobilearn Project Deliverable (2003)
5. Parsons, D., Ryu, H., Cranshaw, M.: A Design Requirement Framework of Mobile Learning Environments. Journal of Computers 2(4), 1–8 (2007)
6. Donnelly, K., Walsh, S.: Mobile Learning Reviewed (2009)
7. Kaikkonen, A., Laarni, J.: Designing for Small Display Screens. In: 2nd Nordic Conference on Human-Computer Interaction. Aarhus, Denmark (2002)
8. Uther, M.: Mobile Internet Usability: What Can The 'Mobile Learning' Learn From The Past? In: The IEEE International Workshop on Wireless and Mobile Technologies in Education, WMTE 2002 (2002)

9. Grasso, A., Roselli, T.: Guidelines for Designing and Developing Contents for Mobile Learning. In: IEEE International Workshop on Wireless and Mobile Technologies in Education (WMTE 2005). ACM Digital Library (2005)
10. Buchanan, G., Farrant, S., Jonnes, M., Thimbleby, H.: Improving Mobile Internet Usability. In: International Conference on the World Wide Web. ACM Press, Hong Kong (2001)
11. Nielsen, J.: Usability Engineering. Academic Press, Boston (1993)
12. Lin, H.X., Choong, Y.-Y., Salvendy, G.: A Proposed Index of Usability: A Method for Comparing the Relative Usability of Different Software Systems. Behaviour & Information Technology 16(4/5), 267–278 (1997)
13. Nielsen, J.: Why You Only Need to Test with 5 Users (2000), [cited 2010], http://www.useit.com/alertbox/20000319.html
14. Su, D.K.S., Yee, V.S.Y., Read, J.: Exploring Text-based and Graphical-based Usable Interfaces for Mobile Chat Systems. International Journal on Human-Computer Interaction 1(3), 37–53 (2007)
15. Colazzo, L., Molinari, A., Ronchetti, M., Trifonova, A.: Towards a Multi-Vendor Mobile Learning Management System. In: World Conference on E-Learning in Corporate, Government, Healthcare, and Higher Education, Chesapeake (2003)
16. Bevan, N.: International Standards for HCI and Usability. International Journal of Human Computer Studies 55(4), 533–552 (2001)
17. Collura, M.: Human-Computer Interaction and Main Principles to Design Practice Human-Centred System. In: Management and Industrial Engineering Department. Universita Della Calabria, Cosenza (2006)
18. Sharp, H., Rogers, Y., Preece, J.: Interaction Design, 2nd edn. John Wiley & Sons, Ltd. (2007)

Game Design Framework: A Pilot Study on Users' Perceptions

Ibrahim Ahmad[1] and Azizah Jaafar[2]

[1] Faculty of Communication and Information Technology,
Universiti Teknikal Malaysia Melaka, Durian Tunggal, Melaka
ibrahim@utem.edu.my
[2] Institute of Visual Informatics, Universiti Kebangsaan Malaysia, Bangi, Selangor
aj@ukm.edu.my

Abstract. Study on computer game design has a lot been carried out. Many researchers stated that the design of the computer game is able to influence users' emotions that play the game. This working paper tries to discuss on framework for the design of a computer game. Analyze and repossession that explained is the pilot study on respondent view on the type of game design that they wanted.

Keywords: Game Design, User Centered Game Design, Visual Informatics.

1 Introduction

Computer game production has begun more than four decades ago with first computer game production that named Spacewar [1]. Nowadays, more digital game provides more interactive experience that are enjoyable and not boring. Study related to user experience plays computer game was being conducted especially in the area of science and technology (as in human-computer interaction's study, psychology field and entertainment computer), social science (such as media psychology, psycho-sociology and communication science).[2]

Computer game is an example of application system that need to provide idea environment for the purpose of the study in artificial intelligence because they used complex simulation and world various agent that dynamic [3,4,5] Furthermore, computer game reputedly offers a basis to cognitive model that is fixed in interactive form. [5]

Computer game also urged to new challenge in studies to various scientific discipline – either existing or emerging. Likely in year 1944, Neumann and Morgenstern are the first researcher that try to discuss on game scientifically in basic mathematical as one science economic.[2] After over the a half centuries old, [6] together with the other researcher friends endeavoured to understand basis of computer game in literature theory. [2,6]

Study on design and computer game application development has a lot been carried out. However, study related to the basic design of computer game development is getting less response. This due to it needs perusal on social aspect, emotion and the association with human life.

When designer wish to use method or technique that fit to design computer game that is associated with human social will, they have space limitations to succeed. They lack of suitable method and technique to develop user centered design that complex apart from doing test and assessment [7,8].

H. Badioze Zaman et al. (Eds.): IVIC 2011, Part II, LNCS 7067, pp. 33–38, 2011.

Computer game is designed so that it could be read, watched, heard but it could also be manipulated with designer includes expectation or without expectation. This is known as human interaction and media. No man need interaction with hardware or software what more interaction with paper, they wish to interact with what is presented on screen with message or order that easy and medium. [9].

A few design models that can be made as foundation to plan computer game is like that are suggested [10]. They conducted survey to 10 years old students in Scotland which used computer game as a learning tool showed themselves as more motivated and enthusiastic in learning something. Their study focused more on computer game design that was developed with prospect in education which followed.

2 Research Methodology

Methodology that is used in this study is the design model that can be found in User Centered Game Design model (UCGD).

In this model, process in designing the game involves the three major phase development namely conceptualization construction, prototyping and playtesting. [11]

From three phases that mentioned [11] just now, [12], explained the process to develop a computer game in UCGD will become

- Particular application
- Ability in method play
- Effects in games

Based on that phases, [12] added another phase in game development process use UCGD contains another extra development phase that received as process in designing a computer game seriously. It is named as observational study phase. Figure 1.1 show model for UCGD.

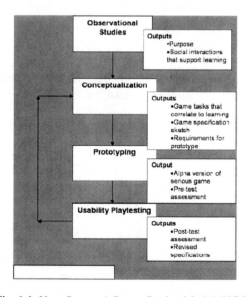

Fig. 1.1. User Centered Games Design Model (UCGD)

In computer game design UCGD model, in game conception phased designer produces game specification which showed beginning for feeling 'look and feel' in game interface provision that produced, identify behavior system for interaction rules and procedure for playing and controlling the game to users in steering virtual world game. [11,13].

[12][14] state that there are a few similarity between UCGD and human-centered game design, A major similarity is both of them begun with the observational phase. However, there is a subtle different between of them which is UCGD observes social interaction associated with game play to identify and leverage the social interaction that support acquisition and application of knowledge.

3 Analysis and Finding

This section discusses on respondent view based on construct needed. There are three constructs that are studied in determine design needed by users before the development process. Those three constructs are information design: Game Strategy, Interface design: Presentation and interaction Design: Computer Game Structure.

In this study, to every mean determination item are predicated to likert scale five whereas value 1 (lowest value) show very respondent disapproved by statement that given and value 5 (highest value) show very respondent agreeing with statement. This means mean value that diperolhi exceeding from value 3 show respondent face the music that prepared

Table 1 show mean value that is achieved as a result of questionnaire conducted for information design construct feedback: Game Strategy. Statement begun with "I like use computer game application that" followed by statement that displayed in the table.

Table 1. Information design : Game Strategy

No	Statement	Means
1	provide story line and situation which challenges thinking such as activity fight, exploration, musing in decide passageway and so on.	4.07
2	Role Playing Games (RPG) genre which provides characters (character) that representing me in that game	3.80
3	provided many character choice or tools that can be used during exploration	4.33
4	provide game level according to easy level, medium and hard in that game.	4.20
5	provide letters that foolproof in keyboard which represents direction of motion and character control such as A, S, D Z and X that the position is near to one another.	4.40
6	may delegate myself in that game such as when I scowl, I can choose tools or character suitably with my emotion.	3.80
7	I express my feelings when I interact with anything that have in game story line.	3.47
8	were capable for me to think creatively and critically in solving problem.	4.13
9	give freedom to determine and choose my own exploration route.	4.00
10	provide facilities that enable me arrange and organized information	4.00

Mean value that attained from this construct shows mean value that more than 4.00 and one of their game design types that they prefer is the one that could make they think creatively and critically in solving problem.

Table 2 show mean value that is attained as a result of the questionnaire that has been carried out to determine design that fit for interface construct design: Presentation. Statement begun with "I like to use computer game application that" followed by statement that displayed in the table.

Table 2. Interface design : Presentation

No	Statement	Means
1	use background colour that soft and harmony such as grey colour, baby blue and beige	3.33
2	use background colour that bright and aggressive such as red colour and yellow	3.33
3	provide access 'help' that easy to help me if I need information and help	4.27
4	It is started with game synopsis but there is 'skip' if I do not need it.	4.20
5	provide image map or route map as exploration route to facilitate me to choose which route easy to be followed.	4.33
6	provide character / hero in games that look great, attractive, and not boring	4.47
7	provide order that not boring and long-winded.	4.47
8	easy and attract and not fibrous with display that overwhelm perception	4.47
9	there is human capital values that nice on the interface display	4.33
10	can distinguish between a level with another level clearly such as simple level in clearing, moderate level in forest and hard level in valley that gap.	4.33

One of the computer game features that students like most is the one which is not boring especially with dangling order that can trouble users' head. Mean value which exceeded value 3.33 show student like simple design but attractive specifically in interface construct presentation.

Table 3 on the other hand show mean value that attained as a result of the questionnaire that has been carried out to determine design that fit for interface construct design: Computer Game Structure. Statement begun with "I like use computer game application that" followed by statement that displayed in the table.

Table 3. Interaction design : Computer Game Structure

No	Statement	Means
1	allow exploration process according to my need	3.93
2	provide more than one way / route to resolve that game	4.33
3	enable me to interact with character with easier and pleasant	4.00
4	Provide facility for me to save my high score in the system to know the score that I have achieved	4.53

5	provide 'life' that have been obtained easily to helps me continue the game	4.33
6	can be customized according to my own will in terms of background, costume, character and others	4.13
7	could save my data when playing that I can continue my game anytime that I want after I stop.	4.53
8	easy to move the game character easily such as running, jump and others	4.27
9	Provide time choice plays according 10 minutes, 30 minutes, 45 minutes or 60 minutes.	3.60
10	provide game structure that is not tangled narration road and the exploration.	4.33

One of the computer game design features that is preferred by the students is the one that could save users' information, score marks, some other data that can be used if they want to play the game again in other day or time.

4 Conclusions

Designing a computer game is not as easy as what is imagined. When a user tries to play a computer game, they often deny other people's work by giving comment that quite negative if the game that that they play do not have a story line that suit their soul.

This working paper explains students' perception in one of the local universities on game design that they like. Three constructs have been used to measure student's perception on game design that they want. For the overall finding, ever retrieval item that questioned give mean value that more than 3. This show that respondents accept statement that asked for producing a game design as they interest. Repossession indicated that most students like game that has many route choices to facilitate them to customize the game according to their own need. Such game design features help all computer game developer to produce a game that able to attract users' interest to use it. Hopefully, that can be used in producing a creative computer game.

References

1. Flemming, J.: Down the HyperSspatial Tube: Spacewar and The Birth of Digital Game culture, http://www.gamasutra.com (retrieved on April 13, 2010)
2. Nacke, L.E.: Affective Ludology Scientific Measurement of User Experience in Interactive Entertainment. PhD Thesis. Blekinge Institute of Technology (2009)
3. Champandard, A.J.: AI Game Game Development. New Riders Publishing (2004)
4. Laird, J.E., Van Lent, M.: Human-level AI's killer application: Interactive Computer Games. In: Proceedings of the Seventh National Conference on Artificial Intelligence (AAAI), pp. 1171–1178. AAAI Press (2000)
5. Yannakakis: Entertainment Capture Through Heart Rate Activity in Physical Interactive Playground. User Modeling and User-Adapted Interaction 18(1-2), 207–243 (2008)

6. Aarseth, E.: Computer game studies, year one. Game Studies—The International Journal of Computer Game Research 1(1) (2001),
    http://gamestudies.org/0101/editorial.html
7. Neilsen, et al.: Visual Congnition and multimedia artifact. In: Danielsen, O., Nilsen, J., Holm-Sorensen (eds.) Learning and Narrativity in Digital Media (2003)
8. Karat, J., Karat, C.M.: The evolution of user-centered focus in human-computer interaction field. IBM Systems Journal 42(4), 532–554 (2003)
9. Thom, G.: Digital Storytelling and Computer Game Design. Tutorial Paper in CHI 1997 (1997)
10. Robertson, J., Howells, C.: Computer game design: Opportunities for successful learning (2008), http://www.sciencedirect.com
11. Fullerton, et al.: Game Design Workshop: Designing, Prototyping and Playtesting Games. CMP Books (2004)
12. Rankin, Y.A., McNeal, M., Shute, M.W.: User-Centered Game Design:Evaluating Massive Multiplayer Online Role Playing Games for Secondary Language Acquisition. In: Sandbox Symposium, Los Angeles
13. Rucker, R.: Software Engineering and Computer Games. Addison-Wesley (2003)
14. Abeele, V.V., Husson, J., Vandeurzen, L., Desmet, S.: A soft approach to Computer Science: Designing and Developing Computer Game for and with Senior Citizens. Journal of Game Development 2, 41–62 (2007)

The Development of History Educational Game as a Revision Tool for Malaysia School Education

A.A.R. Hadi, Wan Mohd Fazdli Wan Daud, and Nurul Huda Ibrahim

School of Multimedia Technology & Communication, UUM College of Arts & Sciences,
Universiti Utara Malaysia, 06010 UUM Sintok, Kedah, Malaysia
{ahadiar,nurul}@uum.edu.my,
onefazdli@yahoo.com

Abstract. Computer game has indisputably become a culture especially among teenagers even in Malaysian community. Through the use of broadband and civilizing of IT usage, teenagers have now been exposed to computer game since at young age. A decade ago, computer game was perceived as only a medium for students to seek pleasure without giving any benefit to them. Recently, various attempts have been arranged to enable computer game to be incorporated into classroom to make learning experience more interesting and enjoyable. As a result, an educational computer game prototype has been developed for the purpose of meeting these requirements. The prototype, which is dedicated for the history subject for Malaysia secondary school, mainly serves as a revision tool for the student. MUDPY model has been employed as the main methodology for the project. The prototype was tested using the black box test to ensure the functionality and PUEU test for the effectiveness. This paper exposes the techniques used for development and the findings resulted from the tests conducted.

Keywords: educational games, history educational game, game prototype, and revision tools, Visual Informatics.

1 Introduction

The most crucial task in learning history subject is to overcome the boring phenomenon among students. Curriculum Development Division reported that history subject is known as a 'dead' and boring subject [2]. Normally, the society assumed that history subject lacks the commercial value. Students also don't show much interest in learning the subject because they assume the history subject is dull and they have to memorize and understand all the facts, concept, time and historical events [14]. Nevertheless, history subject in Malaysia is a core subject in the Kurikulum Bersepadu Sekolah Menengah (KBSM) and must be well educated by all students on an ongoing basis for five years. Thus, the history curriculum was arranged to have continuity from Junior Secondary Schools (SMR) until Senior Secondary Schools (SMA) so that the foundations of knowledge, values, skills and experience gained can be strengthened and developed further [4].

H. Badioze Zaman et al. (Eds.): IVIC 2011, Part II, LNCS 7067, pp. 39–49, 2011.

70.6 % students admitted that the main problem in learning history is the difficulty to memorize historical fact [11]. At the same time, 44.5% student has no interest in history because of teaching media such as dreary textbooks. Another 15.8 % student claimed that they are discouraged due to teachers' unexciting teaching method. Meanwhile lack of teaching aid/material used by the teacher contributed 16.5% of student negative perception in history learning. Student did not get clear description about historical events and cannot understand history context. Deficiency of history references also contributes to the existing problem.

In order to overcome the boring phenomenon, we developed an educational game prototype to integrate fun in history learning. The prototype can be used as teaching aid in class or as a revision tool at home. With the right development and use, an educational game could be a great tool in education [13]. Another study found that game has attractive elements, which include motivation and engagement [3]. Computer game can be exciting, fast paced, appealing, compelling and rewarding compared to classroom-based strategies and it provides an ideal learning environment for students [17].

The educational game prototype represents the history about Japanese invasion on Malaya as in the form 3-history syllabus of SMA. Realizing the positive impacts that educational game may has towards learning history in school, this paper will highlight the development phase in building the educational games prototype to enhance the learning process.

2   Related Research on Educational Game

Game is based on the concept of fun [13] and is a free activity, outside ordinary life, with no profit [18]. It has rules and a defined way of progressing. It may possess social groupings that cloak themselves in secrecy to stress their difference from the common world. Game may create a make-believe element [5] and it is an activity that is executed only for pleasure and without conscious purpose [10].

An educational game, one designed for learning, is a subset of both play and fun. It is a melding of educational content, learning principles, and computer games [13]. An educational game is combining the element of joy and learns in a playable situation. Serious game that is synonym with educational game can be defined as a mental contest, played with computer in accordance with specific rules that use entertainment to further government or corporate training, education, health, public policy and strategic communication objectives [18]. It is called serious game because it is used in a pedagogical way for political, social, marketing, economical, environmental or humanitarian purposes [1]. Serious game has not just a story, art, and software, but also involves pedagogy: activities that educate or instruct, thereby imparting knowledge or skill [18].

Although there are opinions saying game leads kids into violent, but the effectiveness of educational game can't be denied [9]. Many researchers have come out with results that show the positive sides of gaming in education. Game may provide limited superficial information and is not enough to satisfy young people's educational needs, but it may be enough for them to get a grasp on it and that in more overtly educational settings the role of teachers, peers and other supporting materials will be necessary to build on these superficial understandings [7]. Game is effective; not because of what it is, but because of what it embodies and what learners are doing as they play a game. Table 1 shows a portion of recent works by selected researchers . Based on the given evidence, we conclude that game can be effective for educational purposes and learning process becomes more interactive and enjoyable.

Table 1. An Overview of the Studies Related with Effectiveness in using Computer Games in Education [6][7]

Author(s)	Year	Genre	N	Subject	Results
Noble et al.	2000	Action	101	Drug education	Students taught through video games find the experience motivating and want to play the video game again.
Din Feng & Caleo	2000	–	47	Spelling and math	Children who play video games learn (mostly in spelling) better compared to peers who do not use video games.
Turnin et al.	2000	–	2000	Eating habits	Video games can teach students about eating habits and lead to significant change in everyday habits.
Lieberman	2001	Action		Asthma, diabetes,	A review of a number of research projects supports the notion of learning from video games.
Becker	2001	Action	–	Programing	The study testifies to the increased motivation in connection with video games. Games are found to be more effective and motivating than traditional teaching.
McFarlane et al.	2002	–	–	All subjects	The study finds that teachers in general are skeptical towards the learning of content with video games. However, teachers appreciate the learning of general skills.
Gander	2002	Strategy	29	Programing	The study finds that video games are especially effective for teaching specific knowledge.
Rosas et al.	2003	Action	1274	Reading and math	Video games increase motivation, and there is a transfer of competence in technology from using the video game.
Squire et al.	2004	Simulation	96	Physics	Students using the simulation game performed better compared to the control group.
Egenfeldt-Nielsen	2005	Strategy	72	History	Students initially learn the same in history when using video games but have better retention.
Buch & Egenfeldt-Nielsen	2006	RPG	72	Social Studies	60% students on self-assessment found they learned more with Global Conflicts: Palestine than a traditional course. Almost 40% that it was around the same.

3 Educational Game Prototypes: History of Japanese Occupation in Malaya

Development is an important phase in any project lifecycle. This phase determine wheter we can answer the problems that have been addressed in the ealier section. This project development phases are based on the Multimedia Design and Planning Pyramid (MUDPY) model [15]. An educational game prototype involves iterative process during development. The development process also comprises ideas taken from a wide range of fields, including marketing, pedagogy, digital technology, aesthetics, graphics, intellectual property law, and management.

MUDPY model consist of three phases; which are planning, design and production. There were several stages that we adopted in order to develop the prototype and these stages are shown in Figure 1.

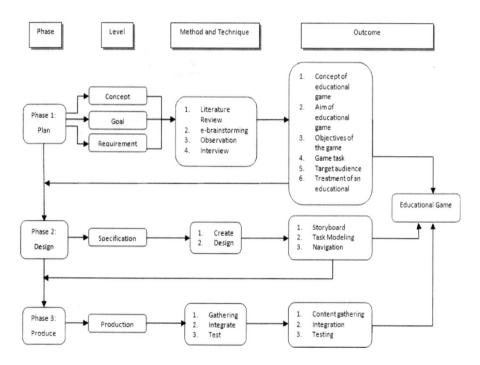

Fig. 1. The development cycle diagram

3.1 Phase 1: Plan

In this stage, concept, goal and requirement were gathered through literature reviews, e-brainstorming, observations and interviews. Based on literature review as explained in previous section, the concept of education game, previous reseacher works and education theories have been identified and integrated as the requirement for the development. Using e-brainstorming method, a set of questions related with educational game has been circulated through email to the teachers in order to gather some input for the development. Several history teachers were selected from all over the country for this reason. Observation was done in several school in Malaysia by sitting at the back of the classroom to experience the history learning process in the school. After the class end, we took several minutes to interview the teacher and selected students. The outcome was used to derive the concept, objectives, aim, task, target audience and game treatment.

e-Brainstorming. From the e-brainstorming, we found that the teachers had a problem with the student attention in the class. They confess that students are not interested in history because they had to memorize all the facts. Lack of teaching aids also contributed to the lack of students attention in the class. Teachers cannot find any good teaching aid to assist them in the class and they are willing to use any possible teaching aids if provided. They also state that multimedia teaching aids would be better compare to the other teaching aids because in the past multimedia was known to attract students attention.

Students perceptions on the teaching methods used had only worsen the current problem. They consider the methods to be outdated and traditional whereas they prefer modern teaching aids and technologies. With combination of better teaching methods and aids, a classroom can be a very conducive place to learn.

Interview. Based on the interview conducted in several schools, the findings are concluded into two parts as stated below.

Teachers. Teachers had good experience in history and teaching, but lack of students initiative to make early preparations was a major drawbacks to the teachers. Teachers also want students to make their own learning aids like mind maps, but students did not take serious action to the task. From the interview teacher also willing to use a new teaching aid like educational game in class to help the knowledge transfer between students and teachers.

Students. From the interview, we found that the most attractive part of learning in school is the way of knowledge being delivered in class. Students ready to learn in a conducive environment. They don't want a teacher that always gave them pressure to study and create unease feeling in the classroom. Students also like to learn something that have impact on their life. From the interview, we also found that students spends an average of 1.5 hours a day to play video game. Sports game is the most favorable game for them. Second most played game is a 3D first person shooter game.

Observation. Based on the observation that had been done, we have concluded that the history class in the school can be more fun by adding some interesting value into the teaching methods. Teachers always used chalk and blackboard as a major tools which is very unexciting. Students only write down the note without understanding the contents. Teacher also don't emphasis on the important facts.

Requirement Derived from Phase 1. In this phase, a set of requirement had been produced based on the information gathered through literature reviews, e-brainstorming, interviews and observation. The requirement list of the educational game prototype is shown in Table 2. This table includes the concept, aim, objectives, task, target audience and game treatment for the prototype development.

Table 2. Requirement for Educational Game Prototype

No	Subject	Outcome
1.	Concept	This educational game is about the invasion of Japanese army in Malaya. Student have to answer question to eliminate enemy and win the game. Mark will be given based on the right answer.
2.	Aim	To make the history learning experience as fun as possible and deliver knowledge at the same time.
3.	Objectives	After playing the game student can: 1. State the reasons for Japan's expanding power. 2. Describe the arrival of the Japanese to Malaya. 3. List the success factors of Japan dominates Malaya.
4.	Task	Student can walk in the game room and shoot the enemy to answer question (multimedia). Student can learn about the facts related to Japan invasion (learning)
5.	Target audience	Form 3 student in Malaysia Secondary School
6.	Game treatment	Game type is first person perspective. Game must have smooth look and high frame per seconds.

3.2 Phase 2: Design

This phase is also known as specification level [15]. In this phase, we designed the character, storyboard, task modelling and also navigations. Specifications for the prototype such as platform, hardware and software have also been identified. The chosen platform for this prototype development is a Windows base due to the student awareness in using Windows platform at home. Any computer using Intel Pentium 4 processor is suitable to run the prototype application. The memory should be 1MB or above and there should be a free space of 500 KB on the hard disk. The computer should be occupied with multimedia devices such as CD-ROM, speaker, monitor, keyboard and mouse.

Character Design. Character design was done through sketching process. Then, the sketches were transfered into a computer through a scanner. Manipulation of the characters was done through Adobe Photoshop. Characters were selected carefully to give an impact to the student while playing this game. The antagonist character was pictured as Japanese army, who invaded Malaya while the protogonist character was pictured as Malay army that secured the Malaya in that particular time.

Storyboard. After the character design, storyboard was created. This storyboard contains the storyline inside the game. The storyboard is a vital document in this game development. The storyboard will determine the flow and elements of the prototype and it becomes the guide for the researchers. The welcome screen was design with simple instructions to ensure students understanding and good performance while playing the game.

Figure 2 shows the screen when the player engages with an enemy. To enable the player to shoot the enemy, the player must answer a pop-up question as show in Figure 3. The player has to pick one correct answer. If the answer was correct then the player will get a bonus mark and if it was incorrect then the player will be given one more chance. If the answer was accurate on the second try, a normal score will be given but if the answer was inaccurate the cumulative score and health will be deducted. If the health value becomes zero after deductions, then the game will be over. The player has to encounter ten enemies and responds to ten questions for the game to be completed. Final score will be shown at the last stage when the game is completed or if the game is over.

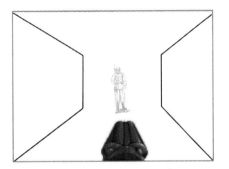

Fig. 2. Player engages with an enemy

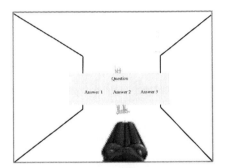

Fig. 3. A pop-up question

Task modelling. Task Modeling techniques provide the means to specify goal-oriented tasks [12]. It describes the window for required interfaces. Task modeling has some influence on the game composition and navigation. Figure 4 shows an example of a task flow for the game. The player must complete the current task in order to get to the next task. In this game prototype, the task is to answer the multiple-choice question. Player is given two chances to answer the question. After answering the question correctly, player can continue playing the game.

Game Navigation. Navigation outlines on how the pages in the game link together. There are several ways of navigation like linear, circular, network and tree structure. For this game prototype, linear navigation was used because there is no upper level. Player can end the game anytime by hitting the escape key. The structure of game navigation is shown in Figure 5.

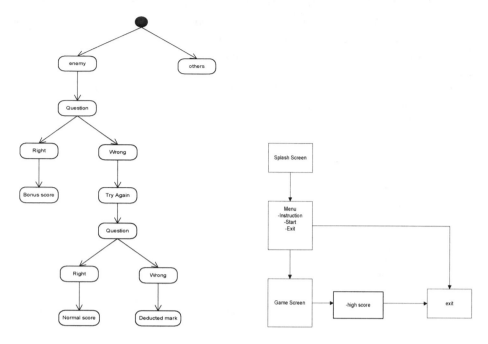

Fig. 4. Task Modeling   **Fig. 5.** Game Navigation

3.3   Phase 3: Produce

In this stage all the components are integrated together to produce a game to fullfill the objectives. The methods used are gathering, integrating and testing. The outcome of every phases are combined to produce the educational game prototype. Components like graphic, audio, animation, video and text are selected to ensure the product greatest functionality.

Content Gathering. The content of the game is gathered through various ways. Most of the content are gathered through the Internet and history textbook. Then the content is integrated together using Game Maker 8.0 software. Before the content can be implanted into the game maker software, some of them have to be built and edited.We used Adobe Photoshop editing software to edit pictures. After that, we integrated all items into the sprites and converted them as objects in the Game Maker 8.0 software. The content were blended properly in order to create useable prototype which meets the initial objectives.

Integration. Sprite is the main component inside Game Maker 8.0; where all the animations and the characters are placed. Sprite is created like an animation to make sure the movement of the character is as smooth as it can be. After that, the sprite was transformed into an object in which we can manipulate it's behavior and condition using some programming codes.

Proper background and wall were used to form the game border. This background and wall were the environments choosen to make sure the condition of the game was synchronized to the storyline. In this game, researchers had decided to used the jungle theme as the game was based on the war in the jungle area. Sound is added and integrated together into the Game Maker software. This sound is edited using Audacity Software and Sony Sound Forge.

In the Game Maker software there is a pane known as a room. Room is the place where all the resources is integrated together. Before the room can be used , we must drew a border through a wall and a background. The room is viewed from the top to make sure we know where was the placed to put the player, object, obstruction and enemies. Finally we were succeed in developing the game prototype. Two screen shots sample of the game interfaces can be viewed in Figure 6 and Figure 7.

Fig. 6. Screen shot of the educational game prototype

Fig. 7. Screen shot for the questions asked

Testing. Testing was done to ensure the prototype fulfilled the user needs and can perform the task properly. For this prototype, black box testing has been used for the functional system testing. Meanwhile for the usefulness of the system the Perceived Usefulness and Ease of Use (PUEU) test has been implemented. Black box testing has been piloted during the development for each phases. This test was rapidly conducted to make sure the prototype was working well and the development process was in the right track. After each test was completed, we made a few adjustments to meet the requirement of the prototype.

PUEU test was conducted at the end of development process, once the prototype was completely produced. A sample of twenty students was selected from various gender to participate in this survey. They were ask to fill up a questionnaire after playing the game prototype. Result of the test will determine whether the prototype had successfully satisfy the initial requirements. PUEU consists of twelve questions with seven scales from unlikely to likely.

To analyze the PUEU test, researchers carried out a descriptive analysis by using Microsoft Excel software. The questions were divided into two parts. The first part, question 1 to 6 related to the perceived of usefulness meanwhile the second part, question 7 to 12 related to the ease of use. Table 3 and 4 describe the results derived from the answered questionaires.

Table 3. Descriptive Analysis of Perceived Usefulness

	Question 1	Question 2	Question 3	Question 4	Question 5	Question 6
Mean	6.25	5.9	5.31	5.75	5.8	6.31
Standard Error	0.25	0.26	0.41	0.28	0.32	0.26
Median	7	6	6	6	6.5	7
Mode	7	7	6	7	7	7

Table 4. Descriptive Analysis of Ease of Use

	Question 7	Question 8	Question 9	Question 10	Question 11	Question 12
Mean	5.15	4.57	5.85	5.63	5.2	5.89
Standard Error	0.43	0.53	0.34	0.32	0.40	0.43
Median	5	6	6	6	6	7
Mode	7	7	7	7	6	7

From the result we can concluded that the average score from the prototype is around 4.5 to 6.3. This is because the users are unfamiliar with the game environment and new to the system. The median of every question is around five to seven. From the result we can conclude that this game will help paced the history revision and the system was easy to use in the process. We also include a few questions inside the questionaires to be fill up by the users. The questions are about the most negative and positive aspect of the game.

From the feedback, we found that the most negative aspect is the violent and the use of gun in the game and it's not really appreciated by the users. Meanwhile the most positive aspect is about the effectiveness of the game to help the users to revise the history subject. They can revise the subject quickly and much more fun compare to the conventional methods. With this feedback, we are confident that this game can make a contribution to help the student to do revision for history subject in school.

4 Conclusion

This prototype has been developed to achieve four main objectives. The first objective is to identify the requirements for an educational game. This objective has been attained by using several methods and techniques such as literature review, e-brainstorming, observation / interview and the requirements have been derived. The next objective of this project is to develop an educational game prototype to help the student to revise history subject. Based on the requirement identified earlier, the prototype has been developed using the Game Maker software and all the processed involved were discussed in this paper.

The third objective is to test the functionality of the educational game prototype. To accomplished this, we used the black box testing method to test the functionality of the educational game. The testing showed us that the educational game prototype is functional and ready to be used. The last objective of the study is to measure the usefulness and ease of use of the prototype. Using PUEU test, the result shows that this educational game has fulfilled the user requirement, easy to be use by the user and it is usefull to the student in learning.

References

1. Arvers, I.: Serious Game. The International Digital Art Magazine, 24–25 (2009)
2. Azwan, A., Abdul Ghani, A., Mohammad Zohir, A., Abd Rahman, A.A.: Kesan Efikasi Kendiri Guru Sejarah Terhadap Amalan Pengajaran berbantukan Teknologi Maklumatdan Komunikasi (ICT). Jurnal Penyelidikan Pendidikan 7, 15–24 (2005)
3. Baek, Y.K.: What Hinders Teachers in Using Computer and Video Games in Classroom? Exploring Factors Inhibiting the Uptake of Computer and Video Games. CyberPsychology & Behaviour 11, 665–671 (2008)
4. Bahagian Perkembangan Kurikulum. Huraian Sukatan Pelajaran KBSM Sejarah. Kuala Lumpur: Kementerian Pelajaran Malaysia (2002)
5. Caillois, R.: Man, play, and games. Glencoe, New York (1961)
6. Egenfeldnt-Nielsen, S.: Overview of Research on the Educational Use of Video Games. Digital Kompetanse: Nordic Journal of Digital Literacy (1), 184–213 (2006)
7. Egenfeldnt-Nielsen, S.: Third Generation Educational Use of Computer Games. Journal of Educational Multimedia and Hypermedia 16(3), 263–281 (2007)
8. Huizinga, J.: Homo Ludens. The Beacon Press, Boston (1955)
9. John, K.C., McFarlane, A.: Literature Review in Gaming and Learning. Futurelab, United Kingdom (2004)
10. Kramer, W.: What is a game, really? From The Games Journal (2000), http://www.thegamesjournal.com/articles/WhatIsaGame.shtml (retrieved November 24, 2010)
11. Nor Azan, M.Z., Wong, S.Y.: Game Based Learning Model for History Courseware: A Preliminary Analysis. In: International Symposium on Information Technology, ITSim 2008, pp. 1–8. Universiti Kebangsaan Malaysia, Kuala Lumpur (2008)
12. Paterno, F.: Human Computer Interaction With Mobile Devices. Springer, Pisa (2002)
13. Prensky, M.: Digital Game based Learning. McGraw Hill, New York (2001)
14. Rozita, N.M., Zaliza, M.D.: Increasing the Skill of Answer Essay Question for History Paper 2 SPM. In: Proceeding Education Research Seminar IPBA, pp. 106–113. Malaysia Examination Syndicate, Kuala Lumpur (2005)
15. Sharda, N.: Creating Meaningful Multimedia with the Multimedia Design and Planning Pyramid. In: The 10th International Multi-Media Modelling Conference, p. 370. Victoria University, Brisbane (2004)
16. Van Eck, R.: Digital game-based learning: It's not just the digital natives who are restless. Educause Review 41(2), 16–30 (2006)
17. Virvou, M., Katsinis, G., Manos, K.: Combining Software Games With Education: Evaluation of Its Educational Effectiveness. Educationai Technology & Society 8(2), 54–65 (2005)
18. Zyda, M.: From Visual Simulation to Virtual Reality to Games. IEEE Computer Journal 38(9), 25–32 (2005)

Ontology Construction Using Computational Linguistics for E-Learning

L. Jegatha Deborah[1], R. Baskaran[1], and A. Kannan[2]

[1] Department of Computer Science and Engineering, Anna University Chennai
blessedjeny@gmail.com, baaski@annauniv.edu
[2] Department of Information Science and Technology, Anna University Chennai
kannan@annauniv.edu

Abstract. The recent explosion in the usage of web services and information technologies had always led to the hot issue of interoperability among heterogeneous systems. Intelligent resources organization in such systems is closely coupled to the principles of Semantic (Intelligent) Web. One of the existing widespread applications of semantic web is Electronic learning (E-learning) service which is deemed to be "Education at all stages". The prerequisite of this semantic-driven resource management and content delivery in E-learning service has been facilitated by building Ontology thus playing a key role in managing and distributing the resources semantically. Out of the several challenging issues present in the construction of ontology, the problem of anaphora resolution (resolving pronouns) has a greater impact on the expressiveness of the constructed ontology. Anaphora resolution in the web documents with highly related sentences has obtained greater importance in the research area of semantic web. The crux contribution of the paper is to present a framework known as DEKA for constructing and visualizing ontology for the web documents based on Computational Linguistics (rule-based model). The paper also addresses the working of some of the automatic ontology construction methodologies. The experimental data sets taken from the web corpus have been found to produce promising results for the performance metrics.

Keywords: Semantic (Intelligent) Web, Web Services, E-learning, Ontology, Computational Linguistics, Anaphora Resolution.

1 Introduction

Semantic Web [1-3] is about managing resources (e.g. Web documents) intelligently especially in heterogeneous systems by describing the properties of the entities (terms) involved and the relationships among them. Such conceptual organization is facilitated by building ontology pertaining to a particular domain [4-5]. Domain ontology provides the contents, essential properties in them and the relationships among the terms present in the knowledge base and they have gained enormous popularity in the areas like semantic web, knowledge representation, knowledge management, information retrieval, information search, etc [10]. One of the major

H. Badioze Zaman et al. (Eds.): IVIC 2011, Part II, LNCS 7067, pp. 50–63, 2011.
© Springer-Verlag Berlin Heidelberg 2011

areas of research in retrieving the web information intelligently is the provision of learning course contents through online (E-learning) [13]. The main motivation to proceed with this work came from several existing educational ontology like EduOnto (An ontology for Educational resources), OntoEdu (Ontology-based Education Grid System for e-Learning), GeneOntology and OntoGeo [12]. The crux of the online learning course contents in an educational system (E-learning) in our input domain are very well represented using ontology. The main scope of building ontology in our work for the learning course contents (posted by an end-user or an instructor) is to organize them semantically and such semantic organization of several individual learning course contents can help in clustering the web documents (learning course contents) with respect to a particular educational domain.

There are several issues which are yet to be solved in ontology construction expressively which includes identifying relationships among terms, hierarchies and mode of visualization [10]. Traditional ontology building methodologies were text-based models and are then replaced by graph-based models in the past [11]. The existing models in ontology construction helped in representing several structural relationships among the terms which were depicted clearly, crisply and in an elegant manner. In the midst of such inventions, identifying and resolving the presence of anaphora and cataphora among the sentences pertained to a particular domain was a milestone to be achieved until 1998 [7-9]. Most of the earlier techniques failed when ontology had to be constructed and visualized for an abstract (web data corpus) with enormous number of related sentences. The existing methodologies presented in literature survey analysis lacked the property of resolving anaphora and cataphora and was found to be a great challenge. In our proposed framework DEKA (based on Computational Linguistics), the construction and visualization of domain ontology automatically for a large corpus is handled by propositional logic-based modeling of knowledge base from a computational perspective. DEKA framework in this paper addresses the problem of anaphora resolution specifically and presents a separate module for resolving intra-sentential and inter-sentential anaphors.

The paper is semantically organized as follows. Section 2 provides the working of the related literature analysis. Section 3 offers the proposed Computational Linguistics Propositional logic-based framework, DEKA for automatic domain ontology construction following the components depicted in the system architecture. Section 4 presents the experimental results evaluation of several web data corpuses and performs a comparative study. Section 5 precisely concludes with the future scope of the work in progress. The paper ends with a list of some of the references.

2 Related Literature Analysis

Building domain ontology for web learning contents from scratch usually satisfies the property of reusability [18]. The constructed ontology could be stored in the ontology library for future references. Ontology construction is an iterative process which normally begins with the initial phase of deciding the domain and the scope. The major phases of the ontology construction has several stages which includes selection of the domain and scope, spotting the important terms, defining classes and class hierarchy, analyzing the properties of classes and creating instances for the classes and considering the property of reuse [4]. The ontology modeling tools have a clear separation between the 'model' part and the 'view' part. The model part designs the hierarchical relationships among the terms and the view part is for visualizing the hierarchy. Several ontology specification languages for building ontology are prevalent and Web Ontology Language (OWL) based on Resource Description Framework (RDF) is the most widely accepted one for representing and sharing knowledge in the semantic web context earlier [5]. However, in the later stages OWL specification language was replaced by XML Path expressions. Linguistics annotation is accessed through an XML-based exchange format. The following section presents an overview of several ontology building tool editors which help in acquiring, organizing and visualizing the domain knowledge intelligently. The surveyed tools are useful for building sometimes for ontology schemas or together with the instances of schema.

2.1 Text-To-Onto

The problem of engineering large and adequate ontology's within short time frames in order to keep costs low had always been a demand. TEXT-TO-ONTO Ontology Learning Environment is a basic learning environment for discovering conceptual structures and engineering ontologies from text [18]. This environment helps in the acquisition of conceptual structures as mapping linguistic resources to the acquired structures. TEXT-TO-ONTO exploits the interacting constraints on the various language levels in order to discover new concepts and stipulate relationships between concepts. The system follows a balanced cooperation approach described in [4], i.e. each modeling task can be done by the user or by a learning tool of the system. This balanced interaction of system and user contributes to the preparation of background knowledge, enhancing the domain knowledge (ontology) and to inspecting the learned knowledge.   The Ontology Engineering Environment ONTOEDIT, which is a submodule of the Ontology Learning Environment TEXT-TO-ONTO supports the ontology engineer in semi-automatically adding newly discovered conceptual structures to the ontology. OntoEdit internally stores modeled ontologies using an XML serialization. The core idea of this approach is to support the knowledge engineer using a balanced cooperative modeling paradigm. The limitation of the system is that the system does not consider a fully automatic ontology acquisition from the natural text and the knowledge engineer is supported with visualization interfaces of conceptual structures.

2.2 TextOntoEx

Most of the existing ontology construction tools fail to support the construction of domain relations and non-taxonomic conceptual relationships. A semantic pattern-based framework TextOntoEx constructs ontology from natural domain text [20]. TextOntoEx analyses natural domain text to extract candidate relations and then maps them into meaning representation to facilitate constructing ontology acting as a chain between linguistic analysis and ontological engineering. TextOntoEx does not discover new relation but discovers instances of known relation. The three main modules in the system are constructing semantic patterns using pattern editor, selecting domain natural text and extracting domain ontology from natural text. Initially, a set of patterns is constructed that describes a particular domain relation between two or more concepts. This is done for assembling the library. The matched process is very simple and easy after including the ontological classes on the converted text. The experimental data was tested against many levels of validation which is also taken for comparison in our framework. The performance metrics had a good level of measure with the precision ratio of 100% and a recall ratio of 54%. The unmatched patterns will be exhibited if there were null semantic patterns obtained from the pattern editor.

2.3 OntoLT

The system provided an integrated environment for the integration of linguistic analysis in ontology engineering through the definition of matching rules. OntoLT is protégé plug-in for Ontology extraction from the text based on linguistic analysis [19]. OntoLT provides a precondition language (implemented as XPATH expressions) with which the user can define some mapping rules. The major strengths of OntoLT plug-in environment is automatic linguistic analysis and annotation, automatic statistical preprocessing of extracted linguistic entities and automatic integration of validated class and slot candidates into an existing or a new ontology. The key limitations of the system are that it lacked the integration of linguistic annotation over a web service and integration of an information extraction approach for ontology population viz. identifying and inclusion of class instances.

3   DEKA - Computational Linguistics Propositional Logic-Based Ontology Construction (Proposed Framework)

Computational Linguistics is considered to be a sub-field of Artificial Intelligence and is a field of study devoted to develop algorithms and software for intelligently processing natural language data. The text data present in the natural language should be carefully organized such that information extraction/retrieval could be done intelligently. For the purpose of such semantic organization, a framework for fully automatic domain ontology construction is proposed which is based on Computational Linguistics. DEKA is based on XML Path expressions. The input text is preprocessed and the output is written in an XML file for further processing of the text in ontology construction. DEKA framework constitutes the following modules acting dependently on each other for ontology construction and visualization. The modules are elaborated as

1. Split Sentences   2. Parse Sentences
3. Resolve Anaphora   4. Recovering Ontological Relationships
5. Visualizing Ontology

The complete framework of the system is shown below

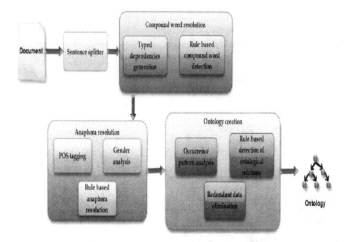

Fig. 1. System Architecture

3.1 Split Sentences

The learning course content for an E-learning domain is posted to an E-learning service provider by the end-user (student or instructor). The contents are posted as a text document. This raw document has to be pre-processed before ontology construction. The statements in the text document are split as individual sentences using Sentence Splitter Tagger which analyzes the stop points using the parser [22]. The output of this module is the individual sentences to be considered for further processing. Each of the individual sentences is given as an input to the next module of Parsing. These stages are considered to be pre-processing stages.

```
Algorithm: Sentence Splitter
Input: Text document (unprocessed)
Output: Individual sentence
Procedure
Begin
do
input the text file document to the parser
document content are split using stop points
while (end of document)
end
```

3.2 Parse Sentences

The document is now ready to be pre-processed completely. The next stage is to provide the document to the parser module. DEKA uses the standard Stanford Parser for parsing the document [22-24]. But the input text from the web corpus is also found to work well on FDG parsers, Charnaik parsers too. The parser generates the parse tree. This parse tree is given as an input to the typed dependencies generator module of the Stanford Parser. The complete typed dependencies of the document is generated and stored in the XML file [23]. The compound words are identified from this document. Once the compound words are identified the other words are lemmatized to resolve the root words by the process of lemmatization [16]. On successfully finding the compound nouns and root words by the process of lemmatization, the entire document is now cleaned by removing the existing prepositional dependencies like det, auxpass, advmod, advcl, rel, expl, prt, mark. These tags mainly give relation between articles and the words and hence could be removed explicitly. These compound words and the root words are replaced in the original document. The complete document is again parsed to get the new typed dependencies for further refinement.

```
Algorithm: Parsing
Input: Set of statements S in Pre-processed Text
Document P, Set of  CompoundWord
             Identification Rules, CWIR
Input Rule 1: If a noun is followed by another noun it
is a compound noun
Input Rule 2: If an adjective is followed by a noun it
is a compound noun
Output: Set of Cleaned Lexical Semantic representation C
Procedure:
Begin
CW is set of Compound Words
For each statement S_i in S do
C_i ← Stanford Parser(S_i)
For each rule CWIRj in CWIR
   CW_{new}+=ApplyRule(CWIR_j,C_i)
i←i+1
  End
  For each statement S_i in S do
    For each word cw_{new} in CW
    If  cw_{new} exists in S_i
      S_i ← Replace(cw_{old},cw_{new})
    End End return C_i    End
```

3.3 Resolve Anaphora

In linguistics, anaphora is an instance of an expression referring to another. The process of anaphora resolution is the problem of resolving what a pronoun or a noun phrase refers to that is previously defined in the complete text document. In other words, the referential entity is called as an anaphor and the entity to which it refers to previously is called an antecedent. The process of determining the antecedent of the anaphor is called as Anaphora Resolution. Anaphora resolution is a complicated problem in computational linguistics and is an active area of research. The existence of several anaphor in the document has a great impact in the construction of correct ontology. Several types of anaphora are exists which includes pronominal anaphora, definite noun-phrase anaphora and One-anaphora [7]. DEKA framework consists of a module "Anaphora Resolution" which concentrates on three categories of nouns which pertain to the gender, person and grammar number resolution of the text. The procedure could find he/she/it and who/where types of words for the replacement of nouns.

```
Algorithm: Anaphora Resolution
Input: Text document (processed - individual sentences)
Output: Resolved Anaphors
Procedure
Begin
Do
{
  Provide identifiers for each sentences,   S₁,S₂,…,Sₙ
   // Anaphora Resolution for he/she/it kind of words
  If there exists word Wᵢ in sentence Sₖ such that
Personal-Pronoun(Wᵢ) is true then
           If there exists word Wⱼ in Sentence Sₖ₋₁ such that
Noun(Wⱼ) is true then
                   Wᵢ is anaphora of Wⱼ
  Else
       Display message "Unknown Phrase"
   // Anaphora Resolution for who/where kind of words
 If there exists word Wᵢ in sentence Sₖ such that POS(Wᵢ)
                                           ="WH" then
   If there exists word Wⱼ in Sentence Sₖ such that
Noun(Wⱼ) is true and Gender(Wᵢ)= Gender(Wⱼ) then
       Wᵢ refers to Wⱼ
  else
       Display message "Unknown Phrase"
}
While (end of document)
End
```

3.4   Recovering Ontological Relationships

The output document obtained from the previous stage is present as lexical semantic representation. The exact hierarchy for the ontology construction is designed in this phase. The relationships among the terms are to be resolved for the generation of ontology. The first-order logic implementation is used in order to write the facts and rules to be applied on the document. From the typed dependencies the prolog facts are obtained. The nouns and verbs from the documents are identified in order to find the relationships using rule-based approaches. The basic facts and rules are applied on these prolog facts. The query processor runs and finds the different kinds of structural relationships among the terms in the document. The results obtained are cleaned and the following six types of structural relationships are obtained [21]. They are categorized as

1. Aggregation relationship (partOf)

2. Attribute relationship (attributeOf)

3. Property relationship (propertyOf)

4. Generalization/specialization relationship (isA)

5. Equivalence relationship (sameAs)

6. Association relationship (associatedWith)

Once these structural relationships are identified, the connectives among the terms could be easily resolved and viewed [21]. The algorithmic steps are given below

```
Algorithm: Ontological Relationships
Input: XML file with typed dependencies
Output: Prolog file with facts and generated
ontological relationships
Procedure
Begin
    Obtain prolog facts from the typed dependencies
    Knowledge base (facts and rules) is written using
      first-order logic extraction rules written in
      sec 3.4.1
    Query processor identifies the six kinds of
      relationships
End
```

3.4.1 Extraction Rules
RULE 1 & 2 – *Object & Relationship*: If x is a noun, then x is an object. If r is a verb, then r is a relationship.

Rule 3 - *Aggregation*: Let r be a special verb relation (e.g., part of, belong to or subdivision of). If a noun x participates in object y with r, then object x is a part of object y.

Rule 4 - *Aggregation*: Let r be a special verb relation (e.g., have, contain, comprise, include, define, consist of, compose of, denote by, identify by, make up of or record with). If a noun x participates in a noun y with r and a noun y also participates in a noun z with another r, then noun y is a part of noun x.

Rule 5 - *Attribute*: If a noun x participates in a possessive relation with another noun y and is mentioned once in the requirements artifacts, then the noun x is an attribute of the noun y.

Rule 6 – *Generalization/Specialization*: Let r be a special verb relation (e.g., be, kind of, type of, classify into or consider as). If a noun x participates in noun y with r, then the noun x is a kind of the noun y.

Rule 7 – *Association*: Let r be a relationship. If a noun x participates in the noun y with r, then the noun x is associated with the noun y with relationship r.

Rule 8 – *Property*: If a noun x is a numeric modifier of another noun y, then the noun x is a property of the noun y.

Rule 9 – *Equivalence*: If a noun x is an abbreviation for another noun y, then the noun x is the same as another noun y.

3.5 Visualizing Ontology

The structural relationships that are obtained are made feasible through any visualization mechanism. For such visualization, a base ontology [21] is used as a premise. The generated relationships are matched with the base ontology and create a new ontology graph. The base ontology is given as a graphViz dot file. The new relationships are matched with the base ontology and written back to graphViz dot file. The new ontology graph is now visualized using graphViz tool [25].

```
Algorithm: Ontology Creation
Input: Relationship file, Base ontology file
Output: Ontology graph
Procedure
Begin
   Base ontology is given as graphViz dot file
   Ontological relationships file are mapped with the
   base ontology mapper
   New ontology is visualized using graphViz tool
End
```

4 Discussions and Evaluation Results

The proposed algorithm encapsulates various implementation language and standard tools for performance evaluation. The implementation languages and tools used in our approach are java, Prolog, graphViz dot, Netbeans IDE 6.9.1, Stanford Parser, tuprolog and graphViz. The input text is taken from the web corpus. The abstracts posted by the end-user or the instructor to the E-learning service providers are used for the evaluation of the performance metrics. The performance efficiency in terms of constructing the right ontology by our algorithm is found to be more than 85% (approx). The sample input data set considered for our approach is University Information System, School Educational System and Library Information System [21].

Evaluation Procedure

When evaluation and testing had to be performed, we obtained the help of some of the domain experts in identifying the ontological relationships. They worked out manually with the help of a paper and pen for the construction of ontology and recovering ontological relationships. Later, the same web document input was given to the several algorithms present in the system. The number of ontological relationships uncovered by both the domain expert and the system were stored for analyzing the performance metrics. DEKA framework is evaluated using a number of web document abstracts. The framework is tested against the traditional performance metrics, precision and recall. It was found that good results were obtained in comparison to the other algorithms explained in the literature survey.

Results Analysis

The values of the performance metrics - Precision and Recall achieve better results when the size of the dataset is less. As the size of the data set increases the values also tend to be low. Hence, the main limitation of our framework is that the algorithm sometimes fails to achieve scalability. In connection to this, the current ongoing work aims at solving the problem of scalability. The graphical results for precision, recall and the performance efficiency is shown below. As a way to this, the formulation for precision, recall and performance efficiency are given below

Assumptions

Let m (integer variable) be the number of ontological relationships uncovered by a domain expert

Let n (integer variable) be the number of ontological relationships uncovered by the system (involving various algorithms)

Let c (integer variable) be the total intersecting number of ontological relationships uncovered by both the domain expert and the system.

Let g (integer variable) be the number of exact (correct) number of ontological relationships present in the web corpus.

Let P, R, E be the variables for precision, recall and performance efficiency output values

The value of precision is given by,

$$P = c / n \tag{1}$$

The value of recall is given by,

$$R = c / m \tag{2}$$

The performance efficiency is calculated as,

$$E = c / g \tag{3}$$

The tabulated input measures for the above metrics are

Table 1. Precision Evaluation

Text Corpus	Algorithms			
	TextOntoEx	OntoLT	Text-To-Onto	DEKA
University Info System (1)	0.96	0.90	0.86	0.96
School Educational System (2)	0.90	0.88	0.83	0.93
Library Information System (3)	0.91	0.86	0.81	0.94

Table 2. Recall Evaluation

Text Corpus	Algorithms			
	TextOntoEx	OntoLT	Text-To-Onto	DEKA
University Info System (1)	0.89	0.87	0.84	0.88
School Educational System (2)	0.87	0.85	0.83	0.86
Library Information System (3)	0.81	0.78	0.75	0.81

Table 3. Performance Efficiency

Text Corpus	Performance Efficiency			
	DEKA	TextOntoEx	OntoLT	Text-To-Onto
University Info System (1)	0.98	0.97	0.93	0.94
School Educational System (2)	0.96	0.95	0.89	0.9
Library Information System (3)	0.92	0.9	0.85	0.87

The visualizations of the results are

1. Precision

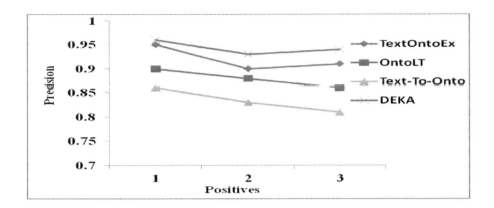

Fig. 2. Precision Evaluation

Fig. 2 provides the graphical results of the performance metric of Precision as given in equ 1. Precision is actually evaluated against the number of Positive Conflicts obtained from the algorithm.

2. Recall

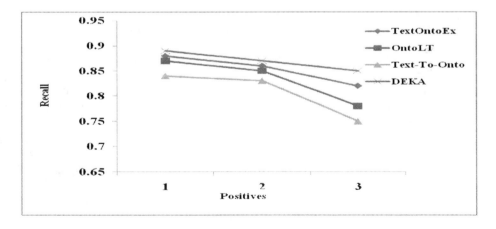

Fig. 3. Recall Evaluation

Fig.3 provides the graphical results of the other performance metric of Recall as given in equ. 2. This is also evaluated against the Positive number of conflicts obtained by the different algorithms.

3. Performance Efficiency

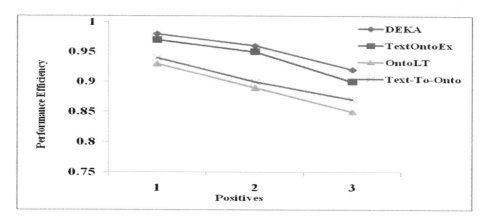

Fig. 4. Efficiency Evaluation

In Fig 4. we have introduced and evaluated a new measure called Performance Efficiency given by equ. 3 and the performance level is high in DEKA framework comparatively.

5 Concluding Remarks

Ontology plays a vital role in clustering the web documents semantically to enhance the performance of many information extraction and information retrieval systems. Section 2 details several methodologies for constructing the ontology automatically using Natural Language Processing. This paper has addressed the sensitive issue of resolving anaphors. A complete framework is designed for parsing, anaphora resolution, uncovering ontological relationships and visualizing the ontology. The future work for the next paper addresses the problem of resolving cataphora (twin domain of anaphora), where the occurrence of the pronoun will be at an initial stage and the nouns (exact meaning of pronouns) shall be occurring later in a sentence.

References

1. Berners-Lee, T., Hendler, J., Lassila, O.: The Semantic Web. Scientific American 284(5), 34–43 (2001)
2. Buitelaar, P., Declerck T.: Linguistic Annotation for the Semantic Web. In: Handschuh, S., Staab, S. (eds.) Annotation for the Semantic Web. IOS Press (2003)
3. Gangemi, A., Mika, P.: Understanding the Semantic Web through Descriptions and Situations. In: Proceedings of the International Conference on Semantic Web (2003)
4. Gómez-Pérez, A., Fernández-López, M., Corcho, O.: Ontological Engineering. Springer, London (2003)
5. Horrocks, I., Patel-Schneider, P.F., van Harmelen, F.: From SHIQ and RDF to OWL: The making of a web ontology language. Journal of Web Semantics 1(1) (2003)

6. Guangzuo, C., Fei, C., Chenhu, L.S.: OntoEdu: Ontology-based Education Grid System for e-Learning. In: International Conference on GCCCE 2004, Hong Kong (2004)
7. Denis, P., Baldridge, J.: A ranking approach to pronoun resolution. In: Proc. of IJCAI 2007 (2007)
8. Markert, K., Nissim, M.: Comparing Knowledge Sources for Nominal Anaphora Resolution. Association for Computational Linguistics 31(3) (2005)
9. Webber, B., Stone, M., Joshi, A., Knott, A.: Anaphora and discourse structure. Computational Linguistics 29(4), 545–587 (2003)
10. Hong Kong, Maedche, Staab, S.: Discovering conceptual relations from text. In: Horn, W. (ed.) Proceedings of the 14th European Conference on Artificial Intelligence, ECAI 2000. IOS Press, Amsterdam (2000)
11. Chein, M., Mugnier, M.: Graph-based Knowledge Representation: Computational Foundations of Conceptual Graphs. Springer, Heidelberg (2009)
12. Fok, A.W.P., Ip, H.H.S.: Educational Ontologies Construction for Personalized Learning on the Web. SCI, vol. 62, pp. 47–82. Springer, Heidelberg (2007)
13. Fok, A.W.P., Ip, H.H.-S.: Personalized Education: An Exploratory Study of Learning Pedagogies in Relation to Personalization Technologies. In: Liu, W., Shi, Y., Li, Q. (eds.) ICWL 2004. LNCS, vol. 3143, pp. 407–415. Springer, Heidelberg (2004)
14. Declerck, T.: A set of tools for integrating linguistic and non-linguistic information. In: Proceedings of the SAAKM Workshop at ECAI, Lyon (2002)
15. Winograd, T.: Understanding natural language. Academic Press, New York (1972)
16. Miller, G.A., Beckwith, R., Fellbaum, C.D., Gross, D., Miller, K.: WordNet: An online lexical database. International Journal of Lexicography 3, 235–244 (1990)
17. Zhang, H., Bonacina, M., Hsiang, J.: Psato: A distributed propositional prover and its application to quasigroup problems. Journal of Symbolic Computation 21, 543–560 (1996)
18. Biébow, B., Szulman, S.: TERMINAE: A Linguistics-Based Tool for the Building of a Domain Ontology. In: Fensel, D., Studer, R. (eds.) EKAW 1999. LNCS (LNAI), vol. 1621, pp. 49–66. Springer, Heidelberg (1999)
19. Arpírez, J.C., Gómez-Pérez, A., Lozano, A., Pinto, H.S. (ONTO) Agent: An ontology-based WWW broker to select ontologies. In: Gómez-Pérez, A., Benjamins, R.V. (eds.) ECAI 1998 Workshop on Applications of Ontologies and Problem-Solving Methods, Brighton, UK, pp. 16–24 (1998)
20. Dahab, M.Y., Hassan, H.A., Rafea, A.: TextOntoEx: Automatic Ontology Construction from Natural English Text. In: AIML 2006 International Conference, Sharm El Sheikh, Egypt (2006)
21. Assawamekin, N., Sunetnanta, T., Pluempitiwiriyawej, C.: Ontology based multiperspective requirements traceability framework. Knowledge and Information Systems Journal (2009)
22. The Stanford Parser: A Statistical Parser (version 1.6). Stanford University (August 18, 2007), http://nlp.stanford.edu/software/lex-parser.shtml
23. de Marnee, M.-C., Manning, C.D.: Stanford typed dependencies manual. Stanford Parser Library (2010)
24. The FDG parser: a statistical parser (version 3.7), http://3d2f.com/download/11-349-parser-generator-free-download.shtml
25. http://www.graphviz.org/Download.php

Eye Tracking in Educational Games Environment: Evaluating User Interface Design through Eye Tracking Patterns

Nurul Hidayah Mat Zain[1], Fariza Hanis Abdul Razak[1],
Azizah Jaafar[2], and Mohd Firdaus Zulkipli[1]

[1] Faculty Computer and Mathematical Sciences (FSKM), University Technology MARA
(UiTM), 40450 Shah Alam, Selangor, Malaysia
[2] Institute of Visual Informatics, University Kebangsaan Malaysia (UKM),
43600 Bangi, Selangor, Malaysia
{nurulmz,fariza}@fskm.uitm.edu.my,
aj@ftsm.uk.my, kast_outz@gmail.com

Abstract. Eye tracking research has been commonly used in human computer
interaction study. Researcher can collect data on user's behavior through their
eye movement by using eye tracking technique. Many company or individual
has taken this technology for overcome usability issues in their website,
application as well as games. It is not easy to design and develop educational
game application. Many aspects must be considered in making a good game.
Educational game needs to have good usability in order to be effective and easy
to learn. In this paper, we analyze of eye tracking patterns (heat map and gaze
plot) to evaluate user interface design in educational game. In addition, we
proposed a user interface design guidelines to the issues that highlighted. We
conducted experiments using Tobii T60 remote eye tracking system and
ManGold software suite to capture and analyze the user's experience when
playing educational game. The findings suggest eye-tracking patterns consist of
a series of metrics, such as 'number of fixations' and 'heat map separation'
correlating with the user interface design issues and ineffective presentation.

Keywords: eye tracking, educational game, usability, user interface design,
Visual Informatics.

1 Introduction

Computer games have become an essential part of social and cultural environment
[1], and have been proposed as a potential learning tool by others educational
researchers [2-3] and game developers [4-5]. Educational game is games that have
been specifically designed to teach people about certain subject, expand concepts,
reinforce development, understand an historical event or culture, or assist them in
learning a skill as they play [6]. One of the goals in educational games and learning is
to create engaging and immersive learning experiences for delivering specified
learning goals, outcomes and experiences. However, there is limited number of
research done on game usability or quality of game interface design. Failure in design

H. Badioze Zaman et al. (Eds.): IVIC 2011, Part II, LNCS 7067, pp. 64–73, 2011.
© Springer-Verlag Berlin Heidelberg 2011

usable game interfaces can interfere with the larger goal of creating a compelling experience for users and can have a negative effect on the overall quality and success of a game [7].

Despite the huge amount of human computer interaction that is taking place there has been little serious research into issues of games design and usability. It's difficult to measure experience when the user is still playing the game. This approach risks their distraction from the game.

Moreover, at the end of the game, the user's memories might have already faded or been re-constructed. Many researchers involved with the assessment of satisfaction have used interviews and questionnaires but then they found that the results may be problematic and subjective due to memory degradation or rational reconstruction by the [8]. However, by using combination of a tool based on the automated collection such as eye tracking system, the researcher able to analyze user experience while playing games.

2 Literature Review

2.1 Eye Tracking

Eye-tracking is a technique whereby eye movement is recorded whilst the user is looking at a stimulus [9]. Individual's eye movements are measured so that the researcher knows both where a person is looking at any given time and the sequence in which their eyes are shifting from one location to another. When these movement can be measured, it helps HCI researcher understand visually information processing and the factors that may impact upon the usability of system interfaces.

Basically eye movement can be categorized in two ways. First is fixation, which is a moment where the eye is relatively motionless. In addition eye fixation were defined as a spatially stable gaze lasting for approximately 200-300 milliseconds, during which visual attention is directed to a specific area of the visual display [10]. Secondly is a saccade, where a quick movement between fixations to another element [9]. Fixations represent the instances in which information acquisition and processing is able to occur, and thus, fixations were the indices most relevant to this current evaluation [11].

2.2 User Interface Design Issues in Educational Game

Many great scholars in education, cognition, and psychology have worked tirelessly on educational games over the years. Researchers have looked at the implications of commercial games on learning, attitudes, and efficacy, the three areas most reported [12-15]. Educational games is one of the games types and genre that being discussed in term of the relevance and potential in education.

Nowadays, there is a wide selection of different computer games. To get an overview, the games can be divided into genres such as action, puzzle, role playing, and so on. Scholars believe educational games can offer many learning benefits for the students based on the highly motivating nature of the computer games itself as well as because of the behaviour of the new generation of learners [16-17].

There are many issues involves in evaluating user interface design in educational game. In any system, interface plays an importance role in order to provide appealing and attractive interface for the users. It implies the same concept for educational game; interface design is the main issue that needs to be taken into consideration in evaluating educational game. Issues of consistency, interactivity, navigation, screen design and pleasant to use are the important elements that need to be evaluate [18].

3 Research Methodology

We conducted an empirical study to collect data from which to evaluate user interface design through eye tracking patterns. In summary, participants undertook tasks with educational game application. We collected verbal protocols (think-aloud technique) and observational data to evaluate user interface design, as well as eye-tracking data from which to derive eye movement patterns.

3.1 Task

For this experiment, one educational game was selected for use in the study: Histogram Processing Educational Game. There are three tasks that the participants need to do.

- Task 1: Participants require collecting keys to access the scholar.
- Task 2: Participants require answering the quizzes.
- Task 3: Participants require accessing the school.

Consequently, these task provided coverage of a range of different kinds of interactions, including scanning text, reading, checkbox input, usage of navigation elements, scanning of pictures, searching and so on that were expected to yield a broad range of evaluation user interface design.

3.2 Participants

Six participants (four female and two male) students from Faculty Computer and Mathematical Sciences (FSKM), UiTM were recruited to participate in this study. No specific recruitment criteria were applied. Several participants had glasses or contact lenses but this was not a barrier to tracking their eye movements. All participants had experience playing computer games; however none had previously participated in an eye-tracking study. Their ages ranged from 22 to 25 years old. The highest level of educations for all participants was Diploma level.

Three participants reported that they played video game once a month, two participants played video game daily basis and one participant played video game weekly basis. Two participants had put themselves in very good interm of skill level of playing computer game, three partcipants in moderately good skill level and one participant in not very skilled level of playing computer game.

3.3 Apparatus

Eye tracking equipment (Tobii T60) was used to record the eye movements of the participants during the playing of selected educational game. The tracker works with two infrared light sources, the reflection of which from the retina is recorded by a camera. Consequently, the participants could move freely in the limited area that the tracking system can record accurately. A webcam and a keyboard were attached to give control to all participants without the needing other more devices. The system was running the Tobii Studio™ Analysis Software on a PC desktop with Windows XP operating system.

There are four cameras in each angle of the lab's room. Each of it has been adjusted so that it can record the activities of the participant clearly. ManGold software suite will showed video from each angle simultaneously. There is one more camera on top of the Tobii to capture the motion of the participant. Besides that, the speaker for the computer also has been adjusted so that the participant can hear the sound clearly. If the volume of the sound is too high it may distract the participant's focus and if the volume of the sound is too low the participant may can't hear anything and don't know what is happening when playing the game.

Fig. 1. Tobii T60 Remote Eye Tracking

3.4 Testing Procedure

Each session began with the participant giving informed consent form. The consent form is to ensure the participants agree with all the terms of experiment. The participants also briefed about the experiment objectives, goals and tasks. A short questionnaire was then administered to collect demographic data. Participants were asked during the sessions to provide details about how they felt during playing the game and that they were to reply using single word expressions such as, fine, great, frustrated and so on which is using think-aloud protocols.

The participants was asked to keep their head as still as possible during the experiment as to minimize inaccuracy caused by head movements. The eye tracking equipment was calibrated for the participant. Once the participants and the eye tracker equipment ready to be start, the test administrator will leave the participant alone at the test room. There is no duration time required for participants to complete their task. However they are free to stop the testing as long as they completed their tasks. After the game had finished, the participants required to answer a post-questionnaire. They have to fill it based on their experience playing the game.

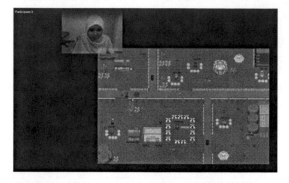

Fig. 2. Screen capture from auto-recorded video while participant playing game

4   Analysis and Finding

4.1   Analysis of Think Aloud Technique

Most participants had difficulty in articulating how they felt as they played the game, "errs and uhms" making up much of the responses. However, the most frequently expressed "proper" words are reported in Figure 3 and Figure 4. The table shows that guessing was the predominantly stated emotion. Based on the emotion gathering, words that are associated with more positive emotions exceed those with more negative ones indicating perhaps the participants didn't feel too much pressure during game play. A summary of negative emotions related with interface design issues identified was presented in Table 2.

However, many of participants feel very happy after they managed to answer the question correctly. They also feel really relieved because they completed the game without any trouble. Some of them enjoyed the game because the game is easy and good for educational purpose.

Table 1. Negative emotions feedback related with user interface design issues

Words Used	User Interface Design Issues
Frustrated	Participants didn't manage to get the quizzes' answer
Bored	Participants feel the game is too easy
Confused	Participants don't know where to go after they completed answering the question.
Annoyed	Participants can't see the font because it is too small and the color is not appropriate.
Lost	Participants don't know where to go after they completed answering the question

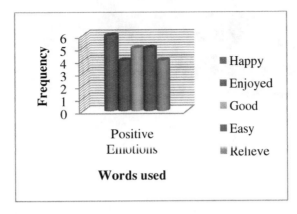

Fig. 3. Words associated with positive emotions

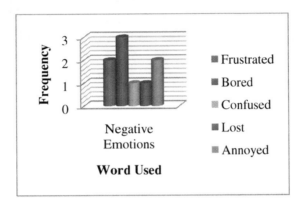

Fig. 4. Words associated with negative emotions

4.2   Analysis of Eye Tracking Patterns

4.2.1   Task 1: Participants Require Collecting Keys to Access the Scholar

Analysis from Eye Tracking Patterns: From the data, there are many fixations in general. Some interface objects draw more attention. From the heat map data, participants look mostly at the center of the screen watching the scholar and also look at top left reading the instruction given.

User Interface Design Issues: *Ineffective presentation and navigation* - Based on Figure 5, P2 didn't even look at the score board. Based on heat map in Figure 6, P2 gives more attention at the top left and middle of the screen. Figure 7 show only P4 looks at the score board. Based on Figure 8, P4 gives more attention on the road and other characters. The game didn't give instructions where to go. There are some participants getting confused where to go first and sometimes hit preventable objects. Some of the players hit objects that they need to avoid.

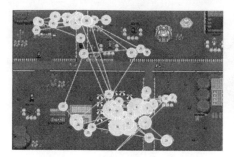

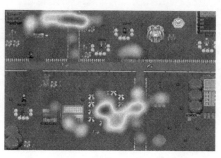

Fig. 5. Gaze plot patterns: P2   **Fig. 6.** Heat map patterns: P2

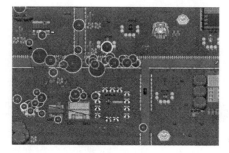

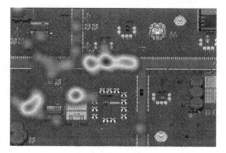

Fig. 7. Gaze plot patterns: P4   **Fig. 8.** Heat map patterns: P4

User Interface Design Guidelines: Any important objects should be blinking, highlight or catch the attention of user so that the participant will know they need to focus on the objects. Any preventable objects should be put a text, example "danger" so that they can know that they need to avoid it. The important location or characters should be put an arrow so that the participant can know that they need to go at that direction.

4.2.2 Task 2: Participants Require Answering the Quizzes
Analysis from Eye Tracking Patterns: From Figure 9 and Figure 11, there are many short fixations on the screen where information is expected and no fixations on problematic element.

User Interface Design Issues: *(1) Expected information missing (on scene, area or subsection)* - A participants goes to an area on the scene, expecting to find specific details which are not provided. The instruction is located at the top left and it gives problem to the participants because it is not suitable as a focus point. *(2) Design of element unclear (layout and color coding)* - The font's color and size of the instruction is not appropriate. The participants find it hard to identify any important information. Most of the participants take a long time to read because it is hard to read.

User Interface Design Guidelines: The instruction should be located at the centre of the screen because it has more spaces and it is suitable as a focus point. Many games

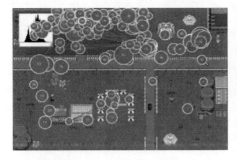

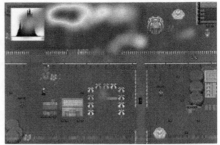

Fig. 9. Gaze plot patterns: P1   **Fig. 10.** Heat map patterns: P1

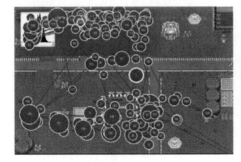

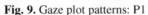

Fig. 11. Gaze plot patterns: P5   **Fig. 12.** Heat map patterns: P5

put instructions at the centre of the screen. The color background of the instruction should be contra with the color of the font. The size of font should big enough for the player to read and any important information should be highlighted.

4.2.3 Task 3: Participants Require Accessing the School

Analysis from Eye Tracking Patterns: Based on Figure 13 and Figure 15, a lot of fixations on area and scene. In addition, there are many fixations across the scene without very long fixations.

User Interface Design Issues*: (1) Non-obvious interaction because of design issues -* Interaction elements was not clear cause problems for the participants who don't seem to be interacting or are delayed in their interaction. Some of the participants got lost because they didn't know where to go next. *(2) Specific information or links not provide -* A participants is coming to an area that does not contain options relevant for his task.

Interface Design Guidelines: There should be instructions notify the player where to go, blink the object or put an arrow showing the location where participants should go. In this task, all participants have finished completely. Since all the participants dealing with difficulties to do next action., this indicated that the content area need to be improved in term of the easy of used and the way it guide participant for easy to understand.

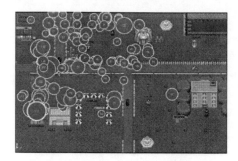

Fig. 13. Gaze plot patterns: P1

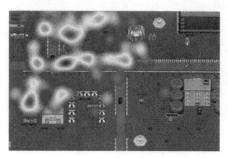

Fig. 14. Heat map patterns: P1

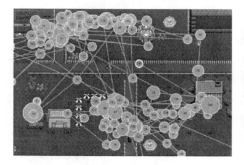

Fig. 15. Gaze plot patterns: P6

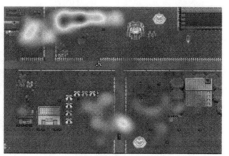

Fig. 16. Heat map patterns: P6

5 Conclusion

This study explored how eye-tracking patterns are linked to specific user interface design issue. The sequences of eye-tracking patterns consist of a series of metrics, such as 'number of fixations' and 'heat map separation' correlating with the user interface design issues and ineffective presentation through unclear instruction. This study also verifies that eye-tracking offered in investigating game design issues and provides the researcher with useful information to design a high-quality user interface. Some technical problems were experienced with the setup of the system and the eye-tracking software. Although this had an effect on some aspects of the study, a comprehensive analysis of the data was conducted and a user interface design guidelines has been suggested. We hope this will benefit others who undertake similar research in the future.

References

1. Oblinger, D.G.: The next generation of educational engagement. Journal of Interactive Media in Education (2004)
2. Gee, J.P.: What video games have to teach us about learning and literacy. Computers in Entertainment (CIE) 1, 20 (2003)

3. Malone, T.W.: What Makes Things Fun to Learn? A Study of Intrinsically Motivating Computer Games. Pipeline (1981)
4. Gibson, D., Aldrich, C., Prensky, M.: Games and simulations in online learning: Research and development frameworks. Information Science Publishing (2007)
5. Prensky, M.: The digital game-based learning revolution. Digital Game-Based Learning (2001)
6. Singh, J., Ling, L., Shanmugam, M., Gunasekaran, S., Dorairaj, S.: Designing computer games to introduce Programming to children (2008)
7. Yue, W.S., Zin, N.A.M.: Usability evaluation for history educational games, pp. 1019–1023. ACM (2009)
8. Lindgaard, G., Dudek, C.: What is this evasive beast we call user satisfaction? Interacting with Computers 15, 429–452 (2003)
9. Ehmke, C., Wilson, S.: Identifying web usability problems from eye-tracking data, pp. 119–128. British Computer Society (2007)
10. Granka, L., Joachims, T., Gay, G.: Eye-tracking analysis of user behavior in WWW search, Citeseer, pp. 25–29 (2004)
11. Rayner, K.: Eye movements in reading and information processing: 20 years of research. Psychological Bulletin 124, 372 (1998)
12. Durkin, K.: Videogames and young people with developmental disorders. Review of General Psychology 14, 122 (2010)
13. Ferguson, C.J.: Evidence for publication bias in video game violence effects literature: A meta-analytic review. Aggression and Violent Behavior 12, 470–482 (2007)
14. Gee, J.P.: Good videogames, the human mind, and good learning (2008)
15. Shaffer, D.W.: Epistemic frames for epistemic games. Computers & Education 46, 223–234 (2006)
16. Chang, W.-C., Chou, Y.-M.: Introductory C Programming Language Learning with Game-Based Digital Learning. In: Li, F., Zhao, J., Shih, T.K., Lau, R., Li, Q., McLeod, D. (eds.) ICWL 2008. LNCS, vol. 5145, pp. 221–231. Springer, Heidelberg (2008)
17. Rajaravivarma, R.: A games-based approach for teaching the introductory programming course. ACM SIGCSE Bulletin 37, 98–102 (2005)
18. Mohamed, H., Jaafar, A.: Conceptual Framework for a Heuristics Based Methodology for Interface Evaluation of Educational Games. Computer and Information Science 3, P211 (2010)

Use of Content Analysis Tools
for Visual Interaction Design

Nazlena Mohamad Ali[1], Hyowon Lee[2], and Alan F. Smeaton[2]

[1] Institute of Visual Informatics, University Kebangsaan Malaysia, Malaysia
[2] CLARITY: Centre for Sensor Web Technologies, Dublin City University, Ireland
nma@ftsm.ukm.my, {hlee,asmeaton}@computing.dcu.ie

Abstract. Automatic media content analysis in multimedia is a very promising field of research bringing in various possibilities for enhancing visual informatics. By computationally analysing the quantitative data contained in text, audio, image and video media, more semantically meaningful and useful information on the media contents can be derived, extracted and visualised, informing human users those facts and patterns initially hidden in the bit streams of data. Insights into how to transform the emerging technological possibilities from these media analysis tools into usable visual interfaces to help people see visual information in novel ways will be an important contribution to visual informatics. In this paper, we outline some of the more promising content analysis techniques currently being researched in multimedia and computer vision and discuss how these could be used to develop visually-oriented end-user interfaces that support searching, browsing and summarization of the media contents in various usage contexts. We illustrate this with a few example applications that we have developed over the years, all of which designed in such a way as to take advantage of the automatic content analysis and to discover and create novel usage scenarios of consuming visually-oriented media contents.

Keywords: content analysis, visual interaction design, visualization, video browsing, Visual Informatics.

1 Introduction

Automatic media content analysis tools and techniques in the field of multimedia are becoming more and more useful as their accuracy and robustness increase as the result of on-going research effort in this area. An emerging research challenge for interaction and visualization community from this is the question of how to take full advantage of the outcomes of these content analysis methods in designing feasible and usable applications. A myriads of technical possibilities in media content analysis bring benefits to users in helping interpret and navigate those rich media in ways that did not exist before. Some of these experimental applications in this line of work went as far as being evaluated most commonly in the back-end technique or algorithm level performance or in user evaluation in a controlled lab setting with group of sample users, but increasingly in the form of deployment via the Web or via App

H. Badioze Zaman et al. (Eds.): IVIC 2011, Part II, LNCS 7067, pp. 74–84, 2011.
© Springer-Verlag Berlin Heidelberg 2011

store in order to reach wider users and to ascertain more realistic usage feedback over long period of time (for example, SportsAnno [4] and NewsBlaster [10] as web-based campus-wide deployments, iTV system [1] on a cable TV network, and PocketNavigator [16] on Android app market). Taking advantage of these automatic content-based techniques, numerous possible real world application scenarios can be imagined and a large number of novel demonstration systems in varying degrees of completeness have been built with aim to emphasize on user interaction (see [11] for more discussion on this aspect). We expect that this direction of research will bring a new perspective into variety of research agenda in visual informatics that extends interaction and communication based on visual interfaces thus could support user in their understanding, knowledge acquisition and sharing.

In this paper, we take a few promising content analysis tools and techniques in multimedia as examples of soon-to-be some of the core back-end engines of many media applications in the future, and illustrate how we developed visual interfaces that particularly take advantage of these tools to guide and shape the future usage of these applications. A number of novel application examples will be introduced in order to demonstrate the ways in which technical advancements are interpreted and represented as user-centred, visually-oriented end-user features.

The paper is organized as follows. In the next section, a selection of multimedia content analysis techniques is introduced that are continuously researched and developed today. In Section 3, some end-user applications developed within our centre highlighting the use of content analysis in its interaction and visualization design are described, and in particular, we explain in each of these applications how they try to leverage the power of these content analysis in such a ways as to support visually oriented user interaction. We end with a conclusion for summarizing the trend of R&D effort in this area and the future work.

2   Multimedia Content Analysis

In this section we introduce some of the influential and potentially high-impacting content analysis techniques that are currently developing in the multimedia research field, some combinations of which could be used to design visually-oriented end-user applications. Many of these tools are currently being investigated and refined in multimedia and computer vision laboratories, with varying stages of their overall development.

Shot Boundary Detection (SBD) and *Keyframe Extraction* have main goal of segmenting broadcast news into individual camera shots and finding most accurate visual representation of each shot, enabling further structuring of the video content and other operations, thus serving as essential precursors to video indexing and retrieval [5]. A video *shot* refers to the basic unit of retrieval – a short, coherent video sequence that serves as the starting point for the semantic analysis and structuring of content – and relates directly to camera shooting boundaries within the video sequence. Most SBD approaches involve measuring the visual similarity between adjacent or near-adjacent video frames and if these are visually similar, within some threshold value, then it is likely that they belong to the same shot [19]. Camera and/or object motion will cause adjacent frames to be slightly dissimilar while shot cuts will generally cause a noticeable increase in this dissimilarity. Sudden changes in shots or hard-cuts are relatively easy to identify.

Once a video sequence has been segmented into a sequence of shots, representative keyframes can be extracted for each shot as keyframes serve as a visual shot summary. What constitutes a *good* keyframe and how to recognize a good keyframe remains an open question and current techniques generally rely on a variety of heuristic methods. For example, the simplest approach often involves selecting the first, middle, or last frame in the shot. More sophisticated techniques, however, can take account of in-shot camera movement by selecting the frame where camera movement stops.

Reliable and accurate shot boundary detection and keyframe extraction techniques are considered an "enabling technology" that can be used as the first step for more sophisticated and advanced administration of content analysis tools to media contents, and so far have led to the development of a number of systems that focus on providing users with more effective sequence navigation and shot browsing features.

Another research on content analysis is related to *face detection and recognition*. Because much of our media consumption is based on people directly known to us (e.g. friends and family) or those from media (e.g. celebrity and politicians), the content analysis tools that automatically detect faces and label their names appearing in the media contents have been considered valuable and have a relatively long history of research. Many of currently researched face detection algorithms are based on classifiers where the system is trained using example face data then the regions of image contents are transformed into feature vectors and determined whether the region falls into the 'face exists' category or not. Detected faces are then compared to each other in terms of their feature vector similarity in order to establish/predict whether two faces are of the same person. While working reasonably well for domain-constrained environment (e.g. comparing frontal faces of crime suspects from a convicts database), the overall accuracy and reliability in general context is not high enough to be used in an unsupervised setting (e.g. comparing faces in Flickr database). Additional contextual cues such as 'body patch', location or time could dramatically enhance the reliability of face detection or recognition algorithms [14].

Other work on content analysis is *scene detection and classification*. Depending on the genre of the media content, different techniques optimised for that particular genre can be used. For example, *news story segmentation* is a special case of scene detection applied to broadcast TV news. TV news is typically very well-structured typically starting with a short highlight of the day's news followed by an anchorperson(s) introducing the first news story then a reporter appearing from the scene then returning back to the anchorperson(s) to start the second news story, and so on. Using some of these news broadcast conventions and a combination of other related detection methods such as shot boundary detection and face detection), a TV news programme can be automatically segmented into individual news stories. *Topic detection tracking (TDT)* then tries to identify the topics in the segmented news stories and establish similarity and relatedness amongst the stories.

The scene detection and classification in a generic video content such as movies try to detect *events* based on a number of audiovisual features from movie creation principles [8,9]. These features were used in the event class detections such as a description of the audio content, where the audio (speech or music) are placed into a specific class; measurement of the amount of camera movement; measurement of the amount of motion in the frame; measurement of the editing pace; and measurement of the amount of shot repetition. For example, work has been done using an approach to detect events in a movie and classified them into three classes based on film grammar as follows:

- *Dialogue*— contains a conversation among characters (one or more people)
- *Exciting* — contains something exciting for the audience (car chase, fighting etc.)
- *Montage* — contains strong musical background as in montage, emotional and musical events

In making a movie, a director follows a certain universal film grammar. For example, he will use a static camera to give the audience a low distraction, relaxed viewing-mode and to give more focus. On the other hand, faster pace editing and high level of camera movement can be used to create an exciting feeling for viewers, give high impact and increased stimulation levels. In addition, background music is used a lot as a medium for creating an emotional response among the viewers. Based on these criteria, a summary of certain measurements are used as the basis in the scene detections.

A work on *concept detection* and *activity identification* focusing on identifying what objects, concepts, events or activities are shown or happening in the visual media contents (e.g. explosion, nature, sunset, people eating food, shopping, etc.) is a difficult challenge because what appears in visual media may not even be agreed by two human viewers or indexers with possibly very ambiguous and subjective interpretation at work in the process. However, using machine learning algorithms to train the system with positive examples (i.e. those parts of video that contain a concept X) and negative examples (i.e. those that don't contain it), reasonable accuracy can be achieved depending on the training data size and the nature of the contents. In the annual TRECVid which aims to advance the automatic indexing of digital video contents, detection of high-level concepts such as "people marching on the street" or "airplane taxing in the airport" have been exercised for a number of years, pushing the level of accuracy each year.

Study of Lifelogging also have utilised concept detection within Lifelog data such as photo collection generated by passive capture devices such as SenseCam [6]. The SenseCam is a small wearable personal device which automatically captures up to about 2,500 images per day. This yields a very large personal collection of images, or in a sense a large visual diary of a person's day. Automatic and intelligent techniques are necessary for effective structuring, searching and browsing of such a large image set for locating important or significant events in a person's life [6]. The identification of the activity can be detected by machine learning techniques, we can classify the lifelog photos in terms of what they contain for example eating, car, people, indoor, shopping or driving.

The techniques described in this section are, even though bearing an enormous potential for future exploitation, simply a selection of technical content analysis without direct link to its potential usage scenarios and possible real-world applications. Because not many of these techniques are currently used in existing applications, how to channel these technical possibilities into feasible and usable end-user visualization tools is a significant question. In the next section, we introduce some of our end-user applications that leverage the power of these content analysis and touch on how the various techniques could be used to visualize the results of these content analysis in user-centred way.

3   Using Content Analysis for Visual Interaction

We believe that in order to develop sound, practical and useful new media applications, the perspective from multimedia technology should not be used alone in terms of its progress and experimentation but be combined and balanced with conventional and established work practices of use and the way human users have been carrying out work tasks. This is because the introduction of a new technology should be used to enhance rather than completely overturn established work methods. The discipline of Human-Computer Interaction and especially a series of techniques, for example in usability engineering [13] has been developed in order to identify existing practices from the end-user point of view and to then guide the development of new (interfaces) technology into established work practice.

We now present a variety of example of visual interfaces that leverage some combinations of the content analysis techniques as introduced in the previous section and explain how those various tools could be used to visualize the results of the content analysis.

3.1   Video Browsing with Fischlar System

The Fischlar Digital Video Library System was developed to support capture, indexing, browsing, searching and summarising of digital video and has been deployed into four separate video content collections for a variety of users and application scenarios [18]. The four versions of the Fischlar system include TV programs [7], TV news [17], TRECVid video track participation [2] and nursing educational videos [3], each designed to support different content type. Information provided to users in the system interface are based on finding and selecting a video program either using text or metadata. Supported interface elements included a keyframe slideshow, a hierarchical keyframe browser, and a timeline browser.

Fischlar-News was one of the collections designed to support an archive to the main evening TV news broadcast. It incorporates a number of multimedia and recommendation techniques and was deployed within a University campus for several years, in which the large scale testing and evaluation (performance and usability) has been carried out [17]. Methods used from video content analysis include shot boundary detection, keyframe extraction, news story segmentation, capture of closed captions, and the system allows for text searching, browsing and playback based on news stories. An example of an interface screen shot is depicted in Fig. 1.

Fig. 1. Fischlar Interface

Using the output of news story segmentation, shot boundary detection and keyframe extraction directly on the user-interface, this application was designed with the expectation that the accuracy and robustness of these content analysis techniques will become high enough in near future so that those detected and segmented units could directly be mapped into visual representation elements on the screen.

3.2 Managing Personal Photo Collection with MediAssist

The MediAssist [15] is a novel application that incorporated a number of content analysis to enable users to efficiently search their personal photo archives. Automatically generated contextual metadata and content-based analysis tools (face and building detection) are used, and semi automatic annotation techniques allow the user to interactively improve the automatically generated annotations. Our retrieval tools allow for complex query formulation for personal digital photo collection management. Fig. 2 shows the interface of the application. The user starts with formulating a search query on the left side of the screen, by selecting location and dragging timeline bar as well as time of the year, number of faces in the photos, weather conditions when the photos were taken, and so on. The result of search is displayed on the right side of the screen as a grid of thumbnail photos, and selecting one of the results then presents an enlarged display of the photo as shown in Fig.2.

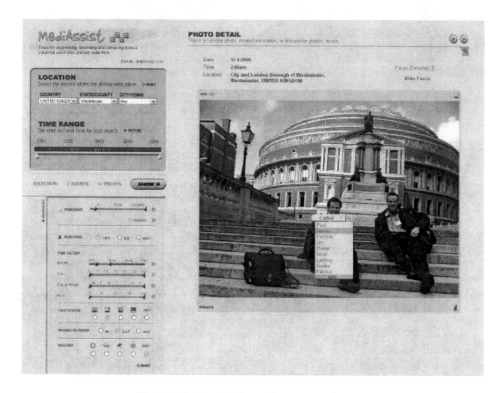

Fig. 2. MediAssist Photo Management System

Recognizing the fact that the detection algorithms incorporated in the system cannot be 100 percent accurate today, a simple user correction mechanism is featured where the user can click on the face of the person and select one of the few predicted names based on the visual similarity of that face within the same event. While content analysis tools are improving steadily, unpredictable photo quality and face orientation, shading, occlusion, and lighting condition inevitably causes incorrect labeling of the faces thus a simple and easy manual correction whenever such an error is noticed by the user becomes an important feature in an application such as this.

3.3   Navigating Scene Types with MOVIEBROWSER2

We developed the MOVIEBROWSER2 [11,12] to incorporate the use of a number of content analysis techniques, particularly those that identify movie scene boundaries and categorise them into exciting, montage and dialogue scenes. MOVIEBROWSER2 uses several recent multimedia technologies to automatically process digital video content but at the same time we used a usability engineering process to relate these techniques to the real tasks of real users in their real environments. The application domain we work in is film studies where students need to study movie contents and analyse movie sequences and was deployed in the university for a duration of a semester. Fig. 3 shows the main interface of MOVIEBROWSER2 application.

When a user selects a movie (i.e. "Shrek" in Fig. 3), the movie's content is visually presented to the user. In Fig. 3, the whole duration of the movie is represented as 3-band horizontal timeline near the top of the screen, in three different colours, each representing different types of scenes. For example, the green band represents those scenes with *Dialogues*; the pink band represents those scenes with *Montage*; the yellow band represents *Exciting* scenes and it is also noticeable the *Exciting* keyframe scenes appear throughout the movie. Clicking on any of these colour blocks on the band will jump the keyframe list (below the timeline) to that scene, and clicking on the keyframe will start streaming the video from that point onwards.

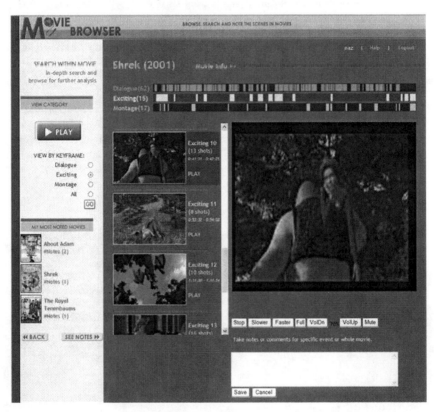

Fig. 3. MOVIEBROWSER2 Main Interface

An experiment has been carried out on how the visual display on automatic content analysis is beneficial to the user as reported in [11]. In this experiment, a film studies students were chosen as a sample users and they were given a task to browse and complete the short essays. The findings from the essay outcome revealed that there are slightly improving or better results which is also supported by the remarks from the module lecturer that shows students have more variability (more opinions, expressions) in their written essay when using MOVIEBROWSER2. Our findings also show that satisfaction levels are higher after using the newly introduced tool with higher mean scores in all aspects of statements given as compared to when using a conventional standard player.

3.4   Reviewing a Day with My Visual Diary

My Visual Diary, a SenseCam image management system, is an application for SenseCam use that resolves some of the problems of managing the exceedingly large number of SenseCam photos [6]. The system employs a number of content-based image analysis techniques to automatically structure and index the captured photos in such a way that the owner of the photos can easily search and browse the large amount of SenseCam photos through a web-based interface.

Usage scenario involves a user wearing the SenseCam over a long period of time (say a few years), and a few nights a week tries to review what happened during the past week. The main challenge of this kind of Lifelogging scenario is the huge number of photos that have to be managed: typically resulting in 2,000 – 3,000 photos per day, or if worn every day, over 1 million photos per year, going through individual photos and manually tagging or annotating them for future access is out of the question. Using our event detection to group the photos into meaningful events and calculating the visual uniqueness of each event, the application automatically compose an appealing visual montage of a day's happenings.   Fig. 4 shows a screen shot where a user selected one particular date from the mini calendar on the top left of the screen, and that day's visual summary is presented on the main part of the screen. Currently 19 most important events of the day are shown, each photo representing a key photo from an event. The size of the photos is in proportion to the uniqueness of the event relative to the rest of the events that happened that day. Thus, for example, the largest photo at the bottom of the screen is the most unique event that happened that day by this user.

Fig. 4. SenseCam Photo Browser Interface

This application allows a very quick glance of a day, not by intensively flipping through thousands of photos of that day, but by intelligently grouping the photos into events, selecting most representative photo from each event, and identifying more important (or unique) events then presenting them in a static, one page template.

4 Conclusion

Automatic content analysis is one of the most dynamic and technically aggressive research area in multimedia. Most of the techniques being researched in this field have been initially conceived from a computational perspective and technical possibilities rather than from an end-user perspective and their needs thus they generally tend to lack the grounding into the real-world scenarios and situations. However, the potential for exploitation as the understanding of these tools grows and matures is staggering. From the perspective of a visual interaction designer, an automatic detection and content analysis can be a significant advantage to help come up with novel ways of supporting the envisaged end-users by creating visual interfaces that otherwise could not be implemented. While understanding the user perspectives and their requirements is an important element for visual informatics, taking advantage of these emerging content analysis tools and techniques and exploring novel visualization provisions that end-users would normally not ask or demand in their conventional usage context could open up many innovative new ways of discovering or creating visual interfaces afforded by these emerging tools. Once a novel visualization is designed, then a series of well-established usability engineering methods could be used to see how these new interfaces could be tailored, adapted and customized for the specific wishes and needs of the users.

Our future work includes refining the applications as described in this paper by more rigorously employing the usability engineering methods, especially longitudinal study methods such as diary method and ethnographic studies in order to understand people's adoption and appropriation of the novel applications in their lives. Such a study will reveal many new challenges back to the content analysis streams of research and guide their future directions and agenda, then the technical tools that come out under those agenda will more likely be valuable and useful for incorporating into subsequent new batch of visual applications.

Acknowledgement. We would like to thank those involved directly or indirectly on the projects that have been carried out in CLARITY: Centre for Sensor Web Technologies, Dublin City University.

References

1. Bernhaupt, R., Obrist, M., Tscheligi, M.: Usability and usage of iTV services: lessons learned in an Austrian field trial. ACM Computers in Entertainment 5(2) (2007)
2. Browne, P., Czirjek, C., Gaughan, G., Gurrin, C., Jones, G., Lee, H., Marlow, S., Mc-Donald, K., Murphy, N., O'Connor, N.E., O'Hare, N., Smeaton, A.F., Ye, J.: Dublin City University Video Track Experiments for TREC 2003. In: Proceedings of the TRECVid Workshop, Gaithersburg (2003)

3. Gurrin, C., MacNeela, P., Smeaton, A.F., Lee, H., Browne, P., McDonald, K.: Físchlar-Nursing, Using Digital Video Libraries to Teach Nursing Students. In: WBE 2004 - IASTED International Conference on Web-Based Education, pp. 111–116 (2004)
4. Lanagan, J., Smeaton, A.F.: SportsAnno: What Do You Think? In: Proc. of Large-Scale Semantic Access to Content (Text, Image, Video and Sound) RIAO (2007)
5. Lee, H., Smeaton, A.F., O'Connor, N., Smyth, B.: User Evaluation of Físchlár-News: An Automatic Broadcast News Delivery System. TOIS - ACM Transactions on Information Systems 24(2), 145–189 (2006)
6. Lee, H., Smeaton, A.F., O'Connor, N., Jones, G., Blighe, M., Byrne, D., Doherty, A., Gurrin, C.: Constructing a SenseCam Visual Diary as a Media Process. Multimedia Systems Journal, Special Issue on Canonical Processes of Media Production 14(6), 341–349 (2008)
7. Lee, H., Smeaton, A.F.: Designing the User Interface for the Físchlar Digital Video Library. Journal of Digital Information 2(4) (2002)
8. Lehane, B., O'Connor, N.E., Lee, H., Smeaton, A.F.: Indexing of Fictional Video Content for Event Detection and Summarisation. EURASIP Journal on Image and Video Processing, 1–15 (2007)
9. Lehane, B., O'Connor, N.E., Smeaton, A., Lee, H.: A System for Event-Based Film Browsing. In: Göbel, S., Malkewitz, R., Iurgel, I. (eds.) TIDSE 2006. LNCS, vol. 4326, pp. 334–345. Springer, Heidelberg (2006)
10. McKeown, K., Barzilay, R., Evans, D., Hatzivassiloglou, V., Klavans, J., Nenkovo, A., Sable, C., Schiffman, B., Sigelman, S.: Tracking and summarazing news on a daily basis with Columbia's Newsblaster. In: Proc. of the Human Language Technology Conference (2002)
11. Mohamad Ali, N., Smeaton, A.F.: Are Visual Informatics Actually Useful in Practice: A Study in a Film Studies Context. In: Badioze Zaman, H., Robinson, P., Petrou, M., Olivier, P., Schröder, H., Shih, T.K. (eds.) IVIC 2009. LNCS, vol. 5857, pp. 811–821. Springer, Heidelberg (2009)
12. Mohamad Ali, N., Smeaton, A.F., Lee, H., Brereton, P.: Developing, Deploying and Assessing the Usage of a Movie Archive System. In: HCI 2009. LNCS, vol. 5613, pp. 567–576. Springer, Heidelberg (2009)
13. Nielsen, J.: Usability Engineering. Academic Press, Inc. (1993)
14. O'Hare, N., Smeaton, A.F.: Context-Aware Person Identification in Personal Photo Collections. IEEE Transactions on Multimedia, Special Issue on Integration of Context and Content for Multimedia Management 11(2), 220–228 (2009)
15. O'Hare, N., Lee, H., Cooray, S., Gurrin, C., Jones, G., Malobabic, J., O'Connor, N., Smeaton, A.F., Uscilowski, B.: MediAssist: Using Content-Based Analysis and Context to Manage Personal Photo Collections. In: Sundaram, H., Naphade, M., Smith, J.R., Rui, Y. (eds.) CIVR 2006. LNCS, vol. 4071, pp. 529–532. Springer, Heidelberg (2006)
16. Pielot, M., Boll, S.: Tactile Wayfinder: Comparison of Tactile Waypoint Navigation with Commercial Pedestrian Navigation Systems. In: Floréen, P., Krüger, A., Spasojevic, M. (eds.) Pervasive Computing. LNCS, vol. 6030, pp. 76–93. Springer, Heidelberg (2010)
17. Smeaton, A.F., Gurrin, C., Lee, H., McDonald, K., Murphy, N., O'Connor, N.E., O'Sullivan, D., Smyth, B., Wilson, D.: The Físchlar-News-Stories System: Personalised Access to an Archive of TV News. In: RIAO 2004 - Coupling Approaches, Coupling Media and Coupling Languages for Information Retrieval, pp. 3–17 (2004)
18. Smeaton, A.F., Lee, H., McDonald, K.: Experiences of Creating Four Video Library Collections with the Físchlar System. International Journal on Digital Libraries 4(1), 42–44 (2004)
19. Smeaton, A.F., Over, P., Doherty, A.: Video Shot Boundary Detection: Seven Years of TRECVid Activity. Computer Vision and Image Understanding 114(4), 411–418 (2010)

Improving Accessibility through Aggregative E-Learning for All Framework

Khairuddin Kamaludin, Noor Faezah Mohd Yatim, and Md. Jan Nordin

Faculty of Information Science and Technology
Universiti Kebangsaan Malaysia
43600 UKM Bangi, Selangor Malaysia
udin2x@gmail.com, {nfmy,jan}@ftsm.ukm.my

Abstract. Common approach to accessible e-learning system are based on following strict guideline and requirement of assistive technology tools, developing alternative interface for user with impairment or separating of user platform and data platform. This paper has identified and discusses three major issues shared in common approaches as difficulty to implement guideline by W3C, accessibility on learning perspective and issues with emerging technology. When most approaches are able to provide contents to be access by user with impairment, the outcome can only be defined as technical perspective. User practices, preferences and ability in learning are affected by their physical disability, thus creating a barrier that demands learning accessibility. This paper has introduced Aggregative E-learning for All Framework that are based on both, technical and learning accessibility. The responsibilities of accessible e-learning are shared by content provider or instructor with system provider. In this framework, the technical components of accessibility become responsibility of system developer, and the learning components of accessibility are accountable to content provider.

Keywords: E-learning accessibility, User with Impairment, Assistive Technology, E-learning Framework.

1 Introduction

Various approaches have been implemented to provide an accessible e-learning system for diverse users to eliminate discrimination and equal access for users with impairment. This paper discusses the similarity issues arise from various approaches, guideline and framework that related to e-learning and people with disability (PWD). Three main issues identified are Implementation of W3C guideline, learning perspective on accessibility and emerging technology. This paper intends to propose new framework that separate accessibility into two perspectives, technical and learning. With shared responsibility, contents providers or instructor are accountable for learning accessibility of the contents to meet learning objectives and goals, and system provider hold the responsibility in technical accessibility of the system in general. The proposed framework is not restricted to follow specific standard organization guideline such as W3C, but also flexible with changes in technology and e-learning practices.

H. Badioze Zaman et al. (Eds.): IVIC 2011, Part II, LNCS 7067, pp. 85–92, 2011.

Three common approaches are by developing an e-learning that follow strict guidelines and requirement required by assistive technology (AT) tools (1), creating alternative interface for PWD (2), and separating user platform with data platform (3).

Among the guidelines that allow access to AT tools is W3C's Web Accessibility Initiative (WAI) that consists of Web Content Authoring Guidelines (WCAG), Authoring Tool Accessibility Guideline (ATAG) and User Agent Accessibility Guidelines (UAAG) and the newly introduced Accessible Rich Internet Applications (ARIA). W3C's CC/PP (Composite Capabilities/Preference Profile) also promoted the utilization of AT devices [1].

An approach of providing alternative interfaces has been applied in Multi-Purpose E-Environment for People with Sight Disabilities by Drigas et al. [2]. Previously, a similar approach for people with audio impairment is also conducted by the same researcher in 2005 [3].

Approached on separating user platform with data platform are implemented in various methods and frameworks such as aDeNu (adaptive Dynamic on-line Educational system based oN User modeling) as part of EU4ALL (European Unified Approach for Accessible Lifelong Learning) [4], IMS's ACCLIP (Accessibility for Learner Information Package) and ACCMD (Accessibility MetaData), Model Driven Architecture (MDA) that combine ACCLIP with W3C's CC/PP [5] and Profiling Learners for Custom Learning Framework [6].

2   Current Issues in Implementing Accessible E-Learning

Current researches have been able to solve multiple issues related to providing access for e-learning to PWD. However, there are similar patents and area where problem related to PWD accessibility in e-learning can be improved. In this section, we will discuss on issues that currently solved and issues that still existing, related to the topic.

Current implemented solutions are proven to be able to provide navigation, data and information to PWD. Different media contents can be transformed to another, for example from text to audio, audio to text, video with close caption and so on. Use of AT has been recognized by system developer, by implementing CC/PP as well as user profile/model as part of the development framework.

Most of the e-learning for PWD approaches are successful in providing access to data from various media to an alternative contains, as well as developing alternative navigation for hypermedia. However, in pedagogical perspective the accessibility of curriculum design and knowledge presentation in learning object is still in question.

2.1 Issues in Implementing W3C Guideline

The motivation for most of the current e-learning accessibility solution is to meet minimum requirement provided by legislation or institution policy. However, it is also common for an e-learning or web-based system not being able to comply with WAI standards as well as other accessibility auditing tools.

A survey in 2004 showed only 58% of 160 UK University online entry point are able to conform with WCAG A and less than 6% for WCAG AA conformant. The result with lower increase as opposed to the same survey made in 2002 where only 43% conformant with WCAG A and only 2% for WCAG AA conformant [7]. Considering the complexity of e-learning, the worse is expected. Discussion within web development community for educational institute in United Kingdom shows that WCAG framework is hard to be implemented [7] due to:

- WCAG are based on W3C perspective and too theoretical for real world.
- Web author have no control over user access facility and practice, Therefore to meet all WAI requirement is impossible.
- Phrases uses in the guidelines are very ambiguous and open to various interpretations.
- Failed to recognize accessibility by vendors and other proprietary guidelines that not based on W3C.

Even if all W3C requirement and consideration are made to allow all access through the system, it could be argued that the system would be the best solution for universal access to all users. Such system is not only limited to certain web technology, it also has to negotiate with all disability, thus it will give less benefit for common students to reach their maximum potentials.

2.2 Accessibility in Learning Perspective

Most of the approaches try to meet only one goal, the technical aspect of e-learning accessibility to PWD. While technical accessibility is important, it should be also conformant to the learning objectives and goal of each course taken by students.

A survey conducted in 2008 by Eric Bel and Emma Bradburn suggest that majority of the respondent from teacher in United Kingdom's Higher Education institute regards accessibility refers to technical access to resources and only some regard accessibility as an opportunity to learn and the provision and access to resources[8]. It is suggested that re-conceptualizing of accessibility as a pedagogical challenge rather than a technical issue [8]. This shows that accessibility practices are limited to technical perspectives.

From current implementation and finding made by Eric Bel and Emma Bradburn, it shows that the learning perspective of accessibility has been overlooked due to the nature of available guidance material provided that concentrates on technical aspect of accessibility [8]. Thus, the accessibility of a system should look at both, technical and learning perspective.

Learning accessibility that focus on usability and the effectiveness of learning process has become the main concern for learning requirement. Some researches argue that reusability and open deployment that have been suggested in various framework discussed earlier are hard to be implemented. Separating user platform and data platform is difficult in practices because of the learning factors of PWD. Compare with normal user, different impairment resulting in different needs of pedagogical approaches, semantic content and interaction characteristics [9].

From a research done by Juozenas et al. three main barriers are providing input, interpreting output and reading supportive material to a level that meet learning outcome and goal [10]. The ability to meet learning outcome and goals are not solely based on user physical ability. Therefore, the elements of human tasks that include cognitive ability, perceptual ability and psychomotor of PWD should be considered as part of e-learning. For PWD, their physical characteristic of impairment may affect their performance, resulting different preferences and learning process.

Using profiling system in implementing e-learning should go beyond providing interface for PWD. It should make the system to be accessible both, technically and pedagogically. For example, a consideration needs for students with hearing impairment are their difficulty on accepting e-learning, especially on adapting text due to the cognitive process of their study and low linguistic competency [11]. Therefore, having it all in text form would make the contents accessible technically but does not necessarily meet learning accessibility.

Current solution that concentrated on technical accessibility of the system does not meet the basic goal of e-learning. User with visual impairment is not equally or more receptive in language skills, comparing with normally sighted individual [12]. Their language development is more self-oriented with limited meaning [13]. With lack of visual references and have reduced integration of information from environment, It is common for them to receive less description on objects and events details in developing communication and learning process [14].

Even if the information is technically accessible in current solution, it still needs improvement in learning perspectives. For both visual and audio impairment, users usually depend on singular memory skills, either visual memory or auditory memory, which would affect their performance during learning. In learning process, students with visual impairment have difficulty to comprehend information derived from tables, chart, graphs or diagram, due to visual references and memory skills. Similar case occurs for auditory memory requirement for people with audio impairment. Different characteristic and level of disability would bring another different preference and learning requirement that should be faced by the developer of e-learning system.

Thus, consideration should be made on making e-learning to be developed not only based on technical accessibility requirement, but learning accessibility as well. A well define requirement should be able to identify if certain content is replaceable for information delivery, or replaceable for alternative learning contents, objective and/or syllabus. This paper proposed a framework that aggregating various elements on technical and learning to meet specific individual needs in e-learning.

2.3 Issues with Emerging Technology

Continuing issues with Assistive Technology are to developed tools and application that can keep up with the latest trends or changes in technology. With the emerging rich web technology, such as web 2.0 and the Semantic web, it is believe that accessibility issues on the web should take a new approach.

Various issues highlighted by Walter Kern in 2008 related to developer perspective of web 2.0 [15] including:

- No relevant and official standard or guideline on web 2.0. Most guideline are on usability and not accessibility. Guideline such as Torab (2007) and Kroski (2007) are concentrating on design, style, visual and social aspect of web 2.0.
- Most of accessibility evaluation tools could not be used to evaluate web 2.0

- Assistive Technology doesn't comply with asynchronous web change, such as no visual progress indicator for AJAX request and website contents that inaccessible when JavaScript's are disable.

Some of the issues raised in web 2.0 are solved by implementing WAI-ARIA guideline. As of 2011, the first version of WAI-ARIA is available as a working draft. Many of the issues related to web 2.0, rich contents and semantic web can be solved by following the editor's draft [16] or W3C's ARIA candidate recommendation [17].

In user perspective, the use of social networking and web 2.0 also revealed the following issues:

- Enormous increase in web video contents, such as video blogs, video instruction and others may cause accessibility issues for user with visual/audio impairment.
- Web becoming more graphics than text and limited visual description resulting accessibility issues to user with visual impairment.
- AT cannot fully handle the web 2.0 technology and practice [18].
- No guarantee that tools and toolkits used by web developer can generate fully accessibility contents [18].

With some of the framework and guidelines that are specific to certain technology, aggregative e-learning framework for all is created to be receptive on new technology and blend with others framework or guideline that related to e-learning.

3 Supporting Learning through Aggregative E-Learning for All Framework

With rapid changes of technology, and the need on open framework that is not limited to specific technology, we introduce Aggregative E-learning For All Framework that based on user profiles and contents profile that look into both technical accessibility and learning accessibility.

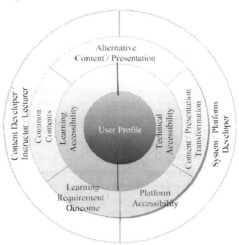

Fig. 1. Aggregative E-learning For All Framework

In Figure 1 we summarized the Aggregative E-learning For All Framework that is based on user-centric profile, and content developer and system developer on the edge. The left hemisphere of the diagram, the relationship between e-learning user and responsibility of content developer (or instructor) in providing e-learning accessibility are defined. The right hemisphere of the diagram shows the relationship between user of e-learning system and system provider. This framework acknowledge that both content developer and system developer, are responsible in providing accessible e-learning, while user are required to have access on assistive tools through user profile.

3.1   Suitable Content in Aggregative E-Learning in All Framework

Content developers are responsible to evaluate learning accessibility which involves learning requirement/outcome and common contents based on subject syllabus and learning goal. With user profile defined, instructor of given subject can provide alternative learning object or outcome to the student. If exemption is required due to user disability, it can be define to either partial exemption of learning object or user are request to take alternative subject due to their incompetency to meet learning outcome for the whole subject. Common contents refers to learning contents that can be shared by all user, regardless their disability.

Learning accessibility in figure 1.0 is located closed to user profile, but still part of content developer responsibility. In this framework, the suggested task is to evaluate the learning contents based on user ability in cognitive, perceptual and psychomotor. The physical characteristic of visual, audio or motor impairment leads to user preferences and ability in those three areas. For example, if the cognitive process required in learning contents is not suitable for user with visual impairment, content developer have an option to either provide alternative contents or alternative learning outcome.

3.2   Suitable System Requirement in Aggregative E-Learning in All Framework

Technical accessibility component in figure 1 includes user system capability, browser capability and assistive tools capability. Some accessibility control available in operating system can be used to manipulate information provided/required by user. The use of operating system design for user with disability should also be recognized by e-learning developer as main preference for matching components. Users with disability also use their preferred browser in accessing internet contents. Some web browser like Mozilla Firefox can be combined with AxsJAX for audio control and screen reader. It is very common for browser to have content enlargement function, color scheme and text preferences and other tools. If user system and browser cannot manipulate information to make it accessible to user, Assistive tools should be able to transform contents into acceptable output to user.

Other than technical accessibility, system developer is also responsible in platform accessibility and contents/presentation transformation. The component in platform accessibility related to vision, hearing and touch requirement to interact with the system. The areas of concerns are during presentation and interaction. Transformability of presentation refers to the ability to transform or control using user tools. Presentation transformation is the ability to change one media to another for user input or control.

3.3   Alternative Contents in Aggregative E-Learning for All Framework

A shared element between system developer and content developer is alternative content and presentation. This is refers to elements which cannot be transformed to user. It can be due to inability of the content to be transformed or the quality of transformed object for learning process. If the content is unable to be transformed automatically, it is a responsibility for both system developer and content developer to find an alternative content or presentation for specific group of user. If the quality of transformed material does not meet the required quality in learning outcome or requirement, content developer are responsible in providing the alternative.

The purpose of this framework is to integrate both aspect of learning accessibility and technical accessibility into implementation of e-learning. It is also use to recognized and acknowledge the responsibility for accessibility should be share by user, system provider and content provider. In order to develop user profile based on technical, current methods such as W3C's Web Accessibility Initiative (WAI) or IMS's AccessforAll, ACCLIPS and ACCMD can be used. The technical accessibility (right hemisphere) of the framework can also work together with available e-learning framework that is concentrated on technical accessibility such as APLE (adaptable Personal Learning Environment), Profiling Learners for Custom Learning Framework or Model Driven Architecture. The suggested implementation for learning accessibility (left hemisphere) of the framework can be done by creating user profile matching. User profile can be created and verified with the help of learning accessibility center, that represented by learning or disability expert and pathologist. It should also be designed to cooperate with institution practices in learning object model.

4   Conclusion

The responsibility of providing accessible e-learning should be shared by system provider and content provider. General principles in designing e-learning system must support teaching staff and technical staff in helping providing the accessible contents and presentation. A technically accessible e-learning contents doesn't necessarily improved user experience and ability in learning process. With the introduction of learning accessibility into one framework, the preferences and ability in learning are well defined to help student in meeting learning objectives and goal.

Acknowledgement. We would like to thank and acknowledge Multimedia and Usability Research Group of Faculty of Information Science and Technology, Universiti Kebangsaan Malaysia.

References

1. Rodriguez-Ascaso, A., et al.: Towards Universal Access to eLearning in TUMAS. In: Conati, C., McCoy, K., Paliouras, G. (eds.) UM 2007. LNCS (LNAI), vol. 4511, pp. 27–31. Springer, Heidelberg (2007)
2. Drigas, A., Koukianakis, L., Papagerasimou, Y.: An E-Learning Environment for Nontraditional Students with Sight Disabilities. In: ASEE/IEEE, 36th Annual Frontiers in Education Conference. IEEE, San Diego (2006)
3. Drigas, A., Vrettaros, J., Kouremenos, D.: An e-learning management system for the deaf people. World Scientific and Engineering Academy and Society, WSEAS (2005)
4. Santos, O.C., Rodriguez-Ascaso, A., Boticario, J.G., Martin, L.: User Modeling for Attending Functional Diversity for ALL in Higher Education. In: Weske, M., Hacid, M.-S., Godart, C. (eds.) WISE Workshops 2007. LNCS, vol. 4832, pp. 301–312. Springer, Heidelberg (2007)
5. Bouraoui, A., Jemni, M., Laabidi, M.: A Model Driven Framework to Provide Accessible E-learning for Students with Disabilities. In: 1st International Conference on ICTA (Information and Communication Technology and Accessibility), ICT & Accessibility, Hammamet, Tunisia (2007)
6. Salomoni, P., et al.: Profiling Learners with Special Needs for Custom E-learning Experiences, a Closed Case? In: ACM, Proceedings of the 2007 International Cross-Disciplinary Conference on Web Accessibility (W4A), pp. 84–92. ACM, Banff (2007)
7. Kelly, B., et al.: Forcing standardization or accommodating diversity?: a framework for applying the WCAG in the real world. In: Proceedings of the 2005 International Cross-Disciplinary Workshop on Web Accessibility (W4A). ACM, Chiba (2005)
8. Bel, E., Bradburn, E.: Reframing Teachers' Conceptions of Accessible E-Learning Designs. In: Proceedings of the 2008 Eighth IEEE International Conference on Advanced Learning Technologies. IEEE Computer Society (2008)
9. Savidis, A., Grammenos, D., Stephanidis, C.: Developing Inclusive E-learning Systems. Universal Access in the Information Society 5(1), 51–72 (2006)
10. Juozenas, A., Kasparaitis, P., Ratkevicius, K., Rudinskas, D., Rudzionis, A., Rudzionis, V., Sidaras, S.: DfA Implementations for People with Vision and Hearing Disabilities: Application and Development for Information Society. In: Stephanidis, C. (ed.) HCI 2007. LNCS, vol. 4554, pp. 686–695. Springer, Heidelberg (2007)
11. Bueno, F.J., et al.: E-learning Content Adaptation for Deaf Students. In: Proceedings of the 12th Annual SIGCSE Conference on Innovation and Technology in Computer Science Education (ITiCSE 2007). ACM SIGCSE Bulletin, Dundee (2007)
12. Fraiberg, S.H.: Insights from the Blind. Basic Books, New York (1977)
13. Andersen, E.S., Dunlea, A., Kekelis, L.S.: Blind Children's Language: Resolving Some Differences. Journal of Child Language 11(3), 645–664 (1984)
14. McConachie, H.R., Moore, V.: Early Expressive Language of Severely Visually Impaired Children. Developmental Medicine & Child Neurology 36(3), 230–240 (1994)
15. Kern, W.: Web 2.0 - End of Accessibility? - Analysis of most common problems with web 2.0 based applications regarding web accessibility. International Journal of Public Information Systems 2, 131–154 (2008)
16. W3C. Accessibile Rich Internet Applications (WAI-ARIA 1.0): Editor's Draft (2011), http://www.w3.org/WAI/PF/aria/complete
17. W3C. Accessibile Rich Internet Application (WAI-ARIA 1.0): W3C Candidate Recomendation (May 9, 2011), http://www.w3.org/TR/wai-aria/complete
18. Yesilada, Y., Harper, S.: Web 2.0 and the semantic web: hindrance or opportunity? In: W4A – International Cross-Disciplinary Conference on Web Accessibility 2007. SIGACCESS Access. Comput., 19–31 (2008)

Exploiting the Query Expansion
through Knowledgebases for Images

Roohullah and J. Jaafar

Department of Computer and Information Sciences
Universiti Teknologi PETRONAS, Malaysia
Roohullah_orc@yahoo.com, jafreez@petronas.edu.my

Abstract. The evolution in the digital technology from the last few decades and different multimedia sources like Broadcast news, Movies, Videos, images, etc. have increased the size volume of the digital media daily. Due to this explosive growth in the digital media volume, it's strongly urged for the system that efficiently and effectively compiles the user demand and retrieving the relevant images. In this paper, the user query will be expanded through an open-source knowledge base WordNet and ConceptNet for retrieves the images on the base of different synonyms and concepts. This technique covers the word mismatch and word sense disambiguation (WSD) problem. Propose method effectively applied on the open benchmark image dataset LabelMe. The experimental results show that of the propose techniques have improved the retrieval performance over the traditional ones and get the accuracy up to 94% for single word and 83% for sentence word queries.

Keywords: Query Expansion, knowledge bases, images corpus, Semantic gap.

1 Introduction

In recently years, there has been a phenomenal growth in technology revolution in digital media. The explosive growth of digital media both online and offline increases the expectation that it will be easily managed and effectively search like a text. Now-a-days, the digital media are the regular part of our digital lives, every moment or places the people can get the pictures and share through online and offline devices or services with friends. It is very difficult for the average users to find the relative images from the large corpus of data. The most popular technique used to find the relevant images from the large corpus is the keyword based search [1]. Sometimes the keyword queries cannot describe what the users really want or mostly the users are not expert in formulating the keyword query. After numbers of studies, mostly the user can enter the queries is too much short, which are not describing the actual content of the information and as a result the poor coverage of relevant information [1]. Secondly, a fundamental problem in information retrieval is wording mismatch, which occurs when the authors of a document and the user of an information retrieval system use different words to describe the same concept [2], [3]. Usually, on relevant words, images in the corpus can be found, typically many irrelevant images are also retrieved, and many relevant images are missed. So the word mismatch problem has

H. Badioze Zaman et al. (Eds.): IVIC 2011, Part II, LNCS 7067, pp. 93–103, 2011.

become one of the increasingly important research topics in IR. Furthermore, sometimes the retrieval has an effect query expression by different users, due to different backgrounds and experiences of different users. The information inquired could ranges from various perspectives [4].

Query expansion [5] is a method to utilize within IR for the remedy of this kind of problem. A user query can expand with additional related terms to the original terms. From the last few decades, different of the query techniques have been introduced by different researchers from the manually constructed thesauri to the open-source knowledge base. All these methods show the effective performance in the IR system.

As much of the work has already done on the query expansion but still the area is worth investigating. In this paper, we are proposing query expansion lexically and semantically via knowledge bases, where first the query is passed through Natural Language Processing (NLP) function for some of the basic pre-processing like Tokenization, Lemmatization and Parts-of-Speech Tagging (POST). After the NLP, the user query will be passed into Candidate Term Selection that selects POST words from the user query; when the candidate term selection is done the selected terms will be passed into a Lexical and semantic expansion that added related synonyms and concepts through WordNet and ConceptNet. During the expansion, the irrelevant words will be also adding to the user query. So to remove these words from the expanded terms the Semantic Similarity Selection will be applied, which is select the related words to the user query from the expanded terms and after this the process completion the selected words will be passed into Ranked and Retrieval for step that retrieves the images from the Image corpus.

Section 2 reviews of the related work. Section 3 includes the new propose algorithm. Section 4 includes the how to evaluate evaluation performance of the algorithm. Section 5 contains the experiments, i.e. to evaluate and compare the propose algorithm with existing ones. In last section 6 includes the conclusion.

2 Related Works

Query expansion is one of the predictive methods for information Retrieval (IR) system. However, sometimes these methods need some techniques that more accurately retrieve the information from the IR system. The vocabulary gap is the problem facing by most of the IR system, where the same concept has been labeled with different words while Word Sense Disambiguation (WSD) is another key factor of poor information retrieval by the IR system. WSD is the proficiency of the system that defines the meaning of the terms and its context. So Query Expansion is specific in using for these problems to reduce the vocabulary gap as well as to solve WSD of the user query by using the WordNet knowledgebase.

From the last few decades, numbers of researchers have been conducted in defining different methods for query expansion to retrieve the data from the IR system. Okabe and Yamada [7] expand the user query with minimal user interaction. They expand the query from the initial retrieval results, and the user can select any terms from the retrieval results, and the search engine can find more information related to this topic. However, this method is too much valuable but fails to get more accurate results. Moreover, Badie et al [10] have expanded the user query from the initial retrieval results and little improvement in Result. XU and Croft [28] compared the performance of utilizing the local and global documents' analysis for QE (Query Expansion), while their experiment shows that the local analysis is more effective than the global analysis. Firstly, time has expanded the user query through a knowledge base by the Voorhees [29]. She expands the user query through the lexical knowledge base by using the WordNet. Their experiments showed that the query expansion can get little improving in the retrieval results. Liu et al [30] also using the WordNet to expand the user query automatically. They performed phrase recognition and define WSD on queries and then selected highly correlated terms of the same sense with query terms. Similarly different researchers have been using the WordNet for information retrieval like from a mini web logs image retrieval [8], log mining techniques for support Web Query [12], Folksonomy tag co-occurrence for Web [13], Compact Concept Ontology (CCO) [22], Abouenour et al [23] have expanded the query of user through WordNet for Arabic language and get a high-precision result from the Retrieval system. Wang and Zhang [11] have expanded the user query through WordNet and then remove the semantic similarity space between the expanded terms and original query. However, all these techniques have increased the Precision of the system but still the problems of the Recall. Which are not increased like a Precision of the IR system? LU et al [9] had expanded the Query by using the snippets' technique that the user's manually select semantic similarity terms from the expanded terms. The experiment work showing little more accurately results. Similarly, Chli and De Wilde [17] had also used Subdivision-based interactive query expansion for information retrieval from the internet. Wu et al [5] study about the ontology based that this query expansion through ontology based [14] is given more effective results. Conesa et al [15] have expanded the WEB query through a semantic knowledge base. Grootjen et al [16] have been using conceptual query expansion for searching and increasing the values of Precision and Recall for the retrieval system.

However, still these techniques need more remedy to effectively and efficiently retrieve information from the large corpus of images, and the user can retrieve the images based on different synonyms and concept.

A thesaurus is defined as a dictionary of synonyms and related words. In most situations, a thesaurus is used to improve retrieval performance by expanding queries with same words that are related to the original keywords [6]. There are two types of building thesaurus in the queries 1) Manually and 2) Automatically. First thesauri is built manually by linguistic and domain experts. A manual thesaurus is often too broad or as well narrow. Mostly manual thesaurus is usually time-consuming and depends on some people, there are a lot of problems to manually thesaurus, which are eventually updated by regularly and also there are a lot of errors according to human kind of different natures. However, the automatically thesaurus had added the synonyms with the user query by itself and there is no interaction of the user query and besides improving the retrieval results of the IR system.

WordNet [31] is a lexical dictionary of English words. It expands the user query for the short and simple queries but for the complex or semantic based queries, it's just outmoded. The WordNet expansion relies merely on the lexical meaning rather than the conceptual meaning of the query.

Query Expansion is still the existing issues to effective retrieve results from the large information corpus. However, the trends now move to the semantic expansion of the user queries. The systems those are heavily relied on lexical analysis, flunks in the complex queries. It does not discover the semantic relatedness or have no possibility for common sense reasoning. Despite the facts of these, that lexical analysis plays a vital role in the extracting the meaning from the user request. The common sense reasoning also plays a main role in the user query. Common sense knowledge includes knowledge about the social, physical, spatial, temporal and psychological aspects of daily life. WordNet has been used ordinarily for the query expansion. It has made some modification, but it was limited. Several studies expose the importance of common sense reasoning in information retrieval, data filtering, data mining, etc. [18].

The proposed method expands the user query through lexically as well as semantically. For lexically query expanded, used WordNet, while for semantic expansion, the ConceptNet is selected. ConceptNet is an Open Mind common sense reasoning system for common sense knowledge representation and processing. ConceptNet is developed by MIT Media Laboratory and is presently the largest commonsense Knowledgebase [19]. ConceptNet has been used by a few researchers to expanding the user query. The Annotation and Retrieval Integration Agent (ARIA) project also used the common sense reasoning to bridge the semantic gap and expand the retrieval efficacy [20]. Comparison between the WordNet and ConceptNet knowledgebase's has already been testing by using TREC-6, TREC-7 and TREC-8 datasets. The result exposes that the WordNet has enhanced the Precision while the ConceptNet has improved the Recall of the IR system [21].

3 Methodology

To optimize the performance of the Information Retrieval (IR) System, propose the novel approach for the IR System where the query is expanded lexically and commonsensical by using knowledge bases. Propose Query expansion includes the seven steps. 1) Natural Language Processing, 2) Candidate Term Selection, 3) Lexical Expansion, 4) Semantically expansion, 5) Average Mean calculation, 6) Semantic Filtration by using semantic similarity technique, and 7) Ranked the Retrieve Results. The overall structure of the propose system is shown in the Figure 1. Where the user input in the form of Query is passes through all-inclusive, the stated steps and retrieves the required images in the form of results from the Image Corpus.

When the user enters the Query into the System in the type of Q, The query may be a type of single word or a sentence query. The query can be represented in the type of Tn.

$$Q = T1, T2, T3, \ldots\ldots\ldots\ldots, Tn. \tag{1}$$

$$Q = \sum_{n=1}^{n} Tn \tag{2}$$

Where Tn is representing the total number of tokens of the user query. Initially, the user query will be passed into Natural Language Processing (NLP) where the user query converted into different tokens. After Tokenization, the user query may be existed in a different suffixes or different morphological form like future, past form or plural. To convert this form into base form by using the lemmatization that converts all the different suffixes into base suffixes. After the lemmatization, we apply

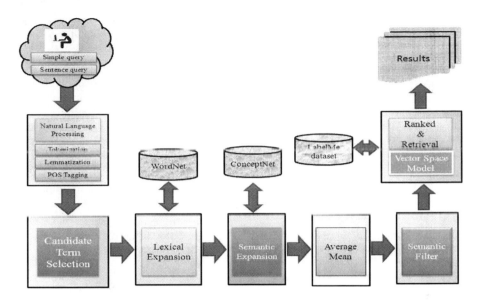

Fig. 1. Query Expansion Through Lexically and Semantically

Montilingua [24] that label the Part Of Speech (POST) from the user query. Montilingua tagger uses Penn Treebank tag set for object of speech tagging [25]. So from the tagging only the appropriate words will be select from the expanded list for further processing. Because there a lot of unusual words in the user query add in expansion, which is decreasing the precision of the IR system? So for candidate term's selection only nouns, verbs and adverbs will be select for further processing and stops the irrelevant words or common words. So the selected candidate terms are represented the following finite set.

$$C= C1, C2, C3, ..., Cn \tag{3}$$

$$C= \sum_1^n Cn \tag{4}$$

Here Cn is representing the total candidate terms' selections of the user query. After the candidate terms' selection, the selected words will be passes into Lexical expansion, which are done through WordNet Knowledge base that attaches the same meaning synonyms known as synsets.

The WordNet has approved the word mismatch problem and improve the precision of the IR system. However, the problem Word Sense disambiguation (WSD) still exists, which are solving through a common sense knowledge base. So after the lexically expansion the candidate terms are also expanding through semantically with the help of an open-source knowledge base ConceptNet, that attaches the semantic knowledge with the candidate terms' selection to solve the WSD and as well increase the Recall of the IR system. The attachments of the Synsets and Semantic to candidate terms selections are representing the following impression.

$$C'= \coprod_{n=1}^n (C(\sum_{m=1}^m LEm, \ \sum_{i=1}^i SEi))n \tag{5}$$

Where LE represents the Lexical expansion while SE represents the semantic expansion that attaches with the candidate terms selection. C' represents the set of the selected Lexical expansion and the Semantic Expansion of the candidate term selection.

From the lexical and semantic expansion, there are lots of concepts will be attaching to the user who increases the recall of the system. However, expansion through ConceptNet and WordNet knowledge base it will be attaching a lot of irrelevant words to the user query which are infecting the precision of the IR system. So to remove or stops the irrelevant word from the expanded terms. We are applying semantic filtration that filter the relevant words from the user query through average means. For finding the average mean of the expanded terms, we are adding all the Lexical and semantic expansion words on run time and find the threshold value that selects those words which are above of this value of equal and remove the other words from the expanded terms. So it will be filters those terms which are semantically relevant to the user query. The set of the filter expanded terms are representing the following equation.

$$Q' = T'1, T'2, T'3, \ldots\ldots, T'n \tag{6}$$

$$Q' = \sum_{n=1}^{n} T'n \tag{7}$$

T' represents the filters expanded terms.

After the semantic filtration, the filter expanded terms will be passed into retrieval and Ranked. The Ranked will be done through the well-known model Vector Space Model (VSM). The VSM has compared the filters expanded terms to Meta's data attach with the images. The VSM has retrieved the images in the basis of concepts attach with it and ranked according to their frequency. The similarity between the filter expanded terms and the images along with user original query will be calculated in the form of cosine measurement.

$$\cos\Theta Ii = similarity(Q', Ii) \tag{8}$$

$$Similarity\ (Q', Ii) = \sum_i WQ, i, WIi\ /\ \sqrt{\sum_j W2Qj}\ \sqrt{\sum_j W2i, j} \tag{9}$$

The Vector Space Model (VSM) will be ranked the results that the largest frequency images will be display before the lower frequency images' similarity related to the user query and so on.

4 Experiments

For the experiments of the propose algorithm to check the efficiency. The algorithm applies it on the open source available dataset for research and academia LabelMe dataset [27]. LabelMe developed by the MIT Computer science and Artificial Intelligence Laboratory (CSAIL) [19], which provides digital images, with different annotations. The corpus consists above 9,000 images. 66,000 annotated images and 30,886 images are still not annotated and remain for tagging.

For the evolution of this algorithm, the two most popular measurements have been applied. Which is Precision and Recall [26]? Precision is defined to the total numbers of retrieved images with all corpuses, while the Recall is the specific related images with retrieval images. The highest value of both measurements is 1.

$$Precision = \frac{[Relevent\ result] \cap [Retrieved\ Result]}{[Retrieved\ result]} \tag{10}$$

$$Recall = \frac{[Relevent\ result] \cap [Retrieved\ Result]}{[Relevent\ result]} \tag{11}$$

On proposed method performed two (2) experiments on the Query Expansion through Lexically and semantically on the LabelMe dataset. The Figure 2 has shown the single query with their expansion through lexically and semantically, and Figure 3 shows their output of this single query with expansion of different terms.

User Single Query	Lexically Expansion	Semantically Expansion	Semantic Filtration
Birds	fowl(1), dame(1), doll(1), wench(1), skirt(1), chick(1), boo(1), hoot(1), hiss(1), raspberry(1), razzing(1), razz(1), snort(1), shuttlecock(1), birdie(1), shuttle(1)	bird(1), bush(0.53), door(0.59), feather(0.46), feather flock(0.44), fish(0.77), hand(0.53), next worm(0.71), paradise(0.31), person 's nest(0.49), predator(0.75), prey(0.75), raptor(0.95), similarity(0.4), swan(0.9), twig(0.4), wind(0.59), wing(0.63), winter(0.38), worth two(0.53)	bird(1),fowl(1),dame(1),doll(1),wench(1),skirt(1),chick(1),boo(1),hoot(1),hiss(1),raspberry(1),razzing(1),razz(1),snort(1),shuttlecock(1),birdie(1),shuttle(1),fish(0.77),next worm(0.71),predator(0.75),prey(0.75),raptor(0.95),swan(0.9),wing(0.63)

Fig. 2. Query expansion through Lexically and Semantically for single Word Query

Figure 2 shows the user query expansion that expands the query "Birds" through Lexically that adds the same meaning words. Which are called synonyms has been adding to the user query from the WordNet. Similarly different concepts of the user query "Birds" like bird wing, bird winter, etc. have been add from the ConceptNet for the purpose that retrieves the images based on where the same query concept had existed. The value of the expanded terms that are showing in the lexical as well as semantic expansion, i.e. fowl (1), dame (1), bush (0.53) etc. represents relevancy to the user query. It shows that 1 is 100% these words are relevant to the user query. Similarly, for 0.53 shows that 53% this word is relevant to the original query and same as for the rest of the word values. These values are provided by default the WordNet and ConceptNet. Through expansion, there are lots of words have been added and also there are chances that some irrelevant words in addition add.

To stops or remove the irrelevant words after the lexical and semantic expansion semantic similarity applies that filters those words, which are the highest value and mostly relevant to the original query and stop the lower value from the expanded terms. Semantic filtration represents that word which is nearest to the user query. The filtration words are now applied for on the LabelMe images' dataset and get the result. The first top three (3) results are shown in Figure 3.

Fig. 3. Show the output of the single word Query Expansion

When applying the word "Birds" and its filters expanded terms for searching on the LabelMe image dataset. So it will retrieve lots of images from the dataset. In the retrieval results from a large number of images related to the word "Birds" while a few numbers of image's non-relevant to the user query. In Figure 3, the first top three (3) images have shown of the retrieval system. Through this method images search and retrieval, the accuracy of the system is very high while the error is too much low. The accuracy of this method has shown in the Figure 6.

Similarly, also gave a query in the shape of a sentence that successfully algorithm has converted into different terms and then expand through lexically and semantically. Figure 4 has shown the sentence query with their expansion and Figure 5 shows the results of this sentence query.

User sentence Query	Lexically Expansion		Semantically Expansion		Semantic Filtration
birds flying	Bird	Fly	Bird	Fly	bird(1),fly(1),fowl(1),dame(1), doll(1),wench(1),skirt(1),chick(1),boo(1),hoot(1),hiss(1),raspbe rry(1),razzing(1),razz(1),snort(1),shuttlecock(1),birdie(1),shuttl e(1),wing(1),aviate(1),pilot(1),f ell(1),vanish(1),flee(1),vanish(1),vaporize(1),fish(0.77),next worm(0.71),predator(0.75),prey (0.75),raptor(0.95),swan(0.9), wing(0.63), air(0.46), airplane(0.53),airplane and moth(0.72),bird(0.59),bunny(0. 48), dog(0.74), fun(0.6),kite(0.71),pilot(1),plan e(0.7),wing(1)
	fowl(1),dame(1),doll(1),wen ch(1),skirt(1),c hick(1),boo(1) ,hoot(1),hiss(1),raspberry(1), razzing(1),razz (1),snort(1),sh uttlecock(1),bi rdie(1),shuttle(1).	wing(1),aviate(1),pilot(1),fell(1),vanish(1),flee(1),take flight(0.7).vanis h(1),vaporize(1) .	bird(1), bush(0.53), door(0.59), feather(0.46), feather flock(0.44), fish(0.77), hand(0.53), next worm(0.71), paradise(0.31), person 's nest(0.49), predator(0.75), prey(0.75), raptor(0.95), similarity(0.4), swan(0.9), twig(0.4), wind(0.59), wing(0.63), winter(0.38), worth two(0.53).	air(0.46), airplane(0.53), airplane and moth(0.72), bird(0.59), bunny(0.48), capability(0.2), danger(0.36), dog(0.74), fly(1), fun(0.6), kite(0.71), pilot(1), plane(0.7), which(0), wing(1).	

Fig. 4. Query Expansion through Lexically and Semantically for Sentence Query

In the Figure 4 represents, the user query in the shape of Multi words that given for searching the images on the LableMe dataset. In this type of query, firstly the propose system has split into an atomic word that each part separately expands through

WordNet and ConceptNet and then filters the relevant words in the semantic similarity filtration. Each atomic word has the same procedure is like for the single query. However, in the sentence query, every separate word has to expand in Lexical and semantic parts by parts but in the semantic filters step, they all be come into combined for searching to be applied.

Fig. 5. Show the output of the sentence Query

The retrieval result of the sentence query is very effective and gets the value of the Precision and Recall is the highest which are showing in Figure 6. However, in the sentence query the rear multiple concepts exist in the user query, so the search engine has retrieved the images, mostly relevant but some of the mare not relevant to the user query. The accuracy of the sentence query represents in the Precision and Recall Curve. In Figure 5, the first three (3) retrieved images represent that retrieved the propose system.

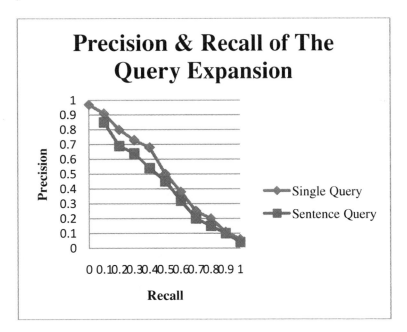

Fig. 6. Show the evolution of single word and sentence user queries. It is clear show that proposed a method succeed in the perceptible improvement in the propose techniques.

The accuracy of the propose system for both queries will be showing in the Figure 6. It shows that propose a system is more efficient and accurately given the results according to the user requirements. The accuracy of the propose system is showing by the two measurements Precision and Recall. Precision represented the total number of retrieval results and Recall represents the relevant images in the total retrieval results. The value of both measurements is 1.

Evaluation of the propose method, that given two (2) query show in the Figure 6 and calculates the Precision and Recall of the retrieval results. For the single word query, the accuracy of the propose system is 94% while for the sentence words query the accuracy is up to 83%. In this method add the ConceptNet knowledge base it has given 25% increase retrieval as compare to LabelMe previous method. However, a difference between the accuracy of the single word and sentence words queries are that, single query represents the single concept while the sentence query represents the multiple concepts. So for it once time multiple concepts' exit in the user query. In contrast, propose a system is given more accurately results over the traditional ones.

5 Conclusions

This paper presents a new query expansion through Lexically and Semantically with the open available Knowledge base WordNet and Conceptnet. The experiments represent of our algorithm is more efficiently and accurately according to the user requires and displays the results through different synonyms and also with a different concept of the user query. The accuracy of the propose system for single word query is 93% while for the sentence, query is 83% achieve from the overall image's retrieval.

References

1. Jin, S., Lin, H., Su, S.: Query expansion based on Folksonomy tag co-occurrence analysis. In: IEEE International Conference on Granular Computing, pp. 300–305 (2009)
2. Kobayashi, M., Takeda, K.: Information on retrieval on the web. ACM Computing Survey 32(2), 144–173 (2000)
3. Nekrestyanov, I., Panteleeva, N.: Text Retrieval system for the web. Journal Programming and Computer Software 28(4), 207–225 (2002)
4. Li, J., Guo, M., Tian, S.: A new Approach to Query Expansion. In: Proceeding of the 4th International Conference on Machine Learning and Cybernetics, IEEE pp. 2302–2306 (2005)
5. Wu, J., Ilyas, I., Weddell, G.: A Study of Ontology-based Query Expansion. Technical Report CS-2011-04
6. Sheng, F., Fan, X., Thomas, G.: A Knowledge-Based Approach to Effective Document Retrieval. Journal of Systems Integration 10(2), 411–436 (2001)
7. Okabe, M., Yamada, S.: Semi supervised Query Expansion with Minimal Feedback. IEEE Transaction on Journal of Knowledge and Data Engineering 19(11), 1585–1589 (2007)
8. Gulati, P., Sharma, A.K.: Ontology Driven Query Expansion for Better Image Retrieval. International Journal of Computer Applications 5(10), 33–37 (2010)
9. Lu, G., Huang, P., He, L., Cu, C., Li, X.: A New Semantic Similarity Measuring Method Based on Web Search Engines. WSEAS Transactions on Computers 9(1), 1–10 (2010)

10. Badie, K., Mahmoudi, M.T., Ghaderi, M.A.: A Framework for Query Expansion Based on Viewpoint-Oriented Manipulation Of The Related Concepts. In: 4th Asia International Conference on Mathematical/Analytical Modeling and Computer Simulation, IEEE, pp. 112–117 (2010)
11. Huang, G., Wang, S., Zhang, X.: Query Expansion based on Associated Semantic Space. Journal of Computers 6(2), 172–177 (2011)
12. Ngok, P., Gong, Z.: Log Mining to Support Web Query Expansions. In: Proceedings of the IEEE International Conference on Information and Automation, pp. 375–379 (2009)
13. Jin, S., Lin, H., Su, S.: Query Expansion based on Folksonomy Tag Co-occurrence Analysis. In: IEEE Conference on Granular Computing (2009)
14. Bhogal, J., Macfarlane, A., Smith, P.: A review of ontology based query expansion. Journal Information Processing and Management 43, 866–886 (2007)
15. Conesa, J., Storey, V.C., Sugumaran, V.: Improving web-query processing through semantic knowledge. Journal Data & Knowledge Engineering 66, 18–34 (2008)
16. Grootjen, F.A., Van der Weide, T.P.: Conceptual query expansion. Journal Data & Knowledge Engineering 56, 174–193 (2006)
17. Chli, M., De Wilde, P.: Internet search: Subdivision-based interactive query expansion and the soft semantic web. Journal Applied Soft Computing 6, 372–383 (2006)
18. Lieberman, H., Liu, H., Singh, P., Barry, B.: Beating Common Sense into Interactive Applications. AI Magazine 25(4) (2004)
19. Liu, H., Singh, P.: ConceptNet: A Practical Commonsense Reasoning Toolkit. BT Technology Journal (2004)
20. Lieberman, H., Rosenzweig, E., Singh, P.: Aria: An Agent for Annotating And Retrieving Images. IEEE Computer (July 2001)
21. Hsu, M.-H., Tsai, M.-F., Chen, H.-H.: Query Expansion with ConceptNet and WordNet: An Intrinsic Comparison. In: Ng, H.T., Leong, M.-K., Kan, M.-Y., Ji, D. (eds.) AIRS 2006. LNCS, vol. 4182, pp. 1–13. Springer, Heidelberg (2006)
22. Zhang, C., Cui, B., Cong, G., Wang, Y.-J.: A Revisit of Query Expansion with Different Semantic Levels. In: Zhou, X., Yokota, H., Deng, K., Liu, Q. (eds.) DASFAA 2009. LNCS, vol. 5463, pp. 662–676. Springer, Heidelberg (2009)
23. Abouenour, L., Bouzouba, K., Rosso, P.: An evaluated semantic query expansion andstructure-based approach for enhancing Arabic question/answering. International Journal on Information and Communication Technologies 3(3), 37–51 (2010)
24. http://web.media.mit.edu/~hugo/montylingua/
25. http://en.wikipedia.org/wiki/MontyLingua
26. Nasraoui, O., Zhuhadar, L.: Improving Recall and Precision of a Personalized Semantic Search Engine for E-learning. In: 4th International Conference on Digital Society, IEEE, pp. 216–221 (2010)
27. Russell, B., Torralba, A., Freeman, W.: The open annotation tool. Computer Science and Artificial Intelligence Laboratory, University MIT (2005), http://labelme.csail.mit.edu/
28. Xu, J., Croft, W.B.: Query Expansion using local and global document analysis. In: Proceeding of the 19th Annual International ACM SIGIR Conference, pp. 4–11 (1996)
29. Voorhess, E.M.: Query Expansion using lexical-semantic relation. In: Proceedings of the 17th Annual International ACM SIGIR Conference, pp. 61–69 (1994)
30. Liu, S., Liu, F., Yu, C.T., Meng, W.: An effective approach to document retrieval via utilizing WordNet and recognizing phrases. In: Proceedings of the 27th Annual International ACM SIGIR Conference on Research and Development in Information Retrieval SIGIR, pp. 266–272. ACM, New York (2004)
31. Fellbaum, C.: WordNet: an electronic lexical database. MIT Press, Cambridge (1998)

Usability Evaluation for 'Komputer Saya': Multimedia Courseware for Slow Learners

Norfarhana Abdollah, Wan Fatimah Wan Ahmad, and Emelia Akashah Patah Akhir

Department of Computer and Information Sciences, Universiti Teknologi PETRONAS

Abstract. Computer-based learning has been proven as an effective tool in education and implemented for its various advantages and capabilities. One of computer-based application is multimedia courseware which has been increasingly developed not only for teaching and learning in normal class setting, but also proven beneficial for those with learning disabilities including slow learners. The aim of this research is to develop a multimedia courseware namely 'Komputer Saya' consists of learning theme of multimedia, as referring to Special Education Syllabus for Learning Disabled. This paper discusses on the courseware evaluation design and the quantitative results for the parts of usability and courseware content evaluations. The evaluations have been conducted involving eight slow learners from special education for learning disabilities for user testing, while four teachers and one parent for heuristic evaluation. The results have shown that the courseware has met the requirement for usability part on engaging of the multimedia elements, ease of learn of the courseware design as well the suitability of the courseware contents for slow learners. This analysis is believed can be beneficial for future reference and improvement for future research.

Keywords: Slow learners, Courseware, Evaluation, Usability.

1 Introduction

Computer-based learning these days has been recognized as an effective instrument that can help both teachers and learners in various levels of education. It has been increasingly used not only for teaching and learning in normal class setting, but can also benefit in assisting slow learners' in their learning as well [1-3]. One of the well known multimedia learning applications is multimedia courseware. Numerous studies on developing the multimedia courseware for special education learners have shown great advantages in improving and facilitating their learning [4, 5]. Study conducted by [5] stated that there is a good match between multimedia technology and learning needs of children with learning disabilities because presentation of information via multiple forms (sound, text, and image) allows them for multiple exposures to the same information. However, to ensure the effectiveness of any multimedia learning that is developed, evaluation must be conducted [6]. Usability evaluations have became an important act in order to ensure the learning resources developed has been designed appropriately in order to facilitate effective learning [7].

H. Badioze Zaman et al. (Eds.): IVIC 2011, Part II, LNCS 7067, pp. 104–113, 2011.

2 Literature Review

To date, numerous studies have already being conducted regarding usability testing of multimedia application designed for learning disabilities learners. Research in [8] conducted a usability evaluation on software tools for people with learning disabilities, he has chosen 15 expert evaluators including computer scientists, educational technologists and special education teachers to evaluate on the usability questionnaire. Usability study by [9] have found that think aloud technique is not a suitable method to test with cognitive disabilities' children. Instead, they have conducted an informal walkthrough to observe the children using the courseware in real situations. In addition, expert evaluation technique using questionnaires has also been conducted in order to find for other usability issues that was overlooked and unexposed using observational technique. Experts found usability issues that were not detected during observations such as perception and recognition part of the screen design while on the other hand also missed some problems can be revealed in an observational study. Combinations of both techniques produce complementary results to cater the usability problems regarding courseware designed for special needs users [9]. However, [10] used user test technique which involve the real users; Down Syndrome's children to test on usability issue of the courseware designed to teach basic reading. User test has been conducted for certain period of time and with specific guidelines to work with the special children. Evaluation of multimedia courseware for Dyslexic children conducted by [4] opt for expert evaluations, observations and user test techniques to collect the usability data. User test was conducted with a small group which consists of 15 dyslexics children to test on procedures required for installation of the courseware in the real class setting. As conclusion, nature and timing of study, costs, availability of test subject and expertise have to be considered in choosing suitable usability evaluation method for particular development situation [11].

3 Research Objectives

General idea of this study is to develop a multimedia learning courseware namely 'Komputer Saya' for slow learners. The courseware is developed with the theme of multimedia learning which is one of learning components in the Special Education Curriculum for Learning Disabled [12] with aim to increase slow learners' motivation in learning by using computer. The objectives of this paper are to discuss on evaluation design for 'Komputer Saya' courseware and to present on the quantitative findings for the usability and courseware content evaluations.

4 Methodology

Evaluations in this study have been conducted using mainly two different methods; 1) Heuristic evaluation which involve teachers and parent of slow learners and 2) User testing technique by carrying out an observation on slow learners. The evaluations were conducted using two different methods because each usability inspection method will produce different type and dimensions of outcomes. For heuristic evaluation, five respondents have been determined. They are four special education teachers and one parent of slow learners' child. In this study, user testing has been conducted using field study technique where the evaluation took place in natural setting (in this case, slow learners' classroom) instead of controlled setting (usability laboratory). Field study can provide a better view of how children interact with and use the technology in their everyday lives [13]. According to reference [13] as well, children are more familiar with school environment instead of laboratory, because location plays a large part on their behaviour. They would behave naturally in their familiar environment and people. As slow learners' behave awkwardly and shy due to their difficulties in learning in their daily class environment, more would come up to if they were required to be in contact with new people and environment. This technique is finally decided as to minimize any unnecessary outcome due to limitations discussed. Figure 1 illustrates the courseware evaluation design of this research study.

4.1 Courseware Evaluation Design

Engaging concerns on how pleasant, satisfying or interesting the interface is to be use by the user [14]. In this study, engaging item is being evaluated by distributing questionnaire checklist of multimedia elements to evaluate on whether the multimedia elements in the courseware engaged the users (heuristic evaluation). This evaluation method was chosen by adopting the suggestion made by [14] for technique to evaluate engaging. Additional data is obtained from observations on user's behaviours and verbal expressions on any courseware's elements that are attractive to them.

Efficiency measures speed with accuracy in which users can complete the tasks while using the product [15]. Timing data has been collected to measure time taken to perform each task (time on task). The tasks have been set to see the difference of time taken by each user to complete the task for several time usages, depending on the task, to see whether there is decrement in time (increase of efficiency). Besides, qualitative data has also been obtained from observations on their interaction with elements such as text, navigational icon, button, sound instruction etc, assistance prompted and any errors or problems that interrupt and slow them down while using the courseware.

Easy to learn being evaluated using two techniques; first is by distributing questionnaire checklist on easy to learn elements (heuristic evaluation). The second evaluation is conducted from observations on overall usage timing (time for tasks completion) recorded and compared between two levels of slow learners (low and achievers) to see whether the courseware is easy to be learn by all slow learners regardless their learning abilities and experiences. This technique has been adopted from reference [14].

Satisfaction attribute was chosen to measure user's satisfaction after using the courseware. Satisfaction being measured qualitatively; using open-ended survey and interview method with teachers and parent, as slow learners are unable to respond to written questionnaire [16]. This technique has been adapted from [17]. Their comment on satisfaction issue after using the courseware were recorded.

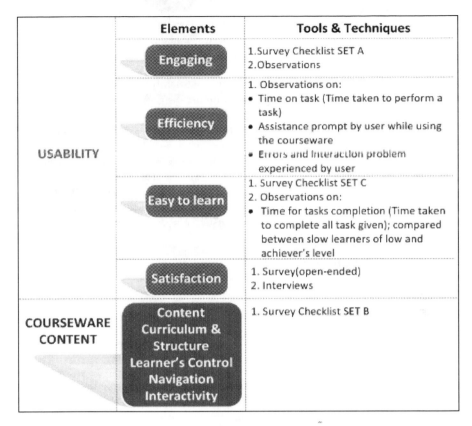

Fig. 1. Courseware evaluation design

The second part of evaluation is to evaluate on courseware content using checklist adapted from [18]. The framework proposed by [18] stated that acceptability of courseware should be evaluated on 'presentation and organization of content' and 'evaluation of learning' because courseware has to be both pedagogically and technically sound. The proposed framework also has been used by [4] to evaluate learning courseware for Dyslexic children. For this study, five constructs have been evaluated; content, curriculum and structure, learner's control, interactivity and navigation.

In this study, combinations of both qualitative and quantitative methods have been used to obtain both types of data. However, this paper only presents the quantitative results of usability on engaging and ease of learn checklists as well as courseware content checklist where all results have been analyzed using *Statistical Package for Social Science (SPSS)* software and Microsoft Excel.

4.2 Experimental Set-Up

Each of the respondents was given one to one and half hour to use and get familiar with the courseware. Then, three sets of questionnaire were distributed where all respondents were required to fill in all sets of questionnaire. For evaluation discuss in this paper, three questionnaire checklists have been used as evaluation tools which are:

- SET A: Questionnaire on Multimedia Elements Evaluation
- SET B: Questionnaire on Courseware Content Evaluation
- SET C: Questionnaire on Easy to Learn Evaluation

For the evaluation of on the engaging attribute of usability, multimedia elements in the courseware were evaluated using questionnaire SET A. Teachers and parent of slow learners were required to respond to the questionnaire. Six multimedia elements were evaluated; text, graphic, audio, animation, interactivity and interface. For the evaluation of courseware contents, teachers and parent of slow learner were required to respond to questionnaire SET B. The questionnaire was designed to evaluate on five elements; content, curriculum and structure, learner's control, navigation, interactivity. Questionnaire SET C was used to evaluate on easy to learn element. For the entire questionnaire sets, five point Likert Scale is used to assess each item; Strongly Agree = 5, Agree = 4, Neutral = 3, Disagree = 2 and Strongly Disagree = 1.

5 Result and Discussion

This section discusses on the summaries of the data recorded from evaluation of usability of engaging attributes of multimedia, ease of learn and courseware content.

5.1 Evaluation on Usability Attributes: Engaging of Multimedia

Usability of engaging in this study concerns on how pleasant, interesting and satisfying the courseware to be used. It concerns on the engagement offered by the multimedia elements offered by the courseware towards user's satisfaction. Figure 2 illustrates mean scores for each multimedia element. Audio and Screen Design both share highest mean value which is 4.8, Interactivity and Graphic with both 4.7 mean value, Animation with 4.6 mean value and text with 4.5 mean value.

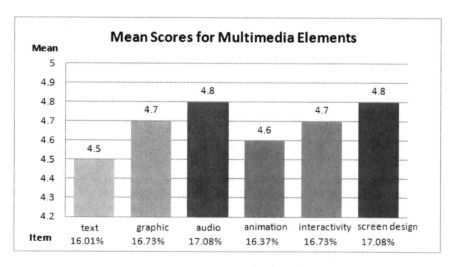

Fig. 2. Mean scores for multimedia elements

One of the effective technique to teach special education learners is to incorporate multisensory learning styles which include visual, auditory and kinesthetic [2], [19], [20]. Table 1 depicted the percentage result of the effect of multimedia elements on slow learners' learning. The results stated that slow learners gained 49.47% from learning through graphic, video and animation, 17.08% from audio, 17.08% from interface and 16.37% from text. The results were then compared to existing research on effectiveness of multimedia components for memory storage that contributes to learning [21].

Table 1. Comparison on effectiveness of multimedia components

Medium of learning	Memory storage used in learning	Engaging of multimedia elements of 'Komputer Saya' courseware
Graphic, video, animation	75%	49.47%
Audio	13%	17.08%
Text	6%	16.37%
Interface	3%	17.08%

From the result, it can be seen that visual or 'seeing' process gained the highest percentage on information retrieval for slow learners (from graphic, video and animation) if compared to other elements. With the existence of suitable graphic, video and animation, the learning content will be able to be demonstrated clearly thus can enhance learners' ability in remembering and understanding the materials [5, 21].

Analysis however shows that the result of audio preferences is 17.08% which is slightly higher than text element with 16.37%. These values also shown significant difference between information retrieval for normal individuals whereby they learn better from text compared to slow learners that require auditory based instruction to support text-based instruction. Slow learners needs additional audio instruction added to normal text instruction because most of them have difficulties in reading and some even can only recognized the simple alphabet and do not know how to spell or read at all [5]. Thus, clear audio instructions are very useful while using the courseware. Along with visual presentation, audio instruction is a useful element because presentation using both visual and verbal forms will allow the slow learners to process information via two channel [5]. As according to [22], the feedback from the courseware system helps users to know their status and at the same time can motivate users to learn and complete the exercises as provided. Accompanying text with audio will also enhance their understanding as they normally have limitation on learning via printed materials.

Interface preferences also gained same result with audio which is 17.08%. Slow learners are attracted more on the visual and fun interface which could boost and motivate their learning process. According to [5], the special needs children will have longer attention span interacting with computer software because the interface and interactivity will make them feel like they are playing games. Suitable interface elements increase their engagement in using the courseware and hence will allow them to retain the learning for a longer period if compared to traditional methods which normally make them easily get bored and exhausted.

5.2   Evaluation on Usability Attributes: Ease of Learn

Ease of learn item from the questionnaire measures how quickly the user can get some work done using the courseware and can use it later after first time use without having to learn everything all over from the start [18]. The mean result which is 4.698 depicted that the courseware is suitable for average performance group of slow learners. This is one important issue to address on limitation of current courseware usage by most special learners in Malaysia that were developed mostly for normal children [5]. Suitable and appropriate design in ease of learn context can make the slow learners make full use of the courseware thus make the process of achieving learning needs and educational goals much easier.

Table 2. Result for Ease of Learn

Item	Minimum	Maximum	Mean
Courseware is easy to learn, user can quickly remember after several time used.	4	5	4.8
Courseware can be used without many technical errors, or if does, it can be easily recovered.	4	4	4.4
Courseware is easy to remember; the casual user is able to return to using it after some period without having to learn everything all over.	4	5	4.8
The structure of courseware is comprehensive and the average performance slow learners' can easily follow it.	4	5	4.6
Users are subjectively satisfied by using courseware.	4	5	4.8
Users find courseware interesting.	4	5	4.8
Mean (n=5)			4.698

5.3   Evaluation on Courseware Content

Figure 3 shows the graph for mean scores gained for each courseware content element. The highest mean is on content aspect with 4.634 mean values, followed by navigation with 4.486, interactivity with 4.45, learner's control with 4.4 and curriculum and structure for 4.24 mean values.

The highest mean score is on the content element which gained 4.634 score. Content element consists of evaluation regarding the correct, suitable and relevant contents for slow learners' level. Correct use of grammar, concepts and vocabulary used in the courseware is related to slow learners' abilities. This is important to cater for their cognitive skills as the slow learners will directly retrieve the information from what they are being taught. So, this validity and suitability issues are important in order to ensure all the learning information delivered to them is accurate and suitable to their learning scope and depth.

The second highest mean score is on the navigation item which gained 4.486 mean values. This mean shows that all respondents agree with all navigational buttons provided in the courseware which consist of links to each learning elements and to important parts of other content such as help, instruction and objective key that available for access on each page in the courseware. Good navigation elements are important to ensure user can make use of the learning contents provided by the courseware wisely without spending too much time to learn on navigation.

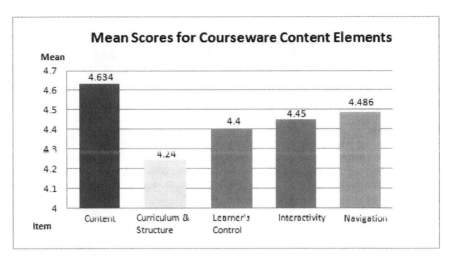

Fig. 3. Mean scores for courseware contents elements

The effectiveness of multimedia learning resources for special education learners depends on the level of interactivity [5]. Interactivity context includes the feedback issue which is also important for learning [5, 18]. From the evaluation, interactivity item which gained 4.45 mean scores shown that respondents agree that the interaction in the courseware are designed appropriately to the maturity level of slow learners. They agree that the interactivity offers by the courseware allow the slow learners to discover and learn through active exploration.

For learner's control item, mean result gained is 4.4. From the result, most of the respondent agree that the courseware have been designed with appropriate learner's control that corresponds to slow learners' age, individual pace, and cognitive capabilities. The result also reported that the courseware considers individual differences of slow learners by providing exercises range from easy to intermediate level depends on their cognitive and psychomotor capabilities.

Curriculum and structure are also important issues in courseware usability evaluation for slow learners. As reported by [5], some of the local multimedia resources in the market were found lacking in pedagogically sound principle which hinder them from fully utilizing the resources. From the result of curriculum and structure, 4.24 mean values have been obtained. This depicts that the courseware has been designed with learning content related to slow learners' curriculum and suitable to be used as one of learning material in their daily learning. Most of the teachers agree that the courseware can be used by the slow learners alone, however, physical and verbal instruction from others (teacher/parent) were initially required to teach them to interact with the courseware.

6 Conclusions

This paper has elaborated on the results of the evaluation of 'Komputer Saya' courseware which has been developed specifically for slow learners. The evaluation has been made to examine the content and usability elements in the courseware. The results have shown that the courseware has met the requirement of usability part on engaging of multimedia elements for slow learners' learning, the ease of learn of the courseware as well the suitability of the courseware content for slow learners.

References

1. Flannigan, S., Groth, K.: Slow Learners,
   http://students.uis.edu/kgrot01s/slowlearners.html
2. Schools, S.P.: A Focused Look at the Slow Learner: The Who the What and the How's,
   http://www.spsk12.net/departments/specialed/slowlearner.htm
3. Abdullah, M.H.L., Hisham, S., Parumo, S.: MyLexics: an assistive courseware for Dyslexic children to learn basic Malay language, pp. 3–9 (2009)
4. Anusuriya, D., Zeratul Izzah, M.Y., Mohd Hafiz, Z., Umawathy, T., X-Leksia: Creation, Assessment, and Implementation. In: International Conference on Teaching and Learning, Putrajaya, Malaysia (2007)
5. Wah, L.L.: Development of Multimedia Learning Resources for Children with Learning Disabilities in an Undergraduate Special Education Technology Course. Malaysian Education Dean's Council (MEDC) 1, 29–36 (2007)
6. Yussof, R.L., Badioze Zaman, H.: Usability Evaluation of Multimedia Courseware (MEL-sindD). In: Badioze Zaman, H., Robinson, P., Petrou, M., Olivier, P., Schröder, H., Shih, T.K. (eds.) IVIC 2009. LNCS, vol. 5857, pp. 337–343. Springer, Heidelberg (2009)
7. Moore, J.L., Dickson-Deane, C., Galyen, K., Vo, N., Charoentham, M.: ELearning Usability Instruments What is being Evaluated? In: E-Learning in Corporate, Government, Healthcare, and Higher Education 2008, Las Vegas, Nevada, USA, pp. 430–435 (2008)
8. Poobrasert, O.: Work in Progress: A Case Study of Usability Testing of Software Toolsfor People with Learning Disabilities. In: Computers and Simulation in Modern Science (2009)
9. Lepistö, A., Ovaska, S.: Usability evaluation involving participants with cognitive disabilities. In: Nordic Conference on Human-Computer Interaction, pp. 305–308 (2004)
10. Yussof, R.L., Zaman, H.B.: Perisian Kursus Bacaan untuk Murid Sindrom Down (MELb-SindD): Metodologi Pengujian Kepenggunaan. In: Visual Informatics Graduate Seminar FIST, UKM 2008, UKM, Bangi, Malaysia (2008)
11. Yussof, R.L., Zaman, H.B.: Usability Methodology of Multimedia Courseware (Mel-Sindd) for Down Syndrome Learner. In: 3rd International Malaysian Educational Technology Convention, Batu Ferringhi, Penang, Malaysia (2009)
12. Khas, J.P.: Huraian Sukatan Pelajaran Pendidikan Khas Bermasalah Pembelajaran Sekolah Rendah & Menengah. Kementerian Pendidikan Malaysia, Kuala Lumpur (2003)
13. Fariza Hanis, A.R., Hanayanti, H., Nadia, S., Nur 'Atiqah, Z., Haryani, H.: Usability Testing with Children: Laboratory vs Field Studies. In: International Conference on User Science and Engineering (i-USEr 2010), Shah Alam (2010)
14. Quesenbery, W.: Dimensions of Usability: Defining the Conversation, Driving the Process. In: UPA 2003 Conference (2003)
15. Quesenbery, W.: What Does Usability Mean: Looking Beyond 'Ease of Use'. In: 48th Annual Conference, Society for Technical Communication (2001)
16. Rahmah, L.Y., Halimah, B.Z.: Usability Methodology of Multimedia Courseware (Mel-Sindd) for Down Syndrome Learner. In: 3rd International Malaysian Educational Technology Convention, Batu Ferringhi, Penang, Malaysia (2009)

17. Travis, D.: Measuring satisfaction: Beyond the usability questionnaire (2009), http://www.userfocus.co.uk/articles/satisfaction.html
18. Elissavet, G., Economides, A.A.: An Evaluation Instrument for Hypermedia Courseware. Educational Technology & Society 6, 31–44 (2003)
19. Hopkins, B.: Teachers Resource Manual: The child who is a slow learner, http://www.drbillsplace.org/images/pdf/slowleaner.pdf
20. Parfitt, L., Jo, J., Nguyen, A.: Multimedia in Distance Learning for Tertiary Students with Special Needs. Presented at the ASCILITE 1998, University of Wollongong, New South Wales, Australia (1998)
21. Mazyrah, M.: The Development and Usability of a Multimedia Black Cat Courseware using Storytelling Approach. In: MSc in Information and Communication Technology, Computer and Information Sciences, Universiti Teknologi PETRONAS, Perak, Malaysia (2009)
22. Norfarhana, A., Wan Fatimah, W.A., Emelia Akashah, P.A.: Multimedia Courseware for Slow Learners: A Preliminary Analysis. In: International Symposium on Information Technology, Kuala Lumpur (2010)

Reconstruction of 3D Faces Using Face Space Coefficient, Texture Space and Shape Space

Sheng Hung Chung and Ean Teng Khor

School of Science and Technology, Wawasan Open University,
Penang, Malaysia
{shchung,etkhor}@wou.edu.my

Abstract. This paper presents a 3D face reconstruction face model by using PCA-based reconstruction model in synthesizing faces of individual. A 3D face reconstruction model is derived by transforming the shape and texture of the training sets into a vector space representation. In this paper, a reconstruction of face model is adapted from 3 Dimensional Face Space (3DFS) with the knowledge of the shape and texture of faces. Faces statistics produced by sampling from Face Space is computed by Principle Component Analysis (PCA) of 100 exemplar 3D faces. 3D face space is formed by two distinctive subspaces: the 3D shape space and 3D texture space which consist of 79-dimensional (79 shape and texture coefficient). The first shape space shows the impact of the shape and texture dimensions and the second texture space shows the influence of the shape and texture dimensions. A vertex is a point where two edges of a 2D polygon or two or more vertices of a 3D polyhedron meet. Face Space Coefficient (FSC) is computed as the input for training in generating novel 3D faces as Wavefront Object files (OBJ). The output 3D face space is computed with the aid of material file (.mtl) and texture file (.jpg, .rgb) and viewed by OBJ viewer to achieve good 3D representation using this approach.

Keywords: 3D face reconstruction, face space, Principle Component Analysis, texture coefficient, texture dimension, Wavefront Object files, 3D representation.

1 Introduction

Three-dimensional (3D) face modeling and reconstruction has become a popular research area in image processing and achieves higher accuracy in face recognition in comparison with two-dimensional (2D) facial images [1]. The process of construction of 3D facial models is an important topic in computer vision which has recently received attention within the research community. Most 3D face reconstruction methods proposed so far are based on artificial 3D face models such as public available avatars [1]. The main contribution of this paper is based on the new approach [2], an automatic 3D face reconstruction system by producing realistic 3D reconstructed faces generate from the shape vector and texture vector of the training sets. Principle Component Analysis (PCA) is applied on the shape vector to compute 3D shape coefficients. The proposed system integrates the training of 100 samples, storing the principle components and standard deviations mainly mean (.mean), sigma

H. Badioze Zaman et al. (Eds.): IVIC 2011, Part II, LNCS 7067, pp. 114–122, 2011.
© Springer-Verlag Berlin Heidelberg 2011

(.sigma) and Echoview (.ev) as the organization tool. The shape space and the texture space have each 79 dimensions and constructed by applying PCA to 100 training heads. Texture mapping with triangle list generated from face model were stored as Wavefront Object files (OBJ) to be presented by using viewer application with the aid of material file (.mtl) and texture file (.jpg, .rgb).

Various approaches for the 3D reconstruction of face data have been as shown in Table 1. The development and application of 3D face reconstruction models is important in visual imaging mainly shape representation, motion tracking and face recognition includes human-robot-interaction, human-computer-interaction, smart cards applications and verification that include driver's license, immigration, national ID, passport, voter registration. This paper is organized as follows. An overview of the proposed 3D Face Reconstruction Systems is presented in Section 2. The PCA computation of face space coefficient is described in Section 3. Implementation with OBJ viewer is shown in Section 4 and the paper is concluded with some comments of future work in Section 5.

Table 1. 3D face reconstruction by different approach and face data in prior work are summarized in Table 1 below

Researchers	Approach	Related Work
Yepeng Guan	Automatic 3D Face Reconstruction based on single 2D Image	• Changes of head pose and facial expression cause a 2D image of a face to become unreliable for identification. • 3D representation suggests all useful features for face classification and recognition. Proposal to overcome the deficiencies of 3D facial model reconstruction from one image by improvements using an affine transformation and a 3D statistical face model.
Jun Wang et al.	3D Facial Expression Recognition Based on Primitive Surface Feature Distribution	• 3D facial geometric shapes to represent and recognize facial expressions using 3D facial expression range data.
Y. Hu, D. Jiang, S. Yan, L. Zhang, H. Zhang	Automatic 3D Reconstruction for Face Recognition	• 2D to 3D integrated face reconstruction approach. • Face Recognition using variant pose, illumination and expression (PIE) with realistic virtual faces to characterize the face subspace.
Mena-Chalco, J.P. et al.	PCA- based 3D Face Photography	• Facial feature points are obtained by an active shape model Active Shape Model (ASM) extracted from the 2D grey-level images. • PCA is used to represent the face dataset defining an orthonormal basis of texture and range data.
Yuxiao, H. et al.	Automatic 3D Reconstruction for Face Recognition	• Features extracted from the parameter estimation approach for face alignment are used to identify the feature points to construct the 3D face shape.

Table 1 lists the 3D face reconstruction approach based on different techniques and face data, namely, statistical face model, primitive surface feature distribution, face recognition using variant pose, illumination and expression (PIE), Active Shape Model (ASM) and PCA-based with extraction of facial feature points which have shown useful results in modeling of 3D faces. The PCA-based approach undertaken by Mena-Chalco, et al. [4] is to obtain 3D faces by using ASM and PCA components. PCA-based 3D face photography [2] approach obtains the geometry representation of given face provided as a texture image, through transformations of texture and geometry spaces. Scan volume specification are: 111 x 84 x 40mm (min) to 1200 x 903 x 400mm (max) (width x depth x height, respectively). Texture images were acquired with 320 x 240 pixels resolution, contains approximately 15000 geometry points. Training of the 3D face data consist of facial landmark (77 landmark points), triangulation and geometry (3D face obtained). In the development of the 3D face models, the evaluation through features extraction, shape modeling techniques mainly, Structure from Motion (SfM) [1] were adapted to identify similar points in different 2D images. Features extracted from the parameter estimation approach [4] for face alignment are used to identify the feature points to construct the 3D face shape. The 2D face image will be feed into the constructed 3D face geometry to build the face texture.

Reconstruction in face surface is one of the model-based techniques which include geometry, physics and approximation theory. Partial Differential Equations (PDE), a deformable model is used in shape recovery and object detection [5] by incorporating data such as points, surfels, images and other visual cues such as shading and optical flow. The computation of disparity map [6] from two face frontal images with vertices extracted from 2D images to align, replacing the coordinates of the vertices of the eyes, eyebrows, mouth, nose and chin. Deformable models are categorized into two categories: explicit models and implicit models which are parameterized shapes that deform due to forces according to physical laws [7]. PDE-an explicit deformable model includes parametric representations and discrete presentations. Other shape approximation techniques have shown effective shape recovery by point matching convex optimization. Scale Invariant Feature Transform (SIFT) is used as a matching algorithm for detecting feature points among 2D facial images. For vision applications, the method for shape estimation [11] is determined from visual cues such as edges in an image. Deformable models are capable in segmenting, matching based on location, size and shape of anatomic structures across every biological structures.

2   3D Face Reconstruction System

Techniques for attaining facial information for 3D reconstruction are broadly categorized into pure image-based techniques, hybrid image-based techniques and 3D scanning techniques [4]. The approach in this paper will be concentrating on hybrid image-based techniques with 3D face data as the input training.

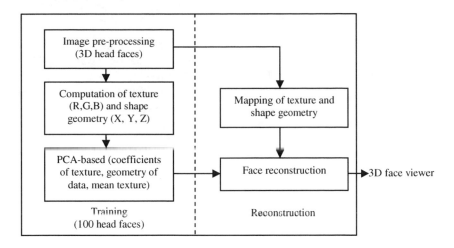

Fig. 1. 3D Shape vector for ten vertices that contains X, Y, Z coordinates

PCA [2] procedures are carried out separately for the geometry L_i^g and texture L_i^t where L represent i-th texture and geometry landmarks respectively. Normalization by Procrustes [2] analysis with landmark aligned in common coordinate system. Mapping of input image onto the average facial landmarks produced by the Procrustes analysis.

The proposed approach is based on learning a 3D face model using texture and geometry of a training face of 100 exemplar 3D faces. An input 2D face image (i.e. only texture) is then reconstructed by projecting it on the trained 2D texture space, decomposing it as weights of the training samples. The obtained weighting coefficients are then used to build a 3D model from the 3D training geometry samples. The training set is composed by pairs of texture and geometry data from a given subject with some different facial expressions. The texture and geometry data are registered and mapped to corresponding geometry coordinates. Figure 2 depict the results obtained [2] as follows: (a) frontal faces with different expressions of one subject, (b) face geometry (c) 3D face with mapped texture:

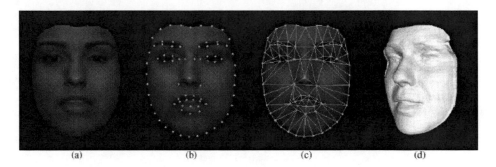

Fig. 2. Shape vector for ten vertices that contains X, Y, Z coordinates

2.1 Data acquisition and Face Model

3D face data is acquired [3] from University of South Florida with faces produced by sampling from Face Space funded by DARPA Information Awareness Office (IAO) under the project of Human ID at a Distance Program. Texture images have been acquired with a 512 x 512 pixels resolution. The 3D geometry associated has one line per vertex, with 75972 vertices. The data is hence composed by registered texture (x, y, z coordinates) for the geometry texture data with the value of R, G, B values. Images from a single subject have been acquired with 7 different facial expressions (one single image per facial expression). The training data has been obtained and presented as Face Space Coefficient (FSC) containing the 's', there must be up to 79 shape coefficient and each of these coefficients is the coefficient of the related principal component of the shape. Following the shape coefficient, there must be a 't' indicating that the texture coefficients follows.

3 Shape, Texture Vector, Face Space Coefficients

In this paper, the shape and texture are derived one line per vertex. For the shape vector the coordinates X, Y, Z are listed and for texture vector the values of R, G, B are listed. Each shape vector or texture vector contains three parameters (X, Y, Z) and (R, G, B) respectively.

```
-55.71  -48.66  -11.30
-55.71  -49.26  -11.16
-55.70  -49.87  -11.09
-55.69  -50.48  -11.06
-55.69  -51.08  -11.02
-55.69  -51.69  -11.01
-55.69  -52.31  -10.99
-55.69  -52.92  -10.98
-55.69  -53.53  -10.97
-55.70  -54.13  -10.95
```

Fig. 3. Shape vector for ten vertices that contains X, Y, Z coordinates

```
111.40  65.06  59.49
111.32  65.11  59.44
111.26  65.13  59.48
111.05  64.93  59.24
111.98  65.47  59.75
112.55  65.71  59.87
112.35  65.44  59.64
112.23  65.17  59.43
112.21  65.18  59.48
112.17  65.10  59.37
```

Fig. 4. Texture vector for ten vertices that contains R, G, B values

The implemented data directory contains the shape and texture 79 principal components, their sigma and the mean. These are stored in the following ASCII files:

pc_xxxy.ev store the principal component number for $FaceHead^n$

pc_y.sigma store the correspond standard deviation
pc_y.mean store the correspond mean

where $FaceHead^n$ is the number of principal components (between 001 and 079) and *y* can be s (for shape) or t (for texture). The files *pc_xxxy.ev* and *pc_y.mean* have the same format: One line per vertex (There are 75972 vertices) where each line contains three white space separated numbers. The shape files are represented by numbers X, Y, Z coordinates, the texture file are represented using numbers R, G, B values.

The file *pc_y.sigma* has 79 lines, one number per line. This number is the standard deviation of the related principle components. The mapping and the reference triangle list are stored in seperated directory as: the texture mapping file (texmap.obj) and the triangle list (trilist.obj). The two files are in the OBJ file format as shown in Section 3.1.

3.1   Wavefront Object Files (OBJ)

Wavefront OBJ files are used to store geometric objects composed of lines. The following keywords are included in an OBJ file. In the list, keywords are arranged by data type followed by a brief description.

Vertex data:
v   Geometric vertices
vt   Texture vertices
vn   Vertex normals
vp   Parameter space vertices

The main *.obj* file functions as storing the X, Y, Z position of the vertices, the triangle list and the texture mapping information. The.mtl material file is used to specify the material properties of the object (i.e. skin reflectance properties).   In this study, we restrict the representation informations about skin reflectance properties to default material. The texture file is an image that can be saved in any image file format (i.e. *.jpg*, *.rgb*).

3.2   Face Space Coefficients (FSC)

A Face Space Coefficients (FSC) file (e.g. train100.fsc) is used as input by the program 3dfs to generate heads. It contains shape and texture PCA coefficients. Its format follows: Any character following a '#' character is ignored (up to the end of line). One line is used to generate one head. The format of a line is: <file name> s <sc1> <sc2> ... <sc100> t <tc1> <tc2> ... <tc100>: The first word of a line is the output file name as shown in structure below:

train_03552_1

s -0.094272 0.670098 -1.393610 0.111603 -1.300562 0.095380 -0.594798
2.321349 -0.692311 0.650755 -0.592134 0.657911 -1.248391 3.115958 -
0.007914 1.027007 -0.233899 0.790300 -0.321136 1.710343 -0.441713
0.816414 -1.671928 0.187761 -1.129272 0.003116 -0.014983 -0.157744 -
0.768711 0.576657 -0.024133 0.207843 -0.136583 2.700135 -0.865121
0.655704 -0.400483 1.442643 -0.841999 0.628456 -0.108721 1.916490 -
0.080467 0.248343 -0.693080 0.051558 -0.568044 0.136050 -1.486663 -
1.610184 0.271899 -0.804094 0.012373 -0.109012 0.245431 -0.710056 -
0.021307 -1.057949 0.032593 0.056661 -0.045943 0.055931 0.251669
1.643154 -1.265350 0.999170 -0.126567 0.258015 -0.350509 0.556197
0.418133 -1.188419 -2.536872 0.743577 -0.622926 1.445501 0.204625
1.606314 -2.019961 1.412338 0.043177 -0.135815 0.711473 -0.733836 -
1.255529 0.322338 1.467858 0.726069 -0.888888 0.304938 1.185616 -
0.239449 -1.169583 1.492903 0.142500 1.112696 1.071626 0.946418 -
1.235367

t -1.323577 0.418075 -0.532380 1.348730 -1.634048 0.816871 -1.304787
1.096121 -1.332300 1.067521 -1.493207 0.363388 0.019430 0.729201 -
0.435562 0.429890 -1.331250 1.217685 -0.538517 2.267194 -1.792312
0.729993 -0.308588 0.527500 -0.801129 0.121089 -0.673094 0.867875 -
0.487893 0.429025 0.128244 1.391387 0.043451 -0.121803 0.216578 -
0.397723 0.146863 -0.453677 1.744690 -1.112286 1.142468 -0.730732 -
1.869387 1.168862 0.174969 -0.724492 0.611632 0.692473 1.223606 0.655633
-0.271460 0.476379 -0.781272 0.661264 -0.278660 -0.179769 -0.553443
0.083362 -0.125071 0.258926 -1.282528 0.215209 -0.864747 0.176212 -
0.272452 0.551889 -1.433417 0.369421 0.410143 0.306466 0.734297 0.132864
-1.063810 -0.192311 -0.779925 0.127990 -0.875888 1.204390 -0.258566 -
0.548146 0.594802 -0.012895 1.750321 -0.393728 0.028485 1.963699 -
0.719728 0.074914 0.654687 0.726493 -3.002158 -0.529711 -2.760086 -
0.425366 0.404691 2.627079 -2.324771 0.067479 0.411612

$<sc^n>$, shape coefficient of particular face
$<tc^n>$, texture coefficient of particular face

4   Implementation and Analysis with Wavefront Object Files (OBJ) Viewer

The Program ObjViewer is a viewer of 3D objects in the Wavefront OBJ format developed using Java Development ToolKit and Java3D (OpenGL) SDK. The 3D viewer prototype is written in Java and can be used on various platforms with the presence of Java Development Kit (JDK) and Java3D API in the workstation.

After loading into the ObjViewer, a 3D face object can be moved, rotated and scaled interactively in Figure 5(a), (b) below:

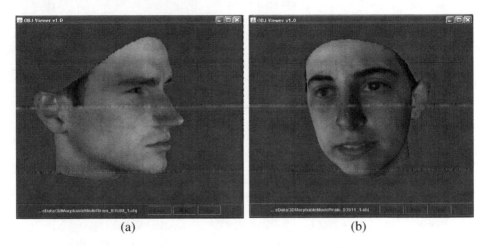

        (a)   (b)

Fig. 5. 3D Faces constructer displayed using OBJViewer

5   Conclusion and Future Work

The present study has shown the reconstruction of 3D face space using texture space and shape space. PCA components were computed, namely mean and sigma and the combination of texture geometry coordinates with correspond shape geometry. In particular, this paper provides the reconstruction of Wavefront Object File (OBJ) for the modeling of 3D faces with the aid of material file (.mtl) and texture file (.jpg, .rgb).

The future implementation will focus on the reconstructions of the deformable 2D facial models and to be incorporated with face recognition techniques using 2D images. Once an initial face shape is constructed, the model can be further refined and evaluate to improve the fitting accuracy. The selection of appropriate features points for estimation and points matching is to provide highly accuracy results. The experimental evaluation of face reconstruction for face recognition will then be compared against experimental data upon which further optimization of the model will be carried out under difficult condition such as PIE.

References

1. Akaydın, A., Kucuktunc, O.: 3D Face Reconstruction from 2D Images for Effective Face Recognition, pp. 25–31 (2009)
2. Mena-Chalco, J.P., et al.: PCA- based 3D Face Photography. In: SIBGRAPI 2008 Proceedings of the XXI Brazilian Symposium on Computer Graphics and Image Processing, pp. 313–320 (2008)
3. Pentland, A., Sclaroff, S.: Closed-form solutions for physically based shape modeling and recognition. IEEE Pattern Analysis and Machine Intelligence 13(7), 715–729 (1991)

4. Hu, Y., Jiang, D., Yan, S., Zhang, L., Zhang, H.: Automatic 3D Reconstruction for Face Recognition. In: Proceedings. Sixth IEEE International Conference on Automatic Face and Gesture Recognition, pp. 843–848 (2004)
5. Duan, Y., Yang, L., Qin, H., Samaras, D.: Shape Reconstruction from 3D and 2D Data Using PDE-Based Deformable Surfaces. In: Pajdla, T., Matas, J(G.) (eds.) ECCV 2004. LNCS, vol. 3023, pp. 238–251. Springer, Heidelberg (2004)
6. Ansari, A.-N., Abdel-Mottaleb, M., Mahoor, M.H.: Disparity-Based 3D Face Modeling using 3D Deformable Facial Mask for 3D Face Recognition. In: 2006 IEEE International Conference on Multimedia and Expo., pp. 981–984 (2006)
7. Metaxas, D., Terzopoulos, D.: Shape and nonrigid motion estimation through physics-based synthesis. IEEE Pattern Analysis and Machine Intelligence 15(6), 580–591 (1993)
8. McInerney, T., Terzopoulos, D.: Deformable models in medical image analysis: a survey. Medical Image Analysis 1(2), 91–108 (1996)
9. Metaxas, D., Terzopoulos, D.: Physics-based modeling and reasoning in computer vision. Computer Vision and Image Understanding 65(5), 111–359
10. Slaroff, S., Pentland, A.P.: Modal Matching for correspondence and recognition. Journal IEEE Transactions on Pattern Analysis and Machine Intelligence 17(6), 308–313 (1995)
11. Wang, J., Yin, L., Wei, X., Sun, Y.: 3D Facial Expression Recognition Based on Primitive Surface Feature Distribution. In: IEEE Computer Society Conference on Computer Vision and Pattern Recognition, pp. 1399–1406 (2006)

Research Finding for Usability Testing on ILC-WBLE

Ming Chee Hoh, Wou Onn Choo, and Pei Hwa Siew

Universiti Tunku Abdul Rahman, Jalan Universiti Bandar Barat,
31900, Kampar. Perak. Malaysia
{hohmc,choowo,siewph}@utar.edu.my

Abstract. The purpose of this research is to develop a dynamic multimedia content creation of Independent Learner Courseware for Web-Based Learning Environment (ILC-WBLE). Usability testing was carried out on the developed system. Evaluation forms with Likert rating and open-ended questions were applied to evaluate the system. Academic staff and students from Universiti Tunku Abdul Rahman (UTAR) took part in this usability testing. The strengths and weaknesses of ILC-WBLE were summarised according to the result obtained from the evaluation.

Keywords: Moodle, Universiti Tunku Abdul Rahman, multimedia courseware, dynamic content creation.

1 Introduction

Moodle is one of the popular Web-based learning environment systems widely used in education [1], [2]. Universiti Tunku Abdul Rahman (UTAR) uses Moodle to create a resource website called WBLE (Web-Based Learning Environment) to facilitate the teaching-learning activities among lecturers and students since year 2005. WBLE, as shown in Fig. 1, can be accessed at http://wble.utar.edu.my.

Fig. 1. Screenshot from the index page of WBLE

H. Badioze Zaman et al. (Eds.): IVIC 2011, Part II, LNCS 7067, pp. 123–134, 2011.
© Springer-Verlag Berlin Heidelberg 2011

Even though UTAR has implemented a resource website called WBLE as the learning management system to facilitate the teaching-learning process between lecturers and students, the masses of features embedded in WBLE are always overlooked by the users, especially the academic staff.

2   Research Background

The core principle of implementing WBLE in UTAR is to facilitate academic staff and students of the university. An abundance of functions can be performed in WBLE because Moodle is the platform system of WBLE. However, most of the academic staff are merely utilising WBLE as a tool to manage learning materials. Academic staff access into WBLE for the sole purpose of uploading learning materials for students and students access into WBLE for the intention of downloading learning materials uploaded by lecturers. Thereby, the development of ILC-WBLE in this research aims to produce an alternative learning tool to WBLE. The contents of ILC-WBLE can be tailored based on the needs of users, specifically the academic staff.

The research aims to achieve the following six objectives [3]:

1. To research on the best Instructional Design Model (ID-Model) which is deemed suitable for developing a dynamic multimedia content creation of Independent Learning Courseware for Web-Based Learning Environment (ILC-WBLE) [3];
2. To design a suitable Instructional Design Model (ID-Model) for developing the ILC-WBLE based on instructional design approach;
3. To develop a prototype of ILC-WBLE;
4. To evaluate usability of the prototype of ILC-WBLE as an alternative learning mode to traditional instruction;
5. To identify the strengths and weaknesses of ILC-WBLE;
6. To develop a framework for effective design and development of Computer Based Learning Modules.

Currently, learning materials that are uploaded into WBLE are not possible to be created directly in WBLE; creation of learning materials must be done using other systems or software. ILC-WBLE is a dynamic multimedia content creation system. Multimedia elements such as graphics, images, audio and video are used in delivering the learning contents prepared by lecturers. In addition, three types of quizzes, i.e. fill in the blanks, drag and drop, and multiple choices, are integrated in the system for students to practice their skills and test their understanding on a learned topic. ILC-WBLE is embedded into a webpage at http://www.hohmingchee.com. Fig. 2. depicts the screenshot from the first page of ILC-WBLE.

Users of the system can be categorised into two types, which are as follow:

- Students: Students are allowed to view created subjects in the system, however, they do not have the authority to create a new subject.
- Administrator and Lecturer: Lecturers are granted with the ability to create subjects. In order to create subjects, lecturers have to log into the system with user name and password provided by the administrator of the system.

Fig. 2. Screenshot from the first page (left), and content page (right) of ILC-WBLE

3 Evaluation Approach

This is the research regarding on the development of ILC-WBLE which is to develop a courseware for the purpose of provides assistance to the instructors in UTAR in using the WBLE system of the institution. Consequently, a qualitative research method by using Heuristic Evaluation will be carried out throughout the research [4]. The experimental research of ILC-WBLE consists of 5 constructs which are (i) easy to use, (ii) easy to learn, (iii) level of interactivity, (iv) presentation of interface (v) error free assessment. Every single construct listed here will be fitted with principles of user interface design accordingly.

Table 3.1. Principles Apply in Constructs of Experimental Research of ILC-WBLE

Constructs	Principles
Easy to use	Visibility of system status
	Consistency and standards
Easy to learn	Match between system and the real world
	Help and Documentation
Level of Interactivity	User control and freedom
	Flexibility and Efficiency of use
Presentation of interface	Recognition rather than recall
	Aesthetic and minimalist design
Error free assessment	Error prevention
	Help users recognise, diagnose, and
	recover from errors

Likert Scaling will be applied for the rating portion of evaluation of ILC-WBLE. There are 5-points scaling from 1 (strongly disagree) to 5 (strongly agree).

The evaluation form consists of 3 parts. Part A refers to personal details of respondents such as gender, current trimester of study, and experience in using computers of a respondent. Part B is made up of 5 sections (Easy to use, Easy to learn, Level of interactivity, Presentation of interface, and Error-free assessment) and each section comprises 5 questions which concern matters of the particular section. Part C will be a place for respondent to provide comments on the system.

The authentication on the reliability of evaluation form used in evaluating ILC-WBLE will be conducted through pilot test. In total 6 academic staff and 25 students were participated in pilot test. Consequently, Cronbach's alpha values generated from the result of pilot test for both categories' participants are 0.894 and 0.948 respectively. According to [5], [6], Cronbach's Alpha value more than 0.7 is considered satisfactory and acceptable, hence, the evaluation form for both academic staff and student are considered reliable and acceptable to be used to evaluate ILC-WBLE.

4 Result

4.1 Student

There are in total 101 respondents who participated in final evaluation. 40.6% of respondents are male students and 59.4% of respondents are female students. They were given 2 weeks' time in accessing the developed ILC-WBLE, after which they were required to fill up an evaluation form which composed of 5 sections (with 5 questions in each section).

Section 1: Easy to Use. Easy to Use refers to the evaluation on the easiness of accessing to the system.

Section 1.1 refers to the awareness of options that can be carried out in the system and as the result, there were 79.2% of respondents who agreed or strongly agreed to this statement.

Section 1.2 refers to the awareness of where to proceed to the next step that respondent wish in the system. In order to create an user-friendly interface of the system, icons such as "Previous" and "Next" buttons can be seen easily in the system to give direction to user to go to previous or next page by clicking on those buttons. Nevertheless, the title of the selected page is highlighted with blue colour sequentially to notify user that this is the current page they have selected, whereas the rest of the titles of pages are in grey colour. As a result, there were 84.2% of respondents who agreed or strongly agreed to the statement of they were aware of where to proceed to the next step that they wish in the system.

Section 1.3 refers to the consistency of the steps to view, read, or answer contents throughout the system and as a result, there were 64.3% of respondents agreed or strongly agreed to this statement but 31.7% of respondents were unable to decide the rating in this section.

Section 1.4 refers to respondents whom were aware of the total pages for a particular subject, and were able to estimate the amount of time needed in accomplishing the particular subject. Consequently, there were 71.3% of respondents who agreed or strongly agreed to this statement. All the pages (with page numbers) are aligned properly at the left frame of the system, thus respondents were always informed of the total number of pages for a particular subject in the system.

Section 1.5 refers to whether all instructions in the system are clearly listed. As a result, 69.3% of respondents agreed or strongly agreed that all instructions in the system are clearly listed.

Section 2: Easy to Learn. Easy to Learn refers to the evaluation on the easiness of learning the system.

Most of the respondents, i.e. 84.2% of respondents, rated either "Agree" or "Strongly Agree" to the easiness to understand the words and phrases used in the system (Section 2.1).

Section 2.2 refers to the awareness on how to proceed to the next step in the system. For example, users have to click on the "Submit" button after answering quizzes in the system to review the correct answers. Based on the result of evaluation, 79.2% of respondents agreed or strongly agreed that they were clear of how to proceed to the next step in the system.

Section 2.3 focuses on whether the location of navigation buttons were placed properly in the system. The result of the evaluation revealed that there were in total 70.3% respondents who agreed or strongly agreed that the navigation buttons were appropriately located.

Section 2.4 refers to the clarity of guidance provided in the system while Section 2.5 enquires whether the location of the "Help" icon can be found easily in the system. As a result of the evaluation, most of the respondents were unable to decide on the rating, in which a total of 32.7% respondents rated "Neutral" for Section 2.4. As for Section 2.5, there were only 57.4% of respondents who rated either "Agree" or "Strongly Disagree" to the easiness of locating the "Help" icon.

Section 3: Level of Interactivity. Level of interactivity is related to the options that can be done in ILC-WBLE. Options such as the sorting feature that allowed the rearrangement of the page sequence in the system, attachments could support various of file format or even the system could support multimedia file or not.

Section 3.1 refers to the sorting feature in the system – whether pages of the subject can be rearranged easily in the system. There were quite a number of respondents (28.7%) whom were unable to decide on the rating in this section.

As mentioned earlier, quizzes can be created in three types of formats, i.e. "Fill in the Blank", "Drag and Drop", and "Multiple Choices". Section 3.2 enquires whether the quizzes of the system are set in various methods. There are in total 74.3% respondents who rated either "Agree" or Strongly Agree" that quizzes could be set in various formats.

Section 3.3 refers to the support of multimedia contents in the system. ILC-WBLE is a system which is not just constrained to the insertion of text and images, it too, can support multimedia file (text, image, audio, video, and animation). This section was anticipated to have a higher rate but surprisingly there were only 75.3% respondents who agreed or strongly agreed that the system could support multimedia contents. This could be due to the limitation of connection speed in UTAR (as respondents tried out the system in UTAR) which led to the failure in viewing multimedia file that had been uploaded into the system.

The similar reason influenced the result for Section 3.4, which refers to the control of playing the video and audio file in the system. 76.3% of respondents rated "Agree" and "Strongly Agree" in Section 3.4.

Nevertheless, the slow connection speed in UTAR also affected Section 3.5, which enquires the availability of supporting materials such as hyperlinks and attachments in the system. As a result, only 71.3% of respondents agreed or strongly agreed that supporting materials could be found in the forms of hyperlinks and attachments.

Section 4: Presentation of Interface. Presentation of interface is the section which refers to the layout design of the system. As usual, there are five sections included in this section. The first four sections produced results of not more than 70% of respondents rated "Agree" or "Strongly Agree", whereas Section 4.5 witnessed a total of 76.2% respondents whom agreed or strongly agreed to the statement.

ILC-WBLE only applied one type of colour scheme, compared to any other system where user could change the colour scheme of the system since the system is embedded with a few colour schemes for user to choose. Although the current system is included with eight types of layout for content page, but most of the lecturers only chose a few of the layout type for the content page they added into the subject, hence, students would not notice most of the layout design of the system. All these reasons led to the results in Sections 4.1 and 4.2, in which only 66.3% respondent rated "Agree" or "Strongly Agree" to the statement that the contents of each page come in various layout design and 65.3% of respondents agreed or strongly agreed that the colour scheme applied in the system is appropriate, respectively.

Section 4.3 refers to the clarity of graphics used in navigation buttons such as, "Previous" and "Next" buttons, background music controller, or video controller in the system. There were only 58.4% of respondents whom agreed and strongly agreed that the graphics used in navigation buttons clearly explained the functions of the buttons.

Section 4.4 is the section which witnessed the highest undecided rating in the whole evaluation of ILC-WBLE, in which a total of 39.6% of respondents were unable to decide the rating for the statement "instructions will be given repeatedly in every section to reduce the use of users' memory".

Section 4.5, which states that each page has a clear and short title to indicate the current location in the system, observed 79.2% of respondents agreed or strongly agreed to the statement. Title of each page is located at the left frame of the system and each page includes a title sequentially to explain the content of each page.

Section 5: Error-free Assessment. Most of the respondents accessed to ILC-WBLE in UTAR's campus either by using computers in computer lab or being connected to UTAR's internet service via their own computers. They experienced slow downloading speed while trying to download attachments from ILC-WBLE, and even videos that were uploaded into ILC-WBLE were failed to be loaded. For those respondents who accessed to the system from their own staying places, they did not have difficulty downloading attachments from the system and or playing videos smoothly without error in the system. Due to the reasons mentioned above, there were two respondents whom commented on the slow downloading speed in the system, and a total of 8.9% of respondents rated "disagree" and 1.0% of respondents rated

"Strongly Disagree" towards the statement that error-free attachments could be downloaded from the system (Section 5.1).

The existence of this phenomenon was due to the reason that UTAR has given the priority of bandwidth to UTAR interrelated websites only, thus other websites would encounter slow accessing speed.

Section 5.2 refers to the accessibility of hyperlinks in the system. Hyperlinks that linked to other sources, like websites, can be added into the content page of the system. Based on the result from the evaluation, there were in total 59.5% of respondents whom rated "Agree" and "Strongly Agree" that the hyperlink feature in the system could be accessed without any error.

Section 5.3 states that pages in the system are sorted properly according to page type. Respondents were able to view the pages of the particular subject either by sorting them according to page type (rearrange all the content pages to the front and quizzes to the back) or remain the original sequence. Based on the result from the evaluation, there were 68.4% of respondents whom were able to sort the page type while 24.8% of respondents were unable to decide the rating of the sorting feature in the system.

Section 5.5 refers to whether all quizzes in the system can be answered without any error. There are 3 types of quizzes which can be created in the system (drag and drop, fill in the blank, and multiple choices). Answering quizzes that were created by using 'fill in the blank' feature in the system would require user to provide answers that are exactly the same (capital letter sensitive) with the preset answers. If user had provided correct answers but in different way compared to the preset answers, responses after submitting the answers would be negative. As result, there were in total 11.9% respondents whom rated "Disagree" and "Strongly Disagree" in this section.

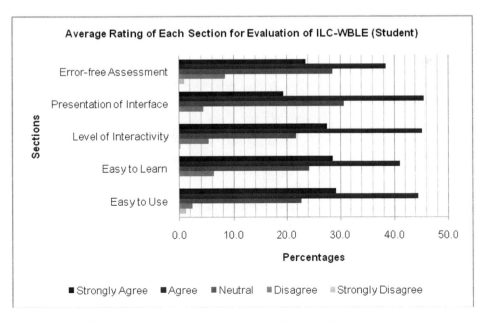

Fig. 3. Summary of average rating of each section from students

Open-Ended Comments. The last part of the evaluation form is an open-ended question enquiring suggestions to the system. There were in total 24 replies which were collected from respondents from the evaluation.

Table 1. Summary of comments from students

Primary Positive Aspects	Primary Negative Aspects
Easy to use and easy to learn.	Colour scheme applied in the system is unattractive.
ILC-WBLE is an informative system.	Loading speed of the content and downloading speed of the attachments are slow.
Contents included in the system could improve the academic performance of student.	Wordings used in the system are not interesting.

4.2 Academic Staff

Second type of targeted respondents involved in this evaluation was lecturers who are lecturing in Foundation level. There were in total 10 respondents who participated in final evaluation. 20% of respondents are male while 80% of respondents are female lecturers.

They were given 2 weeks' time to access the developed ILC-WBLE, after that, they were required to fill up an evaluation form which is composed of 5 sections (5 questions in each section). In total, 12 evaluation forms were distributed to lecturers, and 10 evaluation forms were collected at the end of evaluation (response rate being 83.33%). The total teaching hours per week assigned to lecturers in Centre for Foundation Studies are higher compared to any other faculty in UTAR, thus leading to the imperfect response rate.

Section 1: Easy to Use. Easy to Use refers to the evaluation on the easiness of accessing the system and whether options and features can be utilised easily in the system.

Section 1.1 is related to the awareness of options that can be carried out in the system. There were respectively 40% and 60% of respondents who strongly agreed and agreed that they were aware of the options available in the system.

In order to create a user-friendly interface of the system, icons such as "Previous" and "Next" buttons are included in the system while title of each page of the subject can be viewed readily at the left frame of the content page. As a result, 50% respondents agreed while 40% respondents strongly agreed that they were aware of where to proceed to the next step that they wished in the system.

The main page of lecturer is used to carry out monitoring tasks such as creation, edition, and deletion of subject. Dates created and modified of subjects can be viewed in the main page to facilitate lecturers in knowing the latest modified date of the subject. Consequently, 40% of respondents strongly agreed that date of creation and modification of subjects are easily identified in the system (Section 1.3).

While uploading file into the system, uploading progress bar can be seen in the middle of the page. Thus, 60% respondents agreed and 40% respondents strongly agreed that latest upload progress is being informed while uploading any file in the system (Section 1.4). Last but not least, 50% respondents strongly agreed that all instructions in the system are clearly listed (Section 1.5).

Section 2: Easy to Learn. Easy to learn is a section pertaining how easy user gets familiarised with the system. The mode of the rating in this section is 5 (Strongly Agree) except for Section 2.3 which refers to the consistency of the placement of navigation buttons in the system. The mode of Section 2.3 is 4 (Agree).

Language used in the system is considered easy to understand based on the responses from students and lecturers. There were 100% lecturers participated in the evaluation of ILC-WBLE who strongly agreed or agreed to this statement (Section 2.1).

Section 2.2 enquired whether the user had been able to create and modify the content and quiz page in the system. 70% of respondents strongly agreed and the rest of the respondents agreed that they were able to do so.

Sections 2.4 and 2.5 refer to the guidance provided in the system. "Help" buttons can be viewed in every content and quiz page, users can always refer to the provided guidelines while creating content or quiz pages. As result, both sections witnessed the same number of respondents (50%) who strongly agreed that clear guidance was provided and "Help" button could be easily found within any page.

Section 3: Level of Interactivity. Level of interactivity is related to the options that can be done in ILC-WBLE, such as sorting feature, creating content and quiz page, and inserting multimedia files, attachments and hyperlinks.

Mode of the rating in Section 3 is 4 (Agree). There were 70% respondents who agreed that pages in the system can be sorted easily according to page type (Section 3.1) and 80% respondents who agreed that quizzes can be set in various methods (Section 3.2).

Sections 3.3, 3.4, and 3.5 had the same number of respondents (60%) who agreed to the statements in each section. Section 3.3 stated that the system can support multimedia files and Section 3.4 stated that viewing of video and audio are controllable in the system. Finally, Section 3.5 stated that hyperlinks can be inserted in the system and the system also supports several file formats as the attachments.

Section 4: Presentation of Interface. "Presentation of Interface" is a section which refers to the layout design of the system and the mode of the rating in this section is 4 (Agree).

Eight types of layout design are provided in the system for users to choose while creating a content page. Section 4.1 is related to the various layout designs that can be selected in creating a content page. There were 40% respondents who agreed to the statement. Other than that, 70% respondents agreed that the colour scheme that is applied in the system is appropriate (Section 4.2). Most of the respondents (80%) also agreed that the graphics used in navigation buttons could clearly explain the function of the button (Section 4.3).

Section 4.4 refers to the instructions in the system being given repeatedly in every section to reduce the use of users' memory, which had quite positive responses from the respondents because there were 90% of respondents who agreed to the statement.

There were also 50% of respondents who agreed that each page has a clear and short title to indicate the current location (Section 4.5).

Section 5: Error-free Assessment. "Error-free Assessment" section refers to whether there is any error in the system, and whether solution has been provided to avoid mistake from occurring while using ILC-WBLE.

Users (Lecturers) of the system may carry out deletion of the subjects and pages that were created earlier. In order to avoid from accidentally deleting some of the items in the system, a pop up message will appear to enquire users if they wish to delete the particular item after having clicked on the "Delete" button. Thus, 50% of respondents strongly agreed that they were required to confirm their actions before deleting any unwanted items (Section 5.1).

There were similarly 60% of respondents who agreed that hyperlinks can be created without any error (Section 5.2) and pages can be sorted according to page type without error (Section 5.3).

If an error happens in the system, an error message will appear together with a message that indicates the problem in order to facilitate users to solve the error. Thus 40% of respondents agreed that error message pops out could precisely indicate the problem (Section 5.4) while 50% of respondents agreed that all error messages will be provided with the respective solutions (Section 5.5).

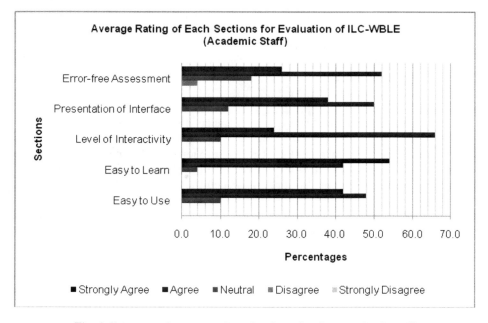

Fig. 4. Summary of average rating of each section from academic staff

Open-Ended Comments. The last part of the evaluation form is an open-ended question regarding the suggestion to the system. There were in total 7 replies from respondents of academic staffs which were collected from the evaluation.

Table 2. Summary of comments from academic staffs

Primary Positive Aspects	Primary Negative Aspects
Easy to access compared to UTAR's WBLE.	Loading of the contents in student section is slow.
Able to create quizzes in the system is useful for lecturers to set up test for students easily.	Font size, font colour, type of bullet and numbering function are not available in the system.
User-friendly interactions in the system.	Unable to create courseware with same subject name that is created earlier in the system.

4.3 Discussion

Strengths and weaknesses of ILC-WBLE are defined according to the outcome of the evaluation. Based on the analysed results from the five sections, the mode of the rating is "4", which means respondents are agreeable upon the easiness in using the system, easiness in learning the system, inclusiveness of various levels of interactions in the system, pleasantness in the interface design of the system, and last but not least, limitedness of errors encountered in the system.

4.3.1 Strengths of ILC-WBLE

As mentioned, evaluation form also includes a section where respondents are able to comment and suggest about the system. The comments collected from the respondents are summarised and used to define the strengths and weaknesses of ILC-WBLE.

The strengths of the system could be categorised into three aspects, which are:

- easiness on accessing the system compare to the current system (WBLE) applied in UTAR,
- ILC-WBLE is a simple yet informative system, and
- level of interaction in creating quizzes.

ILC-WBLE is a simple and easy to use system, especially the feature of creating quizzes online is sufficient to provide exercises for students. Even though functions of ILC-WBLE are not as many as WBLE, yet they are adequate in facilitating lecturers, since ILC-WBLE is easy to use and it enables lecturers to create learning materials online in the system.

4.3.2 Weaknesses of ILC-WBLE

The weaknesses of the system can be categoried into three aspects as well, which are:

- colour schemes and wordings applied in the system are unattractive,
- absence of text editor in the system, and
- the slow loading and downloading speeds of the system.

Features such as text editor and changing of colour schemes for the layout of the system are excluded from the system. Slow loading and downloading speeds that occur in the system are due to the web hosting package that is used to host the system.

Currently, ILC-WBLE is hosted in a shared web server, which means bandwidth assigned to the web site (ILC-WBLE) is shared among many other web sites that are hosted in the same web server. If the system is hosted in a dedicated web server such as UTAR's server, loading and downloading speeds of the system are deemed to be faster.

5   Conclusion

Numerous features integrated in WBLE facilitate instructors and learners in the teaching-learning process. However, not every feature has been fully utilised by the users. Hence, ILC-WBLE is indeed a simple system which fulfills the basic requirements of a user.

Learning comes in many forms, multimedia should always be included in a learning process. ILC-WBLE is a system which supports real-time viewing of multimedia files. Quizzes created in the system are not constrained to be in multiple choices only, however, fill in the blanks and drag and drop are the types of quizzes that can be created in the system as well. All the creations in the system are easily generated, as commented by the respondents of the evaluation.

Moreover, one of the strengths of ILC-WBLE is, ILC-WBLE allows user to create his/her personalised courseware online at anywhere, anytime without installing any external software such as Microsoft Power Points. ILC-WBLE is definitely a straightforward and useful system to facilitate and enhance the teaching-learning process.

Nevertheless, ILC-WBLE is a system which supports multi languages, such as Chinese, Tamil, Hindi, Japanese, Korean, German, and Spanish. Due to this feature, language instructors are deemed to benefit from this great advantage.

With the existence of ILC-WBLE, it is believed that the development of ILC-WBLE would benefit lecturers to gain knowledge in exploiting the system, as well as improving the learning progress of students.

References

1. Dougiamas, M., Taylor, P.: Moodle: Using Learning Communities to Create an Open Source Course Management System. In: Lassner, D., McNaught, C. (eds.) Proceedings of World Conference on Educational Multimedia, Hypermedia and Telecommunications 2003, vol. 2, pp. 171–178. AACE, Chesapeake (2003)
2. Rice, W.: Moodle teaching techniques: creative ways to use moodle for constructing online learning solutions. Packt Publishing (2007)
3. Hoh, M.C., Choo, W.O., Siew, P.H.: Dynamic Multimedia Content Creation for Independent Learner: A Web Based Learning Environment. In: Proceedings of Knowledge Management International Conference 2010, pp. 151–156 (2010)
4. Nielsen, J.: Ten Usability Heuristics. Nielsen Norman Group, Alertbox (2005)
5. Martin, B.J., Douglas, G.A.: Statistics notes: Cronbach's Alpha. BMJ 314, 572 (1997)
6. Santos, J.R.A.: Cronbach's Alpha: A Tool for Assessing the Reliability of Scales. Extension Journal 37 (1999)

Factors Affecting Undergraduates' Acceptance of Educational Game: An Application of Technology Acceptance Model (TAM)

Roslina Ibrahim[1], Rasimah Che Mohd Yusoff[1], Khalili Khalil[2], and Azizah Jaafar[3]

[1] Advanced Informatics School, Universiti Teknologi Malaysia, Jalan Semarak,
54100, Kuala Lumpur, Malaysia
[2] Insitut Teknologi Darul Takzim INSTEDT, Kota Tinggi, Johor, Malaysia
[3] Institute of Visual Informatics, Universiti Kebangsaan Malaysia, Bangi, Selangor, Malaysia
{lina,rasimah}@ic.utm.my, khalili@instedt.edu.my, aj@ftsm.ukm.my

Abstract. Educational games (EG) are seen as a promising educational technology. This is due to fun and engaging nature of games compared to other media. However, little studies have been done to investigate factors that might affect student's acceptance of EG, especially among undergraduate student. Understanding those factors can assist EG designers in designing better games. This study investigated those factors by applying modified technology acceptance model (TAM). Four (4) factors, namely usefulness, ease of use, attitude and learning opportunity were used. An online survey was done with 63 samples from Universiti Teknologi Malaysia. Data was analyzed using structural equation modeling (SEM) as well as descriptive method. Findings shown that usefulness, ease of use and attitude are significant acceptance factors of EG. Hopefully, this study will enrich literatures regarding EG acceptance factors especially among undergraduate students.

Keywords: educational games, user acceptance, unified theory of acceptance and use of technology (UTAUT), Visual Informatics.

1 Introduction

Educational games are regarded as future teaching and learning methods that better suits the preferences of younger generations, as reported by Federation of American Scientists (FAS), [1]. These generations grow up with internet, social networking programs, Sony Playstation (PS), online games, online videos, emails and so on are found to have different preferences in teaching and learning approach [2]. Therefore, integration of these technologies into their education seems to bring about positive effects.

Games are believed to have distinct advantages compared to conventional teaching and learning approach. Gee has proposed that it is able to teach 21st century skills such as problem solving, critical thinking, collaboration and team working [3]. From the perspective of rich games genre and design opportunities, EG developers have lots of opportunities to develop games based on learning outcomes and theories [4], [5], learning styles and learning domain [6], [7], [8].

H. Badioze Zaman et al. (Eds.): IVIC 2011, Part II, LNCS 7067, pp. 135–146, 2011.

Many studies have been done to investigate EG effectiveness as a learning tool. Garris et al [6], have found that EGs are able to help student on various learning domains such as cognitive, affective as well as psychomotor skills. EG is also found to increase learning motivation as demonstrated in [9], [10], [11]. Motivation is among the most important element in learning, intrinsically or extrinsically. A study by Garzotto, [12] revealed that multiplayer online games provide learning benefits on affective level as well as knowledge domain. Other studies also acknowledged the benefits of using games for learning such as in [13], [14], [5] that stated game motivates learning, offer immediate feedback, support skills, and influences changes in behavior and attitudes.

With such promise, EG adoption, however, are still rather slow, Kebritchi [15]. Kebritchi suggested that there are need to investigate EG acceptance factors to further understand the reasons of low adoption rate of EG among schools despite its positive promise. She also stated that there are very much lacks of literatures discussing the matter. Similarly, De-Freitas [16] discussed the barriers for adoption of EG including i) familiarity with games-based software, ii) time to prepare effective game-based learning, iii) learners group who like to use this approach and, iv) cost associated with application. Therefore, we need to understand the factors that affects EG acceptance to help designers design better games.

This study seeks to investigate students' acceptance factors of EG. It can assist EG designers to leverage the knowledge during the design process as well as for decision making process. Students are the most important stakeholders in education but often left with no choice when it comes to teaching and learning approach. It is happened both in school and institutes of higher learning (IHL). Thus, we choose undergraduate student as the samples. Besides, computer infrastructures are more accessible among them.

This paper is organized as follows: Section 2 discuss on theoretical background, followed by research model and hypotheses in section 3. Section 4 presents methodology while section 5 present results. Last section (6) is the conclusion.

2   Theoretical Background

2.1 Technology Acceptance

Dillon and Morris [17] defined user acceptance as "demonstrable willingness within a user group to employ information technology for the tasks it is designed to support". It seeks to understand the contributing factors that affect users in deciding whether or not they will use a system. Those factors can be from both systems' factors as well user's factors. Systems factors are including its usefulness, easy to use, and enjoyment while users' factors are about users' background such as experience, attitude and resources that they have access. User acceptance inquires about why people accept a system so that better methods for design and development will be employed. It seeks to extend beyond usability studies that discussed about designing use friendly interface into much more deeper understanding about other factors contribute to user acceptance. User acceptance research seems to compliment usability studies by looking into wider factors. Also, it is depending on factors such as use setting (voluntary or mandatory) and user background. Lack of user acceptance understanding can impede the success of any new technology.

Technology acceptance theory is derived upon Theory of Reasoned Action (TRA), a social psychological theory that defines relationship between beliefs, attitudes, norms, intentions and behavior. It indicates that individual behavior in using technology is determined by one's intention to perform the behavior. This intention is influenced by several factors or determinants.

In the field of information systems (IS), Technology Acceptance Model (TAM) by Davis [18] is among the most widely used model in IS. It has being extensively applied into many types of information system including job related applications, business, government, e-commerce, internet banking, e-learning, and other online applications. TAM postulated that usefulness and ease of use are the main factors to predict behavioral intention.

Another well known user acceptance theory is unified theory of acceptance and use of technology (UTAUT). Upon the realization of multiple theories that co-exist in the field of IS concerning acceptance or adoption, Venkatesh et al [19] formulated and empirically validated eight relevant theories into a unified theory called Unified Theory of Acceptance and Use of Technology (UTAUT). The theories are i) Technology Acceptance Model (TAM), ii) Theory of Planned Behavior (TPB), iii) Theory of Reasoned Action (TRA), iv) Social Cognitive Theory (SCT), v) Model of PC Utilization (MPCU), vi) Diffusion of Innovation (DOI), vii) Combined TAM-TPB, and viii) Motivational Model (MM).UTAUT have four (4) direct determinants of user acceptance which are performance expectancy, effort expectancy, social influence and facilitating conditions, while two others are dependant variables; behavioral intention and use behavior. UTAUT also have four moderators (gender, age, experience and voluntariness of use) that moderate relationship between independent and dependant variables.

2.2 Educational Game Acceptance

Upon extensive reviews of literatures, it is found that there are still huge gap regarding acceptance studies of educational games. As to date, too little attention has being given on investigation on acceptance factors of EG. As the matter of fact, only a small number of studies have being implemented even on acceptance of common entertainment computer games. Considering the fact that both types of games have different nature and purposes, obviously different factors will influence its acceptance. Therefore, thorough investigation are needed to better leverage design and implementation of EG for educational purposes.

Several studies have identified acceptance factors of entertainment games. Hsu and Lu in [20] studied online gaming acceptance using extended TAM incorporated with social norm and flow experience. The model was able to explain about 80% of the variance. Ease of use was found as key determinants of online game. Meanwhile, Ha et al [21] found that perceived enjoyment was better predictors than usefulness. Age was found as key moderator in acceptance of mobile broadband games. In the case of educational games, Bourgonjon et al [22] found that student preference for educational games are affected by a number of factors, such as perceptions of student regarding usefulness, ease of use, learning opportunities and experience with video games in general. Gender effects are found as well, but mediated by experience and ease of use. Another study of EG acceptance among teachers using DOI theory did by Kebritchi in [15], found that teachers are ready to adopt EG provided that the games meet several requirements such as advantages (indication of game effectiveness, game support features, gender-neutral features and engagement and problem-solving instruction strategies), compatibility (game alignment with the state and national standards, available time for playing the game, available computers for playing the game and the teachers' technology training), complexity (rich content, attractive game context and story, adjustment of the game difficulties), trialability (accessing to a trial version of the game. Very recently, Amri [23] have found that usefulness is significant towards intention to use EG but ease of use was found not significant. Table 1 shows the summary of literature review in games acceptance studies. However, only two of the studies investigated the acceptance of educational game while the others are on entertainment games.

Table 1. Summary of games acceptance studies

Author (Year) Model used	Sample (N)/ Technology/system	Findings
Amri Yusoff (2010) Modified TAM	53 undergraduates students Self developed EG (Unilink)	Usefulness has direct effect on intention while transfer skills, learners control effect usefulness. Situated learning effects ease of use and Ease of Use effects usefulness.
Bourgonjon et al (2010) Extended TAM	858 Flemish schools students/ Educational games/ No system use	Usefulness, ease of use, learning opportunities and personal experience with games have direct effect on preference with gender effect found to be mediated by experience and ease of use.
Kebritchi (2010), Diffusion of innovation (DOI)	3 schools teachers/ Educational games/ Dimenxian	Relative advantage, compatibility, complexity, trialability and observability.
Fang and Zhao (2010) Extended TAM	173 US university students/ Several games genre	Enjoyment and perceived ease of use. Two personality traits (sensation seeking and self-forgetfulness) have positive impact on enjoyment
Fetscherin and Lattemann (2008) Extended TAM	249 second life users/ Virtual worlds/Second Life	Community, attitude, social norms have direct effect on perceived usefulness while anxiety does not, ease of use effect usefulness and intention.
Wang and Wang, (2008) Extended TAM	281 responses/ Online games/ World of Warcraft, Lineage and Maple Story	Perceived playfulness on intention based on gender. Self-efficacy, perceived playfulness and BI were all higher in men while computer anxiety was higher in women. No gender differences on system characteristics

Due to lack of investigation in EG acceptance studies, we seek to explore the perceptions of Malaysian undergraduate on using online EG as one of their learning approach. Online game is one of the most popular technologies among teenagers including as undergraduate's students. This is due to easy access to computer and internet in their daily activities. Almost all students have their own PC or laptop as found by our survey [24]. Thus we seek to investigate students' perceptions towards this technology for our further implementation of educational games.

In this study, we proposed to investigate the direct effects of student intention to use EG based upon revised TAM and UTAUT. We proposed usefulness, ease of use, learning opportunity, and attitude as the independent variables while student preference as the dependant variable. Usefulness and ease of use are from original TAM model while learning opportunity and attitude were originated from other studies.

3   Research Model and Hypotheses

3.1   Independent Variables

Usefulness (Use) is defined as "the extent to which an individual believes that using an information system (IS) will help him or her to attain benefits in job performance". Since this definition is more towards job related environment, we like to note here that job performance here is taken as learning performance. However, education is much more than the outcomes only, but it is also involve the process as well. Bourgonjon et al proposed the learning process can be defined as learning opportunity. We used both usefulness and learning opportunity to describe the process and the outcome of learning. Learning opportunities (LO) defined as "the extent which a person believes that using an online educational game can offer him or her opportunities for learning".

Ease of use (EoU) is defined as "the degree of ease associated with the use of system".It is considered the second most important factor in IS acceptance. Venkatesh et al (2003) formulated this construct from three previous models: TAM, MPCU and IDT.

Attitude (Att) towards using technology is defined as "individual behavior overall affective reaction to using a system". Venkatesh et al (2003) explained that attitude was significant across many studies. Marchewka in [25] proposed that attitude will have direct effect on behavioral intention. Based upon above theoretical supports, the following hypotheses are proposed.

> *H1: Usefulness positively affects preferences for educational games.*
> *H2: Ease of use positively affects preferences for educational games.*
> *H3: Attitude positively affects preferences for educational games.*
> *H4: Learning opportunity positively affects preferences for educational games.*

3.2   Dependant Variable: Preferences for Educational Games

This study is in pre-implementation, whereby the actual use of the system is yet to be implemented. Therefore it is not possible to study the actual use of the educational games by the student. While both UTAUT and TAM used it as a dependant variable, we decided to omit that in this particular stage. This is similar with Bourgonjon et al [22] argument that proposed to investigate only the respondent behavioral intention (BI). BI is seen as capable of predicting future use of system. They further argued that behavioral intention can be a good predictor of actual use. We use preference as the dependant variables as it seem to be more appropriate in pre-implementation stage of use as suggested by Bourgonjon et al [22]. Research model is presented in figure 1.

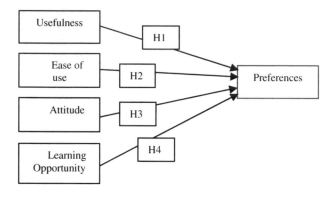

Fig 1. Proposed Model and Hypotheses

4 Methodology

4.1 Instrument and Survey Process

An online survey was developed based on original items developed by Bourgonjon et al [22] and Venkatesh et al [19]. The survey instrument has 21 questionnaire items with 5 constructs, using 5 point Likert's Scale from 1 (strongly disagree) to 5 (strongly agree). Samples are sixty three (N=63) IT students undertaking Diploma in Computer Science course at Universiti Teknologi Malaysia (UTM), Kuala Lumpur with 31 male and 32 female respondents.

Reliability analysis was performed using Cronbach's Alpha on all items (21) with the alpha value of (.92) and on every single construct: Usefulness – 4 items (.85), Ease of Use – 3 items (.73), Learning Opportunity – 7 items (.80), Attitude – 4 items (.85), and preference – 3 items (.83) .All constructs appear to have a good degree of reliability with the value of 0.73 and above. Full list of items is presented in Table 2.

Table 2. Questionnaire items based on construct

Constructs	Items
Usefulness (Use) *Using Online educational games...*	Use1: Would improve my performance
	Use2: Would increase my learning productivity
	Use3: Would enhance my effectiveness
	Use4: Would help me to achieve better grades
Ease of Use (EoU)	EoU1: I would know how to handle online computer educational games
	EoU2: It would be easy to for me to use online computer educational games
	EoU3: My interaction with online computer educational games would be clear and understandable

Attitude (Att)	Att1: Using online educational games would be a good idea
	Att2: Learning with online educational games would be fun
	Att3: Online educational games would make learning a subject more interesting
	Att4: I think I will like learning with online educational games
Learning opportunity (LO)

Online educational computer games offer opportunities to... | LO1: experiment with knowledge |
	LO2: take control over the learning process
	LO3: experience things you learnt about
	LO4: stimulate transfer between subjects
	LO5: interact with other students
	LO6: think critically
	LO7: motivate students
Preferences (Pref)	Pref1: If I had the choice, I would choose to follow courses in which online educational computer games are used
	Pref2: If I had to vote, I would vote in favor of using online educational computer games for learning
	Pref3: I am enthusiastic about using online educational computer games as one of my learning approach

5   Results

5.1 Descriptive Statistic

Findings of descriptive analysis are presented in the following figures by each construct, using percentage (Y axis) and answer of every item (X axis) based on Likert's scale (1 to 5) as the legend.

Figure 2 shows the result for Usefulness (Use) construct. Bar in the chart shown scale 1 (left) up to scale 5 (right) with scale 2, 3 and 4 in between. In general, students agreed that EG would help them to perform better in their learning such as improving performance, increase productivity and enhance their effectiveness. This is an encouraging result as our younger generations shown their preferences of using computer technology - games in particular, for their learning. Even though number of samples in this study are small, the trend among our younger generations are more shifted towards technology and internet are undeniable – hence prompted more studies to fit this technology into their education. Students answers are more towards agree and strongly agree (about 80%), items 1 to 3 shown that they have a positive attitude towards using EG for learning. None of the students strongly disagree with any of the items, with only few (less than 10%) disagreed. Result on helping them achieving better grades is moderated (about half of the sample agreed and another half disagree) – this probably due to no such experience of using EG by the students, hence, no experienced of grade improvement among them.

Figure 3 shown the result for Ease of Use (EoU) construct. It is found that most student are confident that they can easily operated the EG. This is probably due to their own experiences with computer games and other internet applications. This is important when introducing a new application to intended user as it may increase its acceptance rate due familiarity with the computer.

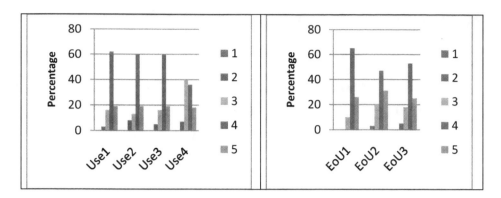

Fig. 2. Result for Usefulness Construct   **Fig. 3.** Result for Ease of Use Construct

Figure 4 shown the result for Learning Opportunity (LO) construct. As can be seen, all items have highest score on scale 4(agree), followed by strongly agree and not sure. Less than 5% choose disagree (in all items). It is not surprised to see some student are not sure about it - given the situation that they never have contextual experience with EG.

Figure 5 present results for Attitude (Att) construct. Most student are having positive attitude towards EG – this is especially on the fun aspect of games. Since games are associated with fun, all of them agree that using EG would be fun. It is important to note that younger generations are more multitasking, less retention, risk taking and adventurous [2], and like to do fun things. Thus, integration of EG into their education would at least help them to be more motivated to learn.

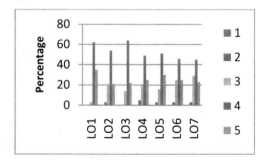

Fig. 4. Result for Learning Opportunity

Figure 6 shown result for Preferences (Pref). It is interesting to note that about 80% of the student agreed on using EG for their learning. This is probably because games are highly motivating and most student play some sort of computer games [24] as their activities. Given the results of this analysis, it is vital for scholars and educators to pay attention to preferences of our students for creating and enhancing our existing education approach for more effective and productive education.

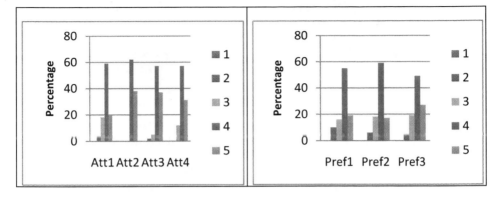

Fig. 5. Result for Attitude   **Fig. 6.** Result for Preferences

Games and gender is a widely discuss issue in literatures, given the interest of males are more interested in games compared to women [26]. Thus, we further explore the differences of some gaming habits between male and female in terms of games playtime, medium of play and reasons for playing. Figure 7 shows the cross tabulation of games playtime between male and female. Students were asked about their frequency of game playing per week. More than half of male students play more than 5 hours per week followed by 1 to 5 hours and 1 hour or less. None of male student stated that they do not play games at all. In contrast, most female students play 1hour or less, or 1 to 5 hours, about 5of them plays more than 5 hours. Small numbers of female students are found not playing games at all.

In terms of games playing medium, students were asked to choose their most favorite medium between computer, TV console, handheld and hand phone. Result shown (Figure 8) that favorite medium for both genders is computer, followed by TV console and hand held. None of male student plays through hand phone while females play using all four mediums.

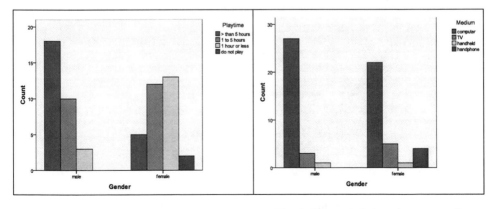

Fig. 7. Cross tabulation of games playtime   **Fig. 8.** Cross tabulation of games medium

For reasons to play games, main reasons for both genders are fun and to fill up free time, followed by challenges. Nice graphic are found not to be the reasons they play games with both genders stated it as the last reason. Thus, it is suggested that games need to be design with fun elements in the first hand, followed by challenges. Even though graphics is important, but the focus should be on other elements as preferred by students.

5.2 Model Validation

For model validation, exploratory factor analysis was done followed by structural model. KMO (Kaiser-Meyer-Olkin) and Bartlett's test. KMO values is .795, which is adequate for factor analysis and Bartlett's test is significant at p < .001. Factor loading for each item which are more than 0.5 were used for further analysis while items LO1 and LO5 were discarded due to low factor loading.

Structural model was developed as shown in Figure 9. Based on model estimates - critical ratios (C.R), three factors were found significant with attitude (Standardized regression weight = .55, C.R =5.892) as the highest predictor for EG acceptance, followed by usefulness (standardized regression weight = .31, C.R =3.397) and ease of use (standardized regression weight = 3.254, C.R = 3.254). This is similar with findings of many acceptance studies such as in Davis [18] and [27]. Learning opportunity however was found not significant. This is probably because of no learning process have been experienced by them using games, therefore it is difficult for them to perceived its opportunity to learn. Bougonjon et al also found this factor moderately significant in his study. The model explained 66% of the variance, which is about similar with research of [27].

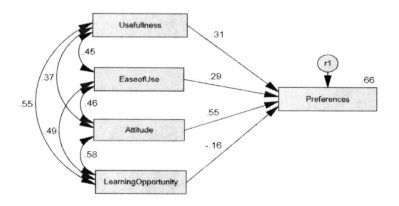

Fig. 9. Structural model

6   Conclusion

This study seeks to understand students acceptance factors in using EG for learning. Descriptive as well as factor confirmation were presented using both SPSS and AMOS. It is interesting to note that undergraduate students from a higher education in

Malaysia are highly interested with using games for their learning. They are also having a very positive attitude towards using EG. Descriptive findings shown that most students prefer to use EG even though they never experienced it before. Their experiences with games were probably being used as a guide in using EG.

Out of four (4) acceptance factors, three were found significant on preferences. Attitude is the highest predictor, shown that the students are highly encouraged to use EG. This should initiate more studies in development of appropriate EG for student learning. Given low motivation to learn as complained by many lecturers, EG for learning is a worth trying to complement existing learning approach. Apart from that, EG designers should leverage usefulness and ease of use elements into their design for better acceptance of EG. Usefulness was found more important than ease of use, thus shown that student will use EG if it is found useful for their learning. This finding is in line with many acceptance studies on utilitarian application.

Due to limited number of samples, this finding should be use with caution. Further studies are needed with more samples from several institutions and if possible, with actual use of developed EG.

References

1. Federation of American Scientists (FAS). Harnessing the power of video games for learning 2006, May 8 (2010)
2. Prensky, M.: Digital Game-Based Learning. Mc Graw Hill, New York (2001)
3. Gee, J.P.: What video games have to teach us about learning and literacy. Palgrave MacMillan, New York (2003)
4. Tan, P.H., Siew, W.L., Choo, Y.T.: Adaptive Digital Game-Based Learning Framework. In: Proceedings of the 2nd International Conference on Digital Interactive Media in Entertainment and Arts 2007, Perth, Australia (2007)
5. Sugimoto, M.: What can children learn through game-based learning systems. In: 1st IEEE International Workshop on Digital Game and Intellignet Toy Enhanced Learning (DIGITEL 2007). IEEE Xplore (2007)
6. Garris, R., Ahlers, R., Driskell, J.E.: Games, Motivation, and Learning: A Research and Practice Model. Simulation and Gaming 33(4), 441–467 (2002)
7. Brandt, E.: Designing Exploratory Design Games: A Framework for Participation in Participatory Design? In: Ninth Participatory Design Conference 2006. ACM, Trento (2006)
8. Wallace, P.: Blending instructional design principal with computer game design: The development of Descartes' Cove. In: Association of the Advancement of Computing in Education, Educational Multimedia and Hypermedia, Montreal, Canada (2005)
9. Jaspaljeet, S.L.L.W., Shanmugam, M., Gunasekaran, S.S., Dorairaj, S.K.: Designing Computer Games to Introduce Programming to Children. In: Information Technology and Multimedia at UNITEN (ICIMU 2008), Uniten, Editor: Selangor, Malaysia, pp. 643–647 (2008)
10. Izam Shah, B.: Perisian Pengembaraan Multimedia: Edutainment Dalam Pendidikan Agama Islam Sekolah Rendah. In: Fakulti Teknologi dan Sains Maklumat. Universiti Kebangsaan Malaysia, Bangi (2007)
11. Norizan, M.D.: Pendekatan Bercerita dan Permainan dalam Pembangunan Perisian Kursus Akhlak Islamiah. UKM, Bangi (2003)

12. Garzotto, F.: Investigating the Educational Effectiveness of Multiplayer Online Games for Children. In: Interaction Design and Children (IDC 2007). ACM Press, Aalborg (2007)
13. Virvao, M.K., Konstantinos, G.M.: Combining software games with education: Evaluation of its educational effectiveness. Educational Technology & Society 8(2), 54–65 (2005)
14. Hill, J.: Impacts of playing video games on learning in children. In: Tollett, M.Y. (ed.) Literature Synthesis for Applying Research. The University of Georgia, Athens, Georgia (2006)
15. Kebritchi, M.: Factors affecting teachers' adoption of educational computer games: A case study. British Journal of Educational Technology 44(2), 256–270 (2010)
16. de- Freitas, S.: Learning in immersive worlds: A review of game based learning. In: JISC Elearning Progrmme, JISC, London (2006)
17. Dillon, A., Morris, M.: User acceptance of new information technology: theories and models. In: Williams, M. (ed.) Annual Review of Information Science and Technology, pp. 3–32. Information Today, Medford NJ (1996)
18. Davis, F.D.: Perceived usefulness, perceived ease of use, and user acceptance of information technology. MIS Quarterly 13, 319–340 (1989)
19. Venkatesh, V., et al.: User acceptance of information technology: Toward a unified view. MIS Quarterly 27(3), 423–478 (2003)
20. Hsu, C.-L., Lu, H.-P.: Why do people play on-line games? An extended TAM with social influences and flow experience. Information & Management 41(7), 853–868 (2004)
21. Ha, I., Yoon, Y., Choi, M.: Determinants of adoption of mobile games under mobile broadband wireless access environment. Information & Management 44(3), 276–286 (2007)
22. Bourgonjon, J., et al.: Students' perceptions about the use of video games in the classroom. Computers and Education 54, 1145–1156 (2010)
23. Amri, Y.: A Conceptual Framework for Serious Games and its Validation. In: School Of Electronics and Computer Science, p. 195. Southampton, Southampton (2010)
24. Roslina, I., Rasimah, C.M.Y., Azizah, J.: Computer Games Playing Activities: Habits of Universiti Teknologi Malaysia Student. In: International Conference on IT and Multimedia (ICIMU). Uniten, Bangi (2008)
25. Marchewka, J.T., Liu, C., Kostiwa, K.: An Application of the UTAUT Model for Understanding Student Perceptions Using Course Management Software. Communications of the IIMA 7(2), 93–104 (2007)
26. Gorriz, C.M., Medina, C.: Engaging girls with computer through software games. Communications of the ACM 43(1), 42–49 (2000)
27. Bourgonjon, J., et al.: Exploring the Acceptance of Video Games in the Classroom by Secondary School Students. In: Kong, S.C., Ogata, H., Arnseth, H.C., Chan, C.K.K., Hirashima, T., Klett, F., Lee, J.H.M., Liu, C.C., Looi, C.K., Milrad, M., Mitrovic, A., Nakabayashi, K., Wong, S.L., Yang, S.J.H. (eds.) 17th International Conference on Computers in Education, pp. 651–658. Asia-Pacific Society for Computers in Education, Hong Kong (2009)

Usability of Educational Computer Game (Usa_ECG): Applying Analytic Hierarchy Process

Hasiah Mohamed Omar[1] and Azizah Jaafar[2]

[1] Faculty of Computer and Mathematical Sciences, Universiti Teknologi MARA,
Sura Hujung, 23000 Dungun, Terengganu
[2] Institute of Visual Informatics, Universiti Kebangsaan Malaysia,43600 Bangi, Selangor
hasia980@tganu.uitm.edu.my, aj@ftsm.ukm.my

Abstract. Evaluation technique for Educational Computer Games (ECG) known as PHEG (consist of 5 heuristics and 37 subheuristics) was developed based on the needs to evaluate the usability of Educational Computer Games (Usa-ECG). Heuristic based concept was used in the development of PHEG. The fundamental issue of PHEG is to help evaluators in evaluating ECG in order to detect Usa-ECG through formative evaluation. At the end of the ECG development, it should be able to integrate educational elements, content, multimedia and it is playable to users with pleasant interface. PHEG was developed through the involvement of expert and verified by prominent experts. To further explore the importance of PHEG, Analytic Hierarchy Process (AHP) was performed by 15 experts from various fields. Result shows that Interface heuristic (40.8%) is selected to be the most important heuristic in evaluating Usa_ECG. The second important heuristic is educational element (25.44%) followed by Content (14.57%), Playability (11.2%) and Multimedia (8%) heuristic.

Keywords: heuristics based, PHEG, usability of educational computer games, evaluation, educational computer games.

1 Introduction

Human Computer Interaction (HCI) is a mature field of study, and usability is one of the main and core concepts that emerged from HCI. Scholars defined usability differently based on their studies. Amongst them are: "the capability to be used by humans easily and effectively" [1], "quality in use" [2] and "the effectiveness, efficiency, and satisfaction with which specified users can achieve goals, in particular environments" [3]. International Organization for Standardization (ISO) defined usability as "the extent to which the product can be used by specified users to achieve specified goals with effectiveness, efficiency, and satisfaction in a specified context of use" [3] and it is one of the widely used definitions by researchers. The evolution of usability has been discussed and researched by various scholars and later, they developed various techniques and criteria to conduct usability studies [4-6]. One of the popular techniques that being developed by [7] is Heuristics Evaluation (HE).

H. Badioze Zaman et al. (Eds.): IVIC 2011, Part II, LNCS 7067, pp. 147–156, 2011.

Heuristic is a design guideline which serves as a useful evaluation tool for booth product designers and usability professional [7]. HE is an inspection evaluation technique that normally being used by an expert to find usability problem in any product or system [7]. HE commonly used for formative evaluation where the product or system is still in a development process. HE involves a small number of evaluators (expert in specific field) who have been assigned to inspect a system according to heuristics or guidelines that relevant and focused on the interface of the system. HE is a light-weight process that can be cheap, fast, and easy to apply in an evaluation process. It can be used both in design and evaluation phases of development and can even be applied to paper-based designs before the first working prototype is created [7]. HCI studies showed that using five evaluators may be enough to find most usability problems, adding more would reduce the benefit to the cost ratio, and suggested that three may suffice [7]. The HE technique has been emerged from evaluation of software (system and products) to one of the most popular applications nowadays that is games [8].

In HE, there is a list of heuristic attributes that covers common criteria for any system that focuses on user interface and interaction elements. These elements cover all perspective of system in general, but in terms of educational computer game (ECG), no specific heuristics cater for all elements in ECG such as educational design and contents. Therefore, it requires having another set of heuristics that focuses on ECG. The argument to the requirement is usability in ECG should cover several elements of education if they are to be applied in teaching and learning formally. Elements of education such as content and educational design should be taken into consideration in evaluation. Specific evaluation technique that cater all the important criteria of educational computer games has been proposed by [9] known as Heuristic Evaluation for Educational Computer Game (PHEG) that caters five heuristics in evaluating usability of educational computer games (Usa-ECG); interface, educational element, content, playability and multimedia.

Development of PHEG is further expended with the integration of Multi-Criteria Decision Model (MCMD) in the evaluation system, particularly Analytic Hierarchy Process (AHP) method. The identified evaluation technique, PHEG is developed based on experts' opinion and later it has been verified by prominent experts. The Analytical Hierarchy Process [10] is a decision approach designed to aid in the solution of complex multiple criteria problems in a number of application domains. AHP is widely used since its introduction in 1972[10]. Example of application in information technology related area that use Analytic Hierarchy Process are software evaluation, evaluation of website performance and software design. This paper describes how AHP can be used to calculate the weights for a set of criteria (heuristic) and indicators (subheuristic) respectively. Through this multi-criteria decision making process, the importance of each heuristics can be determined.

2 Background

Nielsen and Molich [11] introduced a method to be used with their set of usability guidelines. Heuristic evaluation (HE) is a usability engineering method "for finding usability problem in user interface design by having a small set of evaluators examine the interface and judge its compliance with recognized usability principles (the "heuristics"). The 'heuristics' are design guidelines or principles for good interaction design and the aim are to find the problematic aspects of the design in order to improve it. This method uses evaluators to find usability problems or violations that may have a deleterious effect on the user to interact with the system. Typically, these evaluators are experts in usability principles, the domain of interest, or both (so-called "double" experts). Nielsen and Molich [11] described the HE methodology as "cheap", "intuitive", "requires no advance planning," and finally, "can be used development process." Often it is used in conjunction with other usability methodologies to evaluate user interfaces [12].

In an evaluation process, finding flaws earlier rather than later able to reduce usability errors, which may be more costly to rectify once the application or system is complete. This is when the HE is applicable because of its capabilities to detect errors in the early stage with the help of the expert (the evaluators). Indeed, HE also can be used in the spiral or iterative development environment commonly found in the design industry system.

2.1 Heuristic Based Evaluation Criteria

Heuristics evaluation shown a huge potential to be a valuable evaluation tool for computer games since the development of HE related to computer games were recorded increasingly started on 1982 until now. Development of evaluation and design guideline included of guidelines to design enjoyable interfaces, a set of game design principles, three areas of computer games; game interface, game mechanics and game playability, Heuristics for Evaluating Playability (HEP), playability heuristics for mobile games, key factors of heuristics evaluation for game design, key factors of heuristics evaluation for game design and categorized game heuristics on four areas; game interface, game play, game narrative and game mechanic, heuristics evaluation for video game design, usability inspections for games [4] [13] [8, 12] [14-16].

Heuristic for educational element were developed by scholars such as Quinn [17] developed eight heuristics based upon theories, Albion [18] compiled and developed the pedagogical heuristic and content heuristics, Reeves [19] identified 7 instructional design heuristic to evaluate e-learning program, Ssemugabi [20] identified 8 sub-heuristic that relate to instructional design, Nokelainen [21] studied about pedagogical usability criteria for evaluating the digital learning material and Daniel and Wang [22] identified four dimensions in evaluating web-based e-learning system.

2.2 Analytic Hierarchy Process (AHP)

The Analytic Hierarchy (AHP) was developed by Saaty [10] and this method is use to formalizing decision making where there are a limited number of choices but each has a number of attributes and it is difficult to formalize some of those attributes. These are characterised by a choice of criteria, which might be meaningful for an evaluation. These criteria are classified according to their relevance. Problematic situations and for preparing assessments and decisions AHP can be used for both analysing. It was described in detail in the literature (e.g. [10, 23]). The AHP has been used in a large number of applications to provide some structure on a decision making process.

The AHP is based on the pairwise comparison of any items contained in a set of indicators. For the comparisons, Saaty [10] suggested a scale of nine values. These and their related verbal definitions are listed in Table 1. If an expert prefers an indicator with extreme importance compared to another one the value 9 should be used. In the case the expert does not favour one of the two considered indicators value 1 is to be used which means equal importance. All intermediate values represent various degrees of importance. The AHP approach is composed by the following steps:

1. Define the problem and determine its goal.

2. Structure the hierarchy from the top (the objectives from a decision-maker's viewpoint) through the intermediate levels (criteria on which subsequent levels depend) to the lowest level which usually contains the list of alternatives.

3. Construct a set of pair-wise comparison matrices (size NxN) for each of the lower levels with one matrix for each element in the level immediately above by using the relative scale measurement shown in Table 2, represent number of items compared in a matrix. The pair-wise comparisons are done interface terms of which element dominates the other.

4. There are n (n-1) judgments required to develop the set of matrices in step 3. Reciprocals are automatically assigned in each pair-wise comparison.

5. Hierarchical synthesis is now used to weight the eigenvectors by the weights of the criteria and the sum is taken over all weighted eigenvector entries corresponding to those in the next lower level of the hierarchy.

6. Having made all the pair-wise comparisons, the consistency is determined by using the eigenvalue, λmax, to calculate the consistency index, CI as follows: CI = (λmax -n)/(n-1) where n is the matrix size. Judgment consistency can be checked by taking the consistency ratio (CR) of CI with the appropriate value in Table 1. The CR is acceptable, if it does not exceed 0.10. If it is more, the judgment matrix is inconsistent. To obtain a consistent matrix, judgments should be reviewed and improved.

7. Steps 3-6 are performed for all levels in the hierarchy.

Table 1. Scale and definitions of pairwise comparisons according to Saaty (1980)

Weight	Interpretation
1	Equally preffered/important
2	Equally to moderately preffered /important
3	Moderatly preffered /important
4	Moderatly to strongly preffered /important
5	Strongly preffered /important
6	Strongly preffered to very strongly preffered /important
7	Very strongly preffered/important
8	Very to extremely strongly preffered/important
9	Extremely preffered/important

Table 2. Random consistency index (RI)

Saiz Matriks (n)	1	2	3	4	5	6	7	8	9	10
Random Consistency Index (IR)	0.00	0.00	0.58	0.90	1.12	1.24	1.32	1.41	1.45	1.49

3 Methodology

3.1 Conceptual Design

Development of PHEG consists of four phases as shown in Fig. 1. Experts were identified based on their expertise. The involvement of experts was to review, suggest and edit the initial list of PHEG1 provided by researcher. The initial list was developed based on literature review. Once the process of expert review done, researcher compile and restructure the list, PHEG2. In the final phase of developing PHEG, prominent experts were asked to verify the edited version of PHEG, this produce the final version of PHEG. Expert then were asked to perform AHP based on PHEG that being developed.

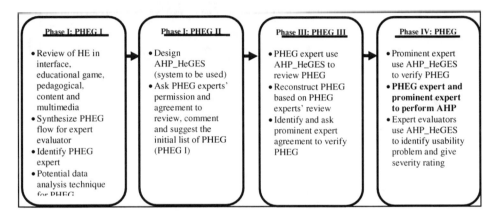

Fig. 1. PHEG Development process

During the process of developing PHEG, development of AHP_HeGES took part. Overall process flow and 3 main modules were identified. The modules are PHEG module, AHP module and PAEG module. All of the data gather from the development of PHEG and evaluation process are stored in the database. Administrator has the authority to access the database and the system is able to produce report based on specific requirement. Fig. 2 shows the conceptual design of the system. There are two types of evaluators involve in the evaluation process; expert evaluator and real users.

3.2 Research Method

Development of the evaluation technique, PHEG produces 5 heuristic with 37 subheuristics (Interface (10), Educational element (6), Content (6), Playability (7) and Multimedia (8)). The first module is for the expert evaluator to perform evaluation of ECG and identified usability problem of ECG. The Second module is regarding the integration of Analytic Hierarchy Process method in the system (AHP_HeGES). This method is important in order to view experts' opinion regarding the importance of heuristics and subheursitics. Fig.3 shows the hierarchy structure of usability for educational computer games.

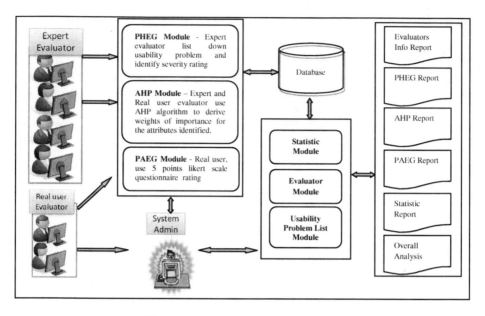

Fig. 2. Conceptual Design of the system

The integration of Analytic Hierarchy Process module in AHP_HeGES is to guide experts to identify the most important heuristics and subheuristics in evaluating usability of educational computer games. Fig. 3 shows the heuristics and subheuristics for Usa-ECG. The goal is rank the heuristics (known as dimensions) and subheuristics (known as criteria).

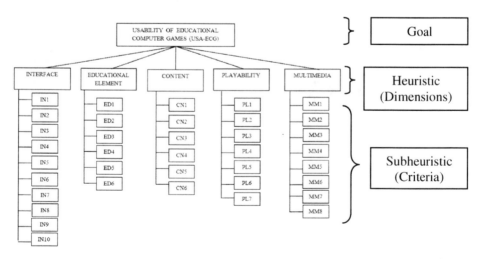

Fig. 3. The hierarchy structure of Usability for Educational Computer Games (Usa_ECG)

3.3 Guided Analytic Hierarchy Process

Guide Analytic Hierarchy Process (GAHP) is adopted from [24], GAHP Model. This model is developed to help the users to perform the evaluation process interface a very simple and guided situation. This follows the second principles of AHP that users need to be guided on how to perform AHP. The design of decision matrix for the criteria involves columns and rows; this may lead users to interpret it differently. In order to perform a sequence of pair wise comparisons for the design matrix, how to read the same level hierarchy of the criteria need to be provided. In order to perform GAHP analysis, the system has to be designed in such a way that both horizontal and vertical criteria in a decision matrix need to be arranged in descending order of importance [24].

3.4 Research Procedure

The main objective is to prioritize the most imporant heuristic in evaluating Usa_ECG. The respondents, who are comprised of 15 experts from various field were contacted through email to perform this AHP through online system, AHP_HeGES. Twentryfive experts were contacted, and 15 replied that they agreed to be paticipated. Three experts from each field were agreed to participate in the study to perform AHP in order to determine the importance of heuristics. The respondent are in the age groups 45-56 years and consist of 5 male and 10 female.

Respondents need to key in their demographic data and continue to perform AHP on the next page. Fig. 4 shows the print screen on how to perform AHP process. Respondents need select the GAHP, based on the instruction given. Submit button lead respondent to view details of the calculation involves in AHP method.

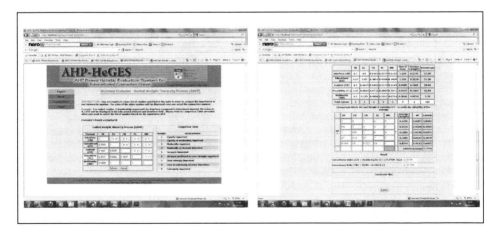

Fig. 4. Print Screen of AHP process

The result of the AHP method can be viewed by administrator of the system as shown in Fig. 5. Result were divided into overall result (before adjustment), consistent (after adjustment) and inconsistent category. Result of the AHP method, performed by 15 experts. AHP_HeGES provide report for Analytic Hierarchy Process module, which is easier for the administrator to view the data.

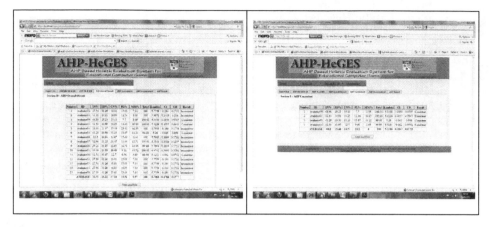

Fig. 5. Administrator view of AHP result

Table 4 shows the overall result (before adjustment) and consistent result (after adhjustment). Results of the AHP are based on average. Both of the results shows that Interface (40.8%) is selected to be the most important heuristic in evaluating Usa_ECG. The second impotant is educational element (25.44%), content (14.57%), playability (11.2%) and multimedia (8%). There are slightly different percentage value for overall result and consistent ratio group. But overall, the ranking of the important heursitic is the same.

Table 3. Weights of heuristic

Heuristic	Before adjustment		After adjustment	
	Weight	Consistency Ratio	Weight	Consistency Ratio
IN Interface	33.52%		40.8%	
ED Educational Element	26.22%		25.44%	
CN Content	17.16%	0.1577	14.57%	0.0755
PL Playability	13.52%		11.2%	
MM Multimedia	9.57%		8%	
Total	100%		100.00%	

4 Discussion

PHEG was developed to help evaluators evaluate Usa-ECG. The involvement of experts and prominent experts in the development of PHEG contribute the importance of PHEG in the formative evaluation process. This evaluation technique that consists of heuristics and subheuristics were rank using Analytic Hierarchy Process method. AHP was performed by 15 experts from various fields of studies (interface, educational technologist, Subject matter expert (content), game developer (playability) and multimedia experts). AHP result shows that Interface heuristic (40.8%) is selected to be the most important heuristic in evaluating Usa_ECG. The second important heuristic is educational element (25.44%) followed by Content (14.57%), Playability (11.2%) and Multimedia (8%) heuristic.

This represent that in any application development, interface plays an important part in order to attract user to use the system. Evaluation process that normally being done during the development or formative evaluation, serious consideration need to be taken into account so that interface of the applications is suitable and attractive enough. The importance of other heuristics plays their own roles in evaluation process of educational computer games. The most important things is developers, educational technologist and subject matter experts know how to merge the element of fun and education in developing educational computer games. For further study, another evaluation can be done to support the result of ranking the heuristics and subheuristics. PHEG can be converted into questionnaires and ask experts or real users to answer and it can be validate using Structural Equation Modeling (SEM). Other than that, PHEG can be used to evaluate ECG and later the result of usability problem found that based on severity rating. AHP can be use to rate the severity rating.

5 Conclusion

Development of PHEG technique to evaluate Usa-ECG based on experts review and prominent experts' verification contribute to the body of knowledge in term of evaluation technique for educational computer games. Evaluation of educational computer games need be performed with specific technique that caters all the important criteria. Five heuristic has been developed based on expert judgment and verified by prominent experts. Debate on the most important heuristic among the developed heuristics need to be highlighted in order to guide developers to improve the educational computer games before it can be released. Fifteen experts involved to perform AHP. Result of AHP is used to rank heuristics and subheuritics of PHEG. The ability of AHP method to identify consistency of the result given by evaluators help to differentiate either the result is consistent or not. Result shows that interface is the most important heuristic in evaluating usability of educational computer games.

References

1. Barendregt, W., et al.: Identifying usability and fun problems in a computer game during first use and after some practice. International Journal of Human-Computer Studies 64(9), 830–846 (2006)
2. Dempsey, J.V., et al.: An exploratory study of forty computer games (COE Technical Report No 97-2). Mobile, Al. University of South Alabama (1997)
3. Ke, F.: Alternative goal structures for computer game-based learning. International Journal of Computer-Supported Collaborative Learning 3(4), 429 (2008)
4. Malone, T.W.: What makes things fun to learn? Heuristics for designing instructional computer games. In: Proceedings of the 3rd ACM SIGSMALL Symposium and the First SIGPC Symposium on Small Systems. ACM Press (1980)
5. Taylor, M.J., Pountney, D.C., Baskett, M.: Using animation to support the teaching of computer game development techniques. Computers & Education 50(4), 1258–1268 (2008)
6. Papastergiou, M.: Digital Game-Based Learning in high school Computer Science education: Impact on educational effectiveness and student motivation. Computers & Education 52(1), 1–12 (2009)

7. Nielsen, J.: Heuristic evaluation. In: Nielsen, J.a.M., Mac, R.L. (eds.) Usability Inspection Methods. John Wiley & Sons, New York (1994)
8. Desurvire, H., Caplan, M., Toth, J.A.: Using heuristics to evaluate the playability of games. In: Computer Human Interaction, CHI 2004, Vienna, Austria (2004)
9. Mohamed, H., Jaafar, A.: Challenges in the evaluation of educational computer games. In: 2010 International Symposium on Information Technology, ITSim (2010)
10. Saaty, T.: How to make a decision: the analytic hierarchy process. European Journal of Operational Research 48(1), 9–26 (1990)
11. Nielsen, J., Molich, R.: Heuristics Evaluation of User Interfaces. In: Proceedings of Human Computer Interaction (1994)
12. Federoff, M.A.: Heuristics And Usability Guidelines For The Creation And Evaluation Of Fun In Video Games. Indiana University (2002)
13. Clanton, C.: An interpreted demonstration of computer game design. In: CHI 98 Summary: Human Factors in Computing Systems, CHI1998. ACM, New York (1998)
14. Hannu, K., Elina, M.I.K.: Playability heuristics for mobile games. In: Proceedings of the 8th Conference on Human-Computer Interaction with Mobile Devices and Services. ACM Press, Helsinki (2006)
15. Song, S., Lee, J.: Retraction notice to Key factors of heuristic evaluation for game design: Towards massively multi-player online role-playing game. International Journal of Human-Computer Studies 20(5), 391 (2007)
16. Pinelle, D., Wong, N.: Heuristic evaluation for games: usability principles for video game design. In: Proceedings of ACM CHI 2008 Conference on Human Factors in Computing Systems (2008)
17. Quinn, C.: Pragmatic evaluation: lessons from usability. In: 13th Annual Conference of the Australasian Society for Computers in Learning in Tertiary Education, Australasian Society for Computers in Learning in Tertiary Education (1996)
18. Albion, P.: Heuristic evaluation of educational multimedia: From theory to practice. In: 16th Annual Conference of the Australasian Society for Computers in Learning in Tertiary Education, Brisbane (1999)
19. Benson, L., Elliott, D., Grant, M., Holschuh, D., Kim, B., Kim, H., Lauber, E., Loh, S., Reeves, T.C.: Usability and Instructional Design Heuristics for E-Learning Evaluation. In: World Conference on Educational Multimedia, Hypermedia and Telecommunications, Chesapeake, VA (2002)
20. Ssemugabi, S., Villiers, R.d.: A comparative study of two usability evaluation methods using a web-based e-learning application. In: Proceedings of the 2007 Annual Research Conference of the South African institute of Computer Scientists and Information Technologists on IT Research in Developing Countries, pp. 132–142. ACM, Port Elizabeth (2007)
21. Nokelainen, P.: An empirical assessment of pedagogical usability criteria for digital learning material with elementary school students. Educational Technology & Society 9(2), 178–197 (2006)
22. Shee, D.Y., Wang, Y.-S.: Multi-criteria evaluation of the web-based e-learning system: A methodology based on learner satisfaction and its applications. Computers & Education 50(3), 894–905 (2008)
23. Saaty, T.: Fundamentals of decision making. RWS Publications, Pittsburgh (1994)
24. Ahmad, F., Saman, M.Y.M., Mohamad Noor, N.M., Othman, A.: DSS for Tendering Process: Integrating Statistical Single-Criteria Model with MCDM Models. In: IEEE International Symposium on Signal Processing and Information Technology (2007)

Visual Learning through Augmented Reality Storybook for Remedial Student

Hafiza Abas[1] and Halimah Badioze Zaman[2]

[1] Advanced Informatics School, Universiti Teknologi Malaysia,
15400 Kuala Lumpur
[2] Institute of Visual Informatics,University Kebangsaan Malaysia, 43600 Bangi, Selangor
hafiza.abas@gmail.com, hbzukm@yahoo.com

Abstract. Remedial students have difficulties in reading either before or during or after the reading session. Before the reading session, they have less interest and motivation to read. During the reading session, they have lack of engagement while after reading session, they do not really remember and understand what they have just read. This research aims to study the development of augmented reality storybook (AR Baca-Pulih) which provides motivation, engagement and enjoyable experience. The development process involves the comprehension of storybook contents and the design of AR flashcards. Stories are based on whole language and related to remedial students' environment. Level of language difficulty is structured in the form of easy, intermediate and advance. The design and development of AR flashcard are based on cognitive load theory. AR Baca-Pulih is evaluated by the experts using heuristics evaluation. Finally, usability study will be implemented to the remedial student for the evaluation.

Keywords: Augmented reality, storybook, visual learning, remedial students, Visual Informatics.

1 Introduction

Reading is a challenging and difficult task for remedial students (RS) who have less interest and motivation. Thus, computer-based applications are being used to change the conventional environment to the new interactive way [1] of learning. Through computer technology, interactive and visual learning are introduced. Illustrations, photos, diagrams, symbols, icon and other visual representative are information through visual learning [2]. Visual learning approach includes visualization, color cues, picture metaphors, concept maps, sketches, diagrams and graphic symbols [3]. With visual learning, students observe the object and its attributes which lead to comprehension and understanding [2] and raise students' performance [4]. For example, [5] nine different experiments were conducted and results showed 89% improvement in learning when relevant visual was presented. In order to ensure the effectiveness of AR storybook, the book and augmented reality contents must adapt with the visual learning concepts which fit RS needs.

H. Badioze Zaman et al. (Eds.): IVIC 2011, Part II, LNCS 7067, pp. 157–167, 2011.
© Springer-Verlag Berlin Heidelberg 2011

Augmented reality (AR) is a new educational tool. It shows potential in education [6].Theoretically, AR is based on visually oriented technique [7]. It is overlaid with virtual objects on real objects between users and the computer [8] and assists them to explore the information at their own abilities [6]. But technology helps with the well design and well organized educational contents [9]; also with proper design of interaction [10]. In order to ensure that the design is accepted for this prototype, heuristic evaluation and user acceptance test were conducted during the design phase. The educational contents were evaluated by the educational experts.

The first part of the paper focuses on development process of AR storybook and AR flash card to support the visualization process in learning. The next section is the brief discussion about RS and related research in AR technology with education, especially using AR book. It is then followed by the development process and discussion on how to apply cognitive load theory (CLT) to the design and development of AR flash card, results and lastly, the conclusion.

2 Literature Review: Remedial Student

Remedial students are special students. They are human capital that can potentially contribute their knowledge and skills to the country. Ministry of Education (MOE) defines remedial students as "a student who has problems in accession with foundation skills in reading, writing and calculating (3M) because of environment factors and not cognitive" [11]. Remedial students are addressed by teachers using diagnostic tests; suggestion from other teachers or request from parents. In the conventional classroom, they learn through flash card, playplastisin, copy a short sentence on the board, read along, do simple exercise and sometimes sing together with friends and teacher.

In the early analysis, it shows that there was no specialized courseware design for RS including a reading courseware for Bahasa Melayu [12]. In order to help RS, a storybook with AR technology was designed, based on Special Remedial Curriculum or *Kurikulum Pemulihan Khas*. It is a creative learning technique to integrate stories and language curriculum as it improves the student level of listening, reading, writing and speaking [13]. Besides the integrating curriculum, other learning strategies and technologies were used such as errorless learning, scaffolding, thematic, whole language, visualization and design approach for children including color, type and size of font, graphics, pesona of interface and avatar. For that, a storybook was chosen because it is a natural way to build literacy skills [14] in order attract and engage RS to read [15].

3 Literature Review: Books with Technology

Physical book is preferred by the user due to its flexibility, robustness, transportability [16]. However, a physical book also has at least five limitations such as static texts, 2D pictures, in black and white color (for low cost books), simple illustrations and non-interactive [17]. In order to enhance the function of physical book, a number of efforts have been done such as adding the audio button and puppet, change the physical design, add the 3D glasses and also equip the book with electronic pen. These factors support us to design and develop the real book with AR technology.

AR has a huge potential to grow rapidly [18] in education through courseware, games, simulation, training and books. Through innovative technology [19], [20], [21] such as AR, it is believed that learning can be fun and attractive [21]. However, innovative technology itself is insufficient. Understanding the user needs, educational contents and the way of delivery knowledge are also the vital elements in creating meaningful learning. There are few researches that have presented educational contents in teaching and learning process. Table 1 summarizes those findings which focus on the innovation and implementation of book with technology, specifically in AR.

Table 1. Augmented reality book in education

Researcher	User	Educational Contents	Research
Hafiza & Halimah [15]	Remedial student	Storybook and courseware	To study the effectiveness of AR storybook for remedial students in reading BahasaMelayu.
Periasamy & Halimah [22]	Remedial student	Courseware	To study the effectiveness of AR courseware in mathematic (negative numbers) for remedial student.
Norziha et.al [7]	Deaf student	Courseware	To use the AR technology in science for deaf student.
Parhizkar & Halimah [23]	Researcher	Application	To developan augmented reality rare book and manuscript for Special Library Collection (AR Rare-BM)
Ajune&Mohd. Shahrizal [24]	Adults	Numerous systems	To study the collaborative AR in urban simulation.
Rasimah & Halimah [25]	Medical student	Mixed reality book	To develop a mixed reality book for tissue engineering.
Roslinda & Halimah [26]	Down sindrom student	Storybook and courseware	To use AR technology in helping down syndrome to learn basic reading in Malay language.
Sin &Halimah [8]	Children	Courseware	To develop an AR application to learn astronomy.
Graset et al. [27]	General user	Storytelling Book	To add the virtual visual and auditory enhancements to a published book. To explore the various alternatives of combining virtual and real content. To add new interactions techniques, and visual effects to enhance immersion. To study the user feedback in using mixed reality book.
Medina et al. [28]	Student	Courseware	To examine how AR helps student in learning and to understand how student learns in AR environments.
Inagawa & Fujinami, [29]	General user	virtual illustration system	To propose a virtual illustration system with two types of add-on devices for the flipping detection: book covers and bookmarks.

Table 1. (*continued*)

Dünser & Hornecker, [30]	Children	Storybook	To observe the AR books pages using animated virtual 3D characters, sound, and interactive tasks for children to read and interact with.
Taketa et al. [31]	Children	virtual pop-up book system	This book displays 3D virtual objects on the real book based on pose and position estimation of the camera but not use any markers.
Gupta [32] &Jaynes,	General user	Multimedia book	To integrate the projected imagery with a physical book as a tangible interface to multimedia data – loaded with images, videos, and volumetric datasets.
Kerawalla [33] et al.	Primary school children	Courseware	To explore the potential of AR in teaching science subject.
Ucelli et al. [34]	Children	Courseware	AR provides a tangible interface metaphor and physical objects are used to communicate meanings.
Camille Scherrer et. al [35]	General user	Poetry book	To use the combination of computer vision and augmented reality in order to animate the illustrations of a poetry book.
Zhou et al. [36]	Children	Storytelling Application	To combine the interface of a foldable physical toy with AR to create a new type of storytelling application.
Siddaharth Singh et.al [37]	Children	Application system using handphone	To enhance reading experience by using handphone and AR Post-It system.
Woods et al. [38]	General user	AR Kiosk	AR Volcano lets user interact with virtual content.
Shibata et al. [39]	General User	Encyclopedia	To transfer inserts in mix reality environment, scale them and observe the insects flying around.
McKenzie & Dernell [[40]	Children	Storybook	To study the effect of AR picture book using handheld visor by animating the 3D content and sound.
Saso et al [41]	Children	Storytelling courseware	To study an augmented reality book using a colour background of a physical book as a playground for a virtual storytelling.
Morten & Benedikt, [42]	Student	Courseware	To reports on some of the advantages of tangible interaction in chemistry education.
Billinghurst [43]	Children	Storybook	To explore the development of interface in a collaborative setting.

AR book is a physical book that offers a multi-sensory learning environment [15] to motivate student with user friendly interaction and brings understanding [9]. It is an empower tool for education that makes learning fun and attractive [29]. Besides, it also gives engagement and motivation [30]; by allowing user to interact with virtual content [44]. It also supports low ability student [30] by reducing the user's cognitive load by extending the human system and information processing [45]. AR can be used as a visualization tool to simplify the complex subject.

4 Methodology for Developing Storybook Contents and Augmented Reality Objects

Analyzing user is the first step in the development AR Baca-Pulih storybook. By studying the RS behavior through observation, interview and reading session, the results we get are remedial student characteristics, behavior and their interest. These factors will be considered and adapted in the design and development process. For example, all of them like cat, and cat will be chosen as an avatar for the AR system. Next is the analysis of Bahasa Melayu syllabus. Sight words, environment which relates to everyday life and whole language are elements that will be used in the design and development of AR storybook. As soon as the design and development process have completed, heuristics evaluation will be done with five experts to evaluate the contents, reading approach and book interface and design. Figure 1 shows the process of development of AR storybook through a flowchart.

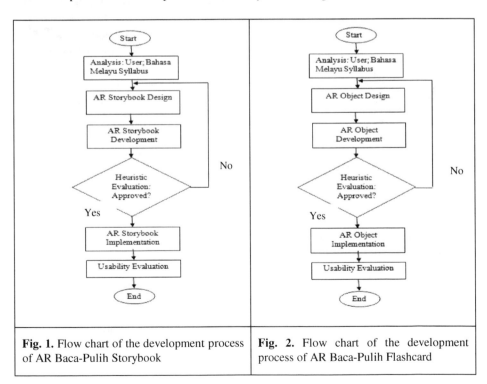

Fig. 1. Flow chart of the development process of AR Baca-Pulih Storybook

Fig. 2. Flow chart of the development process of AR Baca-Pulih Flashcard

The process of development for AR flashcard uses the same flow as the development AR Baca-Pulih Storybook except in the design and development phase. In the design process storyboard, interface and interaction methods are the output from this stage. The development process produces the storyboard contents, program code, 3D graphics and animation for AR flash card. Next, the heuristics evaluation takes place, five experts will evaluate the AR flash card system. Figure 2 shows the development process of AR Baca-Pulih flash card.

5   Applying Cognitive Load Theory to the Design and Development of AR Flashcard

Cognitive load theory (CLT) is a required amount of "mental energy" to process information [46]. It is applied by the researchers in educational research which relates to working memory characteristics and the design of instructional systems [47]. This theory has three assumptions namely i) there are separate and distinct "channels" to process visual and auditory information; ii) each channel has a limited ability to process information; iii) active cognitive process occurs in channels to assemble logical mental representation [48]. Three techniques of CLT are split-attention effect, the redundancy effect and the modality effect. Split-attention effect technique suggest to split-sources of information between graphics and texts [49] because it can delay the skill of acquisition (Feinberg & Murphy 2000). The redundancy effect suggests removal of redundant sources to avoid inefficient used of the working memory [50]. Lastly, modality effect is about the combination between visual and audio modality. It suggests that when dual modality is used, memory capacity will increase [51]. Table 2 shows the implementation of cognitive load theory in AR Baca-Pulih flash card.

Table 2. Cognitive Load theory implementation in AR Baca-Pulih Flash Card

Cognitive Load Theory	Implementation in AR Baca-Pulih Flash Card
Split-Attention Effect	Text is presents on menu while 3D graphic is displays in a camera view mode.
Redundancy Effect	During AR marker displays 3D object, neither text nor narration is presented.
Modality Effect	Visual mode presents the 3D graphic and auditory mode pronounce the word.

Besides the application of CLT in the flash card, multimedia principles are also used in the development of AR Baca-Pulih flash card. For example in visual mode, only graphics and text that relevant to the content are used. In visual and audio mode, only related graphics and audio are used. AR marker also does not display the irrelevant graphics, videos, animation, music, stories and narration. Since RS have a limited working memory capacity or cognitive load, the use of CLT theory and multimedia principles in the AR Baca-Pulih flash card are an accurate way in learning process.

6   Results

Results show the visualization and reading levels of the AR storybook in the Table 3 and AR flashcard in the Table 4.

Table 3. Visualization and reading level in AR Baca-Pulih Storybook

Storybook	Result
Book cover that shows the colorful graphics.	
Graphic in AR Baca-Pulih Storybook. Each story has its own graphic.	
Reading Level: Easy Thematic Stories	*Itu baju biru.* That is a blue shirt
Reading level: Intermediate Thematic Stories	*Ibu membeli rambutan, langsat, durian, cempedak dan nangka.* Mother buys rambutan, langsat, durian, cempedak and a jackfruit.
Reading Level: Advanced Short Stories	**Gigi Bersih** *Aisyah merasa sangat malas untuk memberus gigi. Dia tersengih-sengih di depan cermin untuk melihat giginya. Giginya sudah kuning. Dia telah lupa bila kali terakhir dia memberus gigi.* To be continue …

Table 4. Marker and Flash Card in AR Baca-Pulih Storybook

AR Flashcard	Result
AR marker to display an AR object using web camera detection.	
During AR marker displays 3D object, neither text nor narration is presented. Visual mode presents the 3D graphic and auditory mode pronounces the word.	

7 Conclusions

Visualization plays an important role to bring the RS engagement and enjoyment in reading through AR technology. Visual learning can be applied in the AR storybook using graphics and flash card in a harmony relationships among cognitive load theory, multimedia principles, instructional materials and instructional activities through the design and development process. In order to incorporate the visualization for RS student, RS experience, environment and daily activities are immersed into the design and development of AR Baca-Pulih Storybook. This study is part of the design and development of AR Baca-Pulih storybook and further research needs to be done for more effective reading courseware using AR technology in the future.

References

1. Lundberg, I.: The computer as a tool of remediation in the education of students with reading disabilities: A theory based approach. Learning Disability Quaterly 18(2), 89–100 (1995)
2. Afza Shafie, J.B.J., Ahmad, W.F.W.: Visual Learning in Application of Integratio. In: 1st International Visual Informatics Conference 2009, Bandar Baru Bangi (2009)
3. Armstrong, T.: Multiple Intelligence in the Classroom. Association for Supervision and Curriculum Development, 2nd edn. Stenhouse Publishers, Alexandria (1994)
4. Mazyrah Masri, W.F.W.A., Md. Nordin, S., Sulaiman, S.: The Effect of Visual of a Courseware towards Pre-University Students' Learning in Literature. In: International Visual Informatics Conference 2009. UKM, Bandar Baru Bangi (2009)
5. Mayer, R.E.: The Cambridge Handbook of Multimedia Learning. Cambridge University Press, New York (2005)
6. Eric Woods, M.B., Aldridge, G., Garrie, B., Looser, J., Brown, D., Nelles, C.: Augmenting the Science Centre and Museum Experience. In: GRAPHITE 2004 Proceedings of the 2nd International Conference on Computer Graphics and Interactive Techniques in Australasia and South East Asia. ACM (2004)

7. Mohd. Zainuddin, N.M., Badioze Zaman, H., Ahmad, A.: Learning Science Using AR Book: A Preliminary Study on Visual Needs of Deaf Learners. In: Badioze Zaman, H., Robinson, P., Petrou, M., Olivier, P., Schröder, H., Shih, T.K. (eds.) IVIC 2009. LNCS, vol. 5857, pp. 844–855. Springer, Heidelberg (2009)

8. Sin, A.K., Badioze Zaman, H.: Tangible Interaction in Learning Astronomy through Augmented Reality Book-Based Educational Tool. In: Badioze Zaman, H., Robinson, P., Petrou, M., Olivier, P., Schröder, H., Shih, T.K. (eds.) IVIC 2009. LNCS, vol. 5857, pp. 302–313. Springer, Heidelberg (2009)

9. Chen, C.J.: The design, development and evaluation of a virtual reality based learning environment. Australian Journal of Educational Technology 22(1), 39–63 (2006)

10. Zulikha Jamaludin, H.H., Aziz, F.A.: An IxD support model with affective characteristics for dyslexic children's reading application. In: 3rd International Conference on Computing and Informatics, Bandung, Indonesia (2011)

11. Kementerian Pelajaran Malaysia, Garis Panduan Pelaksanaan Program Pemulihan Khas Jabatan Pendidikan Khas (2008)

12. Abas, H., Badioze Zaman, H.: Digital Storytelling Design with Augmented Reality Technology for Remedial Students in Learning Bahasa Melayu. In: Global Learn Asia Pacific Global Conference on Learning and Technology. AACE Global Learn, Penang (2010)

13. Wenli Tsou, W.W., Tzeng, Y.: Applying a multimedia storytelling website in foreign language learning. Computer and Education 47, 17–28 (2006)

14. Kozlovich, B.: By word of mouth: Storytelling tools for the classroom In: HI: Resources for Education and Learning, Pacific, Honolulu (2002)

15. Abas, H., Badioze Zaman, H.: Augmented Reality Storybook for Remedial Student using Whole Language Approach. In: The International Conference on Early Childhood and Special Education, ICECSE 2011. Universiti Sains Malaysia, Pulau Pinang (2011)

16. Marshall, C.C.: Reading and Interactivity in the Digital Library: Creating an experience that transcends paper. In: CLIR 2005, Kanazawa, Institute of Technology Roundtable (2005)

17. Abas, H., Badioze Zaman, H.: Augmented Reality: A Technology in Helping Reading Disabilities Student. In: The 1st International Conference on Educational Research and Practice, ICERP 2009, Bangi, Selangor (2009)

18. Senthil Kumaran, G., Santhi, K.R., Rubesh Anand, P.M.: Impact of Augmented Reality (AR) in Civil Engineering. Advanced Materials Research 18-19(63), 63–68 (2007)

19. Ronald Azuma, Y.B., Behringer, R., Feiner, S., Julier, S., MacIntyre, B.: Recent Advances in Augmented Reality. IEEE Comput. Graph. Appl. 21(6), 34–47 (2001)

20. Kaufmann, H.: Collaborative Augmented Reality in Education. In: IMAGINA 2003 Conference CD, Monte Carlo, Monaco (2003)

21. Ralph Martin, C.S., Franklin, T., Gerlovich, J.: Teaching Science for All Children: An Inquiry Approach, 4th edn. Pearson, US (2009)

22. Periasamy, E., Badioze Zaman, H.: Augmented Reality as a Remedial Paradigm for Negative Numbers: Content Aspect. In: Badioze Zaman, H., Robinson, P., Petrou, M., Olivier, P., Schröder, H., Shih, T.K. (eds.) IVIC 2009. LNCS, vol. 5857, pp. 371–381. Springer, Heidelberg (2009)

23. Parhizkar, B., Badioze Zaman, H.: Development of an Augmented Reality Rare Book and Manuscript for Special Library Collection (AR Rare-BM). In: Badioze Zaman, H., Robinson, P., Petrou, M., Olivier, P., Schröder, H., Shih, T.K. (eds.) IVIC 2009. LNCS, vol. 5857, pp. 344–355. Springer, Heidelberg (2009)

24. Ismail, A.W., Sunar, M.S.: Collaborative Augmented Reality: Multi-User Interaction in Urban Simulation. In: Badioze Zaman, H., Robinson, P., Petrou, M., Olivier, P., Schröder, H., Shih, T.K. (eds.) IVIC 2009. LNCS, vol. 5857, pp. 382–391. Springer, Heidelberg (2009)
25. Mohd. Yusoff, R.C., Badioze Zaman, H.: Mixed Reality Book: A Visualization Tool. In: Badioze Zaman, H., Robinson, P., Petrou, M., Olivier, P., Schröder, H., Shih, T.K. (eds.) IVIC 2009. LNCS, vol. 5857, pp. 326–336. Springer, Heidelberg (2009)
26. Ramli, R., Badioze Zaman, H.: Augmented Reality Technology in Helping Down Syndrome Learner in Basic Reading. In: Regional Conference on Special Needs Education, Kuala Lumpur (2009)
27. Raphaael Grasset, A.D., Billinghurst, M.: Edutainment with a mixed reality book: a visually augmented illustrative childrens' book. In: Proceedings of the 2008 International Conference in Advances on Computer Entertainment Technology, ACM, Yokohama (2009)
28. Eliana Medina, Y.-C.C., Weghorst, S.: Understanding Biochemistry with Augmented Reality, vol. 5 (2008)
29. Inagawa, N., Fujinami, K.: Making Reading Experience Rich with Augmented Book Cover and Bookmark. In: Lee, S., Choo, H., Ha, S., Shin, I.C. (eds.) APCHI 2008. LNCS, vol. 5068, pp. 157–166. Springer, Heidelberg (2008)
30. Andreas Dünser, E.H.: An observational study of children interacting with an augmented story book (2007)
31. Taketa, N., Hayashi, K., Kato, H., Noshida, S.: Virtual Pop-Up Book Based on Augmented Reality. In: Smith, M.J., Salvendy, G. (eds.) HCII 2007. LNCS, vol. 4558, pp. 475–484. Springer, Heidelberg (2007)
32. Shilpi Gupta, C.J.: The Universal Media Book: Tracking and Augmenting Moving Surfaces with Projected Information (2006)
33. Kerawalla, L., Luckin, R., Seljeflot, S., Woolard, A.: Making it real: Exploring the potential of augmented reality for teaching primary school science. Virtual Real 10(3), 163–174 (2006)
34. Giuliana Ucelli, G.C., De Amicis, R., Servidio, R.: Learning Using Augmented Reality Technology: Multiple Means of Interaction for Teaching Children the Theory of Colours. Springer, Heidelberg (2005)
35. Camille Scherrer, J.P., Fua, P., Lepetit, V.: The Haunted Book (2005)
36. ZhiYing, Z., et al.: An interactive 3D exploration narrative interface for storytelling. In: Proceedings of the 2004 Conference on Interaction Design and Children: Building a Community. ACM, Maryland (2004)
37. Siddaharth Singh, A.D.C., Ng, G.L., Farbiz, F.: 3D augmented reality comic book and notes for children using mobile phones. In: IDC 2004. ACM, Maryland (2004)
38. Eric Woods, G.A., Billinghurst, M.: AR Volcano (2004)
39. Shibata, F., Yoshida, Y., Furuno, K., Sakai, T., Kiguchi, K., Kimura, A., Tamura, H.: Vivid Encyclopedia: M.R Pictorial Book of Insects. In: The VR Society of Japan Annual Conference the 9th (in Japanese), pp. 611–612 (2004)
40. McKenzie, J., D.D.: The eyeMagic Book. In: A report into Augmented Reality Storytelling in the Context of a Children's Workshop 2003. New Zealand Centre for Children's Literature and Chrischurch College of London, Chirstchurch (2004)
41. Saso, T., I.K., Inakage, M.: Little red: storytelling in mixed reality. In: SIGGRAPH Sketches and Applications (2003)
42. Morten, F., Benedikt, M.V.: Augmented Chemistry: An Interactive Educational Workbench. In: Proceedings of the 1st International Symposium on Mixed and Augmented Reality. IEEE Computer Society (2002)

43. Mark, B., Hirokazu, K., Ivan, P.: MagicBook: transitioning between reality and virtuality. In: CHI 2001 extended abstracts on Human Factors in Computing Systems. ACM, Seattle (2001)

44. Woods. E, Billinghurst, M., Looser, J., Aldridge, G., Brown, D., Garrie, B.: Augmenting the Science Centre and Museum Experience. In: Proceedings of 2nd International Conference on Computer Graphics and Interactive Techniques in Australia and SouthEast Asia, Singapore (2004)

45. Ulrich Neumann, A.M.: Cognitive, performance, and systems issues for augmented reality applications in manufacturing and maintenance. In: VRAIS 1998 Proceedings of the Virtual Reality Annual International Symposium 1998, pp. 4–11 (1998)

46. Susan Feinberg, M.M.: Applying cognitive load theory to the design of web-based instruction. In: Proceedings of IEEE Professional Communication Society International Professional Communication Conference and Proceedings of the 18th Annual ACM International Conference on Computer Documentation: Technology & Teamwork. ACM (2000)

47. de Jong, T.: Cognitive load theory, educational research, and instructional design: some food for thought. Springer, Heidelberg (2009)

48. Mayer, R.E.: Multimedia learning. Cambridge University Press, New York (2001)

49. Paul Chandler, J.S.: Cognitive Load Theory and the Format of Instruction. Cognition and Instruction 8, 293–332 (1991)

50. Chong, T.S.: Recent Advances in Cognitive Load Theory Research: Implications for Instructional Designers. Malaysian Online Journal of Instructional Technology (MOJIT) 2(3), 106–117 (2005)

51. Penney, C.G.: Modality effects and the structure of short term verbal memory. Memory and Cognition 17, 398–422

Preliminary Study on Haptic Approach in Learning Jawi Handwriting Skills

Maizan Mat Amin, Halimah Badioze Zaman, and Azlina Ahmad

Institute of Visual Informatics,
Universiti Kebangsaan Malaysia,
43600 Bangi, Selangor
maizan@unisza.edu.my, {hbzukm,azlinaukm}@gmail.com

Abstract. This paper presents the findings of preliminary study on haptic approach in learning Jawi handwriting skills in the Malaysian educational setting. This paper explores current problems, teaching and learning methods used, frequent mistakes done by pupils, and related issues in learning Jawi handwriting skills. The results show that the current approach is too reliant on skills and presence of teachers in the learning and assessment process. The visual haptic approach can be considered as having a very promising potential to aid primary school pupils in teaching and learning Jawi handwriting skills. The results provide important input for future works on *Haptik-Visual Jawi* (HV-Jawi) application design and development.

Keywords: Handwriting skills, Jawi, Teaching and learning, Visual haptic, Visual informatics.

1 Introduction

Media and technology are constantly being introduced in schools as they are said to have a positive impact on teaching and learning. Reeves stated that there are two main approaches in using media and technology in schools [1]. First, students can learn "from" the media and technology such as computer-based instruction and integrated learning systems. Second, students can learn "with" the media and technology, which refers to the cognitive tools and learning environments based on constructivist approach.

The importance of use of computers and Information and Communication Technology (ICT) cannot be denied, as they have a great influence and potential to the world of education. Innovative teaching using various methods such as multimedia courseware, online teaching and learning resources, Internet, virtual reality [31][32], haptic technology, and many others is important for pupils to learn more intensively and to attract them to keep learning.

Visual haptic technology is part of visual informatics (another branch of ICT) that can be explored to be used by pupils in improving teaching and learning process [30]. Haptic systems have great potential and they can be applied in many fields such as simulation, teaching and learning aids, medical procedures and training, assistive and

H. Badioze Zaman et al. (Eds.): IVIC 2011, Part II, LNCS 7067, pp. 168–179, 2011.

rehabilitative devices, and scientific visualisations. Haptic systems and equipment are new additions to multimodal systems. For example, a combination of visual displays with haptic technology can be used to teach or train a person a task that requires hand-eye coordination, such as surgical operations, vessel operations, handwriting [2], [28] and learning [3], [4].

Several visual haptic applications have been developed for training or teaching and learning handwriting of various language characters such as for cursive Latin [5], [6], [7], [8], [9], Japanese [10], [11], [12], Chinese [13], [14], Arabic [12], Tamil [15] and Persian [16]. Yet, no study has been done on visual haptic application in Jawi script. For that purpose, a preliminary study was conducted to investigate the problems and related issues in the current process of teaching and learning Jawi handwriting skills. Subsequently, how haptic approach can help and the benefits of haptic approach are highlighted in this paper.

The remainder of this paper is organised as follows: Section 2 presents related works on advantages and potential of visual haptic technology in teaching and learning handwriting skills. In Section 3, the preparation of materials and methods for this preliminary study is discussed. Section 4 discusses the results of the preliminary analysis and Section 5 highlights our findings and potential future works.

2 Related Works

Several studies have shown that visual haptic technology can be extended and applied in teaching and learning writing skills for pupils between five to ten years old [7], [8], [2], [28], [29]. Figure 1 describes the conventional and haptic approach in learning handwriting skills. Hands-on learning or training method with the teachers will lead to reliance on teachers' skills [14] and the learning process will take time [7], [17]. Meanwhile, practical writing according to the provided letter template makes pupils to be bored for repeating the same letters or words [14]. These conventional methods need a new approach to enhance the learning process and to reduce the reliance on teachers. With the haptic technology, teachers' skills can be replicated in the teaching of writing skills. It can also decrease the time consumed and provide the equivalent opportunity for all pupils or trainees to learn under the same instructions [16].

The potential of haptic force feedback in controlling the movement of pupils to learn how to write correctly has also been proven [18]. Bluteau et al. conducted an experiment involving two Japanese alphabets and two Arabic alphabets to compare three training techniques of haptic guidance to analyse the criteria of speed (kinematic) and shape [12]. The findings showed that haptic guidance force feedback generally improved the smoothness of the trajectory tracking of a visual-manual. This guidance is important as pupils can be self-reliant and not to rely too much on teachers or classes. Besides, the pupils can learn at their pace and they can have their own self-advancement.

Bara et al. used a visuo-haptic and haptic exploration in the Latin alphabet exercises designed to develop phonemic awareness, knowledge of letters and related letter/sound in children aged 5 years on the understanding and application of the principle characters [8]. Study by Eid et al. also showed that combining haptic

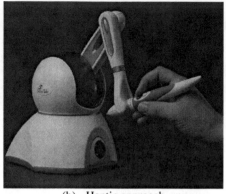

(a)   Conventional approach   (b)   Haptic approach

Fig. 1. Conventional vs. haptic approach in handwriting skills learning

sensory modalities to enhance the ability to learn and a smooth writing letters in different languages: English, Chinese, Japanese, French and Arabic [17, 19]. On the other hand, Boroujeni and Meghdari reviewed the full haptic guidance mode and half haptic guidance mode for the Persia handwriting [16].

In addition, teachers are able to check pupils' writings through the forms of the letters the pupils write. However, teachers are not able to assess the correct stroke order. Dix et al. explained that the most significant information in handwriting is not the forms but the stroke information [20]. Law et al. also reported the results of studies in Chinese characters where pupils often wrote letters in the wrong sequence and caused stroke production mistakes including missed stroke, overdone stroke, broken stroke, and connected stroke [21]. Tang et al. also developed a web system that contained Automatic Feedback and Analysis (AFA) tool that can check a few types of writing errors and provide useful feedback to the users [22]. However, the AFA tool did not use haptic technology but it used the animation template provided by the teacher. Meanwhile, a study by Wang et al. showed that the use of haptic feedback in Chinese calligraphy training system was proven to help in reducing the errors in writing and in improving writing speeds [14]. In this case, haptic technology can mimic the role played by teachers in teaching and evaluating the correct way of writing.

This study focuses on visual haptic approach as a potential teaching and learning aid in Jawi handwriting skills in the Malaysian educational setting. Jawi is a script derived from Arabic alphabets and it is adopted for the use of Malay language writing [27]. Jawi writing skills are essential to be acquired by all Muslim pupils to enable them to read and study in Islamic Education and to learn the language of the Al-Quran. Primary school pupils who are weak in Jawi subject should be the focus at early stage to ensure that no group is left behind in the national education system.

Pupils need to master Jawi, as the textbooks and examinations in the Islamic Education are developed using Jawi script [24]. A review by Nik Rosila has demonstrated that the mastery of Jawi skills among pupils is weak and it is significantly correlated with pupils' achievement in Islamic Education [25]. This situation is very worrying because the pupils will experience drop-out and it will be difficult for them to understand the syllabus in the higher Islamic Education. The failure or inability of some primary school pupils to acquire basic skills in Jawi is among the challenges in education today.

According to Vinter and Chartel, the problem of learning to write can be found in pupils, methods of teaching or interaction between them [23]. According to them also, some researchers have also questioned the contents of handwriting teaching method or time (period) allocated to teaching. Based on these literature reviews, a huge potential for haptic technology in education and the problems in teaching and learning handwriting skills have attracted this research to be conducted. Therefore, a preliminary study was conducted that focused on the current problems, teaching and learning methods used, frequent mistakes done by the pupils, and related issues in learning Jawi handwriting skills in the Malaysian schools. Then, the results that highlight the potential of haptic approach in teaching and learning Jawi handwriting skills are introduced.

3   Materials and Methods

This section describes the matters related to the method used in the preliminary study such as population and sampling, data collection procedure, and material design as well as measurement. For the purpose of this preliminary study, an approval to conduct this study was obtained from Bahagian Perancangan dan Penyelidikan Dasar Pendidikan, Kementerian Pelajaran Malaysia and Jabatan Pelajaran Negeri Terengganu.

Two-phase analysis was done to study the current problems and related issues faced by the pupils in learning Jawi handwriting skills. Phase one involves the teachers engaging in questionnaires and interviews with experts. Next, phase two involves observation in the classroom. This study involves mostly respondents from three primary schools. Three instruments were used in this study: one questionnaire (SKMJ) for teachers, one interview schedule named *Skedul Temu Bual Dengan Pakar Rujuk* (STBPR) for Jawi experts, and one observation checklist or *Senarai Semakan Pemerhatian* (SSPP) for pupils.

3.1   Questionnaire

The data of this study were collected by using personally administered approach. The data were collected using a pre-tested questionnaire that contained closed-ended questions, thus respondents were able to make quick response to choose among the listed options. The questions focused on problems in learning Jawi handwriting skills, frequent mistakes done by pupils in learning Jawi handwriting, and current methods in teaching and learning Jawi writing skills. The respondents were required to indicate their opinion using the five-point Likert scale where 1=strongly disagree, 2=disagree, 3=moderately agree, 4=agree, and 5=strongly agree on the statements given. Complete questionnaires were reviewed and the results were analysed using basic statistics, which is descriptive statistics.

3.2 Interview

Interview schedule named *Skedul Temu Bual Dengan Pakar Rujuk* (STBPR) was used to conduct the interview. In the interview session, the experts were given questions related to these three matters: Jawi teaching methods, current materials used, and disadvantages of current method of teaching and learning Jawi writing skills in particular. The results were analysed and summarised into a table.

3.3 Observation

Observation on pupils during their class in Jawi handwriting skills was carried out. The way of writing and mistakes made by pupils were observed accordingly by using observation checklist or *Senarai Semakan Pemerhatian* (SPP). Teacher was in the class to assist and highlight the mistakes done by pupils. Photographs and video recordings were also transcribed for the purpose of observation. Besides, the interaction between teachers and pupils was also observed and analysed.

4   Results

4.1   Questionnaires

In the present study, reliability of the questionnaires was measured using Cronbach's coefficient alpha. This statistics reflects the consistency of respondents' answers compared to all the items measured. A Cronbach's alpha of 0.50 or greater is generally considered acceptable [26]. The closer Cronbach's alpha to 1, the higher the internal consistency of the measure is. Table 1 shows that the Cronbach's alpha exceeded the minimum requirements for reliability in all domains of the questionnaire.

A total of 14 teachers from three schools answered the questionnaires (see Table 2). Table 3 presents the respondents' demographic profiles in details. The respondents who participated in this questionnaire were 85.7% female and 14.3% male. This study also indicated that 57.1% teachers involved in Jawi Subject and 42.9% of them involved in Jawi Remedial. For academic qualification, most of the respondents have degree (57.1%), 28.6% have certificate, and 14.3% have diploma. In term of years of service, 58.7% of the respondents have 1-10 years of experience in service, 28.4% have 11-20 years of experience in service, and 14.2% have 21 years and above of experience in service.

Table 1. Reliability analysis of the questionnaire

Category	Items	Cronbach's alpha
Problems of learning the skills to write Jawi	6	0.607
Frequent mistakes made by pupils in learning Jawi handwriting skills	5	0.790
Methods of teaching and learning Jawi handwriting skills	5	0.910

Table 2. Involvement of the teachers from the selected schools

School	No. of teachers	Percent (%)
A	7	50.0
B	3	21.4
C	4	28.6
Total	14	100.0

Table 3. Demographic profiles of the respondents

Category	Items	Frequency	Percent (%)
Gender	Male	2	14.3
	Female	12	85.7
Type of Jawi Class	Jawi Subject	8	57.1
	Jawi Remedial	6	42.9
Academic	Certificate	4	28.6
qualification	Diploma	2	14.3
	Degree	8	57.1
Years of	0-10	8	57.4
experience in	11-20	4	28.4
teaching Jawi	21 and above	2	14.2

The results pertaining to general problem faced by pupils in learning Jawi handwriting skills are as shown in Table 4. The results reveal majority of the respondents agreed, the most common problem is that Jawi script is not a daily routine for pupils (mean=4.4). Then, this is followed by the conflict between Roman and Jawi writing ways (mean=4.1), and seldom read Jawi script (mean=4.1), and seldom write Jawi script (mean=4.0). The results also showed that the other common problems faced by pupils are they have less interest in Jawi (mean=3.8) and no prior knowledge or skills in writing Jawi (mean=3.6).

Table 5 presents the descriptive statistics for items related to the frequent mistakes done by pupils in learning Jawi handwriting. It shows that the most frequent mistakes done involves writing from left to right (mean=4.2) followed by writing incomplete form of letters (mean=4.1) and incorrect sequence of writing letters (mean=4.0). Other mistakes are inconsistent size of letters (mean=3.9) and reversal of letters or words (mean=3.9).

Table 4. General problems faced by pupils in learning Jawi writing skills

Problems	Mean
Conflict between Roman and Jawi writing ways	4.1
Seldom write Jawi script	4.0
Seldom read Jawi script	4.1
Jawi script is not a daily routine	4.4
No prior knowledge or skills in writing Jawi	3.6
Pupils have less interest in Jawi	3.8

Table 5. Frequent mistakes done by pupils in learning Jawi handwriting

Mistakes	Mean
Incomplete form of letters	4.1
Incorrect sequence of writing letters	4.0
Writing from left to right	4.2
Inconsistent size of letters	3.9
Reversal of letters or words	3.9

Table 6 describes the current methods in learning Jawi writing skills. The most commonly used approaches are writing letter sketches in the right direction (mean=4.5), connecting broken lines of the letters or syllables of Jawi in the right way (mean=4.4), and sketching forms that are similar to Jawi letters in the right way (mean=4.3). Other approaches are rewriting from the examples provided (mean=4.1) and tracing letters in the order (mean=3.9).

Table 6. Current methods in learning Jawi writing skills

Learning methods	Mean
Sketching forms that are similar to Jawi letters in the right way	4.3
Writing letter sketches in the right direction	4.5
Rewriting from the examples provided	4.1
Connecting broken lines of the letters or syllables of Jawi in the right way	4.4
Tracing letters in the order	3.9

4.2 Interview

Interviews were conducted with five Jawi experts from a few institutions and experienced teachers in Jawi teaching. Table 7 summarises the results from the interview sessions. In the category of teaching methods, the two most commonly used methods in teaching Jawi writing skills are pupils repeatedly trained to learn to write Jawi and pupils learn through observation and imitate the way the teacher writes. Teachers also hold pupils' hand to help them to write in the correct way. However, some experts commented that for those pupils who did not concentrate, they might just write by following the form of letters without considering the correct way and the sequence of writing the letters. Therefore, teachers can only assess based on the form of letters and not on the sequence of writing the letters.

The results also show that there is no courseware or tool developed specifically for learning handwriting skills. Some experts commented that it depends on teachers' skills and initiatives to prepare the material for learning Jawi handwriting. Meanwhile, the respondents agreed that less emphasis on the correct way of writing Jawi is the main weaknesses of the current teaching and learning Jawi writing skills. They also highlighted that some teachers were only concerned on the output and not on the process in writing. Then, this is followed by teachers and pupils who do not write according to the Enhanced Jawi Spelling, and lack of skilled teachers to teach Jawi writing.

Table 7. Interview results on methods of teaching, materials for teaching, and current teaching and learning weaknesses in learning Jawi writing skills

Category	Comments by Interviewees
Methods of teaching	Pupils repeatedly trained to learn to write Jawi
	Pupils learn through observation and imitate the way the teacher writes
	Pupils' hands are held by teachers to help them write in the correct way
Material of teaching	No courseware or tool developed specifically for learning handwriting skills
	Teachers' initiatives
Current teaching and learning weaknesses	Less emphasis on the correct way of writing Jawi
	Teachers were only concerned on the output and not on the process in writing
	Teachers and pupils do not write according to the Enhanced Jawi Spelling
	Lack of skilled teachers to teach Jawi writing

4.3 Observation

Observations have been conducted on 12 seven years old pupils. They were Year One pupils from selected primary school. Table 8 shows the results of the observation. The mistakes made by most pupils are writing incomplete form of character (75%) and writing without following the correct sequence (75%). These are followed by mistakes of writing with inconsistent size of letters (58.3%). It was found from the observation that there were many mistakes made by pupils when writing mechanically. In addition, there were also pupils who were still confused between Jawi script and Iqra'. They

Table 8. Mistakes done by pupils based on observation

Pupil	Incomplete form of letter	Incorrect sequence of writing letters	Write from left to right	Inconsistent of the size of letter	Reversal of letters or words
1	√	√		√	
2	√		√		
3	√	√	√	√	
4	√	√			√
5	√	√	√		
6	√			√	√
8		√			
9	√			√	
10	√	√		√	√
11		√		√	√
12		√		√	
Total	9	9	3	7	4
Percent (%)	75.0	75.0	25.0	58.3	33.3`

added lines in the reading of Jawi like in Iqra'. The issue of right-handedness and left-handedness also influenced the pupils to write Jawi correctly, where left-handed pupils would find it hard to follow the right-handed teachers.

It was also found from the observation that the teachers had to keep repeating the instruction to ensure the pupils gained the skills needed. The pupils were reminded constantly by the teachers to write from right to left, about the form of the letters, and so forth. Some pupils had their hands to be held by the teachers to write in the correct way. Teachers also concentrated more to the weak pupils.

5   Discussions and Recommendations

From the analysis, it shows that the current practice in teaching and learning Jawi handwriting skills is teacher-reliant. Teachers' skills and presence were essential in the process of learning Jawi handwriting. The teachers' skills can be replicated using haptic technology to reduce the reliance of the pupils to the presence of teachers. Table 9 summarizes the current approach and the potential offerred by visual haptic approach.

Practices and repetition of Jawi writing activities with the right skills will help pupils better. The presence of teachers is important in the current learning and assessment of Jawi subject. Pupils learn from the mistakes done and corrected by the teachers. Haptic technology can be used to replicate teachers' skills. Pupils can keep practicing without or less supervision from the teacher as the haptic application can be developed to guide and evaluate the learning of Jawi handwriting skill.

Teachers' guide is very important at this stage to ensure that pupils master the basic skills in writing Jawi. The teachers' guide can be replicated using a new tool such as haptic approach and it will be very helpful to the teachers and pupils. Visual haptic application can be developed in full guidance mode, half-guidance mode, and no guidance as implemented in current approach of learning Jawi.

Table 9. Summary of the current approach and potential offers by haptic approach

	Conventional approach	Haptic approach
Practices	With the help from teachers	With the help from haptic devices
Teaching methods	Teacher-reliant	Visual-haptic application tool and self-reliant
Learning methods	Teachers hold pupils' hands Dotted line, tracing Imitating teachers' handwriting	Full guidance mode Half guidance mode No guidance
Assessment of mistakes	Teachers' assessment Assessment by output	Haptic application's evaluation Assessment by output or/and process of writing
Instructions	Teachers concentrate more to weak pupils	The haptic application provides equivalent opportunity for all pupils to learn under the same instructions
Advancement	Group advancement	Individual advancement

Pupils tend to do mistakes in learning Jawi writing as most of the characters in Jawi have various curvatures and forms. Besides, some Jawi letters have different forms according to their location at the start, middle, or end of word. Mistakes will be repeated if there is no guide and assessment from the teachers. Teachers can only assess by the output and not by sequences of writing, unless they are present at all time. By using haptic application, it can mimic the role played by teachers in assessing the correct way of writing.

An effort to help pupils in learning Jawi handwriting skills has prompted the researchers to develop a visual haptic application called *Haptik-Visual Jawi* (HV-Jawi). Based on previous works, visual haptic applications can be a good learning medium to support the learning of handwriting skills. It is expected that visual haptic application can enhance Jawi handwriting skills.

5   Conclusion

This research aims is to develop a visual haptic application called HV-Jawi to enhance Jawi handwriting skills for primary school pupils. The preliminary study with the purpose of acquiring data for software requirement specification (SRS) was conducted using various instruments such as SKMJ, STBPR, and SSPP. From the analysis, it shows that the current practice in teaching and learning Jawi handwriting skills is teacher-reliant. All the teachings and assessment need to be done with the presence of the teachers. Haptic approach is going to be introduced to replicate the teachers' skills and to mimic the role of the teachers.

Previous studies have proven that visual haptic brings a lot of benefits in learning environment of the handwriting of other languages and scripts [12, 13, 14, 16, 19]. Therefore, visual haptic technology can be a promising application in the process of learning Jawi handwriting skills. The *Haptik-Visual Jawi* application (HV-Jawi) is going to be designed and developed based on the results of this preliminary study. The application expectantly attracts pupils to Jawi subject and they can pursue in Islamic Education subject more effectively.

Acknowledgements. This research is supported by the National University of Malaysia (UKM) under the grant of Projek Arus Perdana entitled Multi-Display Interactive Visualisation Environment on Haptic Horizontal Surface (Grant No: UKM-AP-ICT-16-2009) by the Institute of Visual Informatics. Their support is greatly appreciated. Special thanks to Ministry of Higher Education (KPT), Ministry of Education (KPM), and University of Sultan Zainal Abidin (UNISZA) for the help and support in this research. We would also like to thank the schools, teachers, pupils, and individuals who participated to this study.

References

1. Reeves, T.C.: The impact of media and technology in schools. A Research Report prepared for the Bertelsmann Foundation. University of Georgia. Partnership for 21st Century Skills (2003). Learning for the 21st Century: A Report and a Mile Guide for 21st Century Skills, Washington (1998)

2. Mullins, J., Mawson, C., Nahavandi, S.: Haptic Handwriting Aid for Training and Rehabilitation. In: IEEE International Conference on Systems, Man and Cybernatics. IEEE (2006)
3. Gillenwater, C., Kumar, A., Moynihan, B., Van Drimmelen, J.: Running Head: Haptics, Presence, & HCI (2008)
4. Williams II, R.L., Chen, M.Y., Seaton, J.M.: Haptics-Augmented High School Physics Tutorials. International Journal of Virtual Reality 5(1) (2002)
5. Wang, J., Wu, C., Xu, Y.Q., Shum, H.Y., Ji, L.: Learning-Based Cursive Handwriting Synthesis (2002)
6. Hennion, B., Gentaz, E., Gouagout, P., Bara, F.: Telemaque, a New Visuo-Haptic Interface for Remediation of Dysgraphic Children. IEEE (2005)
7. Palluel-Germain, R., Bara, F., Hillairet de Boisferon, A., Hennion, B., Gouagout, P., Gentaz, E.: A Visuo-Haptic Device-Telemaque - Increases Kindergarten Children's Handwriting Acquisition. Proceedings of IEEE World Haptics 2007, 72–77 (2007)
8. Bara, F., Gentaz, E., Colé, P., Sprenger-Charolles, L.: The Visuo-Haptic and Haptic Exploration of Letters Increases the Kindergarten-Children's Understanding of the Alphabetic Principle. Cognitive Development 19(3), 433–449 (2004)
9. Steinherz, T., Doermann, D., Rivlin, E., Intrator, N.: Offline Loop Investigation for Handwriting Analysis. IEEE Transactions on Pattern Analysis and Machine Intelligence 31(2), 193–209 (2008)
10. Henmi, K., Yoshikawa, T.: Virtual Lesson and Its Application to Virtual Calligraphy System. In: Proceedings of the IEEE International Conference on Robotics and Animations. IEEE Press (1998)
11. Solis, J., Avizzano, C.A., Bergamasco, M.: Teaching to Write Japanese Characters Using a Haptic Interface. IEEE Computer Society (2002)
12. Bluteau, J., Coquillart, S., Payan, Y., Gentaz, E.: Haptic Guidance Improves the Visuo-Manual Tracking of Trajectories. PLoS ONE 3(3) (2008)
13. Teo, C.L., Burdet, E., Lim, H.P.: A Robotic Teacher of Chinese Handwriting. In: Proceedings of 10th Haptic Interfaces for Virtual Environment and Teleoperator Systems (2002)
14. Wang, D., Zhang, Y., Yao, C.: Stroke-Based Modeling and Haptic Skill Display for Chinese Calligraphy Simulation System. Virtual Reality 9(2), 118–132 (2006)
15. Li, X., Srimathveeravalli, G., Singla, P., Kesavadas, T.: A Novel and Robust Algorithm to Model Handwriting Skill for Haptic Applications. IEEE (2009)
16. Boroujeni, M.M., Meghdari, A.: Haptic Device Application in Persian Calligraphy. In: International Conference on Computer and Automation Engineering (2009)
17. Eid, M.A., Mansour, M., El Saddik, A.H., Iglesias, R.: A Haptic Multimedia Handwriting Learning System. In: Proceedings of the International Workshop on Educational Multimedia and Multimedia Education (EMME 2007). ACM Press (2007)
18. Morris, D., Tan, H., Barbagli, F., Chang, T., Salisbury, K.: Haptic Feedback Enhances Force Skill Learning. IEEE (2007)
19. Mansour, M., Eid, M., El Saddik, A.: A Multimedia Handwriting Learning and Evaluation Tool. In: Proc. Intelligent Interactive Learning Object Repositories (I2LOR), Montreal, QC, Canada (2007)
20. Dix, A., Finlay, J., Abowd, G., Beale, R.: Human Computer Interaction, 3rd edn. Prentice Hall (2004)
21. Law, N., Ki, W.W., Chung, A.L.S., Ko, P.Y., Lam, H.C.: Children's Stroke Sequence Errors in Writing Chinese Characters. Reading and Writing 10(3), 267–292 (1998)

22. Tang, K.-T., Li, K.-K., Leung, H.: A Web-Based Chinese Handwriting Education System with Automatic Feedback and Analysis. In: Liu, W., Li, Q., Lau, R. (eds.) ICWL 2006. LNCS, vol. 4181, pp. 176–188. Springer, Heidelberg (2006)
23. Vinter, A., Chartrel, E.: Effects of Different Types of Learning on Handwriting Movements in Young Children. Learning and Instruction (2009) (in press, corrected proof)
24. Nordin, A.L., Ahmad, M.Y.: Penilaian Dalam Pendidikan Islam. In: Seminar Penyelidikan Jangka Pendek 2003, Universiti Malaya, Kuala Lumpur, Malaysia, March 11-12 (2003) (unpublished)
25. Yaacob, N.R.N.: Penguasaan Jawi dan Hubungannya dengan Minat dan Pencapaian Pelajar dalam Pendidikan Islam. Malaysian Journal of Educators and Education 22, 161–172 (2007)
26. Sekaran, U.: Research Methods for Business: A Skill Building Approach, 4th edn. John Wiley & Sons Publications, New York (2003)
27. Mohammad Faidzul, N., Khairuddin, O., Zakaria, M., Liong, C.Y.: Handwritten Cursive Jawi Character Recognition: A Survey. IEEE (2008)
28. Bara, F., Gentaz, E.: Haptics in Teaching Handwriting: The Role of Perceptual and Visuo-Motor Skills. Human Movement Science (2011)
29. Pernalete, N., Edwards, S., Gottipati, R., Tipple, J., Kolipakam, V., Dubey, R.V.: Eye-Hand Coordination Assessment/Therapy Using a Robotic Haptic Device. IEEE (2005)
30. Badioze Zaman, H.: Simbiosis Seni, Sains dan Teknologi Berasingan ke Multimedia-Fusion. Penerbit UKM, Bangi (2009) ISBN 978-967-942-896-4
31. Parhizkar, B., Badioze Zaman, H.: Development of an Augmented Reality Rare Book and Manuscript for Special Library Collection (AR Rare-BM). In: Visual Informatics: Bridging Research and Practice, pp. 344–355 (2009)
32. Badioze Zaman, H., Bakar, N., Ahmad, A., Sulaiman, R., Arshad, H., Mohd. Yatim, N.F.: Virtual Visualisation Laboratory for Science and Mathematics Content (Vlab-SMC) with Special Reference to Teaching and Learning of Chemistry. In: Badioze Zaman, H., Robinson, P., Petrou, M., Olivier, P., Schröder, H., Shih, T.K. (eds.) IVIC 2009. LNCS, vol. 5857, pp. 356–370. Springer, Heidelberg (2009) ISSN 0302-9743, ISBN-13 978-3-642-05035-2

Scaffolding in Early Reading Activities
for Down Syndrome

Rahmah Lob Yussof[1] and Halimah Badioze Zaman[2]

[1] Faculty of Computer Science and Mathematics,
Universiti Teknologi Mara, Kampus Kuantan 1, Pahang
25200 Kuantan, Pahang Darul Makmur, Malaysia
[2] Institute of Visual Informatics,
Universiti Kebangsaan Malaysia,
43600 Bangi, Selangor Darul Ehsan, Malaysia

Abstract. The learning difficulties of Down Syndrome students are often related to limitation of their short term memory. They have constraints in separating the information received by the brain. This leads to difficulties in reading process. Therefore, they fail to focus when learning. Scaffolding is a systematic assistance used to ease the burden of the short term memory of the Down Syndrome students. The Scaffolding models are integrated in the development of the early reading multimedia courseware called MEL-SindD in order to give confidence and motivation to them in their early reading stage.

Keywords: Scaffolding, Courseware, Down Syndrome, Visual Informatics.

1 Introduction

Down syndrome children learn using the same learning strategy as normal children but the learning stage develops slowly [1][2]. Interaction through the language used at school, home and with community is a possible method that can be used for Down Syndrome children to learn about the surrounding world. They also have a weak mental ability, difficulty in pronunciation and delay in understanding the reading process. Nevertheless, they can still learn to read [2] even though at the beginning of the reading stage, they can only master a few common words.

1.1 The Learning Process of Down Syndrome Children

Each individual can obtain information by seeing, hearing, touching, tasting and smelling or combining any of the natural senses together. Usually, each individual can discard the unnecessary information and focus to the most significant object and event at one time [3]. During that time the individual is depending on the discarding system that helps him to distinguish the most significant information or knowledge, so that it can be stored in the memory. Some of the information enters the memory automatically and the rest of the information needs some form of rehearsal before it can be stored. When the information enters the memory, it has to be arranged

H. Badioze Zaman et al. (Eds.): IVIC 2011, Part II, LNCS 7067, pp. 180–192, 2011.

beforehand then only be stored. This process aims to give assistance in order to recall the information when it is needed [3].

Down syndrome children have difficulty in each process mentioned. They may possess unsound sensory input due to poor eye sight and hearing. Besides, down syndrome children have problem in their perception. This means, each object and taste does not give any meaning to them. They also have less understanding on the concept of each object and event that surrounds them as they have limited vocabulary about the object or event stored in their sensory input. The discarding system obtained by the down syndrome children is not automatic where they have less intuitive motivation to know and choose the important information in their surrounding at one time. Besides these children do not have enough time and information to arrange and store the object and event in their memory. This makes it difficult for them to recall the information and therefore the information becomes insignificant.

Many studies conducted on memory ability of Down Syndrome children focused on short term memory skilsl. Down syndrome children are different from the normal children in terms of their short term memory. The weak short term memory is a barrier to master the reading skill but they can still learn through similar strategies as the normal kids. According to [4], the research on the memory exercise shows that the short term memory ability can be enhanced. The short term memory ability can give a lot of benefits in their reading process. There are many activities that uses auditory exercises which can improve their phonological coding. Short term memory is related to the vocabulary stored, communication, reading and understanding [4].

Some down syndrome children do not have ability to understand the meaning of each object or event through concept. Besides they have difficulty to combine the present and past information so that it can be reused. [5] suggests that assistance has to be given to them in order to learn the skill of arranging information so that they can store and recall the information from their memory.

1.2 Scaffolding

Scaffolding has been widely used since two decades ago by educators and researchers [6][7]. They use the scaffolding concept as a metaphor to picture the roles of adults or knowledgeable people in giving guidelines or support towards the development and the learning process of the children [8]. [9] claims that scaffolding is "the precise help that enables a learner to achieve a specific goal that could not be possible without some kind of support". The developed scaffolding will be eliminated once the desired learning skill is obtained [10][11].

Wood et al.[12], used the term 'zone of proximal' development in the formation of scaffolding. Nevertheless, many researchers relate zone of proximal development with scaffolding [9][13]. [14:86] believes zone of proximal development as:

"the distance between the actual developmental level as determined by independent problem solving and the level of potential development as determined through problem-solving under adult guidance or in collaboration with more capable peers. The zone represents the potential for a child's development when aided by others."

Scaffolding acts as an assistant needed for students to succeed in zone of proximal development. The effectiveness of the scaffolding can be determined if the students are placed in their zone of proximal development boundary. The overwhelming assistance or support will make each task less challenging, while lack of support and assistance will lead to low confidence, doubts and frustrations to the students [15].The scaffolding metaphor has been applied in various learning courses. For example, [16] has analyzed the roles of scaffolding in teaching English as the second language. Whereby [17] conducted a research on the characteristics of scaffolding in mathematics. Donovan, & Smolkin, [18] on the other hand, explores various scaffolding aspects in the teaching of reading and writing. The use of scaffolding metaphor by researchers has increased [19]. Researchers such as [20] and [21] have encouraged the development of multimedia courseware that includes scaffolding in its application.

Based on cognitive theory, the information processing occurs in the short term memory [22]. Cowan[23], on the other hand claims that the short term memory has limitations and down syndrome children also have similar problem with their short term memory. They have low ability in dividing the information received by their memory. For instance, learning to read is a task that burdens their memory. In order to overcome this shortcoming, scaffolding is needed to ease the burden of the short term memory capacity [24].

Scaffolding application in the teaching and learning process can assist the down syndrome children to build their confidence [11]. They also need additional support and motivation to carry out tasks that they are unfamiliar with. The scaffolding metaphor that is instilled in the multimedia courseware can help them by giving support and assistance through the designed functions. [25]. Barry & Pitt [20] claim that the scaffolding metaphor that is instilled in the multimedia courseware can assist students with different background, learning styles and skills. The assistance or support given through the system will be slowly reduced until the students no longer need the support [21].

Nowadays, computer assisted learning has become a need in schools. This makes the efforts to integrate scaffolding in the teaching and learning environment increase [26]. Guzdial in [27] believes there are a few types of scaffolding base on multimedia courseware:

- Communicating: The formation of performance and demonstration of each skill following the contexts through the system.
- Coaching: Students receive support or assistance to enhance their achievement in completing each task step by step through the system
- Eliciting articulation: Students use multimedia courseware to gain thorough understanding of what is learnt. The level of understanding determines the number of assistance or support that should be given to the students.

Jackson et al. in [28] has explained three types of scaffolding used in the multimedia courseware that include:

- Supporting scaffolding: scaffolding in support form like advice or coach when the task is completed. For example, the next step that students should take. Once the scaffolding is slowly reduced, students will understand the rules of the concept that is supported by the same tasks.

- Reflective scaffolding: support to think such as making prediction or evaluation
- Intrinsic scaffolding. the internal scaffolding will lessen the difficulty of each task (difficult task becomes easy), and attract students' attention. Once the support is slowly reduced, the tasks will change, but students will still manage to do simple tasks to a more complex ones.

According to [29], there are two scaffolding application concepts in the electronic learning environment like multimedia:

- The aim of the support or assistance given through multimedia courseware is students will be independent in completing the task at the end of the learning session. The support or assistance exists in a form of modeling, providing hints and asking leading questions.
- The support which will gradually fade is used once the students have shown skill in completing the given task and when they do not need any more assistance [21].

According to [25] the use of scaffolding is seen as providing benefits to students with learning difficulties if it gives impacts as listed below:

- The reduction to the number of instruction needed in achieving the learning objectives.
- The reduction to the number of errors made by the students in the learning process.
- The reduction to negative feeling and frustration related to learning difficulties.

Beale has done a research on the integration of scaffolding in a courseware assisted by computer. His study instills six scaffolding principles as an instructional design (ID) concept as a strategy to teach reading skill for students with learning difficulty. The scaffolding concepts include: to reduce errors, maximize motivation and prepare prompt responses, instill errorless learning approach, consider the cognitive load, give attention to information preparation, and take consideration on teaching and models. According to [10] and [30], the scaffolding strategy discussed can be a beneficial model to design multimedia courseware.

This paper will discuss the three scaffolding models instilled in the MEL-SindD multimedia courseware modules in order to help students to interact with the system and explore the modules. The scaffolding models are to explore the courseware module (MSMkMP), a model to hear and read story (MSDBC) and a sub module to explore the mind (MSsmJM).

2   MEL-SindD Scaffolding Models

Down syndrome students need a well planned and systematic support to do unfamiliar task. The scaffolding concept prepared in the MEL-SindD multimedia courseware is to assist down syndrome students to interact with the system and to explore the courseware modules step by step with some assistance. Support or assistance given through the courseware is to make sure students will be independent in completing each task at the end of the learning session. The aims of including the scaffolding in the MEL-SindD multimedia courseware is to reduce errors made by students, prepare prompt responses and instill errorless learning approach.

Based on the scaffolding concept, three scaffolding models are designed to give support to down syndrome student in using the courseware. The models include:

- Scaffolding model to explore the courseware module (MSMkMP)
- Scaffolding model to hear and read stories (MSDBC)
- Scaffolding model using sub modules to explore the minds (MSsmJM)

2.1   The Scaffolding Model to Explore the Courseware Module (MSMkMP)

The model from Figure 1 includes three elements which are: screen, scaffolding strategy and action. The screen is a model that consists of three introduction screens in the courseware; whereas the scaffolding strategy is a form of support and assistance from the system for users to complete navigation tasks. The scaffolding will slowly be reduced once the down syndrome students understand the navigation procedure. The action element refers to the next steps given by the system base on students' responses.

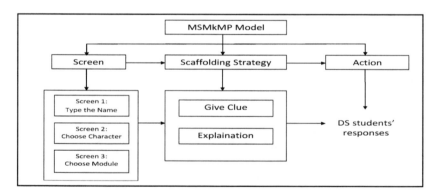

Fig. 1. Scaffolding Model: Explore the Courseware Module (MSMkMP)

2.2   The Scaffolding Model to Listen and Read Stories (MSDBC)

The model includes four elements as can be seen in Figure 2 which are: module, scaffolding strategy, guidelines and action. The module in this model refers to the listening to stories and reading together modules; the scaffolding strategy refers to a form of support and assistance from the system for the down syndrome students to do the tasks while listening and reading the stories with the system. Whereas guideline is the assistance given by the system when the down syndrome students press the button or words while listening or reading with the system. The action element on the other hand refers to next support given by the system base on students' responses.

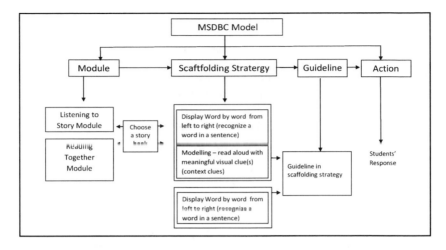

Fig. 2. Scaffolding Model: Listen and Read Stories (MSDBC)

2.3 Scaffolding Model of the Sub Module to Explore the Mind (MSsmJM)

This model consists of three elements as can be seen in Figure 3 which are: the sub module, scaffolding strategy, guideline and action. The module in this model refers to listening to stories and reading together modules; the scaffolding strategy on the other hand is a form of support and assistance from the system for the down syndrome students to perform task on listening and reading together with the system. Whereas guideline refers to the assistance given by the system when the down syndrome student presses the button or words while listening or reading with the system. The action element on the other hand refers to next support given by the system base on students' responses.

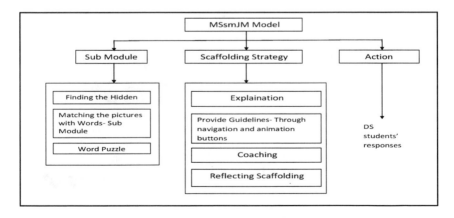

Fig. 3. Scaffolding Model: Sub Module to Explore the Mind (MSsmJM)

3 Scaffolding in Reading Activities

The MEL-SindD courseware starts with an introduction screen and has five main modules which are Flash Cards, Hearing Story, Reading Together, Exploring the Mind and Learning ABC modules.   The scaffolding concept is instilled in the modules through the development of scaffolding models.

3.1 User interaction through Model Scaffolding MSMkMP

The scaffolding model built, instill errorless learning approach through delay assistance concept by words, to enable the down syndrome students to explore from screen to screen or to courseware model (MSMkMP) through the introduction screen. On the screen, the student is asked to type his name at the given place; the student will be helped to prepare hand animation pointing to the name box as seen in Figure 4. The process of typing the name can be seen as impossible for the student who just starts to learn. However, the function is good when the student can acquire the skill. Meanwhile, the assistance from teacher or adult is needed, especially when the down syndrome student uses the package for the first time. The scaffolding strategy developed can assist the student to overcome learning difficulty such as fear of failure and lack of cognitive ability. The Scaffolding model also aims to give support to students in order to navigate with confidence. The support will be reduced slowly when the down syndrome student understands and remembers the navigation courseware procedure as seen in Figure 5.

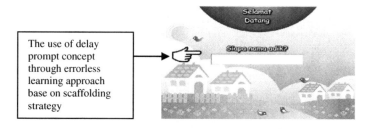

Fig. 4. Instilling MSMkMP Scaffolding Model

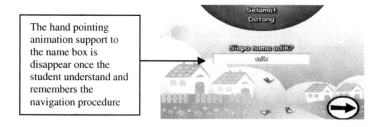

Fig. 5. Instilling MSMkMP scaffolding Model

3.2   User Interaction through Model Scaffolding MSDBC

The listening to story module shows the text narration story with graphic and animation. Story reading by the system is done using one word to another with the slow display by delaying the word assistance concept and instills the scaffolding concept through MSDBC model. The step is to assist the down syndrome student to see and hear words mentioned in a slow pace. This is to match the learning style of down syndrome students which is at slow pace compare to normal kids. Each sentence and text narration includes four words in maximum, so that the information can be delivered clearly and easy to comprehend. This is in line with the suggestions by Oelwein (1995) and Thomas (1996), related to the learning characteristics of down syndrome students who have weak memory, attention, fear of failure, and weak metacognition and learning skills. So when the word in the text narration is shown individually, the font size of the word will be enlarged and the world will be pronounced by the system to stimulate their eye sight. The students will only have to listen and observe the graphic and animation shown.

When the sentences in the text narration is read by the system, the student has to press the stop navigation button then click on the play navigation button in order to continue with the reading stories activity. The stop and play navigation buttons are also prepared to instill the assistance application base on the scaffolding model MSDBC developed as seen in Figure 6. Assuming that after repeating it several times, the use of navigation button can be reduced once the down syndrome students succeed in making use to the story reading system.

Fig. 6. Mapping of MSDBC scaffolding model in "Listen to Story" module

3.3   User Interaction through Model Scaffolding MSsmJM

The mind exploration module consists of a help button aims to give assistance to solve each exercise activity provided in animation form. The down syndrome student can repeat the animation to distinguish the movement of the mouse until he is able to use it on his own. The demonstration on how to do the activity is displayed by the system. This is in line with the instillation strategy in MSsmJM scaffolding model. The help button on the other hand instills the errorless learning through scaffolding strategy.

(a) Finding Hidden Words Sub Module

This sub module is represented by navigation button in a form of graphic icon. Part of the "car" word is hidden behind the graphic of a car (Figure 7). When the student moves the mouse towards the button, all of the word of "car" will appear in front of the car graphic (Figure 8). This step can help the cognitive ability by using clue and metacognitive exercise in the activity that is carried out. This is in line with the scaffolding strategy mentioned in the MSsmJm scaffolding model.

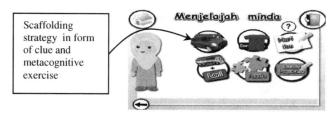

Fig. 7.

Fig. 8.

The start screen will be displayed once the student clicks on the finding hidden words sub module. This is to enable the down syndrome students to be in a ready mode and start paying attention to it. The step is the instillation of scaffolding strategy in clues and explanation forms. The system will pronounce the word "ready" and there will be an animation of the "ready" navigation button aims to coach student to move to another screen and get prepared for the learning session (Figure 9).

Fig. 9. Scaffolding Strategy of coaching, explanation and clue in MSsmJM

(b) Matching Pictures and Words Module

The interface matching pictures with words module will be displayed when the down syndrome student clicks on the navigation button of the graphic icon of "lorry" and the lorry graphic as can be observed in Figure 10. This step helps the cognitive ability by preparing the scaffolding strategy mentioned in the MSsmJm scaffolding model that is giving explanation, clue and metacognitive exercise on the activities that have to be done.

Fig. 10. The Inculcation of scaffolding Strategy in Explanation, Clue and Metacognitive Exercise

   The activity that has to be done by the student is to match the graphic pictures with the words. The matching, choosing and naming techniques can be assisted by teacher or parents when student interacts with the module. The background of the graphic pictures and the matching words are similar in colours in order to give guideline or clue for the down syndrome student to choose the correct information and therefore remember what is seen in Figure 11. This is in line with the instillation of the scaffolding strategy in a form of assistance. If the student makes the incorrect match, the system will say 'oops' as a clue that the choice is incorrect. But if he makes the correct match, complimentary remark, hand clap and graphic icon in a form of medal animation will be displayed. This step on the other hand instills the coaching scaffolding strategy. Here, the student will receive support or help to improve his achievement in doing the step by step task through this sub module.

Colour as a clue and metacognitive exercise

Fig. 11. The background colour of the graphic pictures and the matching words are similar in colours

(c) Words Puzzle Sub Module

Word Puzzle sub module will be displayed once the student clicks on the icon navigation of puzzle word. Two pieces of puzzle in graphic form is used as an intuitive metaphor as can be seen in Figure 12, in line with the scaffolding strategy in giving explanation and clues as stated in MSsmJm scaffolding model. The learning outcomes in this module are intellectual and motor skill abilities through activities to recognize and distinguish words as a whole.

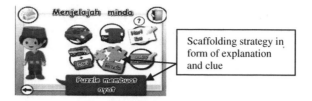

Fig. 12. The two puzzle is used as intuitive metaphor

This interface module prepares three activities that train competency which is related to psychomotor, hearing and visual. The techniques of choosing, matching and naming are used by teacher or parents when interacting with the student. The displayed screen includes the navigation button to the Main Menu, to exit from the system and to the mind exploration module. There are three words that have to be matched with three pieces of puzzles in the middle of the screen which are located in the lower middle screen as can be observed in Figure 13. The down syndrome student has to click one word at one time and match it with a piece of puzzle in the lower middle screen. The coaching strategy and metacognitive exercise are instilled in the module during the matching process. Once the student clicks on the word, the word will stick to the mouse and the student will only have to bring the mouse to the matching puzzle. The word will stick to the mouse until the student is able to place it on the correct puzzle.

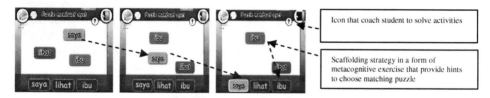

Fig. 13. Mapping of activities that instill the MSsmJM Scaffolding Model

4   Conclusion

The development of the three scaffolding models which include exploration to the courseware (MSMkMP), listening and story reading (MSDBC) modules and the mind exploration sub module have taken into account the learning process of the Down Syndrome children that have problem with their short term memory. Scaffolding on the other hand, is used to help this shortcoming and is found effective in teaching and learning process especially for students with learning difficulty. This study has instilled scaffolding concept based on opinions of [10][27][30][25][21] and [29]. Usability testing on learnability and ease of use has been carried out in the modules that instill the scaffolding strategy as stated above. (Usability testing is not discussed in this paper). The outcome of the study showed that the scaffolding models developed had successfully enhanced Down Syndrome students' confident level. At the same time they were able to participate actively in the learning process through the use of MELSindD.

References

1. Wishart, J.G.: Motivation and learning styles in young children with down syndrome. Down Syndrome Research and Practice 7(2), 47–51 (2001)
2. Bayliss, P.: The reading skills of children with down syndrome. In: International Special Education Congress, ISEC 2000, University of York (2000)
3. Groome, D., Brace, N., Dewart, H., Edgar, G., Edgar, H., Esgate, A., Kemp, R., Pike, G., Stafford, T.: An Introduction to Cognitive Psychology: Processes and Disorders, ke-2 edn. Psychology Press, East Sussex (2006)
4. Buckley, S., Bird, G.: Memory development for individuals with Down syndrome– An overview. Down Syndrome Issues and Information (2001), http://www.down-syndrome.org/information/memory/overview/?page=1 (February 10, 2009)
5. Oelwein, P.L.: Teaching reading to children with Down Syndrome: A guide for parents and teachers. Woodbine House, Bethesda (1995)
6. Pentimonti, J.M., Justice, L.M.: Teachers' use of scaffolding strategies during read alouds in the preschool classroom. Early childhood Education Journal 37(4), 241–248 (2009)
7. Kim, M.C., Hannafin, M.J.: Scaffolding 6th graders' problem solving in technology-enhanced science classrooms: a qualitative case study. Instructional Science, 1–28 (2010)
8. Graves, M.F., Graves, B.B.: Scaffolding reading experience: Design for student success. Christopher-Gordon, Norwood (2003)
9. Sharpe, T.: 'Unpacking' scaffolding: Identifying Discourse and multimodal strategies that support learning. Language and Education 20(3), 211–231 (2006)
10. Beale, I.L.: Scaffolding and integrated assessment in computer assisted learning (CAL) for children with learning disabilities. Australian Journal of Educational Technology 21(2), 173–191 (2005), http://www.Ascilite.org.au/ajet/ajet21/beale.html
11. Pahl, C.: An Evaluation of scaffolding for virtual interactive tutorilas. Paper Presented at E-Learn 2002, Montreal, Canada, October 15-19 (2002), http://odtl.dcu.ie/wp/2002/odtl-2002-03.html (December 12, 2008)
12. Wood, D., Bruner, J., Ross, G.: The role of tutoring in problem solving. Journal of Child Psychology and Psychiatry 17, 89–100 (1976)
13. Shepard, L.: Linking formative assessment to scaffolding. Educational Leadership 63(3), 66–70 (2005)
14. Vygotsky, L.S.: Mind in society: The development of higher psychological processes. Harvard University Press, Cambridge (1978)
15. McNeill, K., Lizotte, D.J., Krajcik, J.: Supproting students' construction of specific explanations by fading scaffolding in instructional materials. The Journal of the Learning Science 15(2), 153–191 (2006)
16. Hammond, J.: Scaffolding Teaching and Learning in Language and Literacy Education. PETA Convention, San Francisco, Newtown, Australia (2002)
17. Siemon, D., Virgona, J.: Identifying and describing teachers' scaffolding practices in mathematics, NZARE/AARE Conference, Auckland, New Zealand (2003), http://www.aare.edu.au/indexpap.htm (December 13, 2007)
18. Donovan, C., Smolkin, L.: Children's Genre Knowledge: An Examination of K-5 Students Performance on Multiple Tasks Providing Differing Levels of Scaffolding. Reading Research Quarterly Newark 37(4), 428–465 (2002)
19. Merill, D.: First principles of instruction. Educational Technology Research and Development 50(3), 43–59 (2002)

20. Barry, M., Pitt, I.: Interaction design: a multidimensional approach for learners with autism. In: Prosiding konferens Interaction design and children, Tampere Finland, pp. 33–36 (2006)
21. Jackson, S.L., Krajcik, J., Soloway, E.: The design of guided learner-adaptable scaffolding in interactive learning environment (2005), http://www.sj.umich.edu/umdl/chi98paper.pdf (December 20, 2007)
22. Bruning, R.H., Schraw, G.J., Norby, M.M., Ronning, R.R.: Cognitive Psychology and instruction, ke-4 edn. Pearson Prentice Hall, Upper Saddle River (2004)
23. Cowan, N.: Working memory capacity. Psychology Press, New York (2005)
24. Kirschner, P.A., Sweller, J., Clark, R.: Why minimal guidance during instruction does not work: An analysis of the failure of constructivist, discovery,problem-based, experiential, and inquiry-based teaching. Educational Psychologist 41, 75–86 (2006)
25. Ubaidullah, N.H.: Perisian kursus multimedia dalam literasi matematik (D-Matematika) untuk pelajar disleksia. Tesis Dr Fal. Universiti Kebangsaan Malaysia, Bangi (2007)
26. Guzdial, M., Kehoe, C.: Apprenticeship-based learning environments: A principle approach to providing software-realized scaffolding through hypermedia. Journal of Educational Multimedia and Hypermedia 9(3/4), 289–336 (1998)
27. Hwa, S.P.: Pembangunan Dan Keberkesanan Pakej Multimedia Interaktif (CITRA) dalam Pendidikan Moral untuk Murid Sekolah Rendah. Tesis Dr. Fal. Universiti Kebangsaan Malaysia (2005)
28. Ali, B.B.: Kejuruteraan Perisian Kursus Multimedia Matematik Berasaskan Model Kecerdasan Pelbagai (MI-MathS). Tesis Dr Fal. Universiti Kebangsaan Malaysia, Bangi (2008)
29. Winnips, J.C.: Scaffolding-by-design: A model for WWW-based learner support. Tesis Ph.D. University of Twente (Disember 24, 2001),
http://www.ub.utwente.nl/webdocs/to/1/t000000e.pdf
30. Quintana, C., Fishman, B.J.: Supporting science learning and teaching with software-based scaffolding (Disember 22, 2006),
http://hi-ce-org/papers/2006/AERA06-Scaffolding-FINAL-pdf

EduTism: An Assistive Educational System for the Treatment of Autism Children with Intelligent Approach

I. Siti Iradah[1,*] and A.K. Rabiah[2]

[1] Department of Information Technology, Center for Diploma Programme,
Multimedia University. 75450 Ayer Keroh Melaka, Malaysia
`iradah.ismail@mmu.edu.my`
[2] Department of Multimedia, Faculty of Computer Science and Information Technology,
Universiti Putra Malaysia. 43400 Serdang Selangor, Malaysia
`rabiah@fsktm.upm.edu.my`

Abstract. This paper presents the development of an assistive educational system with intelligent approach which can be a basic electronic training and treatment tool to assist children with high-functioning autism. The plan is to bring these changes through the use of rules based algorithm as an approach to decide which level difficulty of the system should go according to the autism student performance based on the percentage of score. By applying this approach, the system will be able to monitor and analyze the performance of intelligent of autism student's capabilities. The system is capable to control the particular level of the autism students should play. It is capable to replace the teacher's responsibilities in terms of monitoring the student's progress and performance. Testing was conducted in Autism Intervention Programme of The National Autism Society of Malaysia (NASOM) at Malacca branch. Results and findings from this testing support the idea that educational software may be one of an effective and practical tool for teaching academic skills to autism children. Having programs such as *EduTism* can improve effectiveness and efficiency of data collection tracking and reporting for the teachers and parents.

Keywords: High-Functioning Autism, E-Learning, Assistive Educational System, Intelligent Approach, Rule - Based Algorithm, Multimedia System.

1 Introduction

Nowadays, computers are increasingly present at the early stage of education settings. Since computers have become popular, many educational system resources have been developed which can be categorized into animations, simulations, games, computer based training, web-based learning, intelligent tutorial systems and pedagogical agents [1]. Most of the educational system offers the unique advantages in teaching and learning. The unique advantage that form by computers and learning approach could emphasized practical learning, where teachers and students were trained to use

---

* Corresponding author.

H. Badioze Zaman et al. (Eds.): IVIC 2011, Part II, LNCS 7067, pp. 193–204, 2011.

various teaching aids, namely computer based training, integrated into the educational curriculum in such a way improving the teaching and learning process. However, in Malaysia, current practice in schools and autism intervention center such as National Autism Society of Malaysia (NASOM) center uses traditional classroom teaching treatments, manual textbooks, blackboard and pieces of paper to conduct activities and games in class. The instructors or teachers are currently using traditional ways of teaching. Since the disorder qualifies as learning disability, a treatment and therapy progress especially in their educational process is necessary to assist them.

The specific aim of this study is to design the monitoring control of the game difficulty levels for the autism children should play. Rules based algorithm is used to decide which level difficulty of the system should go according to the autism student performance according to the percentage of score. By applying this approach, *EduTism* will be able to monitor and analyze the performance of intelligent of autism student's capabilities by individually basis. The system is capable to control the particular level of the autism students should play. Moreover, the system is capable to replace the teacher's responsibilities in terms of monitoring the student's progress and performance. This system also reduces the teacher's administrative and paperwork burden. At the end, the system will be able to generate a report to conclude the overall performance of the students in terms of excellent, good, moderate and weak based on the total percentage for the whole learning sessions.

In the following we first review on the recent trends and approach to new technology tools for the support of individual suffering from Autistic Spectrum Disorders (ASD). Then we describe the design and architecture of the *EduTism* in Section 3. Section 4 describes the discussions on testing and analysis of results that have been conducted. Finally, section 5 summarizes our conclusions.

1.1 Problem Statements

Autism can be defined as a pervasive developmental disorder characterized by impairments in social interaction, communication, and restricted, repetitive, and stereotypic patterns of behaviors, interests, and activities [2]. As own efforts to get clear understanding, autism is a lifelong developmental disability that blocks the learning, language communication, emotional and social development of a child. Basically, there two types of autism children which high functioning autism and low functioning autism. For low functioning autism, they are not able to care for their needs, and they have no hope of living on their own independently. For example, teachers or instructors need to take care for their toileting, foods and drinks. While for high functioning autism, they are able to communicate with words somewhat, and they are able to do some tasks independently.

Statistics show that one in every 150 children born today has a typical autism. The number of children with autism has increased by a staggering 30% over the last three years [3]. There is no cure for autism. More efforts should be carried out to address issues affecting children with autism [4]. In Malaysia, awareness of autism has increased in the last few years but more research is needed to assess the situation and to draft an efficient support system to address it [5]. According to experts, they must have a minimum of 40 hours a week of therapy. The cost of living is much lower but the additional cost to raise an autistic child is a burden on the average family.

Diagnosis and assessments such as speech therapy cost as much as RM100 per session and autism child needs at least one session a week [5].

Therefore, *EduTism* is developed to assist the high functioning autism children to learn and help special education teachers more effectively deliver the lessons at no costs. Teachers do not have to spend lots of time at the particular student, in order to maintain the focus of the autism children, repeat the same lesson many times, and re-ask or restate the same questions.

2 Literature Reviews

At the moment, the teaching and learning process is using conventional methods. Teachers usually use books, blackboard and pieces of papers to do some exercise or activities in class in teaching special needs children at school. It is very difficult to find in Malaysia current market because developers only focus for the normal children. To make matters worse, not many individuals or organizations are interested in working with children with special needs, especially autistic children. In contrast, there are many technology and system available for autism children have been developed in abroad. However, the similar ways of learning techniques and approach to new technological developments are used here in making some getting ideas, comparison and evaluation on the related researches and cases.

Different disabilities require different assistive technologies. Assistive technology includes products and services to help people who have difficulty speaking, typing, writing, remembering, pointing, seeing, hearing, learning, and walking. Educational system can be developed to help people with autism to learn. However, since good educational design requires good communication with users, designing for children with Autism Spectrum Disorder requires a special approach. Therefore, the proposed educational system is focused on the specialized learning materials and instructional aids for individual with autism in order to assist them in learning and teaching process.

One of the examples of technology for autism is vSked, an interactive and collaborative visual scheduling system for autism classrooms [6]. The vSked system provides interfaces for creating, facilitating, and viewing progress of classroom activities based around an interactive visual schedule. The vSked system provides logs features to log every action during a user's interaction with the system. They can also recognize particular concepts with which particular students consistently struggle. Upon successful completion of a task, students are individually presented with a reward chosen specifically for them, such as an animation of fireworks travelling across the screen. Staff can generate reports on individual student progress or the entire class across individual activities or days and week.

Using vSked, however, the researchers observed improvements in student-specialist communication, particularly asynchronous. In addition to the added awareness that use of vSked enabled, the researchers found that the school professionals were able to document and share information with one another more formally through vSked.

Second example is Affective Computer-Aided Learning Platform for Children with Autism, known as ACALPA, is developed using an affective avatar, synthesized speech and multimedia content such as videos, images and sounds. The main goal of the platform is to facilitate the teacher-child learning scheme where the users will be both the teachers and the children with autism [7]. ACALPA is developed based on various interaction procedures according to the disability level of the autistic person in question. The instructions and the difficulty level can be personalised for each user. Other than that, an educator may register specific educational or personality data for each autistic person. The printable format of all the records enables easy monitoring and analysis of the learning process.

Third example is TeachTown software. It is a computer assisted education program that teaches six learning domains which are adaptive skills, cognitive skills, language art, language development, mathematics, social and emotional skills for student with autism with developmental age 2 to 7 years old [8]. It was designed based on best-practices from applied behavior analysis (ABA) presented within a developmental framework. Special education students, especially children with ASD, tend not to respond well to traditional teaching strategies. As children with ASD tend to respond well to things that interest them and because children with ASD often respond well to treatments that use visual supports computers are a logical choice for intervention. Benefits of using TeachTown are that non-experts can rely on the program artificial intelligence to select which lessons the student should learn [9]. For expert or classroom teacher can select the lessons and rewards to present to the autism student.

By comparing the existing system that have been, the similar ways of learning styles in the TeachTown can be integrate here for developing an assistive educational system for autism children. It is used an applied behavior analysis (ABA) to always provide appropriate prompts and reinforcement consistently. However, the content syllabuses of the technology available are not suitable for student environments for autism children in Malaysia since they are different in the contents and syllabuses of the teaching and learning, while students in abroad have different education whereas they have different syllabuses and language styles. Most of the technologies provide the learner monitoring progress so that reports could be provided to caregivers with detailed feedback on the learners' strengths and areas of difficulty. Other than that, most of the researchers have applied the intelligent approach into the technology for example in TeachTown they provide auto-adjusting lessons to select which lessons the autism student should learn. Therefore, the proposed system, *EduTism* will be designed based on special education syllabuses contents used in Malaysia for special needs education. This paper presents the use of rules based algorithm as an approach to decide which level difficulty of the system should go according to the autism student performance according to the percentage of score.

3 *EduTism* Project

As stated before, *EduTism* is a platform designed to support educational activities for high-functioning autism children. This section will explain the features and elements provided by *EduTism*,. The main function of the system can be divided into two modules, which is module for autism students and module for teachers or parent of autism children. All activities and games enabled in *EduTism* platform have been designed having in mind children with autism. The module for student consists of five difficulty levels focusing on the academic and cognitive skills learning domain. Autism students will learn to recognize people in their environments which are family members.

The student module is aimed to develop cognitive skills such as attention, memory, and categorization and teaches early academics. A new player is registered in the system. At the beginning, the system will indicate that she or has no knowledge on the domain.The system will automatically move the level forward or back depending on their actual performance based on the total percentage of score in order to jump, proceed or stay at the current level. The system then save the game level that contains data such as levels that have been resolved, score, date and time start, date and time end. Positive and negative feedback will be provided by the system to the user under question to indicate correct answer or wrong answers. When all the levels have been accomplished, the user has finished the lesson. She or he has reached the end by getting reward. Reward is given to build motivation by rewarding performance of completion of tasks with activities like going to the playground. When the user cannot accomplish the level the system will reload a previous level. This action symbolizes the user performing an exercise incorrectly, and she or he must try again.

In teacher module, the system has the ability to register new student. Autism student's progress was tracked, and then the data is displayed for teacher or parent when they choose to view the student's performance. The printable format of all the records enables easy monitoring and analysis of the learning process. All these features are very important to verify the effectiveness of games and to monitor report for each autism student.

3.1 System Architecture

The system will automatically move the level forward or backward depending on the student's actual performance based on the total percentage of score. If the student gets 100 percent of score for a particular level, he or she will be able to jump to next level, for example level 1 jump to level 3. If the student gets greater or equal to 80 percent of score for a particular level, he or she will able to proceed to the normal sequence of level, for example level 1 to level 2. However, if the student gets below that 80 percent of score for a particular level, he or she cannot proceed to any level, which is the system will reload the same previous game level.

When the user cannot accomplish a particular level, the system will reload a previous level. For example, if the student gets below than 80 percent of score for a particular level, this indicates that the student is failed. If the student continue for next learning session, the system will able to decide which level the system should go. The system will go to the particular level that she or he cannot accomplish. This represent as the intelligent approach of the system, which is the system, can replace the teachers or parents' responsibilities in monitoring the autism children's learning progress based on the total percentage of score and learning status of the student whether pass or fail. Fig. 1 shows an example of the overall system architecture.

Rule-based algorithm is a set of rules consists of if-then rules statements. The rules are simply patterns and able to do inference to search for patterns in the rules to predict what next the system should play. The system is able to load a game level by retrieving the autism player's accomplished levels. If the student's status is excellent, the system will go to the current level+2.If the student's status is passed, the system will go to the current level+1, while if the student's status is failed, the system will go

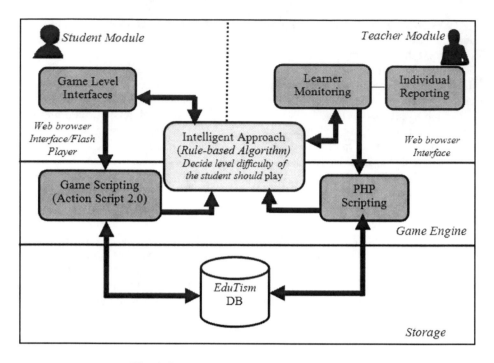

Fig. 1. System Architecture of *EduTism* project

to the current level. If the student has completed all level or did not start any level, the system will automatically go back to the first level (level 0). By using this rules, the system are capable to reload a previous level that student cannot accomplish.

The implementation stages involve the process of integration of all modules. Adobe Flash with action script 2.0 is used to create the interface of games module activities, while PHP scripting is used to integrate flash interface and database. PhpMyAdmin is used to handle the administration of MySQL.

3.2 Interface Design

Designing an assistive application such *EduTism* involves selecting or generating information as well as representing the structure and the content to the user through the interface. In this section, a brief explanation of the game and system's interfaces are presented. Examples of user interface design will be described in terms of student module and teacher module. Fig. 2 shows an example interface of student's login interface. If the student clicks on login without entering any username, the system will pop up a message asking them to enter their username. The username of each autism students must be registered first by the teacher.

Fig. 3 shows the example of popup design to indicate the student can jump based on the percentage of score is equal or greater than 80 percent. Scoring is important to measure the overall performance of autism children. A scoring subsystem is responsible for processing response objects, calculating scores and status standings

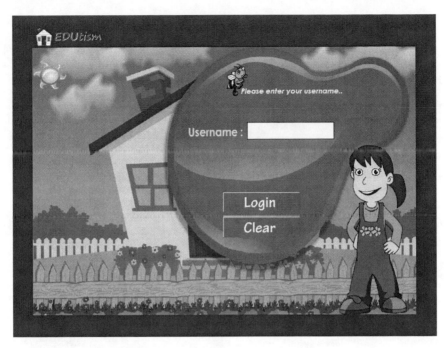

Fig. 2. Example of Student Login Interface

Fig. 3. Example of pop up design interface to indicate the student can jump based on the total percentage

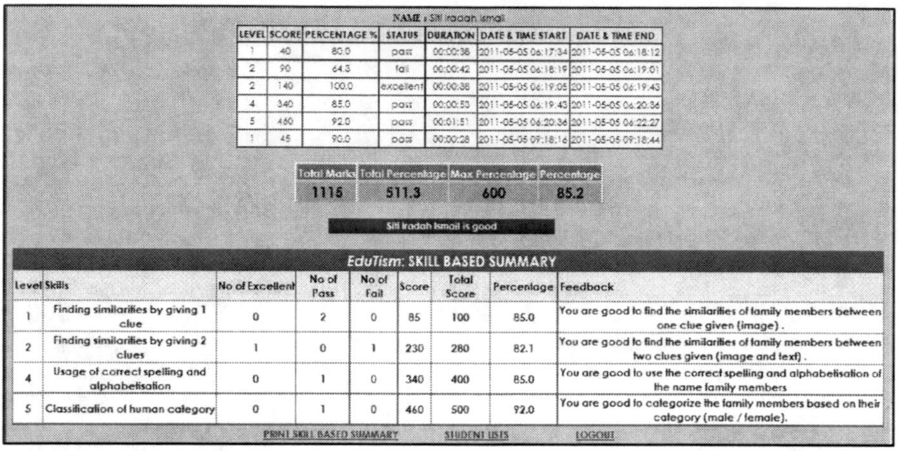

NAME : Siti iradah ismail

LEVEL	SCORE	PERCENTAGE %	STATUS	DURATION	DATE & TIME START	DATE & TIME END
1	40	80.0	pass	00:00:38	2011-05-05 06:17:34	2011-05-05 06:18:12
2	90	64.3	fail	00:00:42	2011-05-05 06:18:19	2011-05-05 06:19:01
2	140	100.0	excellent	00:00:38	2011-05-05 06:19:05	2011-05-05 06:19:43
4	340	85.0	pass	00:00:53	2011-05-05 06:19:43	2011-05-05 06:20:36
5	460	92.0	pass	00:01:51	2011-05-05 06:20:36	2011-05-05 06:22:27
1	45	90.0	pass	00:00:28	2011-05-05 09:18:16	2011-05-05 09:18:44

Total Marks	Total Percentage	Max Percentage	Percentage
1115	511.3	600	85.2

Siti Iradah Ismail is good

EduTism: SKILL BASED SUMMARY

Level	Skills	No of Excellent	No of Pass	No of Fail	Score	Total Score	Percentage	Feedback
1	Finding similarities by giving 1 clue	0	2	0	85	100	85.0	You are good to find the similarities of family members between one clue given (image).
2	Finding similarities by giving 2 clues	1	0	1	230	280	82.1	You are good to find the similarities of family members between two clues given (image and text).
4	Usage of correct spelling and alphabetisation	0	1	0	340	400	85.0	You are good to use the correct spelling and alphabetisation of the name family members
5	Classification of human category	0	1	0	460	500	92.0	You are good to categorize the family members based on their category (male / female).

PRINT SKILL BASED SUMMARY STUDENT LISTS LOGOUT

Fig. 4. Example interface of learner monitoring progress module

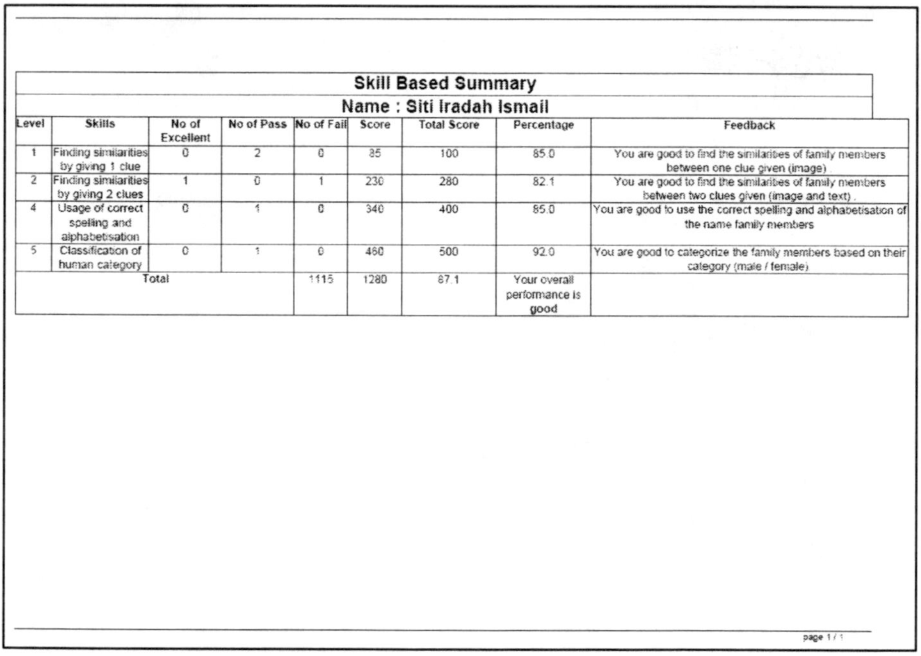

Skill Based Summary

Name : Siti Iradah Ismail

Level	Skills	No of Excellent	No of Pass	No of Fail	Score	Total Score	Percentage	Feedback
1	Finding similarities by giving 1 clue	0	2	0	85	100	85.0	You are good to find the similarities of family members between one clue given (image).
2	Finding similarities by giving 2 clues	1	0	1	230	280	82.1	You are good to find the similarities of family members between two clues given (image and text).
4	Usage of correct spelling and alphabetisation	0	1	0	340	400	85.0	You are good to use the correct spelling and alphabetisation of the name family members
5	Classification of human category	0	1	0	460	500	92.0	You are good to categorize the family members based on their category (male / female)
Total					1115	1280	87.1	Your overall performance is good

page 1 / 1

Fig. 5. Example of student's skills based summary report

for current game and written back to the database. Fig 4 shows an example of output for learner monitoring progress module. Learner monitoring progress module are capable to track the autism student's interaction during learning session such as total score, total percentage of score, duration to complete each level and date taken. The system is also able to give feedback for a particular level. The learner monitoring progress also allow teacher to see areas where the child has success and areas where he or she struggle more, whereas the system will count the number of pass and fail for each level.

Fig. 5 shows the example of student's skills based summary report. This reduces the teacher's administrative and paperwork burden. At the end, the system will conclude the overall performance of the students in terms of excellent, good, moderate and weak based on the total percentage for all levels.

4 Testing and Results

For this project, testing was conducted using a personnel desktop with high performance to support multimedia elements. Fig. 6 shows the setup during testing was conducted at NASOM Malacca. Two types of testing were conducted which usability testing and user acceptance testing. The main objective of the usability testing is to test the content of the prototype used is efficient to be delivered to the high-functioning autism students. Usability testing involved 3 special education teachers since only these teacher teaches academic skills at NASOM Malacca. They were tested on the usability of the learning application either the prototype can assist the high-functioning autism children in their learning process. They were asked on their opinion and feedback about the content design whether it appropriate with the autism students or need support of technical person to use the prototype wisely. They were also asked whether the difficulty levels are suitable for autism children level of understandings. Furthermore, they were also asked whether the learning monitoring designs can help them and parents to more frequently and effectively assess high-functioning autism student progress.

User acceptance testing involved five autism students between 5 to 8 years old. The objective of user acceptance testing is to test the understanding of the high-functioning autism students during using the prototype. Only five high-functioning autism students involved since these students were selected by their teachers based on their current learning performances and know how to use the computer. Special education teachers have to do the observations based on their attitudes and behaviors during using the prototype. The observations and evaluations are made based on the criteria for example the students are able to complete all levels or not without any problem or mistake and decided to use it again. They also need to observe whether the autism students can pay attention to the system more than 10 minutes or not.

There are guidelines to conduct the test so that the testers will know what level to determine the prototype. All the classes of result will be given by the criteria that are relevant to the prototype application. The testers were provided by a set of testing form and they need to evaluate based on the criteria given. There are levels of the evaluation as guidelines for tester in order to conduct testing wisely. The levels of test were divided in to five scales which are strongly agreed, agreed, neutral, disagreed and strongly disagreed.

The findings and results from the usability testing imply that most of the teachers agreed that learning through *EduTism* can be one of the attractive and effective educational tools for autistic learning disability. They are all agreed that the lessons and activities are well integrated for autism children to learn in order to improve the

Fig. 6. Example of computer setup during testing was conducted

autism children level of understanding. However, according to Ruzaila Hamzah, the interfaces of the *EduTism* must put in more space for the autism student to easily understand and catch up for the learning session. Besides that, she also suggests that to use the real pictures of family members for the learning contents in level 5. This is because the students are hard to categorize the male and female pictures of the family members. In order to differentiate male and female pictures, the uses of real pictures with give clear representations of physical appearance for male and female. She also suggests that the system should enable the teachers to upload the real pictures of family members of each autism children to help them to recognize the faces of their family members.

They are also agreed that the learning automatic monitoring designs help them to more frequently and effectively assess autism student progress. This would be reducing their burden since they do not need to repeat the same lesson many times and re-ask or restate the same questions to train the autism students to learn. They also suggest that the system should enable them to generate report by monthly basis or weekly basis. Other than that, most of the autism students need support of technical person to be able to use the prototype at the first time, but when the teacher or developer demonstrates to them, they can do by their own. This means that they need training at first in order to use the system.

The findings of user acceptance testing imply that the autism students are exciting to use this prototype and they are enjoyed learning using the prototype. Overall, most of the students could pay attention to the prototype more than 10 minutes, but only for those who are very excellent. Two students, who are very excellent, able to complete all levels less than 10 minutes, making the prototype is very easy to them. Thus, the prototype should add more level by increasing the level of difficulty for those who are very excellent. Most of the students except student number 4 ended this system without any problem or mistake and decided to use it again.

As the conclusion for this section, results and findings from this section support the idea that educational software or computer aided-learning may be one of an effective and practical tool for teaching academic skills to children with ASD in a classroom environment. *EduTism* will significantly help special education teachers more effectively deliver the lessons. Teachers do not have to spend lots of time at the particular student, in order to maintain the focus of the autism children, repeat the same lesson many times, and re-ask or restate the same questions. Having programs such as *EduTism* can improve effectiveness and efficiency of data collection tracking and reporting for the autism children, but more features are needed on reporting progress in making the prototype more efficient.

5 Conclusion

Since testing phase has been conducted, therefore observation on the weaknesses and strengths of the prototype are identified. First, and probably most important, it is not yet known whether skills learned on the computer will generalize to the natural environment. Computers also are not available in every environment. For instance, classrooms at NASOM do not even have a computer available, whereas they only provide two computers, and some families do not have a computer

Other than that, some people worry that using computers at a young age may have negative effects that is similar to television. Computers may be hard for some people to use. This is a real problem, as not all parents, teachers, and clinicians, and so on have computer skills themselves. To address this issue, the burden falls on the developers of these programs and on researchers to provide better training and implementation programs that are cost-effective and that result in rapid and effective implementation by the end-users. This could be done through better design of the programs themselves by making them more user friendly, providing video trainings, providing strategy guides, and providing communication systems for addressing issues quickly as they come up.

The contribution of this system is in educational fields for autistic learning disabilities. This prototype is about developing an assistive educational system application that demonstrates and promotes the use of various multimedia learning applications through computer for autistic learning disabilities. Although results from this study are preliminary and further research is needed, it is important to consider the impact of this kind of intervention on educating children with Autism Spectrum Disorder.

References

1. Fernado, P.M., Ricardo, C.P., Angel, G.: MAS: Learning Support Software Platform for People with Disabilities. In: MSIADU 2009, October 23. ACM, Beijing (2009)
2. Bryna, S.: Helping Children with Autism Learn, p. 90. Oxford University (2003)
3. The National Autism Society of Malaysia, http://www.nasom.com.my

4. The Star Online: Focus More on Autism,
   http://thestar.com.my/news/story.asp
5. The Star Online: The Burden of Autism,
   http://thestar.com.my/news/story.asp
6. Sen, H.H., Michael, T.Y., Gabriela, M., David, H.N., Lou, A.B., Gillian, R.: vSked: Evaluation of a System to Support Classroom Activities for Children with Autism. In: CHI 2010, Atlanta, Georgia, USA, April 10–15 (2010)
7. Evdokimos, I.K., Magda, H., Andrej, L., Maria, M.N., Panagiotis, D.B., Maria, N.M.: Using Affective Avatars and Rich Multimedia Content for Education of Children with Autism. In: Petra 2009, June 9–13. ACM, Corfu (2009) ISBN 978-1-60558-409-6
8. Teachtown Software, http://www.teachtown.com/
9. Whalen, C., Moss, D., Ilan, A.B., Vaupel, M., Fielding, P., Macdonald, K., Cernich, S., Symon, J.: Efficacy of TeachTown: Basics computer-assisted intervention for the Intensive Comprehensive Autism Program in Los Angeles Unified School District, Autism. The International Journal of Research and Practice (2010)

Investigating the Roles of Assistance in a Digital Storytelling Authoring System

Jumail, Dayang Rohaya Awang Rambli, and Suziah Sulaiman

Universiti Teknologi PETRONAS,
Computer and Information Science Department,
Bandar Seri Iskandar, Tronoh,
31750 Perak, Malaysia
jumail.wastam@gmail.com, roharam@petronas.com.my,
suziah@petronas.com.my

Abstract. Assistance giving or guided learning refers to a condition where assistance is needed to motivate and encourage student understanding on the idea of story creation. Tutored approach is one form of guided learning condition designed to create a balance between giving and withholding assistance. This condition then allows learners to get helps, hints, and feedback anytime they need it without disturbing their ability to build knowledge on they own. G-Flash, an authoring tool, was developed based on a flashcard-based guided digital storytelling design framework for digital storytelling which highlights illustrated flashcards and tutored condition as important features of framework. Both illustrated flashcards and 2D animated character were designed as assistance providers in this framework. A study on the story creation process was conducted to examine the roles and usefulness of the assistance giving in encouraging student understanding of the story to be created.

Keywords: Digital Storytelling, Tutored Approach, Flashcards, Assistance, Authoring Tool.

1 Introduction

An authoring tool developed based on flashcard-based guided digital storytelling design framework, G-Flash was designed to support children discovery learning through creation of digital stories [1]. The main idea of this paper is to explore the roles of assistance in the process of story creation in a learning-based storytelling approach. The use of storytelling approach as the platform for creating story among children is encouraged for them to communicate their own experiences freely [2]. Assistance giving allows children as the potential target users to move forward when they are struggling and truly need help in the process of story creation; yet a major concern is when its presence limits their motivation to learn on their own. Assistance withholding on the other hand encourages students to think and learn for themselves, yet it may cause frustration when the children are unsure of what to do next [3]. Thus, a better condition of assistance is to allow the children to receive help through a balance of assistance giving and withholding [3], [4] without affecting their motivation.

H. Badioze Zaman et al. (Eds.): IVIC 2011, Part II, LNCS 7067, pp. 205–216, 2011.
© Springer-Verlag Berlin Heidelberg 2011

Each storytelling approach usually uses and explores the use of media and interaction method to support storyteller roles for examples the use of Moving Images, voice recording, 2D character, 3D modeling, Text, Video, and Narration. The method of interaction of storytelling can additionally be diverse influenced by presence of interactive and non-interactive media. The media acts as a medium to support children in collaborative learning, experience sharing, encouraging self communication, and other else through drawing, writing, recording, talking or even chatting [5], [6], [7], [8]. The proposed design of this work explores a different media that is flashcards specifically digital illustrated flashcard to support creation of digital storytelling [1].

Flashcards has been used as an effective medium to support children [9], [10] in encouraging and motivating their learning. In the proposed framework, the digital illustrated flashcards can be considered as a passive assistance in which the illustrations on the card indirectly can act as a reference to initiate and encourage generation of ideas for story creation. Conversely, the presence of virtual instructor directly interacting with the user when needed provides an active assistance. Guided learning or assistance giving within this proposed G-Flash authoring conceptual framework allow the children to get helps, hints, and feedback on their story creation anytime they need via a 2D animated instructor character.

The layout of this paper describes the roles of assistance used in the conceptual framework design of G-Flash prototype as a digital storytelling authoring system. To maintain the balance of giving and withholding assistance, tutored condition decided to allow the user to request helps only when needed. The results of a study investigating the usefulness of these assistance roles in helping and encouraging young users to generate more focused idea of story creation based on the instruction and illustration on the cards are presented.

2   Assistance Dilemmas

Borek and colleagues [3] explains that assistance giving or guided learning can be divided into three continua based on the condition how assistance is given. The first continuum is a minimal assistance known as inquiry-learning approach in which children get no hint and minimal feedback. The second one is a mid-level assistance or tutored approach in which the children received intelligent tutoring hints and feedback. Children in this condition get helps based on request and feedback on incorrect steps. Meanwhile the third one is a high level assistance known as a direct-instruction approach in which the children were coaxed to follow the specific set of steps given by the instructor [3].

However, how much assistance is needed to support an optimal learning condition referred to as "Assistance Dilemma" has being an ongoing issue [3], [4]. It was thus described as a central issue in the learning science that has been being debated for some time. The extreme position of assistance giving is usually called as a direct-instruction or guided learning. Supporters of this guided learning or assistance giving position [11], [12], [13] agree that higher assistance example such as direct and tutored condition could lead to better learning results for providing information that child cannot create on their own. Supporters of the opposing "withholding assistance" position [14], [15], [16], [17] advocate a much lower assistance approach, often called discovery or inquiry learning. Here they agree that assistance withholding encourages students to construct knowledge on their own. As such, the later idea is adopted as a part of the design framework for the development of the G-Flash authoring tool.

2.1 Condition of Assistance

Guided learning is often referred to assistance giving or directed-instruction [18]. According to [19], it is a type of learning where the subject matter has been reduced to the steps which the learner will find them manageable and most of the learning will be acquired by the learner himself by way of instructional activities themselves. Similarly, guided learning could be perceived as the instructional sequences for the small group of students to provide a bridge between teaching and independent work [18].

Based on the amount of assistance given, guided learning can be categorized into three approaches of conditions [3] as follows:

1. *Inquiry-learning* approach. This provides a minimal guidance whereby students are doing activity without any hints and work receiving minimal feedback; feedback provided only on correct solution.
2. *Tutored-approach* It is a mid level of assistance in which student receives intelligent tutoring hints and feedback while interacting with the system. Feedback provided on incorrect steps and hints are given upon student request only.
3. *Direct-instructional* approach. This is a high-level of assistance. Children were coaxed to follow a specific set of steps with immediate yes/no feedback on every correct and incorrect step. Explicit instruction and explanations are on each incorrect step and before each action, containing explanations of the goal. One additional explicit hint is also available upon request, specifying the instruction in more details. Explicit instruction is given automatically before the student takes each step. One additional hint is available upon request only.

Tutored approach is context sensitive in which the tutor takes the pedagogical initiative and guides the student through the system with a structured agenda, uses some explicit instructions and makes sure that the user is learning [20]. A benefit of the tutored approach listed by Jaako Hakkulinen and colleagues includes [21]:

- Learning occurs in a meaningful context.
- Students can try things out right away and learn by doing.
- Students can develop their thinking and understanding through the tutoring approach.
- Students can get supporting feedback on their performance.

2.2 Assistance Design

In this study the use of assistance giving is intended to encourage user understanding through helps, hints, and feedback given. The tutored condition as one of the better approaches of assistance was implemented as part of the conceptual design framework in which its concept was translated through incorporation of 2D animated instructor as an active assistance provider and illustrated flashcards as a passive assistance provider. Students can select their own instructor based on the gender and instructor ID, and choose a topic of the story as the theme of their story according to the Topic ID. Both items were designed and implemented using Action Script as per the following:

```
var frmTopicID; ——————  Passive Assistance defined based on Topic ID
var frmSoundID;
var frmGender;      ———————————    Active Assistance defined
var frmInsNameID;      ——————       based on Gender and
....                                 Instructor Name ID

btnSubmit.onRelease = function (){
    _level0.currentInsNameID = frmInsNameID;
    _level0.currentInsGender = frmGender;
    trace(frmInsNameID  +  "/"  +  frmGender  +  "/"  +
frmTopicID + "/" + frmSoundID);
    dtToPHP.childID = _level0.currentID;
    dtToPHP.frmInsName = frmInsNameID;
    dtToPHP.frmInsGender = frmGender;
    dtToPHP.topicID = frmTopicID;
    dtToPHP.soundID = frmSoundID;

    dtToPHP.sendAndLoad(_level0.localhostName          +
"update_child.php", dtFrPHP, "POST");
    }
```

From the given codes above, the program will allow student to get assistance and helps from the instructor; yet they must register the instructor gender *(frmGender)* and instructor id *(frmInsNameID)* first to define the selected instructor (See Fig. 1). As an active assistance giver, the instructor will assist student with the required information according to the topic of the story *(frmTopicID)* selected by the student during the story registration phase. The topic of the story is implemented through a series of illustrated flashcards by which students need to select and arrange the cards into a story. The illustrations on the cards were designed as a passive guide to encourage student to think, jog their memory or recall ideas to facilitate the storytelling process. For example, by the topic of "My family", images of family members and activities or personalities of the members provided on the card; students just need to select the relevant cards for their story. As described earlier, for tutored approach, a help would be given only upon user's request. Thus this would require the student thinking on the story creation process and provide the opportunities for the student to be creative.

Fig. 1. A screenshot of the G-Flash Authoring Tool on assistance and story registration with the instructor preferred was female and selected topic of the story was My Family

Figure 2 further illustrates the story creation process through the proposed concept of assistance. The guided digital storytelling tool, G-Flash will allow user to select their own topic of the story from the list, then register one preferred instructor as a required assistance support to provide helps during the process of creating a digital story. When needed, the instructor will provide the children during the process of creation of digital story hints, audio instruction, and text narration just by a click of a help button. The illustrated flashcards [22], [23] will provide a passive assistance, which encourages student to recall ideas according to the illustration on the cards functioning both as a guide for the story flow (card arrangements) and as a story description (card descriptions).

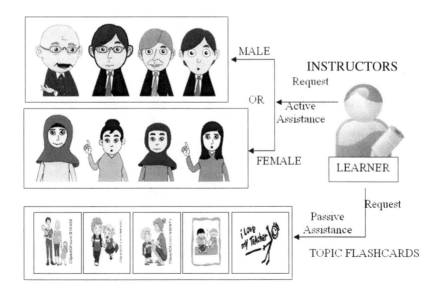

Fig. 2. A conceptual design of assistance

3 The Application

A digital storytelling authoring application called G-Flash is a computer-based interactive learning tool that encourages children to generate idea and communicate experience into a digital story creation. G-Flash was developed to support a storytelling to be an assisted interactive learning approach. The creation process is through some steps or flow of creation including defining a topic of the story, arranging the cards, and describing the illustration on the cards into a digital storyline.

To design and create their own story, each of children as a young storyteller has to select an idea of story by defining a topic of the story at the beginning, define the instructor character for the assistance provider, and then choose a suitable background sound to put into their plan digital story. Active assistance design called as the instructor will assist them in each stage of story creation process (See Fig. 3 as a sample). Digital story as an experience or an event told through technological means facilitates the children to tell their likes, dislikes, curiosities [6] and to express their own experience freely within a storyline concept. G-Flash was performing such concept to encourage children to express and communicate their own experience into a storyline by understanding the topic of the story as a theme of idea.

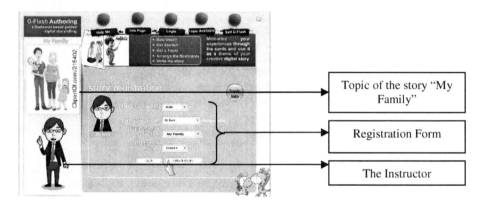

Fig. 3. A screenshot of the G-Flash Authoring Tool

4 Story Creation Test

A test has been done to explain the roles of the assistance which is used within the learning process of the story creation.

The rates of the task score are defined based on the *score criteria* of the student to complete each task presented in each screen page display. According to the rates of score criteria, the task presenting each process of story creation was performed in *easy* level when the students can pass it at the first try. The task then was performed in *medium* level when the students were *observed difficulty* to pass the task at *second* or *third* trying. For the *third* or *fourth* trying it can be considered that the task was performed in *hard* level, meaning the student will *express difficulty* in

Table 1. Scoring criteria for task performance test

Scoring Criteria (for tasks)		
Menu label	**Pass/Fail**	**Description**
Easy	Pass	1st try - no problem
Medium	Pass	2nd/3rd try - observed difficulty
Hard	Pass	3rd/4th try - expressed difficulty
Assist	Pass	Succeeded with assistance
Fail	Fail	Failed or gave up

passing the task. *Assist* is the condition when the task was performed successfully with *helps* or *assistance*. While, *Fail* means the users have given up and failed to perform the task given, it scored fail then.

Here are the lists of the tasks which are representing the process of a digital story creation.

Table 2. Shows the task of each phase of the story creation process

#	Task *(aka Scenario/Question)*	Chart Label	Scored
1	Describe the objective of study and the purpose of the system, usability within 10 minutes, and try out the application within 5 minutes		No
2	Open the application	Explain	No
3	Understand the function of character of the instructor	Roles	No
4	Understand start the application for the new / current user	Introduction	Yes
5	How to start the process of story creation	Reg Story	Yes
6	How to begin the arrangement	Arrangement	Yes
7	How to arrange story	Drag n Drop	Yes
8	Understanding result of the arrangement	Feedback	Yes
9	Process option	Deciding	Yes
10	Describing the illustration of the card	Describing	Yes
11	Save the story creation	Saving	Yes
12	End the application	Ending	Yes

Each task performed in each phase of story creation will be identified as *pass* or *fail* depending on how they perform the task as explained at preceding elaboration. However, the assist will be identified when the student does clicking on the "*help me*", or other *help* buttons to get assistance during creation process.

As shown at Table 2 there are 9 tasks that are scored that each participant should inclusively go through some activities from the beginning phase of *introduction* section, start the story composing by *register / login*, *arrange* the flashcards, use *drag and drop* interaction method, understand the *feedback* of interaction result, *decide* the option e.g. Yes / No, *describe* the illustration, *save* the story creation, and *end* the application. All tasks represent the steps of creating story by using the G-Flash authoring tool.

4.1 Test Conditions

Students have been given 30 minutes for exploring and composing a digital story using the proposed version of G-Flash authoring application. The test involved by 8 participants from the private primary school, ranging from 9 to 11 years old. The test is divided into 4 group of test and each group consists of 2 students with the same age level.

At the early phase of study the students get an explicit explanation from the observer about the purposes and usability of the proposed system, and to the way to use the system. The students then are directed to explore and test the system freely in 5 minutes in constraint. During the test, student interaction and expression are recorded by an external camera device (See Fig.4). As the test session begins, the student is not allowed to ask the teacher, tutor, friend or observer. The result then is analyzed by using data logger v.5.1.1 to create the graph form.

Fig. 4. The student during the story creation test

5   Results

Chart 1 (See Fig. 5) displays the distribution of the different scoring criteria per task such that the criteria total 100% for each task. On the chart 1 it is seen that the tasks inclusive some activities from the beginning phase of *introduction* section, the story composing by *registering / logging*, arranging the flashcards, *dragging and dropping* interaction, responding *feedback*, *deciding* Yes / No option, *describing* the illustration of the cards into a storyline, *saving* the story creation, and *ending* the application. 100% participant entirely passed the task performance test. 55.55% of the tasks totally were succeeded performed on they own with easy and medium performance level. However, 44.45% of the tasks were succeeded performed with assistance.

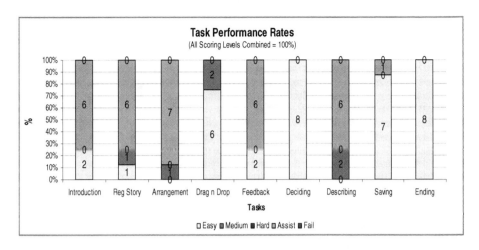

Fig. 5. Shows the chart of task performance result

The result shows that the students actually like to perform and do the activity on their own; yet in some condition they feel stuck and do not know what to do. They will prefer to find some helps to solve the problem. For example, for the process student is not required to consult such as clicking "exit" button for exit or deciding "Yes" or "No" button to proceed the process they can confidently perform on they own (e.g. task "deciding" and "ending"). However, for more advance task (e.g. task "Reg Story"), which student need to understand how to work with the tasks, most of them need to find an assistance and help to perform the process successfully.

Furthermore, the use of the illustrated flashcards as a passive assistance providing a theme of idea through a design of the topic of the story could encourage the student to create a focus idea according to the selected topic. As shown from the examples (See Fig.6) of the story those students successfully save into the database.

+ Options

			childID	ins_name	ins_gender	topicID	soundID	materialID	theStory
□	✎	X	nurain	3	2	2	6	6#1#15#11#14#5#13	At morning i go to the school using a school bus.#...
□	✎	X	aisyah	1	1	1	2	1#2#6#4#0#0#0	Keluarga saya ada ayah, mak, dan adek. Adek saya b...
□	✎	X	hamid	2	1	3	2	5#1#3#2#15#0#0	My mother is very beatiful, she is the best mother...
□	✎	X	munirah1	2	2	2	3	1#2#3#4#7#11#9	I think this is my best school. I like to school o...
□	✎	X	wawa2	4	1	1	6	1#4#3#15#6#2#13	this is my family. there is father, mother, and si...
□	✎	X	nurul izzah	1	2	3	1	1#3#2#0#5#0#0	saya mempunyai seorang ibu yang baik.ibu saya seor...
□	✎	X	alnmaz	2	2	3	1	8#4#5#1#2#11#10	My mom name is Saliza,she is the best mother in th...
□	✎	X	muhammad	1	1	2	6	1#3#2#4#10#5#8	Kami sekolah dekat Taman Maju #Bila kami tiba di s...
□	✎	X	aida comel	2	2	2	1		
□	✎	X	aida cantik	2	2	2	5	2#14#1#4#15#2#6	cikgu saya suka mengajar bayak sabjet#saya suka me...
□	✎	X	sawdah	1	1	1	4	13#2#3#4#6#6#7	my name is Muhammad. I am 12 years old########

⌐ Check All / Uncheck All *With selected:* ✎   X   ▤

Fig. 6. The saving story that student successfully create

Participant 1 (P1):*"At morning i go to the school using a school bus.#my school in taman maju#in the school i am study with my teacher.#in the class.#I am study.#To learn to read ABC#and i also learn mathematic in the class."*

From the example of story P1 shows that she creates a story based on the topic *"My School"* with which the instructor selected was ID number 3 namely *"Miss Suhaida"*, and some flashcards was arranged as *"6#1#15#11#14#5#13"* with detail of story contained as:

Illustration #6: *At morning i go to the school using a school bus.*
Illustration #1: *my school in taman maju.*
Illustration #15: *in the school i am study with my teacher.*
Illustration #11: *in the class.*
Illustration #14: *I am study*
Illustration #5: *To learn to read ABC*
Illustration #13: *and i also learn mathematic in the class.*

The result of digital story is that P1 was successfully created as shown in Fig.7.

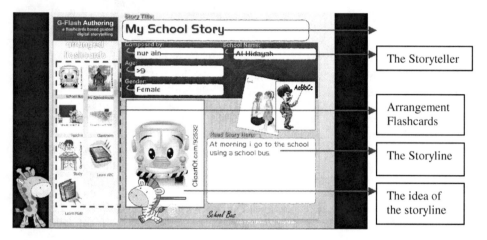

Fig. 7. P1 story creation result with the story titled My School Story, composed by Nur Ain

6   Conclusion

The use of storytelling approach as the platform for creating story among children is encouraged to communicate their own experiences freely. Roles of assistance within the process of story creation provide digital storytelling to be more guidable to create a focus idea of story creation. G-Flash is a digital storytelling authoring tool designed to adapt that concept. The concept allows children to get helps, information, and feedback during the process of creating story. According to the test result, assistance can encourage student to understand the idea that they have to explain into their storyline. It shows from the example of story created by P1, from the story she successfully creates a story with the topic "My School" and she shows the focus idea according to the selected topic to be filled into the storyline.

References

1. Wastam, J., Rambli, D.R.A., Sulaiman, S.: A guided digital storytelling prototype system using illustrated flashcards. In: 2010 International Symposium on Information Technology (ITSim), June 15-17, vol. 1, pp. 1–6 (2010)
2. Barrett, H.: Researching and Evaluating Digital Storytelling as a Deep Learning Tool. In: Crawford, C., et al. (eds.) Proceedings of Society for Information Technology and Teacher Education International Conference, pp. 647–654. AACE, Chesapeake, VA (2006)
3. Borek, A., McLaren, B.M., Karabinos, M., Yaron, D.: How Much Assistance is Helpful to Students in Discovery Learning? In: Cress, U., Dimitrova, V., Specht, M. (eds.) EC-TEL 2009. LNCS, vol. 5794, pp. 391–404. Springer, Heidelberg (2009)
4. Koedinger, K.R., Aleven, V.: Exploring the Assistance Dilemma in Experiments with Cognitive Tutors. Educ. Psychol. Rev. (2007)
5. Hourcade, J.P., Baderson, B.B., Druin, A., Taxen, G.: KidPad: Colaborative Storytelling for Children. In: Proc. Human Factor in Computing System (CHI 2002), pp. 500–501. ACM Press (April 2002)
6. Widjajanto, W.A., Lund, M., Schelhowe, H.: Wayang Authoring: A Web-based Authoring Tool for Visual Storytelling for Children. In: Proc. MoMM 2008, pp. 464–467 (November 2008)
7. Vaucelle, C., Jehan, T.: Dolltalk: A computational toy to enhance children creativity. In: Short Talk: Portporri: Children and Virtual Reality, CHI 2002, Minneapolis, Minnesota, USA, CHI, April 20-25 (2002)
8. Landry, B.M., Guzdial, M.: ITELL: Supporting retrospective storytelling with digital photo. In: DIS 2006, June 26–28. University Park, Pennsylvania (2006)
9. Hayter, S., Scott, E., et al.: The Use Modified Direct Instruction Flashcards System with Two High School Students with Developmental Disability, June 28 (2007)
10. Tan, A., Nicholson, T.: Flashcards revisited: training poor readers to read word faster improves their comprehension of text. Journal of Educational Psychology 89, 276–288 (1997)
11. Klahr, D., Nigam, M.: The Equivalence of Learning Paths in Early Science Instruction Effects of Direct Instruction and Discovery Learning. Psychological Science, 661–667 (2004)
12. Mayer, R.E.: Should There Be a Three-Strike Rule Against Pure Discovery Learning? The Case for Guided Methods of Instruction. American Psychologist, 14–19 (2004)
13. Kirschner, P.A., Sweller, J., Clark, R.E.: Why Minimal Guidance During Instruction Does Not Work: An Analysis of the Failure of Constructivist, Discovery, Problem-Based, Experiential and Inquiry-Based Teaching. Educational Psychologist, 75–86 (2006)
14. Bruner, J.S.: The Art of Discovery. Harvard Educational Review (31), 21–32 (1961)
15. Barrows, H.S., Tamblyn, R.M.: Problem-based Learning: An Approach to Medical Education. Springer, New York (1980)
16. Jonassen, D.: Objectivism vs. Constructivism. Educational Technology Research and Development 39(3), 5–14 (1991)
17. Steffe, L., Gale, J.: Constructivism in Education. Lawrence Erlbaum Associates, Inc., Hillsdale (1995)

18. Valinho, P., Correia, N.: oTTomer: An interactive adventure system for children. In: SRMC 2004, New Tork, New York, USA, October 15, pp. 71–74 (2004)
19. Bers, M.U., Cassell, J.: Interactive Storytelling System for Children: Using Technology to Explore Language and Identity. Journal of Interactive Learning Research 9(2), 183–215 (1998)
20. Department for Education and Skill.: Pedagogy and Practice: Teaching and Learning in Secondary School (2004),
    http://www.sjl.herts.sch.uk/teachingtoolkit/PDF/GuidedLearning.pdf
21. Hakulinen, J., Turunen, M., et al.: Tutor Design for Tutor Based Speech Interfaces. In: DIS 2004, Cambridge, Massachusetts, USA, August 1-4 (2004)
22. ESL Flashcards.com. Free ESL Flashcards, http://www.eslflashcards.com/
23. ClipartOf,
    http://www.clipartof.com/gallery/clipart/flashcards.html

MYNDA - An Intelligent Data Mining Application Generator

Zulaiha Ali Othman, Abdul Razak Hamdan, Azuraliza Abu Bakar, Suhaila Zainudin,
Hafiz Mohd Sarim, Mohd Zakree Ahmad Nazri, Zalinda Othman, Salwani Abdullah,
Masri Ayob, and Ahmad Tarmizi Abdul Ghani

Faculty of Information Science and Technology
University Kebangsaan Malaysia (UKM)
Bangi, Selangor D.E., Malaysia
{zao,arh,aab,suhaila,hafiz,mzan,zalinda,salwani,masri,
tarmizi}@ftsm.ukm.my

Abstract. Development of a Decision Support System (DSS) based on data mining is expensive. It consists of three main phases: produce quality input data, develop quality knowledge models and developed an application based on the model, which needs experts in the domain, data mining and software development respectively. Current commercial data mining tools, such as Insightful miner, aims for the development of quality knowledge models which are conducted by data mining expert. The knowledge model is not meaningful to the end user without the development of a DSS application based on the knowledge model. Mynda is a web-based data mining tool for domain expert users to generate knowledge models from client's data (model generator) and also generate a data mining application from the knowledge model (application generator). The user only provides input data sets (for example in Excel format) and set the mining technique profile. Mynda will automatically develop the knowledge model and generate an executable data mining application based on the profile. The data mining application can be run independently as a stand alone application. Mynda has reduced the complexity of the development of data mining based DSS applications.

Keywords: Data Mining tools, Application Generator, Mynda.

1   Introduction

A Decision Support System (DSS) is a cutting edge tool which can supply the business intelligence needs of everybody, especially managers. Currently, most organizations store their valuable business information electronically. The utility of the stored business information can be increased through the use of data mining, a well known technique for knowledge discovery [1]. However, development of a DSS application based on data mining is a complex process. The development process consists of three main phases: produce quality input data, develop high-quality knowledge models and develop a DSS application based on the model.   In relation to this, the development process involves three types of experts: the data domain expert, the data mining expert and a software development expert, who will collaborate among each other to develop

H. Badioze Zaman et al. (Eds.): IVIC 2011, Part II, LNCS 7067, pp. 217–230, 2011.

a DSS data mining application. A domain expert is the person who has expertise in the domain of data. This person has complete understanding on the data and knows what kind of DSS application could be produced based on the knowledge. The end user is the user who used the DSS data mining application developed by the domain expert.

The second phase involves the data mining expert's tasks to produce the best knowledge model. The data miner has to communicate with the domain expert in order to model the correct knowledge model. Currently, there are more than 50 data mining domain tools available in market which can be categorized as commercial [8] such as Insightful Miner [4], Clementine [5], and others; and free tools such as Weka [6], and Rosetta [7]. The tools provide many data mining techniques either for specific or generic domains. It aims to generate the best knowledge model from the data. It also provides various data preprocessing techniques to produce quality input data. The tools are suitable for the data mining experts who have a good understanding on the concept of data mining in depth. In practice, the data miner uses these data mining tools to perform a series of various preprocessing and mining technique to produce the best model. However, conducting experiments to produce the best model using the tools is a complex process, especially when mining using 10-fold cross validation processes [1]. Setting up preprocessing and mining profile would reduce the need for data mining experts when conducting the experiments.

Having the best model is meaningless without turning it into a usable DSS application. The current practice is assigning an expert software developer to develop the DSS application based on the model, by using an appropriate programming language. This phase involves a complex software development process and which can become expensive.

Based on the discussion above, we conclude that the current data mining tools has limitations when producing a DSS data mining application. Therefore, this paper presents an intelligent data mining application generator named Mynda. Mynda, an acronym for "Make Your Own Data Mining Application (DSS)", aims to allow the owners of expert domain data to develop their own data mining DSS applications easily, by eliminating the task of the data miner expert and software developer expert. The primary price determinant of current commercial data mining tools is based on the number of the users. Mynda is a web based data mining tool for the use of the domain expert, to develop DSS data mining applications. Mynda will consist of two components: generate knowledge models from client's data (model generator) and also generate a data mining application from the knowledge model (application generator). Mynda's business model is either based on subscription or usage. A registered user can use Mynda to produce the best knowledge model. It is also used to generate a data mining DSS application which can be readily used by the end user. The data mining DSS application can run online, and can also be distributed to the end user as a stand-alone application. The use of Mynda has reduced the complexity of developing data mining-based DSS applications.

This paper discusses the features of the current data mining tools and its limitations, the features or Mynda and its components, a snapshot of the Mynda implementation, and a snapshot of a sample "Breast Cancer Prediction System" built using Mynda. The system can propose the type of breast cancer, either benign or malignant, based on attributes given. Lastly, the paper present the experiment result of best model prediction system for 30 data sets collected from UCI.

2 Development Process in Mynda versus Current Data Mining Tools

As stated earlier, the development of a DSS data mining application consists of three phases: prepare raw data prove by the expert, developed a knowledge model and develop the data mining application based on the knowledge model. Figure 1 shows the process of developing DSS data mining applications using Mynda versus using the current data mining tools. As mentioned earlier, current data mining tools largely function as general data mining tools to develop a knowledge model which provides various methods of preprocessing and mining. Domain experts would usually not be able to develop the knowledge by themselves, but require the assistance of data mining experts to develop the best model by conducting various experiments using any data mining tools. Later, depending on type of knowledge model, the programmer develops the data mining application according to the software engineering development process.

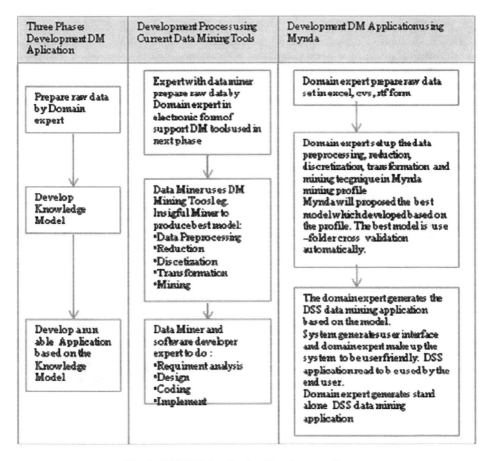

Fig. 1. DSS DM Application Development Process

Mynda is designed in such a way suitable for domain expert to develop it own data mining application.   Domain expert knows the trustworthiness, reliability and completeness of the data to be used for decision making. Mynda provides default profile preferences for developing data mining applications. As an example, for users who want to developed prediction systems, when preparing the data, the system enforces the choice of class attributes. Upon chosing the type of system, the system will provide the default preprocessing task and techniques. For example, the discretization and/or transformation technique, which the user can choose, along with other techniques that are made available as well. The default preprocessing techniques suggested are based on the best practices of past researchers. The knowledge model is developed after performing the preprocessing task. Mynda will propose the mining task based on the type of system chosen. For example, if user selects a classification based Prediction system, Mynda will list the suitable data mining techniques for the system, such as neural network, Decision tree, Bayesian, etc. However, Mynda sets the default data mining techniques as neural network.

Lastly, Mynda generates the data mining application which consists of two parts: the user interface and the knowledge model. The user interface is designed based on attribute sets after preprocessing task, while the knowledge model is developed on the predefined data mining algorithm used in the system. For example, when modelling knowledge based on neural networks, the weight parameters for the best model is selected and set into the neural network algorithm, as later it used as an independent application.

3   Mynda Framework

MYNDA consists of four components namely data cleaning, data pre-processing, model generator and application generator. Figure 2 shows the Mynda general framework. Using this framework, raw data acquired is converted into a usable DSS DM Application. The main differences between Mynda with other data mining tools is the fact that Mynda is be able to perform generate data mining application automatically based on raw data and preferences.

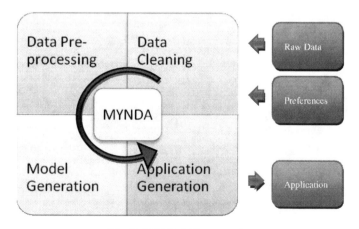

Fig. 2. MYNDA Framework

Raw data is the user's original source data or exported data from user databases which consist of attributes and records. This raw data contains very large data sets, most of which may not be usable for application generation. The data is stored in a comma separated value format or a .xls spreadsheet file for MS Excel. The raw data is pre-preprocessed into clean and prepared data to be consumed by the model generator. The model generator consists of several subtasks in order to generate the best model. The application generator constructs the user interface, controller and combines models to form a DSS data mining application.

A Profile is the setup the preferences of data mining task, which are used during the development of the data mining application. It includes the preprocessing, discretization, reduction, normalization and mining techniques. Mynda provides several techniques in each data mining task. These techniques are hard coded in the Mynda. The user needs to select the techniques to set the data mining preferences profile. The best knowledge model is build based on setting up of the profile preferences.

Mynda is developed using component based approach which apply the criteria using the *plug-and-play* concept. Each Mynda component is defined as a module and each module consists of sub-modules. Each module is developed in the form of a .dll file, which communicates with each other using predefined API. Similar approach is used for the sub-module. The preprocessing or classification techniques are hard coded in the system as a sub-module. Using this approach any additional technique is easy to add in Mynda.

In order to optimize the data mining development process, Mynda applies parallel processing methods in preprocessing task, if and only if the user select more than one preprocessing techniques to apply in the preprocessing profile. Mynda also apply the parallel processing while performing robust experiment such as 10-fold cross validation.

A. Data Cleaning

Several processes are conducted in the data cleaning stages. First, the attribute extraction process which converts the raw data in the attributes matrix and extracts the attributes information. The attributes matrix will then be filtered using the data cleaning process.

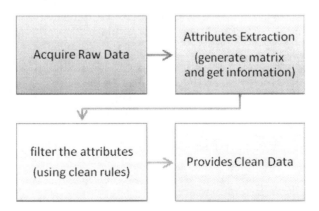

Fig. 3. Data Cleaning Process

1)   Attributes Extraction

Raw data contained in a text file in comma separated value (CSV) data types are lined up in row and columns format. This format makes data dependable, and matches difficult to handle data with the relevant attributes. Therefore, data is placed into the attributes matrix. The attributes matrix is created by detecting the number of columns and its information as attributes information. Each row of column is filled into the attributes matrix as string values.

The main purpose of data extraction into a matrix of attributes instead of the rows and columns schema is to enable parallel processing of attributes independently, which improves computation times, simplify and improves the overall process to generate models, and to select the best model respectively.

2)   Basic Cleaning Process

The attributes matrix generated still contains noisy and invaluable data such as missing, invaluable, unique and repeatable attributes. The data cleaning process performs missing value marking and data dictionary generation against the attributes. This process produces similar data frequency information for each attribute. This information is used to filter the attributes and replaced missing values.

Rules of the frequency of the instance values are constructed to decide which attributes are proposed to be considered invalid which are subject to be removed.   The output of this process is a set of meaningful attributes and records. The domain expert is responsible to agree upon the output. The system will identify meaningful attributes and records. The data cleaning component will provide clean data to be prepared by the pre-processing process for the model generation process. Each of the problems during the data cleaning process is subject to the criteria. This criterion is used to propose attributes to be ignored or marked as invalid attributes. Invalid attributes will be discarded from further processes.

The basic cleaning rules used are as follows [1]:

i.   *Missing value*: Several attributes sometimes have no value or become null because the attributes is optional or data is not entered or information is missing. A missing value will be very difficult to handle as it will introduce problems during model generation. Therefore, if the number of missing value is more than 60% of total rows in the attributes, the attributes are considered invalid or the missing value have to be replaced with possible or closest value. There are several methods in replacement of missing values, currently we use the average values to replace the missing value.

ii.   *Invaluable*: This condition happens when 70% of the rows in the attributes have similar values. The invaluable attributes are considered invalid.

iii.   *Unique Value*: The attributes are considered have unique value when 90% of it rows is unique and the attributes are considered invalid.

iv.   *Repeated data*: If the two or more attributes are identical or have 100% similar rows values. Both attributes are considered repeated, therefore the attributes are considered invalid.

B. Data Pre-processing

The clean attributes from data cleaning result is free from problematic data which could potentially introduce problems during further processing. This data is ready to be modeled by the model generator to create the application. However, the variation and the ranges of values of the data will reduce the model performance as the model generated is less effective.

In order to produce quality models, the pre-processing task are conducted. Nowadays, there are more than 70 pre-processing techniques available. However, currently Mynda only provides techniques which are most commonly used by practitioners; such as Boolean reasoning, min-max, etc. The techniques are available during profile setup which could be changed by the user before generating the application.

C. Model Generation

The model generator follows the standard data mining process. It uses prepared data from the data cleaning process, and data pre-processing. In the model generation process, the data is partitioned into ratios of ten cross validation processes and is evaluated to generate the best models. This process is shown at Figure 4.

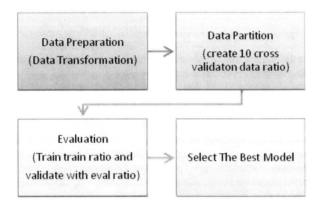

Fig. 4. Process in Model generator

The models generator creates the knowledge models from the dataset. For example, for Mynda to be able to generate models for classification or prediction, it provides a Multi Layer Perceptron (MLP) Neural Networks models generator as the default setting in preferences. In order to reduce computation times and improve model performance, the model generator uses several pre-processing steps in order to remove noisy and invaluable attributes or instances. The best model selection process is lead by the partition of models into several models for 10-fold cross validation processing. These models are trained and evaluated.

Each process in the model generator involves several data mining process, therefore this model generator is actually a common process found in most data mining tools. Important information is extracted in the above process. This information is required to integrate models with applications.

1)   Data Preparation

Before parted into 10-fold cross validation sets, data is transformed into more concise representation using selected normalization techniques. This transformation is required to optimize neural networks model generation.

2)   Partition

Partitioning involves generating 10 randomized duplicated data sets using 10-fold cross validation process (90:10; 80:20,..). Each data set produces models. A randomizing process assists in reducing evaluation bias.

3)   Evaluation

This process generates several models for ten cross validation process to select the best models. Each training ratio is trained until converged, and then evaluated against the evaluation ratio. The results is means square error, accuracy, specificity and sensitivity. The result will be used to select the best models.

4)   The best model selection

From the evaluation results for each ten cross validation models, the best model is selected using selection rules based on means square error, accuracy, specificity and sensitivity of the model. The models are then exported to be used in the application stages.

D. Application Generation

At this stage, the complete application which is ready to be used by the user is generated. The application consists of a user interface, model and profile. The user interface is constructed using a template generator which is common or generic for each application generated using profile. It includes customized branding, navigation, themes, the authentication modules as part of application permission and policy, and the prediction interface as a core component of user interface which bridges with model. This model specification is abstracted in order to support multiple models types. MYNDA provides functionality to edit and manage the user interface look and feel. The profile is first generated from the template profile and then constructed from the data.

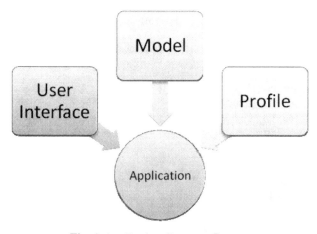

Fig. 4. Application Generator Process

4   Mynda Implementation

Mynda is a web-based system with three level access. Admin, the DSS DM application creator, and the DSS DM application's users.

The admin manages all access and control in Mynda. DSS DM application creator is the company/domain expert who subscribes to Mynda to develop the DSS DM application based on their data, and later invites their end users to use the DSS DM application. The following sub-section shows some of the interfaces of Mynda tools used to develop and run DSS DM applications.

Mynda is developed using the component based approach. All data mining task techniques is developed as a component (in a form of .dll, which communicate using APIs)

E.   Setup profile

The most common preprocessing and mining techniques is set up as a default profile. The user can modify the profile according their preferences. Figure 5 shows the interface for setting up the profile.

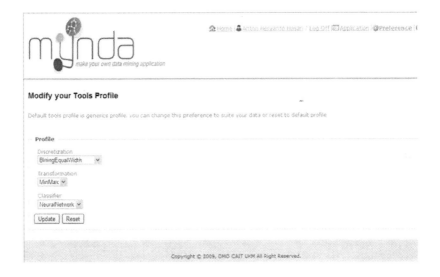

Fig. 5. User Interface Mining Profile

F.   Creating DSS DM Application

DSS DM application is automatically generated when the domain expert has developed the knowledge model. Figure 6 shows the interface for creating DSS DM application. It contains of the name of the application, application description, load the data set, agreement of license and category data.

Fig. 6. Mynda Creating Model and Application Setup

G. Result Best Model

The accuracy of each fold of data sets is calculated automatically. Figure 7 shows the accuracy and error rate of each fold. The blue color shows the best model selected. For the meantime, the selection of the best model is based on the accuracy.

Fig. 7. Accuracy Model of each 10-cross validation

H. Executable DSS DM Application

The DSS DM application is created when the user clicks the button 'Summary' as shown in Figure 7. The new DM application is added in the DM application list as shown in Figure 8. The figure shows some data mining prediction system created using Mynda.

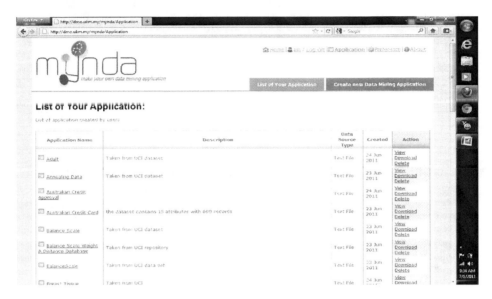

Fig. 8. the list of DSS DM Applications

I. An Example of A Prediction System

Figure 9 shows a sample user interface of the Breast Cancer Prediction System, which generates from the data set Breast Cancer from UCI[3].

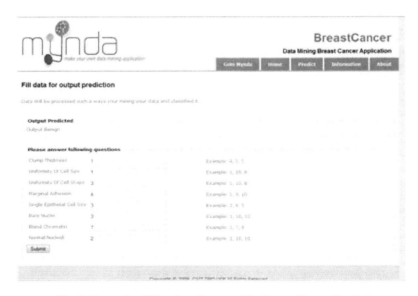

Fig. 9. Example of User Interface used for Breast Cancer Prediction

The system can be used to predict the type of cancer, either benign or malignant, based on 8 types of attributes, such as size of clump thickness, uniformity of the cell size, uniformity of the cell shape, marginal adhesion, epithelia cell size, nuclei size, clomatine size and nucleoli normal [3]. Based on the input given, the Breast Cancer Prediction system will propose the type of cancer.

5 Result

Table 1 shows the result of execution time to develop Data Mining Application from data set taken from UCI, the fold of the best model and the accuracy. The execution time is mainly dependent on the size of data set. The execution time is based on the time taken when start uploading the data set until the development of the Data mining application.

Nama Data	Name of Data Mining System	Number of Record	Execcution Times (sc)	Best Model in Mynda	Accuracy (%)
Annealing (T1)	Annealing Prediction System	798	148.7	70:30	78.07
Australian Credit approval (T3)	Autralian Credit Approval Prediction System	690	56.2	70:30	86.96
Car(T7)	Car Prediction System	1354	153.2	60:40	79.70
Mammographic Mass Data(T9)	Mammographic Mass Prediction System	961	122.5	60:40	80.21
Data Credit Card CRX(T11)	CRX Prediction System	690	55.7	70:30	86.47
Echocardiogram (T13)	Echocardiogram Prediction System	132	23,0	80:20	73.08
Flag Database(T15)	Flag Prediction System	194	39.5	80:20	61.54
Glass Identification (T17)	Glass Identification Prediction System	214	55.0	80:20	48.84
Heart Disease(T19)	Heart Diseases Prediction System	270	24.3	90:10	88.89
Horse Colic(T21)	HorseColic Prediction System	368	27.0	70:30	88.18
Thyroid Disease(T23)	Thyroid Disease Prediction System	9173	2271.2	30:70	60.16
Iris Plants(25)	Iris Plants Prediction System	150	10.5	90:10	100.00

Database for Fitting Contact lenses(T27)	Lenses Prediction System	24	2.3	70:30	80.00
BUPA Liver Disorders(T29)	Liver Disorder Prediction System	345	70.7	90:10	61.76
Lymphography Domain(T31)	Lymphography Domain Prediction System	148	10.4	90:10	93.33
Water Treatment(T33)	Water Treatment Prediction System	527	198.7	90:10	45.28
E.Coli Promoter gene sequences (DNA)(T37)	E.Coli Prediction System	336	52.9	20:80	72.49
Cylinder Band(T39)	Cylinder Band Prediction System	512	88.9	90:10	74.07
Teaching Assistant Evaluation(T43)	Teaching Assistant Evaluation Prediction System	151	40.8	90:10	40.00
Vehicle Silhouette(T45)	Vehicle Silhouette Prediction System	846	181.9	70:30	60.24
Contraceptive Method Choice(T47)	Contraceptive Method Choice Prediction System	1473	396.5	50:50	46.74
Protein Localization Site @ Yeast(T49)	Yeast Prediction System	1484	469.4	90:10	45.95
Zoo	Zoo Prediction System	101	18.1	90:10	90.00
Lung Cancer	Lung Cancer Prediction System	32	5.3	50:50	75.00
Coil 2000	Coil 2000 Prediction System	85	25.7	60:40	99.05
Cleveland	Cleveland Prediction System	304	35.9	90:10	80.00
Diabetes	Diabetes Prediction System	768	115.7	90:10	76.62
Nursery	Nursery Prediction System	10344	1332.7	30:70	78.03

The table also shows how fast the data mining application is developed using mynda for end users, compared with the traditional process using the current data mining tools. The traditional data mining tools provides longer time as the data miner experts have to discuss with the user by conducting several experiments, especially the 10-fold cross validation process to select the best model, and later assign the programmer to develop the decision support system using the data was given.

6   Conclusion

This paper has presented an intelligent data mining application generator that is able to develop DSS DM applications easily. The use of Mynda has reduced the complexity and cost of developing DSS DM applications. Mynda is a web based data mining tools that uses the subscription based model which is cheaper. DSS DM applications which have been developed from Mynda can run either as an online web-based application or run as a standalone DSS DM application. Currently, Mynda allows user to select the pre-processing and mining profile in order to develop the knowledge model. In the future, Mynda aims to improve its ability to be able to propose the best knowledge model by performing various mining experiments using various preprocessing techniques without having the user specify the preprocessing profile using an agent based approach, which will produce a more robust model evaluation process to select the best model, and develop an application installer for easier deployment.

Acknowledgement. Thanks to Universiti Kebangsaan Malaysia for sponsorship of this research.

References

[1] Han, J., Kamber, M.: Data Mining: concepts and techniques. Morgan Kaufman Publishers, San Francisco (2006)
[2] Liu, H., Hussain, F., Tan, C.L., Dash, M.: Discretization: an enabling technique. Data Mining and knowledge Discovery 6, pp. 393–423 (2002)
[3] UCI Repositories of Machine Learning and Domain Theories, http://archive.ics.uci.edu/ml/dataset.html
[4] Insighful Software Informer, http://insightful.software.informer.com/
[5] IBM SPSS Modeler Profesional, http://www.spss.com/software/modeling/modeler-pro/
[6] Weka 3 Data Mining with Open Source Machine Learning Software, http://www.cs.waikato.ac.nz/ml/weka/
[7] Rosseta: A Rough Set Toolkit for Analysis of Data, rosetta.lcb.uu.se/
[8] Elder IV, J.F., Abbott, D.W.: A Comparison of Leading Data Mining Tools. In: Fourth International Conferences on Knowledge Discovery and Data Mining, New York (1998)

Scaffolding Poetry Lessons Using Desktop Virtual Reality

Nazrul Azha Mohamed Shaari[1] and Halimah Badioze Zaman[2]

[1] Faculty of Information Science and Technogy
[2] Institute of Visual Informatics,
Universiti Kebangsaan Malaysia, Malaysia
nash@tmsk.uitm.edu.my, hbzukm@yahoo.com

Abstract. This paper discusses the development of a courseware which is able to facilitate attractive and quality lessons in learning poetry for Form 1 students, based on the technology of computer graphics. The need for the development of the courseware was based upon a survey conducted in 2006 in which English Language was then a national issue. This lead to an idea to develop four learning modules which are presented in the form of an interactive virtual environment, called Interactive 3D Poem (I3DP). In order to make this courseware capable of meeting users' needs, several steps were taken, which began by identifying suitable learning theories which could help to design the presentation of knowledge, collecting media resources related to the content and developing the prototype of the courseware. This paper also discusses the construction of its core components of instruction which is capable of increasing students' independence and self- reliance, and also in enhancing students' interest in learning poems.

Keywords: Visual informatics, Desktop VR, Virtual Reality, Learning Poetry, visual learning.

1 Introduction

According to Towndrow & Vallance [1], computers have become very much a part of an educational institute's infrastructure. The potential of computers to enhance learning has also regenerated the imagination and enthusiasm of many educators. People have also been suggesting that well-designed simulations generated from virtual reality could provide access to learning experiences that are simply unavailable via normal means [2]. Consider students' presence at a virtual gallery of William Shakespeare, touch virtual boxes, sculptors and see vibrant colors. Many desktop VR or PC-based simulations have pursued this dream with varying results [2], [3]. Therefore, learning poetry using desktop VR, is not only feasible but in fact, is capable to motivate them to move into the art of symbolic words and meaning.

2 Related Studies

2.1 Virtual Reality Technology

Virtual Reality (VR) technology, is both interactive and immersive. It is a high end user-computer interface that involves real-time simulation and interactions

H. Badioze Zaman et al. (Eds.): IVIC 2011, Part II, LNCS 7067, pp. 231–241, 2011.

through multiple sensorial channels. These sensorial modalities are visual, auditory, tactile, smell, and taste [4]. According to Stanney & Zyda [5],VR is driven by the technology that is used to design and build these systems. This technology consists of human-machine interface devices that are used to present multimodal information and sense the virtual world, as well as the hardware and software used to generate the virtual world.

Chaoshun [6] categorized VR into desktop VR, immersive VR system, distributed VR system and augmented reality. Fully immersive VR are displayed via a Head Mounted Display (HMD), and interaction may be controlled using a tracked hand-held input device such as Data Gloves [7].

Desktop VR is the most basic VR technology which allows users to immerse in unifying realistic realities with artificial reality [8], [4]. The immersion is generated via a simulation in which computer graphics being used to produce a realistic-looking world. According to Burdea & Coiffet [4], the synthetic world is not static, but responds to the user's input. In this type of set up, users need only to have a desktop monitor as the output device and key board and mouse as the input device in order to get involved in the environment. Thus, desktop VR retains the benefits of real-time visualization and interaction within a virtual world, but without many of the inherent problems still associated with immersion systems [9]. Since it is cheaper than other virtual reality systems mentioned above, desktop VR is mainly used for CAD / CAM, education, teaching and other fields.

2.2 Learning Poetry

In 2003, the Malaysian English language curriculum of secondary schools had advocated the use of literary text in the language lesson. This is needed because literary texts are able to enhance the learning of English language which is a strong second language in Malaysia [10]. As a result, this demanded English language teachers to think of effective ways and techniques to ensure that the curriculum met its purpose [11].

On the contrary, Nazrul [12] found that literary text was the most problematic topic to learn among Form 1 students. Huzaina [13], found that students faced difficulties in understanding the poem "Life's Brief Candle" which was one of the poems taught in the previous syllabus. According to Iasevoli [14], constructing meanings from the ambiguous words in a poem is a very difficult task for most students. This is true to non-native English language speakers and in fact most of them perceived learning poetry as a routine of encoding text for the purpose of getting its literal meaning [14]. Students who evade analysing poetry, often hinder themselves from comprehension. Most times, they fear such an open-ended concept where there are no guaranteed approaches to bring about the "right" answer. Therefore, something has to be put into place, so that the positive idea as advocated in the Malaysian English language curriculum is achievable. This also implied that the ways poems were delivered in the classroom needed to be changed, so that students'interests became priority. If students were motivated, they would engage more actively, in the learning activities given to them in the poetry classes.

3 Proposed Design and Development

A number of researchers have proposed methods of teaching poetry but Allie [15], stated that there is no systematic equation to yield a definite solution for teaching poetry. Moreover, no pattern can be attributed to poetry comprehension.

Thus, the poetry scaffoldings framework which acts as the instructional sequences in this paper is designed based on a combination of few methods suggested by Huda [16], Kelly [17], Kovalcik & Certo [18], Mager [19], Mager, [20], Tarleton [21], and Fleming [22].

3.1 Scaffolding Students in Learning Poetry

The I3DP scaffolding framework can be observed in Fig. 1. Generally, the framework can be divided into three (3) stages : Foundation Stage, Attending Stage and Exploration Stage. The purpose of making its instructional sequence into stages is to impart confidence to students gradually. This is important, because it will draw upon students' attention and motivation in order for them to be engaged actively in learning a poem. According to Woolfolk [23], teachers should have a well planned strategy to encourage motivation and thoughtful learning.

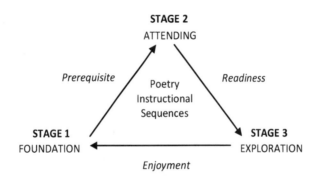

Fig. 1. The I3DP Scaffolding Framework

Breaking instruction into stages can be seen as a way to organize information to be learned and also able to create a necessary condition of learning. The goals of sequencing instruction are to inflame students' interest in learning poetry, keep motivation high, and to make sure they have accomplished the course objectives by the time they leave school. In an observation conducted by Nazrul [12] and Huda [16], implemented her lesson plan of teaching poetry by breaking them into three (3) learning activities.

During the Foundation stage, the general concept of poetry and its purpose will be presented to students first. Indrakaran [24], proposed a brief introduction on poetry first before putting down the guidelines on analysing a poem. He began by prompting students with questions such as, What is poetry? and What to look for in a poem?" In another situation, Tarleton [21] and Fleming [22], focused on secondary-aged students' perceptions of poetry. Fleming's study of Year 9 students involved offering them texts to identify as poems, ranging from an extract from the two-times table, to shopping lists, to riddles, to haiku. A semi-structured interview questions were used also presented to them such as, What do you think poetry is?, What's the difference between a poem and a story? Do you think poetry is important? What kinds of things do people write poetry about? This is the most basic step which teacher should consider because responding to children's perceptions about poetry starts to give them, and their teachers, a more rounded, inclusive view of poetry and a richer poetic language and meta-language than one predicated on form alone [17]. Building background before reading and responding to poems are really an exemplar of instructional sequences for students [25]. This is to say that by providing students a foundation early in this stage will motivate them to get involve in poetry learning activities. It acts as the prerequisites for them to attend the actual text of a poem.

In the Attending stage, students will be given an opportunity to get to know the poet. Students should be given time to explore biography of the poet before they start reading the poem. A biography of the poet will have a special appeal for students because they frequently come to care about a person while learning about him or her. Apart from that, students will learn about the times of the poet [26]. This is an opportunity for students to form emotional ties along with new understanding. Besides that, it will help generate students' enthusiasms for continuing attending the poem with better levels of insights and emotions.

Reading aloud is another element that will take place in the attending stage. Huda, [16] called upon students to come in front of her poetry class to perform reading aloud a poem. According to Lenz [20], every mini lesson should begin with a reading-aloud of poetry. This is vital because listening to poetry help students develop a consistent pattern of fluent reading [27], a feel for the texture and power of language.

Guidelines in analysing a poem is another vital element that should be introduced to students. It opens up students minds and teaches them that they are some form of steps in understanding poems. Westerhof, [28] shows students on how to attend to a poem by providing them guidelines in analysing it in the form models such as New Critical and Reader Response Methods. The idea is to emphasize that Westerhof [28], put effort on students, helping them to read or make meaning of text, what is important in a poem, what students should pay attention to and encourage them to see that the meaning of a reader is what a poem is made of. Indrakaran [24] also proposed a list of guidelines in analysing a poem before introducing poems for students to start reading.

In the Exploration stage, there are four (4) learning activities designed in this study. The activities can be seen as Vocabulary, Background or Historical Setting, Literary Meaning and Interpretation.

Vocabulary is the first element that students should embark at this stage. Coming from various language backgrounds, and being at various levels of competence in reading, students need to develop an understanding of vocabularies or words used in the poem. For this purpose, students were given ample time to get meanings of the difficult words in the poem. Kovalcik & Certo [18], provide vocabulary and interpretation sessions within a double-period time of teaching. Since English is taught as a second language in Malaysia, most of the poems studied in the class rooms, contained vocabularies that students do not know. To lessen the burden, teachers should introduce activities that give students a chance to get the meanings of new words gradually. If students learn vocabularies, this could help to make them 'strong' in the language slowly [27]. This can also be seen as a prerequisite lesson in helping them comprehend the messages conveyed by the poets in the poems. Once, students had achieved a basic comprehension of the poem, they are ready to use that advantage to analyze the text, make connections between persona's actions and the idea of the poems.

The background or historical setting is also essential in helping students prepare their venture into the enchanter world of poetry. Yin & Whatt [29] and Morais & Kay [30], provide a background to the poem in the form of illustration and text to students, in order to help them understand the settings of the poem. In this manner, students will be able to imagine the situation and identify reasons why the poem is written. Setting plays an important role [25] in helping students appreciate the messages from the poet. According to Westerhof [28], students usually became interested in researching background information to help them situate the text.

Literal meaning is another element included in this stage where students usher into words that are taken from the poem and its meaning. Yin & Whatt [29] and Morais & Kay [30], provide activities for students to understand the literal meaning of words used by a poet in a poem. This can also be seen as a device that help students comprehend the surface meaning of the poem. Once, the students are able to get the meaning, then only are they ready to move into the interpretation part of this stage.

Arriving into this final part of the scaffolding framework, students were seen ready to give their personal response to the poem. This is where they are encouraged to relate poems they read to the life of today generally, and to their own life specifically. Yin & Whatt [29] and Morais & Kay [30], provide many activities for students to get involved in giving opinions as their interpretations. These activities were in the form of structured questions and multiple choice questions to be answered by students pertaining to the meaning of the text. These activities can be looked not only as a way to respond to a poem but also help them to familiarize with examinations questions which they will encounter in their tests and examinations. Fig. 2 shows de at each stage.

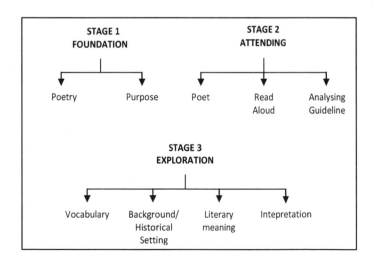

Fig. 2. Elements of the Stages in the I3DP Scaffolding Framework

3.2   Bringing in VR technology into Poetry Instruction

It's never a bad idea to provide students opportunity to learn poetry in a world which is built with interactive 3D objects. Generating poetry learning activities into virtual environment will motivate students to engage in most learning activities which all this while were bored to them [12], [13]. Burdea & Coiffet [4], pointed out and discussed on designs of virtual reality in domain areas such as education, military and business.

Three (3) types of softwares have been identified as an easy to learn and use to create the virtual environment. Autodesk 3DMax is used to create the 3D environment while 3DVia is used to create interactivity behaviors needed for students to walkthrough and interact within the virtual world. Adobe Dreamweaver is used to create the interface of presenting the learning content. Therefore, the content of the VR can be assessed by students via browser and for best results, students should use Internet Explorer (IE) for viewing and using the courseware. The process of transforming the I3DP scaffolding framework into VR content is shown in Fig. 3.

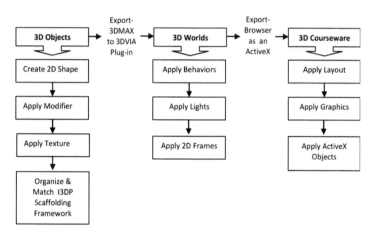

Fig. 3. Transformation of I3DP Scaffolding Framework into VR Content

Referring to Fig. 3, the construction of the three (3) worlds was based on the I3DP scaffolding framework. Objects are created from 2 Dimensional shapes and then transformed into 3 Dimensional objects with the help of a function provided in the software called modifier. As its name implied, the modifier was responsible in modifying 2D shapes into 3D objects. Almost all objects created in this courseware were created by using modifiers.

Texture mappings were also applied, so that it gave a realistic impression of the objects to the students. For example, an image of wood was needed to be applied on to an object box and this helped students to recognize easily the object as a wooden box. Once all of the objects needed in the courseware were built and made to appear realistic, they were exported into a file format (.vmo) which was compatible to the 3D authoring software (3DVIA). In this case, a plug-in was installed and placed into the 3D program (3DMAX).

After a successful process of bringing in 3D objects into the 3D authoring environment, only then features such as camera movements that allow students to walk through the 3D world and interact with some of them were programmed. Programming process was done in the 3D authoring tools (3DVIA) using functions called, Behaviors Building (BB) Scripts. For example, in this context, a few functions created, allowed users to change their view according to the mouse movement and also key press. In order to impress students and attract their attention, particles system were also used as special effects.

Lastly, the scripted 3D scene which was an output of the 3D authoring tools were exported into a format which was compatible to most browsers. Adobe Dreamweaver was used to organize the 3D scene and other related objects that acted as the interface for students to interact with. The 3D scene or the (.vmo) file format was imported into Dreamweaver as ActiveX objects. With the use of a plug-in, which could be downloaded from the Internet, students were able to see and interact with the courseware via browser.

4   I3DP Interfaces

In this study, the prototype consists of four (4) learning modules developed using the I3DP scaffolding framework (Fig.2) which has been discussed above. The modules can be seen as:

i)   Module *"Who am I"* is based on stage 1 in which students learn basic knowledge on poetry.

ii)   Module *"Recite It"* is based on stage 2 in which students are able to identify skills needed in reading aloud and analyzing an poem.

iii)   Module "*Unfamiliar Words"* is based on stage 3 in which students are be able to acquire meaning of difficult words used by poets in a poem.

iv)   Module "*Understand It*" is based on stage 3 in which students are able to give personal response to a poem.

To begin the lesson, students are invited into the virtual building that acts as the main menu of the system. Students see three (3) different doors which takes them into three (3) different rooms where biographies of poets are presented in the form of exhibitions. For this prototype, modules were developed based on the poem entitled "Life's Brief Candle" and its poet. Fig.4 (a) and (b) shows the interface where students can walk through and make their options. Fig. 4 (a) also shows thet information regarding the poetry is placed on the walls for students to read and develop the required foundation.

For this prototype students will then go into a room which exhibits information Students learn about William Shakespeare in the form of multimedia elements such as text, animations pictures, audio and video. Fig. 4 (b) shows a screen shot of the room where information regarding the bard is placed.

Once students have completed wondering around and learned the background of the poet, they are ready to move into another section of the virtual environment where three (3) learning modules are available for them to choose from. Students who are new in using the courseware are advised to use learning modules according to the

Fig. 4 (b). Screen shot of the room of   **Fig. 4 (a).** Screen shot of the main menu
William Shakespeare

Fig. 5. Screen shot of the numbered sub   **Fig. 6.** Screen shot of the Module "Recite It"
menu

number written on each door of the virtual building as can be seen in Fig. 5. Access to learning modules can be done when students click the doors that are attached to the walls of the virtual building.

Fig. 6 shows how wooden boxes which contain important information regarding the guideline on analysing a poem are stored inside them are organized. Students are required to find them by clicking on the box with the mouse. Besides that, video presentations on 'read aloud' on the poem are also provided for students to observe and analyse. Here again, students need to find the right objects to click on in order to start watching the videos.

Fig. 7 shows several cubes which students are required to touch and rotate, in order for them to find important information regarding the meaning of difficult words found in the poem. Students are also required to arrange those scrambled words found on cubes to form the correct match or meaning to the words. It is expected that at the end of the activity, students will acquire skills needed for them to move into the next module.

Finally, Fig. 8 shows a screen shot of the Module "Understand It". In this module, there are four (4) activities designed for students to practice their understanding of the poem. Activity lessons in this module are presented in a virtual area which has two levels. In level one, information regarding the background of the poem is placed on the wall for students to access them easily. Students will able to develop their understanding on why the poem is created by the poet after they have completed reading and understanding that information. Information in the form of videos and animations on Macbeth is also presented to the students upon request.Therefore, students need to find the correct objects to enable the presentation to show up. There are three (3) more activities placed on the second level of the virtual building of this last module as can be seen in Fig 8. To practice their understanding on how to react to text used by the poet, students need to make a correct choice on questions asked by the system. The choices which represent answers to the questions asked, are presented to students in the form of clickable objects. Students can easily notice whether they have made correct answers or vice-versa by looking on feedbacks given by the system. Students can repeat all of the modules as they like at anytime based on their own learningpace.

Fig. 7. Screen shot of the rotatable cubes   **Fig. 8.** Screen shot of the Module "Understand It"

5 Discussions

This prototype was designed and developed for 13 year- old students to use and undergo an experiential learning on poems in the virtual world. Students need go through all the four (4) modules designed and discussed earlier. From the usability point of view, students' feedback should also be collected once they have finished using it. Issues such as user factors, task factors and system functionality should be identified and made known once students have completed the activities in the modules.

To gauge whether this desktop VR method really help students to learn poetry, experiments will be conducted. Experiments can be done by comparing the dimension aspects of the visuals used in conveying the poetry instructions. Since VR technology is still new in Malaysian schools, students' perceptions should also be analysed. This can be done by seeking their responses on how they can accept desktop VR as part of their learning tools in learning poems. Gender aspect of students' acceptance towards VR technology should also be conducted because it is assumed that most male students are very keen and familiar with 3D game technology. It would then be interesting to study how female students would fair in this aspect, although indications have shown that it would have a positive effect too. Thus, the authors' are of the opinion that by implementing interactive virtual worlds into learning poetry which have a combination of perceptual effects, the tendencies are strong that it would motivate students' (both genders) better understanding of poetry.

6 Conclusion

In conclusion, this paper presents the I3DP scaffolding framework which becomes the basis of adopting VR technology into the environment of learning poetry. By implementing a simple set up of VR system such as desktop VR, students can spend time individually at their own pace, instilling interest in learning poetry. With the power of interactivity and dynamic visuals of VR, students can more actively engage in learning activities, compared to the same type of activity conducted in a conventional classroom. As far as learning poetry is concerned, engagement plays an important role since learning will be more effective if they are allowed to be responsible for and are in control of their own learning.

It is the authors' hope that by adopting and implementing desktop VR as an alternative method in learning poetry in Secondary Schools, will be the beginning of an innovation to improve the learning of poetry and English language in Malaysian schools generally.

Acknowledgement. The authors acknowledge Universiti Kebangsaan Malaysia and Ministry of Higher Education (MOHE) for the Arus Perdana grant (UKM-AP-ICT-16-2009). The authors would also like to acknowledge Puan Nurul Huda of Sekolah Menengah Seksyen 9, Shah Alam for helping to demonstrate her poetry lesson plan which become the basis of the study.

References

1. Towndrow, P.A., Vallance, M.: Using IT in the Language Classroom, Longman, Singapore (2004)
2. Moshell, J.M., Hughes, C.E.: Virtual Environment As a Tool for Academic Learning. In: Handbook of Virtual Environments: Design, Implementation, and Applications. Lawrence Erlbaum Associates, New Jersey (2002)
3. Weller, H.G.: Assessing The Impact of Computer-based Learning on Science. Journal of Research in Computing in Education 28(4), 461–485 (1996)
4. Burdea, G.C., Coiffet, P.: Virtual Reality Technology, 2nd edn. John Wiley Hobeken, New Jersey (2003)
5. Stanney, K.M., Zyda, M.: Virtual Environments in the 21st Century. In: Handbook of Virtual Environments: Design, Implementation, and Applications. Lawrence Erlbaum Associates, New Jersey (2002)
6. Chaoshun, W.: Application of Virtual Reality Technology in Environment Art Design Teaching, pp. 1012–1014. IEEE Xplore (2010)
7. Daghestani, L., Ward, R.D., Xu, Z., Al-Nuaim, H.: The Design, Development and Evaluation of Virtual Reality Learning Environment for Numeracy Concepts Using 3D Virtual Manipulatives. In: Fifth International Conference on Computer Graphics, Imaging and Visualization, pp. 93–100. IEEE Xplore (2008)

8. Codella, C.R., Jalili, L., Koved, L.J.: A Toolkit for Developing Multi-User, Distributed Virtual Environments. In: IEEE Virtual Reality Annual International Symposium, Seattle, pp. 401–407 (1993)
9. Tait, A.: Desktop Virtual Reality. In: IEE Colloquium on Using Virtual Worlds. IEEE Xplore (2002)
10. Ibrahim, S.: Literature in English for Lower Secondry Schools. Selected Poems and Short Stories Form 1. In: Kementerian Pendidikan Malaysia & Dewan Bahasa dan Pustaka, Pustaka. Ampang Press, Kuala Lumpur (2003)
11. Wan, M.O.: Experiential Learning: An alternative approach to teach poetry in a training room. English Language Journal 3, 57–66 (2009)
12. Nazrul, A.M.S.: Multimedia Courseware (3DIPoem) for Form One English Language Instruction: An Interactive 3D Approach Based on Scaffolding Technique. In: FTSM, UKM, Graduate Seminar 2007: Innovative Research in Multimedia System Towards Globalization, Hotel Palm Garden, Putrajaya (2007)
13. Huzaina, A.H.: Student's Preferences in Learning Literature Component of the Malaysian Secondary School English Language Syllabus. Jurnal Pendidikan, 141–155 (2006)
14. Iasevoli, D.: Nobody Knew Where I Was and Now I am No Longer There: Two Case Studies of Aesthetic and Ambiguity in Reading Poetry. PhD Thesis. Columbia University, USA (2002)
15. Allie, A.: A Constructivist Approach to Analyzing Figurative Language in Poetry by Drawing and Mapping (2003), http://www.chatham.edu/pti/curriculum/units/2003/Allie.pdf
16. Huda, N.: An Interview. Sekolah Menengah Seksyen 9, Shah Alam (2006)
17. Kelly, A.: Poetry? Of course we do it. In: It's in the National Curriculum: Primary Children's Perceptions of Poetry. Literacy, pp. 129–134 (2005)
18. Kovalcik, B., Certo, J.L.: The Poetry Café Is Open! Teaching Literary Devices of Sound in Poetry Writing. The Reading Teacher 61(1), 89–93 (2007)
19. Mager, R.F.: Making Instruction Work or Skillbloomers. Golden Books Centre, Kuala Lumpur (1995)
20. Lenz, L.: Crossroads of literacy and orality: Reading Poetry Aloud. Language Arts 69, 597–603 (1992)
21. Tarleton, R.: Children's Thinking and Poetry. English in Education 17(3), 36–46 (1983)
22. Fleming, M.: Pupils' Perceptions of the Nature of Poetry. Cambridge Journal of Education 22(1), 31–41 (1992)
23. Woolfolk, A.E.: Educational Psychology, 7th edn., Allyn and Bacon, USA (1998)
24. Indrakaran, Y.S.: 1001 Nota & Soalan Bahasa Inggeris Sukatan Pelajaran KBSM Baru. Pustaka Sistem Pelajaran, Kuala Lumpur (2003)
25. Kucan, L.: "I" poems: Invitations for Students to Deepen Literary Understanding. International Reading Association 60, 518–524 (2007)
26. Zarnowski, M.: Learning About Biographies: A Reading and Writing for Children. National Councils of Teachers of English and National Councils for Social Studies, Illinois (1990)
27. Sekeres, D.C., Gregg, M.: Poetry in third grade: Getting Started. International Reading Association 60, 466–474 (2007)
28. Westerhof, P.: Teaching Poetry in Secondary English Classroom. Master Thesis. University of Toronto, Canada (2004)
29. Yin, Y.F., Whatt, T.C.: Let's Explore: Literature Component Made Simple. Selected Poems and Short Stories. Setia Emas, Petaling Jaya (2006)
30. Morais, C., Kay, G.: Light on Lit Form 1. Selected Poems and Short Stories. Pearson Longman, Kuala Lumpur (2009)

Augmented Reality Remedial Worksheet for Negative Numbers: Subtraction Operation

Elango Periasamy and Halimah Badioze Zaman

Institute of Visual Informatics, Universiti Kebangsaan Malaysia, Bangi, Selangor
{surensutha,hbzukm}@yahoo.com

Abstract. Augmented Reality Remedial Worksheet for Negative Numbers Subtraction Operation (AR^2WN^2) is a negative numbers subtraction operation worksheet involving two integers for students that need help in subject domain. AR^2WN^2 provides visualization of correct thinking process for remedial students of negative numbers subtraction operation with a useful meta-cognitive learning tool that helps them to follow, analyse and construct it as their own thinking via an algorithm. AR^2WN^2 include explanatory texts that support the algorithm which is animated step-by-step through the visualization of correct thinking process. Thus, this paper introduces a suite of visualizations spanning an algorithm for negative numbers subtraction operation, offering to stimulate discussion and debate on the pedagogical merits of this technique.

Keywords: Visual informatics, Augmented Reality, Negative Numbers, Visualization, Subtraction, Remedial.

1 Introduction

Augmented Reality (AR) technology is not new, it's potential in education is just beginning to be explored and unlike other computing technologies, AR interfaces offer seamless interaction between the real and virtual world, a tangible interface metaphor and a means for transitioning between real and virtual worlds and urges that educators should work with researchers in the field to explore how these characteristics can best be applied in a school environment [1]. The range of AR interfaces are as traditional approach (AR as information browser), spatial (3D AR interfaces), augmented surfaces and tangible interfaces, tangible AR interfaces or transitional AR interfaces [2]. Furthermore, he asserted that AR Reality is preferred for co-located collaboration, tangible object interaction or enhanced interaction in the real world [1].

As AR is a newly emerging technology by which the user's view of the real world is augmented with additional information from a computer model [3]. It means that the user can see the real world around him, with computer graphics superimposed or composite with the real world and instead of replacing the real world, we supplement it and ideally, it would seem to the user that the real and virtual objects coexisted [4] and the information is presented three-dimensionally integrated into the real world

H. Badioze Zaman et al. (Eds.): IVIC 2011, Part II, LNCS 7067, pp. 242–252, 2011.
© Springer-Verlag Berlin Heidelberg 2011

[4];[3], which can be either in 2D images or 3D objects [4];[5]. Nevertheless, research in this area of AR is still maturing, with few papers available on AR in education [1];[6].

According to [7], the Lower Secondary Examination (PMR) report from the Malaysian examination Board shows that students were unable to master the skills and understanding the abstract concepts that involves negative number operation in fraction, transformation and algebra. Moreover, in the 2002 PMR examination, 47% showed clear weaknesses in operation involving negative number such as (-17+14), (-17+22+8), (-17-14) and (-17+30) [8]. Such that, a study with 124 students aged 14 year from two secondary schools in Malaysia was carried out by [9] which revealed the existence of difficulties in solving negative numbers subtraction operation involving two integers. Such phenomenon is explained by [10] as situations whereby negative numbers extend our number line and greatly simplify our calculations, but sometimes students struggle with the concepts. Nevertheless, according to [11] it is also important for students to determine what things are as well as what they are not, if we are to help them avoid arising at incorrect assumptions, conclusions, thought processes and generalization.

A review of literature showed that teachers were very creative and innovative in teaching the concept of subtraction and addition operation involving negative numbers by integrating various communication tools such as line graph, coloured stones, coloured chips, gain-owe techniques and computer courseware in their effort to help students acquire the knowledge of solving negative numbers subtraction and addition operation. These efforts shows that the commitment and creativeness of teachers that should be acknowledged as an ongoing process that are continuously evolving in searching ways and mean to help students to acquire knowledge related to subtraction and addition operation in negative numbers. Thus, to help students avoid arising at incorrect assumption, conclusions, thought process and generalizations which are also important for them to determine what things are as well as what they are not [11]. Moreover, a study conducted by [9];[12] indicated that the need for students to recall basic negative number subtraction operation skills from what they have learnt from their Mathematics teachers in classroom were essential for further study because even though some students' memory have its potential which can be sufficient for capturing and allowing access to salient information and important details taught by Mathematics teachers but study shows that the mathematics classroom learning environment is such that students need to combine their visual, auditory and writing capability and use them simultaneously and non repeatable which created misconception among others.

Therefore, this study was narrowing the gap in school remedial learning environment by introducing an AR^2WN^2 subtraction operation involving single and double digit integers. AR^2WN^2 is a useful learning accompaniment in negative numbers subtraction operation by constructing animations or visualizations of correct thinking process (CTP) via an algorithm which is named as an algorithm visualization of correct thinking process (AVCTP) which is created based on the meta-cognitive study carried out by [9];[12];[13] which actually predicts on how an expert thinking process when confronted with such sentence questions. The process of solving through this algorithm is common and always done in experts' minds is an actual fact.

In conjunction, the actual purpose was to illustrate in a way impossible in the print medium, including the classroom blackboard, the operation of this AVCTP. Rather than considering many problems from negative numbers subtraction operation, we have attempted to develop visualization for one algorithm for just one problem in subject domain. The process of remedial uses a special remedial worksheet, adobe flash player 10 and a camera. Here, the users are still experiencing the physical worksheet, so believability is achieved. Then by adding simple graphical animation of CTP on to the worksheet creates a better user experience as a help guide while the users are still seeing a familiar worksheet. Thus, it is the replacement of the user's physical reality particularly that which is experienced through sight and it is repeatable. This paper introduced here a suite of visualizations spanning an algorithm for negative numbers subtraction operation, offering thereby to stimulate discussion and debate on the pedagogical merits of this technique for remedial purposes.

2 Related Works

According to [5], AR has a wide variety of uses, as it can clearly demonstrate spatial concepts, temporal concepts and contextual relationships between both real and virtual objects. They further asserted that the factors that make AR a powerful educational powerful tool is the main advantage of using virtual objects is that they can be animated, respond to the users actions and are not constrained by the costs and practical or physical limitations of real objects which includes 2D images, 3D objects, animated 2D images (i.e. videos), animated 3D objects and sound (both background sound and narration) virtual media in their BlackMagic Book projects. Furthermore it was interesting to note that with their BlackMagic Book they observed that many users made no attempt to read the text on the left of each page.

According to [14] in their research titled "Lessons from AR Book Study" observed children reading an augmented book aimed at early literacy education. They explored how children aged six to seven experiences and interact with these novel instructional media. They focused on issues arising from the tangibility of interface elements, the integration of physical and digital elements, on-screen and paper elements, and of text and interactive sequences. With an interactive book, a range of factors contribute to the user experience: the story itself, the visuals, the interactive sequences and how the user interacts with these, how 3D elements, interactive sequences and traditional text relate to each other, and the handling of the overall augmented book. Nevertheless, the children repeatedly had issues navigating from page to page and sequence to sequence, especially when switching between text pages (on the computer screen and navigated by mouse) and interactive sequences (physical pages, sometimes in sequence). Although most did learn how to handle this, it required close assistance in the beginning and there were episodes of insecurity of how to go on. Children often attempted to use the wrong button or continued to flip physical pages waiting for something to happen. Added complexity was created by sometimes having two buttons for 'next' and 'close window' to start interactive sequences. They recommend keeping navigation as simple, explicit and consistent as possible. An on-screen button might simply say 'next' and *always* continue to whatever is the next logical element (if linear sequence). Added complexity is introduced by different navigation styles when on screen and paper. Making use of the AR technology, this could be simplified by providing a paper sheet for each screen page and flipping pages (showing markers) telling the system to move on, using the book metaphor for navigating through the story. In this case, the creators of the stories deemed pattern recognition to be too unreliable in uncontrolled lighting conditions, running the risk of the system jumping to the wrong page or starting a scene all over again. Careful consideration should furthermore be given to visibility of instructions and additional visual cues when the book is distributed across screen and paper. Children that looked to the screen often did not notice additional cues on the paper pages (e.g. 'hot spots' for putting the paddle). Thus, according to them navigation turned out to be an important issue when combining paper and on-screen elements, in particular if these are not integrated in one visual area and deploy tangible *and* desktop-based input devices.

According to [15], *'constructionism'* is based on constructivism and promotes that learning takes place when students can construct things. Sometimes students have problems understanding the physical concepts of mechanics. It might be that physics in the traditional sense is sometimes taught in an abstract, jejune way and is therefore not very motivating for students. The result is that theoretical models behind physical phenomena are often misunderstood. It is not necessary to stress that conveying these concepts correctly is of utmost importance since they are fundamental to physics. Many theoretical models are based on Newton's laws of motion. Therefore the authors developed an educational AR application called PhysicsPlayground [16] that is supposed to support students in studying and finally understanding the concepts of mechanics. In this three-dimensional virtual environment learners and educators are able to freely create physical experiments that can be simulated in real time. They considered the analyzing functionality an important strength of a virtual laboratory like PhysicsPlayground. It offers possibilities that are far superior to what can be done in a real physics lab. A direct connection between simulated reality and physical data is supposed to help students grasp the theoretical basics of mechanics. To establish a direct link to students pre-knowledge, physical data that can be acquired through the application is presented in a way so that it closely relates to formulas and equations of school mechanics.

Construct3D [17] is a three dimensional dynamic geometry construction tool that can be used in high school and university education. It uses augmented reality to provide a natural setting for face-to-face collaboration of teachers and students. The main advantage of using VR and AR is that students actually see three dimensional objects which they until now had to calculate and construct with traditional (mostly pen and paper) methods. Furthermore, by working directly in 3D space, complex spatial problems and spatial relationships may be comprehended better and faster than with traditional methods. Three usability studies with more than 100 students have been conducted since 2000 [18] and guidelines have been formulated regarding how to design AR applications for geometry education [19]. Anecdotal evidence supports their claim that Construct3D combines four research areas: geometry, pedagogy, psychology and augmented reality is easy to learn, encourages experimentation with geometric constructions, and improves spatial skills [17]. Although usability of Construct3D is high and teachers as well as students are highly motivated to use the application, practical usage in schools is hindered by hardware costs, support of a low number of users and technical complexity of the whole setup (requiring dedicated personnel for maintenance).

According to [2], designing AR system is equivalent to interface design which uses different input and output technologies as in fig 1. The important aspects in designing AR Interfaces are i) goal that makes the computer invisible and enhance the user experience (Augmentation is a tool not the final goal) ii) objective is a high quality of user experience in terms of appropriateness to tasks and applications, ease of use, iii) learning of interface and performance and satisfaction and iv) usability evaluation necessary to measure quality of experience [2]. Therefore, in designing an AR system, the needs to consider various aspects such as its navigational aspect, interface aspect, pedagogical aspect and content aspect and how it would compliment each other in achieving our goal is important.

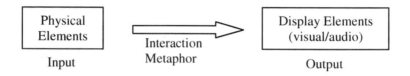

Fig. 1. AR Design Principles: Interaction Components [2]

3   Methodology

An early analysis of this research revealed how teachers' conduct the remedial in a school setting are as follows: i) Worksheets distributed, ii) Students asked to complete the task, iii) hand over to teacher when completed task and iv). Teachers' checks and explains their mistakes or misconception with a step by step solution. Nevertheless, as impressive as it may appear, further instigation revealed that the first three steps were done but the fourth step was done in manner that did not addressed specifically to each students' misconception which could vary tremendously. Furthermore, according to those teachers, in Malaysia school setting is a fact that student teacher ratio did not permit one to one remedial process which would be the best way in identifying and rectifying misconception of remedial students. This is an ongoing research which is based on the five stages of optimal learning, introduced by [20] as follows:

i.   Preparation - Provides a framework for the new learning and primes the learner s' brain with possible connections. The more background learners have in the subject, the faster they will absorb and process the new information.

ii. Acquisition - is achieved through either direct means (eg providing handouts) or indirect means (eg putting up related visuals). Both approaches can work, and they complement each other. Acquisition stage involves making connections that is, getting neurons to "talk" to one another. The sources for acquisition are endless. They may include discussion, lecture, visual tools, environmental stimuli, hands on experiences, role modelling, reading, manipulative, videos, reflection, group project and pair share activities. But remember that this first step of making a connection is highly dependent on prior knowledge.

iii. Elaboration - Explores the interconnectedness of topics and encourages depth of understanding. An enormous gap exists between what a teacher explains and what learners understand. To reduce this gap, teachers need to engage students' deeper understanding and feedback with implicit and explicit learning strategies. Nevertheless, if you do not know what students do not understand, how can you elaborate effectively? Making corrections as we go along is a critical approach for teaching with the brain in mind. Once a learner is lost and the brain somehow switches off. Experiences brain based instructors adjust their course before this happens. In the elaboration process, students learn to review and evaluate their own and others' work and receive constructive feedback in a productive way. This is the step that ensures learners are not merely regurgitating rote facts but are developing complex neural pathways that connect subjects in meaningful ways. This stage is a precursor of remembering.

iv. Memory Formation - Cements the learning so that what was learned on Monday is retrievable on Tuesday.

v. Functional Integration - reminds us to use the new learning so that it is further reinforced and expanded upon.

This study is about the second and the third stages which are the acquisition and elaboration stage whereby it happens after incorporating the preparation strategies. Nevertheless, in this study, even if the process of manually conducting remedial learning environment as stipulate about is applicable but the cost and time needed to recruit a remedial teacher to monitor each student personally is practically impossible to be implemented. The acquisition stage involves making connections that is, getting neurons to "talk" to one another and the sources for acquisition are endless [20]. Furthermore, they may include discussion, lecture, visual tools, environmental stimuli, hands on experiences, role modelling, reading, manipulative, videos, reflection, group project and pair share activities but remember that this first step of making a connection is highly dependent on prior knowledge [20]. Acquisition aspect of AR^2WN^2 was achieved through both direct means (remedial worksheet) and indirect means by putting up related visuals (simulation of CTP). Both approaches are integrated and they complement each other. In the elaboration process, students learn to review and evaluate their own and others' work and receive constructive feedback in a productive ways and this is the step that ensures learners are not merely regurgitating rote facts but are developing complex neural pathways that connect subjects in meaningful ways which is a precursor of remembering [20]. The elaboration aspect of AR^2WN^2 is achieved through how remedial students explore the interconnectedness of type A, B, C and D which encourages depth of understanding. Therefore, in developing this remedial software, the main aspect was to eliminate stress onto the meta-cognitive strategy of remedial student so as to give an awareness and control over their thinking process so that a new memory is formed and discover the depth of their learning, thus the following questions are addressed:

i.   How to achieve the direct and indirect means of acquisition aspect?

ii. How to achieve the elaboration aspect?

4 Finding

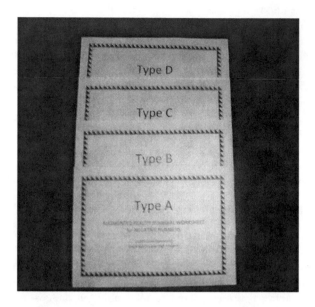

Fig. 2. AR Activity Worksheets

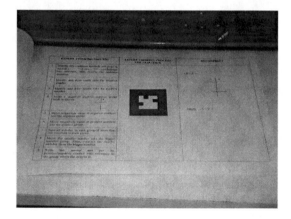

Fig. 3. Example of Worksheet B

Commonly, the experiment requests remedial student to manipulate typical computer documents and applications being projected onto an ordinary worksheet. Figure 2 consists of four types of remedial worksheet (A, B, C and D). Worksheet A consists of questions regarding "Subtraction Operation Involving Two Positive Integers". Worksheet B consists of questions regarding "Subtraction Operation Involving Negative Integer with Positive Integer". Worksheet C consists of questions regarding

"Subtraction Operation Involving Positive Integer with Negative Integer". Meanwhile, Worksheet D consists of questions regarding "Subtraction Operation Involving Two Negative Integers".

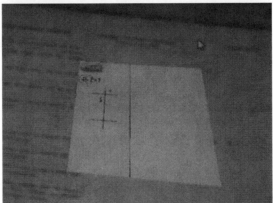

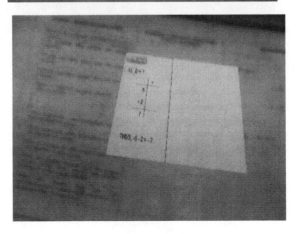

Fig. 4. AR Animation of CTP

Figure 3 shows an example of question in worksheet B. The layout of the worksheet is such that it is divided into three columns. The first column consists of the 9 steps of CTP needed in solving subtraction operation involving two integers. The second column consists of a marker which would show step by step solution simulated when a camera is pointed onto it as shown in Figure 4 based on the 9 steps listed. Then, the third column consists of partial of the CTP for remedial student to fill in by writing which would promote constructivism by writing aspect. Thus, giving remedial students two choices that are to learn from verbalized technique as in first column or/and when the remedial students struggle, they can watch the simulated answer from the marker to help guide them to adapt the CTP. These aspects are the same for all the rest of the worksheet. Meanwhile, figure 4, shows three pictures of how the simulated answers are augmented on a worksheet. In conjunction, the process of how remedial activity is conducted as mentioned would constitute the acquisition aspect of AR^2WN^2. Meanwhile, how remedial students explore the inter and intra connectedness of questions in worksheet A, B, C and D would encourages depth of understanding which constitute the elaboration aspect of AR^2WN^2.

5   Discussions

This research is to create a remedial worksheet that integrates digital help which takes place in a real environment. Such combination of physical object and digital help can only be achieved through an AR technique which would be a new technology in the remedial process of Mathematics. According to [21] the extensive development of new technologies has marked influence on education by facilitating the design of new learning and teaching material that can improve the attitude of learners towards mathematics and the plausibility of advanced interactive personalized learning process. AR has considerable educational potential because it can assist in letting a student explore the information at their own pace (helping construct a knowledge framework) and can also enable critical analysis to assist in challenging this framework [5]. Basically, applications of this technology use the virtual objects to aid the user's understanding of his environment [4] by manipulating and examining real objects and simultaneously receive additional information about them or the task at hand [5]. Nevertheless, fundamentally, AR is about augmentation of human perception in supplying information not ordinarily detectable by human senses [4]. With AR^2WN^2, a range of factors contribute to the user experience: the content itself, the visuals, the interactive sequences and how the user interacts with these, how 2D elements, interactive sequences and traditional text relate to each other, and the handling of the overall augmented digital help onto a remedial worksheet. Furthermore, it would be interesting to investigate further into the usability of this AR^2WN^2 the following features:

i.   No attempt to Read the Text: According to [5], it was interesting to note that with their BlackMagic Book they observed that many users made no attempt to read the text on the left of each page.
ii. Tangible Elements: According to [14], they focused on issues arising from the tangibility of interface elements, the integration of physical and digital elements, on-screen and paper elements, and of text and interactive sequences.

iii. Construct Things: According to [15], '*constructionism*' is based on constructivism and promotes that learning takes place when students can construct things. Sometimes students have problems understanding the physical concepts of mechanics. It might be that physics in the traditional sense is sometimes taught in abstract, jejune way and therefore not very motivating for students.

iv. Far superior to what can be done in real settings: According to [15], it offers possibilities that are far superior to what can be done in a real physics lab. A direct connection between simulated reality and physical data is supposed to help students grasp the theoretical basics of mechanics. To establish a direct link to students pre-knowledge, physical data that can be acquired through the application is presented in a way so that it closely relates to formulas and equations of school mechanics.

v. Methods: The main advantage of using VR and AR are that students actually see three dimensional objects which they until now had to calculate and construct with traditional (mostly pen and paper) methods [17].

6 Conclusions

This study was about augmentation of remedial students' perception by supplying meta-cognitive analysing and synthesizing process in solving negative numbers subtraction operation involving two integers. The AR^2WN^2 described in this study was performed in the context of an application that aims to use AR techniques in a negative numbers subtraction operation remedial worksheet environment and tried to avoid create a new interaction paradigm that require a lot of learning from users. Thus, simplicity was the key element we considered during the development process which combines navigation aspect, pedagogy aspect, interface aspect and content aspect as a whole.

7 Future Works

According to [2], the usability evaluation is necessary to measure quality of experience. To investigate further into the usability of AR^2WN^2 in real setting with Mathematics teachers and remedial student in a secondary school in Malaysia will be interesting as well as challenging.

References

1. Billinghurst, M.: Augmented Reality in Education, New Horizons for Learning (2002), http://www.newhorizons.org/strategies/technology/billinghurst.htm (January 20, 2009)
2. Billinghurst, M., Grasset, R., Looser, J.: Designing augmented reality interfaces. SIGGRAPH Comput. Graph 39(1), 17–22 (2005)
3. Bauer, M.: AR Forum - Discussion on Augmented and Virtual Reality Technology: What is augmented reality? Retrieved From (2006), http://campar.in.tum.de/ARForum/AugmentedReality (September 27, 2008)

4. Azuma Ronald, T.: NSF/ARPA Science and Technology Centre for Computer Graphics and Scientific Visualization: Registration Errors in Augmented Reality. Retrieved From (1995), http://www.cs.unc.edu/~azuma/azuma_AR.html (September 27, 2008)
5. Woods, E., Billinghurst, M., Looser, J., Aldridge, G., Brown, D., Garrie, B., Nelles, C.: Augmenting the science centre and museum experience. In: Spencer, S.N. (ed.) Proceedings of the 2nd International Conference on Computer Graphics and Interactive Techniques in Australasia and South East Asia, GRAPHITE 2004, Singapore, June 15-18, pp. 230–236. ACM, New York (2004)
6. Kaufmann, H., Schmalstieg, D.: Mathematics and geometry education with collaborative augmented reality. In: ACM SIGGRAPH 2002 Conference Abstracts and Applications, SIGGRAPH 2002, San Antonio, Texas, July 21-26, pp. 37–41. ACM, New York (2002)
7. Lembaga Peperiksaan Malaysia, Laporan Prestasi PMR. Kementerian Pendidikan Malaysia, Kuala Lumpur (1993)
8. Lembaga Peperiksaan Malaysia, Laporan Prestasi PMR. Kementerian Pendidikan Malaysia, Kuala Lumpur (2002)
9. Periasamy, E., Badioze Zaman, H.: Augmented Reality as a Remedial Paradigm for Negative Numbers: Content Aspect. In: Badioze Zaman, H., Robinson, P., Petrou, M., Olivier, P., Schröder, H., Shih, T.K. (eds.) IVIC 2009. LNCS, vol. 5857, pp. 371–381. Springer, Heidelberg (2009)
10. Naylor, M.: Integrating Math in Your Classroom. Accentuate the Negative. Teaching Pre K-8. ERIC 36(4), 34–35 (2006)
11. Brumbaugh, K.D., Rock, D.: Teaching secondary Mathematics, 3rd edn. Lawrence Erlbaum Associates, New Jersey (2006)
12. Periasamy, E., Badioze Zaman, H.: Predict Incorrect Thinking Process: Negative Numbers Subtraction Operation Second Category. International Journal on Advanced Science, Engineering and Information Technology 1(2), 145–149 (2011)
13. Periasamy, E., Badioze Zaman, H.: Augmented Reality Remedial Paradigm for Negative Numbers: AVCTP. In: Mohamad Zain, J., Wan Mohd, W.M.b., El-Qawasmeh, E. (eds.) ICSECS 2011, Part IV. CCIS, vol. 179, pp. 188–198. Springer, Heidelberg (2011)
14. Dunser, A., Hornecker, E.: Lessons from an Ar Book Study. In: Proceedings of the 1st International Conference on Tangible and Embedded Interaction. ACM, Baton Rouge (2007)
15. Kaufmann, H., Meyer, B.: Simulating Educational Physical Experiments in Augmented Reality. In: ACM SIGGRAPH ASIA 2008 Educators Programme. ACM, Singapore (2008)
16. Meyer, B.: Physics Education in the Field of Mechanics with Virtual Reality. Master's thesis, University of Applied Sciences Deggendorf and Vienna University of Technology (2007)
17. Kaufmann, H., Schmalstieg, D.: Mathematics and geometry education with collaborative augmented reality. Computers & Graphics 27(3), 339–345 (2003)
18. Kaufmann, H., Dünser, A.: Summary of usability evaluations of an educational augmented reality application. In: Shumaker, R. (ed.) HCII 2007 and ICVR 2007. LNCS, vol. 4563, pp. 660–669. Springer, Heidelberg (2007)
19. Kaufmann, H., Schmalstieg, D.: Designing immersive virtual reality for geometry education. Proceedings of IEEE Virtual Reality Conference 2006, 51–58 (2006)
20. Jensen, E.: Brain-Based Learning: The New Paradigm of Teaching, 2nd edn. Corwin Press, California (2008)
21. Badioze Zaman, H., Bakar, N., Ahmad, A., Sulaiman, R., Arshad, H., Mohd. Yatim, N.F.: Virtual Visualisation Laboratory for Science and Mathematics Content (Vlab-SMC) with Special Reference to Teaching and Learning of Chemistry. In: Badioze Zaman, H., Robinson, P., Petrou, M., Olivier, P., Schröder, H., Shih, T.K. (eds.) IVIC 2009. LNCS, vol. 5857, pp. 356–370. Springer, Heidelberg (2009)

Developing Conceptual Model of Virtual Museum Environment Based on User Interaction Issues

Normala Rahim[1], Tengku Siti Meriam Tengku Wook[2], and Nor Azan Mat Zin[2]

[1] Faculty of Informatics (FIT), University of Sultan Zainal Abidin (UniSZA),
21300 Gong Badak, Terengganu, Malaysia
normalarahim@unisza.edu.my
[2] Faculty of Technology & Information Science (FTSM),
The National University of Malaysia (UKM), 43600 Bangi, Selangor, Malaysia
{tsm,azan}@ftsm.ukm.my

Abstract. This paper discusses the development of a conceptual model of Virtual Museum Environment (VME) using Image-based Model. The case study of this model is Terengganu Museum. In the early stage of the development, user needs were identified by observing the existing applications and collecting data through interviews and questionnaires. Virtual Reality Panoramic technique was found suitable to be implemented in this environment. The conceptual model can be used as a guideline in designing and evaluating virtual museum. To validate the conceptual model, factors such as easy to use, efficiency and satisfaction are used as the benchmark of the usability factor in virtual museum.

Keywords: Image-based model, VR Panoramic, User interaction, User-centered design, Visual Informatics.

1 Introduction

The important issue in this research is about the user interactions in a virtual museum using the Image-based Model. User interactions play an important role to enhance the sense of presence when users explore the Virtual Museum Environment (VME). The main purpose of this research is to develop a conceptual model of virtual museum by identifying the user requirements based on the element of user interactions and to determine the appropriate virtual reality techniques to be applied in this environment.

There were many virtual museums that had been developed either in or outside of Malaysia, but the emphasis on the user interactions element were still low, because of the development was not following the needs of the real users [1], [11], [15]. User interactions that consist of navigation elements, manipulation and control systems have been identified as suitable components to be incorporated in the conceptual model of virtual museum [8]. Navigation element was an exploration of the VME with features such as styles, techniques, spatial knowledge and features that helped users in exploring the environment more easily and efficiently. Manipulation was an element of interaction that could manipulate objects and consisted of a few classification metaphors and variables that affected the performance of a user. Control system which is also known as graphical interface design was crucial to attract users

H. Badioze Zaman et al. (Eds.): IVIC 2011, Part II, LNCS 7067, pp. 253–260, 2011.

to use the application. The interface design model developed by [6] was adapted in designing the interface of virtual museum. This model can be used as principles and guidelines to acquire the criteria that required by the users.

All of above issues are important to achieve a usable virtual museum that emphasizes on aspects of user requirements. Part 2 of this paper will discuss on the methods of conceptual model development.

2   Method in Development of Conceptual Model

Figure 1 show the method employed in the development of a virtual museum conceptual model of which takes into consideration the user interactions. The two phases involved are:

a)   **Initial Investigation:** preliminary study is done based on existing applications of virtual museum to identify research problems.
b)   **Data Collection:** the collection of data is done through interviews and questionnaires to acquire the users requirement and the suitable application.

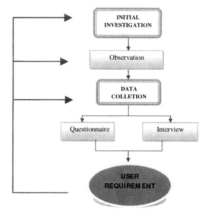

Fig. 1. Method of Conceptual Model Development

The method involves using iterative user-centered design to meet the needs of real users.

2.1   Initial Investigation

The observations of existing applications are carried out in initial investigation to determine the research problems.

2.1.1   Observation

The researchers had conducted observation by doing comparisons on existing virtual museums. Four virtual museums either in or outside of Malaysia were selected. Two of them were Sarawak Virtual Museum and Malacca Virtual Museum. The other two were Virtual Museum NMAI and The Virtual Smithsonian. According to [3], Virtual

Museum Sarawak focuses on the exploration of the panoramic while Virtual Museum Melaka was based on full immersion environment. NMAI and The Virtual Smithsonian were the best examples of Virtual Museum that used Image-based Model [5]. Although they were the best, a few problems regarding interaction still exist, such as lack of interface design that had aesthetic values and the interface design that had no functions on artifacts manipulation.

The user interactions in virtual museum were still at a low level [6], [11]. In addition, there are still problems in interface design of virtual museum [11], [15], [15] stated that the presentation of the exhibition by the museum institution is still not steady enough and lack of acceptance from the users. Moreover the research on usability of virtual museum still lacks seriousness [3].

The issues regarding the low levels of ICT utilization by museum institution brought challenges especially on improving the quality of museum services in delivering accurate information in a way that is more interesting [4]. In his research, [7] stated that 74.1% of museum visitors wanted to see an exhibition that has interactive concepts, however reality many museums still retained the traditional concept in presenting their exhibitions. So, a virtual museum can be an alternative to convey information and to provide real experience as in the real locations to interact through virtual environments [1], [2], [3].

2.1.2   Analysis and Findings

Table 1 shows the problem statements identified through observation technique.

Table 1. Problem statement of research

VIRTUAL MUSEUM	INITIAL INVESTIGATION	PROBLEM STATEMENTS
Sarawak	1. Limited user interactions 2. User could not manipulate artifact 3. Quality of images were low 4. Lack of information	1. User interactions are not incorporated in the virtual museum. 2. No guidelines in designing the interface of virtual museum.
Malacca	1. User cannot interact with environment 2. Only showing environment (full immersion) 3. Quality of images were low 4. No user interactions 5. Lack of information 6. User could not manipulate artifact	3. The assessment of usability in virtual museum is not done in serious manner.
NMAI	1. Lack of interface design that had aesthetic values. 2. Small display of information	
The Virtual Smithsonian	1. User could not manipulate artifact in 360^0, only showed still image	

As shown in Table 1, the development of existing virtual museum is not based on the user requirements such as element of user interactions, graphical interface design and usability of virtual museum. From the problem statements that have been formulated, the researchers have determined the need of the users through data collection such as interviews and questionnaires.

2.2   Data Collection

In the data collection phase, the questionnaires technique is used to obtain the need of the users in developing virtual museum. The questionnaire used Likert scale of 1-5. Items were modified QUIS instrument [10]. In addition, interviews were also carried out with the museum officers in the case study.

2.2.1   Questionnaire

The instrument was administered online and 12 actual users who were randomly selected completed the questionnaire. The respondents provided the feedbacks based on existing applications online. They were given instructions to access the virtual museum of Sarawak and Malacca and then answered the questionnaire based on their browsing experience on both virtual museums. This questionnaire consisted of four parts, the respondent demographics, navigation, manipulation and graphical interface design.

2.2.2   Interview

The interview session was conducted with Information Technology Officer and Assistant Curator of Communication and Marketing Department at Museum Terengganu with work experiences of 5 to 12 years. The findings from the interview are the requirements content of virtual museum which are Fishing Gallery, Craft Gallery and Islamic Gallery. These where organized as modules and should be made the icons of Museum Terengganu that need to be presented to the public.

2.2.3   Analysis and Finding

Figure 2 shows the findings of user requirement through questionnaire technique.

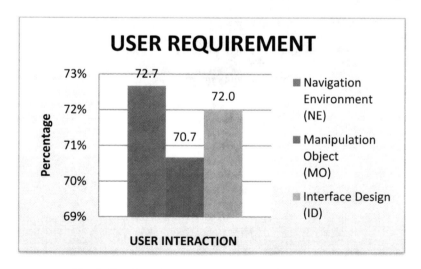

Fig. 2. User Requirement in Developing Virtual Museum

The figure shows that the navigation element consist of 73% of total requirement. Then the interface design element of 72% while manipulation element of 71%. The findings of this study concur with that of [8] which found that the elements of user interaction are needed in developing virtual museum.

3   Application Technique

The appropriate application techniques are determined through the literature reviews and are to be coordinated with the need of the users. Virtual Reality Panoramic (VRP) is a technique categorized as Image-based Model in virtual reality technology [1], [9], [12], [13], [14]. VRP represent a virtual reality system because it could help users to interact and to enhance their feeling as in a real environment [2]. This technique can show a virtual environment that allows users to see the environment and objects in 360 degrees either from left to right or from top to bottom. VRP consists of four types; horizontal, cylinder, cube and sphere [16]. Cylinder Panoramic is produced by using wide-angle lens that is taken as single-row. VRP is the result of a combination of several images [2]. To get the combination of panoramic images, stitching process is done. The process is carried out by incorporating multiple images with overlapping fields of view (FOV) either vertically or horizontally [1], [2].

The process of image stitching is also known as a process that combines a collection of small FOV images to produce panoramic images with larger FOV. A large FOV is required to obtain the virtual reality panoramic because a very large view can be produced and it can let the users to feel like they are in real environment. So, it is necessary to ensure a high level of reality when users explore the virtual environment [2]. The total percentages of FOV are between 20% to 50% [1]. However, according to Zakirah et al. (2002) the total percentages of overlapping FOV also depend on the VPR software used.

Virtual environment has two components, the environment and the object. The technique to produce the environment component is the inside-out views technique. The concept of this technique is that the designers need to stand in the middle and look around with the maximum or less than 360 degrees of display. Meanwhile for the object component, the outside-in views technique is used. In this technique, the camera will be placed outside the object in static position but the camera will be at in static rotating in 360 degrees around the object or the camera will be instatic position but the object will be rotating by using a turntable that can be rotated at 360 degrees [9].

3.1   Analysis and Finding

Virtual Reality Panoramic (VRP) technique has been identified as a technique that can be used in the development of Virtual Museum. VRP technique was determined to be used in the study because it can presents a real museum in the form of a virtual reality that allows users to interact in three dimensions. This technique requires only a source of original images that can reflect better the actual visualization of the museum. Implementation of these techniques can save time and costs. Thus, VRP techniques suitable for use in the study. Figure 3 shows the process of VRP technique in virtual museum development.

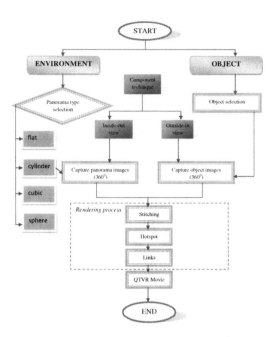

Fig. 3. Virtual Reality Panoramic (VRP) Technique

In this technique there are two components involved namely environment and object. In VME prototype, the environment component shows the panoramic in Museum Terengganu. Cylinder Panoramic has been selected in VME. The process of capturing image is realized by photographing objects in 360 degrees. The inside-out views technique is used to create the environment component. Then the object component can show the artifacts that can be found in the gallery and can be manipulated in 360 degrees. Image can be produced by capturing the image in 360 degrees. For this component, the outside-in views technique is used. When the images have been produced, the rendering process will be conducted to create QTVR movie. In this process, the images from the environment component and object component will be merged through stitching process. Thereafter, every movie will be included in hot spot according to the needs of each panoramic movie and object, and finally, every movie will be linked together by using node to form a complete panoramic movie.

4   Result

Results from this research are the development method and application technique used to formulated conceptual model of Virtual Museum Environment (VME) using Image-based Model. There are several advantages through the implementation of image-based model which is can provide a high quality of images and the rendering process is much faster than geometric based and hybrid based model. It is also can provide interactive panoramic environment with rich sense of presence. In addition, using this model can allow user to experience the situation as real. Furthermore, the use of image based model has a high-density of reality, multi access simplicity and low cost and compatibility.

This conceptual model is useful as a guideline to designing and evaluating virtual museum. The user interactions that which consist of navigation elements, manipulation and control systems are the main issues that contribute to usable application of virtual museum. The conceptual model was formulated based on results from three main activities namely initial investigation, data collection and technical specifications. Figure 4 shows the model which illustrated various components and their relationship;

- Virtual Reality Panoramic (VRP) technique; using cylinder panoramic is identified as a suitable technique in development of virtual museum.
- The inputs are environment component and object component.
- Every component uses different techniques; specifically inside-out views technique is used for environment and outside-in views technique for object.
- User interactions are the main component that should be applied in developing of virtual museum.
- The validation of the conceptual model; factors such as easy to use, efficiency and satisfaction are used as the benchmark of the usability factor in virtual museum.

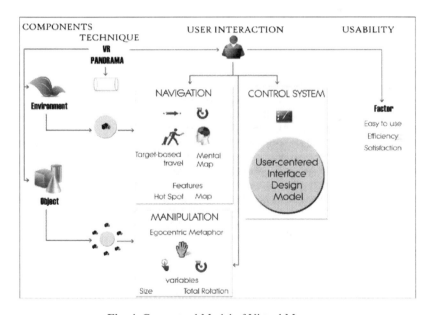

Fig. 4. Conceptual Model of Virtual Museum

5   Conclusion

This paper has discussed the development of conceptual model for virtual museum. The model consist of four main items; components, techniques, user interaction and usability. VRP technique using cylinder panoramic is used in the model. There are two main components which is environment that used inside-out view technique and the object component used outside-in view technique. Three elements of user interaction consist of easy to use, efficiency and satisfaction are used as the benchmark of the usability factor. Future related research will be the development of virtual museum based on this model and usability of the virtual museum prototype to validate the model.

References

1. Othman, Z., Yaakub, A.R., Zulkifli, A.N.: Virtual environment navigation using an image based approach. In: Student Conference on Research & Development Proceeding, Shah Alam, Malaysia (2002)
2. Wan Abd Arif, W.N., Wan Ahmad, W.F., Nordin, S.M., Abdullah, A., Sivapalan, S.: Designing 3 Dimensional Virtual Reality Using Panoramic Image. In: Badioze Zaman, H., Robinson, P., Petrou, M., Olivier, P., Schröder, H., Shih, T.K. (eds.) IVIC 2009. LNCS, vol. 5857, pp. 404–414. Springer, Heidelberg (2009)
3. Awang, N., Yaakub, A.R., Othman, Z.: Accessing user acceptance towards virtual museum: The case in Kedah State Museum. In: Sixth International Conference on Computer Graphics, Imaging & Visualization, Malaysia (2009)
4. Bakar, J.A.A, Kassim, P.S.J., Mahmud, M.: The level of information and communication technology use by museum in Malaysia (2010)
5. Jones, D., Christal, M.: The future of virtual museums: on-line, immersive, 3d environments (2002)
6. Yang, G.: A study on the user-centered interface design for virtual museum (2009)
7. Hertzun, M.: A review of museum websites: in search of user centered design. Archives & Museum Informatics: Cultural Heritage Information Quarterly 12(2), 127–138 (1998)
8. Bowman, D.A., Kruijff, E., Laviola Jr., J.J., Poupyrev, I.: An introduction to 3D user interface design. Presence 10(1), 96–108 (2001)
9. Fleishman, S., Chen, B., Kaufman, A., Cohen-Or., D.: Navigating through sparse views (1999)
10. Chin et al. Questionnaire for User Interface Satisfaction (1988), http://hcibib.org/perlman/question.cgi?form=QUIS
11. Kjeldskov, J.: Interaction in Virtual Reality: comparing use of full and partial immersive displays (2001)
12. Xiao, D.Y.: Experiencing the library in a panorama virtual reality environment. Library Hi Tech 18(2), 167–184 (2000)
13. Dorta, T.: Drafted Virtual Reality-A new paradigm to design with computers. In: Proceedings of the CAADRIA 2004 Conference, pp. 829–843 (2004)
14. Tzavidas, S., Katsaggelos, A.K.: A Multicamera Setup for Generating Stereo Panoramic Video. IEEE Transactions on Multimedia 7(5), 880–890 (2005)
15. Zara, J.: Virtual Reality and Cultural Heritage on the Web. In: From Proceedings of the 7th International Conference on Computer Graphics and Artificial Intelligence (3IA 2004), Limoges, France, pp. 101–112 (2004) ISBN 2-914256-06-X
16. Andrew, P.: 360^0 photography (2003)

Use of RSVP Techniques on Children's Digital Flashcards

Siti Zahidah Abdullah[1] and Nazlena Mohamad Ali[2]

[1] Faculty of Information Science and Technology,
University Kebangsaan Malaysia
[2] Institute of Visual Informatics,
University Kebangsaan Malaysia
ctz1986@gmail.com, nma@ftsm.ukm.my

Abstract. Rapid Serial Visual Presentation (RSVP) is an effective tool for image representation. We applied the RSVP technique for image representation in the context of flashcard learning for children 6-8 years old. An evaluation was carried out to investigate the acceptance of RSVP modes in digital flashcard learning for the children. Two groups of children have been tested; there are children from a normal class and another group from the LINUS program class. In the evaluation, *keyhole mode*, *shelf mode*, and *carousel mode* were used in representation flashcard learning to give a comparison between these three modes. The highest choice between these three modes of RSVP was found. The finding shows that children from the normal class prefer to choose the *carousel mode* and children from the LINUS program prefer to choose the *keyhole mode* as a representation technique in their digital flashcard learning. This experiment provides us an early insight into use of RSVP techniques in the digital flashcard context. Future work is to conduct an experiment for more samples of users and using this technique in relation to the flashcard learning context.

Keywords: Rapid Serial Visual Presentation (RSVP), flashcard learning, children preference, Visual Informatics.

1 Introduction

In recent years, researchers have explored the effectiveness and efficiency of techniques for imparting basic literacy skills to children with and without disabilities. Flashcards are often used to teach basic facts such as the names and sounds of the letters of the alphabet [26]. When students were taught words using a traditional flashcard method, they increase the number of words they are able to read [12].

Based on previous studies in the field of educational psychology of children [2], [7], [17], [19], flashcards had played an important role in the early education of children in kindergarten or at school. Therefore, the approach using a digital flashcard by applying the RSVP technique in children's learning have been done to see the acceptance of children involved in some of the RSVP modes.

H. Badioze Zaman et al. (Eds.): IVIC 2011, Part II, LNCS 7067, pp. 261–272, 2011.
© Springer-Verlag Berlin Heidelberg 2011

In NKRA Education, the government will focus on four sub-NKRAs to expand access to affordable and quality education. One of the sub-NKRAs is the Literacy and Numeracy Programme (LINUS) at primary school level through which every student will be able to acquire basic literacy and numeracy after three years of primary education by the year 2012. The LINUS program had been implemented in all primary schools by March 2010. Students are selected in this program through a screening test in school before entering the first year class in primary school. Based on the screening test, students who do have problems in learning are identified. These students will be placed in the LINUS program class. This program will use a variety of approaches and methods of teaching and learning such as the Teaching and Learning Module, LINUS Programme Module and pedagogical comforted.

Thus, the purpose of this study is to investigate the acceptance of RSVP techniques in this group of children and to identify the children's preferred modes in RSVP techniques. This paper is divided into several sections. Section 2 describes the related works on RSVP techniques pertaining to image representation and related applications. Then an experiment is conducted as defined in section 3, followed by the results and discussion in section 4. Finally, the conclusions and future work are included in section 5.

2 Related Work

2.1 RSVP Techniques in Image Representation

In general, the RSVP technique trades time for space when presenting a set of images. Recent well-publicized uses of RSVP in computer interfaces include Apple's "Coverflow" and Windows Vista's "Flip 3D" [8]. Rapid Serial Visual Presentation (RSVP) offers a powerful presentation technique for digital photo. Studies conducted by De Bruijn & Spence [4], [5] explain that the technique of RSVP has been identified as a potential technique, particularly involving limited display space and images. Wittenburg et al. [22], [23] described RSVP interfaces that explore trade-offs in temporal and spatial layouts as offering one avenue to improve on the basic paradigms. This method also has priority in the simplicity of control and offers a great benefit to designer's devices for the customers.

Spence [18] states that, RSVP has its own objectives, namely to support efficient formation of a mental model of some data, using the method of displaying information (text, images, and video) in the limited space in which every part of the information is displayed only briefly. This is achieved, for example, by scanning through the contents of a folder labelled to remember or to find a particular image.

According to Spence [18] the earliest RSVP techniques in the context of electronic information is the *carousel-mode*, which comprises the flow of images that emerged from one side of a container and follows a circular route around it, disappearing into the opposite side of the container. This mode is used in Web Navigation [5]. The second mode in RSVP is the *collage mode*. This mode is suitable for sale on the

Internet [5]. It displays images one by one, but quickly, a short distance apart so that as many as possible can be seen simultaneously before the image is hidden by the latest image. The third mode of RSVP is the *floating-mode*, where each image is displayed initially set in the middle of the screen, then moves towards the edge of the display, the image size growing at the time. The fourth mode is the *shelf-mode*, in which the initial presentation of a picture is "full size" and is located in the lower right corner of the screen, is there for a while and then moves towards the opposite corner and shrinking size. It is suitable to display on-line products [5]. Next RSVP mode is the *keyhole mode*, like the slide-show technique in which the image displayed is at the same location and time. The *Keyhole mode* is a static presentation mode and also known as the *slideshow mode* [3].

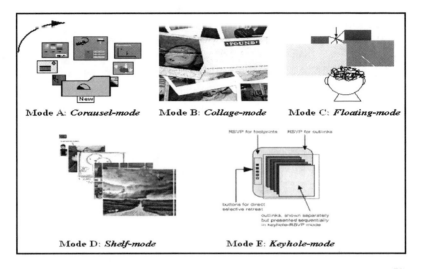

Fig. 1. Modes of RSVP technique; source De Bruijn & Spence [5]

Meanwhile, four other modes of the RSVP techniques are dynamic presentation modes which are a combination of 'spatial' and 'temporal presentation', while the mode is 'purely temporal' [5]. In addition, a number of different modes in the techniques of RSVP were also compared to determine the effectiveness in identifying the image, by observing the trends and users' acceptance [3]. Comparison of physical characteristics between the four dynamic modes of the RSVP technique can be seen in Table 1 below.

Table 1. Comparison between the physical characteristics of the four dynamic modes of RSVP, source De Bruijn & Spence [5]

Parameter	RSVP Modes			
	Carousel	**Collage**	**Floating**	**Shelf**
Trajectory	Circular	Circular	Linear	Linear
Image Size	Growing/Shrinking	Constant	Growing	Shrinking
Image Position	Dynamic	Static	Dynamic	Static/Dynamic

According to the literature review conducted, we have found that the RSVP technique has more benefits and advantages over some other techniques. Referring to some of the findings made by previous researchers [4], [18], [22], [23], we found that this technique has great potential in visualizing digital images. Through the experiment they conducted it was also shown that users are more likely to use this technique which is also more effective in relation to the activities performed.

Spence [18], gave an overview of the RSVP technique, which has several modes that include the *carousel, floating, collage, keyhole,* and *shelf modes.* However, each mode also has its own advantages and disadvantages. According to Bruijn & Spence [5], the *keyhole mode* is found to be of the highest ranking compared to other modes. The experimental results of studying the "pattern of eye gaze" by the researchers also found three other modes in the RSVP technique which are less effective because it involves the movement of the eye (eye gaze) especially in image recognition. Cooper *et al.* [3] also studied the comparison between static images and moving images to present a collection of images. The experimental results showed that the percentage of accuracy for the recognition of static images is higher than a moving image.

Since previous studies have not seen how far this technique can be applied in the children's learning, the investigation will be broadened to include children in acceptance of the RSVP technique. In this study we purpose to investigate only three modes of the RSVP techniques which are the *shelf mode,* the *carousel mode* and the *keyhole mode.* These three modes have been selected due to the literature review has been done [3], [5], [18], [23]. Previous study on a comparison of static and moving presentation modes [3], found that the *keyhole mode* as a static mode had higher rates of user preference. The result from the experiment conducted show that 50% of subjects prefer the static mode and only 25% of subjects preferred a moving mode. Spence [18], also stated that human performance as measured by the *keyhole mode* is more effective than using the *carousel mode* in image recognition tasks. Besides, in the pattern of eye gaze studied by Bruijn & Spence [5] the *carousel mode* as a unique characteristic to be investigated. The circular motions in the *carousel mode* require eye movements. Eye tracking, or gaze tracking, is a particularly useful technique for determining which features in a display attract a user's attention [5]. Based on these studies we choose the *keyhole mode* and *carousel mode* to be compared in the context of children's preference and children's learning environment. A study by Wittenburg et al. [23], applied the *shelf mode* to display digital video to consumers. The user from the experiment conducted commented that by using this mode it is easier for them to distinguish scenes compared to the traditional television broadcasts. They also applied this mode for digital photo collections. Figure 2 shows the experimental setup for digital photo collections. According to this finding, the *shelf mode* becomes an interesting mode to be applied in the digital flashcard representation technique.

An obvious question which arise are, "Do the children accept the RSVP as a representation technique?" and "Which mode in the RSVP technique is more preferred by the children?" The purpose of this study is to investigate the acceptance of the RSVP technique among children. With the potential value of the modes in the RSVP technique they can be applied in representations of children's digital flashcard learning.

Fig. 2. Experimental setup by using shelf mode, source Wittenburg et al. [23]

2.2 RSVP Applications

The earliest RSVP applications were handled manually and combined with the *'bifocal'* concept had been used for a collection of video images of a large poster (Figure 3), as reported by Lam & Spence [11]. Wittenburg *et al.* [22] also used the *floating mode* and *collage mode* in RSVP techniques to display book cover images in the online bookstore (Figure 4).

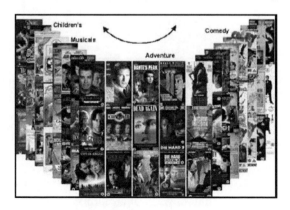

Fig. 3. RSVP technique in representation of a collection of video images of a large poster; source Cooper *et al.* [3]

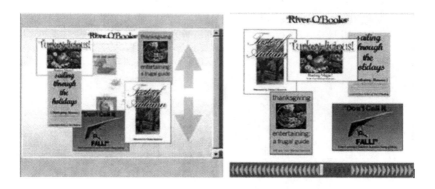

Fig. 4. *Floating mode* and *collage mode* to display images in the online bookstore; source Cooper *et al.* [3]

Another example by Witkowski *et al.* [21] describes a scenario in kiosks (Figure 5) where customers can view images of products (e.g. bottles) from a large database (nearly 450 images) as fast as displayed on a shelf (using *shelf mode*).

Fig. 5. *Shelf mode* application in kiosk scenario; source Cooper *et al.* [3]

As potential applications for watching television, Wittenburg *et al.* [23] suggest the *'diagonal'* or *'time tunnel mode'* in RSVP. Besides that, RSVP techniques have a potential to and capability of improving image representation in a small and limited screen, in a study conducted by De Bruijn & Tong [6]. An example is to enable a news channel to be reached via phone. Different applications using RSVP [10], [20], [23], gave rise to the development of the application involving the search for a video or movie to watch without having to watch it at normal speed. According to research conducted by Wittenburg *et al.* [23], each video is displayed by using the *timetune mode* and the *carousel mode*.

Various studies and applications developed using RSVP techniques ware found to have potential and obtained a positive response from the users. RSVP by using *trade-offs in temporal* and *spatial layouts* could be a way to improve the existing basic techniques [23].

With the positive outcomes and the potential value of modes in RSVP techniques, this study has extended previous research findings in presenting digital flashcard learning for children. One experiment has been carried out to investigate which modes in RSVP techniques are more acceptable for children in representation of digital flashcard learning.

3 User Experiment

This section describes the experimental procedure conducted to test each of the three presentation modes in order to know which modes in RSVP technique are more preferred by the children in representation of digital flashcard learning. From inspiring paper [23], it has been shown that the *shelf mode* in RSVP techniques has been applied in representing consumer digital video and elicited positive results from the users. Our hypothesis is that children will prefer to choose a dynamic mode like the *shelf mode* and the *carousel mode* rather than the *keyhole mode*.

Subject - Eighteen out of twenty five children aged 6-8 years from e-Xra Learning Centre Bangi have been tested in this experiment. The children in this learning centre come from two groups; they are either children from normal classes or children from the LINUS program classes at school.

Design and Procedures - The first interface in the form of a digital flashcard learning tool has been developed to test the children (Figure 6-8). This testing application was written using Flex Builder 3.0 with the flash plug-in and was presented on an Intel Pentium-M computer using Adobe Flash Player 10. The application used a few selected modes of RSVP techniques to represent the flashcard images. Three different RSVP modes have been chosen in this experiment, which are the *shelf mode* (MODE A), the *carousel mode* (MODE B) and the *keyhole mode* (MODE C). The experiment sessions took place in a classroom. Subjects were seated in front of a computer and they had been asked to see and play with the application. After the task is finished, they will answer a questionnaire (under the teacher's guidance) to get their feedbacks regarding their experience. The figures below show the application interfaces.

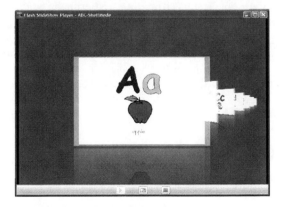

Fig. 6. Digital flashcard in *shelf mode* representation technique (MODE A)

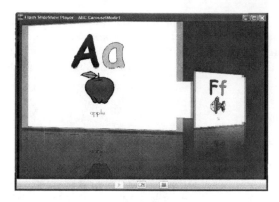

Fig. 7. Digital flashcard in *carousel mode* representation technique (MODE B)

Fig. 8. Digital flashcard in *keyhole mode (thumbnail)* representation technique (MODE C)

4   Results and Discussion

This section describes our results from our experiment with sample users. We consider this experiment as tough as it included children as our subjects who were unfamiliar with the digital flashcard tools and most importantly some of them had come from the LINUS program class which comprised children with learning disabilities. In our main target from this experiment children will accept the use of RSVP techniques as a part of their learning tools. The findings from this experiment gave the positive results. Overall, these groups of children really enjoyed with this technique and from our observation, this technique has the potential of improving their attention to learning.

In the earlier experimental question, we believe that participants will choose the *shelf mode* (MODE A) as their favourite's technique as inferred from paper [23]. The introduction of new images in a circular motion could have resulted in child preference. Feedbacks given by some children from the normal class contend that the *carousel mode* is more challenging to them. It was common for these children to focus their attention while looking for the movement of the flashcard image.

However, the majority of children from the LINUS program class commented that the carousel interfaces made them dizzy. This is because this group of children has difficulties in focusing and recognizing the moving image. Some images that move fast (*shelf mode* and *carousel mode*) compared to the eye gaze direction cause most activity and result in limited recognition of visual images [8]. In particular for modes like the *shelf mode* and the *carousel* mode the movement of the images may have caused some strain on the visual system in requiring smooth pursuit eye movements to keep the images in foveal vision [5]. With the *keyhole mode*, the image is present on screen at any one time and children commented that this was quite easy for them. One child did comment that she enjoyed the *keyhole mode* due to its simplicity. Figures 9 and 10 show the summaries of the result.

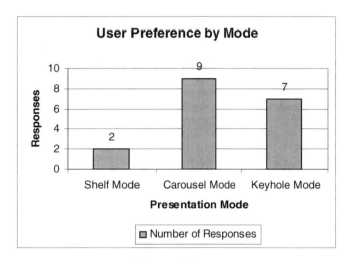

Fig. 9. User preference by mode

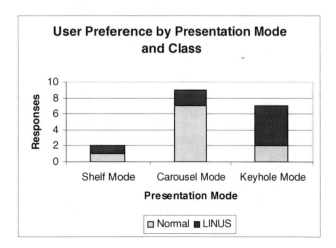

Fig. 10. User preference by presentation mode and class

The result in Figure 9 shows that nine of the children chose the *carousel mode* as their favourite, seven children chose the *keyhole mode* and two of them chose the *shelf mode* as their favourite representation techniques. Figure 10 below shows the finding of differential choice.

We can see that 50% of the children chose the *carousel mode* as their favourite and the majority of them are from the normal class. Meanwhile, 39% of children from the LINUS programme class preferred to choose the *keyhole mode* and only 11% of them chose the *shelf mode*. In any event, what seems clear is that there is a differential choice between children in the normal class and children in the LINUS program class. The children from the normal class preferred to choose the dynamic mode whereas children from the LINUS program class are more inclined to choose the static presentation mode. The result obtained shows that RSVP modes of representation in flashcard learning could bring potential benefits in learning but we need to test on different groups of users to see their preferences in particular contexts.

There are a few limitations during the experiment. We had communication difficulties with the group of children from the LINUS program class who had learning disabilities. During data collection, the data might have been influenced and affected by the children's environment. Due to this constraint, the next experiment will involve their teacher's cooperation to facilitate the work.

5 Conclusions and Future Work

This study investigated the acceptance of RSVP modes for children in the application of digital flashcard learning. RSVP had already been shown to have potential in the general field of information visualization, and our evaluation showed that it has potential in the field of image browsers as well as application on children's digital flashcard learning. From the results we can see that the children can accept the RSVP mode technique in their learning environments. Indeed, the results of the present experiment are not that consistent as we have pointed before but our finding seems to be that under certain situations RSVP modes have differential acceptance for the users. The experiment report in this paper shows that there had been a differential choice between children from the normal class and children from the LINUS program class. Future work will involve specific groups of users in the learning context and another experiment to evaluate in terms of users' eye gaze by using eye tracker tools.

References

1. Akyurek, E.G., Hommel, B.: Memory Operations in Rapid Serial Visual Presentation. European Journal of Cognitive Psychology 18(4), 520–536 (2006)
2. Burns, M.K., Dean, J.D., Foley, S.: Pre-teaching unknown key words with incremental rehearsal to improve reading fluency comprehension with children identified as reading disabled. Journal of School Psychology 42, 303–314 (2004)
3. Cooper, K., De Bruijin, O., Spence, R., Witkowski, M.A.: Comparison of Static and Moving Presentation Modes for Image Collections. ACM, 1-59393-353-0/06/0005 (2006)

4. De Bruijn, O., Spence, R.: Rapid Serial Visual Presentation: A Space-Time Trade-off in Information Presentation. In: Proceedings of the Working Conference on Advanced Visual Interfaces (AVI 2000), di Palermo, Italy, pp. 189–192 (2000)
5. De Bruijn, O., Spence, R.: Patterns of eye gaze during Rapid Serial Visual Presentation. In: Proceedings of Advanced Visual Interfaces (AVI 2002), di Trento, Italy, pp. 209–217 (2002)
6. De Bruijn, O., Tong, C.H.: M-RSVP: Mobile Web browsing on a PDA. In: O'Neill, E., Palanque, P., Johnson, P. (eds.) People and Computers – Designing for Society, pp. 297–311. Springer, Heidelberg (2003)
7. Ehri, L.: Learning to read words: Theory, findings, and issues. Scientific Studies of Reading 9(2), 167–188 (2005)
8. Forlines, C., Balakrishnan, R.: Improving Visual Search with Image Segmentation. ACM Visualization, 978-1-60558-246-7/09/04 (2009)
9. Houten, R.V., Rollder, A.: An Analysis of Several Variables Influencing the Atficacy of Flash Card Instruction. Journal of Applied Behavior Analysis 22(1), 111–118 (1989)
10. Komlodi, A., Marchionini, G.: Key Frame Preview Techniques for Video Browsing. In: ACM Proceedings of Digital Libraries, pp. 118–125 (1998)
11. Lam, K., Spence, R.: Image Browsing –a spacetime trade-off. In: Proceeding INTERACT 1997, pp. 611–612 (1997)
12. MacQuarrie, L.L., Tucker, J.A., Burns, M.K., Hartman, B.: Comparison of Retention Rates using Traditional, Drill Sandwich, and Incremental Rehearsal Flash Card Method. School Psychology Review 31, 584–595 (2002)
13. Potter, M.C., Fox, L.F.: Detecting and Remembering Simultaneous Pictures in a Rapid Serial Visual Presentation. J. EXP. Psychol Hum. Percept Perform 35(1), 28–38 (2009), doi:10.1037/a0013624
14. Raymond, J.E., Shapiro, K.L., Arnell, K.M.: Temporary Suppression of Visual Processing in an RSVP Task – An Attentional Blink. Journal of Experimental Psychology – Human Perception and Performance 18, 849–860 (1992)
15. Russel, M.C., Chaparro, B.S.: Exploring Effects of Speed and Font Size with RSVP. In: Proceeding of the Human Factors and Ergonimics Society 45th Annual Meeting (2001)
16. Sabol, V., Kienreich, W., Granitzer, M.: Visualisation Techniques for Analysis and Exploration of Multimedia Data. Computational Intelligence (SCI) 101, 219–238 (2008)
17. Skinner, C.H., Fletcher, P.A., Henington, C.: Increasing Learning Rates by Increasing Student Response Rates: A summary of research. School Psychology Quarterly 11, 313–325 (1996)
18. Spence, R.: Rapid Serial and Visual: A Presentation Technique with Potential. Information Visualization 1(1), 13–19 (2002)
19. Stanovich, K.E.: Constructivism in Reading Education. The Journal of Special Education 28, 259–274 (1994)
20. Tse, T., Marchionini, G., Ding, W., Slaughter, L., Komlodi, A.: Dynamic Key Frame Presentation Techniques for Augmented Video Browsing. In: ACM Proceeding Conference on Advanced Visual Interfaces, pp. 185–194 (1998)
21. Witkowski, M., Neville, B., Pitt, J.: Agent Mediated Retailing in the Connected Community. Interacting with Computers 15, 5–32 (2003)
22. Wittenburg, K., Chiyoda, C., Heinrichs, M., Lanning, T.: Browsing through Rapid-Fire Imaging: Requirements and Industry Initiatives. In: Proceedings of Electronic Imaging 2000: Internet Imaging di San Jose CA, USA, pp. 48–56 (2000)

23. Wittenburg, K., Forlines, C., Esenther, A., Harada, S., Miyachi, T.: Rapid Serial Visual Presentation Techniques for Consumer Digital Video Devices. In: UIST 2003, Vancouver, BC, Canada, vol. 5(1), pp. 115–124 (2003)
24. Wolfe, J.M., Horowitz, T.S., Michod, K.O.: Is Visual Attention Required for Robust Picture Memory? Vision Research. Vision Research 47, 955–964 (2006)
25. Wong, A.C.-N., Qu, Z., McGugin, R.W., Gauthier, I.: Interference in Character Processing Reflect Common Perceptual Expertise Across Writing Systems. Journal of Vision 11(1), 1–8 & 15 (2011)
26. Young, C.C., Hecimovic, A., Salzberg, C.L.: Tutor-tutee Behavior of Disadvantaged Kindergarten Children during Peer Teaching. Education and Treatment of Children 6, 123–135 (1983)

Cultural Learning in Virtual Heritage: An Overview

Nazrita Ibrahim[1], Nazlena Mohamad Ali[2], and Noor Faezah Mohd Yatim[3]

[1] College of Information Technology, Universiti Tenaga Nasional
[2] Institute of Visual Informatics, Universiti Kebangsaan Malaysia
[3] Faculty of Information Science and Technology, Universiti Kebangsaan Malaysia
nazrita@uniten.edu.my, {nma,nfmy}@ftsm.ukm.my

Abstract. The aim of this paper is to present the overview of cultural learning in virtual heritage. In the past, works done on virtual heritage were mostly focused on replicating and visualizing heritage objects for presentation using virtual reality. However, accurate and realistic representation of heritage objects is not enough when it comes to cultural learning in virtual environment. This paper attempts to identify issues that impede cultural learning in virtual environment. In order to develop a virtual environment that is able to facilitate cultural learning, we argue that there is a need to understand what the end users really want to know when it comes to learning culture. We propose a thorough user study to be carried out at the beginning of virtual heritage project development and discuss the outline of our intended approach.

Keywords: Virtual Heritage, Virtual Environment, Cultural Learning, Visual Informatics.

1 Introduction

Cultural heritage, by UNESCO (1972) definition, refers to monuments, architectural structures and sites which are of outstanding universal value from the historical, aesthetic, ethnological and anthropological point of view. Virtual Heritage on the other hand refers to works that involved replicating or visualizing cultural heritage entity using virtual reality [1].

The initial motivation of Virtual Heritage research is to facilitate conservation, historical research, reproduction, representation and display of cultural evidence with the use of virtual reality. However, efforts have been made to shift the direction of virtual heritage research, from creating 3D models of heritage objects merely for display to creating a virtual environment that is able to facilitate the teaching and learning of culture [2]. It is suggested that the accumulation of 3D heritage objects in virtual environment is not supposed to be like a dead museum, but to enable users to feel and understand another culture [3].

This paper intends to identify the issues that impede cultural learning in virtual heritage and proposed an action that would help to improve present condition. The rest of this paper is organized according to the following: Section 2 briefly presents the background study on virtual heritage domain; Section 3 discusses current issues for cultural learning in virtual heritage; Section 4 outlines our proposed approaches and discusses the reasons behind the proposal, and Section 5 presents the conclusion of this paper.

H. Badioze Zaman et al. (Eds.): IVIC 2011, Part II, LNCS 7067, pp. 273–283, 2011.
© Springer-Verlag Berlin Heidelberg 2011

2   Virtual Heritage

2.1 Domains of Virtual Heritage

Virtual Heritage is a term used to define works that deal with cultural heritage and virtual reality [1]. Rahaman and Tan define Virtual Heritage as the instance of cultural heritage properties within a technological domain [4]. Among all the definitions, we feel that the definition suggested by Toast and Champion is the most comprehensive in describing what Virtual Heritage should be: *"...the use of computer-based interactive technologies to record, preserve, or recreate artifacts, sites and actors of historic, artistic, religious, and cultural significance and to deliver the results openly to a global audience in such a way as to provide formative educational experiences through electronic manipulations of time and space."* [5].

According to Addison [6], there are three major domains in Virtual Heritage as shown in Fig. 1.

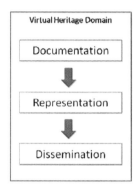

Fig. 1. Virtual Heritage Domain

3D documentation involves gathering data, as accurately as possible, about cultural heritage object under study ranging from site investigation, measurement taking, sketching to epigraphy. There are many techniques available to capture the data for heritage objects. Among them are using 3D laser scanning, laser triangulation, topography, photogrammetry, empirical, stereophotogrammetry and structured light technique [7,8,9]. Each of these techniques requires certain devices and hardware to work with, and also suitable for different types of object and monument. Some of the data collected also comes from sources such as ancient map, photograph, period painting, and written document [10, 11].

3D Representation involves either the 3D replication of heritage object that still exists, or visualization of heritage object that has been badly damaged, lost or does not exist anymore. Research in this domain mostly focused on the technical aspect of heritage object digitization such as effective 3D modeling technique [12, 13], computational lighting, effective texturing, faster rendering and processing of raw data from 3D scanning.

3D dissemination of virtual heritage content refers to how the recreated 3D models being displayed to the users. In most of the projects, virtual reality is used as the medium to present the 3D content to the users. Some of the researches in this domain focus on securing data validity and preserving its authenticity while transferring the 3D heritage content between computer networks, archive system for the 3D heritage content created [14], and content retrieval [15].

Table 1 presents a short list of the various type of virtual heritage project. As we can see from the table, the type of projects in virtual heritage varies, ranging from the reconstruction of architecture building to the simulation of intangible heritage.

Table 1 Type of Projects in Virtual Heritage

Project Type	Example
Reconstruction of Historical Building	19th Century of Italian Theatre [16]
	Gassho-zukuri house [17]
Reconstruction of Historical monument, relic or object of cultural value	The Great Buddha Project [18]
	Anyang Xinyu Project [19]
Historical site based on archeological finding	DentroTrento Project [20]
	Roman Cologne Project [21]
Historical site based on existing ancient town	Ancient city of Hue, Vietnam [22]
Simulation of the intangible heritage	Royal Dance of Chu performed in Royal Palace of Zhongshan [10]
	Namaz Prayer performed in the Sergius & Bacchus Mosque [23]

2.2 Research in Cultural Learning

From literature review, we observe that there are five (5) important research areas when it comes to cultural learning in virtual heritage, as summarized by Fig. 2. The five (5) research areas are:

- Navigation or wayfinding.
- Interpretation of cultural heritage content in virtual environment.
- Evaluation of virtual heritage project.
- Cultural Presence in virtual environment.
- Creation of meaningful content expressing cultural value in virtual environment.

Research in navigation or wayfinding within the virtual environment is what we regard as a 'classic virtual reality problem' inherited by virtual heritage. Lots of works have been done in this area (with regards to virtual reality) and many suggested solution to the problems can be applied to the design of virtual heritage environment.

Interpreting virtual heritage is another research area that focuses on the method of communicating cultural heritage content to the users to increase their awareness and enhance understanding of cultural heritage site [4]. There is also a need to define suitable evaluation method for virtual heritage environment since there has no satisfactory standard of methodology yet been developed [5].

Cultural presence is another interesting area in virtual heritage research [5] that focuses on defining the elements that constitute cultural presence in virtual heritage environment. The last research area is the study to create meaningful content expressing cultural value.

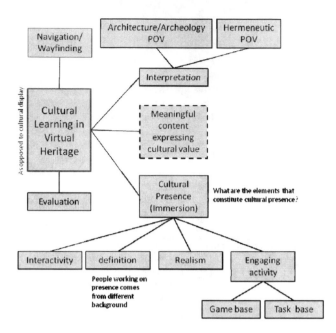

Fig. 2. Research areas for Cultural Learning in Virtual Heritage

3   Issues

Earlier projects in virtual heritage focused more on creating an accurate and realistic representation of heritage objects, which is a vital component for heritage preservation. However, the accumulation of those 3D heritage objects has become nothing more than becoming a collection merely for cultural display. While the main reason for virtual heritage project is to preserve the past by reconstructing or reproducing heritage object, the real goal in virtual heritage study should actually to understand past culture [3]. Designing virtual environment that encourage cultural learning still poses a great challenge for virtual heritage designer.

Some studies have been made to address this challenge. Laycock et al. developed an environment which is capable of displaying the evolution of particular heritage content over time [24]. Jacobson and Holden created an abstraction of Egyptian temple which has three level of interpretation suited for three different types of users [3]. Valtolina et al. introduced the concept of guided tour based on a predefined script and storyboard [16]. Papagiannakis et al. developed character-based virtual heritage, where real time character simulation is used to recreate ceremonies of past culture so that users can see how ceremonies were performed back then [23]. Champian also suggested the use of game and thematic activities to improve user engagement factors in virtual heritage [25], while Rahaman proposed a new heritage interpretation model that incorporates multiplicity viewpoint [4, 26].

Although many studies have been made in this area, we observe some issues that are still quite apparent and hindering the process of cultural learning in virtual environment. These issues are discussed in the following sections.

3.1 Cultural Heritage Learning

In order to understand what is required for cultural learning to take place, we need to understand the motivation for people to learn culture. Why do people go to the museum? Or why do people go to any historical places around the world? The motivation for people to learn culture is different from those learning formal academic subjects done in the classroom. They do not learn culture because they want to earn a degree or to get a passing grade. Most of the time, people learn culture for personal gain, with most of the time to satisfy their personal curiosity.

Learning culture should not be treated in similar fashion as when ones learn other subjects. Cultural Heritage is not a static concept but is defined by the society in question [27]. The meaning of heritage evolves and is updated by subsequent generations [4]. A study conducted by Wedgwood [28] showed that cultural value is not only perceived by what ones can see, but also by what ones retained in the memory (i.e. what they remember about the past).

The aim of cultural learning should be emphasized for historical and cultural awareness, directed to informal learning instead of mentally challenged. Unfortunately, many virtual heritage projects have taken the approach that is more towards pedagogical in nature. The design of the virtual environment is treated like designing a courseware or teaching plan, while the 'learning part' is evaluated as if someone is taking an exam – through memory recall. Example of memory recall are the use of Multiple Choice Question (MCQ) to gauge users understanding about the 'culture' through their visit to the virtual environment, or puzzle game where users need to rearrange the jigsaw puzzle until it forms the correct image. More serious games include finding the answer to the clue given by a game master in order to proceed to the next level, where the answers to the clues is embedded within the environment or even more, from external resource such as books or the internet.

3.2 Content Development Approach

We observed that some virtual heritage projects were initially carried out for preservation purpose. It is only when the recreation of the past has been completed that the developers start to think how the 3D environment could be used for cultural learning. As the result of this approach, users are left out from the development cycle. They only function as the *consumer* of the product, but not part of the development process.

Hence there is an issue that the existing virtual heritage projects are still not able to provide for cultural learning. One of the suggested reasons for this is that the users do not feel as if they are connected to the past. It is recommended that in order for the users to feel the past, the virtual environment should:

- look realistic,
- have engaging activities, and
- utilizes multi-sensory interaction (e.g. visual, haptic, audio).

Could it be possible the reason that the users could not feel connected to the past is because there is not much information for them to comprehend? Or the kind of information that they are looking for is not provided? The analogy of this assumption is like having someone looking for information over the web. By visiting an exciting looking website but with no relevant information or with not much information will make the users leave feeling that his search is unfulfilled, not matter how interesting the website is constructed.

The same thing goes with the development of virtual heritage project. At the moment, the decision on what the users *should see and know* is based on expert assumption (i.e. archeologist, historian and 3D designer). From the literature review, almost none of the papers actually discussed having asking the actual users of the system (museum visitors or general public interested in ancient history) what they really want to know when it comes to cultural learning. Most works carried out mainly based on *user survey* of a *completed project*. To our knowledge, no proper user study has been made *prior* to project commencement.

There is however, one interesting work that includes users as part of project development. Rahaman et al. [26, 29] proposed a new non-linear interpretive framework that incorporates multiplicity of viewpoint. An online platform was developed to allow multiple users to share their experience and memories of a recreated historical site. Although users are included as part of the process, the users only get to feed their interpretative view of the historical site only AFTER the historical site has been reconstructed (in this case, it is the 3D view of Sompur Mahavihara, in Bangladesh). This approach is quite different from what we would like to propose where users' view are taken into account at the very beginning of the project.

3.3 Every Culture Is Unique

Since cultural heritage is defined by the society in question, it is important for us to know how that society perceives its own culture. Generalization that every culture is perceived as the same is no longer appropriate here. There are aspects that seem to be important to one culture but it is not to another. Vecco [27] highlighted that western philosophical approach regards *'conservation manifests itself in the preservation of the historic monument'*, while the oriental *'tries to use the monuments to preserve the very spirit they present'*. For example, to some culture, conserving heritage means preserving the very remains of the architecture, while to some other, preserving the knowledge and technique link to the creation of the architecture is more important than preserving the architecture itself.

4 Proposed Approach

From the issues discussed above and from the observation made from literature review, we conclude that there is a need for proper user study being carried out for virtual heritage project. In order to develop a virtual heritage project that facilitates cultural learning, we believe that users should not be treated merely as the consumer of the product but as the shareholder of the project development. Their view should be taken into account at the very early stage of any virtual heritage project development. Therefore, we proposed a comprehensive user study to be included as part of the process in virtual heritage project development.

4.1   User Study

The objective of this study is to understand how cultural elements are seen by the users. Our approach is based on the assumption that different users want to know different things when it comes to learning culture, based on their individual interest, prior knowledge and their association with the culture. Hence, in order to determine *what kind of information should be incorporated in the virtual environment*, it is important for us to capture everyone's view on what they perceive and expect a culture should be made of. In order for us to do that, we would like to identify (as shown by Fig. 3):

1. What kind of information that the end users want to know when it comes to cultural heritage learning?
2. How the society perceives a particular culture?

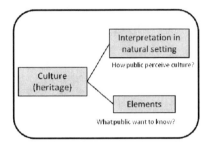

Fig. 3. Culture and Heritage study from end user perspective

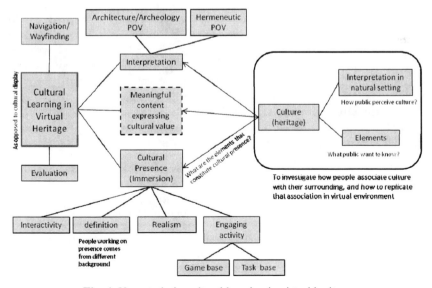

Fig. 4. User study in cultural learning in virtual heritage

Fig. 4 shows how our research fit into current research direction. It is our intention and hope that the result from this study to be used to complement the three important researches areas described in section 2.2: Identifying elements of cultural presence, complementing existing heritage interpretation model and providing guideline for content creation.

For this study, we plan to conduct in depth interview. Interview is chosen as the data gathering method because it gives us the opportunity to probe for more detail and specific answer from the respondents.

Type of questions to be asked to the respondent will be based on the following objectives:

Objective 1: Finding out the respondent knowledge about …
Objective 2: Finding out what the respondent would like to know more about…
Objective 3: Finding out the elements that the respondent thinks are important, if s/he wants to promote the culture to others.

Each of the questions asked will be based on a specific cultural heritage object, for example, architecture, monument or historical relic.

4.2 User Groups

We have identified 4 user groups as the respondents for this user study, as follows:

1. Expert: someone who have an in-depth knowledge about a particular culture.
2. Ethnic: the ethnic belongs to the culture under study.
3. Non Ethnic: people who live within the community long enough to understand the culture under study.
4. General Public: anybody picked at random.

As for our research, since *Budaya Melayu* or *Malay Culture* is chosen as our case study, the **expert** group will consists of those who have in-depth knowledge in Malay Culture, and also those who work in preserving the heritage with regards to Malay Culture (e.g. museum curator). The **ethnic** group will be the Malays (Bangsa Melayu). The **non ethnic** group will consist of any other races that have been living closely with the Malay community (in our case, we anticipated that the non ethnic group will mostly comes from the Chinese and the Indian races).

The **general public** group is a special group targeted to study people perception about learning another culture that they do not know anything about. In this study, the general public will be represented by two groups of user:

• People living outside Malaysia who have no prior knowledge about the Malay Culture, and
• Malaysian people, whom we will ask about another distant culture that we hope they never have heard of, for example, the Mayan Culture.

The reason why we need to gather data from these four different groups is because each of this group represents different set of user's needs and requirements, and data gathered from each group will complement each other. Expert view might provide guideline of what a particular culture should have. Even though experts have a deeper understanding and knowledge of a specific culture, they might dismiss anything that seems trivial as not important, and hence not including it in their answers. The ethnic group will recount based on what they remember, what being told to them by their ancestor, and based on how they lived the culture themselves. The non-ethnic will give their answers based on what they assumed the culture has to be based on their observation, and the general users will give their answer based on the universal understanding of what constitute culture.

The finding from this user study will provide us an insight of cultural elements as seen by the users. Fig. 5 summarizes our proposed user study.

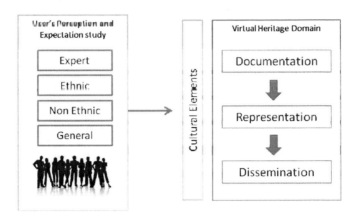

Fig. 5. Proposed user study for cultural learning in virtual heritage

5   Conclusion

In this paper, we have presented an overview of virtual heritage particularly in learning culture. Some issues and challenges have been discussed and the direction of the research has been laid out in a diagram mapping. We argue that in order to encourage cultural learning, we need to understand what the users really want to know when it comes to learning another culture or even understanding culture of their own. We have also discussed three issues that could impede cultural learning in virtual environment. We proposed for a proper user study to be included as part of virtual heritage development process. Our next plan is to carry out the user study as outlined in this paper and to develop a prototype of virtual environment based on the findings of the study.

References

1. Roussou, M.: Virtual Heritage: from the research lab to the broad public. In: Virtual Archeology, pp. 93–100 (2002)
2. Ott, M., Pozzi, F.: ICT and Cultural Heritage Education: Which Added Value? In: Lytras, M.D., Damiani, E., Tennyson, R.D. (eds.) WSKS 2008. LNCS (LNAI), vol. 5288, pp. 131–138. Springer, Heidelberg (2008)
3. Jacobsen, J., Holden, L.: Virtual Heritage: Living in the Past. J. of the Society for Philosophy and Technology 10(3) (2007)

4. Rahaman, H., Tan, B.K.: Interpreting Digital Heritage. In: 15th International Conference on Computer-Aided Architectural Design Research in Asia CAADRIA 2010, pp. 93–102 (2010)
5. Tost, L.P., Champion, E.: A Critical Examination of Presence Applied to Cultural Heritage. In: 10th Annual International Workshop on Presence, PRESENCE 2007 (2007)
6. Addison, A.C.: Emerging trends in virtual heritage. Multimedia, IEEE 7(2), 22–25 (2000)
7. Pavlidis, G., Koutsoudis, A., Arnaoutoglou, F., Tsioukas, V., Chamzas, C.: Methods for 3D digitization of Cultural Heritage. Journal of Cultural Heritage 8, 93–98 (2007)
8. Pieraccini, M., Gabriele, G., Carlo, A.: 3D digitizing of cultural heritage. Journal of Cultural Heritage 2(1), 63–70 (2001)
9. Cignoni, P., Roberto, S.: Sampled 3D models for CH applications: A viable and enabling new medium or just a technological exercise? J. Comput. Cult. Herit. 1(1), 1–23 (2008)
10. Cheng, Y., Peng, D., Sun, S.: Creating a Virtual Activity for the Intangible Culture Heritage. In: 16th International Conference on Artificial Reality and Telexistence–Workshops, ICAT 2006, pp. 636–641 (2006)
11. Yahedu, E.K.: Preserving cultural heritage through digital media. In: Yehuda, E.K., Kvan, T., Affleck, J. (eds.) Hew Heritage: New Media and Cultural Heritage, pp. 1–10. Routledge (2008)
12. Rafi, A., Salleh, A., Paul, A., Noraisah, S., Jun, Y., Hanif, R., Mahadzir, M.: Modeling optimization for real-time virtual heritage visualization content: A research on e- Warisan SENIBINA. In: International Symposium in Information Technology (ITSim), pp. 1–7 (2010)
13. Ibrahim, N., Azmi, K.A., Salleh, F.H.M., Yussof, S.: Cultural Heritage Preservation: 3D Modeling of Traditional Malay House using Hidden Surface Removal Approach. In: Proceeding of International Conference on Software Engineering and Computer Systems, ICSECS 2009 (2009)
14. Koller, D., Frischer, B., Humphreys, G.: Research challenges for digital archives of 3D cultural heritage models. Journal on Computing and Cultural Heritage (JOCCH) 2(3) (2009)
15. Chen, C.-c., Wactlar, H.D., Wang, J.Z., Kiernan, K.: Digital imagery for significant cultural and historical materials. International Journal on Digital Libraries 5(4), 275–286 (2005)
16. Valtolina, S., Franzoni, S., Mazzoleni, P., Bertino, E.: Dissemination of Cultural Heritage Content through Virtual Reality and Multimedia Techniques: A Case Study. In: Multimedia Modelling Conference (MMM 2005), pp. 214–221 (2005)
17. Hirayu, H., Ojika, T., Kijima, R.: Constructing the historic villages of Shirakawa-go in virtual reality. Multimedia, IEEE 7(2), 61–64 (2000)
18. Ikeuchi, K., Oishi, T., Takamatsu, J., Sagawa, R., Nakazawa, A., Kurazume, R., Nishino, K., Kamakura, M., Okamoto, Y.: The Great Buddha Project: Digitally Archiving, Restoring, and Analyzing Cultural Heritage Objects. International Journal of Computer Vision 75(1), 189–208 (2007)
19. Xinyu, D., Baoqing, G., Chuangming, S.: Virtual Exploration Application of Cultural Heritage for Anyang Yinxu. In: Second Workshop on Digital Media and its Application in Museum & Heritages, pp. 237–241 (2007)
20. Conti, G., Piffer, S., Girardi, G., De Amicis, R., Ucelli, G.: DentroTrento: a virtual walk across history. In: Proceedings of the Working Conference on Advanced Visual Interfaces, pp. 318–321 (2006)

21. Trapp, M., Semmo, A., Pokorski, R., Herrmann, C.-D., Döllner, J., Eichhorn, M., Heinzelmann, M.: Communication of Digital Cultural Heritage in Public Spaces by the Example of Roman Cologne. In: Ioannides, M., Fellner, D., Georgopoulos, A., Hadjimitsis, D.G. (eds.) EuroMed 2010. LNCS, vol. 6436, pp. 262–276. Springer, Heidelberg (2010)
22. Pugnaloni, F., Issini, G., Minh, N.D.: 3D City Model of the Ancient Hue, Vietnam; Reconstruction of the City Environment for the Cultural Heritage Identity Conservation. In: Wyeld, T.G., Kenderdine, S., Docherty, M. (eds.) VSMM 2007. LNCS, vol. 4820, pp. 13–23. Springer, Heidelberg (2008)
23. Papagiannakis, G., Foni, A., Magnenat-Thalmann, N.: Real-Time recreated ceremonies in VR restituted cultural heritage sites. In: CIPA XIXth International Symposium, pp. 235–240 (2003)
24. Laycock, R.G., Drinkwater, D., Day, A.M.: Exploring cultural heritage sites through space and time. Journal on Computing and Cultural Heritage (JOCCH) 1(2) (2008)
25. Champion, E.: Heritage Role Playing - History as an Interactive Digital Game. In: Interactive Entertainment Workshop, pp. 47–53 (2004)
26. Rahaman, H.: Interpreting Digital Heritage: Interaction, Dialogue and Multiple Perspectives of the Past. In: SMARTdoc 2010: Heritage Recording and Information Management in the Digital Age, Pennsylvania (2010)
27. Vecco, M.: A definition of cultural heritage: From the tangible to the intangible. Journal of Cultural Heritage 11(3), 321–324 (2010)
28. Wedgwood, T.: History in Two Dimensions or Three? Working Class Responses to History. International Journal of Heritage Studies 15(4), 277–297 (2009)
29. Rahaman., H., Rashid, M.M., Rahman, M.: Heritage Interpretation – Collective Reconstruction of Sompur Mahavihara, Bangladesh. In: 16th International Conference on Virtual Systems and Multimedia (VSMM), pp. 163–170 (2010)

i-JEN: Visual Interactive Malaysia Crime News Retrieval System

Nazlena Mohamad Ali[1], Masnizah Mohd[2], Hyowon Lee[3], Alan F. Smeaton[3],
Fabio Crestani[4], and Shahrul Azman Mohd Noah[2]

[1] Institute of Visual Informatics
[2] Faculty of Information Science and Technology,
University Kebangsaan Malaysia, Malaysia
[3] CLARITY: Centre for Sensor Web Technology, Dublin City University, Ireland
[4] Faculty of Informatics, University of Lugano, Switzerland
{nma,mas,samn}@ftsm.ukm.my,
{hlee,asmeaton}@computing.dcu.ie, fabio.crestani@usi.ch

Abstract. Supporting crime news investigation involves a mechanism to help monitor the current and past status of criminal events. We believe this could be well facilitated by focusing on the user interfaces and the event crime model aspects. In this paper we discuss on a development of Visual Interactive Malaysia Crime News Retrieval System (i-JEN) and describe the approach, user studies and planned, the system architecture and future plan. Our main objectives are to construct crime-based event; investigate the use of crime-based event in improving the classification and clustering; develop an interactive crime news retrieval system; visualize crime news in an effective and interactive way; integrate them into a usable and robust system and evaluate the usability and system performance. The system will serve as a news monitoring system which aims to automatically organize, retrieve and present the crime news in such a way as to support an effective monitoring, searching, and browsing for the target users groups of general public, news analysts and policemen or crime investigators. The study will contribute to the better understanding of the crime data consumption in the Malaysian context as well as the developed system with the visualisation features to address crime data and the eventual goal of combating the crimes.

Keywords: interaction design, visualisation, content analysis, crime news, Visual Informatics.

1 Introduction

Crime in Malaysia has been steadily increasing in the past few years. The national crime rates last year increased by 15.74% with every states reporting an increment in 2006[1]. The Index Crime statistic has proved that the crime situation in Malaysia is critical and newspaper reporting shows that the public continues to see crime as one of the most pressing problems in society [21]. In a layman's term Index Crime

---

[1] Malaysia Crime Watch (accessed May 2011)
http://malaysiacrimewatch.lokety.com/malaysia-crime-rate-up-15-per-cent-in-2006/

H. Badioze Zaman et al. (Eds.): IVIC 2011, Part II, LNCS 7067, pp. 284–294, 2011.
© Springer-Verlag Berlin Heidelberg 2011

represents those offences that are regular and common in occurrence thus it can be later used to compare general crime situation between countries.

The journalists and the general public mainly depend on resources reported by the media production in investigating or monitoring crime topics. Therefore a huge amount of crime news needs to be organized in an effective way such as mining the crime news should provide information on the crime pattern and to discover new information. It would be good to have a crime news system that will be able to automatically track the crime topics and detect new news for a specific crime. This is beneficial to users such as the journalist in writing news or to the police in monitoring the crime news, as well as general public in their day-to-day news consumption.

This paper is organised as follows. Section 2 elaborates some related works on event crime model and crime data visual interfaces. It is followed in Section 3 by our approaches in designing and developing Malaysian crime news system which consist of technical possibilities and visual interaction design. Finally we conclude our approaches in designing the system and some future work in Section 4.

2 Related Works

This section discusses the related works on event crime model and crime data visualization.

2.1 Event Crime Model

The notion of "event" is highly associated with a crime. When crime news such as 'Sosilawati murder' was reported, we tend to investigate and to know on 'who killed her?', 'when did she die?', 'where was she killed?' 'what happened?'. It was observed that when hearing a crime, what we concern about most may be its participants, time and location it happen and probably the instruments used and goods involved. The questions on the *Who, Where and When* are more to the factoid or facts finding meanwhile the *What* question is more on the associative discovery or finding the chronology of the murder case.

Brown [5] has constructed a software framework for mining data in order to catch professional criminals. He thought that the analyst needs to get the details of data such as where and when the incidents occurred. Nath [17] outlined a new approach for crime pattern discovery. In his method, each record is composed of many attributes describing the crimes, such as date/time, location, outline, demographic and weapon.

An event is identified by event triggers, and is associated with participants, time, location and others, and is a larger semantic unit compared with a concept. There is an intrinsic link between events. It is a new attempt to apply the semantic analysis technology of events to mine web crime information on the web.

Cunhua et al. [7] have explored cyber crime in Chinese web pages by event ontology construction. In particular, they define event ontology and demonstrate how it can be used to describe cyber crimes on the level of event, relation and event class. Promising techniques such as SVM-based text classification was employed in the implementation of their prototype system. Some researchers have proposed ideas of event-oriented ontology for processing events. Although Sánchez and Moreno [19] did not mention the notion of events, he actually applied an event triple model to assist the construction of ontology. Lin and Liang [12] presented the method of information retrieval based on event ontology. Han [10] constructed a character ontology model based on events, in which a character will relate to some special events, and events are attributes of characters. But his ontology is still limited to the character ontology..

In the context of Topic Detection and Tracking (TDT) which is an area aims to effectively retrieve and organise broadcast news (speech) and newswire stories (text) into groups of events, Nallapati et al. [16] have modelled the news topic based on event and their dependency. They named the process of recognizing events and identifying dependencies among them as *event threading*, an analogy to email threading that shows connections between related email messages. Although their corpus are the general news and not the crime news, we believed it would be interesting to model crime news topics by considering a relational structure of events interconnected by dependencies. Again, the crime news such as '*Sosilawati murder*' starts with the missing event, followed by kidnapping and finally the killing event. Therefore event dependency could support the associative discovery or finding the chronology of a crime case.

2.2 Crime Data Visualization

A number of works has been done in applying visualization techniques for crime data, mostly focusing on either or both of geographic map views with crime locations plotted and timeline views with temporal frequency of crime events over time. Oakland Crimespotting[2] provides an exploration tool for crime data. The system supports panning and zooming on the geographical map representation and filtering the crime type. The application also has a feature to dynamically browse both based on time and day of the crime and temporal form of data visualization. Fig. 1 shows the interface of Oakland Crimespotting.

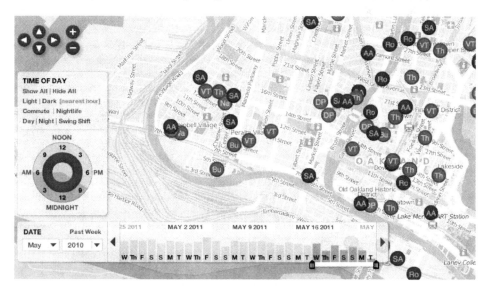

Fig. 1. Oakland Crimespotting interface

---

[2] http://oakland.crimespotting.org

Fig. 2. New York Homicides Map interface

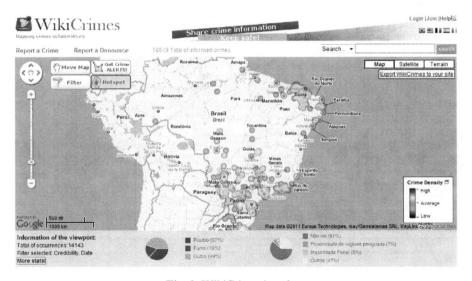

Fig. 3. WikiCrimes interface

Another similar application is the New York Homicides Map[3] as shown in Fig. 2. The interface includes the geographical map representation and plots the locations of the crimes, and supports searching and browsing of crimes by type and time, and also features temporal view of crime data.

WikiCrimes[4] is another related work in crime data visualization. It is a typical Web 2.0 application that allows users to access and register criminal events on the

---

[3] http://projects.nytimes.com/crime/homicides/map
[4] http://www.wikicrimes.org

computer directly in a specific geographic location represented by a map. Fig. 3 shows the main screen of WikiCrimes, which offers a crime search function that enables users to view the registers of crimes, filtered by crime type and view statistics about the visualized area.

Relatively a large number of crime-related visualisation systems are available using the similar concepts as the examples described above.   While there are many visualisation ideas that have been explored in the past such as cone-tree, treemaps, Document Lens or Hyperbolic for different domain of data. Many specific techniques from these can be customised to be adopted to support the crime data visualisation. For example, dynamic query preview, zoomable, fish-eye lense, and small multiples are some of the techniques that can help visualising data while confirming the well-known information visualisation mantra "overview first, zoom and filter, then details on demand" [20].   It was also believed that visualizing a huge amount of document in cluster form helps user to understand news in a relatively fast and efficient manner [15],[22]. In addition, the use of advanced back-end processing of data (see Section 3.1) could result in more novel visualisation possibilities which currently we are not aware of.

3   An Interactive Malaysia Crime News Retrieval System (i-JEN)

i-JEN system is an interactive crime news monitoring system with the ability to track the crime news. It is a novel news system that applies the-state-of-the-art techniques in classification and clustering approach. This is a ground-breaking study which investigates Malaysia crime news where the focus is on the interactive crime data visualization, designed to help the general public, news analysts and the police to monitor the crime news. Fig.4 illustrates the conceptual framework of i-JEN.

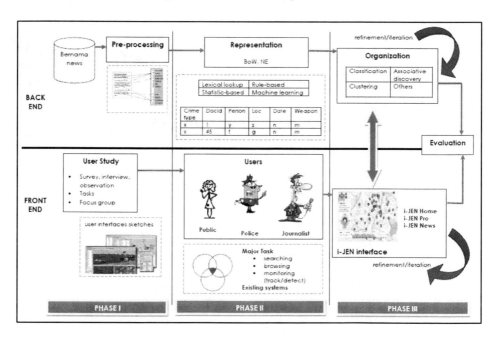

Fig. 4. i-JEN conceptual diagram

3.1 Technical Possibilities

There are three phases involved in i-JEN development approaches from the back end perspective as depicted in Fig. 4.

Phase I: Data Preparation and Preprocessing

This phase involve understanding the data provided by Bernama[5] news agency and preparing the crime news corpus and data preprocessing.

Characterizing and collecting the data - Understanding the characteristics of the crime-related information that needs to be organized and detected is important. This will ensure that the appropriate data will be collected and used to achieve good features in document representation. The data understanding activity starts with an initial data collection and proceeds with exploratory activities necessary to get familiar with the data, to identify data-quality problems, to gain an initial insight into the data or to identify interesting subsets, and to form hypotheses from the hidden information.

During this phase consideration is given to the quality of the data and how that will impact the results obtained. Consideration is also given to how we will access the data and address confidentiality and privacy issues. At this phase, considering additional information such as data from the police dataset or from judiciary, may be warranted. Table 1 shows some examples of the Malaysian high profile crime news topics that we have constructed into the solved case and unsolved case. Solved topic refers to the crime case that has gone through the prosecution and the sentence has been determined. On the other hand, unsolved topic refers to the ongoing crime case which is still under investigation process. Bache and Crestani have constructed the police dataset and they treated some of the solved case as the unsolved case [1].

Table 1. Construction of the high profile crime topics

Crime topic	Solved topic	Unsolved topic
Murder	Mona Fendy (**Maznah Ismail**) Noritta Samsuddin Canny Ong	Dato' Sosilawati Nurin Jazlin Jazimin
Kidnap	Dato' Sosilawati	Nurin Jazlin Jazimin Sharlinie Mohd Nashar

The researchers who are working in crime domain, used to build their own corpus by collecting data from multiple resources such as news portals and police databases [6]. Hence, the need for standard crime news corpus is on demand. This will be a challenge in i-JEN project since there is no Malaysia crime news corpus available and therefore, one of the contributions of the project is to collect, define and make accessible a set of Malaysia crime data for future researchers.

---

[5] http://www.bernama.com/bernama/v5/index.php

Data preprocessing - Data preprocessing mainly involves the elimination of the noisy data which may contribute to inaccurate results [23]. The first steps in data preprocessing phase is to remove the redundant stories and then the stopwords [3]. We believe that identifying a list of stopwords for crime domain will reflect significant improvement on feature selection process. Other techniques are also applied in this phase such as words stemming and tokenization [23].

Phase II: Data Representation

Data representation phase is important since the crime stories are represented in different formats. Researchers have modified and improved techniques in data representation such as finding new similarity distance measure, calculating similarity between objects and better data representation [4].

Each story in this phase is represented by a set of terms which is called *features*. Selecting the features from the indexed words is considered as a real challenge. This is because more than one feature or combinations of features are considered in this phase. Usually, the high score terms are selected as features, where the score of each term is calculated based on some predefined criterion such as TF-IDF weight [9]. This weight is a statistical measure used to evaluate how important a word is to a document in a collection or corpus.

Phase III: Data Organization

Data mining techniques have been used to extract useful information from a huge amount of unstructured data. Clustering analysis plays an important role in topic detection field [8]. The clustering techniques represent the process of segmenting a collection of various stories into subset where each subset groups the most similar documents together based on their similarity.

Clustering is widely used in TDT field, aiming to describe and construct the actual hierarchical of the news contents in simplifying the process of topic detection. In consequence, the clustering processes enhance the IR systems by speeding up the process of browsing and detecting the information needed [2].

3.2 Interaction Design and Visualization

While the accuracy and the speed of the processing and retrieval of relevant pieces of information are the key for the back-end of the system (top row in Fig. 4), the usability of the user-interaction and visualisation in terms of ease of use and the ability to reveal the patterns in the data are the key for the front-end of the system (bottom row in Fig. 4). Taking a strongly user-centred design approach in implementing the front-end element of the system, we start with our target user groups (general public, news analysts and the police) and their needs while being cognisant of the new technical possibilities that might arise from the back-end development.

Among the approaches to the user centred design is a Usability Engineering (UE). UE approach to system development is an iterative design process [18]. Nielsen recommended a Usability Engineering lifecycle as compared to a Waterfall model in building a system. His point of view is that linear progression in a development process from one set of specifications to another set will not succeed because most users cannot read specifications. Nielsen suggested development should be divided into three main stages, namely: Pre-design (i.e. field studies, usability test); Design (i.e. iterative design, prototyping); and Post-design stages (i.e. real-use data collections and feedback). Example of work that have implemented the UE throughout its system design and development is MovieBrowser2 with a user evaluation carried out with a film studies students in Dublin City University [13],[14]. By utilizing UE approaches, a system can be design and developed tailored to end users need and requirement. On the other hand, the technical possibilities for the back-end engine will follow a model define by Jesus Mena [11] in which the objective is to establish more efficient and reliable crime data detection and classification. This model defines the generic data mining processes which are: Understand the investigation's objective; Understand the data; Data preparation; Modeling; Evaluation and Deployment.

Our main goal in designing i-JEN interface for Malaysian crime news content is to enhance user interaction in information access and in exploitation of a user tasks. News information is inherently temporal while the instances of the information could take various types (i.e. text, video, images), elements (i.e. who, where, when), relation (i.e. cause and effect, chronology) and events category (i.e. murder, kidnap). This information can possibly be encoded in a variety of interactive visual display in which a user can exploit for different types of cognitive tasks such as retrieval, analysis, comparison, and summarization. In this work, we will adopt the user-centered approached in the system design and development in order to ensure the specific needs of the target users are accommodated. A number of issues that will be addressed in our initial user study are as follows:

- Visualization techniques - Our main consideration is to find out the most efficient ways of encoding crime data and a better way to represent clustering and classification. These will relate to the types of data or documents used, and will be applied by using some of the techniques mentioned in Section 2.2.

- User Interaction - Most of the applications regarding crime data interaction design facilitate the function of filtering, searching, exploration and browsing. Thus our application will highlight these tasks in its design.

- Cognitive tasks – The design of the visualization and user interaction will also consider ways to support the users' cognitive tasks such as identification, comprehension or abstraction of the crime data.

- Evaluation - The application will be evaluated in term of its effectiveness of the visualization components, usability and the system performance. An experiment will be conducted in two forms which is longitudinal study of the deployment system and also as a controlled lab experiment with a sample group of users.

Our approach in designing the application will be based on simplified version of UE process as illustrated in our conceptual diagram shown in Fig. 4. We divided the tasks into three phases. In the first phase, we will conduct a user requirement study on potential group of users in the three groups of public users, news editors/journalists and the policemen as mentioned earlier. We began our work with the identification of user needs through observations, extensive document reviews, in-depth interviews and the focus groups. It will involves qualitative data analysis. We will soon commence sketching and prototyping a system that incorporates some functional features that might be useful for each focus group of users. A number of designs of low-fidelity system prototype will be used to gauge and capture initial user's opinion and feedback. The initial sketches that come from technical stream will emphasise on the technical possibilities in order to engage our sample users in a more open-ended brainstorming and discussions rather than fixated on the current practice only: illustrating technical possibilities that our users had not thought of will help the users see their work in different lights, allowing novel features to be conceived. Our main objectives at the first phase are to understand how the end user carries out their task particularly in managing crime data and help them see how those tasks might be conducted in different ways.

At the second phase, we will manage and analyse the data that we gathered from the first phase. At this phase, user needs for each of the different groups will be identified and categorised. It will then map into an intersection of user needs and requirement. An identification of the similarities or differences between user needs will be used as guidelines in designing future visualization tools. Our main focus will be the identification of their major tasks and grouping them into the features for searching, browsing or monitoring (i.e. tracking and detecting) of crime data. An extensive exploration of the state-of-the-art visualization tools will also be carried out.

The outcome of the second phase will be used to design and developed the application and the system will have another iteration and refinement based on user evaluation and feedback. Integration with the back-end engine and data processing will be performed. These are the identified design framework that will be used in design and developing Malaysia crime data visualization tool.

4   Conclusion

In this paper we presented our conceptual framework, work done so far and the plans for designing and developing an interactive visual Malaysian crime news retrieval system. By strongly focusing on the specific target user groups in the context of Malaysia and thus adopting user-centred design approach to rigorously ascertain their needs and requirements, we believe that the i-JEN project should be very useful and practical for the community in various ways: the crime data collected and organised will be useful for continuing research and development in information retrieval and management for the crime-related corpus; understanding the specific needs and requirements of the currently practice in crime information consumption in Malaysia will be useful to help guiding and directing future research and policy-making in this area; tailoring and customising the technological tools to the Malaysian crime context will help identify new possible ways to support the user tasks in crime data usage and will open various avenues for further investigation.

Once the fully-working i-JEN system becomes operational, we will conduct a series of extensive longitudinal experiments with real users in order to understand the various features of the system we built and to see the ways those features are put into practice.

Acknowledgement. The work was supported by the University Kebangsaan Malaysia Arus Perdana research grant (UKM-AP-ICT-21-2010).

References

1. Bache, R., Crestani, F.: An Approach to Indexing and Clustering News Stories Using Continuous Language Models. In: Natural Language Processing and Information Systems, pp. 109–116 (2010)
2. Bouras, C., Tsogkas V.: Assigning Web News to Clusters. In: Proceedings of Conference on Internet and Web Applications and Services, pp. 1–6 (2010a)
3. Bouras, C., Tsogkas, V.: Improving text summarization using noun retrieval techniques. In: Lovrek, I., Howlett, R.J., Jain, L.C. (eds.) KES 2008, Part II. LNCS (LNAI), vol. 5178, pp. 593–600. Springer, Heidelberg (2008b)
4. Brants, T., Chen, F., Farahat, A.: A system for new event detection. In: Proceedings of the 26th Annual International ACM SIGIR Conference on Research and Development in Informaion Retrieval, pp. 330–337 (2003)
5. Brown, D.E.: The regional crime analysis program (RECAP): A frame work for mining data to catch criminals. In: Proc. of the IEEE International Conference on Systems, Man, and Cybernetics, pp. 2848–2853 (1998)
6. Chandra, B., Gupta, M.: A multivariate time series clustering approach for crime trends prediction. In: Proceedings of International Conference on Systems, Man and Cybernetics, pp. 892–896 (2008)
7. Li, C., Yun., H., Zhaoman., Z.: An event ontology construction approach to web crime mining. In: Seventh International Conference on Fuzzy Systen and Knowledge Discovery, (FSKD), vol. 5, pp. 2441–2445 (2010)
8. Dai, X., Chen, Q., Wang, X., Xu, J.: Online topic detection and tracking of financial news based on hierarchical clustering. In: Proceeding of International Conference on Machine Learning and Cybernetics, pp. 3341–3346 (2010)
9. Hao, X., Hu, Y.: Topic detection and tracking oriented to BBS. In: Proceeding of International Conference on Computer, Mechatronics, Control and Electronic Engineering, pp. 154–157 (2010)
10. Han, Y.: Reconstruction of People Information based on an Event Ontology. In: Proc. of International Conference on Natural Language Processing and Knowledge Engineering, pp. 446–451 (2007)
11. Jesus, M.: Investigative Data Mining for Security and Criminal Detection. B-H Publisher (2003)
12. Lin, H.F., Liang, J.M.: Event-based Ontology design for retrieving digital archives on human religious self-help consulting. In: Proc. of 2005 IEEE International Conference on e- Technology, e-Commerce and e-Service, pp. 522–527 (2005)
13. Mohamad Ali, N., Smeaton, A.F.: Are Visual Informatics Actually Useful in Practice: A Study in a Film Studies Context. In: Badioze Zaman, H., Robinson, P., Petrou, M., Olivier, P., Schröder, H., Shih, T.K. (eds.) IVIC 2009. LNCS, vol. 5857, pp. 811–821. Springer, Heidelberg (2009)
14. Mohamad Ali, N., Smeaton, A.F., Lee, H., Brereton, P.: Developing, Deploying and Assessing the Usage of a Movie Archive System. In: Jacko, J.A. (ed.) HCII 2009, Part IV. LNCS, vol. 5613, pp. 567–576. Springer, Heidelberg (2009)
15. Mohd, M., Crestani, F., Ruthven, I.: Design of an Interface for Interactive Topic Detection and Tracking. In: Andreasen, T., Yager, R.R., Bulskov, H., Christiansen, H., Larsen, H.L. (eds.) FQAS 2009. LNCS, vol. 5822, pp. 227–238. Springer, Heidelberg (2009)
16. Nallapati, R., Feng, A., Peng, F., Allan, J.: Event threading within news topics. In: Proceedings of the Thirteenth ACM International Conference on Information and Knowledge Management (CIKM 2004), pp. 446–453. ACM (2004)

17. Nath, S.V.: Crime pattern detection using data mining. In: Proc. of the 2006 IEEE/WIC/ACM International Conference on Web Intelligence and Intelligent Agent Technology, pp. 41–44 (2006)
18. Nielsen, J.: Usability Engineering. Academic Press Inc. (1993)
19. Sánchez, D., Moreno, A.: A methodology for knowledge acquisition from the web. International Journal of Knowledge-Based and Intelligent Engineering Systems, 453–475 (2006)
20. Shneiderman, B., Plaisant, C.: Designing the User Interface: Strategies for Effective Human-Computer Interaction, 5th edn. Addison-Wesley (2009)
21. Sidhu, A.S.: The Rise of Crime in Malaysia: An academic and statistical analysis. Journal of the Kuala Lumpur Royal Malaysia Police College 4 (2005)
22. Spence, R.: Information Visualization: Design for Interaction, 2nd edn. Prentice-Hall (2007)
23. Yang, Y., Pierce, T., Carbonell, J.: A study of retrospective and on-line event detection. In: Proceedings of the 21st Annual International ACM SIGIR Conference, pp. 28–36 (1998)

Measurement Model to Evaluate Success
of E-Government Applications
through Visual Relationship

Norshita Mat Nayan [1], Halimah Badioze Zaman[2],
and Tengku Mohd Tengku Sembok[1]

[1] Faculty of Information Science and Technology,
[2] Institute of Visual Informatics, Universiti Kebangsaan Malaysia
{norshita_nayan,hbzukm}@yahoo.com, tmts@ftsm.ukm.my

Abstract. The evaluation on the success of E-Government applications through visual relationship measurement model using Structural Equation Modeling (SEM) was conducted on 157 public user. Thus, the objective of this paper is to discuss the implementation of e-government in Malaysia, based on the findings of public user assessment conducted on Malaysia's electronic government applications such as E-services, e-procurement, Generic Office Environment (GOE), Human Resources Management Information System (HRMIS), Project Monitoring System (PMS), Electronic Labor Exchange (ELX), e-tanah, e-pbt (local authority), e-kehakiman and e-syariah. The study adopted a cross-sectional survey research approach and a three-round Delphi for ascertaining the definition of information system project success. Findings of the study showed that there was evidence from public user's perspective that the e-government applications were generally successful. Data were analyzed using exploratory factor analysis via SPSS and confirmatory factor analysis via visual relationship shown through AMOS, to validate the hypothesis model.

Keywords: Visual measurement model, Electronic Government, Definition of success, Public user.

1 Introduction

Government around the globe is striving to deliver effective and efficient services to their citizens. In late 1990's, the Malaysia government introduced seven flagship project as part of Multimedia Super Corridor (MSC) initiatives to spur the growth of information and communication technology in Malaysia. The objectives of MSC to achieve the goals of Malaysia's vision 2020, leapfrog Malaysia into leadership in the information age and to build global bridges between Malaysia and other intelligent cities[1]. Electronic government (EG) was one of the projects. Electronic government is defined as the use of Internet and other digital devices in public sector to deliver services and information [2],[3],[4]. The common focus is on the application of ICT to improve the internal management of the government, to offer more flexible and convenient services to the public and to enhance public participant and democracy [2],[5],[6],[7],[8].

The government flagship initiative will be the basis for enhancing efficiency and service delivery to the public while fostering partnership between the government,

H. Badioze Zaman et al. (Eds.): IVIC 2011, Part II, LNCS 7067, pp. 295–304, 2011.
© Springer-Verlag Berlin Heidelberg 2011

citizens and businesses [9]. In Malaysia, one of the government agencies, Malaysia Administrative Modernization and Management Planning Unit (MAMPU), has been entrusted to plan, implement and monitor the e-government initiative. Re-inventing government services within the government itself and to the public and business is one of the key elements for the success of e-government implementation in Malaysia. Ten applications were designed in Malaysia's electronic government namely e-services, e-procurement, Generic Office Environment (GOE), Human Resources Management Information System (HRMIS), Project Monitoring System (PMS), Electronic Labor Exchange (ELX), e-tanah, e-pbt (local authority), e-kehakiman and e-syariah. The governments entrusted a particular agency to lead the implementation for each of these application as can be observed in Table 1.

Table 1. Malaysia's E-Government Projects and Implementation Agencies

E-G APPLICATIONS	AGENCIES
HRMIS	Public Service Department
GOE	Prime Minister's Office
PMS	Implementation Coordination Unit at the Prime Minister's Office
ELX	Ministry of Human Resources
e-service	Road Transport Department
e-procurement	Ministry of Finance
e-syariah/e-kehakiman	Islamic Justice Department at the Prime Minister's Office
e-tanah	Ministry of Natural Resources and Environment
e-pbt	Ministry of Housing and Local Government

In Ninth Malaysia plan, the government spent RM2.2 billion on the development of ICT for the public sector in 2005 [10]. This figure is projected to grow at 10% annually. Based on this huge amount, public users' assessment is crucial in order to help government agencies in implementing successful ICT projects. The literature review related to electronic government will be discuss in section 2; whilst the methodology will be discussed in section 3 next of this paper; Findings and discussion will be discussed in section 4 and section 5 will involve the discussion and conclusion of this paper.

2 Literature Review

2.1 Malaysia's Electronic Government Applications

The public sector in Malaysia is going through a period pf rapid change. The government's leading role in spearheading the surge forward into the information rich digital age has compelled the public sector to lead the way [11]. In the last ten years, the public sector has become a major investor and user of information technology. The Malaysian government launched electronic government (EG) as one of the MSC flagship applications to employ Information Technology to the conventional methods used in the government operations. E-government was anticipated to improve government operations internally and the way it delivers its services to the general public. The EG applications launched under e-government flagship since 1997 are: e-services, e-procurement, Generic Office Environment (GOE), Human Resources Management Information System (HRMIS), Project Monitoring System (PMS), Electronic Labor Exchange (ELX), e-tanah, e-pbt (local authority), e-kehakiman and e-syariah. They all use IT and multimedia technologies to transform the way government operates, including coordination and enforcement[12],[13]. Table 2 summarizes the projects and their respective functions.

Table 2. Pilot Project Under E-Government Flagship

PROJECTS	FUNCTIONS
Generic Office Environment (GOE),	Provides a new paradigm of working in a collaborative environment where government agencies communicate, interact and share information.
Electronic procurement (EP)	• Links government and suppliers in an online environment. • Government agencies as buyers, procure goods/services by browsing catalogues advertised by suppliers. • Aimed at best value for money, timely and accurate payment.
Project Monitoring System (PMS)	Provides a new mechanism for monitoring and implementation of development projects, incorporating operational and managerial functions, and knowledge Repository.
Human Resources Management Information System (HRMIS)	Provides a single interface for government employees to perform human resources department functions effectively and efficiently in an integrated environment.
Electronic services (e-services)	Enables direct, online transactions between public, government and large service providers via electronic means.
Electronic Labor Exchange (ELX)	A one-stop-centre for labour market information, accessible to government agencies, business sector and citizens.
E-syariah	• Introduces administrative reforms that upgrade the quality of services in Syariah courts. • To enhance the Islamic Affairs Department's effectiveness- better monitoring and coordination of its agencies and 102 Syariah courts.
E-Kehakiman	• Introduces administrative reforms that upgrade the quality of services in courts. • To enhance the process more effective, fasters and make the case easy to handle.
E-PBT (local Authority)	E-PBT (*Elektronik Pihak Berkuasa Tempatan*) system is an end-to-end integrated web-based solution with its key objective to IT-enabled the processes of Local Authorities and provisions electronic public delivery services to its community.
E-Tanah	To improve the delivery of land administration services in Peninsular Malaysia by utilizing IT integratively.

Source: MDeC[13]

2.2 IT Project Success Model

Several research on the success factors of IT projects have been conducted [14],[15],[16],[17]. The researchers analyzed the successful projects and explained the success factors based on individual project. The success of an IT project depends on its capability and strategies to complete according to plan, based on estimated cost. Researchers considered this factor as fundamental to the success of IT projects. This factor must be closely monitored to avoid unforeseen problems that could disturb the smooth running of the projects. Success factors of a project normally begins with the ability to control cost and milestones. Due to that, care has to be taken to ensure that the timeframe is monitored well to avoid cost surplus.

This study defines success of projects on information system as projects that do not over time and cost or systems that fulfill users' requirements and project objectives achieved. These could caused proper management and/or organized system development process. This was attained through a three-round Delphi. Detail findings of the Delphi study will not be included as it has already been discussed in a previous paper by Norshita, Halimah & Tengku M. [18]. Measuring IT success is recognized as a difficult task. Therefore, researchers turned to surrogate measures of IT success. One commonly used surrogate measure is user satisfaction. User satisfaction refers to the successful interaction between the information system itself and its user [19]. User satisfaction measure has been used since 1980s until the present day. Besides user satisfaction, other measures of information system success factors may include system quality, information quality, use, individual impact and organization impact [19]. System quality is concerned with whether or not there are bugs in the system;   consistency of the user interface; ease of the use; response rate in the interactive system; documentation and quality and sustainability of the program code. Information quality is concerned with issues such as: timeliness, accuracy, relevance and format of the information generated. Use examines the use of information system and the extent of use on the information systems at specific user jobs. Individual impact examines the effect of the information system on the users' performance. Organizational impact is concerned with the influence on the information system on overall organizational performance [20]. This study used the

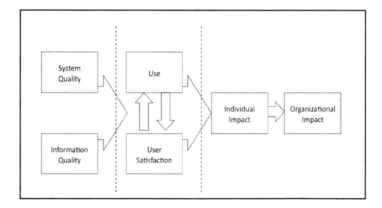

Fig. 1. DeLone and McLean's model of information system success

DeLone and McLean model [19] of information system success which is in line with the definition acquired through the 3-round Delphi approach. Consequently, based on the DeLone and McLean model, a research framework was developed as shown in Figure 1. The framework shows the relationship between organizational factors and four Information System success dimensions.

3   Research Methodology

This study used the 3-Round Delphi method for the definition on success of projects on information systems and a cross sectional survey as a method of data collection on user satisfaction. The sample size was determined by the general guidelines of Structural Equation Modeling (SEM). Several literature have suggested that a large sample is much better when conducting SEM and examining the model fit. Anderson and Gerbing [21] suggested a sample size of 150 or more typically will be needed to obtain parameter estimates that have standard errors small enough to be of practical use. Hair et al. [22] on the other hand, suggested a sample size that range from 150 to 400, to avoid problems of misspecification [22]. Ten e-government flagship applications - e-services, e-procurement, Generic Office Environment (GOE), Human Resources Management Information System (HRMIS), Project Monitoring System (PMS), Electronic Labor Exchange (ELX), e-tanah, e-pbt, e-kehakiman and e-syariah were used for the evaluation of this study. The population of the study consisted of the general public that uses the e-government (EG) applications as an end user.

As a real test requirements, 3,000 invitations through email were sent to respondents asking them to participate in an online survey that was developed in http//www.penilaian-egov.org.   Approximately 11.5 % of the invitations were answered.   350 responded the invitation. However, only 157 were actual users of EG. Thus, the evaluation of this study was based on 157 respondents. Respondents were required to evaluate agreement to statements that used a seven point Likert scale. The seven point represents: 'strongly agree' while a one point represents :'strongly disagree'. Measures of service quality were borrowed and adapted accordingly from Sherman (1997). Ten questionnaires were distributed to information system lecturers in three universities in Malaysia for pretest. They were asked to critically evaluate the questionnaire with regards to its objective, content clarity and ease of completion. All respondents responded and the feedback was incorporated accordingly.

4   Findings of the Study

The study used online questionnaire survey to measure the usefulness of the electronic government application by public users. Three thousand online questionnaires were distributed randomly by email to respondents in January 2010. The respondents were asked to evaluate the e-government applications that they frequently used: irrespective of use for work or personal matters. Based on the public user assessment conducted, majority of the usable responses were on e-service. The E-service application involved   multiple daily tasks as indicated in Table 3. The least number of usable responses were on e-syariah, PMS (project monitoring system) and GOE (generic office environment). This is due to the fact that these three applications were not really related to their daily needs   (refer to Table 2 for functionality of the system).

Table 3. E-Service Application Task

Agency	Task
Road Transport Department	a. Information services b. Summon payment c. Driving lesson d. Driving license e. Renew road tax
Kuala Lumpur City Hall	a. Bill payment b. Tax payment
Malaysia Telecommunication Department	a. Bill payment b. Information services
Tenaga Nasional Berhad (electricity)	a. Bill payment b. Information services
Insolvency Department	a. Searching bankrupt status for individu and company

In this research, a more holistic approach to model evaluation was employed, whereby several fix indices were examined instead of relying only on a single criterion. It is widely accepted and recognized that the chi-square statistics represent an impractical an unreliable goodness-of-fit indicator [23]. Thus, the inclusion of the chi-square statistics in this article is merely for informative purposes. Alternatively, the measurement model was observed for overall fitness by referring to several other fit indices suggested by various researchers such as Hair et al. [22], Kline [23], Byrne [24] and Medsker, Williams and Holahan [25]. Two important steps were undertaken in order to validate the measurement model and indicators, namely the Exploratory Factor Analysis (EFA) and Confirmatory Factor Analysis (CFA).

4.1 Exploratory Factor Analysis

The exploratory factor analysis (EFA) is crucial in assessing the measurement model prior to the confirmatory factor analysis[25]. EFA is a process to define underlying structure among the variable in the analysis [22]. The items in this study were analyzed using principal axis factoring with Direct Oblimin rotation to examine their dimensionality. The reliability coefficients (measured using Cronbach's Alpha) for user satisfaction, system quality, information quality, usefulness and organization context were 0.91, 0.94, 0.96, 0.95 and 0.92 respectively, which were above the acceptance value of 0.7 [22]. The Kaiser-Meyer-Olkin (KMO) values were 0.767 (user satisfaction), 0.867 (system quality), 0.9 (information quality), 0.802 (usefulness) and 0.880 for organization context, exceeding the recommended value of 0.6, reached the statistical significance and supports the factorability of the correlation matrix [26],[27].

In order to understand the strength of the relationship between the measures, correlation analysis was conducted. The association between the four information system success dimension employed in the study: system usefulness, information quality, system quality, user satisfaction and organization context are presented in Table 4. The results showed that the five variables are highly correlated with one another. The value of Pearson correlation matrix ranges from r = 0.59 to r = 0.88. The highest correlation value was between information quality and system quality. This suggests that users were concerned with the quality of the information systems presented to them and the quality of the information presented to them. This can be a factor that contributes to the system being considered by the users to be more of a quality and thus will be used more frequently.

Table 4. Correlation Analysis Between the Factors

Item	User satisfaction	System quality	Information quality	Usefulness	Organization context
User satisfaction	1	$.857^{**}$	$.845^{**}$	$.763^{**}$	$.666^{**}$
System quality	$.857^{**}$	1	$.880^{**}$	$.740^{**}$	$.643^{**}$
Information quality	$.845^{**}$	$.880^{**}$	1	$.716^{**}$	$.718^{**}$
Usefulness	$.763^{**}$	$.740^{**}$	$.716^{**}$	1	$.590^{**}$
Organization context	$.666^{**}$	$.643^{**}$	$.718^{**}$	$.590^{**}$	1

**. Correlation is significant at the 0.01 level (2-tailed).

The cut off value for highly correlated factors is 0.5 as suggested by Hair [28]. The high correlation value suggests the five IS suggested dimensions were significantly related with each other.

4.2 Confirmatory Factor Analysis

The confirmatory Factor Analysis (CFA) was done to statistically test the significance of the hypothesized model. The proposed hypothesized measurement model was tested using Structural Equation Modeling (SEM) with AMOS version 5.0. In this study, the proposed model consisted of the visual relationships between the constructs and the indicators. The measurement model was analyzed using first order and second order CFA. The measurement combined five constructs together, which were: user satisfaction, system quality, information quality, usefulness and organization context.

These constructs needed to be run concurrently for CFA due to the small number of items for each construct.

In SEM, the chi square (X^2) is the statistical measure of difference which is often used to compare the observed and estimated covariance matrices. Researchers have addressed the chi square (X^2) limitations by developing goodness-of-fit indexes that makes a more pragmatic approach to the evaluation process [24]. Some of the alternative indexes of-fit are Tucker-Lewis index (TLI), Comparative Fit index (CFI) and root mean square error of approximation (RMSEA). The results for the measurement model are shown in Figure 2. The p-value associated with this result is 0.000 and CMIN/DF (X^2/df) =2.0. By looking at a holistic view, the model was acceptably fit with TLI=0.84 and CFI=0.92, which were exceeding the cut-off point of .90. The values of RMSEA=0.06. In addition, the value of CMIN/DF=2.0 was within the suggested range between 2.0 and 5.0 [22].

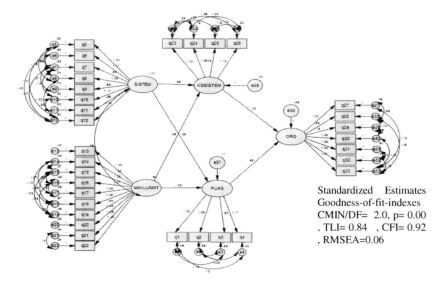

Standardized Estimates
Goodness-of-fit-indexes
CMIN/DF= 2.0, p= 0.00
, TLI= 0.84   , CFI= 0.92
, RMSEA=0.06

Fig. 2. CFA for Public User Assessment of Malaysia E-Government Applications

The CFA results suggested that holistically, the user satisfaction, system quality, information quality, usefulness and organization context measurement model provides a reasonably good fit and thus it is necessary to use it as a guideline in the development of information system project in Malaysia. Generally, the majority of public users were satisfied with the e-government flagship applications. For system quality, the public users who responded to the survey perceived that the e-government applications had system quality value and also information quality value. Beside that, CFA results also show that majority of the public users were used the system for personel or work matters. All variables that measure organization context show that majority of users perceived that most organization in Malaysia support the e-government application.

5   Conclusion

The main objective of the research is to investigate the public users assessment of Malaysia's e-government applications. In order to answer the research question , the study had used the DeLone and McLean success theory to evaluate Malaysia's e-government applications. The research finding demonstrate that public users who used the system were generally satisfied with the system. The proposed hypothesized measurement model was tested using SEM with AMOS version 5.0. The study has achieved its objective to develop and validate a measurement model of the five dimensions which can be used as guidelines by policy-makers in the development of information system project in Malaysia. The public users who responden to the survey perceived that the e-government applications had system and information quality value for them. Additionally the system very useful and the most organization in Malaysia support the e-government initiatives. It can be concluded from this study that e-government applications were successful from the public users' perspectives. This research contributes to theoretical knowledge in that finding from correlation analysis and measurement model show that model of information systems success can be used to evaluate Malaysia's e-government application. Further studies should focus to evaluate internal user either for lead agencies or other related government agencies perceptive in e-governments application. Beside that, future studies could also take case studies and interview or observation approach to evaluate or understand reasons or specific issues that relate for variability in user or system developer perception of each application.

Acknowledgments. The authors wish to thank the Ministry of Higher Education Malaysia (MOHE) and Universiti Kebangsaan Malaysia for the grant given (UKM-TT-02-FRGS-0003-2006) as well as University of Malaya to enable the project to be conducted successfully.

References

1. Raiz, M., Nazariah: E-government in Malaysia. Pelanduk Publications, Kuala Lumpur (2003)
2. West, D.M.: Global e-government. Brown University (2004), http://www.insidepolitics.org/egov04
3. Hart, T.: E-government: The next American Revolution, 2001. Council for Excellence in Government (2009), http://www.excelgov.org/egovpoll/index.htm
4. Howard, M.: E-government across the globe: How will 'e' change Government. Government Finance Review 17(4), 6–9 (2009)
5. Seifert, J.W., Relyea, H.C.: Considering e-government from U.S. federal perspective: A evolving concept, a developing practice. Journal of E-Government 1(1), 7–16 (2004)
6. Ancarani, A.: Toward quality e-services in the public sector: the evolution of web sites in the local public service sector. Managing Service Quality 15(1), 6–23 (2005)
7. Maniam, K., Halimah, A., Hazman, S.A.: Citizens Expectations for Electronic Government Services: Malaysian Perspectives. The e-government Asia Conference in Bangkok, Thailand (2006)

8. Maniam, K.: Technology Acceptance for Government Procurement: A Study on e-Perolehan in Malaysia. Unpublished PhD Thesis. University of Malaya, Kuala Lumpur (2008)
9. Malaysian Administrative and Manpower Planning Unit (MAMPU).: The Malaysian public sector ICT strategic plan (2004),
    http://www.mampu.gov.my/mampu/bi.program/ict/ISPlan/ISPlan.htm
10. EPU, Prime Minister Office.: End year report (2009),
    http://www.epu.jpm.my/rm9/English
11. Hazman, S., Ala-aldin, A.: A Study of the Use of Information Technology and its Impact on Service Quality in the Malaysian Public Sector. EROPA Hong Kong Conference (2000)
12. Malaysian Administrative and Manpower Planning Unit (MAMPU).: Malaysian Public Sector ICT Strategic Plan (2003),
    http://www.mampu.gov.my/mampu/bi.program/ict/ISPlan/ISPlan.htm
13. Multimedia Development Corporation (MDeC).:Flagship Applications (2006),
    http://www.mscmalaysia.my/topic/12073046901815
14. Al Neimat, T., Taimour, T.: Why IT project Fail. The project prefect white paper collection (2005)
15. Coley Consulting.: Reducing your acceptance testing risk: Why project fail (2005),
    http://www.coleyconsulting.co.uk/failure.htm
16. Glen, L.: Understanding information technology system project failure. Dublin Institute of Technology (2004)
17. Goulielmos, M.: Outlining organisatinal failure in information system development. Disaster Development and Management Journal, 319–327 (2002)
18. Norshita, M.N., Halimah, B.Z., Tengku Mohd, T.S.: Defining Information System Failure in Malaysia: Result from Delphi Technique. In: Information Technology International Symposium, vol. 3, pp. 1616–1621 (2010)
19. DeLone, W.H., McLean, E.R.: Information System Success: The Quest for the Dependent Variable. Information Systems Research 3(1), 60–95 (1992)
20. Norshida, M.: Internal user self-assessment of Malaysia e-government flagship applications in lead implementation agencies. Journal of Electronic Government 2(1) (2008)
21. Anderson, J.C., Gerbing, D.W.: Structural equation modeling in practice: A review and recommended two-step approach. Psychological Bulletin 103(3), 411–423 (1988)
22. Hair, J.F., Black, W.C., Babin, B.J., Anderson, R.E.: Multivariate data analysis, 7th edn. Pearson Prentice Hall, Upper Saddle River (2010)
23. Kline, R.B.: Principles and practice of structural equation modeling. The Guilford Press, New York (2005)
24. Byrne, B.M.: Structural equation modeling with AMOS: Basic concepts, applications and programming, 2nd edn. Routledge, New York (2010)
25. Medsker, G.J., Williams, L.R., Holahan, P.J.: A review of current practices for evaluating causal models in organizational behavior and human resources management research. Journal of Management 20(2), 439–464 (1994)
26. Pallant, J.: SPSS survival manual: A step by step guide to data analysis using SPSS. Allen & Unwin, Crows Nest (2007)
27. Tabachnick, B., Fidell, L.: Using multivariate statistics, 5th edn. Pearson Education, Inc., Boston (2007)
28. Hair, J., Anderson, R., Tatham, R., Black, W.: Multivariate Data Analysis, 5th edn. Prentice Hall, New Jersey (1998)

A Conceptual Design for Augmented Reality Games Using Motion Detection as User Interface and Interaction

Azfar Bin Tomi and Dayang Rohaya Awang Rambli

Computer and Information Sciences Department
Universiti Teknologi PETRONAS

Abstract. Augmented Reality (AR) is a technology that provides the seamless interaction between real and virtual environment. Since its emergence, AR has been gaining wide acceptance in various fields of application including the gaming industry. Its unique interface allows for integration of difference user interface and interaction techniques to create immersing and fun gaming experience. Motion detection which is related with visual user interface (UI) and gesture recognition is one such example. With the introduction of devices such as Microsoft Kinect and Nintendo Wii Remote, motion based technique has been fast gaining popularity as a more natural mean of user interface, which can be referred as natural user interface (NUI). This paper presents a conceptual design framework for motion detection based AR games. A physical prop is introduced as a reference point to enhance the game experience. A case scenario of a simple game will be presented to illustrate the concept. Potential design and implementation challenges will be highlighted and discussed.

Keywords: Augmented Reality, Natural User Interface, Motion Detection, Visual Informatics.

1 Introduction

Nowadays, many types of video game have been developed since a decade ago. The researchers have investigated several ways and approaches to enhance video game in such a way to create the most experiencing game ever for the gamers around the world. One of the ways is the use of Augmented Reality (AR) technology into video game; currently gaining popularity as it has the ability to give the user the sense of the real world while interacting with the virtual and physical object [1].

When it comes to the user interface and interaction, AR has several types of user interface of itself [12]. One of the user interfaces and interaction is visual user interface (UI) and gesture recognition and it can be related with the motion detection. Motion detection is one of the AR user interfaces and can be referred as natural user interface. The term natural user interface (NUI) is the common phrasing used by designers and developers of computer interfaces to refer to a user interface that is effectively invisible or becomes invisible with successive learned interactions to its users. The approach is to develop an AR games with controller-free, which means full body play by detecting the motion of the player to control the game.

This paper is aimed to present a conceptual design for AR games using motion detection. The objective of the proposed design is to create an AR game space which

H. Badioze Zaman et al. (Eds.): IVIC 2011, Part II, LNCS 7067, pp. 305–315, 2011.
© Springer-Verlag Berlin Heidelberg 2011

is uses motion detection as user interface and interaction technique. The posibility of using motion detection that can be referred as NUI will be explore more especially on how body motion detection can enhance the AR experience and give more interactive in AR games rather than using the most current user interface and interaction technique in AR which is tangible UI and 3D pointing (which can be referred as Graphical User Interface (GUI)). A physical prop is introduced in the design to provide a reference point during game.

The motivation behind the proposed design is to explore more on the used of motion detection as user interface and interaction technique in AR games due to the recent technology advancement. Motion based technique has been fast gaining popularity as a more natural mean of user interface after the introduction of devices such as Microsoft Kinect and Nintendo Wii Remote, which are referred as NUI. From the term NUI itself, it will be expected to enhance the experience of AR games. It also give a promising direction for the research of markerless detection and tracking of generic object. There are several researches on markerless AR [17] but nobody applied it sucessfully in AR games [9].

The background of study about AR, NUI, and motion detection will be discussed in Section 2, included with related work. Section 3 will demonstrate the conceptual design of motion detection AR in gaming that implementing NUI. Section 5 will explain about a case scenario based on conceptual design followed by Section 6, explaining about challenges and design issues. Finally, Section 7 will conclude the overall research element in this paper and the future work.

2   Background and Related Work

This section will explain about the background of study of the research area for this topic including the related work. The paper will cover the aspect of AR in games, the user interface, the AR user interface that can be referred as a NUI and the motion detection as the user interface.

2.1   Augmented Reality

AR is a new technology which allows the virtual and physical world to coexist. Virtual Reality (VR) allows the totally immersed of the user into the virtual world but unlike AR, user is not able to see the real world environment. [1] [2] As the most cited definition given by Azuma, 1995, he defined that AR is the technology which combines the virtual object and real world environment and it runs, allows interaction at the real time and register the physical and virtual object together. [2] In general, AR technology consists of input device to capture the real environment and output device to display the virtual graphics such as 3D object over some specific calculated position to make it coexist in the real time by using the computer to process the information and display it. The user can view AR through Head-Mounted Display (HMD), monitor based interface, projection display or by using mobile and others. [2]

Others view of AR is a continuum that spans from real environment to a pure virtual environment. In between there are Augmented Reality (closer to the real environment) and Augmented Virtuality (closer to the virtual environment) [16]. Figure 1 shows the reality and virtually (R/V) continuum with examples from games.

Fig. 1. The Reality / Virtuality Continuum as applied to games

2.2 User Interface

A user interface is one part of a system that allows users to interact with the system behind the interface [3]. Basically, user interfaces combine two channels which are:

• Input – allowing a user to manipulate a system's state

• Output – allowing a user to perceive the effects of a user's manipulation

In the proposed conceptual design, the input is using user's motion to manipulate a system state and the output will be the effects of user's manipulation. It is based on user interface and interaction that has been used in AR user interface and interaction.

There are several types of user interfaces that has evolved since the early beginnings of human-computer interaction which are command-line interface (CLI), graphical user interfaces (GUI) and natural user interfaces (NUI). Figure below illustrates the three user interfaces to their origination time and denotes their main characteristic.

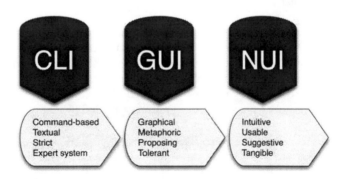

Fig. 2. The historical appearance of user interfaces (from left to right: eldest user interface to most recent terminology) [3].

CLI is based on command-based approach that provides the user specific set of commands. These commands were typed by the user using a physical keyboard as input device and the textual input commands were afterwards interpreted by the system. It was many years before since nowadays we are using the modern user interfaces which is mostly using the GUI and it cannot be used in AR due to CLI is a command-based and textual.

Unlike CLI that make of use of manual command input, GUI provides a richer set of graphical output exceeding mere textual output. Most GUI's are based on the desktop metaphor and try to emulate a real desktop itself using graphic, due to the familiar to most users. From what we can see in the most interfaces around the world currently, these graphically enriched systems and applications are based on the WIMP paradigm (Window, Icon, Menu, Pointer).

From this paradigm, it can be related with the AR user interface and interaction. One of the AR user interfaces is new user interface (UI) paradigm. This user interface is referring to WIMP, but it does not apply well to AR system due to AR system needing six degrees of freedom (6DOF) rather than 2D. Like in WIMP that can be referred to GUI, AR interfaces have to support selecting, positioning, and rotating of virtual objects, drawing paths or trajectories, assigning quantitative values and text input, but AR interaction must include the selection, annotation, and possibly direct manipulation of physical objects. This computing paradigm is still a challenge [4].

It is possible to solve the problem by using a new UI paradigm which is more 'natural', when it comes to interaction between real and virtual environment. It can be said that, AR user interface fall after the GUI and currently moving toward the NUI bringing the objective of enhancing the AR experience.

NUI is the common phrasing used by designers and developers of computer interfaces to refer to a user interface that is effectively invisible, or become invisible with successive learned interactions, to its users [3]. The word natural is used because most computer interfaces uses artificial control devices whose operation has to be learned. A NUI relies on a user being able to carry out natural motions, movements or gestures and let them quickly discover how to control the computer application. The displacement of physical keyboards and mouses is the most descriptive identifier of NUI.

Based on [5], Robert Jacob et al. tries to interpret such acquired skill for post-WIMP interfaces (that can be referred as a new UI paradigm in AR user interface and interaction [12]) emerging from virtual, mixed and augmented reality, tangible interaction, ubiquitous and pervasive computing, context-aware computing, handheld or mobile interaction, perceptual and affective computing as well as lightweight, tacit or passive interaction. From this, AR user interface can be referred to as NUI but still not reaching it. Thus, AR user interfaces are moving toward NUI from GUI based on growing technologies. Figure 3 below illustrated the changing eras of computers starting from the early beginning of the mainframes in 1960 [6].

Fig. 3. A sketch of Harper et al. [6] emphasizing past decades of computing and giving a short prediction of ubiquitous computing in the year 2020.

2.3 Motion Detection as AR User Interface and Interaction

Currently, there exist different types of AR user interfaces [12] which are post WIMP interface, tangible UI and 3D pointing, haptic UI and gesture recognition, visual UI and gesture recognition, gaze tracking, aural UI and speech recognition, text input, hybrid UI, context awareness and human-machine symbiosis. Motion detection can be referred as one of the AR user interface which is visual UI and gesture recognition.

Motion Detection in 3D-Computer Graphic, Mixed Reality and Augmented Reality is often referred to as Tracking [7]. Motion detection can also be one of the ways for the user to interact with the system. Motion detection can be referred to as NUI due to the motion of the user act as the user interface and it leads to a successive learned interactions to the user itself.

The Nintendo Wii, Sony Move and Microsft Kinect are all proving that for the average person, motion is a compelling and natural way to interact with the digital data. Thus, motion detection as interaction techniques in gaming can become a good idea when it comes into a game design. The game that has the ability to used motion detection as player's controller will give a great benefit in AR due to its seamless interaction between real and virtual environment.

Besides registering virtual environment with the user's real environment perception, the system needs to provide some kind of interface with both virtual and real objects. One of the ways is using visual UI and gesture recognition. Besides using other trackers such as hand-worn trackers, haptic devices, etc., hand movement may also be tracked visually, leaving the hands unencumbered. A head-worn, collar-mounted camera or motion detection device pointed at the user's hands can be used for gesture recognition. Through the gesture recognition, AR could automatically draw up reports of activities [13]. Handy AR system can also be used for a simple hand gesture in the initialization of markerless tracking, which estimates a camera pose from a user's outstretched hand [14]. Nowadays, Zugara has implemented a motion capture AR software which is ZugMO [10], as also can be considered as visual UI and gesture recognition.

2.4 AR in Games

Games are often recognized as the best application of AR technologies. Games are well-known for bringing new technology to the masses and the game industry is a huge and expanding industry that attracts an enormous number of consumers [8]. Games can be broadly classified into either entertainment games or serious games [9]. Table 1 shows the AR games that have been developed since year 2000 until 2010 based on the entertainment/serious classification.

2.4.1 Technology in AR Games
Technology is not based on hardware and software due to AR games are currently still primarily dependent on the choice of hardware based on the user interface and interaction itself. The software program is still very much built around the hardware that are chosen. Based on [9], C.T. Tan et al. mentioned that the work done in earlier years mainly make use of highly specialized hardware like HMDs, gloves and motion sensors. In recent years, marker-driven detection and tracking through a simple web

Table 1. AR games (year 2000 – 2010) classified based on entertainment/serious classification, technology and, interface and interaction technique.

AR games	Entertainment / Serious	Technology	Interface and interaction technique
AR Defender	Entertainment	Marker-based + camera	Tangible UI and 3D pointing
Invizimals	Entertainment	Marker-based + camera	Tangible UI and 3D pointing
Art of Defense	Entertainment	Marker-based + camera	Tangible UI and 3D pointing
AR Squash	Entertainment	Marker-based + camera, Motion sensor	Tangible UI and 3D pointing
Augmented Coliseum	Entertainment	Other	Tangible UI and 3D pointing
CurBall	Entertainment	Marker-based + camera, Motion sensor	Tangible UI and 3D pointing
Butterfly Effect	Entertainment	HMD, Motion sensor	Visual UI and gesture recognition
AR Battle Commander	Entertainment	HMD, VR Gloves, Motion sensor, GPS	Tangible UI and 3D pointing
AR Quake	Entertainment	HMD, Motion sensor, GPS, Other	Context awareness
Tangible Cubes	Serious	HMD, Marker-based + camera	Tangible UI and 3D pointing
Learning Words	Serious	HMD, Marker-based + camera	Tangible UI and 3D pointing
Shelf Stack	Serious	Marker-based + camera	Visual UI and gesture recognition
AR Racing	Serious	HMD, VR Gloves, Marker-based + camera	Visual UI and gesture recognition
Environmental Detectives	Serious	GPS	Context awareness
Gen Virtual	Serious	Marker-based + camera	Aural UI
Mah-Jongg	Entertainment	HMD, Marker-based + camera	Tangible UI and 3D pointing
NetAttack	Entertainment	HMD, Motion sensor, GPS, Other	Context awareness
Epidemic Menace	Entertainment	HMD, Motion sensor, GPS, Other	Context awareness
TimeWarp	Entertainment	HMD, Motion sensor, GPS, Other	Context awareness
AR Ve	Serious	Marker-based + camera	Tangible UI and 3D pointing
Cannonballz	Entertainment	Motion sensor	Visual UI and gesture recognition

camera or phone camera has become popular. Basically, in AR games, the technology that involved in the system mostly are HMD, VR gloves, motion sensor, GPS, marker-based and camera, and other technology that can be applied. The motion sensor device is related with motion detection as for the visual UI and gesture recognition. Table 1 shows the AR games classification based on technology such as HMD, VR gloves, motion sensor, GPS, marker-based with camera and others. From Table 1, very few games in AR use motion sensor technology.

2.4.2 AR Games Based on AR User Interface and Interaction

Refer to [12], D.W.F. van Krevelen et al. mentioned that AR user interface and interaction consists of post WIMP interface, tangible UI and 3D pointing, haptic UI and gesture recognition, visual UI and gesture recognition, gaze tracking, aural UI and speech recognition, text input, hybrid UI, context awareness and human-machine symbiosis. Table 1 shows the AR games based on AR user interface and interaction. From table 1, not many games in AR are using visual UI and gesture recognition as the game's interface and interaction technique. It shows that there are very few AR games using motion detection but its still there. Thus, it can be said that motion detection is currently being explored to unlock the possibility in enhancing not only in AR gaming experience, but in general AR application experience.

2.4.3 Motion Detection in AR Games Recently

ZugMo [10] is one of the motion detection AR software. This software has the ability to turn people's webcam into a data input device, thus will create a more NUI. It turns a standard webcam into an input device that translates a person's motion in front of the camera into data in application that want to be utilized. Cannonballz is one of the motion based game that has been developed using this software.

Recently, the interest in AR games grows further with the release of Microsoft's motion detection/sensor, Kinect [15]. Microsoft marketed the Kinect sensor as a "controller-free gaming and entertainment experience" for the Xbox 360 game console. It can track full-body motion and provides facial and voice recognition. Kinect can eliminates the physical boundaries between physical world and virtual world, thus give oppurtunity in developing any AR games due to the ability of seamless interaction between real and virtual environment in gaming. However, most of Kinect games are currently toward to VR.

In 2006, Nintendo released the Wii that features its wireless controller, the Wii Remote [11]. The Wii Remote is capable of motion detection that allows users to interact between physical world into virtual world using gestures powered by optical sensor technology. It is the same as the Kinect which is more to VR.

3 The Proposed Conceptual Design

This section will present the proposed conceptual design for AR games using motion detection as user interface and interaction. Thus, the conceptual design focusing more on AR aspect in games that can be referred to as NUI by using motion detection as AR user interface.

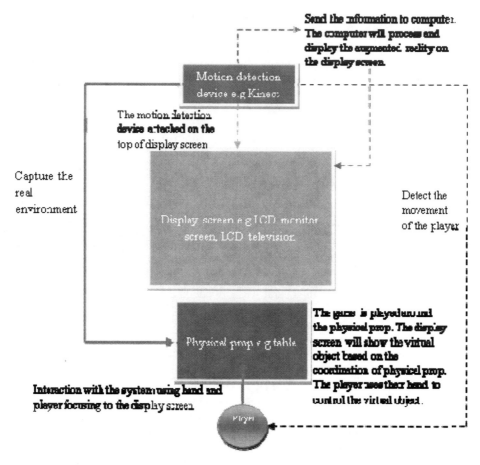

Fig. 4. Illustration of the proposed conceptual design for AR games using motion detection as user interface and interaction

The design basically based on the previous related work's setup which is required to use a motion detection device/camera that capture the player's motion [10][11][15]. The player will uses his/her body motion to interact with the game that can be seen at the display screen. However, most of games using this design, focus on interaction between player and VR environment, rather that AR environment. Thus, the proposed conceptual design promoting the AR environment toward the previous related work's setup. The term NUI can be reffered when the player use their body motion to interact within the AR game space. A physical prop will be introduced to create more natural mean of interaction in that game space. As mentioned before, motion detection can be reffered as visual UI (optic). Visual UI can be devided into marker-based system and markerless tracking system [12][18]. The proposed conceptual design practically implementing the markerless tracking system. Motion detection device is used to track body motion of the player. Then, the motion data will be presented in AR game space.

The illustration of the conceptual design is in Figure 4. The display will be a display screen such as LCD monitor screen or LCD television. The motion detection device will be attached at the top of the display screen. Both display screen and motion detection device will be connected to a computer. There will be a physical prop in front of the display screen. The physical prop here is introduced to provide the player with a reference point during game and it is expected to enhance the game experience. This hypotesis will be tested once prototype is ready. The player facing the display screen and the motion detection device. In game session, the player will focus on the display screen and uses their hand to control the virtual objects.

The aim of conceptual design is to enhance the AR experience in playing AR games and make it more interactively as referred to NUI. The player can feel that the game was played around the physical prop. Thus, instead of point freely, waving or gesturing the hand in the air, the physical prop act as an "anchor" point or reference point for the player. The seamless interaction will be real object (which is the physical prop) and virtual object (which is the 3D objects that appear based on the coordination of physical prop). The motion detection device will capture the real environment including the physical prop. The motion detection device will also detect the player's motion as the controller for the games. All the data/information will be gathered by the motion detection device. It will be send to computer to be processed and the computer will display the AR environment on the screen. The player is facing to the display screen and focusing on the screen while his/her motion controls the game. A case scenario will be presented in Section 4 for further information on how the AR game will be played based on the this proposed conceptual design.

4   Case Scenario: A Simple Ball Game

A simple game as putting a ball in a single hole can be implemented using this conceptual design. Based on the Figure 4 in the previous section, the player of the game is sitting in front of the table that virtually has a hole in any part of the surface on the table that will be shown in the display screen.

When the game start, a virtual ball will falling to the surface of the table and bounce a little bit to make the game more challenging. The player must hit the ball using their hand to make sure the ball is going inside the hole. If the player hit the ball to much or, let the ball bouncing and not hit it, the ball can falling down from the table. Every five seconds, the next ball will drop and bouncing. The next ball can collides with the first ball and there will be more bouncing. Thus, it will be more challenging when the player failed to put the first ball into the hole and both ball can falling down from the table. The next five seconds will be for the third ball to drop and so on. The game will be set for one minute. The score is based on how many balls inside the hole. The score will be deducted based on how many balls falling down from the table.

Based on the conceptual design, the game is played on table (physical prop) and the player manipulating the virtual objects (the balls and the hole) using their hand. The motion detection device will detect the motion of the player's hand and send it to computer for processing. The computer will display the AR environment on the display screen. The player will focusing the display screen while their hand control the game. The design will be expected to enhance the AR experince in AR games that can be reflected with the seamless interaction between real and virtual environment. It also promoting AR environment in the previous related work's setup. In this case scenario, controlling the virtual objects using player's hand can be reffered as a more natural mean of interaction, which is NUI.

5 Challenges and Design Issues

The challenge and issue in user interface and interaction of the design are based on how 'natural' the user interacts with the game using this design. It is concerning on NUI that will be applied. The user interface and interaction technique is using motion detection. It will make the game as controller-free. The question is on how does the user's interaction on playing the game using this conceptual design. Thus, the design will be challenging when it comes to consider the NUI aspect, as to create a user interface that is effectively invisible or becomes invisible with successive learned interactions to its user [3]. From that, it will raise other issues on how the design will be effectively invisible and interactive to the user when they play the game using this conceptual design.

One of challenge for the motion detection device is to make the device itself not only tracking the user's motion, but to track some of the physical prop that will be used during the gaming. The other challenge and issue is on the implementation of design's setup. The setup basically based on Figure 4 which is requiring to used a large display screen with the motion detection device itself. The overall design consumes a large space for a game to be played.

6 Conclusion and Future Work

The paper has presented a conceptual design for AR games using motion detection as the user interface itself. When it comes to user interface, AR interface is in between the GUI and moving toward to NUI. Motion detection is related with visual UI and gesture recognition, and can be referred as AR user interface and interaction. In the proposed conceptual design, the user is using their hand to control the game while playing it. It can be referred to NUI which is the user interface becomes invisible with successive learned interactions to its users. A physical prop is introduced in the design to provide a reference point during game. So, this conceptual design will be expected to enhance AR experience and give more interactive in AR games as referred to NUI. Future work including prototype development of an example case scenario based on this conceptual design will be the research activities.

References

1. Azuma, R.: A Survey of Augmented Reality. Presence: Teleoperators and Virtual Environments 6(4), 355–388 (1997)
2. Kaufmann, H.: Collaborative Augmented Reality in Education. Position Paper for Keynote Speech at Imagina 2003 Conference, Monte Carlo, Monaco (February 3, 2003)

3. Radle, R.: Squidy: A Zoomable Design Environment for Natural User Interfaces, Master Thesis for the degree. Master of Science (M.Sc.) in Information Engineering. Department of Computer and Information Science. Universität Konstanz (2010)
4. Azuma, R.T., Neely III, H., Daily, M., Leonard, J.: Performance analysis of an outdoor augmented reality tracking system that relies upon a few mobile beacons. In: ISMAR 2006: Proc. 5th Int'l Symp. on Mixed and Augmented Reality, Santa Barbara, CA, USA, October 22-25, pp. 101–104 (2006)
5. Jacob, R.J.K., Girouard, A., Hirshfield, L.M., Horn, M.S., Shaer, O., Solovey, E.T., Zigelbaum, J.: Reality-based interaction: a framework for post-WIMP interfaces. In: CHI 2008: Proceeding of the Twenty-Sixth Annual SIGCHI Conference on Human Factors in Computing Systems, pp. 201–210. ACM, New York (2008)
6. Harper, R., Rodden, T., Rogers, Y., Sellen, A.: Being human: Human-computerinteraction in the year 2020 (2008)
7. Drab, S.A., Artner, N.M.: Motion Detection as Interaction Technique for Games & Applications on Mobile Devices. In: Interaction Devices (PERMID 2005) Workshop (2005)
8. Anderson, N.: Video gaming to be twice as big as music by 2011 (statistics from pricewaterhousecoopers) (2009)
9. Tan, C.T., Soh, D.: Augmented Reality Games: A Review. In: Proceedings of GAMEON-ARABIA, EUROSIS (2010)
10. ZugMO, Motion Capture Augmented Reality Software, Zugara, http://www.zugara.com/augmentedreality/motion-capture
11. Wii remote, Wii at Nintendo, http://www.nintendo.com/wii
12. van Krevelen, D.W.F., Poelman, R.: A Survey of Augmented Reality Technologies, Applications and Limitations. The International Journal of Virtual Reality 9(2), 1–20 (2010)
13. Merten, M.: Erweiterte Realität-verschmelzung zweier Welten. Deutsches Ärzteblatt 104(13), A–840–A–842 (2007)
14. Liarokapis, F., Mourkoussis, N., White, M., Darcy, J., Sifniotis, M., Petridis, P., Basu, A., Lister, P.F.: Web3D and augmented reality to support engineering education. World Trans. Engineering and Technology Education 3(1), 1–4 (2004)
15. Microsoft Kinect, http://www.xbox.com/kinect
16. Milgram, P., Takemura, H., Utsumi, A., Kishino, F.: Augmented reality: A class of displays on the reality-virtuality continuum. In: Telemanipulator and Telepresence Technologies, pp. 42–48 (1994)
17. Ferrari, V., Tuytelaars, T., Van Gool, L.: Markerless augmented reality with a real-time affine region tracker. In: Proc. Intl. Symposium on Augmented Reality, pp. 87–96 (2001)
18. Huang, C., Harwood, A., Karunasekera, S.: Directions for Peer-to-Peer based mobile pervasive augmented reality gaming. In: 2007 International Conference on Parallel and Distributed Systems, December 5-7, vol. 2, pp. 1–8 (2007)

FaceSnap: Game-Based Courseware as a Learning Tool for Children with Social Impairment

Y.Y. Chen, Wan Fatimah Wan Ahmad, and Nur Zareen Zulkarnain

Universiti Teknologi PETRONAS
Bandar Seri Iskandar,
31750, Tronoh, Perak Darul Ridzuan, Malaysia
{chenyokeyie,fatimhd}@petronas.com.my,
zareenzul@gmail.com

Abstract. Gaming has been viewed as a way of making education fun and is able to engage children in the learning process longer. This paper presents a development of a game-based courseware for children with social impairment. This courseware focuses on helping children with Asperger's Syndrome to learn facial expression and social behavior. Six children are divided into two groups; Asperger's Syndrome group and a control group consisting of normal children are tested in playing this game. The result shows that there is an improvement in the former group's scores which indicates that this courseware is effective in helping children with social impairment to learn facial expressions and social behavior.

Keywords: Game-based learning, courseware, social impairment, Asperger's Syndrome, Visual Informatics.

1 Introduction

Social impairment is a disorder that includes but not limited to attributes such as inability to interact with peers, lack of appreciation of social cues, socially and emotionally inappropriate behavior and limited facial expression. Social impairment often exists in people with Autism Spectrum Disorder (ASD) such as Asperger's Syndrome as well as for people with Attention-Deficit Hyperactivity Disorder (ADHD). These people usually have an average or above average intellectual ability thus they can be educated [1].Currently, children with social impairment overcome their problem by learning through pen and papers. This could sometimes be boring and does not encourage much interactivity. Through game based learning, these children will be able to observe and learn appropriate social behaviors and facial expressions while practicing it along the way.

The objective of this study is to present a development of a game- based courseware for children with social impairment to learn facial expression and social behavior. It is hope that through learning facial expression and social behavior, children with social impairment is able to communicate and interact more successfully with other children. The target group for the courseware is children with Asperger's Syndrome between 7 to 11 years old. A game has common characteristics,

H. Badioze Zaman et al. (Eds.): IVIC 2011, Part II, LNCS 7067, pp. 316–322, 2011.
© Springer-Verlag Berlin Heidelberg 2011

this includes identifiable player, set of rules, player interaction, organized method of play and desirable goals or outcome [2]. Therefore, it is important to identify the children's learning behavior before determining the type of games that is suitable for them.

2 Related Works

2.1 Gaming and Asperger's Syndrome

Nearly half of a child's mental capacity is developed before the age of 4. Another 30 percent before the age of 8, and the remaining 20 percent by the time he or she reaches 17 [2]. At their early age, most education comes from playing games, in example; a game of Hide-and-Seek can teach a child to overcome separation anxiety. Asperger's Syndrome is described as a cluster of related symptoms primarily involving problems with social interaction despite average to above-average intellectual and expressive language ability [1]. A lack of social understanding and limited ability to have a reciprocal conversation are the core of this syndrome [3]. Currently, these children learn through pen and papers which is less interesting and mundane. It is important for them to have a strong interest in education. The use of interactive multimedia on young children's behavior has been explored and proves that it could engage children in their learning for a longer period of time [4].

2.2 Facial Expressions and Human Emotions

Each and every human being has emotions. These emotions are being expressed through words, actions and also facial expressions. Children with Asperger's Syndrome and other Autism Spectrum Disorder (ASD) have problems in expressing and understanding emotions through facial expressions and this puts barrier in their social life. There are six basic human emotions which include happiness, sadness, fear, anger, disgust and surprise [5].

Each emotion is represented with its own facial expressions. Normal people learn to understand the relation between a person's facial expressions and the feelings of emotion at young age. This knowledge is acquired naturally without needing to have formal classes for it [5]. Normal people can also guess how another person is feeling even if the other person does not express it because they have a theory of mind. However, this is different with Aspies (people who identified with Asperger's Syndrome). They could not read other people's feeling even though it is being expressed through facial expressions. This is because they lack theory of mind. They lack the ability of reading people's emotion based on situation rather than expressions.

There are several ways to teach children with Asperger's Syndrome on facial expressions and the emotions they signify. This includes using real photograph, video or animation of a human being. However, the effectiveness of these media on learning facial expression is dependent on the children themselves as each child is individual in their ability to recognize emotions [6]. Thus, it is hypothesized that Aspies facial emotion processing strategies would require greater processing time [7].

2.3 Recognizing Facial Expressions

Facial expressions are nonverbal communicator that results from one or more motions or positions of the muscles of the face. It is used to represent various states of emotions. Therefore, the way to recognize emotion is by looking at the facial clues given by the facial expression [8]. Different people have different facial expressions when they express certain emotions. However, the facial expression usually follows certain guidelines provided by facial cues from our eyes, eyebrows and mouth. Normal people usually look at a face and can simply guess the emotion. Aspies on the other hand, recognize facial expression by looking at these facial cues. It was hypothesized that individuals with Asperger's Syndrome would perform best at tasks related to verbal content when asked to identify emotion and perform poorly with regard to prosody and facial expression [9]. This resulted in their biased recognition towards emotion as verbal content only would not give the truth. A person could verbally say he is happy but his facial expression may differ.

To determine a happy expression, it is said that the eyebrows are relaxed and the mouth is open with its corners pulled back toward ears. Sad expression on the other hand can be seen with the inner eyebrows being bent upward, eyes slightly closed and the mouth relaxed. If the inner eyebrows are pulled downward and together with the eyes wide open and lips pressed against each other or opened to expose teeth then, it is giving out an angry expression. In designing a game that educates children, it is important to know the learning content to find the best game styles. For children with Asperger's Syndrome, the learning content would be behaviors, reasoning and communication. Table 1 shows the possible game styles for each.

Table 1. Relationship between learning content, learning activities and possible game styles [10]

Learning Content	Learning Activities	Possible Game Styles
Behaviors: supervision, self-control, setting example	Imitation, feedback, coaching, continuous practice	Role play games (RPG)
Reasoning: strategic and tactical thinking, quality analysis	Problems, examples	Puzzles
Communication: Appropriate language, involvement	Imitation, practice	RPG, reflex games

3   Research Methodology

NASOM is a nonprofit organization that helps providing intervention to people with Autism including Asperger's Syndrome. In order to determine the type of games to be developed, interviews and observations were carried out with students of National Autism Society of Malaysia (NASOM) training centre. A few rounds of interviews were conducted with people who are associated with Aspies such as their parents, trainers, doctors and experts. These interviews were aimed to share their experience with children who have Asperger's Syndrome in order to understand these children's learning behavior. These interviews were also to elicit their opinion on the best type of games that are suitable to the children's learning style. Observations were made on their interactions with friends and instructors as well as the way they react in every learning situation.

4   Results and Discussions

4.1   Game Design and Storyline

Using role play game with hybrid of puzzle and strategy game style, FaceSnap gives the children a chance to play the role of a photographer to help another character in the story to collect pictures for her book. The game will start in a playground with a character explaining the background of the story and the objective that the user need to achieve. Then, a map will be presented with three different locations, namely Happy Slide, Sad Swing and Angry Seesaw, where the user needs to get the pictures. Next, the users will be directed to the first location, 'Happy Slide', where they will learn about happiness and the facial expression corresponding to it. The next location can only be played if they finished the game in current location.

At each location, a character will teach the child about the emotion and facial expression. Following this, they are required to solve a puzzle. Real pictures and videos were used so that the child can see the real expression. When the game is over, users can snap a picture of a character portraying the facial expression and complete their goal.

Fig. 1. Snapshot of different stages in FaceSnap

Children with Asperger's Syndrome learn well through repetitive task. Thus, the lessons for each location can be repeated many times. When all pictures were taken, the first character will read the story from the book she's writing. She will stop at a certain point in the story to show a scenario and the child will put a picture of the facial expression that fits the scenario. Through this social story, the child will not only learn about appropriate social behavior but also to put all the knowledge into use. Snapshot of different stages in the courseware is shown in Fig. 1.

4.2 Game Testing

Testing was conducted at National Autism Society of Malaysia (NASOM) in Penang. Six children participated, in which three of them were in Asperger's Syndrome group (child A, B and C) and another three in the control group (child D, E and F). Four test sessions were performed and each session tested on the 3 stages of game in FaceSnap namely, Happy Slide, Sad Swing and Angry Seesaw. It is found that there are significant improvements in every child's score as the child progress from test session 1 to 4. The time taken for them to finish the 'Happy Slide' game has become shorter after each session (See Fig. 2a). The scores collected from the 'Sad Swing' and 'Angry Seesaw' game also showed improvements (See Fig. 2b and 2c). From the graphs in Fig. 2, it is observed that children with Asperger's Syndrome child (A, B and C) showed bigger improvements as compared with normal children (child D, E and F).

Based on the testing that has been conducted, a few observations have been made. Different child with Asperger's Syndrome have different set of capabilities. Some of them are able to read at the age of 7 to 11 years old while some could not. Some have good motor skills and able to control the mouse well while some could not. Therefore, it is important that the game needed to be flexible in a way that it could provide narration for children who could not read. However, the game should also allow turning off the narration f the children is able to read. It was also observed that for children with less motor skills, it is better for them to play the game on a touch-screen computer making it easier for them to position the cursor and consequently play the game well.

Different types of games in FaceSnap have shown different results. Games that is more predictable gives better result because the children are able to remember the facial expression as well as the location of the facial expressions. However, games that require them to focus and response quickly in order to get better score are actually much better though it sometimes gives lower scores. This is because, children would not just remember the location but can actually understand and remember the expression until they can detect it in whatever situations. From the testing, feedbacks are shown to be positive as the children showed great interest in playing the games. None need to be forced to play the game and many wanted to play the game all over again after the game is over. The children were also asked to mimic the expressions they learned once they finished the game. Child B who was always happy found it hard to mimic the sad expression. However, with the real image of a child showing sad expression, he somehow managed to mimic it.

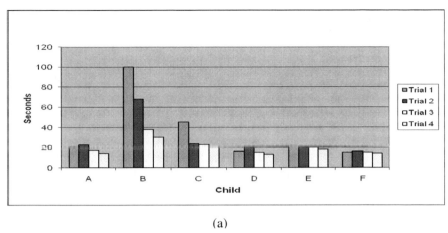

(a)

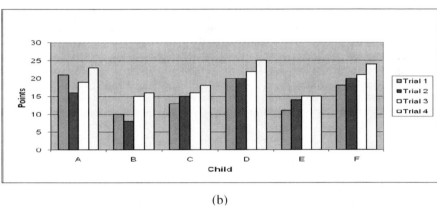

(b)

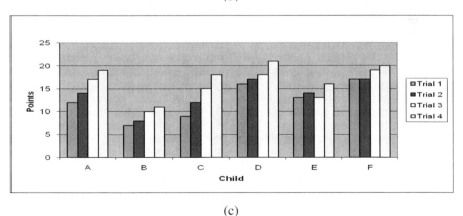

(c)

Fig. 2. Results of each child from (a) 'Happy Slide' (b) 'Sad Swing' and (c) 'Angry Seesaw' game

5 Conclusion

Social impairment is a common problem among children with Autism Spectrum Disorder (ASD). However, they should not be left behind because they have their own abilities and have average to above-average intellectual ability. Through computer based games, they may learn to overcome their social impairment and blend in with their peers. They can learn how to express emotions through facial expressions and learn appropriate social behavior. Focusing on children with Asperger's Syndrome, this study proposed a game based method is best suited for them. It can be concluded that FaceSnap is effective in teaching facial expressions and social behavior to children with social impairment.

References

1. Myles, B.S.: An Overview of Asperger Syndrome. In: Baker, J.E., Myles, B.S. (eds.) Social Skills Training for Children and Adolescents with Asperger Syndrome and Social-Communication Problems, ch.2. Autism Asperger Publishing Co, Kansas (2003)
2. Attwood, T.: The Complete Guide to Asperger's Syndrome. Jessica Kingsley Publishers, London (2007)
3. Saulter, J.: Introduction to Video Game Design and Development. McGraw-Hill, New York (2007)
4. Min, L.: An Exploratory Study of How Pre-kindergarten Children Use the Interactive Multimedia Technology: Implications for Multimedia Software Design. University of Texas, Austin (1996), http://www.eric.ed.gov/PDFS/ED396713.pdf
5. Ekman, P.: Basic Emotions. In: Dalgleish, T., Power, M. (eds.) Handbook of Cognition and Emotion, ch.3, John Wiley & Sons, Sussex (1999)
6. Elzouki, S., Fabri, M., Moore, D.: Teaching Severely Autistic Children to Recognize Emotions: Finding a Methodology. In: British Computer Society Conference on Human-Computer Interaction, vol. 2, pp. 137–140 (2007), http://portal.acm.org/citation.cfm?id=1531407.1531443
7. Grossman, J.B., et al.: Verbal Bias in Recognition of Facial Emotions in Children with Asperger Syndrome. Journal of Child Psychology and Psychiatry 41, 369–379 (2000)
8. Shah, M.: Recognizing Facial Expressions, Presentation given at Department of Electrical Engineering and Computer Sciences. University of Central Florida (February 20, 2008), http://www.cs.ucf.edu/courses/cap6411/spr2008/notes/Lecture-13.pdf
9. Lindner, J.L., Rosen, L.A.: Decoding of Emotion through Facial Expression, Prosody and Verbal Content in Children and Adolescents with Asperger's Syndrome. Journal of Autism and Developmental Disorders 36, 769–777 (2006)
10. Rapeepisarn, K., Wong, K.W., Fung, C.C., Khine, M.S.: The Relationship between Game Genres, Learning Techniques and Learning Styles in Educational Computer Games. In: Pan, Z., Zhang, X., El Rhalibi, A., Woo, W., Li, Y., et al. (eds.) Edutainment 2008. LNCS, vol. 5093, pp. 497–508. Springer, Heidelberg (2008), http://www.springerlink.com/content/j826834q456j1906/

A Visual Measurement Model on Human Capital and ICT Dimensions of a Knowledge Society (KS) Framework for Malaysia towards an Innovative Digital Economy

Halimah Badioze Zaman[1], A.H. Norsiah[2], Azlina Ahmad[1], S. Riza[1],
M.A. Nazlena[1], J. Azizah[1], and M.C. Ang[1]

[1] Institute of Visual Informatics (IVI), Universiti Kebangsaan Malaysia
[2] Universiti Utara Malaysia
hbzukm@yahoo.com, norsiah@uum.edu.my

Abstract This paper outlines the research conducted to test a visual measurement model of the Human Capital and ICT dimensions to develop a framework of a Knowledge-based Society for Malaysia towards an Innovative Digital Economy. Based on an initial analysis on Knowledge-based Society (KS),it was found that Human capital and ICT represent important enabling dimensions in a KS framework. The content domain to measure both these dimensions were developed based on empirical data and literature available. It was then tested using a sample of 450 respondents from both government and private sectors as well as NGOs. Four factors were extracted from the exploratory factor analysis based on 44 items proposed in the survey questionnaire. For the Human Capital dimension, 42 items were loaded into the four factors, and 2 items were deleted due to loadings less than 0.3; whilst for the ICT dimension, 39 items were loaded into the four factors and 2 items were also deleted due to loadings less than 0.3. The visual measurement model was validated using the Structural Equation Modelling (SEM).The confirmatory factor analysis results indicated that generally, Human Capital and ICT dimensions provided a reasonably good fit measurement model, thus necessary to be used as a guide in the development of a KS framework in Malaysia.

Keywords: Visual informatics, visual measurement model, human capital dimension, information technology and communication dimension, knowledge-based society, innovative digital economy.

1 Introduction

Malaysia embarked on a long-term 'visual' plan called Vision 2020, which provides to the 'government of the day' a guide towards achieving a developed society by 2020. This vision, introduced in February 1991 (and still relevant today), aims to transform the Malaysian society into a knowledge-based society based on 'its own mould' [22]. The 'mould' signifies that Malaysia will endogenously develop its knowledge society based on its own terms and criteria, without duplicating any other country. The approach to be taken shall be a holistic one, covering various aspects: economic and social, politics, cultural norms, spiritual values and psychology [22].

H. Badioze Zaman et al. (Eds.): IVIC 2011, Part II, LNCS 7067, pp. 323–339, 2011.
© Springer-Verlag Berlin Heidelberg 2011

All these aspects are crucial in ensuring that the development of the Knowledge Society (henceforth KS) is on the right track. In a KS, the important inputs are technology, knowledge as well as research and development (R&D), which represents what is also known as quaternary industry [1]. On the other hand, in an industrial society, traditional inputs such as land, labour, capital and entrepreneurship were used, which represents what is known as tertiary industry. The development of a nation however, involves human beings as the major player in the process, and there lies the concept of 'human capital'. Naisbitt et al.[25] opined that the technological and knowledge growths are not beneficial unless related to human beings. The word 'technology' has emerged and it does not exist in a vacuum. Thus, they stressed that high technology (including ICT) also termed as 'high tech' expands its meaning from 'a thing' to 'interrelationship' to 'consequences', which means powerful technology have powerful consequences. The essence of their idea is to balance the material wonders, i.e. 'high tech' (including ICT), with the spiritual demands of human nature or termed as 'high touch'. In any KS, not only the means ('high tech') is needed to be taken into account, but also the ends - a value-based ('high touch') human capital development, in order to make it effective [25].Thus, the reason for these two dimensions: Human capital and Information and communication Technology (ICT) given the impetus in this study.

2   Objective of Research

The main objectives of this research are as follows:

i.   To conduct a Five-round (R5) Delphi technique to ascertain a general Knowledge Society (KS)   Framework to suite the Malaysian setting.
ii.   To conduct a semi-structured interview with prominent experts to verify the KS Framework.
iii.   To conduct an empirical study (public survey) to acquire a visual measurement on the Human Capital (HC) and Information Communications and Technology (ICT) dimensions of a general Knowledge Society (KS) Framework suitable for Malaysia based on the Structural Equation Modeling (SEM).

3   Methodology of Research

The research methodology adopted in this research is the mixed method (Triangulation) approach in order to acquire the best results for this type of study. In order to ascertain the Knowledge Society (KS) framework for the Malaysian setting, a Five-round (R5) Delphi technique was conducted amongst nine experts in the field of Knowledge Society and ICT. On the other hand, to study the importance of the Human Capital (HC) and Information Communications Technology (ICT) dimensions in a Knowledge Society suitable for the Malaysian setting, a face-to-face semi-structured interview with prominent experts and an empirical public survey with the government and private sectors, as well as NGOs   were conducted. To observe visual relationships between variables of the two dimensions, the Structural Equation Modelling   (SEM) approach was adopted.

4   Human Capital and ICT Dimensions in KS Framework

The Human Capital (HC) dimension implies empowering humans with knowledge and skills needed to survive in a society that continuously changes; whilst the Information and Communication Technology (ICT) dimension implies enabling technologies that is a powerful driver for social change [7],[24],[33];economic growth and competitiveness [19]. Humans has certain underlying characteristics embodied in them. Human Capital can be defined as "knowledge, skills, competencies and attributes embodied in individuals which facilitate personal, social and economic well-being"[33]. ICT too, has characteristics described of them in this modern society and they include: interactivity, permanent availability, global reach and reduced costs for many[25].

5   Elements of Human Capital and ICT Dimensions

HC and ICT in the context of this study is viewed based on various elements: knowledge, skills, competencies, and attributes, and   significant activities related to it such as education, training, R&D, various knowledge activities, and support from the government and private sectors. Education implies the transfer of knowledge using technology (including ICT) and expansion of the learner's mind; from both the use new technologies and conventional methods. Some empirical studies of growth and its related documents have attempted to assess the role of HC and ICT as the determinants in long-term performance using measures of HC and ICT based on literacy rates [3],[23]; school enrolment rates [17]; tertiary enrolment; expenditure on education and training; years of schooling; and level of education of the labour force and usage of ICT, policy, infrastructure, infostructure, ICT application, e-Government, content, ICT provision and skills and ICT adoption, respectively. However, these measures are subject to considerable data limitations and only capture certain aspects of HC and ICT [21]. In fact, HC incorporates knowledge of an individual, which includes competence, know-how, education, innovativeness, capabilities and abilities.

Jussawalla [18] and O'Hara [28], on the other hand, recognised ICT for its multiple roles: as an enabler and facilitator in the creation and development of a knowledge-based society. Some empirical works have shown that human capital and ICT has a positive influence on organisational performance [5],[34],[36]; and societal growth [6],[12],[30]. Advancement in ICT has also caused the explosive rate of increase in knowledge production [13].

6   Knowledge Society (KS) Framework

In order to determine a nation's holistic growth, many existing KS models and measurements in the Digital Economy focused on the development of HC and ICT. In the former, emphasis is not limited to social growth measurements, such as those mentioned in the Millennium Development Goals or MDGs but also the economic growth measurements [6]. In the latter, emphasis is on the technological growth measurements such as the Technology Achievement Index (TAI) [9]; the ArCo Technology Index [3]; Digital Access Index [17] and Digital Divide Index [17] and the e-Readiness Digital Economy Index [10].

Training and professional development are priorities in the KS models used to form KS frameworks. These include infrastructure for training, training of teaching staffs and adult education. In order to develop and sustain the knowledge of humans, there is a need for continuous training and it is considered key to developing human skills. Helping individuals to develop knowledge, skills and competencies also increases HC of a society [8]. In examining skills, it is essential to develop measures that indicate the state of readiness to expand and enhance the use of information and enabling technologies to develop knowledge. The pre-eminent indicator of such readiness is the basic literacy level/illiteracy level [10],[22], where 'illiteracy is a fundamental barrier to participation in KS.

In order to be competitive in the Innovative Digital Economy and a developed nation by the year 2020, skilled knowledge workers in Malaysia, need to be considered as another important indicator, as emphasised by former Prime Minister of Malaysia, Tun Dr. Mahathir Mohamad, *"our workers must be highly qualified and be trained in higher skills…Training of the workers must be done at specialised training centres. Computer programs will be needed to do this"* [22].

In a KS framework, intellectual capital (IC) is an important part of human capital. The concept of IC includes all *traditional* references to intellectual property such as patents, trademarks registered designs, copyright and trade secrets, and also the *modern* organisational perspective that includes knowledge, experiences, organisational technology, relationships and networks, professional skills, ideas, processes, customers and market share or any form of intangible assets that are classified as a wealth creating resource [23]. Meanwhile Nonaka and Takeuchi [26], defined IC as "the stored knowledge possessed by an organisation, which may be *tacit knowledge* – personal knowledge possessed by an employee, and may be *explicit knowledge* – codified and stored by the organisation and available to individuals throughout the structure". The attributes of IC of an organisation can be summarised to include human capital, structural capital and relational capital.

Sharma et al. [30], claim that a successful KS framework, is one where there is extensive R&D activities which aim at acquiring knowledge and learning for common public good and competitive private advantage. Research activity is an integral part of the knowledge generation process [4]. Thus, research and development is a major source for KS ([1],[2], [4], [32]. The R&D activity creates new knowledge and thus, has potential for facilitating and contributing to the digital economy and a nation's growth.

7   Findings Based on HC and ICT Dimensions to Develop KS Framework

Findings of the study on Human Capital (HC) as well as the Information Communications Technology (ICT) dimensions of the Knowledge Society (KS) framework, will be discussed based on the findings of the Five-round (R5) Delphi, the semi structured interview with prominent experts and the empirical study (public survey) on the two dimensions based on the Structural Equation Modelling approach.

7.1 Findings from Delphi Study

Results from the Round-One (R1) Delphi, were analysed and tabulated as a list of statements based on three sub-sections: (i) General statements on KS, (ii) statements on ICT dimension, and (iii) statements on Human Capital dimension. This was done so that it would be easier to classify which item belongs to which dimension, and to ease the process of finalising the definition of KS in the Malaysian setting. The proposition and verification of the KS definition was based on a multiple-stage process involving review of literature as well as the qualitative and quantitative data analysis of the Delphi study. The data were based on comments, input, phrases, keywords and opinions from the nine (9) experts involved in the Delphi study. The identification of the quantitative data was based on statements that reached 'high consensus' and 'moderate consensus' in Round 2 (R2), Round 3 (R3) and Round 4 (R4) of the Delphi study. The definition was finally verified by the panel of prominent experts in Round 5 (R5).

After the Round 4 (R4) Delphi, all 90 items were analysed based on confirmation by the experts for each item. The refinement of KS definition and development of KS indicators were partly based on the literature reviewed, and on findings of the Delphi study and semi-structured face-to-face interviews with the experts. The analysis involved the use of median score, and inter-quartile range (IQR) and quartile deviation (QD) to identify the level of consensus and importance of each item. A narrow IQR [and also QD] indicated that there was a fairly close consensus among respondents. This is supported by the work conducted by Zuraidah [37]. The items were classified as "high importance and high consensus" and "high importance and moderate consensus" to be used as guidance and benchmark to develop the KS framework and indicators.

Table 1 shows the list of items that can be classified as high importance ($M \geq 4$) and high consensus ($QD \leq 0.5$). The items were sorted from the highest to the lowest scores of median and QD. The total is 62 items, of which 15 items were from the General Statements of KS, 12 items from Knowledge dimension, 22 items from ICT dimension and 13 items from Human Capital dimension. The first three items in the 'General Statements of KS' [A01, A02 and A03] ranked at top five. Therefore, it can be summarised that the two dimensions proposed, namely 'ICT' and 'Human Capital' are crucial in the development of KS indicators in this study.

The next part of this study was pertaining to the items which scored **high importance** ($M \geq 4$) and **moderate consensus** ($0.5 < QD \leq 1.0$). This can be observed from Table 2. There were 21 items that fell into this group, of which 9 items were from the General Statements of KS sub-group, 4 items from ICT dimension, and the remaining 2 items from the Human Capital dimension. With regards to the classification of items with 'high importance' and 'no consensus', it was revealed that not even one item could be sorted into this group after the Delphi Round 4 (R4) was conducted. There was no item that achieved a median of 4 and above and QD of more than 1.0.

Table 1. Items Classified as High Importance and High Consensus

General Statements on KS		MEDIAN	QD
A01	Knowledge Society should comprise of knowledge dimension.	5.0	.0
A03	Knowledge Society should comprise of human capital dimension.	5.0	.375
A05x	KS encourages access to information anytime.	5.0	.375
A02	Knowledge Society should comprise of ICT dimension.	5.0	.5
A04	KS should comprise of a balanced combination between knowledge, technology and human capital.	5.0	.5
A05iv	KS should comprise of social dimension.	4.5	.5
A07	Ethical values are crucial in KS.	4.5	.5
A11	Social well-being is vital towards formation of KS.	4.5	.5
A16	KS will benefit the whole nation through the improvement of the quality of life.	4.5	.5
Statements on ICT Dimension		**MEDIAN**	**QD**
C25	ICT should be fairly distributed among all Malaysians.	5.0	0
C14	ICT infrastructure is crucial in KS.	5.0	.375
C15	ICT infostructure is crucial in KS.	5.0	.375
C17	Local content is crucial in ICT application.	5.0	.375
C22	The government is one of the key users of ICT.	5.0	.375
C26	Digital divide is an obstacle towards KS.	5.0	.375
C07	ICT measurement should consist of ICT access.	5.0	.5
C09	ICT measurement should consist of ICT usage.	5.0	.5
C11	ICT measurement should consist of the value to society's life.	5.0	.5
C13	ICT sector comprises of services.	5.0	.5
C19	The government is one of the key contributors of ICT.	5.0	.5
C23	The private sector is one of the key users of ICT.	5.0	.5
C24	The community is one of the key users of ICT.	5.0	.5
C03	ICT is an enabling technology towards KS.	4.5	.5
Statements on Human Capital Dimension		**MEDIAN**	**QD**
D07	Basic literacy is an important criterion in KS.	5.0	.5
D01	Human capital is the driver towards KS.	4.5	.5
D02	Human capital is the input towards KS.	4.5	.5
D05	Education is an important criterion in KS.	4.5	.5
D06	Training is an imperative criterion in KS.	4.5	.5
D08	ICT literacy is an important criterion in KS.	4.5	.5
D13	Knowledge workers play an important role in enhancing the KS development in Malaysia.	4.5	.5

Note: Items were sorted from highest value to the lowest.

Table 2. Items with High Importance and Moderate Consensus

General Statements on KS		MEDIAN	QD
A05ii	KS should comprise of religious dimension.	4.5	.875
A05v	KS should comprise of regulation dimension.	4.0	.875
A05vii	KS should comprise of higher e-inclusion dimension.	4.0	.875
A05xi	KS increases productivity.	4.0	.875
A06	Strong moral is crucial in KS.	4.0	.75
A09	Self-regulating is crucial towards formation of KS.	4.0	1.0
A12	A Malaysian KS should be related to the concept of the Creator and religious principles.	5.0	.875
A13	The concept of Malaysian KS should be related to the socialization of ICT as everyday habit.	4.5	.875
A17	There is a need to focus Malaysian KS in a 'systems view' because knowledge is itself dynamic and interactive.	4.0	.875
Statements on Human Capital Dimension		**MEDIAN**	**QD**
D03	Human capital should be measured in a quantitative manner.	4.0	1.0
D04	Human capital should be measured in a qualitative manner.	4.0	1.0

Note: Items were sorted from highest value to the lowest.

Thus, it can be summarised that based on the Delphi study, all items showed a high and moderate consensus. However, on a few items, opposite opinions coexist. The cut-off point of items that were classified as high importance was set as the benchmark to be considered for KS indicators. Therefore, out of the 90 items proposed in the Delphi study, 83 items were retained and used as guidelines for KS indicators, and the remaining seven items were discarded. Results from the Delphi study showed evidence that human capital and ICT are major dimensions of a Knowledge Society.

7.2   Findings from Semi-structured Interview

The semi-structured interviews were conducted with two prominent experts to enrich and support the results obtained from the Delphi study. These two experts are prominent in the field of Knowledge Society and well-versed with Malaysian policy planning and implementation.   The first prominent expert (Expert A) is a male and a former Prime Minister of Malaysia. He was the one who introduced the long-term Vision 2020 for Malaysia, to achieve a value-based knowledge society by the year 2020. The second prominent expert (Expert B) is a female and the former Executive Director of an international NGO, and had previously worked with NITC. She has tremendous experience in KS and on the Malaysian policy especially in ICT and human development. The interview sessions with the two experts were conducted separately and voice-recorded.

Expert A stated that the term 'Malaysian KS' should be defined in its own way and the target to become a developed country by the year 2020 is stressed on 'its own mould', and not to simply follow the definition or framework created by other developed countries. Expert A emphasised that for the Malaysian KS, Human Capital (HC) dimension should encompass knowledge itself. He believes that with knowledge, KS can be achieved by human capital itself:

> *What we mean by KS is a society that is highly educated in the modern knowledge... which will contribute towards his capacity to improve his quality of life. So the moment he improves his knowledge, he is in the position to improve his quality of life.*

He further stressed that *"Human development actually also involves knowledge of the workings of society."* Expert B supports the argument of Expert A.   Thus, she is of the opinion that:

> *Knowledge is an input. You use knowledge to produce something, a better way of life, solutions for different challenges or problems. ....*

All the statements pertaining to the human capital support the earlier findings of the Delphi that human capital is crucial in the development of the Malaysian KS Framework.

7.3   Findings from Empirical Study (Pubic Survey)

This section discusses results obtained from the questionnaire, which seeks to identify the perceived importance of KS indicators from two of the seven dimensions of the

KS Framework namely: Human Capital (HC) and ICT based on 450 respondents. The other dimensions   are discussed in other papers.

Table 3. Human Capital - Factors emerged from EFA with Loading Coefficients

Item Code	Item Description	Factor Loadings			
		Factor 1	Factor 2	Factor 3	Factor 4
Factor 1 - Education and Training					
B9	Number of tertiary enrolment	.801			
B8	Number of pupils completing school education	.627			
B10	Number of tertiary graduates	.625			
B7	Number of school enrolment	.602			
B11	Tertiary students in Science, Mathematics and Engineering	.568			
B2	Total expenditure on education	.534			
Factor 2 – R&D					
B30	Number of research projects awarded grant by foreign/ international agency		-.793		
B31	Number of patents awarded to local researchers		-.772		
B29	Number of research projects awarded grant locally		-.770		
B32	Number of copyrights awarded to local researchers		-.756		
B27	Researchers in R&D		-.746		
B28	Number of research institutions/centres		-.726		
B26	Total expenditure for R&D		-.615		
Factor 3 - Skills					
B24	Intra-personal skills (e.g. motivation/perseverance, problem solving, self-discipline, capacity to make judgments based on goals in life)			.749	
B23	Communication competency			.625	
B17	Fair and equitable distribution of information and knowledge sources among citizens			.493	
B19	Application of mobile learning			.457	
Factor 4 – Knowledge Sharing & Dissemination					
B39	Number of locally sold educational magazines				.745
B36	Number of locally published journals				.727
B35	Number of locally printed educational books sold				.720
B15	Number of local professional workers migrating to other countries (brain drain)				
Total Eigenvalues		13.616	2.881	2.407	2.164
Percentage of variance explained		30.945	6.547	5.471	4.919
Total variance explained		47.882			
KMO		.908			
Bartlett's Test of Sphericity		11857.203			
df		946.00			
Sig.		.000			

Extraction Method: Principal Axis Factoring. Rotation Method: Oblimin with Kaiser Normalization.
a.   Rotation converged in 17 iterations. Note: Only loadings >.30 were displayed (except B15 and B22).

A. Human Capital Dimension

The Exploratory Factor Analysis (EFA) was used to group together items for HC dimension. Then, the process of item parcelling was undertaken to minimise the items into fewer parameter estimations and create a more optimal variable to sample size ratio. After that, the parcelled items were submitted to EFA to ensure that they fall into the general concept of Human Capital (HC). For HC, 44 items that belong to this dimension, fourteen items were loaded under Factor 1, ten items under Factor 2, eleven items under Factor 3 and seven items were loaded under Factor 4. There are two items, B15 and B22 which have loading values far less than 0.30; therefore they were deleted from this dimension. The factors that emerged from this process were then labelled as: (i) Education and Training, (ii) Research and Development, (iii)

Table 4. ICT - Factors emerging from EFA with Loading Coefficients

Item Code	Item Description	Factor Loadings Factor					
		1	2	3	4	5	6
Factor 1 – ICT Usage							
B75	Number of Internet/online transaction (services)	.924					
B74	Number of Internet/online transaction (goods)	.868					
B76	Number of Internet banking users	.829					
Factor 2 – Electronic Government							
B51	Government readiness towards electronic government (infrastructure)		.829				
B52	Government readiness towards electronic government (application)		.814				
B54	Implementation of electronic government by the government		.667				
B53	Implementation of ICT law by the government		.635				
Factor 3 – ICT Application							
B57	Number of web sites for women			.682			
B58	Number of web sites for marginalised groups			.601			
Factor 4 – Content							
B61	Number of local electronic books published				-.718		
B63	Number of public service portals providing information and knowledge				-.699		
B62	Number of online local educational journals published				-.697		
Factor 5 – ICT Provision and Skill							
B47	Total expenditure on ICT infrastructure					-.864	
B48	Total expenditure on ICT infostructure					-.858	
B49	Number of Internet hosts per 1,000 population					-.504	
Factor 6 – ICT Adoption							
B71	Number of radio listeners						.759
B70	Number of TV viewers						.744
B68	Number of registered users for cellular/mobile telephone services						.721
B67	Number of registered users for fixed line telephone						.649
Total Eigen values		15.663	3.247	2.130	1.560	1.391	1.192
Percentage of variance explained		40.162	8.325	5.460	3.999	3.567	3.056
Total variance explained		64.570					
KMO		.931					
Bartlett's Test of Sphericity		13523.574					
df		741.000					
Sig.		.000					

Extraction Method: Principal Axis Factoring. Rotation Method: Oblimin with Kaiser Normalization.
a. Rotation converged in 13 iterations.

Skills, and (iv) Knowledge Sharing and Dissemination. Table 3 shows that out of 44 items that belong to this dimension, fourteen items were loaded under Factor 1, ten items under Factor 2, eleven items under Factor 3 and seven items were loaded under Factor 4. There are two items, B15 and B22 which have loading values far less than 0.30; Therefore, they were deleted from this dimension. The factors that emerged from this process were then labelled as: (i) Education and Training, (ii) Research and Development, (iii) Skills, and (iv) Knowledge Sharing and Dissemination. Table 3 also indicates that the KMO value of .908 shows the marvellous measure of sampling adequacy and Bartlett's test of Sphericity value of 11857.203 as significant at $p<.05$. These two values proved that the correlation matrix was not an identity matrix, thus EFA could be conducted [16].

B. ICT Dimension

Similar to the Human Capital dimension, the EFA was also used to group together items for the ICT dimension. Then, the process of item parcelling was undertaken to minimise the items into fewer parameter estimations and create a more optimal variable to sample size ratio. After that, the parcelled items were submitted to EFA to ensure that they fall into the general concept of ICT. Prior to the exploratory factor analysis, the ICT dimension comprised 39 items. After the EFA was conducted, the KMO value was .931, which is considered excellent. Six factors were extracted that explained 40.16%, 8.32%, 5.46%, 3.99%, 3.56% and 3.05% of the total variation in the 39 items. As shown in Table 4, seven items were loaded into Factor 1, six items into Factor 2, six items into Factor 3, seven items into Factor 4, five items into Factor 5 and six items into Factor 6. There were two items (B45 and B46) which have loading values of less than .30, while two items (B81 and B82) were cross-loaded into two factors: Factor 1 and Factor 6. Even though items B45 and B46 have loading values $<.30$, it was decided that both items be retained since they were deemed important in the ICT construct. Items B81 and B82 however, were dropped from the list. The six factors that emerged from this process were then labelled as: (i) Usage, (ii) Electronic Government (E-G), (iii) Application, (iv) Content, (v) Provision and Skill, and (vi) Adoption. This labelling process took place with assistance from the experts during the verification stage.

All items loaded on the targeted factor with strong factor loadings, ranging from 0.619 to 0.835, and exceeding the cut-off point of 0.30; for an item to be considered as contributing in explaining the construct. The percentage of total variance of the factor explained by the parcelled items was 56.958%. There were also evidences of sampling adequacy for conducting the analysis with KMO value of 0.895 and the Bartlett's test of Sphericity resulted in the value of 5767.96 which was significant at $p<.05$, to show that the correlation matrix was not an identity matrix [16]. Since all parcelled items loaded on a single factor, indicating that the six factors actually belong to a general factor of ICT; thus it supports the proposed second-order measurement model for ICT.

8   Measurement Model of Visual Relationship : SEM

The Structural Equation Modelling (SEM) approach adopted in this study was based on a two-step procedure: (i) the analysis of the measurement models through

Confirmatory Factor Analysis (CFA) followed by (ii) the analysis of the Structural Equation Modelling (SEM). Since the objective of this research is to develop a general model of a Malaysia's KS, the structural model was not performed. Analyses were only done for the measurement models.

8.1   Measurement Model 1 and 2 : 1st and 2nd Order CFA for Human Capital Dimension

The first measurement model on HC was hypothesised to comprise four factors: (i) Education & Training (EDU_TRAIN) (ii) R&D (R&D) (iii) Skills (SKILL) and (iv) Knowledge Sharing and Dissemination (K_SHDIS). In specifying a first-order CFA model, there were double-headed arrows linking the four factors to one another. All item parcels were submitted to a CFA to test the first order measurement model of Human Capital. The fit indices, particularly the Tucker-Lewis Index – TLI, Comparative Fit Index – CFI, Root Mean Square Error of Approximation – RMSEA, Standardised Root Mean Square Residual – SRMR, and Chi-square/Degree of Freedom – X^2/df or CMIN/DF, were examined to test its fitness to the data collected in this study. Figure 1 exhibits that the model was acceptably fit since all the indices fulfil the criteria of model fit, in which TLI=.974 and CFI=.980. The CMIN/DF value equals 2.545 (X^2=150.18 with DF=59, and p=0.000). The values of RMSEA=.059 and SRMR=.0312 also indicated that the model was a good fit. Factor loadings were all significant at p<.05, ranging from β=.72, t=15.22 to β=.96, t=33.56; hence, convergent validity was established for this measurement model. In addition, the correlations between the human capital factors ranged from the lowest value, r=.56, t=9.2, p<.05 (between EDU_TRAIN and K_SHDIS) to the highest value, r=.69, t=11.19, p<.05 (between R&D and K_SHDIS), indicating that the human capital factors were discriminant between one another (John & Benet-Martinez 2000). It should also be noted that the correlations among the four factors were all positive.

The second measurement model for Human Capital was hypothesised as having a second order, comprising four lower order factors: (i) Education & Training (EDU_TRAIN); (ii) R&D (R&D); (iii) Skills (SKILL) and (iv) Knowledge Sharing and Dissemination (K_SHDIS). In specifying a second-order CFA model, there was no double-headed arrow linking the four lower order factors to one another. This indicates that the correlations between the four lower order factors were accounted for by the higher order factor of Human Capital. In addition, there were arrows from the higher order factor of Human Capital, leading to the four lower order factors, indicating that the higher order factor was hypothesised as having to predict the lower order factors of Education & Training, R&D, Skills, and Knowledge Sharing and Dissemination. Besides the usual error terms which were postulated for the indicators, other error terms which were labelled as 'r' (for residual) were also observed with the four lower order factors.

Good-fitting model was established with CMIN/DF=2.584 (X^2=157.648, DF=61) with p=0.000, TLI=.974, CFI=.979, RMSEA=.059 and SRMR=.036. The loadings ranged from β values of β=.71 to β=.96, with all loadings significant at p<.05, as shown in Figure 2. These values indicated that convergence validity was evident for the instrument used. The lowest critical ratio of all items on the model was 10.74, meaning that critical ratio values for all items exceeded the suggested minimal value of 1.96 [16].

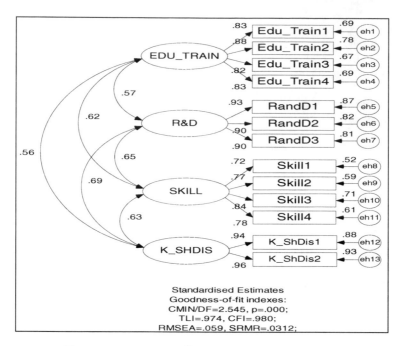

Fig. 1. AMOS Output - 1st Order CFA for Human Capital

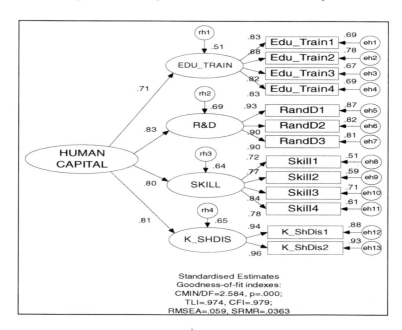

Fig. 2. AMOS Output - 2nd Order CFA for Human Capital

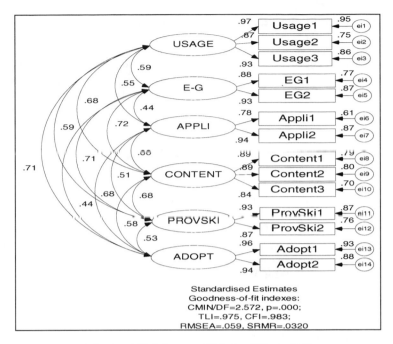

Fig. 3. AMOS Output - 1st Order CFA for ICT

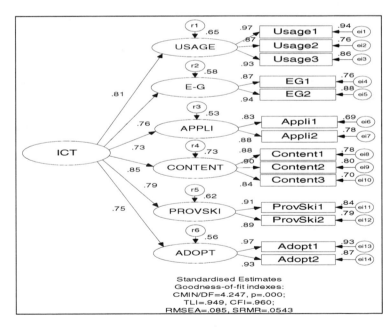

Fig. 4. AMOS Output - 2nd Order CFA for ICT

8.2 Measurement Model 1 and 2 : 1st and 2nd Order CFA for   ICT Dimension

After the EFA process, the ICT dimension was submitted for CFA. This dimension was hypothesised to have a second order measurement model.The ICT dimension was measured based on a total of 37 items. The results for the first order CFA for ICT are shown in Figure 3. The model was acceptably fit with the value of CMIN/DF=2.572 (X^2=159.468, DF=62) with p=.000, which is less than 3 [16].In addition, values of TLI= .975, CFI=.983, RMSEA=.059 and SRMR=.032 are within the suggested fit values. The factor loadings ranged from β= 0.78, t=17.12 to β=0.97, t=40.68, and were significant at p<.05; hence convergent validity was established for this 1st order measurement model. Furthermore, the correlations between the ICT factors ranged from the lowest value, r=0.44, t=7.86 (between E-G and ADOPTION) to the highest, r=0.72, t=10.99 (between E-G and CONTENT), indicating that the ICT factors were discriminant between one another [35].

A second order CFA for ICT was hypothesised in this measurement model, with six factors in the first order: (i) ICT Usage (ii) Electronic Government (iii) ICT Application (iv) Content (v) ICT Provision and Skill and (vi) ICT Adoption. Items were parcelled out, resulting in a total of fourteen item parcels. Similar to the specifications of the model for Human Capital, there was no double-headed arrow linking the five lower order factors of this measurement model. The higher order factor of ICT was hypothesised as having to predict the lower order factor of Usage (measured by three indicators or parcelled items), Electronic Government (measured by two parcelled items), Application (measured by two parcelled items), Content (measured by three parcelled item), Provision and Skill (measured by two parcelled items) and Adoption (measured by two parcelled items). In addition, all errors were postulated as uncorrelated.

As indicated in Figure 4, the model was found to be acceptably fit with the values of the incremental indexes well above .95 (TLI=.949 and CFI=.960). The value of CMIN/DF=4.247 (X^2=301.509, DF=71) with p=.000, is within the suggested range of 2 to 5, and RMSEA=.085 was slightly above the cut-off point of .08. Having mentioned that, the overall magnitude of error was still acceptably low because of the small standardised root mean residual value, SRMR=.0543. In addition, the loading values were all significant at p<.05, ranging from β-values of β=.73, t=12.79 to β=.97, t=40.45; thus establishing convergent validity of the instrument.

9 Conclusion

In conclusion, this paper contributes to the enrichment of existing literature on Knowledge Society (KS) through the refinement of a KS framework for Malaysia. The framework which comprises nine imperative dimensions of which only two of them is discussed in this paper, can act as a guideline to a country in achieving the KS status. The major contributions of this study can be summarised in threefold. Firstly, this study contributes to the formulation, refinement and verification of a new KS framework in the Malaysian context. Secondly, it adds to the body of knowledge on the general model of KS which comprised significant dimensions (specifically HC and ICT dimensions) of the KS framework. Lastly, it contributes to the awareness and readiness of the Malaysian society with respect to the achievement of KS in the country. This paper therefore, provides evidence that the two dimensions, i.e. Human Capital and ICT are important to the development of a Knowledge Society (KS) framework in Malaysia towards an innovative digital economy.

Acknowledgement. We would like to thank Universiti Kebangsaan Malaysia and Ministry of Higher Education for the financial support given through the UKM Fundamental Research Grant (UKM-TT-05-FRGS0013-2006) and MOHE Long Term Research Grant Scheme (LRGS /TD/2011/UKM/ICT/04) to ensure the success of the study undertaken.

References

[1] Rahim, A., Jamaludin, Z.: Agenda ICT ke arah pembangunan k-ekonomi Malaysia. Penerbit Universiti Utara Malaysia, Sintok (2005)
[2] Al-Hawamdeh, S., Hart, T.L.: Information and knowledge society. McGraw-Hill, Singapore (2002)
[3] Archibugi, D., Coco, A.: Measuring technological capabilities at the country level: A survey and a menu for choice. Research Policy 34, 175–194 (2005)
[4] Bakry, S.H., Al-Ghamdi, A.: A framework for the knowledge society ecosystem: A tool for development. In: Lytras, M.D., Carroll, J.M., Damiani, E., Tennyson, R.D., Avison, D., Vossen, G., Pablos, P.O.D. (eds.) The Open Knowledge Society. A Computer Science and Information Systems Manifesto. Springer, Heidelberg (2008)
[5] Bontis, N., Keow, W.C.C., Richardson, S.: Intellectual capital and business performance in Malaysian industries. Journal of Intellectual Capital 1(1), 85–100 (2000)
[6] Chen, C.: Construct model of knowledge-based economy indicators. Journal of American Academy of Business 13(1), 215–222 (2008b)
[7] Commission of the European Communities. Building the knowledge society: Social and human capital interactions (2003)
[8] Cunningham, I.: Developing human and social capital in organisations. Industrial and Commercial Training 34(3), 89–94 (2002)
[9] Desai, M., Fukuda-Parr, S., Johansson, C., Sagasti, F.: Measuring the technology achievement of nations and the capacity to participate in the network age. Journal of Human Development 3(1), 95–122 (2002)
[10] Economist & IBM. E-readiness rankings. Digital Economy Index (2010)
[11] Gao, S.: China's transformation into a knowledge-based economy. In: WBI Global Innovation Policy Dialogue: India and China. World Bank Institute, Ahmadabad (2005)
[12] Zaman, H.B., Ahmad, A., Parhizkar, B., Onn, C.W.: Voice recognition systems for the visually impaired: Virtual cognitive approach. Paper read at International Symposium on Information Technology 2008. IEEE, New York (2008); IEEEXplore
[13] Halimah, B.Z., Azlina, A., Sembok, T.M., Sufian, I., Sharul Azman, M.N., Azuraliza, A.B., Zulaiha, A.O., Nazlia, O., Salwani, A., Sanep, A., Hailani, M.T., Zaher, M.Z., Azizah, J., Nor Faezah, M.Y., Choo, W.O., Abdullah, C., Sopian, B.: Multi-Tiered S-SOA, Parameter-Driven New Islamic Syariah Products of Holistic Islamic Banking System (HiCORE): Virtual Banking Environment. In: Badioze Zaman, H., Robinson, P., Petrou, M., Olivier, P., Schröder, H., Shih, T.K. (eds.) IVIC 2009. LNCS, vol. 5857, pp. 288–301. Springer, Heidelberg (2009) ISSN 0302-9743, ISBN-13 978-3-642-05035-0

[14] Nayan, N.M., Badioze Zaman, H.: Information System Development Model: Theories Analysis and Guidelines. In: Badioze Zaman, H., Robinson, P., Petrou, M., Olivier, P., Schröder, H., Shih, T.K. (eds.) IVIC 2009. LNCS, vol. 5857, pp. 894–904. Springer, Heidelberg (2009) ISSN 0302-9743, ISBN-13 978-3-642-05035-0

[15] Halimah, B.Z., Azlina, A., Sembok, T.M.T., Sufian, I., Sharul Azman, M.N., Azuraliza, A.B., Zulaiha, A.O., Nazlia, O., Salwani, A., Sanep, A., Hailani, M.T., Zaher, M.Z., Azizah, J., Nor Faezah, M.Y., Choo, W.O., Abdullah, C., Sopian, B.: Evaluation of HiCORE: Multi-tiered Holistic Islamic Banking System based on User Acceptance Test. In: Visual Informatics, ITSim 2010, vol. 1. IEEE, Piscataway (2010) ISBN 978-1-4244-6716-7

[16] Hair, J.F., Black, W.C., Babin, B.J., Anderson, R.E.: Multivariate data analysis, 7th edn. Pearson Prentice Hall, Upper Saddle River (2010)

[17] ITU. World telecommunication/ICT development report (2010)

[18] Jussawalla, M.: Bridging the "global digital divide". In: Jussawalla, M., Taylor, R.D. (eds.) Information Technology Parks of the Asia Pacific: Lessons for the Regional Digital Divide. M.E. Sharpe, Armonk (2003)

[19] Kuppusamy, M., Shanmugam, B.: Information-communication technology and economic growth in Malaysia. Review of Islamic Economics 11(2), 87–100 (2007)

[20] Kwong, H.C.: Being critical on ICT and development. Paper Read at The 6th International Malaysian Studies Conference (MSC6), Kuching, Sarawak, August 5-7. Organised by Malaysian Social Science Association (2008)

[21] Laroche, M., Merette, M., Ruggeri, G.C.: On the concept and dimensions of human capital in a knowledge-based economy context. Canadian Public Policy/Analyse de Politiques 25(1), 87–100 (1999)

[22] Mohamad, M.: Malaysia: The way forward. Centre for Economic Research & Services. Malaysian Business Council, Kuala Lumpur (1991)

[23] Mansell, R., When, U.: Knowledge societies: Information technology for sustainable development. United Nations Commission on Science and Technology for Development, New York (1998)

[24] McElhinney, S.: Exposing the interests: Decoding the promise of the global knowledge society. New Media & Society 7(6), 748–769 (2005)

[25] Naisbitt, J., Naisbitt, N., Philips, D.: High tech high touch: Technology and our search for meaning. Nicholas Brealey Publishing, London (1999)

[26] Nonaka, I., Toyama, R., Konno, N.: SECI, Ba and leadership: A unified model of dynamic knowledge creation. Long Range Planning - International Journal of Strategic Management 33(1), 5–34 (2000)

[27] Hamid, N.A., Zaman, H.B.: Kriteria dan indikator masyarakat berpengetahuan di kalangan masyarakat Malaysia. Paper Read at Seminar Kebangsaan 2007 Merapatkan Jurang Digital: Inisiatif Malaysia, December 10-11. Organised by E-Community Research Centre. Universiti Kebangsaan Malaysia, Kuala Lumpur (2007)

[28] O'Hara, M.: Strangers in a strange land: Knowing, learning and education for the global knowledge society. Futures 39(8), 930–941 (2007)

[29] Sayed, H., Cheng, M.Y.: An introduction to knowledge economy: Concepts and issues, 2nd edn. McGraw-Hill, Kuala Lumpur (2004)

[30] Sharma, R.S., Ng, W.J., Dharmawirya, M., Samuel, E.M.: A policy framework for developing knowledge societies. International Journal of Knowledge Society Research 1(1), 23–46 (2010)

[31] Shariffadeen, T.M.A.: Knowledge and ICT for development and poverty eradication. Paper Presented at Workshop on Science and Technology for Development: Poverty Eradication, Kuala Lumpur (2008)

[32] Shapira, P., Youtie, J., Yogeesvaran, K., Zakiah, J.: Knowledge economy measurement: Methods, results and insights from the Malaysian knowledge content study. Research Policy 35(10), 1522–1537 (2006)

[33] Toffler, A.: The third wave. Bantam Books, London (1980)

[34] Ulku, H.: R&D innovation and economic growth: An empirical analysis. In: International Monetary Fund (2004), http://ssrn.com/abstract=879010 (October 23, 2008)

[35] Walker, D.C.: Exploring the human capital contribution to productivity profitability and market evaluation of the firm, Webster University (2001)

[36] Youndt, M.A.: Human resource management system, intellectual capital and organizational performance. Doctoral thesis. Pennsylvania State University (1998)

[37] Manaf, Z.A.: Establishing the national digital cultural heritage repository in Malaysia. Library Review 57(7), 537–548 (2008)

Visualization of the Hadith Chain of Narrators

Zarina Shukur, Norasikin Fabil, Juhana Salim, and Shahrul Azman Noah

Fakulti Teknologi dan Sains Maklumat, Universiti Kebangsaan Malaysia,
43600 Bangi, Selangor, Malaysia
{zs,samn,js}@ftsm.ukm.my, norasikin@upsi.edu.my

Abstract. The large amount of classic books needs to be explored during the activity in studying the Science of Hadith. In brief, Science of Hadith is a study related to the knowledge about Prophet Muhammad (peace be upon him) in Islamic believe. The main aim of the study is to verify the authentication of the story. Hadith contain not just the story, but also record the narrators (or transmitter) of it. One story can have several chains of narrators. This also means that one narrator can transmit several different stories about Prophet Muhammad. This paper describes preliminary results of our work on an Information Visualization approach to view the chain of Hadith narrators, which indirectly show the flow of story about the Prophet in interesting view. We developed a prototype of Chain of Hadith Narrators Visualizer (CHN) and tested it with 20 students of Islamic Education Programme. The findings of this study showedthat the information visualization approach is an appropriate tool to support the learning of Science of Hadith.

Keywords: Information Visualization, Science of Hadith, Domain Intellectual Visualization.

1 Introduction

The benefits of using Information Visualization (IV) techniques cannot be denied. Spence (2007) stated that one of the benefits of information visualization is the ability to understand about information from different perspective in order to gain new knowledge. Whilst by having a tool that can visualize information, it can be used in learning environment and as an analysis tool in the respective area (Sedig et al., 2003).

Azami (1988) defines hadith literature as the literature which consists of the narrations of the life of the prophet and the things approved by him. Whilst in brief, Science of Hadith is said by IbnHajr as the knowledge of the principles by which the condition of the narrator and the narrated are determined. In this work, we are interested to observe the chain of narrators of hadith by using IV technique. The main related work that has inspired us in applying this technique in the Science of Hadith domain is by Chen and Paul (1999). The latest IV applications that have motivated us is the Historical Archives research by Katifori et. al (2008) and the citation patterns of 113 years of physical review by Herr et. al (2008).

H. Badioze Zaman et al. (Eds.): IVIC 2011, Part II, LNCS 7067, pp. 340–347, 2011.

The rest of the paper is organized as follows: Section 2 describes about the domain knowledge that is hadith, section 3 is a short description of the technique that we used, section 4 shows the prototype that have been developed, section 5 shows the findings based on the feedback of activities in studying the Science of Hadith and, we conclude the paper in the last section.

2   Knowledge Domain: The Hadith

The collection of hadith can be found in six major hadith collections that are: SahihBukhari, Sahih Muslim, SunanAbiDa'ud, Sunan al-Tirmidhi, SunanSughra, SunanIbnMaja. Collections such as SahihBukhari is a collection of hadith by a great scholar name Muhammad ibn Ismail al-Bukhari (popularly known as Imam Bukhari). SahihBukhari records about nine thousand hadith, that are put into order based on different issues. However, if only the unique hadith is counted, it will be around two thousands unique hadith in the collection. After the compilation of hadith by these great scholars, there is no more need to record new narrators. Scholar like Bukhari, is only about 220 years time difference after the death of Prophet Muhammad.

The structure of hadith can be seen in the following example (Figure 1). The example is a hadith taken from the collection of 40 hadith by Imam Nawawi, which he referred from SahihBukhari and Sahih Muslim:

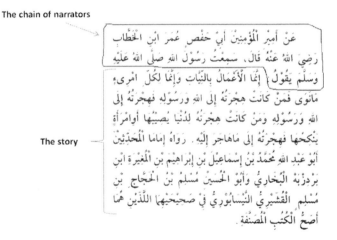

Fig. 1. Sample of a recorded Hadith

Translated in English:

It is narrated on the authority of AmirulMu'minin, Abu Hafs 'Umar bin al-Khattab, radiyallahu 'anhu, who said: I heard the Messenger of Allah, sallallahu 'alayhiwasallam, say:

"Actions are (judged) by motives (niyyah), so each man will have what he intended. Thus, he whose migration (hijrah) was to Allah and His Messenger, his migration is to Allah and His Messenger; but he whose migration was for some worldly thing he might gain, or for a wife he might marry, his migration is to that for which he migrated."

Azami (1988) gave an example to show how the chain of narrators proliferated:

Abu Hurairah reported that Rasululllah (peace be upon him) said when anyone amongst you wakes up from sleep, he must not put his hand in a utensil till he has washed it three times, for he does not know where his hand was during sleep.

(The complete chain of narrators is not written in this paper. However it can be referred in the six major hadith collections.) According to Azami (1977) there were at least thirteen students of Abu Hurairah that transmitted this hadith from him, and there were sixteen scholars who transmitted this hadith from the students of Abu Hurairah. One of the approaches in studying the veracity of hadith is to analyse the reliability of the chain of narrators. The information of hadith's narrators can be found in biographical dictionaries such as IbnHajar al-Asqalani's "Tahdhīb al-Tahdhīb" or al-Dhahabi's "Tadhkirat al-huffāz." The information includes:

- The narator's name.
- Their date and place of birth.
- Familial connections.
- Teachers-students relationship.
- Religiosity.
- Moral behaviour.
- Literary output.
- Their travel
- Their date of death.

One hadith can be found in more than one place in a hadith collection, for example in page X and Y of SahihBukhari. It means that it might have different chain of narrators. The same hadith can also be found in different collection such as SahihBukhari and Sahih Muslim, which might have different chain of narrators as well. One chain of narrators will have a number of narrators, starting from companions. Information of one narrator can be found in several biographical dictionaries. As a result, the study in Science of Hadith is quite labor intensive. The main reason to this is one has to search and collect information from several collections of hadith and biographical dictionaries.

3 The Visualization Approach

Shneiderman (1996) has summarized the user interface for information visualization based on the type of concern data i.e. temporal, dimensional, hierarchical, network or workspace. He also list out some systems that have been developed by various institutions. Based on the data type, he proposed Information Visualization Interface Taxonomy.

Since the chain of Hadith narrators proliferates like a tree structure, therefore we employ hierarchical approach to visualize the chain of narrators for our prototype.

However, we found out that multi-dimensional is suitable if the biographical information of the narrators (such as geography, date of birth etc.) is taken into consideration.

4 The Prototype

The main function of the prototype is to aid in accessing the information related to hadith. At the moment, the prototype implements the first three hadiths in the collection of Hadith 40 of Imam Nawawi. Based on these three hadiths, several chains of narrators were obtained from the six canon of Hadith collection. Based on narrator biographical dictionaries, the information of those narrators can be recorded.

4.1 Prototype

Figure 2 shows the prototype of Chain of Hadith Narrators Visualizer (CHNV). This prototype can support Science of Hadith researchers to obtain information about each narrators of a hadith and its chain. The interface of the prototype is divided into two areas; the visualizer area and the text area. The visualizer area displays the narrator's information and its chain in the form of graph, whilst the text area displays individual Hadith narrator information and its chain in text form. Additional and yet significant information such as the story itself, is also displayed.

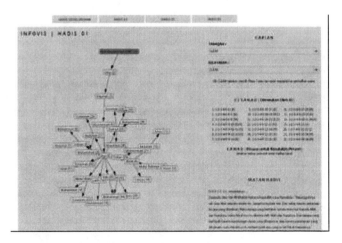

Fig. 2. The interface of CHNV prototype

4.2 Example of Output

By using this visualizer, one can obtain a chain of hadith narrators for one specific narrator as shown in Figure 3. From the figure, the focus narrator is Abdullah. In the text area, it displays the chain that involves Abdullah, as well as detail information about him. The chain of hadith narration through Abdullah is visualized in blue that is:

Abdullah→Yazid→Yahya→Muhammad→Alqamah→Umar→Muhammad s.a.w.

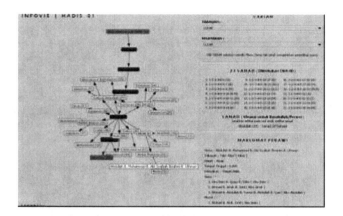

Fig. 3. Visualization of One Narrator in One Chain

Besides that, an analysis of six major hadith collections can also be displayed, as in Figure 4. The figure shows the searching of generation for the whole narrators in hadith one, two and three. Generation of narrators refers to whether he is a companion of Prophet, follower of the companion, or follower of the companion follower, and so on. Sayuti in his book Tabaqat al-huffaz recorded about 24 level of narrators generation. The generation analysis shows that there are only two narrators who are also companions and they are Umar and Abdullah.

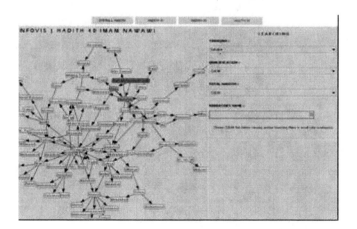

Fig. 4. Visualization of Chain of Narrators for Three Hadith

A student can also obtain one level chain of a specific narrator, as shown in Figure 5. For example, Abdullah's chain relation with Kasmah, Matar and Uthman as a transmitter (teacher) is coloured in green and his relation with Humaid and Yahya as a receiver (student) is coloured in blue.

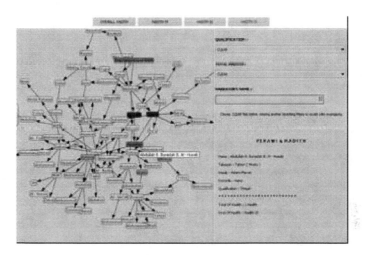

Fig. 5. One Level Information of a specific narrator

5   Findings

In this work, we have implemented a hierarchical information visualization method to visualise the chain of narrators in hadiths. Aspects of context + focus method were also implemented in the sense that user can focus on specific narrator in order to obtain further information on his relationships with other narrators in other hadiths. A prototype was developed in order to illustrate the effectiveness of the method. The prototype has been tested by 20 students of the Islamic Education Programme. The aim of this test is to get feedback on the activity in studying the Science of Hadith using the prototype and the traditional materials. A set of question was asked orally to the respondents and they have to answerby using the prototype and the traditional materials. An example of the question asked is shown below:

Could you define how many chains of narrators through the narrator's name "Hamad"?

The question had been written based on the main activities in studying the Science of Hadith. The finding is shown in table 1.

Table 1. Findings on activities in studying the Science of Hadith

Activity		1	2	3	4	5	Mean	Interpretation
1. Identify the chain of narrators	System	0 0%	0 0%	0 0%	1 5%	19 95%	4.95	Easier
	Traditional	0 0%	1 5%	10 50%	6 30%	3 15%	3.45	Easy
2. Identify the narrators in the chain given	System	0 0%	0 0%	0 0%	0 0%	20 100%	5	Easier
	Traditional	0 0%	0 0%	14 70%	1 5%	5 25%	3.55	Easy
3. Identify the relationships between the narrators.	System	0 0%	0 0%	0 0%	0 0%	20 100%	5	Easier
	Traditional	0 0%	1 5%	10 50%	6 30%	3 15%	3.55	Easy
4. Do analysis of the chain for three hadith based on the narrator given	System	0 0%	0 0%	0 0%	1 5%	19 95%	4.95	Easiest
	Traditional	15 75%	3 15%	1 5%	0 0%	0 0%	1.2	Very Difficult
5. Remember the chain of narrators	System	0 0%	0 0%	1 5%	2 10%	17 85%	4.8	Easiest
	Traditional	0 0%	8 40%	8 40%	4 20%	0 0%	2.8	Difficult
Overall Means	System						4.94	Easiest
	Traditional						2.91	Difficult

1= Very Difficult, 2= Difficult, 3=Easy, 4=Easier, 5=Easiest

Table 1 shows the differences on the level of performingthe activities instudying the Science of Hadith. Some of the activities are easily done by using the traditional material. However, it also showed that students faced difficulty in doing analysis involving more than one hadith. On contrary, the activities became easier when students used the prototype. To support this result, we also did think aloud process to get the respond from the users on usability of the prototype. Table 2 shows the summarization of the think aloud process.

Table 2. Summarization of think aloud on usability of the prototype

Item	Component	User's responds
1.	Interface	a. Match the knowledge domain b. Feel happy but strange with the new interface c. Highly applicable to deliver the chain information.
2.	Interactivities	a. Interesting b. Fast in respond c. Easy to understand the interaction d. Enjoy using the prototype.
3.	IV Approach	a. Support the usage of IV approach for visualizing the chain. b. Good in handling system although do not very well understand about IV.
4.	Usability in Science of Hadith	a. Most appropriate as a tool for studying Science of Hadith b. It helps to understand and to memorized the chain c. Very useful d. Extend for a larger number of narrators. e. Happy with the new and alternative method in doing activities in Science of Hadith

The summarization of the think aloud showed that there is positive respond from the users on the ability of the prototype. Moreover, based on the test given earlier, it showed that the information visualization approach is an appropriate tool to help the activity in studying the Science of Hadith.

6 Conclusion

Visualizing the chain of Hadith narrators seems a straight forward effort. By having this tool, we hope to support the learning of Science of Hadith. The application of graph view visualisation technique in representing the domain of hadith knowledge enables the visualization of huge amount of hadith narrators data and complex link between list of hadith narrators which has never been done before. The context + focus method on the hand allows focusing on specific narrators and explore his contextual links with other narrators.In addition, this proposed technique visualizes the sender and receiver involved in hadith passing and structure the list of narrators in hadith passing. However, as a prototype, we have not implemented the detail information about each narrator. Once we implement the details, the knowledge of the 'chain' itself will be more appealing. For example, the date of death of the transmitter must be after the date birth of the immediate receiver. In addition, the age of receiver must be 'akilbaligh' (adult) at the time of receiving the message. Once we have this, the multi-dimensional approach is one of the possible approach to visualize the chain.

Acknowledgments. The authors would like to thank brotherAzhar Abdul Shukur, Bachelor of Science of Hadith, Universiti Abu Bakar, Pakistan for checking the technical aspect of the hadith term in this writing.

References

1. Azami, M.M.: Studies in Hadith Methodology and Literature. American Trust Publications, Indiana (1977)
2. Herr II, B.W., Duhon, R.J., Borner, K., Hardy, E.F., Penumarthy, S.: 113 Years of Physical Review: Using Flow Maps to Show Temporal and Topical Citation Patterns. In: Proceeding of 12th International Conference Information Visualization, pp. 421–426 (2008)
3. Chen, C., Paul, R.J.: Research Future: Visualizing a Knowledge Domain's Intellectual Structure. Computer 34, 65–71 (1999)
4. Katifori, A., Torou, E., Vassilakis, C., Halatsis, C.: Supporting Research in Historical Archives: Historical Information Visualization and Modeling Requirements. In: Proceeding of 12th International Conference Information Visualization, pp. 32–37 (2008)
5. Shneiderman, B.: The Eyes Have It: A Task by Data Type Taxonomy for Information Visualizations. In: Proceedings of IEEE Visual Languages, pp. 336–343 (1996)
6. Spence, R.: Information Visualization: Design for Interaction, 2nd edn. Prentice Hall (2007)
7. Sedig, K., Rowhani, S., Morey, J., Liang, H.-N.: Application of information visualization techniques to the design of a mathematical mindtool: a usability study. Information Visualization 2, 142–159 (2003)

A New Framework
for Phylogenetic Tree Visualization

Wan Mohd Nazmee Wan Zainon,
Abdullah Zawawi Talib, and Bahari Belaton

School of Computer Sciences, Universiti Sains Malaysia,
11800 USM, Penang, Malaysia
{nazmee,azht,bahari}@cs.usm.my

Abstract. This paper focuses on tree structured data visualization. The impetus for the work will be in the domain of phylogenetic classification, which is used by the biologists to describe possible evolutionary relationships between species or individuals based on their DNA or protein sequences. It examines current tree visualization and comparison techniques and proposes a new framework that display fully resolved binary trees in a way that facilitates their visual comparison. A prototype interactive tool named VCPT (Visual Comparison of Phylogenetic trees) is developed to explore the proposed framework and issues in regard to visual comparison and manipulation of phylogenetic trees. Preliminary evaluation suggests that the proposed framework and the prototype application are helpful for the users to easily understand and interpret their tree structured data

Keywords: Phylogenetic Trees, Bioinformatics Visualization, Tree Structured Data.

1 Introduction

Phylogenetics is a field with a growing impact on a variety of science areas and can benefit greatly from the use of visualization techniques. It presents a number of visualization challenges. Biologists and geneticists use phylogenetic trees to represent the evolutionary interrelationships between collections of related species or genes. The discovery and analysis of those relationships may help in many practical applications such as drug discovery, forensics, disease control, and ecological modelling. As Hall [1] plainly stated 'Evolution is important because not only does it provide a scientific answer to the question of human existence but it also forms a framework for understanding the biological diversity we observe around us'.

Biologists construct phylogenetic trees by examining the phenotypes or genotypes of a collection of organisms and attempting to infer the evolutionary process by which the organisms came to be. For example, a geneticist might obtain DNA sequence data from a range of species or from individuals within a population. Then, by comparing the sequences, she could infer how the sampled organisms might have evolved via a series of mutations, each caused by one change in the DNA sequence. This

H. Badioze Zaman et al. (Eds.): IVIC 2011, Part II, LNCS 7067, pp. 348–359, 2011.
© Springer-Verlag Berlin Heidelberg 2011

hypothesised evolutionary history is then represented as a "tree of life" showing how possible ancestors could have led to the current organisms.

Biologists have devised a range of algorithms, based on strategies such as Maximum Likelihood and Maximum Parsimony [2], for computing such phylogenetic trees. However, there is no "gold standard"; current practice dictates that several different methods be applied to the sequence data [3]. Different theories and methods about the evolutionary relationship of the same set of species also result in different phylogenetic trees. A similar situation arises when several species have evolved in close association (co-evolution); the biologist might be interested in understanding how the phylogenetic tree for one species compares with that for the co-evolved species. A fundamental problem in computational biology is to determine how much the two theories have in common. To a certain extent, this problem can be solved by visually comparing these phylogenetic trees to get a more complete picture of the relationships involved.

While some numerical measures are currently being used as a basis for tree comparison, these tasks usually require extensive visual inspection. Numerous applications have been developed in this field to address these issues to varying degrees. However, while phylogenetic inference methods are comparatively well developed, tools in this domain are characterized by a lack of effective visualization techniques. It is not uncommon for biologist to "(fall) back on paper, tape and highlighter pens" due to current deficiencies in phylogenetic visualization programs [4].

The comparison between the trees derived from various experimental data is necessary in order to find the best model for a given set of species. This is where computer science comes into the picture by providing the algorithms and applications that will give such results. Such application should be interactive; that is, it should be capable of various tree manipulations, in order to maximise the discovery of knowledge about the given data.

It should address two major issues that have risen in currently available applications:

- how to efficiently and effectively compare phylogenetic trees, and
- how to visually present the results of the comparison

2 Background and Related Work

2.1 Phylogenetic Analysis and Phylogenetic Trees

Phylogenetic analysis is the field of biology that deals with identifying and understanding the evolutionary relationships among the many different kinds of life on earth, both current and extinct. Evolutionary theory states that similarity among individuals or species is attributed to common descent or inheritance from a common ancestor. This means that the relationships established by phylogenetic analysis can be described as a species' evolutionary history. Understanding this history has been the focus of much research in biology.

Phylogenetic trees allow biologists to organize their thinking about an organism or gene of interest in terms of its relationship to other organisms or genes, and may allow them to draw conclusion about its biological functions that would not otherwise be apparent.

A phylogenetic tree is a mathematical structure that is used to model the actual evolutionary history of a group of sequences or organisms [5]. Fig. 1 illustrates some terminology used to describe phylogenetic trees.

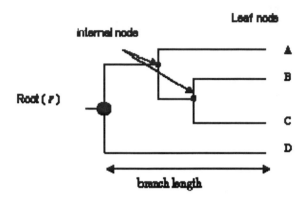

Fig. 1. Example of (fictitious) phylogenetic tree

- **Leaf nodes** represent sequences or organisms for which the data is available.
- **Internal nodes** represent hypothetical ancestors inferred by phylogenetic analysis.
- A **branch** connects nodes together. It defines the relationship between the species in term of descent and ancestry. **Branch length** (when stated) represents the number of evolutionary changes that separate the nodes connected by the branch.

2.2 Tree Comparison

Phylogenetic data is characteristically noisy and incomplete [7]. When dealing with such data, users always face the problem of determining which method is going to be used to construct phylogenetic trees from sequence data. There is no "gold standard" for constructing phylogenetic trees; current practice dictates that several different methods be applied to the sequence data [3]. When this happens, users sometimes need to compare the trees in order to get their required results.

The phylogenetic trees that are compared usually contain conceptually the same information. The information may be derived from different laboratories, created using different methods, or simply collected from different areas. Because of the different ways in which the information can be generated, the difference between the trees is important to understand. Tree comparison techniques aim to examine these differences in order to fully understand the evolution of the given species. During the development it is assumed that the compared trees are more similar than different. This make sense, because comparing trees that represent totally different information serves no purpose. Although, the trees may have a high degree of similarity, there is still a challenge in understanding the difference, as the trees may be very large in size. That is why the aim is, once the comparison occurs, to visually enhance the derived results.

There are several tree comparison methods currently being used to analyse the similarities and differences between two trees, including **consensus trees**, **agreement subtrees**, **triplets**, and **nearest neighbor interchange** (NNI). This section illustrates these techniques as applied to two (fictitious) trees that suggest two possible ways in which 4 present-day species might be related, as shown in Fig. 2.

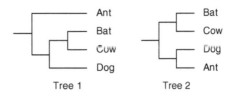

Fig. 2. Example of two fictitious phylogenetic trees

Tree 1 implies that Bat and Cow diverged recently from a common ancestor, that the Bat/Cow ancestor and Dog share a more distant common ancestry, and finally that the whole Bat/Cow/Dog tree split from the Ant branch even further in the past. Tree 2, on the other hand, suggests that a common ancestor split into two branches, one ultimately leading to Bat and Cow and the other to Ant and Dog.

Consensus Trees- Consensus trees are widely used to summarise the agreement between a set of trees. A consensus tree is made by combining multiple trees into a single tree that represents the clades (species) that are common to all the input trees [8]. There are several methods for creating a consensus tree; strict consensus, majority rule consensus, semi-strict consensus, Nelson consensus, and Adams consensus are five of the most common. Bryant [5] provides a detailed discussion on various methods of consensus tree generation.

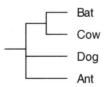

Fig. 3. Strict consensus tree for trees in Fig. 2

Fig. 3 shows the example of the strict consensus tree of the trees in Fig. 2. The consensus tree indicates that both trees agree that Bat and Cow had a recent common ancestor, but disagree about how Ant and Dog fit into the picture. The best that can be said is that both agree that Ant and Dog shared a common ancestor with the Bat/Cow ancestor at some time in the past.

Note that a consensus tree includes all of the original leaf nodes, but is normally not fully resolved; areas of disagreement generally result in interior nodes with more than two branches.

An **agreement subtree** is a subtree that is common to two or more trees. Conceptually, a subtree can be obtained by pruning leaf nodes (and collapsing the parent internal nodes) from the original tree. An agreement subtree is a subtree that can be extracted in such a manner from all of the trees. A greatest agreement subtree (GAS) is an agreement subtree with the greatest number of leaf nodes. For example, the trees in Fig. 2 have two greatest agreement subtrees as shown in Fig. 4.

Fig. 4. Greatest agreement subtrees for trees in Fig. 2

A **triplet** is the smallest possible informative subtree of a rooted tree [8]. The structure of a tree is fully characterised by enumerating the structure of its triplets. A rooted tree with n leaves contains **n(n − 1)(n − 2)/6** triplets. For example, the 4-leaf tree 1 from Fig. 2 will have 4 triplets, as shown in Fig. 5.

Triplets can be used as a basis for quantifying the difference between rooted trees. Using this approach, the structural difference between two trees is the number of triplets whose structure is different in the two trees. For example, Tree 2 from Fig. 2 has the following triplets shown in Fig. 6. Since 2 triplets (the second and third) are different from the corresponding triplets in Tree 1, the structural triplet difference between the two trees is 2.

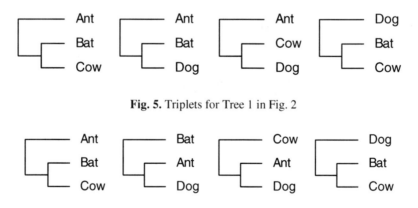

Fig. 5. Triplets for Tree 1 in Fig. 2

Fig. 6. Triplets for Tree 2 in Fig. 2

The **nearest neighbour interchange** (NNI) technique [6] is also used to quantify the difference between trees. A nearest neighbour interchange is an interchange of two "nearest neighbour" branches. The NNI difference between two trees is the minimum number of such interchanges needed to convert one tree into the other.

NNI is usually applied to unrooted trees, but can be adapted for rooted trees. For rooted trees, the "nearest neighbour" of a branch is one of the sub-branches (if they exist) of its sibling. For example, in Tree 1 the nearest neighbours of the Dog branch are the Bat and Cow branches, and the nearest neighbours of the Ant branch are the Dog branch and the (unlabelled) common Bat/Cow ancestor branch.

All of the tree comparison methods discussed above have their own advantages and disadvantages depending on what aspect of tree structure users are interested in comparing. In this paper, the main interest however is not on structural similarities and differences but more on understanding the visual similarities and differences in order to present the users with more detailed results that are easy to understand.

2.3 Existing Framework

Current comparison techniques produced different types of results based on the comparison methods that is being used. The results can either be presented as numerical data, or displayed as a tree with some of the originals data has been lost/deleted in order to understand the differences [7]. These results are sometimes difficult to understand especially for novice users as they requires a full understanding of the original data. Fig. 7 shows the existing framework for comparing phylogenetic trees.

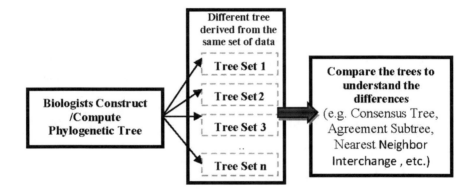

Fig. 7. Existing Framework

3 Visualizing Tree Differences

Our approach to visualizing trees similarities and differences makes use of the fact that a tree with unordered branches can be drawn in many arrangements. In a phylogenetic tree, the order in which branches appear is usually less important than the structural relationships between nodes. In such cases, we can take advantage of this flexibility to draw a pair of trees to highlight both their similarities and differences.

3.1 Proposed Framework

The proposed framework has three main stages (as illustrated in Fig. 8).

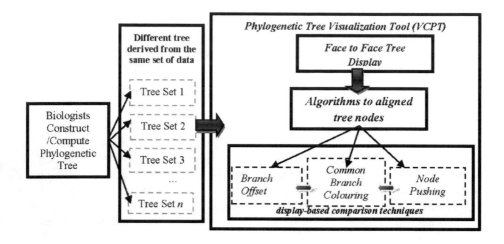

Fig. 8. Proposed Framework

3.1.1 Face to Face Tree Display

The first approach in visually comparing two phylogenetic trees is to draw them "face-to-face" with leaf nodes aligned. Fig. 9 shows an example of two simple trees. In reality, the nodes would be labelled with organisms or gene identifiers; for simplicity in this discussion the labels will be replaced with numbers.

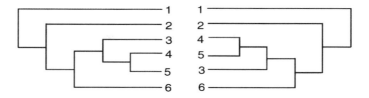

Fig. 9. Example of two simple trees

Having this in mind, the right tree from Fig. 9 can be redrawn in order to visually align its leaf nodes (see Fig. 10). In general, exchanging the branches of any internal node changes the visual appearance of the tree but its structure stays intact. In this case exchanging the highlighted node in the right tree achieves perfect alignment with left tree; the trees are now both visually and structurally the same.

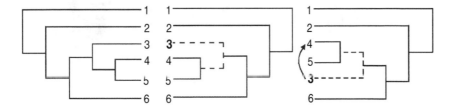

Fig. 10. Creating visually identical presentation of phylogenetic tree

3.1.2 Tree Alignment Algorithms

Typical phylogenetic trees can often have 50 or more nodes, and since the number of possible arrangements of a fully resolved tree of size n is 2^{n-1} it is usually impractical to manually determine the best arrangement. To help in the process we have considered several algorithms for automatically arranging the trees.

- The *minimum triplet difference (MTD) algorithm* computes arrangements of two trees for which the difference, as measured by triplet arrangement pattern, is minimised.
- The *maximum branch similarity (MBS) algorithm* arranges one tree so that its branches have as many leaf nodes as possible in common with the corresponding branch in the other tree.
- The *all-but-n (ABn) algorithm* attempts to arrange the common structures of the two trees so that the nodes that differ can be drawn in alignment.

3.1.3 Display-Based Comparison Techniques

Aligning nodes makes it easier to see which leaf nodes match in the two trees and provides a good starting point for further examination of the trees. In order to further understand the data, we have also developed several additional display-based techniques that will help in identifying the tree structure similarities and differences.

Branch Offset (Gap)

Gaps can be inserted to offset node branches so as to maximise the number of nodes that are aligned when perfect alignment of nodes is not possible. The technique helps to distinguish the common nodes by grouping some nodes closely together. It can also be used to locate and understand the difference between the two trees.

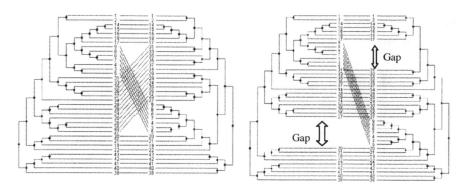

Fig. 11. Example of before and gaps are inserted

Fig. 11 show how offsetting branches can increase the alignment of the leaf nodes. It shows the original trees and the display results after the gaps have been inserted. The final display emphasises that most of the nodes are aligned, but that a small subset is located at a different point in the two trees.

Common Branch Colouring

Colour is a powerful and often-used visual feature. The application of colour to visualisations plays an important role in data representation and analysis. We use colour to highlight the common structures between two trees. In order to identify the common structures, for each of the leaf nodes in Tree 1, we find the corresponding node in Tree 2. If a node in Tree 1 has the same sibling as the corresponding node in Tree 2, the nodes and their parent are considered as structurally identical and will be coloured. The algorithm then recursively considers the common parent nodes.

Fig. 12 shows the two trees with the colour scheme applied. Node 1, Node 2 and Node 3 are coloured because they are considered to be structurally similar. Colouring the nodes that have common structure makes it easier to identify the structural similarity between the two trees, particularly for trees that are much larger in size and complexity.

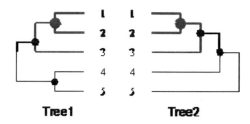

Fig. 12. Example of two trees with the similar nodes coloured

Node Pushing

The "push" method is used to change the location at the point where a parent node attaches to its children. The push up option will push the parent up to the top of the crossbar and the push down option will push the parent to the bottom. The idea is to position the parent of similar nodes at the same height in each of the trees, so that the agreement subtree will have an identical appearance in each tree. The benefit is that the similarities and difference will become more apparent. Fig. 13 shows how the common ancestor will move using this method.

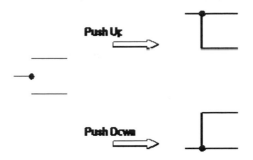

Fig. 13. Push up and push down of the common ancestor

For example, Fig. 14 show how the "push" techniques can be used to highlight the tree differences. It shows the trees before and after the "push" technique is applied.

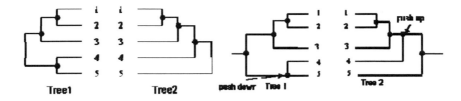

Fig. 14. Example of before and after the "push" technique is applied

In this example, the agreement subtree is Nodes 1, 2, 3, and 5. Pushing Node 4 down in Tree 1 and up in Tree 2 makes the agreement subtree identical in both trees. It is then easier to see how the differing node attaches to the agreement subtree.

4   Evaluation

We have implemented a prototype application known as VCPT (Visual Comparison of Phylogenetic Trees) for and used it as a vehicle for developing and evaluating our ideas. The application is implemented in Java using the Swing components.

The framework and visualization techniques described in this paper were tested by conducting a small usability testing and visualization evaluation in a controlled experiment. The results are helpful to fully understand the potential and limitations of the approach. The evaluation consisted of a group of volunteers carrying out a series of tasks using the prototype application and then completing a series of exercises related to the different display techniques proposed.

Sixteen (16) subjects participated in the evaluation. Each session lasted for about one to two hours. Subjects enrolled on a voluntarily basis and did not directly benefit from taking part in this exercise. They were free to withdraw from the exercise at any time and they were also free to decline to answer any particular question. All subjects were computer science postgraduate students that could be assumed to have a high level of comfort with computers and tree structures.

4.1 Summary of Results

Overall our hypotheses were partially supported, but the careful observation of users during the exercise was very helpful in understanding differences in the way that users interpreted the displays. There were wide differences between participants in terms of speed, and because of the small number of participants, the results are not statistically significant.

All the participants agreed that the alignment of nodes, highlighting the common structures and "pushing" nodes to emphasise agreement subtrees provides a lot of help in visualizing pairs of trees. Fig. 15 shows the result of combining all the three techniques.

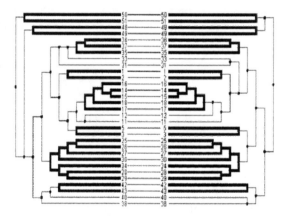

Fig. 15. The result of combining node alignment, highlighting the common structures and "pushing" the common ancestor methods

5 Conclusion

Phylogenetic trees are one of the important graphical notations for representing the evolution of species. Indeed, tree structured data in general are used to represent information graphically in many different domains. The aim of this work was to visually present the similarities and differences between pairs of binary trees. The primary contribution of this work is the development and demonstration of display techniques that are able to compare the trees visually.

Preliminary evaluation suggests that the proposed framework and the prototype application will help the users such as biologists to easily understand and interpret their data. Although the techniques have been developed specifically for the bioinformatics domain, many of these techniques could also be applied to other domains that use similar tree structures.

Acknowledgments. We thank Universiti Sains Malaysia (USM) for providing the funding (Short Term Grant - no. 304/PKOMP/6310021) through which this article was produced.

References

1. Hall, B.G.: Phylogenetic Trees Made Easy: A How-To Manual. Sinauer Associates, Inc., Sunderland (2007)
2. Lesk, A.M.: Introduction to Bioinformatics, 3rd edn. Oxford University Press Inc., New York (2008)
3. Farach, M., Thorup, M.: Fast comparison of evolutionary trees. In: Proceedings of the Fifth Annual ACM_SIAM Symposium on Discrete Algorithms (SODA 1994), pp. 481–488. ACM Press, Arlington (1994)
4. Munzner, T., Guimbretiere, F., Tasiran, S., Zhang, L., Zhou, Y.: TreeJuxtaposer: Scalable tree comparison using focus+context with guaranteed visibility. ACM Transactions on Graphics 22(3), 453–462 (2003)
5. Bryant, D.: Building trees, hunting for trees and comparing trees: Theory and methods in phylogenetic analysis. PhD Thesis. Department of Mathematics, University of Canterbury, New Zealand (1997)
6. Robinson, A.J., Flored, T.P.: Novel techniques for visualizing biological information. Intelligent System in Molecular Biology 5, 241–249 (1997)
7. Carrizo, S.F.: Phylogenetic trees: An information visualization perspective. In: Proceedings of the Second Asia-Pacific Bioinformatics Conference (APBC 2004), pp. 315–320. Australian Computer Society, Dunedin (2004)
8. Page, R.D.M.: GeneTree: Comparing gene and species phylogenies using reconciled trees. Bioinformatics 14, 819–820 (1998)
9. Wan Zainon, W.M. N., Talib, A.Z., Belaton, B.: Display-based Approaches for Phylogenetic Tree Visualisation. In: Proceedings of the 2nd International Conference on Distributed Frameworks and Applications (DFmA 2010), Yogyakarta, Indonesia, pp. 53–59 (2010)
10. Shipman, M.S.: Visualizing trees. Lecture notes, http://www.cs.arizona.edu/icon/docs/ipd275.htm (retrieved July 10, 2010)

Technical Skills in Developing Augmented Reality Application: Teachers' Readiness

Norabeerah Saforrudin[1], Halimah Badioze Zaman[2], and Azlina Ahmad[2]

[1] Teacher Training Institute Malay Language Campus, Kuala Lumpur
[2] Institute of Visual Informatics, Universiti Kebangsaan Malaysia, Bangi
{norabeerah,azlinaukm}@gmail.com, hbzukm@yahoo.com

Abstract. This preliminary study is intended to obtain the background of basic ICT skill required for teachers to develop the Augmented Reality (AR) application using available AR authoring tool. The AR technology enables the virtual world to be in real world concurrently. These features have been identified to be able to accommodate the learning experience in order to promote learning. The samples are comprised of nine AR application developers and forty four teachers. Interview schedule, questionnaire and demonstration are used to collect data. The findings revealed that teachers have low technical skills in order to develop the AR application using available authoring tool according to the requirement listed by the AR application developer. This indicates that there is a need to develop the AR authoring tool which is easy to use in the perspective of teachers. It shows that it is difficult for them to develop their own AR application because of the technical skill required, although they are very interested in the technology and agreed that the technology can help to enhance the students' cognitive process.

Keywords: augmented reality, education, teacher, readiness, visual informatics.

1 Introduction

Due to the blooming of ICT today, various new technology have been explored and one of the technologies in education that been researched is the application of the Augmented Reality (AR) technology. The AR technology enables users to see synthetic object in the real world, which combines the virtual reality and real world [1-5]. This technology has been discovered since the last 40 years but the term Augmented Reality was introduced by Tom Caudell in 1992. Since that, research in the AR started to expand. Literatures have shown that the AR support is a useful visualization technique [6]. This technique in visual informatics used visualization to increase understanding and learning [7]. Therefore, this technology has been applied to various domains such as engineering, architecture, medicine [8], robotics [9], army [10], automotive, education [11-12], entertainment [13], sports, game [14-15] and others.

H. Badioze Zaman et al. (Eds.): IVIC 2011, Part II, LNCS 7067, pp. 360–370, 2011.
© Springer-Verlag Berlin Heidelberg 2011

2   Augmented Reality in Education

The AR technology is suitable to be adopted in education[16]. There are studies conducted to investigate the use of the AR in education either in formal education based on curriculum such as science [17-19], biology [20], mathematics [21-22], chemistry [23-25], physics [26], geometry [22, 27], geology [28], geography [29-30] and engineering [31], or informal education such as astronomy [32-33], reading [34-35], storybook [36-38] and colour theory [39].

Past literatures proved that the AR is able to enhance the student's motivation level, giving positive impacts to learning experiences especially for weak students [40]. On the other hand, it assists the development of creative thinking, increases understanding and changes the paradigm of learning curve in learning any subject [18]. On top of that, it is able to give new learning experience which is fun [20] and promote students to do self exploration with the topic that they are learning [22]. Therefore, this helps to reduce time in mastering knowledge. Furthermore, by using this technology in teaching and learning, it is an alternative for teachers to use as an interactive, attractive and effective learning aid [18].

These positive impressions are revealed because the AR has certain characteristics such as enabling users to move the virtual object and see it in different angles as if they are holding a real object [16]. It supports the seamless interaction within the virtual and reality environment. It also uses the real world metaphor interface to manipulate, replacing input devices such as the mouse and keyboard. Furthermore, this technology enables the transition between the reality and virtual smoothly.

Previously, computers are popularly used as simulation and visualization to help students understand the concepts in teaching and learning [41], especially in subjects such as chemistry, physics and biology. Although it used the 3D model to present, it was still difficult for students to comprehend the abstract visualization, and the AR is an option in this situation [23].

3   Objectives of Preliminary Study

This preliminary study intended to get the background of basic ICT skill required for teachers to develop the Augmented Reality (AR) application using available AR authoring tool. This is the first phase of the major study of developing an Authoring Tool for teachers. This article only discusses four objectives which is part of the objectives of the preliminary study. The objectives are,

1. To identify the basic requirement of technical skills to develop AR application.
2. To reveal the teachers ability to develop the AR application from the AR application developer perspective using available AR authoring tool.
3. To identify the simple or easy to use of AR authoring tool for teachers to develop the AR application.
4. To identify the level of teachers' ICT skill due to the requirement skills to develop AR application based on AR application developer list (from objective 1).

4   Methodology

4.1 Research Design

This case study is held to obtain the information in order to achieve the objectives. This study involved two groups of sample. First, an interview with AR application developer is conducted and then, the questionnaires are distributed to teachers to collect data. Demonstration of AR application and showcase of a movie revealing the application of the AR in education from previous researches are conducted in three sessions according to the teachers' group of classes.

4.2 Sample

First group consisted of nine active AR application developers in Malaysia. They are selected by the judgemental sample technique. Three of them have been interviewed face-to-face, whereas the rest were given open ended questionnaire through email. The email method is used because of the location and time constraint of informants. All informants have been contacted again to clarify their responses.

Meanwhile, the second group consisted of forty four teachers from secondary and primary schools. They attended part-time diploma in education courses during school holidays at the Teachers Training Institute Malay Language Campus.

4.3 Instrument

For the first group, the instrument used for the face-to-face interview was the semi-structure interview schedule whereas, for the email interview, an open ended questionnaire was provided. These instruments consisted of eleven main questions but for this article, only three questions are being discussed.

For the second group, the questionnaire is given to the respondents. It consisted of a four constructs but for this article only two constructs which are the ICT skill construct and AR Awareness construct will be discussed. ICT skill construct consisted of six items using the five likert scale to measure the perception of ICT skill of teachers (Unskilful, Least Skilful, Moderate, Skilful and Most Skilful). On the other hand, AR Awareness construct consisted of four open ended questions.

4.4 Data Analysis

Qualitative data are analyzed using the nViVo software and quantitative data analyzed using SPSS software.

5   Findings

Table 1 tabulates the distribution of AR application developer demographics' involved in the interview. The minimum experience in using the AR is six months and the maximum experience is three years. They are active AR application developers who have experiences with several AR applications. Their perceptions on the levels of programming skill are Moderate (44.4%), Skilful (44.4%) and only one Most Skilful in the programming language.

Table 1. Distribution of AR Application Developer Demographics

D	Gender	Qualification	Specialization	Experiences in Developing AR Application	Level of Programming Skill
D1	M	Master	Information Technology	2 years	Moderate
D2	F	Master	Multimedia in Education	3 years	Skilful
D3	F	Master	Computer Science	6 month	Moderate
D4	F	Master	Software Engineering	1 years	Moderate
D5	F	First Degree	Multimedia	2 years	Skilful
D6	F	Master	Information Technology	1 years	Moderate
D7	M	Master	Information Technology	2 years	Skilful
D8	M	Master	Multimedia	2.5 years	Skilful
D9	M	First Degree	Interactive Multimedia	6 month	Most Skilful

Meanwhile, Table 2 tabulates the distribution of the teachers demographics' involved. They are from secondary (68%) and primary (32.8%) schools. Most of them have experiences in teaching more than 5 years (62.3%). Only one of them is in Information Technology field/option while the rest are in Malay Language option/field. As they are studying at the Teacher Training Institute Malay Language Campus, the main field/option is Malay Language.

Table 2. Distribution of teachers demographics' (n=44)

Demographic factor	Factor	Frequency	Percentage (%)
Gender	Male	7	15.9
	Female	37	84.1
School	Secondary	30	68.2
	Primary	14	31.8
Field / Option	Malay Language	43	97.7
	Information Technology	1	2.3
Teaching Experiences (year)	less 5	21	47.7
	5 - 15	21	47.8
	more 20	2	4.5

5.1 Basic Technical Skill Requirement to Develop AR Application

Findings from the interview with all nine AR application developers have been grouped by themes in order to identify the basic technical skills required [42] to develop the AR application. Table 3 lists the basic technical skill requirement needed to develop the AR application according to AR application developer.

Table 3. Skill to develop AR Application

Skill/AR Application Developer	D1	D2	D3	D4	D5	D6	D7	D8	D9
Programming	✔	✔	✔	✔	✔	✔	✔	✔	✔
3D modelling Software	✔	✔	✔	✔	✔	✔	✔	✔	✔
Graphic Software	✔		✔	✔	✔			✔	
Multimedia element base Software		✔	✔				✔		
Software to change marker format				✔					

Table 3 identifies that one who wants to develop the AR application should have basic technical skills requirement such as programming skill (e.g. C, C++, java or flash), in order to use AR authoring tool available (e.g. ARToolkit, FlarToolKit, Qualcomm AR), and 3D modelling software (e.g. 3DStudioMax, Unity or Sketchup). On top of that, AR application developer also needs to have other software skills which support in editing multimedia elements such as graphic software, video editing software, animation software, audio editing software and others depending on their application requirement which is usually used in multimedia authoring tool software. Furthermore, they also need to have skills in converting the marker format to .patt which is used by the AR system.

5.2   The Ability of Teachers to Develop AR Application

All informants (AR application developers) agreed that the AR application is difficult to be developed by teachers because the AR technology requires teachers to have basic technical skills as listed in Table 3.   The followings are the responses given.

"Not easy. 3DMax is difficult, depends of the software. Programming is difficult. Using Virtools is also difficult." (D1)

"...long time to develop and need in-depth skill in various software" (D4)

"Teachers are not exposed to this technology. Moreover, learning the technology takes a lot of time." (D6)

"... AR needs core and much experience in programming... " (D7)

"No, too many things to learn." (D8)

5.3   A Simple or Easy to Use AR Authoring Tool for Teachers to Develop the AR Application

Based on their experiences, all informants (AR application developer) agreed that currently it is no simple or easy to use AR authoring tool for teachers to develop the AR application.

5.3 Teachers' ICT Skill Regarding to Basic Requirement Which Listed by AR Application Developer

Table 4 shows the teachers' perception on their ICT skills. 56.8% of the teachers assumed that they have moderate skill in using ICT in general. None of the teachers think that they have no skill in ICT in general and one of them claimed to have the most skills in using ICT in general. As we refer to Table 2, it shows that one of the teachers has field/option in ICT. It also shows that, only 2.3% skilful in 3D Modelling Software, 9.1% skilful in Graphic Software, 2.3% skilful in Computer Programming and 4.5% skilful in Animation Software. The result also shows that teachers who have no skills in 3D Modelling Software (15%), Computer Programming (22.7%) and Animation Software (25%).

Table 4. Teachers' ICT skill in Teaching and Learning

ICT Skill	Unskilful		Least Skilful		Moderate		Skilful		Most Skilful	
	Freq	%	Freq	%	Freq	%	Freq	%	Freq	%
In General	0	0	7	15.9	25	56.8	11	25	1	2.3
3D Modelling Software	7	15.9	18	40.9	18	40.9	1	2.3	0	0
Graphic Software	6	13.6	15	34.1	19	43.2	4	9.1	0	0
Computer Programming	10	22.7	21	47.7	12	27.3	1	2.3	0	0
Animation Software	11	25.0	12	27.3	19	43.2	2	4.5	0	0

Referring to Table 5, the skills have been divided into two categories, Low and High Skill. Moderately Skilful and below are categorized as Low Skilled where as Skilful and above are categorized as High Skilled. It shows that 97.7% of the teachers fall in the Low Skilled category in 3D Modelling Software and Computer Programming.

Table 5. Teachers' Basic Skill to Develop AR Application

ICT Skill	Low Skill		High Skill	
	Frequency	%	Frequency	%
3D Modelling Software	43	97.7	1	2.3
Graphic Software	40	90.9	4	9.1
Computer Programming	43	97.7	1	2.3
Animation Software	42	95.5	2	4.5

For more detailed information, Table 6 illustrates the ability of ICT of teachers regarding to this two basic technical skill requirements. It shows that none of the teachers fall under the Most Skilful category in both basic technical skills requirement. Only one teacher is considered as skilful in Computer Programming but moderate in 3D Modelling Software and only one teacher who is skilful in 3D Modelling Software but moderate in Computer Programming. Seven of them are unskilful in both technical skills.

Table 6. Computer Programming Vs 3D Modelling Software Skill

		Computer Programming					Total
		Unskilful	Least	Moderate	Skilful	Most Skilful	
3D Modelling Software	Unskilful	7	0	0	0	0	7
	Least	3	14	1	0	0	18
	Moderate	0	7	10	1	0	18
	Skilful	0	0	1	0	0	1
	Most Skilful	0	0	0	0	0	0
Total		10	21	12	1	0	44

Due to basic skills requirement to develop the AR application, one must have at least two skills which are skilful in using 3D Modelling Software and Computer Programming. As mentioned in Table 3, there are no teachers who have both these skills. Either they have one of the basic requirement or they have both skills but in moderate skilful or less.

6 Discussions

Many researchers tried to expand the use of this technology and giving the chance to various users and not only to programmer [43-45]. Due to the basic skills required such as 3D modelling and computer programming skill, the possibility to use this technology to develop AR application is too technical to make it available to be used easily by teacher.

Although there are many researches that proved that the use of the AR technology is suitable for education [16, 18, 22, 32, 46], but the authoring tool available which enables one to develop the AR application is difficult to learn and use because it involve C programming [47-48], Flash or Java. According to the findings of this study (Table 4, Table 5 and Table 6), these skills are very low among teachers.

Referring to the syllabus in education technology [49] which is a compulsory subject to trainee teacher or pre-service teacher in Teacher Training Institute in Malaysia, both skills (3D modelling software and computer programming) are not included in the syllabus. Both skills are only taught for teachers in ICT field/option. Furthermore, it is not necessary for the teachers' preparation in teaching and learning material. Therefore, no wonder the findings showed that teachers have low skill in both skills.

In order to develop the AR application, one needs to have technical skills [42] as listed by AR application developer in this case study such as skilful in computer programming, enable to produce 3D model, animation and other computer software skills needed depending on the multimedia element required in any AR application. Hence, it's difficult for teacher to develop their own teaching and learning material using AR technology due to these constraints.

Due to this situation, Sauer, Osswald et al. [50] dan Lee, Kim et. al. [51] suggested an AR authoring tool with graphical user interface (GUI), without any programming needed in the process of developing the AR application and although AR authoring tool with GUI base is still few [50-51] and many enhancements are required [48, 50]. This literature also supports the findings in this study, where all AR application developer agreed that there is no AR authoring tool which can be easily used by teachers.

Teachers prefer to use less technical software and economize their time in preparing every teaching and learning material because certain learning aid is suitable for different student with different capability. They used the technology to enhance learning process, understanding and helping student to expand their cognitive capabilities [52]. Although they are very interested with the AR technology and agree that it may help to enhance the students' cognitive process through visualisation, they acknowledged that they are incapable to use this technology if high technical skills are needed.

7 Conclusion

This study concludes by suggesting developing AR authoring tool which is easy to use by teachers. The intended authoring tool should avoid any scripting or programming involvement. Furthermore, it should also provide iconic or graphical user interface authoring tool. The system should include access to free 3D model from internet or provide capability for teachers to use the 3D model without having skills in producing 3D modelling.

In order to have AR authoring tool for teachers, information and analysis of the favourable authoring tool and the nature of teachers' usage of the authoring tool should be discovered and considered. Therefore, the future works are to obtain the data from the lecturers who teach teachers in University or Teacher Training Institute. Hopefully this step will help teachers to use this technology, in order to help the students' cognitive process through visualization.

References

1. Wikipedia. Augmented Reality, http://en.wikipedia.org/wiki/Augmented_reality
2. Feiner, S., MacIntyre, B., Seligmann, D.: Knowledge-based augmented reality. Communications of the ACM 36(7), 52–62 (1993)
3. Azuma, R., et al.: Recent advances in augmented reality. IEEE Computer Graphics and Applications 21(6), 34–47 (2001)
4. Bimber, O., Raskar, R.: Spatial Augmented Reality: Merging Real and Virtual Worlds. AK Peters, Ltd. (2005)
5. Azuma, R.: A Survey of Augmented Reality. Presence: Teleoperators and Virtual Environments 6(4), 355–385 (1997)
6. Yu, D., et al.: A Useful Visualization Technique: A Literature Review for Augmented Reality and its Application, limitation & future direction. In: Huang, M.L. (ed.) Visual Information Communication, Springer Science + Business Media, pp. 311–337 (2010)
7. Medicherla, P.S., Chang, G., Morreale, P.: Visualization for increased understanding and learning using augmented reality. In: Proceedings of the International Conference on Multimedia Information Retrieval. ACM, Philadelphia (2010)

8. Marescaux, J.: Augmented-Reality–Assisted Laparoscopic Adrenalectomy. Journal of the American Medical Association 292(18), 2214–2215 (2004)
9. Collett, T.H.J., MacDonald, B.A.: Developer Oriented Visualisatin of a Robot Program. In: ACM Conference on Human-Robot Interaction (2006)
10. Livingston, M.A., et al.: An Augmented Reality System for Military Operation in Urban Terrain. In: Interservice/Industry Training, Simulation, and Education Conference (2002)
11. Kerdvibulvech, C., Saito, H.: Guitarist Fingertip Tracking by Integrating a Bayesian Classifier into Particle Filters. In: Advances in Human-Computer Interactionp, pp. 1–10 (2008)
12. Maqableh, W.F., Sidhu, M.S.: From boards to augmented reality learning. In: 2010 International Conference on Information Retrieval & Knowledge Management, CAMP (2010)
13. Pair, J., et al.: The Duran Duran project: the augmented reality toolkit in live performance. In: The First IEEE International Workshop on Augmented Reality Toolkit (2002)
14. Uematsu, Y., Saito, H.: Visual Enhancement for Sports Entertainment by Vision-Based Augmented Reality. In: Advances in Human-Computer Interaction, pp. 1–14 (2008)
15. Uchiyama, H., Saito, H.: AR Supporting System for Pool Games Using a Camera-Mounted Handheld Display. In: Advances in Human-Computer Interaction, pp. 1–13 (2008)
16. Billinghurst, M.: Augmented Reality in Education,
    http://www.newhorizons.org/strategies/echnology/
    billinghurst.htm
17. Chen, Y.-C.: A Study of Comparing the Use of Augmented Reality and Physical Models in Chemistry Education. In: VRCIA 2006, pp. 369–372. ACM, Hong Kong (2006)
18. Rosli, H.W., et al.: Using Augmented Reality for Supporting Learning Human Anatomy in Science Subject for Malaysian Primary School. In: Rahman, K.N.A., et al. (eds.) Regional Conference on Knowledge Integration in ICT (INTEGRATION 2010), pp. 44–51. Kolej Universiti Islam Antarabangsa Selangor (KUIS), Putrajaya (2010)
19. Megat Mohd. Zainuddin, N., Badioze Zaman, H., Ahmad, A.: Learning Science Using AR Book: A Preliminary Study on Visual Needs of Deaf Learners. In: Badioze Zaman, H., Robinson, P., Petrou, M., Olivier, P., Schröder, H., Shih, T.K. (eds.) IVIC 2009. LNCS, vol. 5857, pp. 844–855. Springer, Heidelberg (2009)
20. Juan, C., Beatrice, F., Cano, J.: An Augmented Reality System for Learning the Interior of the Human Body. In: Eighth IEEE International Conference on Advanced Learning Technologies, ICALT 2008 (2008)
21. Periasamy, E., Badioze Zaman, H.: Augmented Reality as a Remedial Paradigm for Negative Numbers: Content Aspect, pp. 371–381 (2009)
22. Kaufmann, H.: The Potential of Augmented Reality in Dynamic Geometry Education. In: 12th International Conference on Geometry and Graphics (ISGG), Salvador, Brazil (2006)
23. Chen, Y.C.: A study of comparing the use of augmented reality and physical models in chemistry education. In: Proceedings of the 2006 ACM International Conference on Virtual Reality Continuum and its Applications, pp. 369–372. ACM, Hong Kong (2006)
24. Fjeld, M., Voegtli, B.M.: Augmented Chemistry: an interactive educational workbench. In: Proceedings of International Symposium on Mixed and Augmented Reality, ISMAR 2002 (2002)
25. Medina, E., Chen, Y.C., Weghorst, S.: Understanding Biochemistry with Augmented reality. In: Montgomerie, C., Seale, J. (eds.) World Conference on Educational Multimedia, Hypermedia and Telecommunications 2007, pp. 4235–4239. AACE, Vancouver (2007)

26. Gillet, A., et al.: Augmented reality with tangible auto-fabricated models for molecular biology applications. In: IEEE Visualization (2004)
27. Kaufmann, H., Schmalstieg, D.: Mathematics and geometry education with collaborative augmented reality. In: ACM SIGGRAPH 2002 Conference Abstracts and Applications, pp. 37–41. ACM, San Antonio (2002)
28. Liu, F., Stapleton, C.: Using augmented reality and virtual reality to improve geology study for adult learners. In: Sanchez, J., Zhang, K. (eds.) World Conference on E-Learning in Corporate, Government, Healthcare, and Higher Education 2010, pp. 214–217. AACE, Orlando (2010)
29. Shelton, B.E.: How augmented reality helps students learn dynamic spatial relationships. University of Washington, Seattle (2003)
30. Shetty, R.C.: Augmented Reality Training Kit Can Offer Novel Teaching Solution For Future Cardiac Surgery And Other Medical Professionals. Internet Journal of Medical Simulation 2(1), 1 (2006)
31. Liarokapis, F., et al.: An Interactive Augmented Reality System for Engineering Education. In: 3rd Global Congress on Engineering Education (UICEE 2002), Glasgow, Scotland (2002)
32. Sin, A.K., Badioze Zaman, H.: Tangible Interaction in Learning Astronomy through Augmented Reality Book-Based Educational Tool. In: Badioze Zaman, H., Robinson, P., Petrou, M., Olivier, P., Schröder, H., Shih, T.K. (eds.) IVIC 2009. LNCS, vol. 5857, pp. 302–313. Springer, Heidelberg (2009)
33. Soga, M., et al.: Interactive Learning Environment for Astronomy with Finger Pointing and Augmented Reality. In: Eighth IEEE International Conference on Advanced Learning Technologies, ICALT 2008 (2008)
34. Abas, H., Badioze Zaman, H.B.: Rekabentuk dan Pembangunan Penceritaan Digital dan Teknologi Realiti Tambahan (Augmented Reality) untuk membantu Pelajar Pemulihan Membaca Bahasa Melayu. In: Regional Conference on Knowledge Integration in ICT (INTEGRATION 2010), Kolej Universiti Islam Antarabangsa Selangor, KUIS (2010)
35. Ramli, R., Badioze Zaman, H.: Augmented Reality Basic Reading Courseware for Down Syndrome Learner: A preliminary Analysis. Malaysian Journal of Information & Communication Technology, MyJICT 1 (2009)
36. Raphael, G., Dunser, A., Mark, B.: Edutainment with a Mixed Reality Book: A Visually Augmented Illustrative Childrens' Book. In: Advances in Computer Entertainment Technology 2008, pp. 292–295. ACM, Yokohama (2008)
37. Zhou, Z., et al.: Magic Story Cube: an Interactive Tangible Interface for Storytelling. In: ACE 2004. ACM, Singapore (2004)
38. Grasset, R., et al.: The mixed reality book: a new multimedia reading experience. In: CHI 2007 Extended Abstracts on Human Factors in Computing Systems, pp. 1953–1958. ACM, San Jose (2007)
39. Ucelli, G., et al.: Learning Using Augmented Reality Technology: Multiple Means of Interaction for Teaching Children the Theory of Colours, pp. 193–202 (2005)
40. Freitas, R., Campos, P.: SMART: a System of Augmented Reality for Teaching 2nd grade students. In: Proceedings of the 22nd British CHI Group Annual Conference on HCI 2008: People and Computers XXII: Culture, Creativity, Interaction, vol. 2, pp. 27–30. British Computer Society, Liverpool (2008)
41. Zagoranski, S., Divjak, S.: Use of augmented reality in education. In: EUROCON 2003. Computer as a Tool. The IEEE Region 8 (2003)
42. Wang, M.-J., Tseng, C.-H., Shen, C.-Y.: An Easy to Use Augmented Reality Authoring Tool for Use in Examination Purpose. In: Forbrig, P., Paternó, F., Mark Pejtersen, A. (eds.) HCIS 2010. IFIP AICT, vol. 332, pp. 285–288. Springer, Heidelberg (2010)

43. Jinhyuk, C., et al.: k-MART: Authoring tool for mixed reality contents. In: 2010 9th IEEE International Symposium on Mixed and Augmented Reality (ISMAR) (2010)
44. Lee, G.A., Kim, G.J.: Immersive authoring of Tangible Augmented Reality content: A user study. Journal of Visual Languages and Computing 20(2), 61–79 (2009)
45. Radu, I., MacIntyre, B.: Augmented-reality scratch: a children's authoring environment for augmented-reality experiences. In: Proceedings of the 8th International Conference on Interaction Design and Children, pp. 210–213. ACM, Como (2009)
46. Juan, M.C., et al.: The memory book. In: Proceedings of the 2005 ACM SIGCHI International Conference on Advances in Computer Entertainment Technology, pp. 379–380. ACM, Valencia (2005)
47. Wang, Y., et al.: An Authoring Tool for Mobile Phone AR Environments. In: NZCSRSC 2009: New Zealand Computer Science Research Student Conference, Auckland (2009)
48. Hampshire, A., et al.: Augmented reality authoring: generic context from programmer to designer. In: Proceedings of the 18th Australia Conference on Computer-Human Interaction: Design: Activities, Artefacts and Environments, pp. 409–412. ACM, Sydney (2006)
49. Instititut Pendidikan Guru Malaysia and Bahagian Pendidikan Guru: Buku Panduan Program Ijazah Sarjana Muda Pendidikan dengan Kepujian Sessi 2007/2008, K.P. Malaysia, Editor (2007)
50. Sauer, S., Osswald, K., Wielemans, X., Stifter, M.: U-Create: Creative Authoring Tools for Edutainment Applications. In: Göbel, S., Malkewitz, R., Iurgel, I. (eds.) TIDSE 2006. LNCS, vol. 4326, pp. 163–168. Springer, Heidelberg (2006)
51. Lee, G.A., Kim, G.J., Billinghurst, M.: Immersive authoring: What You eXperience Is What You Get (WYXIWYG). Commun. ACM 48(7), 76–81 (2005)
52. Mayer, R.E.: Multimedia Learning. Cambridge University Press, New York (2001)

Scenario-Based Learning Approach for Virtual Biology Laboratory (VLab-Bio)

Murniza Muhamad[1], Halimah Badioze Zaman[2], and Azlina Ahmad[2]

[1] Teachers Training Institute, International Languages Campus, 59200, Kuala Lumpur
[2] Institute of Visual Informatics, University Kebangsaan Malaysia, 43600, Bangi, Selangor
{murniza_m,hbzukm}@yahoo.com, azlinaukm@gmail.com

Abstract. Virtual technologies generally, and Scenario-based Learning approach specifically, when integrated into a system in enhancing teaching and learning, have shown to be a promising tool to help students acquire knowledge in science. In teaching and learning of Biology, some abstract concepts and dangerous experiments are not conducted in schools due to it being costly or time consuming. The sub-topic chosen: "To describe the application of knowledge on mitosis" was based on results of an earlier survey conducted using the questionnaire technique on teachers and students, to identify the most difficult topic in form four Biology syllabus. An interview was also conducted on teachers to acquire their perception on current teaching aids used in teaching Biology. The proposed VLab-Bio Scenario-based learning tool consists of six modules. This paper describes the process of designing and developing a scenario-based thematic situations, that relates to the experiment module, to be integrated into the VLab-Bio learning tool. Hence, the prototype: Virtual Laboratory for Biology (VLab-Bio): Scenario-based Learning Approach, meant as a learning support tool to learn the topic in Biology, on the application of knowledge on mitosis in cloning was developed.

Keywords: Virtual Learning, Scenario-based Learning, Virtual Laboratory, Biology Teaching and Learning, Scenario Based Design, Visual Informatics.

1 Introduction

It is a good start to integrate the use of information and communication technologies (ICT) in doing practical work in the laboratory for teaching science subjects such as Physics, Chemistry and Biology. Conducting experiments in science laboratories can expose students to danger especially when it involves the use of chemical reagents or animal samples. Some accidents that might occur when conducting experiments in science laboratories are burns, electrical shocks, gas leaks, adverse chemical reactions and infections [1]. Hands-on activities in doing experiments is considered crucial in training in the laboratory that students need to go through in order to accomplish the task given. However, using computers as learning materials including web sites, computer learning packages for tutorial and revision, virtual field trips and virtual laboratories (VL) also allow students to take part in the activities which are not available in the lab. VL is considered as a new teaching strategy that is cheaper, easier

H. Badioze Zaman et al. (Eds.): IVIC 2011, Part II, LNCS 7067, pp. 371–381, 2011.
© Springer-Verlag Berlin Heidelberg 2011

and can attract students' attention in the learning process. It is reported that only a few biology teachers use ICT in laboratory work, which is recognized as a cornerstone of teaching science [2]. Meanwhile many researches also proved that simple forms for representation learning material are not effective for teaching [3]. Scenarios used in virtual learning for teaching of Science have proven to be effective [4]. By integrating the use of scenarios based on specific themes in conducting experiments in science subjects, can help students understand the topics learned in a more meaningful manner. This is due to the fact that they can relate real scenarios to the topics learned. Teaching strategies that mimic real situations through scenarios in a virtual laboratory environment through context, simulation, visuals and audio is expected to create more creative students [5], [4]. Hence, a combination of scenario-based learning approach and virtual laboratory simulations are effective tools in training students when involved the use of sophisticated as well as complicated instruments. In a scenario-based learning approach too, virtual field trips such as a trip to a tissue culture centre can also help students to develop ideas and skills on the subject matter before they visit the actual site.

1.1 Biology Curriculum Specifications

The 21st century has brought greater challenges to the education system in Malaysia. There is a need to prepare ourselves to overcome these challenges in order to remain competitive. In order to ensure that the citizens of Malaysia can face the challenges ahead on par with citizens of developed nations, the need for excellent higher education calls for an "education revolution" [6]. In consonance with the National Education Philosophy, science education in Malaysia nurtures a science and technology culture by focusing on the development of individuals who are competitive, dynamic, robust and resilient and able to master scientific knowledge and technological competency [7]. In a curriculum specification the teaching of science subject also aims to develop a concerned, dynamic and progressive society with a scientific and technological culture that values nature and works towards the preservation and conservation of the environment. Conventional teaching practices all too often consists of memorization and pattern recognition, rather than concept mastery, which can leave both student and teacher with a false sense of subject mastery. To learn, students need an environment in which to learn and virtual learning takes place in virtual environment [8], [4]. Due to this, to gain a confident understanding, one needs to work with and apply abstract concepts to real-life scenarios [9]. In this paper, we focus on the design and development of short story scenarios to motivate or trigger students' enthusiasm in completing the following tasks in the VLab-Bio learning tool.

2 Design and Development of a Scenario-Based Learning Approach for VLab-Bio

The scenario-based learning approach was adopted in the design and development of the modules in VLab-Bio. We started the process by using the findings obtained from the preliminary studies conducted earlier which indicated the sub topic: *Application of Knowledge on Mitosis in Cloning*, to be focused in the VLab-Bio learning tool.

2.1 Some Findings on Preliminary Study Used in the Design and Development of VLab-Bio

The revolution of the technology provides the possibility of extending the classrooms to any part of the globe. Therefore, education systems should look into strategies to meet today's learning requirements with the technology. Modes of delivery and teaching methods must be made flexible [10] and related to real life situations [4]. At that point, teaching using the scenario-based learning approach in virtual laboratory emerged as an alternative solution for the problems of instruction of courses such as Biology.

As an initial step, we used findings of the earlier preliminary study conducted to decide on the topic that would best be adopted to design our scenario-based virtual laboratory exercises. Findings from the survey to identify the most difficult topics conducted among 72 students and 10 teachers from two secondary schools showed that Cell Division was considered difficult to understand, based on their perceptions. We also conducted a test on the topic which consists of 15 multiple choice questions. From the graph plotted, it can be observed that question number six scored the lowest correct answer, i.e. 6%, as shown in Fig.1. The learning outcome for this question was to "describe the application of knowledge on mitosis in cloning'. Fig.1 shows a comparison of students' answers in the test.

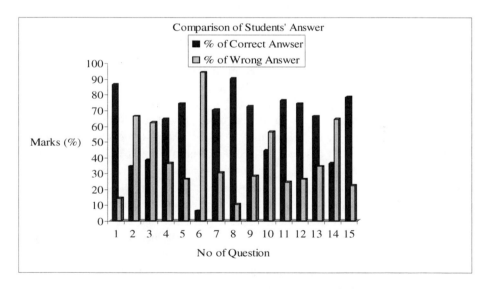

Fig. 1. Column Graph of Test Result

We also conducted an interview among 10 Biology teachers in order to conclude whether there is a need to support the current teaching aids used in teaching Biology. The result of the interview showed that teaching aids currently used by teachers are still restricted to PowerPoint presentation and multimedia CD-Rom supplied by the

Curriculum Development Centre (CDC) and Educational Technology Division (ETD) [11]. Table I below lists the teaching aids which are currently used in teaching Biology.

Table 1. List of Teaching AIDS Used in Biology Teaching

Item	Current Teaching aids used
Teaching Aids	• CD-Rom (supplied by CDC & ETD)
	• Model
	• Video from ETD
	• Power Point Presentation

Then, we also examined the syllabus contents and previous examination performance reports to identify important concepts that were amenable and practical to be created into a scenario-based virtual experiments. We concluded that scenario-based experiments related to describe the application of knowledge on mitosis in cloning would be best for inclusion in the virtual laboratory exercises.

Based on these findings, a scenario-based learning approach in virtual laboratory for biology (VLab-Bio), was considered to be an important element to be included in the support tool to be developed, for learning Biology which consists of real situations or scenarios based on themes integrated with interactive activities, exercises and information on application of knowledge on mitosis in cloning. This VLab-Bio can complement the current teaching aids that are being used for teaching Biology. The scenario-based learning approach VLab-Bio is aimed to help students simulate and visualize the process in acquiring knowledge on mitosis in cloning. Using the scenario-based learning approach in virtual laboratory would simulate students to conduct real experiments and operations instead of in real lab environment, due to limitation of time, safety or cost [12], [4]. Still, scenario based learning in virtual labs also suggest that learning can take place in cyberspace, in an environment that is one step removed from a real one. It also conveys the learning potential of role-playing or goal-based scenarios, live production of real work situation like in the classroom or laboratory. Here, students can learn faster, cheaper safer and more meaningful in a scenario-based virtual laboratory. In VLab-Bio, one of the modules was designed based on the scenario-based learning approach, to provide students with real experience while conducting a virtual experiment. Fig. 2 shows an example based on the process of preparing the medium for tissue culture experiment to be conducted by students after observing a related scenario in the previous module. Here, students can simulate the process by pouring distilled water into the beaker and visualize changes on the pH value on the pH meter. This also means students can understand better the reasons for conducting the experiment.

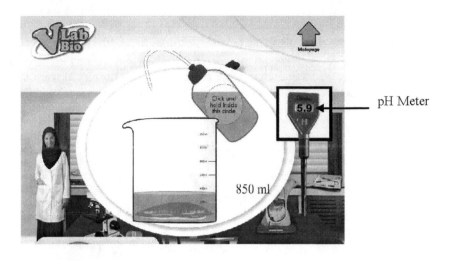

Fig. 2. Screenshot of the learning environment showing the example of the process of preparing the medium for tissue culture experiment

2.2 Scenarios in the VLab-Bio

Scenarios are neither predictions nor forecasts, but rather attempts to reflect on or portray the way in which a system is used in the context of daily real life situations. In Human Computer Interaction, scenarios are stories about people and their activities [13]. Scenarios aid comprehension and create applications as artifacts of human activity – as things to learn from, as tool to use in one's work and a media for interacting with other people [14]. The scenario may describe a currently occurring use, or a potential use that is being designed and may include text, video, pictures and story boards. Central to most scenario-based learning designs is a textual description or narrative of a use of episodes [15]. In this study, the scenario-based learning approach is based on real situations embedded in the tool using not just textual description and narration but also videos and graphics.

In the process of teaching and learning, a scenario-based learning approach is usually incorporated as a set induction where it is about preparation, which is about getting students ready and inducing them into the right mind-set. It also helps to create *clarity* about what is expected happen (both what you will do and what they should do), and to create *motivation* for what will students do next to occur [16], [4]. In designing VLab-Bio scenarios, we create an episode based on real problems and situations related to the application of knowledge on mitosis in cloning. The episode relates to the reason for doing the following tasks, namely animal cloning and plant tissue culture. In this paper we will focus on the design and development of one of the episodes in the scenario-based learning approach in a virtual experiment module for VLab-Bio, i.e. scenario 2 (Plant tissue culture). The following section explains the process involved in creating the scenario-based learning episode.

2.3 Descriptions of VLab-Bio Contents

A virtual laboratory can be used to study the items of apparatus, collecting and assembling items of the apparatus, familiarize themselves with laboratory techniques and procedures [17]. With this in mind, the proposed VLab-Bio virtual learning tool comprises of six modules. Fig. 3 shows the screen navigation of the six modules and sub-modules in VLab-Bio.

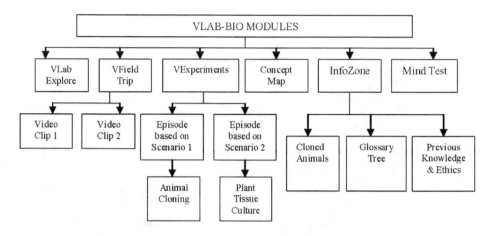

Fig. 3. Screen navigation of VLab-Bio

The modules are: 1) *VLabExplore,* ii) *VFieldTrip, iii) VExperiments,* iv) *Concept Map,* v) *InfoZone* and vi) *MindTest.* The *VLabExplore* module is where students can explore the active and inactive icon to visualize and read the function of the apparatus/equipments in the VLab-Bio. Next, we prepared a scenario-based learning on *VFieldtrip* module that showed a real matched experimental work performed in a real laboratory. The video clips which depicts real situation in virtual form gives a higher degree of realism and makes understanding more accurate, where as animations are perceived to be faked, although they may be equally accurate [18]. The *VExperiments* module related to the scenario-based learning approach, is an interactive activity for students to imitate the process in animal cloning and plant tissue culture process. Here the scenario is created as a set induction or anticipatory set to get learners thinking and ready for the lesson. The approach used to involve learners in the learning process, is the design and development of episodes based on real scenarios. The next module is *InfoZone* where it displays information on photos of Cloned animals, Glossary tree, and Previous knowledge and Ethics. The Glossary tree contains bilingual meanings of words that are related to the topic where certain words are equipped with associated graphics. We also developed the *mind test* module which contains quiz questions to test the students' achievement after using VLab-Bio. There is also a *Concept map* module to give students an overview of the relationship of the topics in VLab-Bio based on the main topic of Cell Division. After the modules were identified, specific contents for each module were developed.

2.4   Identifying an Episode Based on the Scenario-Based Learning Approach

The real situation or scenario for VLab-Bio was developed through an episode based on suggestions given by experts on the subject matter. Prior to the development of the scenarios, an episode that relates to the objective of the learning modules was identified. The specific episode was also identified with the assistance of subject matter experts. The scenario was divided into two episodes to provide scaffolding for the learner to understand the learning modules.

3   Developing a Storyboard for VLab-Bio Episodes

Scenarios based on episodes describe the motivations and experiences of users as well as the events of human-computer interaction [19]. Thus, scenario-based design can be a means for designers to manage the task-artifact cycle in order to achieve greater usefulness and usability [20]. Scenario-based learning for VLab-Bio is designed to put learners in a situation or context, introduce them to the issues and challenges in that context, and gives them an opportunity to apply the knowledge and skills relevant to the situation. In our case, two episodes relevant to the issues were created to relate to the objective of completing the tasks in VLab-Bio learning tool. The episodes based on the scenario-based learning approach, will be used to motivate students to continue doing the following tasks in VLab-Bio.

3.1   Theme for the Episodes

An episode is a fact wrapped in an emotion that can compel us to take action and so transform the world around us [21], [4]. Hence, for each scenario we devised an episode that relates to the goal-task in VLab-Bio virtual experiment. In the case for designing and developing episodes for VLab-Bio, we created a simulation through role-playing for students to experience the event or task prepared in VLab-Bio learning tool, as if it were really happening in real life based on the theme chosen for the scenario. The theme for the episode was the result of a problem faced by six entrepreneurs who attended a short course on learning the process of tissue culture at the Malaysian Agricultural Research and Development Institute (MARDI). An example of the episode is : "A banana orchard is the location. Virus infection and loss is the theme. The farmer and his friend are objects who play a part in the episode". The full episode was written out in the storyboard template form. Fig.4 shows one of the sketched scenes in the storyboard template.

From this template, we started to visualize and sketched a plot and the actors on the storyboard template based on Episode 1. The permission was obtained from the actors identified and a few photos were taken. Images that were deemed suitable for incorporation into the episode were identified. Much effort was devoted to identifying

Storyboard

Scenario: 2   scene: 1

Episode 1

Dialog/text/animation: Visual

A farmer owns a banana plantation. He uses the traditional rails sword or cleavage method to plant the trees. One day, all of his banana trees were infected by Fusarium wilt or Panama disease. He was very upset because this disease is the most dangerous of diseases that attack banana plants. The symptoms can be observed when the leaves become yellow; beginning from the edges, causing the banana plants to wither and eventually die. One of the farmer's friends, who has learnt a new technique called tissue culture, suggested that the farmer consult a MARDI officer and learn the technique which can help him get banana seedlings of a high quality and quantity with high resistance to diseases.

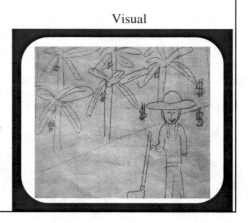

Fig. 4. Example of sketched scene in the Episode 1

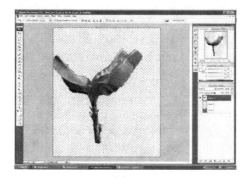

Fig. 5. Example of scenes in the development of the episode in the scenario-based learning approach

the images needed at each scene to suit the storyboard. Following the theme in the storyboard and based on the sketches, the images needed were then cropped using Adobe Photoshop CS3 where the background was omitted. The cropped images were then created into a new scene to suit the theme of the episode in the storyboard. Then, we add up an animation to the picture using flash CS3 to present the episode as a visualization scenario like a movie after the process of rendering. The process was applied to all actors needed.

The scenario-based learning approach was prescribed as an important element of the design methodology. This will be as an initial motivation to induce and engage students in the learning process. Consequently, this approach is to initiate students' understanding as why they should continue with the next module which is tissue culture in VLab-Bio. This leads to scenarios that use text, storyboards, video, and other media to provide open-ended descriptions of the activities that learners might engage in their learning process. Fig. 5 shows an example of scenes in the development of the episodes in the scenario-based learning approach.

4 Discussions

The VLab-Bio learning tool based on the scenario-based learning approach is intended to function as a learning tool for teaching and learning of Biology. The approach was adopted due to the fact that previous research showed that the current materials used by Biology teachers were restricted to educational compact discs prepared by the educational technology division, models, videos and PowerPoint presentation slides prepared by teachers. Thus, the proposed VLab-Bio based on the scenario-based learning approach is expected to help in enhancing the learning and teaching of Biology, especially on the topic of Cell Division. The modules developed in VLab-Bio would help to provide a particular advantage over conventional teaching and learning technologies. This approach is also expected to make learners more active and can improve their skills and understanding through step by step practices based on real situations or scenarios [22], [4]. The scenario-based learning activities in virtual environment can create potential for increasing the standard of safety and reducing time and training cost in conducting experiments. Based on this paper, we also described the process of design and development of the episode for the scenario-based learning, which is used as a motivation to trigger students' interest in why they need to learn the specific experiment related to animal cloning and tissue culture. Thus, the approach adopted in the development of VLab-Bio is expected to help students understand and visualize the experiments to be conducted in real labs later, which would help them acquire better prior knowledge related to the application of knowledge on mitosis in cloning.

5 Conclusion

The scenario-based learning approach of the virtual laboratory (VLab-Bio) is meant to enhance and support the teaching and learning of Biology for form four students. Based on the problems indicated in each scenario, students will know why they have to continue doing the exercises and make specific scientific decisions. Students will be able to actively participate in a virtual laboratory exercises based on real situations that requires them to make decisions based on each scenario given. Students who make correct decisions and answer questions correctly will be able to progress through the scenario; whilst students who give incorrect answers will be provided with feedbacks on their choice of answers and will automatically be required to repeat that portion of the scenario that they are unable to solve. The ability to instantly see the result of an experiment is an advantage over the conventional laboratory practice, which can extend over several days, and can allow students to forget experimental details or lose interest in the results of a particular experiment [22]. Therefore, the use of episodes in scenario-based learning is included in the Virtual Biology Laboratory (VLab-Bio) Learning Tool.

Acknowledgements. We would like to thank the Ministry of Science of Technology and Innovation (MOSTI) on the ScienceFund grant (01-01-02-SF0094) and Universiti Kebangsaan Malaysia (UKM) for the Arus Perdana grant (UKM-AP-ICT-16-2009). We would also like to thank Dr. Norzihan Abdullah and Dr. Mussadin Kamaruddin from, Malaysian Agricultural Research and Development Institute (MARDI) for the themes of the episodes suggested and the permission for attending the tissue culture course at MARDI. We also would like to thank Assc. Prof. Dr. Zamri Zainal, Mr. Choo Wee Kian and Mr. Aziz Kadir from Plant Biotechnology Centre for providing access to the Plant Biotechnology Centre.

References

1. Kurikulum, P.P.: Siri panduan ke arah peningkatan mutu pendidikan sains pengurusan dan keselamatan makmal sains sekolah. Kementerian Pendidikan Malaysia, Kuala Lumpur (1999)
2. Špernjak, A., Šorgo, A.: Recent usage of computer-supported laboratory in the Biology classroom: is virtual laboratory an alternative? In: MIPRO 2010, Croatia, May 24-28 (2010)
3. Morozov, M., Tanakov, A., Gerasimov, A., Bystrov, D., Acirco, V.: Virtual Chemistry 3. Laboratory for School Education. In: The 4th IEEE International Conference on Advanced Technologies (ICALT), pp. 605–608 (2009)
4. Shanck, R.: Virtual Learning; A Revolutionary Approach to Building a Highly Skilled Workplace. Mc Graw Hill, USA (1997)
5. Bakar, N.: Pendekatan Pembelajaran Maya. Universiti Teknikal Malaysia, Melaka (2010)
6. Badioze Zaman, H., Bakar, N., Ahmad, A., Sulaiman, R., Arshad, H., Mohd. Yatim, N.F.: Virtual Visualisation Laboratory for Science and Mathematics Content (Vlab-SMC) with Special Reference to Teaching and Learning of Chemistry. In: Badioze Zaman, H., Robinson, P., Petrou, M., Olivier, P., Schröder, H., Shih, T.K. (eds.) IVIC 2009. LNCS, vol. 5857, pp. 356–370. Springer, Heidelberg (2009)
7. Ministry of Education Malaysia, Integrated Curriculum for Secondary Schools Curriculum Specifications Biology Form 4, Curriculum Development Centre (2005)
8. Bakar, N., Badioze Zaman, H.: Development of VLab-Chem for Chemistry Subject Based on Constructivism-Cognitivism-Contextual Approach. In: Proceedings of the International Conference on Electrical Engineering and Informatics, Bandung, Indonesia, pp. 567–570 (2007)

9. Browne, S.I.: Virtual laboratories - Socratic biology simulators, Unpublished, http://www.virtuallaboratory.net/ (accessed June 23, 2009)
10. Said, H.: Education in Malaysia: Enhancing Accessibility. In: International Conference on Capability and Quality, Bangkok (2011), http://www.Worldedreform.Com/Intercon/Kedre15.Htm (accessed May 12, 2011)
11. Muhamad, M., Badioze Zaman, H., Ahmad, A.: Virtual Laboratory for Learning Biology: A Preliminary Investigation. World Academy of Science, Engineering and Technology 6(71), 775–778 (2010)
12. Mahdavi, A., Metzger, A., Zimmermann, G.: Towards a Virtual Laboratory for Building Performance and Control, http://es.cs.uni-kl.de/publications/datarsg/MaMZ02a.pdf (accessed July 29, 2009)
13. Carroll, J.M., Rosson, M.B.: Deliberated Evolution: Stalking the View Matcher in Design Space. Human-Computer Interaction 6, 281–318 (1991)
14. Caroll, J.M.: Five Reasons for Scenario-based design, interacting with computers, vol. V13, pp. 43–60. Elsevier (2000)
15. Carroll, J.M., Rosson, M.B., Chin, G., Koenemann, J.: Requirements Development in Scenario-Based Design. IEEE Transactions On Software Engineering 24(12) (1998)
16. Cheryl Grable, Teacher Education, http://ualr.edu/crgrable/id99.htm (accessed May 12, 2011)
17. Dalgarno, B., Bishop, A.G., Adlong, W., Bedgood, D.R.: Effectiveness of a Virtual Laboratory as a preparatory resource for Distance Education chemistry students. Journal of Computers & Education 53(3) (2009)
18. Robinson, J.: Virtual Laboratories as a teaching environment A tangible solution or a passing novelty (2003), http://mms.ecs.soton.ac.uk/mms203/papers/5.pdf (accessed September 14, 2009)
19. Wagner, R.: Educational technology: Using computer-based scenario authoring tools in athletic training education. Athl. Train Educ. J. 5(1), 40–44 (2010)
20. Tatli, Z., Ayas, A.: Virtual laboratory applications in chemistry education. In: Procedia Social and Behavioral Sciences. World Conference on Learning, Teaching and Administration, pp. 938–942 (2010)
21. Chuah, K.M., Chen, C.J., Teh, C.S.: ViSTREET: An Educational Virtual Environment for the Teaching of Road Safety Skills to School Students. In: Badioze Zaman, H., Robinson, P., Petrou, M., Olivier, P., Schröder, H., Shih, T.K. (eds.) IVIC 2009. LNCS, vol. 5857, pp. 392–403. Springer, Heidelberg (2009)
22. Breakey, M.K., Levin, D., Miller, I., Kathryn, E.: The Use of Scenario-Based- Learning Interactive Software to Create Custom Virtual Laboratory Scenarios for Teaching Genetics. In: Innovations in Teaching and Learning Genetics, The Genetics Society of America (2008)

Towards a Multimodality Ontology Image Retrieval

Yanti Idaya Aspura Mohd Khalid, Shahrul Azman Noah,
and Siti Norulhuda Sheikh Abdullah

Centre for Artificial Intelligence Technology, Faculty of Information Science & Technology,
Universiti Kebangsaan Malaysia, 43600 UKM, Bangi, Selangor, Malaysia
{P51455,samn,mimi}@ftsm.ukm.my

Abstract. Ontology based retrieval is gaining popularity due to the limitation posed by the conventional bag-of-words retrieval system. To semantically search for images, textual descriptions are usually used since low level features provide little meaningful information. As such conventional searching and retrieving of images are currently being employed. Complex querying and enhanced semantic search still remain the issues to be solved in image retrieval systems. We proposed an ontology driven framework for supporting image retrieval with particular emphasis on the sport news domain. Furthermore, we look into the possibility how multimodality ontology can be integrated in the framework and shows how open knowledge-bases such as the DBpedia play an important role in this area.

Keywords: Ontology based retrieval, Multimodality ontology, Image Retrieval, Semantic search.

1 Introduction

The collection of digital image requires tools for extracting knowledge from the contents to enable effective and efficient image organization, filtering, browsing, searching and retrieval. The use of knowledge model such as ontology is beginning to gain interest among image retrieval researchers. Emphasis in ontology-based information retrieval work is currently on single modality ontology and [11]. Research in content-based image retrieval (CBIR) mainly focuses on low level features like colour, texture and shape [10] with little attention of integrating domain knowledge and textual content. Due to this, the concept of multi-modal information has replaced the original concept of single-modal information. With the establishment of multi-modal information, the development of many sources of information has resulted in the use of ontology and semantic match in image retrieval. Most research on multi-modality ontology tries to bridge the semantic gap between low-level features and high-level concepts [5][7].

This paper presents our framework on multimodality ontology approach to image retrieval. It is part of our on-going work in developing an ontology-driven image retrieval system. The proposed multi-modality ontology was developed by interlinking data in DBpedia which can enrich the concepts in the ontology. The scope of our work is on on-line sport news images. These images are usually associated with captions describing their contents as well as associated textual news content. Further analysis of such content contributes in associating images with multimodality ontology model.

H. Badioze Zaman et al. (Eds.): IVIC 2011, Part II, LNCS 7067, pp. 382–393, 2011.
© Springer-Verlag Berlin Heidelberg 2011

2   Background and Related Research

Ontology is a key element of semantic knowledge and is the solution to the problem of semantic annotation. It involves the concepts and relationships that interlink entities. Ontology is widely used as a solution to the problem of semantic heterogeneity among domains, and provides shared knowledge. Its effectiveness was proven in a study by Wang et al. [6], in which it is used as a middle-level to connect low-level features with high-level human concepts. In a study done by Hyvonen et al. [7], ontology was adopted for image retrieval to solve the problem of knowledge encapsulation in seman tic annotation. Current research on ontology is leading it into a relationship with linked data technology such as Wikipedia, DBpedia, YAGO and FreeBase. Wang et al. [5] adopted Wikipedia as a guideline to create a large-scale multi-modality ontology concept. This ontology concept is able to extract additional information from web pages and increases detection accuracy. They used a method of automatic extraction from web pages to increase entities in the multi-modality ontology.

This research aims at building multi-modality ontology derived from both domain knowledge and low level features. Instead of using Wikipedia as illustrated in the work of [5], we explore DBpedia as a knowledge source to extract domain concepts in order to increase the efficiency of our multi-modality description. An ontology image retrieval system is intended to be developed in order to show the potential of Linked Data Technology like DBpedia [1]. Being semantically rich, the ontology is seen as one of the many alternative solutions to moderate the semantic gap inherits in image retrieval systems.

Images in current CBIR systems are retrieved without using externally provided metadata describing their content. The contents used to represent images include features such as colour, texture, shape and face. So that, content based image retrieval is in fact focused on the visual features. The example of CBIR systems include Pic-SOM system [17], QBIC [19], Virage [18] etc. For this work, the multi-modality ontology is derived from the domain knowledge and the extraction of image features. As mentioned earlier, the scope is on the sports news domain. This research not only looks at sports knowledge, but also focuses on the news as source of information. It combines both sport and news concepts into textual information in order to enhance the textual description ontology.

3   Proposed Framework

The proposed work centred on the use of ontology as vocabulary instead of the normal bag-of-words approach. In any ontology based retrieval model [6][7][11][14], a pre-specified ontology is mapped (or annotated) to documents using available automatic or semi-automatic matching mechanisms. As most of researches mainly focussed on single ontology, their approaches are mainly an adaption of the conventional retrieval model such as the vector space model. As domain specific news images such as 'sport' can be described by more than a single ontology, a multimodality ontology framework is proposed as illustrated in Figure 1. The framework is divided into three main modules: *Domain Knowledge Building*, *Textual Content Analysis* and *Semantic Interpretation for Image Contents*. These three main modules respectively relate with the sport domain ontology, textual description ontology and visual description ontology which form the multimodality ontology driven to image retrieval proposed in this work. The Semantic Matching module shown in the framework matches user queries with these ontologies and obtained a set of related images which is then ranked and produced as an output by the Retrieval module. The following section provides further explanation of these modules.

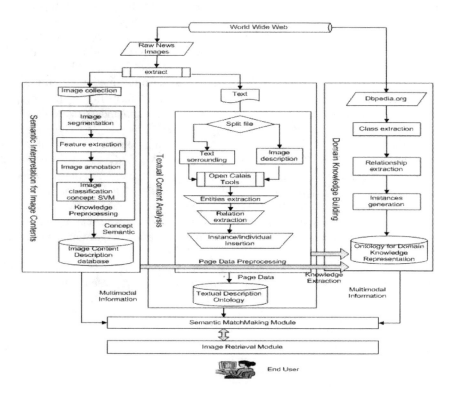

Fig. 1. An approach of a multimodality ontology driven image retrieval system

Domain Knowledge Building. The Domain Knowledge Building module concerns with building the domain knowledge of the stored images. Domain knowledge ontology can either be modelled from scratch or from existing one. For the sport domain used in this study, we model the ontology from various sources which is discussed in the next section.

Textual Content Analysis. The textual content analysis concerns with extracting and analysing textual description relating to images. As shown in Figure 3, the textual data extraction concerns with two types of text: the surrounding text and the textual image description. For our study on news images, the surrounding text relates the news itself whereas the textual image descriptions relates to the image caption. It is necessary to divide them since most content in image descriptions only describes the image attached and often does not associate the image with the news itself. Entities and relationships will be extracted from the textual content by using Open Calais [2]. These entities and relationships are then based on regularity patterns. The entities and relationships is then transformed to RDF syntax to formally represent classes, attributes and relationships. The textual ontology is manually mapped with the domain knowledge base. In examining the textual information, a domain knowledge base is formed to provide a high-level description for terms and their correlations. This knowledge was then encapsulated into a well-defined ontology. Having only textual information was not sufficient; it was also necessary to extract the semantic interpretation from the image collection.

Semantic Interpretation for Image Contents. This module concerns with representing the low-level features of images. Image segmentation is necessary to extract the colour layout, dominant colour and edge histogram descriptors. The low-level features of each image are then used in the image retrieval module to determine what categories they fit under. For example, an image could be classified as an outdoor scene with a green colour object in the foreground. In this phase, the M-Ontomat-Annotizer [8] tool is used to determine the low-level features. Then, the same images are annotated and classified using Label Me Annotation Toolbox [9]. After the annotation and classification, each image is assigned a set of labels to describe its content, which are to be matched with the concepts defined in the knowledge base. This way, the low-level concepts assigned to images can be utilized by semantic matchmaking, thus incorporating the high-level textual information with low-level image attributes. The output results are stored in the image content description database.

Semantic Matchmaking and Image Retrieval Module. This module provides a matching mechanism of the input query with the various ontologies. Inference mechanisms such as those provided by Pellet semantic reasoner [15] will be used. The result of the semantic matching is the retrieval of relevant images.

4   Ontology Construction

This section discusses how the multi-modality ontology was developed from image content using shared semantic interpretation. Multi-modality ontology has three main components: the sport news ontology, textual description ontology and visual description ontology. The sport news domain ontology has two ontologies, sport ontology and news ontology. This ontology is based on formal taxonomy and the category of sport, including relationships and classification. Second, the textual description ontology described the high-level textual information. The information contained descriptions of sport news in the surrounding text and image description. This information was converted into classes and properties. Third, the visual description ontology was derived from the visual annotation and encapsulated low-level image features. In the following part, an elaboration of how each part of the ontology was built is given, including an example of a part of the ontology structure at the end.

4.1   Domain Ontology

Sport news was used to establish this domain ontology. This ontology consists of two different sections: the sport ontology and the news ontology.

4.1.1 Sport Ontology

An ontology is viewed as an agreed knowledge structure of some domains which is usually created by an expert of group of experts. Few methods for building ontology has been discussed in [20]. In this research we modelled the sports ontology by analysing content from various reputable sources such Wikipedia, Basile [3] and Nicols [4]. Analysing various description about sports such as baseball and tennis enable us to identify abstract concepts such as *equipment, grouping of players* and size from Wikipedia. Furthermore Basile [4] provides seven classifications of sport which are team versus individual, qualitative versus quantitative, absolute versus relative, automatic versus judgment, external versus human, physiology versus precision and competition versus leisure. The other classification scheme for sport considered is those suggested by Nicols [4], which classified games according to three major categories: the game's physical requirements (i.e. what the game requires in addition to the players — equipment, size and nature of playing field, and so forth), the structure of the game (i.e. number of players, groupings of players, strategies, and so forth), and the game's personal requirements (i.e. what the game requires of the player — motor skills, fitness levels, numeracy, social skills, and so forth). The aforementioned classifications were used to model the sports ontology used in this research. Figure 2 and Table 1, shows the resulting ontology from this process.

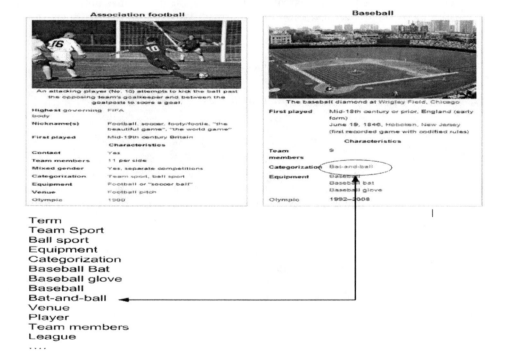

Fig. 2. Example of term analysis from Wikipedia

Table 1. Class of Sport

Super-Class	Sub-Class	Instances
ball game	bat and ball	baseball
		cricket
	club and ball	golf
	2 goal games	basketball
		rugby
		football (soccer)
	target games	bowling
		snooker
auto-racing game		Formula One
		MotoGP
racquet game		badminton
		tennis

Our method of building the sport ontology is quite similar to the one employed in [16].

During experiments, we used the news and images of BBC Sport News published between January to December 2009. During this period 13 types of the most popular sports were chosen to be included in the ontology represented in Figure 3 which forms the ABox of the domain ontology. For example, *baseball* is type of *ball games* (hyponyms), so baseball is defined as an instance of ball games in the sport domain ontology.

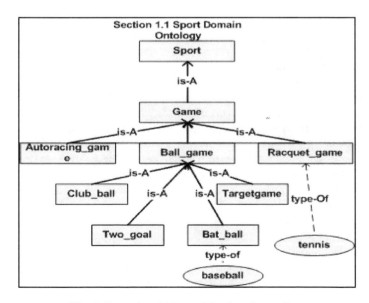

Fig. 3. Example of ABox of the domain ontology

The information about baseball is enriched by using the *owl:sameAs : http://dbpedia.org/resource/Baseball* syntax. Users can access detailed information about the game of baseball. The efficiency of matchmaking between user's query and concepts is maximized in the knowledge base. In the example of image retrieval for racquet games, an image can be retrieved even without the word "racquet" being presented in its description. This is because badminton is defined as a subclass of racquet games. This enables the system to match and adjust the user's query to not only a single category of sport but also the group or class of sport.

4.1.2 News Ontology

The news ontology was produced by looking at the information contained on news extracted from the BBC Sport website. Entities that exist can be seen clearly, because articles are direct and static. A data set that directly focuses on the sport issues was selected. While the selection of articles was based on images showing the action of real sports, such as football player kicking a ball, or basketball players are throwing the ball into nets. All common entities existing in each sample news article in the collection were examined. From the common entities, patterns were reviewed by analysing the relationships. News concepts in DBpedia were extracted to facilitate the preparation of a list of entities and relationships. For example, title, author, date, URL, source and abstract are the basic metadata that should be on every news article. Therefore, only the news ontology inherent in DBpedia needed to be imported.

4.2 Textual Description Ontology

Textual information is a clear indication of image retrieval. However, in most cases the textual information is often restricted by isolated and inappropriate use of keywords in query and retrieval. The keyword-based retrieval system has proven inefficient in matching users' queries with a single keyword. Many incorrect results are returned because polysemy arises in a different context. Therefore, to solve this problem, semantic interpretations are needed to produce correct results. Therefore, the establishment of a formal ontology is important for both domain experts and end users. In this study, BBC Sport was chosen as a category data set to extract the class and relationship definitions. This was chosen because it already classified sport into the type of sport by using standard descriptions of the various aspects of more than 30 types of sports. BBC Sport also has images, text description and surrounding text for all sport news descriptions. The narrative description of sports news was converted into class and property. BBC sport description pages were downloaded, and content was extracted to further facilitate construction of the ontology. The process was done by hand, and OpenCalais Submission Tool [2] was used to extract the entities and relationships. Most general sports descriptions, such as category, physical requirements, league, location and athlete, were available. In the next step, entities were collected and statements containing narrative descriptions were manually generated to build up the ontology. A high level of information was collected and summarized into classes and properties for textual description ontology. Several classes were defined, such as *Category, League, SportPerson and PhysicalRequirement*. Then, semantic relationships were generated to connect different concepts including *hasCategory, hasLeague, hasLocation, hasPhysicalRequirement and hasPerson*. By defining this ontology, certain sport concepts can be correlated with the sport domain knowledge. This provides a more detailed semantic interpretation of sport news keyword, and helps the image retrieval system to identify whether a specific keyword in the document is relevant to user queries or not. Once the textual description ontology is created, the generated classes in the domain ontology are associated with the corresponding textual information by using the properties defined above. With the help of OpenCalais Tools, almost 300 concepts and relationships were collected, which helped to build the textual ontology. The next step was to build up the visual ontology description, which uses image annotation and low-level descriptions. The low-level descriptions were mostly done automatically. It was necessary to annotate each image by hand.

A detailed example is provided in Figure 4 on how an image is mapped, in addition to the matchmaking process.

4.3 Visual Description Ontology

After processing and analysing the textual information, domain knowledge is generated for the high-level descriptions and their correlations, and then the knowledge is encapsulated into a well-defined ontology. However, textual information is not enough in semantic matchmaking image retrieval. There is a lack of connections between web images and textual information. Textual descriptions are unable to represent content of images correctly. Due to that, there is a need to generate the knowledge from the low-level feature of each image to enhance the performance of semantic matchmaking. Semantic matchmaking cannot be directly performed from low-level features. A knowledge base capable of extracting textual information from low-level features is needed. In this research, knowledge generated from high-level textual information and low-level features are incorporated and used for semantic matchmaking.

To build the knowledge base for low-level features, raw images were annotated using the LabelMe toolbox [9]. Each image was manually annotated with a standard set of terms relevant to the image content. Polygon X and Y were used to train the tool to generate semi-automatic terms for each image. For example, an image of a *ball* is a circle. Each imaged needed a specific term example: *tennis ball, football, basketball, and golf ball.* From the annotation, images were classified accordingly. The problem of extracting knowledge from the low-level features of images was solved by using supervised learning technology. Low-level features such as edge histogram, dominant colour, colour structure and region shape provided the colour and texture description for images. Then, the image classification system was manually developed. The class labels used in classification were associated with the terms defined in the knowledge. For example, in sport image analysis, images were first classified as *RGB* or *greyscale* images. Since *greyscale* does not provide as much information as *RGB* images, there was a need to distinguish between them. Images were also classified into *Outdoor* and *Indoor* categories. All *Outdoor* images were further classified into *field* and *OpenAreaScene* categories. *Indoor* images were classified into *court* and *CloseArea* categories. Images were further classified as *physical equipment,* and the individual examples *shuttle, tennis ball, racquet, ball, net, bat* and *bat.* After classification, each image had a set of labels to describe its content. These were used to match concepts defined in the knowledge base. Through this process, low-level features of images were converted into a set of terms that could be utilized by semantic matchmaking, thus incorporating high-level textual information with low-level image attributes.

After extracting high-level information from low-level image attributes, the information needed to be incorporated into a knowledge base. Therefore, an ontology was created from the visual concepts extracted. The visual concepts became a component of the sport description ontology system. To build the visual ontology, the image classification scheme was extracted and then classified into categories under the classification as its subclasses. For instance, *ContentType* is defined as a class under visual ontology, and then based on the classification scheme for *ContentType*, the image is classified as either an *Indoor* image or an *Outdoor* image. Further, *Indoor* images are split into *court* and *CloseArea* classifications. Therefore, *Indoor* and *Outdoor* are defined as subclasses of *ContentType*, and *court* and *CloseArea* are subclasses of *Indoor* images. Next, generative classes were associated under the sport ontology with corresponding visual concepts. For this stage, human experts generated the relationship between the sport and visuals since it could not be generated automatically. The relationship between domain knowledge and the textual ontology and visual ontology was also produced manually. After this, the semantic relationship can be determined from low-level features such as *hasPixColor*, *hasEnvironment*, *hasContent* and *hasPhysicalEquipment*. Every sport image then had high-level description generated from textual information and low-level image attributes. Thus, the performance of the semantic matchmaking system was enhanced, providing more accurate semantic interpretations.

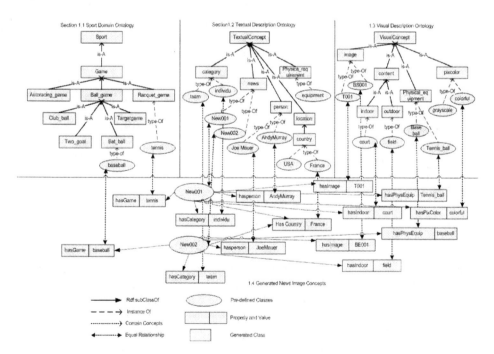

Fig. 4. The structure of the Sport News Description Ontologies

Figure 4 shows the structure of the sport news ontology. In this figure, ovals and ellipses were used to show the predefined class and generated class respectively. Only some of the ontology is shown due to limited space. Two sample types of sports, *tennis* and *baseball,* are shown to demonstrate how concepts are constructed and defined. The ontology is open to further construction. As shown in Figure 3, tennis and baseball are two generated classes under the super-class of game. From the textual description ontology, it is seen that tennis belongs to the category "individual," whereas baseball belongs to the category "team." The visual description ontology shows that the physical equipment for tennis is a *Tennis Ball* and the physical equipment for baseball is a *Base Ball*, even though they share the keyword "ball." The visual description ontology helps to filter a majority of inaccurate results. Visual description ontology supports a lot of content and annotates all the concepts including the low-level features. Last, *owl:sameAs* http://dbpedia.org/resource/Raqibul_Hasan was added. The sample output for the ontology can be seen in Figure 5 in the form of a graph.

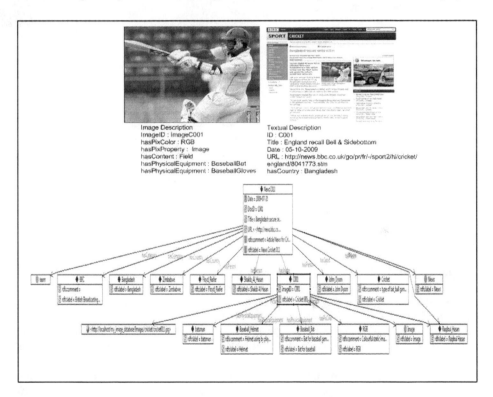

Fig. 5. Ontology of News and Image of Cricket

5 Conclusion

This study has proposed a new alternative to enhance image retrieval by means of multimodality ontology. We proposed a framework by which a multimodality ontology driven to image retrieval can be supported. In our proposed framework, the images' semantic information is based on three main ontologies; the text based ontology, which is the description and text from the news; the visual description from image annotation and feature extraction; and lastly, the domain ontology, extracted from the DBpedia ontology. The multimodality ontology was constructed to provide shared semantic interpretations of image content. From the general classification of sport collected from the web, classes of sports were determined and details were defined to give meaning to the sport images in our collection and connect the concepts with the news ontology.

The proposed framework is part of our on-going effort in developing an ontology-based image retrieval system. As research that integrates textual content in image retrieval is still focusing on bag-of-words and single modality [12][13], the proposed framework is seen as a major step towards multimodality ontology that exploits knowledge sharing communities such as DBpedia in creating and supporting domain knowledge. Therefore, our on-going work includes transforming the proposed framework into a working prototype.

References

1. Dbpedia, http://wiki.dbpedia.org
2. Opencalais Submission Tools, http://www.opencalais.com
3. Basile, http://www.imnc.univ-paris7.fr/basile/sportsclass.html
4. Nicols, http://en.wikipedia.org/wiki/Game_classification
5. Wang, H., Jiang, X., Chia, L.-T., Tan, A.-H.: Wikipedia2onto – Building Concept Ontology Automatically, Experimenting with Web Image Retrieval. Informatica 34, 297–306 (2010)
6. Wang, H., Liu, S., Chia, L.-T.: Image Retrieval with a Multi-Modality Ontology. Multimedia Systems 13(5), 379–390 (2008)
7. Hyvönen, E., et al.: Museumfinland-Finnish Museums on the Semantic Web. Web Semantic 3(2-3), 224–241 (2005)
8. Petridis, K., Anastasopoulos, D., Saathoff, C., Timmermann, N., Kompatsiaris, Y., Staab, S.: M-Ontomat-Annotizer: Image Annotation Linking Ontologies and Multimedia Low-Level Features. In: Gabrys, B., Howlett, R.J., Jain, L.C. (eds.) KES 2006. LNCS (LNAI), vol. 4253, pp. 633–640. Springer, Heidelberg (2006)
9. Russell, B., et al.: Labelme: A Database and Web-Based Tool for Image Annotation. International Journal of Computer Vision 77(1), 157–173 (2008)
10. Smeulders, A.W.M., Worring, M., Santini, S., Gupta, A., Jain, R.: Content-Based Image Retrieval at the End of the Early Years. IEEE Pattern Analysis and Machine Intelligence 22(12), 1349–1380 (2000)
11. Vallet, D., Fernández, M., Castells, P.: An Ontology-Based Information Retrieval Model. In: Gómez-Pérez, A., Euzenat, J. (eds.) ESWC 2005. LNCS, vol. 3532, pp. 455–470. Springer, Heidelberg (2005)
12. Mohd. Noah, S.A., Sabtu, S.B.: Binding semantic to a sketch based query specification tool. Int. Arab J. Inf. Technol. 6(2), 116–123 (2009)
13. Shahrul Azman, M.N., Azilawati, A., Tengku Mohd, T.S., Tengku Siti Meriam, T.W.: Exploiting Surrounding Text for Retrieving Web Images. Journal of Computer Science 4(10), 842–846 (2008)

14. Fang, W.-D., Zhang, L., Wang, Y.-X., Dong, S.-B.: Toward a Semantic Search Engine Based on Ontologies. In: Proceedings of 2005 International Conference on Machine Learning and Cybernetics. Ed. (2005)
15. Sirin, E., Parsia, B., Cuenca Grau, B., Kalyanpur, A., Katz, Y.: Pellet: A Practical Owl-Dl Reasoner. Journal of Web Semantics 5(2), 51–53 (2007)
16. Lenat, D.B., Guha, R.V., Pittman, K., Pratt, D., Shepherd, M.: Cyc: Toward Programs with Common Sense. Communications of the ACM 33(8), 20 (1990)
17. Koskela, M., Laaksonen, J., Laakso, S., Oja. E.: The PicSOM retrieval system: description and evaluations. In: The Challenge of Image Retrieval, Brighton (2000)
18. Bach, J.R., Fuller, C., et al.: The Virage Image Search Engine: An Open Framework for Image Management. In: Proceedings of the SPIE - The International Society for Optical Engineering: Storage and Retrieval for Still Image and Video Databases IV, pp. 76–87 (1996)
19 Niblack, C W , Barber, R., Equitz, W., Flickner, M.D., Glasman, E.H., Petkovic, D., et al.: QBIC project: querying images by content, using color, texture, and shape. Paper Presented at the Storage and Retrieval for Image and Video Databases, San Jose, CA, USA (1993)
20. Gómez-Pérez, A., Fernández-López, M., Corcho, O.: Ontological Engineering: With Examples from the Areas of Knowledge Management. In: E-Commerce and the Semantic Web. Springer, Heidelberg (2004) (print)

A Visual Art Education Tool to Create Logo (APH-Pensil) Based on the Fundamental Design Theory Approach

Halimah Badioze Zaman[1], H. Ridzuan[2], Azlina Ahmad[1], S. Riza[1], M.A. Nazlena[1],
J. Azizah[1], M.C. Ang[1], and Haslina Arshad[3]

[1] Institute of Visual Informatics, Universiti Kebangsaan Malaysia
[2] Universiti Pendidikan Sultan Idris
[3] Faculty of Information Science and Technology, Universiti Kebangsaan Malaysia
hbzukm@yahoo.com, ridzuan@upsi.edu.my

Abstract This paper outlines the research conducted to develop and evaluate a Visual Art Education tool (APH-Pensil), based on the fundamental design theory. This tool consists of six modules. The Art element module help students acquire skills in creating lines, space and colour; the Design module, help students acquire skills to identify harmony, balance, emphasis, contrast, rhythm, variations and integration of design that is created; the Design process module, enable students to redesign available logos; the technique module on the other hand, help students in colour selection and recognition; whilst the Logo HSR module, help students to differentiate different types of logos; and the Fundamental design application module, enable students to design 2D and 3D Logos. The evaluation of the Visual Art Education tool (APH-Pensil), was conducted on the quasi-experimental method to test for effectiveness and creativity of the users using the visual art tool. Data was collected based on instruments such as pre and post tests, specific tasks administered and observational checklist. The *Torrance Test for Creativity Thinking* (TTCT) and the creativity formula was used to measure the outputs of the students. The best creative measurement is one that can produce logos based on the original works sketched on paper and transferred using the system. Findings of the study showed that there was a significance difference in the achievement of students from the experimental group, based on the tasks undertaken by them as compared to the control group. Generally, the findings also showed that the use of the Visual Art Education Tool was effective in the teaching and learning of Visual Art Education amongst the secondary school children tested, and that the tool is capable of motivating students to be creative in the design of Logos based on the fundamental visual art design theory.

Keywords: Visual informatics, visual arts, visual art design, visual art education tool, logo design.

1 Introduction

The New Integrated Curriculum of Secondary Schools or *Kurikulum Bersepadu Sekolah Menengah* (KBSM) that has been conducted for the last two decades, has not

H. Badioze Zaman et al. (Eds.): IVIC 2011, Part II, LNCS 7067, pp. 394–407, 2011.

changed the perception of society in Malaysia on the subject of Visual Art. In most schools the subject on Visual Art concentrates merely on drawing and colouring. This phenomenon has been strengthened further by Mustafa [23] and Mohd Johari [21], who found that Visual Art Education has been looked upon as 'second class' or a subject that is 'unimportant' and to be undertaken only by weak students. Awang Had [1], was of the opinion that this phenomena needs to be revisited and revaluated to reascertain its true value and benefits to students. Standkiewicz [25], stressed that *"students need an art education that goes beyond drawing and painting, beyond technique or formal analysis, toward functional visual literacies that will them shape and understand visual cultures in which they live..."* This is supported by Zakaria [27] ... *"the teaching of art now remains pretty much the same...students need to be motivated...We must tackle their sense of curiosity by showing and doing."* Awang Had [1] however, stressed that it has never been the problem of the teaching of the subject. The problem is due to the exam oriented approach of the education system in the schools that have made the teaching of subjects generally, and the teaching of Visual Art specifically, not interactive and interesting. Students are forced to remember facts for examination purposes to attain good grades and thus are not concerned about understanding and acquiring of certain skills through an enjoyable learning process.

During the time of the British era, the subject on Visual Art in the country was known then as Drawing (*lukisan*). Later the name was changed to Art (*seni lukis*) and craft (*pertukangan tangan*) [1]; and later to Art Education (*pendidikan seni*)[1]. Today the subject is called Visual Art Education (*Pendidikan Seni Visual*) [11]. With its new name, new teaching aids (apart from conventional approaches), such as computer softwares and hardwares will have to be prepared by the schools specifically for the teaching and learning of Visual Art Education. Initial analysis we conducted found that the teaching methods conducted by the teachers were outdated; teachers used text books when they were supposed to show how certain art techniques need to taught practically; teachers did not have the right skills or knowledge in visual art education; teachers were not competent in using the latest technology in teaching the subject on visual art education.

2 Objectives

The main objectives of this research are as follows:

i.   To design a visual art education tool (APH-Pensil) based on fundamental design theory for form four students.

ii.   To design and develop a visual art education tool (APH-Pensil) based on the fundamental design theory.

iii.   To conduct prototype testing on the visual art education tool (APH-Pensil) based on its effectiveness and creativity.

3 Methodology

The research methodology adopted in this research is based on the Prototyping Hybrid-Visual Art Education (APH-Pensil) Life Cycle [10], based on the standard software development life cycle process. The methods involve in conducting this study involves two components: the development methodology component and the usability testing component. The former involved a five phase life cycle approach and the latter involved a product testing based on its effectiveness and creativity by users on the visual art education tool.

4   Fundamental Design in the Development of Visual Art Education Tool

The theory on fundamental design began in 1919 in Bauhaus [3],[7], at a school in Dessau, Germany by an architect named Walter Gropius. The theory on fundamental design is related to the elements and principles of design. The elements involved aspects such as: lines, look, shape, spatial, connection and colour; whilst the principles involved are aspects such as harmony, contrast, balance, concentration, rhythm, variation and integration. Understanding the elements and principles of design based on the 'Theory of Fundamental Design' can help students in the process of creating an art piece. The enhancement of knowledge on the elements and principles of visual art can also help students create a creative visual art piece using new techniques and media through computer.

4.1   Discipline-Based Art Education (DBAE) Model

Discipline-based Art Education (DBAE) Model is an academic curriculum concept in the field of Visual Art Education. The Visual Art Education (VAE) curriculum based

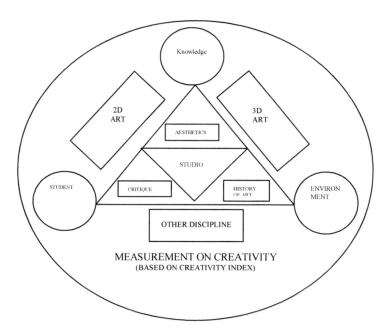

Fig. 1. Adapted DBAE Model

on the DBAE model began in the United States of America by a group of experts in Visual Art Education sponsored by the Getty Foundation. Ken [17], mentioned that the objective of the DBAE Model was to generate the understanding of students in the field through four main aspects in the discipline namely: historical art, aesthetics, critical art and studio art. All these four aspects need to be exposed to the students in the process of learning holistically. Art is fundamentally important to the process of learning generally, as well as it being a subject of learning by itself [17]. Iberahim [14], is of the opinion that the DBAE model can be applied in the process of learning to ensure the understanding of visual art amongst students. Through this model, students will be introduced to art works by various artists in order that they can broaden their perspectives and produce creative works. Figure 1 shows the adapted DBAE model that we used in this study.

From Figure 1, it can observed that the four main aspects: History of Art, Aesthetics, Critique, and Studio are influenced by other entities surrounding it as indicated in the diagram. At the end, what matters would be the measurement on the tasks undertaken by the student. For this study the creativity was measured based on the creativity index [9] formulated by Hafsah et al. [8].

4.2 Elements of the Adapted DBAE Model

As mentioned earlier, the Adapted DBAE model encompasses aspects on History of Art, Aesthetics, Critique, and Studio. According to D'zul Haimi [6], history of Art involves research on the development and changes in visual culture through historical evidences. These evidences can be in the form of animated film, comic, computer graphics, and 2D or 3D images as well as holographics. Iberahim [14], stresses on the other hand that history of art allows students to understand different cultural civilizations and arts that goes beyond time and space. This is supported by Ken's [17] earlier work, that found that students can understand time and place based on a piece of art work. He stressed that there is no piece of art work that does not have a history behind it.

The term 'aesthetics' comes from the 'Yunani' language, pronounced as *'aisthesis'* which means appreciating something. Aesthetics too is related to beauty [2]. Levinson [20], in his study found that there are three important components in the philosophy of aesthetics :an activity that involves the appreciation of art; an attribute of an object that reflects beauty; an attitude, experience or perception that can be labeled as aesthetics. Levin's work also found that aesthetics involve the philosophy which appreciates, analyses and discusses on beauty and dynamics of nature and artists. However, Halimah [9], stated that the philosophy of aesthetics involve harmony that should be embedded in the design of multimedia coursewares that are developed. The goal of Visual Art Education (VAE) is to enhance students' ability to appreciate art through their five senses based on strong aesthetic values.

Critique (Particularly on art), is a response either in written or verbal form, on a piece of art work that involves intellectual insights, and enhances the person's sensory experience. A critique on art is generally the public's reaction to a work of art in a form of emotional interpretation, analysis and evaluation on that piece of work. It has been simplified that a critique on art involves detailed observation done on an art work. Thus, a critique on art involves a knowledge base activity that is systematic, using appropriate technique to acquire reason and evidences on a piece of art work.

Mohd Johari [21], stated that art works such as sculptures, models, artifacts, weaving, pottery and the like are art works created in the studio. Iberahim is of the opinion that such works can help students to think intelligently on the visual image created. This thinking acquired, can later help them to create works of their own that are expressive and coherence based on the previous insights.

5 Principles of Fundamental Design

Principles of fundamental design in the context of this study involve aspects such as: elements in design, harmony, balance, contrast, rhythm, concentration, integration, coherence and index on beauty or creativity[4],[18],[19],[21]. Elements of design incorporates aspects such as lines, look, shape, texture and space. All these elements are interconnected to one another in any piece of art work. This means that in any work of art, there is not just a concentration of one element, but an integration of many. A good piece of art work will integrate various elements of art coherently in an effective manner. Lines [5] in an image, alphabet or symbol can create interesting tones that is bright or dark. Look or appearnce [22], can be a visually perceived area created by an enclosed area or space using colour or lines. It is very much related to shape or form. However, shape or form can be abstractive or otherwise. This means that it can be in a form of a concrete 3D object or an illusive object. It can be in an augmented or holographic form that can be seen but cannot be felt unless a special device is applied. Yet, there could be signs of concentration due to effects created on the surface of the work resembling nature. Rhamat's [24] work, showed that these concentrations in the form of textures on the surface can sometimes be seen and touched. This makes the work more interesting and realistic. Space is another element in design that important in any creation of art. Space is basically the distance between an object (be it in 2D or 3D) that exists in the real world and in the visual art work. Space in the work would show difference in the size, distance and colour based on the perspective of the object. The distance of eye contact of the individual with the object in the piece of art work would indicate the exact position of the line base on perspective. Space can be divided into: real physical space (pottery, sculpture, ceramic and the like and illusion space (painting, print and the like). Itterns [15], indicate in his study that the wheel of colour encompasses 12 basic colours. Holtzshcue [13], on the other hand, states that all colours originate from black and white or dark and light (Aristotle 348-322 AD) and this hypothesis was accepted and used until the 18th century.

The principle on harmony reflects the arrangement of the various elements of design in the creation of a work of art. In VAE, harmony is fundamental requirement that can portray cohesiveness in the application of the elements [24]. Balance is when elements of art are distributed evenly in the design of an object or work of art. Leonardo da Vinci [18], used this principle in his work particularly when his work involves the human body. There is two types of balance: symmetrical and asymmetrical. The former, gives a sense of stability and harmony in a piece of work. The latter on the other hand, gives a sense of tension, concentration and focalisation.

The principle on concentration and focalisation, is particularly applicable to this study as it is most suitable for the creation of logo (of which this visual tool is concentrating upon). The emphasised visual element in a design of a logo will be able to attract the viewer's attention first [3].The principle on contrast releases a feeling of excitement and eludes boredom [5]. It creates an environment of extreme (such as black against white; an empty space against a crowded space). This condition is able to attract the public to the piece of art work more effectively.

Rhythm is another principle in fundamental design that links with repetition of elements (motives) that gives a sense of movement form one element to another, that can be observed on the objects (such as lines on a zebra or on an old bark of tree) [5]. Variation is another principle in fundamental design that involves sometimes different styles of art (collage and text or painting and collage) that can produce a high sense of aesthetics. Cohesiveness in terms of integration of the right elements of art in a piece of work is one of the principles in fundamental design of an art work.

The principle on creativity or beauty index is most crucial in any tool or systems built for the purpose of visual art education. Many of the systems created does not take this into consideration. It is for this reason that the Visual Art Education tool created in this study incorporates a previous work on a formulae for creativity index [8] to measure creativity on the tasks conducted by the students on the topic of Logo creation.

6 Design and Development of Visual Art Education Tool (APH-Pensil)

In order to ensure that the Visual Art Education tool (APH-Pensil) was designed based on sound software engineering process, the Prototyping Hybrid-Visual Art Education (APH-Pensil) Life Cycle was adopted. Basically, the methodology (PHVAE-Life Cycle) incorporated the standard five (5) phases in software development life cycle : analysis, design, development, implementation and evaluation, but with special concentration on entities such as users needs, tasks analysis, content requirement mapping, teaching and learning approaches, and evaluation.

The ID model of the Visual Art Education Tool (APH-Pensil) is as indicated in Figure 2. Basically, the Instructional Design (ID) model for APH-Pensil comprised of six elements: i) Teaching & Learning theory, which takes into consideration theories of learning that can help in a tool such as this to help students not just learn the theoretical aspects of Logo but the 'artistic' and 'creative' skills to create their own logo. Thus, the theories had to incorporate the Behaviourist theories (Torndike, Skinner and Bandura); Cognitive theories (Gestalt) and Constructivist theories (Ausubel and Pattern Recognition). ii) Curriculum, which involves translating the curriculum to specific objectives and activities that involves in the topic involved: Logo. iii) Approach involves way of presentation of the content instruction in the tool. In this context, multimedia elements such as text, graphics, video, audio and animation. iv). Moduled interactivity refers to interactivity that is controlled through navigation in specific modules. This means that students are navigated to specific flows of the module in order to undergo specific skills required in creating logos. They are controlled in terms of the navigation in the system. v). Strategy and technique is another element embedded in the ID model. Various techniques suitable for student-centred learning were adopted in the model to ensure that students have the opportunity to carryout hands-on activities in creating real logos. Creativity or beauty index was incorporated to ensure student achieved a minimum level of creativity. vi). Teaching was felt to be another element to be singled out apart from learning in the ID model. This is due to the fact that certain information need to be taught but must be in a student-centred approach. This also means that teaching activities designed would have to involve tasks that students need to apply concepts and skills taught to create logo of their own. Generally, the fundamental design principles and fundamental design theory as well as the Discipline-based Art Education (DBAE) model were also incorporated into the elements in the ID Model.

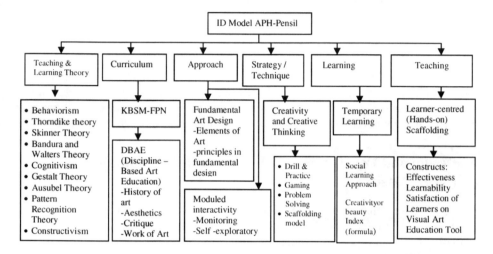

Fig. 2. ID Mdel of Visual Art Education Tool (APH-Pensil)

7   Findings of Study on Visual Art Education Tool (APH-Pensil)

Findings of the study will be presented in two sections: development of the visual art education tool (APH-Pensil) based on appropriate print screens of the system; and the usability testing of the visual art education tool conducted on 51 form four students.

7.1   Findings on Development of Prototype APH-Pensil

The prototype developed for the teaching of Visual Art Education (VAE), was based on the ID model created earlier. The fundamental design theory and principles based on aspects related to lines, shapes, integration, space, colour, were interspersed with text integrated in harmony, balance and rhythm in a cohesive manner. Figure 3 shows the introduction screen of the visual art education tool via a video clip.

The study by Holgate et al. [12], found that video can be successfully applied as induction set to motivate students to interact with the system. Jones & McNamara [16], is also of the opinion that video can create a positive learning environment. However, according to Wahidin et al. [26], the situation can be just the opposite, if video only allows students to watch the video without any interactivity. APH-Pensil allows students to interact with the video by clicking of the objects on the screen.

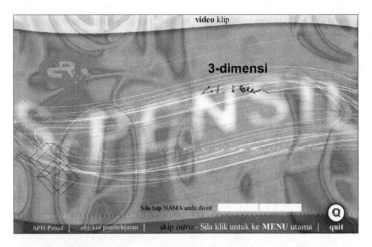

Fig. 3. Screen on Induction Set Screen (Montaj) of Visual Art Education Tool (APH-Pensil)

Fig. 4. On Main Menu of Visual Art Education Tool (APH-Pensil)

Figure 4 shows the main menu of APH-Pensil which encompass six modules: elements of Art module, design principles module, design process module, techniques module, Logo module, and Fundamental art design application module.

When students enter the main menu, an animation in the form of a butterfly can be seen on the screen. This is related to the transformation theory in fundamental design theory where a real image will be transformed to another image (in this case a logo). This also involved the pattern recognition theory based on the cognitive learning theory. The words in the background: shows the focus of the learning of logo that will be concentrated upon in the teaching and learning of the topic: Logo.

Figure 5 shows the *Design Principles Module*. There are seven design principles taught in this module. Among them are: aspects on harmony, balance, concentration, contrast, rhythm, variation and cohesiveness. When students enter this screen they can see the purple bee which gives an indication of independence and self-reliance in selecting and creating the right elements to produce the best logo creation. The objective of this module is to allow students to make the right selection of the design principles to create the best creative logo. Students then navigate the *Design Process module*, built to allow students to choose the right colour and font type: serif or sans-serif and the design a creative logo. The exercises in the Design Process module helps the short term memory of the students to retrieve concepts learned in the design process of logos to design their own.

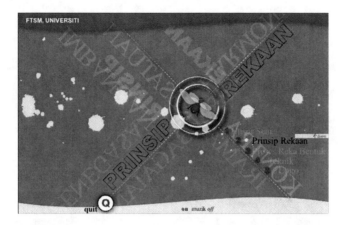

Fig. 5. On Design Principles Module of Visual Art Education Tool (APH-Pensil)

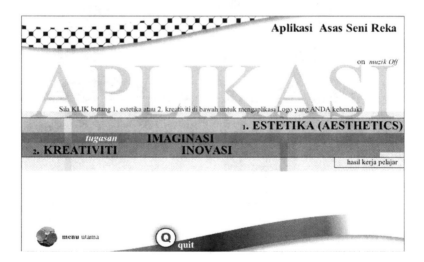

Fig. 6. Screen on *Fundamental Art Design Application Module* of Visual Art Education Tool (APH-Pensil)

Figure 6 shows the *Fundamental Art Design Application Module*. This module reflects the creativity, aesthetics, imagination and innovation. This module is the 'hands-on' activity module that requires students to conduct a task of creating a logo on their own based on the fundamental art design theory. In this module, students can use the various sub-modules: Elements of art sub module (allows students to select the right font types, lines, shape, space, integration and colour); Principles of Design sub-module (allows students to select aspects such as harmony, balance, contrast, variation, rhythm and cohesiveness.

The outcome of the task is then measured based on the creativity or beauty index. The formulae [8], of the index is as follows:

$$K_{hlr} = \frac{\{no.R(p)accuracy + no.R(1^c)\ accuracy\} + \{no.R(c)accurate + no.R(1^c)accuracy\}}{\{no.p + no.1^p\} + no.c + no.1^c\}}$$

The shapes of the logo created are measured based on its accurateness (the lines, curves and joints) based on the original drawing (either sketched conventionally on a piece of paper or straight through the system.

$$I^p, I^c = \begin{cases} 1 & \text{when there is accurate and cohesive integration} \\ 0 & \text{vice versa} \end{cases}$$

The best design is when the student is able to create the logo using the system (APH-Pensil) as accurate as the original sketch drawn conventionally with pen or pencil.

0   K_{hlr} 1

Difficult to learn and use   Easy to learn

Fig. 7. on Element of Art Sub module of the *Fundamental Art Design Application Module* of Visual Art Education Tool (APH-Pensil)

When the student is able to create the logo as accurate as the sketch drawn conventionally (see Figure 7), it also means that they found it easy to learn and create a creative Logo through APH-Pensil)

7.2 Findings of Prototype Testing on the Visual Art Education Tool (APH-Pensil)

The usability testing on Visual Art Education tool (APH-Pensil) was conducted on 51 Form Four students, where 26 were grouped a the experimental group (X1) and 25 grouped as control group (X2).More than 53% (27) were female and 47% (24) were male. The usability testing were conducted based on its effectiveness and creativity by users on the visual art education tool (APH-Pensil).

On the first construct: effectiveness, a pre and post test was conducted on the samples and the results are as indicated in Table 1 and Table 2.

Table 1. Results of Usability Testing: Construct Effectiveness for Experimental Group (X1)

Sample	Marks of Pre Test (100%)	Marks of Post Test (100%)	Improvement (100%)
M1	73.0	73.0	0.0
M2	70.0	76.6	6.6
M3	60.0	66.7	6.7
M4	73.0	63.3	-9.7
M5	66.7	83.3	16.6
M6	66.7	90.0	23.3
M7	73.0	76.6	3.6
M8	70.0	60.0	-10.0
M9	80.0	76.6	-3.0
M10	80.0	66.7	-13.3
M11	46.7	66.7	20.0
M12	53.3	63.3	10.0
M13	56.6	53.3	-3.3
M14	80.0	76.6	-3.4
M15	66.7	80.0	13.3
M16	80.0	66.7	-13.3
M17	66.7	80.0	13.3
M18	76.6	70.0	-6.6
M19	66.7	73.0	6.3
M20	60.0	73.0	13.0
M21	50.0	73.0	23.0
M22	80.0	80.0	0.0
M23	73.0	76.6	3.6
M24	70.0	76.6	6.6
M25	63.3	83.3	20.0
M26	60.0	66.7	6.7
Average	65.5	70.2	4.7

Based on both the tables, it can be observed that the average achievement of students' understanding of the topic being taught by the experimental group (X1) was 65.5%, whilst the control group (X2) scored 66.8% , thus with a difference of 1.8%. The post test results showed that the former achieved 70.2% whilst the latter achieved 66.7% with a difference of 3.5%. This means that students from the experimental group (X1) showed an improvement of a higher score compared to the control group (X2). From both the tables too, it can be observed that the lowest marks from X1 that of student (M11) with 46.7% compared to X2, that of students (K11 and K16) with

50.0%; whilst the highest score from X1 was achieved by students (M9, M10,M14,M16 and M22) with 80.0% compared to X2 which was achieved by student (K3) who also achieved 80.0%. The passing marks was based on the actual exams is 60.0% and the marks for excellence is between 80-100%. This means that the percentage of passes from the post-test conducted:X1 achieved an average of 96%, whilst X2 achieved an average of 92%; there were six (6) students from X1 that achieved excellent scores compared to X2 where none of the students achieved excellent score. Therefore it can be inferred that the Visual Art Education Tool (APH-Pensil) was effective in improving students' achievement compared to the conventional method.The test on creativity was conducted based on a task to design a logo. The same task was given to all students from group X1 and X2. Before the evaluation was conducted, the indicators of scale was created using the *Torrance Test for Creativity Thinking* (TTCT) that concentrates on fluency of ideas, flexibility, originality, and elaboration of design (total marks is 240); then the design was also measured based on the creativity or beauty index that also takes into consideration its accuracy in design based on the original sketch using the formula created.

Table 2. Results of Usability Testing: Construct Effectiveness for Control Group (X2)

Sample	Marks of Pre Test (100%)	Marks of Post Test (100%)	Improvement (100%)
K1	76.6	73.0	-3.6
K2	73.0	70.0	-3.0
K3	80.0	70.0	-10.0
K4	53.3	63.3	10.0
K5	73.0	66.7	-6.3
K6	56.6	66.7	10.1
K7	73.0	66.7	-6.3
K8	76.6	66.7	-9.9
K9	60.0	63.3	3.3
K10	66.7	76.6	9.9
K11	50.0	66.7	16.7
K12	73.0	60.0	-13.0
K13	73.0	70.0	-3.0
K14	63.3	66.7	3.4
K15	70.0	66.7	-3.3
K16	50.0	63.3	13.3
K17	53.3	56.6	3.6
K18	56.6	63.3	6.7
K19	70.0	70.0	0.0
K20	73.0	60.0	-13.0
K21	73.0	60.0	-23.0
K22	76.6	53.3	-10.0
K23	70.0	60.0	-10.0
K24	70.0	63.3	-13.3
K25	60.0	63.3	3.3
Average	66.8	65.0	-1.8

Table 3 shows the results on creativity element in the design of Logo conducted on the two groups (X1 and X2) based on t-test to answer the Hypothesis (H_o1) *"There is no significant difference of marks between students from group X1 and X2 based on the element of creativity."* It can be observed that X1obtained mean scores that were higher than X2 based on : fluency of ideas M=3.62; flexibility M=3.69; Originality M=3.96; and elaboration of design M=4.48. The mean score of X1is more than mean score of X2 and the significant two-tail value for fluency of ideas; flexibility;

Originality; and elaboration of design are p>0.774, p>0.364, p>0.336, dan p>0.616, respectively. This means that the null hypothesis is accepted. Evaluation based on the creativity test based on TTCT and the creativity index also showed that X1 obtained better results than X2 although results of both tests for X1 too can be further improved.

Table 3. Results of t-Test two independent variables for $H_0 1$ for element on creativity between groups: X1 and X2

Variables	Group	N	Mean	sp	dk	t	sig
Fluency of	X1	26	3.6154	0.2153	49	0.288	0.774
Ideas	X2	25	3.5200	02524			
Flexibility	X1	26	3.6923	0.2131	49	0.916	0.364
	X2	25	3.4000	0.2380			
Originality	X1	26	3.9615	0.1708	49	0.972	0.336
	X2	25	3.6800	0.2360			
Elaboration	X1	26	4.6538	0.2349	49	0.505	0.616
of Design		25	4.4800	0.2524			

8 Conclusion

The development of the Visual Art Education Tool (APH-Pensil) for the topic on 'Logo Design' is a positive answer to a new way of teaching and learning of Visual Art subject in secondary schools, particularly for form four students in Malaysia. APH-Pensil which was designed based on the Fundamental Art Design theory, meant that basic philosophy and principles involved in the design of Logos was embedded in the system. Students went through an almost a 'step-by-step' method of creating creative logos through modules based on fundamental principles of visual art design. The interactive tool which is designed to ensure 'hands-on' experience of students showed positive results on effectiveness of the system as well as capability of the system to instil creativity elements in students when designing logos.

Acknowledgement. We would like to thank Universiti Kebangsaan Malaysia and Ministry of Higher Education for the financial support given through the UKM Arus Perdana Grant (UKM-AP-ICT-16-2009), to ensure the success of the study undertaken.

References

[1] Salleh, A.H.: Warisan bersama wawasan. In: Prosiding Konvensyen Kebangsaan Pendidikan Seni Visual. BLSN, Kuala Lumpur (2000)
[2] Beardsley, M.C.: Aesthetics problems in the philosophy of criticism. Hancourt, Brace & World Inc., NY (1958)
[3] Brainard, S.: A design manual, 4th edn. Prentice Hall, New Jersey (2006)
[4] Bowers, J.: Introduction to 2Dimensional Design: Understanding form and function. John Wiley, New York (1999)
[5] Chee, K.: Pendidikan seni tingkatan 1. Penerbitan Pelangi Sdn Bhd., Johor Baharu (2000)

[6] D'zul Haimi, M. Z.: Pensejarahan seni visual dalam konteks sejarah seni di Malaysia. BSLN, Kuala Lumpur (2000)

[7] Feidler, J., Feierabend, P.: BAUHAUS. Konemann Verlagsgesellschaft mbh., Cologne (2000)

[8] Majid, H.A., Zaman, H.B., Abdullah, A.R.: Usability study on Simple CAD System (S-CAD) for schools: a preliminary study. The New Review of Children's Literature and Librarianship 4, 45–55 (1998)

[9] Zaman, H.B.: Simbiosis seni, sains, teknologi berasingan ke multimedia-fusion. UKM, Bangi (2009)

[10] Zaman, H.B., Ahmad, A., Pathizkar, B., Onn, C.W.: Voice recognition systems for the visually impaired: Virtual cognitive approach. In: International Symposium on Information Technology 2008. IEEE, New York (2008); IEEEXplore

[11] Sulaiman, H.: Peningkatan standard kualiti pendidikan seni: perspektif Naziran. Prosiding Konvensyen Pendidikan Seni Visual, BSLN, Kuala Lumpur (2000)

[12] Holgate, E.K., Donnan, P., Meacham, D. (eds.): Distance education: design, development and delivery. Charles Sturt University, Melbourne (1995)

[13] Holtzshcue, L.: Understanding Colour: An introduction for designers. John Wiley, New York (2006)

[14] Hassan, I.: Isu memartabatkan mata pelajaran pendidikan seni visual untuk sekolah menengah: Perlu Kajian semula. Prosiding Konvensyen Kebangsaan Pendidikan Seni Visual. BLSN, Kuala Lumpur (2000)

[15] Itterns, J.: Design and form the basic course at the BAUHAUS. Thames and Hudson, London (1997)

[16] Jones, L., McNamara, O.: The possibilities and constraints of multimedia as a basis for critical reflection. Cambridge Journal of Education 34(3), 279–295 (2004)

[17] Ken, S.: A study comparing effects of LOGO turtle graphics and Paint graphics on the response of students to color, line and shape (1988),
http://proquest.umi.com/pqdweb?did=745788831&sid=1&Fmt=2&clientId=60729&RQT=309&VName=PQD

[18] Knobler, N.: Dialog seni tampak (Translation) Zakaria Ali. DBP, Kuala Lumpur (1985)

[19] Lauer, D.A., Pentak, S.: Design basics, 5th edn. Harcourt Brace College Publishers, Orlando (2000)

[20] Levinson, J.: The Oxford handbook of aesthetics. Oxford University Press, Oxford (2003)

[21] Mohd Johari, A.H.: Asas seni visual. UPSI, Tanjong Malim (2006)

[22] Mohd Fauzi, S.: Bentuk dan makna dalam penghasilan seni visual. In: Mohd Johari, A.H. (ed.) Pendidikan Seni Vsual Dan Muzik. UPSI, Tanjung Malim (2004)

[23] Mustafa, M.G.: Pendekatan penyelidikan dalam bidang seni visual. Prosiding Konvensyen Kebangsaan Pendidikan Seni Visual. BLSN, Kuala Lumpur (2000)

[24] Rhamat, S.: Teks lengkap pendidikan seni visual. Penerbit Fajar Bakti Sdn Bhd., Shah Alam (2004)

[25] Standkiewicz, M.A.: Between teknologi dan literacy. The International Journal of Art and Design 22(3), 316–323 (2004)

[26] Wahidin, K.S., Mohd Meerah, T.S.: Penggunaan peta konsep dan peta vee dalam meningkatkan sikap pelajar terhadap Kimia. Jurnal Pendidikan 29, 125–144 (2004)

[27] Ali, Z.: Globalisation and Art Education. UPSI, Tanjung Malim (2004)

Different Visualization Types in Multimedia Learning: A Comparative Study

Riaza Mohd Rias[1] and Halimah Badioze Zaman[2]

[1] Faculty of Computer and Mathematical Sciences, Universiti Technology Mara (UiTM), Shah Alam
[2] Institute of Visual Informatics, Universiti Kebangsaan Malaysia, Bangi
riaza@tmsk.uitm.edu.my, hbzukm@yahoo.com

Abstract. Visualization techniques is said to be beneficial to learning compared to static visuals, especially when the learning material demands visual movements. The emergence of 3-Dimensional animated visuals has extended the presentation mode in multimedia learning. A case study on a computer science subject was used to test the effect of different visualization types in learning. The field of computer science, especially in operating systems concepts uses an array of abstract concepts such as virtual memory, paging, fragmentations etc to describe and explain the underlying processes. Various studies together with our own observations strongly indicate that students often find these concepts difficult to learn, as they cannot easily be demonstrated. This study investigates the effects of different visualization types on student understanding when studying a complex domain in computer science, that is, the subject of memory management concepts in operating systems. A multimedia learning system was developed in three different versions: static visuals, 2-D animated visuals and 3-D animated visuals. Fifty five students took part in this study and they were randomly assigned into one of these three groups. All the students who took part in this experiment had low prior knowledge in this subject and after viewing the treatment, they were asked to take a test which tested them for recall and transfer knowledge. This test was used to determine if, in fact, improved learning actually occurred and to compare which visualization type produced the better learning outcome. Initial analysis of results indicates no statistical difference between the scores for the three versions and suggests that visualization types, by themselves, do not necessarily improve student understanding.

Keywords: multimedia learning, visualization, 3-D animated visuals, memory management, Visual Informatics.

1 Introduction

Learning with computer generated visualizations has become a topic of major interest in recent years [1]. With the increasing use of digital technologies, it has become possible to display dynamic visuals in the form of animation, video, virtual reality, to name a few. Various researches have been carried out to study the effects and outcome of learning using different instructional conditions ([2],[3],[4]). However,

H. Badioze Zaman et al. (Eds.): IVIC 2011, Part II, LNCS 7067, pp. 408–418, 2011.
© Springer-Verlag Berlin Heidelberg 2011

still little is known with regard to how we learn from different visualization formats and how these processes are related to learning outcomes [5].According to Mayer [6], multimedia learning is learning from words and pictures and multimedia instructional message or multimedia instructional presentation (or multimedia instruction) is presentation involving words and pictures that is intended to foster learning.

Research has shown that computer-based instruction and multimedia presentations enhances learning and fosters positive attitudes towards instruction [7]. In accordance with Schnotz and Lowe [8], dynamic visualization such as animations are depictions that change continuously over time and represent a continuous flow of motion, whereas static visualizations do not show any continuous movement, but only specific states taken from such a flow of motion. Over the years, there have been some contradictions on whether dynamic visualization really helps learning as compared to static pictures. A recent meta-analysia Hoffler & Leutner [9] revealed a medium-sized overall advantage of animation over static visualizations. In contrast, in a review by Tversky, Bauer-Morrison, and Betrancourt [10], most of the studies failed to show any advantages of animations (dynamic) compared to static visualizations. To account for this consistency, it has been recommended to consider when and why dynamic and static visualizations might be best suited ([11],[8]).

The present study is aimed at deepening some findings on the benefits of visual instructions whether in a 2 Dimensional or a 3 Dimensional form. A theoretical framework on multimedia learning [6] was used as basis for this study. Mayer's theory [6] is based on three primary assumptions: i) Visual and auditory experiences or information are processed through separate and distinct information processing 'channels'. ii) Each information processing channel is limited in its ability to process experiences or information, and iii) Processing experiences or information in the channels form an active process designed to construct coherent mental representations [12]. This theory also states that a learner has to select, organize and integrate new information to make sense of the instructional material. Selecting and organizing verbal information leads to the construction of a verbal mental model, whereas the selection and organization of pictorial information results in a pictorial mental model. In order to achieve a deeper understanding of the content learners need to integrate the information from these two mental models by building connections between them based on their structural correspondences [6], [5].

The subject taught in this multimedia presentation is a topic from operating systems, memory management. Operating Systems (OS) is an important course in many Computer Science, Information Science and Computer Engineering curricula. Some of its topics require a careful and detailed explanation from the lecturer as they often involve theoretical concepts and somewhat complex calculations, demanding a certain degree of abstraction from the students if they are to gain full understanding [13], [14].

Animated visuals are used in multimedia environments to represent the dynamic aspects of complex subject matters in an explicit way [15]. According to Schnotz and Rasch [16], animations have two different positive functions in learning. First, they enable learners to perform more cognitive processing (enabling function) by providing them with additional information that cannot be displayed by static pictures. Second, they help learners to build a dynamic mental representation by giving them an external support for simulating the behavior of the system depicted.

Although there is some evidence that animations have positive effects on the understanding of dynamic situations (e.g., [17]), research failed to establish systematic benefits of using animated graphics instead versus static ones (e.g., [18]). In some cases, animations may even prejudice learning [15]. Lowe [15] suggested two different types of problems to explain these negative results, i.e., overwhelming and underwhelming. First, given the limited capacity of working memory, learners may not be able to meet the additional processing demands associated with animations. When learning from dynamic visualizations, they have to select relevant elements (for the purpose of the task) for a larger amount of information provided by multiple frames in a very limited time. They have also to keep in memory and integrate information distributed spatially across the display area or temporarily through the different frames of the animation impose a cognitive load that leads learners to reduce their cognitive resources available for learning [19].

In Mayer's generative theory of multimedia learning ([6], [12]), one assumption is that humans are limited in the amount of information that can be processed in each channel (auditory/verbal or visual/pictorial) at one time. Complex illustrations enhance the cognitive load. In contrast to two dimensional animated visuals, three dimensional images or simulations can relieve cognitive load. Spatial structures are better demonstrated and easier to conceive [20]. Another assumption of Mayer's theory interprets learning as an active process. Interactive three dimensional visuals encourage active learning better than static figures.

In the context of this research, we also wanted to know if 3-D animated visuals are any better than the 2-D version. Cockburn and McKenzie [21] compared the use of 3-D interfaces with their traditional 2-D counterpart. The study describes the comparative evaluation of two document management systems that differ only in the number of dimensions used for displaying and interacting with the data. The primary purpose of this experiment was to see if there were any differences between the 2-D and 3-D interfaces in the efficiency of storing and retrieving web page thumbnail images. Also, they wanted to know how performance in these tasks might be affected by increasing densities of data ('clutter') within the displays. The 3-D system supports users in sorting, organizing and retrieving 'thumbnail' representations of documents such as bookmarked web-pages. Results showed that the subjects were faster at storing and retrieving pages in the display when using 2-D interface, but not significantly so. Retrieval times significantly increased as the number of thumbnails increased. Despite the lack of significant differences between the 2-D and 3-D interfaces, subjective assessments showed a significant preference for 3-D interface.

2 Method

Total of 56 students were randomly selected from the list of first year students from the Faculty of Computer and Mathematical Sciences at UiTM, Shah Alam. These students were than divided randomly into three groups [nineteen, eighteen, and nineteen]. However, one student was not included in this study for not being present during the experiment day; therefore, the group was reduced to 55 students in three groups (nineteen, seventeen, nineteen).

All of them were in their first semester and they had no prior knowledge in the subject of operating systems since all computer sciences students are supposed to take this subject in their third semester only. These students were assumed to be homogenous in terms of age, education and cultural background. To be certain, a prior knowledge survey and demographic survey questions were filled out by these participants. A similar methodology was used by Moreno (2003) to conduct a research on cognitive load and student understanding. In the prior knowledge survey, the students were asked some basic questions on operating system and memory management. All the students involved in this experiment had either none or very little knowledge in the area of operating systems and memory management concepts.

Group 1(G1) viewed the static graphic version accompanied with text. Group 2 (G2) viewed the version with 2-D animated visuals and the third group (G3) viewed the 3-D animated version. All the text contents in the three versions were the same and in accordance with the syllabus for the subject taught in the faculty [24].

All students were given two hours to view the multimedia learning system and then they need to answer the recall and transfer questions within that hour. This test procedure followed the conventional paradigm used to evaluate the mental model constructed during multimedia learning (Mayer & Anderson, 1992). All the course materials and test questions were validated by the course matter experts from the Faculty of Computer and Mathematical Sciences, UiTM, Shah Alam. The tests were divided into two parts, which are, the recall test and transfer test. Recall test asked questions which required them to recall or remember some basic facts mentioned in the slides.

The transfer test required them to solve some problems based on the knowledge learned in the multimedia system. The recall test had some fill in the blanks and multiple choice questions whereas, the transfer test had only multiple choice questions. The transfer test required the students to really understand the calculation method and formula to solve the problem stated.

A descriptive analysis was used to explain the number of students involved in this study. The first and third group has 19 students each per group while the second group has 17 students. The total numbers of students involved in this study were 55 students.

The self-paced multimedia-based instruction explains on the memory management concepts which consist of background on memory management, swapping technique,

Table 1. Display of the results for the three groups

Experimental Group	Recall Knowledge Score Test		Transfer Knowledge Score Test	
	Mean	Std. Deviation	Mean	Std. Deviation
Static (G1)	67.9	16.5	30.8	15.9
2D Animated Visuals (G2)	63.5	16.2	34.4	14.3
3D Animated Visuals G(3)	69.6	16.7	35.3	20.9

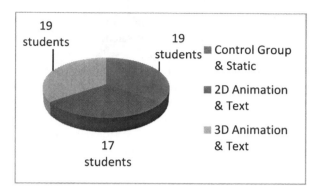

Fig. 1. Pie chart shows the number of participants in each treatment group

contiguous allocation technique and paging technique. Then the students were asked to view the multimedia instructions which were installed in each computer in the computer lab. The animation was self-paced and interactive. Students could view the animation with the play button and they could rewind, pause or stop according to the needs. After the treatment, each participant had to take a test.

The system with 2-D animation and text version (G2) had animation designed using Macromedia Flash and concepts of swapping, contiguous memory allocation and paging techniques were explained using animated form in 2-D. For example, the use of geometric shapes and arrows to show movements of data from memory to backing store as shown in Diagram 1.

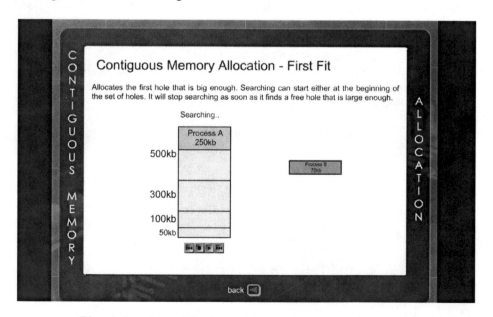

Diag. 1. Snapshots of Contiguous Memory Allocation in 2-D visuals

Diag. 2. Snapshot of Contiguous Memory Allocation in 3-D visuals

The system with 3-D animation and text version (G3) had animation designed using 3D Max and the concepts of memory management were explained using animated form in a 3-D realistic version. For example, the concept of contiguous memory allocation was explained using a forklift to carry large chunks of data to be put into empty spaces in the memory as shown in Diagram 2.

The static graphic version (G1) had non-animated pictures which were similar to the 2-D version and the text was the same for all the three groups.

3 Results

At the beginning of the analysis, the mean score for each test was calculated to give a first overview to the participant's performance. Three different aspects or presentation modes were chosen for analysis. Table 1 shows the summary of mean score and standard deviation for recall test and transfer test for each experimental group. The higher the mean score test, it will give a better result on recall and transfer test. Students would give a higher score on the recall questions by using 3D Animation & Text with the mean recall score test, 69.64%. When they were answering transfer knowledge questions, 3D Animation & Text also will give better results with the mean transfer score test, 35.34% compared to the other experimental groups. Unfortunately, the percentage of transfer score test is worst compared with recall test since all the percentage in each group is below 50%.

The presentation mode was the independent variable and the recall and transfer score were the dependent variables. An ANOVA test was run to get the results. Based on the ANOVA table, it can be concluded that the three experimental groups are significantly difference and may effect on the recall test. ANOVA can tell us only "at least one pair of the treatment means is different" but which particular pairs are different is not specified. So, we proceed to conduct multiple comparisons test to find out which pairs are different.

Table 2. ANOVA results for the experiment

	Sum of Squares	df	Mean Square	F	Sig
Between Groups	1678.176	2	839.088	3.091	0.045
Within Groups	14114.551	52	271.434		
Total	15792.727	54			

From the multiple comparisons test, we can say that there is no differences in using Static or 2D Animated visuals since the p-value is equal to 0.709 which is greater than $\alpha=0.05$. Similar results were found when there was no significant difference when using Static or 3D Animated visuals as a medium in student learning, both produced similar results because the p-value is equal to 0.225. But, there is a difference between 2D animated visuals or 3D animated visuals. Students who took the treatment on 3D produced better result in recall test compare to the group who took the treatment on 2D with the mean difference of 13.31%.

Table 3. Multiple Comparisons of the Recall Test

Multiple Comparisons

Dependent Variable: Recall Knowledge Score (%)
Tukey HSD

(I) Experimental Group	(J) Experimental Group	Mean Difference (I-J)	Std. Error	Sig.	95% Confidence Interval	
					Lower Bound	Upper Bound
Control Group + Static	Control Group + Static					
	2D Animation + Text	4.36533	5.50024	.709	-8.9045	17.6352
	3D Animation + Text	-8.94737	5.34528	.225	-21.8434	3.9486
2D Animation + Text	Control Group + Static	-4.36533	5.50024	.709	-17.6352	8.9045
	2D Animation + Text					
	3D Animation + Text	-13.31269*	5.50024	.049	-26.5826	-.0428
3D Animation + Text	Control Group + Static	8.94737	5.34528	.225	-3.9486	21.8434
	2D Animation + Text	13.31269*	5.50024	.049	.0428	26.5826
	3D Animation + Text					

*. The mean difference is significant at the .05 level.

The 3D animated visuals version produced a higher score on the recall test for the students, or we can recommend using 3D animated version as a medium in learning process for recall test.

For Transfer Test, the ANOVA (Table 4) shows that there is no significant difference between the three experimental groups. All the experimental groups gave the same result or effect on the transfer score test since the p-value is equal to 0.697

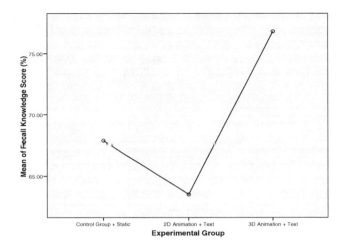

Fig. 3. Main Effect Plot

Table 4. ANOVA for Transfer Test

	Sum of Squares	df	Mean Square	F	Sig
Between Groups	215.420	2	107.710	0.364	0.697
Within Groups	15383.838	52	295.843		
Total	15599.258	54			

Table 5. Multiple Comparisons for Transfer Test

Multiple Comparisons

Dependent Variable: Transfer Knowledge Score (%)
Tukey HSD

(I) Experimental Gr	(J) Experimental Gr	Mean Difference (I-J)	Std. Error	Sig.	95% Confidence Interval	
					Lower Bound	Upper Bound
Control Group + Sta	Control Group + Sta					
	2D Animation + Tex	-3.62671	5.74223	.803	-17.4804	10.2270
	3D Animation + Tex	-4.51128	5.58045	.700	-17.9746	8.9521
2D Animation + Tex	Control Group + Sta	3.62671	5.74223	.803	-10.2270	17.4804
	2D Animation + Tex					
	3D Animation + Tex	-.88456	5.74223	.987	-14.7382	12.9691
3D Animation + Tex	Control Group + Sta	4.51128	5.58045	.700	-8.9521	17.9746
	2D Animation + Tex	.88456	5.74223	.987	-12.9691	14.7382
	3D Animation + Tex					

which is greater than α=0.05. Result on the ANOVA table is consistent with the multiple comparisons test in Table 5 since all the p-value on the Tukey HSD is greater than α=0.05 for transfer score question. So we can conclude that the animated visuals does not help student to improve their understanding on the multimedia learning, when answering transfer or problem solving tests. It appears at first glance, that more correct answers were achieved by group 3 (G3). Nevertheless, students performance overall in the recall test was better than the transfer test.

4   Discussion and Conclusion

The lack of improvement for students who had learned with the assistance of animated visual diagrams in the experiment above supports the view that 'continuous visualization offers no real advantage' to achieve more effective student understanding of complex computer concepts ([25],[26]). It is therefore considered possible that visualization in Compact Disc included with textbooks, or on-line links to multimedia resources, will not necessarily improve student understanding above that expected from a static visual.

The results were in accordance with many previous literature and visualization-related studies. Mayer [27] justified the effect of using coordinated presentation of explanation in visual format (illustrations). Wilson [28] found a general tendency of the mean score for the static treatment produce somewhat better results than any of the dynamic treatments. Owen [29] found a trend that the students' performance decreased as animation strategies were added to the instructional screens. Kuhl et al. [5] observed no differences between the dynamic and static condition concerning any of the learning outcome measures.

We had expected that the 3-D visualization version would provide better understanding especially in recall and transfer. The total score was in favor of the 3-D visual version (G3) but the score difference was not significant to the static version (G1) with a difference of 4.35% only. This study therefore shows that the usage of 2D and 3D visualization requires more development and quantitative evaluation to determine if an improvement in learning can be achieved over a static visual. Kuhl et al.[5] in their recent study concluded that whether dynamic visualization lead to better learning outcomes than static visualizations may depend on the type of learning activities deployed, such as retrieving static visualizations more frequently. However, in our research, time taken to view each treatment was not measured and frequency of each page viewed was not noted, therefore, these are some instruments that need to be considered for future improvements.

A possibility of the results outcome could also be because the participants had no prior knowledge in this subject and therefore found it difficult to absorb some important concepts and ideas from the multimedia learning software. Further research would be carried out on students who have high prior knowledge in this subject as a comparison to this study.

Practically, the results of the study has raised some questions to the practice of instructional designer, is it really worth it to design and develop instructions utilizing visualization strategies versus simply using static visuals if static visuals have been shown to be at least as effective as their animated counterparts? It is known that static visuals are more cost- effective and cost-efficient than animated visualization. In future design, maybe it is better to utilize static visuals as much as possible and use animations only when the use of animation is justified [30].

References

1. Badioze Zaman, H., Bakar, N., Ahmad, A., Sulaiman, R., Arshad, H., Mohd. Yatim, N.F.: Virtual Visualisation Laboratory for Science and Mathematics Content (Vlab-SMC) with Special Reference to Teaching and Learning of Chemistry. In: Badioze Zaman, H., Robinson, P., Petrou, M., Olivier, P., Schröder, H., Shih, T.K. (eds.) IVIC 2009. LNCS, vol. 5857, pp. 356–370. Springer, Heidelberg (2009)
2. Rias, R., Zaman, H.B.: Investigating the Redundancy Effect in Multimedia Learning on a Computer Science Domain. Paper Presented at International Symposium on Information Technology (ITSIM 2010), June 15-17. IEEE Xplore, Kuala Lumpur (2010)
3. Mohd Rias, R., Badioze Zaman, H.: Using 3-D Animation in Multimedia Learning for Memory Management Concepts. In: Proceedings of the International Conference on Signal Processing Systems, Singapore, May 15-17, pp. 748–753. IEEE Computer Society (2009) ISBN: 978-0-7695-3654-5
4. Rias, R., Badioze Zaman, H.: Multimedia Learning in Computer Science: The Effect of Different Modes of Instruction on Student Understanding. Paper Presented at International Symposium on Information Technology (ITSIM 2008). IEEE Xplore, Kuala Lumpur (2008) ISBN: 978-1-4244-2327-9
5. Kuhl, T., Scheiter, K., Gerjets, P., Gemballa, S.: Can differences in learning strategies explain the benefits of learning from static and dynamic visualizations? Computers & Education 56, 176–187 (2011)
6. Mayer, R.E.: Multimedia Learning. Cambridge University Press, Cambridge (2001)
7. Hanim, F., Zaman, H.B.: Development of interactive multimedia courseware using Problem based learning for Mathematics Form 4 (PBL Math-Set). In: Proceedings of the International Symposium on Information Technology 2008 (ITSim 2008), August 26-29. KLCC, Kuala Lumpur (2008)
8. Schnotz, W., Lowe, R.K.: A unified view of learning from animated and static graphics. In: Lowe, R.K., Schnotz, (eds.) Learning with Animation: Research and Design Implications, pp. 304–356. Cambridge University Press, New York (2008)
9. Hoffler, T.N., Leutner, D.: Instructional animation versus static pictures: a meta-analysis. Learning and Instruction 17, 722–738 (2007)
10. Tversky, B., Bauer-Morrison, J., Betrancourt, M.: Animation: can it facilitate? International Journal of Human-Computer Studies 57, 247–262 (2002)
11. Betrancourt, M.: The animation and interactivity principles in multimedia learning. In: Mayer, R.E. (ed.) The Cambridge Handbook of Multimedia Learning, pp. 287–296. Cambridge University Press (2005)
12. Mayer, R.E.: Multimedia Learning, 2nd edn. Cambridge University Press, Cambridge (2009)
13. Park, O., Gittleman, S.S.: Selective Use of animation and feedback in computer-based instruction. Educational Technology Research and Development 40, 27–38 (1992)
14. Maia, L.P., Machado, F.B., Pacheco Jr., A.C.: A constructivist framework for operating systems education: A pedagogical using the Sosim. Paper read at ITiCSE 2005, June 27 - 29, Monte de Caparica, Portugal (2005)

15. Lowe, R.K.: Animation and Learning: Value for money?. In: Beyond the comfort zone: Proceedings of the 21st ASCILITE Conference, Perth, pp. 558–561 (2004)
16. Schnotz, W., Rasch, T.: Enabling, facilitating and inhibiting effects of animations in multimedia learning: why reduction of cognitive load can have negative results on learning. Educational Technology; Research and Development 53, 47–58 (2005)
17. Mayer, R.E., Anderson, R.B.: The instructive animation: Helping students build connections between words and pictures in multimedia learning. Journal of Educational Psychology 84, 444–452 (1992)
18. Chandler, P.: Dynamic visualization and hypermedia: Beyond the 'wow' factor. Computer Human Behavior 25(2), 389–392 (2009)
19. Sangin, M., Molinari, G., Dillenbourg, P.: Collaborative learning with animated pictures: The role of verbalization. In: Proceedings of the 7th International Conference on Learning Sciences at Bloomington, Indiana (2006)
20. Schanze, S.: Do computer-based three-dimensional simulations help chemistry beginners to understand chemical structures? A preliminary study (on-line) (2003), http://www1.phys.uu.nl/esera2003/programme/pdf%5c149s.pdf
21. Cockburn, A., McKenzie, B.: 3D or not 3D? Evaluating the Effects of the third dimension in a document management system. Paper read at CHI, Anyone Anywhere (2001)
22. Huk, T.: Who benefits from learning with 3D models? The case of spatial ability. Journal of Computer Assisted Learning 22, 392–404 (2006)
23. Wu, K., Shah, P.: Exploring visuospatial thinking in chemistry learning. Science Education 88, 465–492 (2004)
24. Silberschatz, A., Galvin, P., Gagne, G.: Operating System Principles, 7th edn. John Wiley & Sons, NJ (2006)
25. Naps, T., Robling, G., et al.: Exploring the role of visualization and engagement in computer science education. ACM SIGCSE Bulletin 35, 131–152 (2002)
26. Mohd Rias, R., Badioze Zaman, H.: 3-D versus 2-D Animation in Multimedia Application: Is the Extra Effort Worth it? Presented at International Conference of Digital Information Processing and Communications (ICDIPC), Ostrava, Czech Republic (July 2011)
27. Mayer, R.E.: Multimedia learning: Are we asking the right questions? Educational Psychology 1, 1–19 (1997)
28. Wilson, F.S.: The effect of time and level of visual enhancement in facilitating student achievement of different educational objectives. Unpublished doctorial dissertation: The Pennsylvania State University (1998)
29. Owens, R.: An investigation to explore the effects of cueing strategies that complement animated visual imagery in facilitating student achievement of different educational objectives. Unpublished doctorial dissertation: The Pennsylvania State University (2002)
30. Reiber, L.P.: Animation in Computer-Based Instruction. Educational Technology Research and Development 38, 77–86 (1990)

Optimal Command and Control Method for Malaysian Army Small Units in a Malaysian Forest Environment: Small Unit Tactical Management System (SUTaMs)

Syed Nasir Alsagoff

Computer Science Department, Faculty of Science and Defence Technology,
National Defence University of Malaysia
syednasir@upnm.edu.my

Abstract. Military section will communicate verbally or visually in the battlefield. Before engaging the enemy, section leader will give commands visually as not to alert the enemy. Once the enemy is engaged, all commands will be verbal. Shooting might cause for some of these commands to be lost due to the noise and confusion. In addition to that, upon engagement by the enemy, soldiers will try to go behind cover to avoid getting shot at. Hiding behind cover will cause the soldier to loose situational awareness. The section leaders might also not be able to give commands effectively to the soldiers. The Small Unit Tactical Silent Communication System (SUTACSICS), a module to be integrated into the Malaysian Army Small Unit Tactical Management System (SUTaMS), was developed using Network Centric Technologies to ensure that section leaders in the battlefield are able to communicate with their soldiers silently and effectively without using either the visual or verbal method of communication. Commands to be sent are selected from a preset list and vibration to alert the soldiers on arrival of the command.

Keywords: Communication, Command and Control, Information Security, Tactical, Silent, Network Centric.

1 Introduction

Tactics are the employment of units in combat. It includes the ordered arrangement and maneuver of units in relation to each other, the terrain and the enemy to translate potential combat power into victorious battles and engagements [1]. A battlefield is a fluid and changing environment and required constant command, control and communication among all the soldiers involved. The concepts of small unit tactics are universal with all the armies of the world. Small units will only consist of about 10 soldiers which is a squad or section [2]. The section leader will need to be aware of the location of his soldiers and of the battlefield (battlefield situational awareness [2]).

The Malaysian forest is a dipterocarp forest as indicated in Figure 1. It is populated by trees from the Dipterocarpaceae family. The dipterocarp forest occurs on dry land just above sea level to an altitude of about 900 meters [3]. The lower level

H. Badioze Zaman et al. (Eds.): IVIC 2011, Part II, LNCS 7067, pp. 419–427, 2011.

Fig. 1. The Dipterocarp Malaysian forest

of the forest is made up of small trees and vegetations. With its various flora and fauna, the Malaysia forest command and control will be difficult to maintain. The environment might affect the sightings of fellow soldiers and also visual signals. The longer the distance, the less likely soldiers are able to see or be alerted by visual signals.

The forest might also affect the communications conducted during a combat, as it will be disorientating to be able to hear commands and not know where the commands are coming from. Proper training will go a long way in alleviating these issues.

1.1 Background Study

In combat, the mission of a military unit will be to close in with the enemy by means of fire and maneuver and to destroy or capture the enemy. Despite all the technological advances of war, close combat is still necessary to win the battle. Close combat means that the unit will be in direct contact of the enemy. The unit can see the enemy, and at the same time the enemy can see the unit. If one side can see each other, then both sides can shoot at each other. Any mistakes in the maneuver can cause casualties and even wipe out the whole unit.

Small units will need to maneuver, to close in on the enemy. To do so, they will have to do a fire and maneuver sequence [2] as shown in Figure 2. A unit will be split into two teams. There is the assault team and the suppressing fire team. The suppressing fire team will fire upon the enemy's location, either to defeat them or to ensure they cannot shoot back. During this time, the assault team will maneuver closer towards the enemy's position. Once reaching a designated area, the role of the teams will switch. This will continue until the enemy's position has been seized or the enemy has been totally defeated [2].

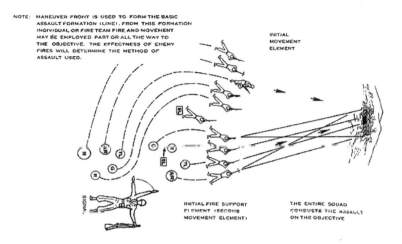

NOTE: MANEUVER FRONT IS USED TO FORM THE BASIC
ASSAULT FORMATION (LINE). FROM THIS FORMATION
INDIVIDUAL OR FIRE TEAM FIRE AND MOVEMENT
MAY BE EMPLOYED PART OR ALL THE WAY TO
THE OBJECTIVE. THE EFFECTNESS OF ENEMY
FIRES WILL DETERMINE THE METHOD OF
ASSAULT USED.

INITIAL
MOVEMENT
ELEMENT

INITIAL FIRE SUPPORT
ELEMENT (SECOND
MOVEMENT ELEMENT)

THE ENTIRE SQUAD
CONDUCTS THE ASSAULT
ON THE OBJECTIVE

Fig. 2. Fire and maneuver

1.2 Objective of Study

This objectives of the study are as follows:

   i). To develop a Malaysian Army Small Unit Tactical Management System
   (SUTaMS) for purposes of combat in a Dipterocarp Malaysian forest.
   ii). To design and develop the Small Unit Tactical Silent Communication System
   (SUTACSICS).
   iii). To test SUTaMS during the Malaysian Army small unit training exercise
   sessions conducted in Malaysian Dipterocarp forest environment.

1.3 Scope of Study

This study will be for the Malaysian environment and will be for small unit tactics
only. Only the communication aspect of a battlefield environment will be discussed
in this paper. Thus this paper will only discuss on the development of the Small Unit
Tactical Silent Communication System (SUTACSICS), which is part of the module
in the Malaysian Army Small Unit Tactical Management System SUTaMs.

1.4 Significance of the Study

The Malaysian Army Small Unit Tactics is already well established through various
real world combat encounters with the Communist Party of Malaysia's guerrillas
during the Malaysian Emergency. The battlefield is a confusing place with many
obstacles. Even if the tactics are well established, there are reports of many soldiers
killed by friendly or enemy fire. Any mistake by the section leader might also cause
the whole unit to be killed. It is anticipated that the significance of this study is the
ability to increase the effectiveness of communication between the section leaders and
soldiers of the Malaysian Army Small Units through silent communication approach.

2 Literature Review

Currently, all command and control of the arrangement and maneuver of units are conducted through either visual or verbal communication [1]. Before engaging the enemy, soldiers will communicate visually as not to alert the enemy. Once the enemy is engaged, all signals will be verbal. Commands will be shouted out for both sides.

Visual signals have certain limitations [4]:

- The range and reliability of visual communications are significantly reduced during periods of poor visibility and when terrain restricts observation.
- They may be misunderstood during a chaotic combat situations.
- They are vulnerable to enemy interception and may be used for deception purposes.

Figure 3 shows samples of the battlefield or combat visual signals.

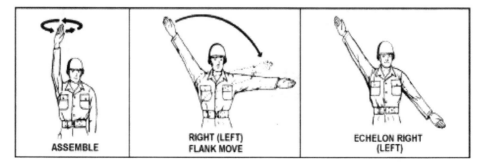

Fig. 3. Sample battlefield visual signal

Shooting might cause for some of these commands to be lost due to the noise and confusion. The sound from a rifle being fired is very deafening. Sounds above 85 decibels will cause ear damage while 5.56 rifles being fired will generate 150+ decibels sound [4]. In addition to that, upon engagement by the enemy, a soldier will try to go behind cover to avoid getting shot at. Hiding behind cover will cause the soldier to lose situational awareness. The section leader might not be able to communicate with the soldier in this situation. Thus, the Malaysian Army Small Unit Tactical Management System (SUTaMS) was studied, designed and developed. One of the modules that will be discussed in this paper is the Small Unit Tactical Silent Communication System (SUTACSICS).

3 Small Unit Tactical Silent Communication System (SUTACSICS)

To overcome the problem of visual and verbal communication problem in a battlefield environment, SUTACSICS : Small Unit Tactical Silent Communication System was designed and developed. Figure 4 shows the conceptual systems design of SUTACSICS.

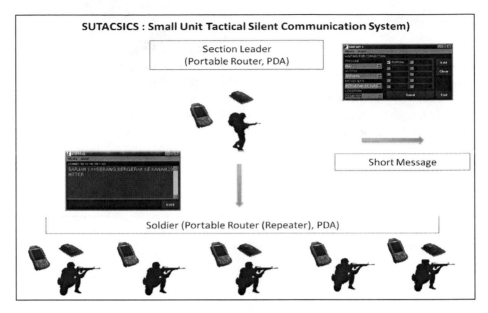

Fig. 4. Conceptual Systems Design of the Small Unit Tactical Silent Communication System SUTACSICS

The main purpose of SUTACSICS is to allow a section leader to deliver commands to the soldiers in the section using short message silently and effectively. This will overcome the visual and verbal communication problems mentioned faced by section leaders and soldiers during a battlefield or combat.

Some of the features of SUTACSICS are as follows:

- Commands are sent without visual or verbal method of communication using short message delivery system.
- Section leader is able to send command s individually, to several or to all soldiers of the section.
- Soldiers will receive command from the section leader instantly.
- Sections leader can choose preset commands without typing.
- New commands can be added easily.
- Vibration will alert soldiers the arrival of the command.
- All command transmissions are secured using RC2 encryption algorithm.
- Commands sent/received are saved in log file for further mission analysis.
- System access is protected by the password.
- Password is transmitted in hash form to avoid from being sniffed by the enemy.
- System utilizes an efficient and effective user interface.
- Applicable to all military and law enforcement units worldwide.
- Ensure the safety and security of all personnel during missions.
- Uses commercial off-the-shelf(COTS) hardware and software solution so development and production cost is kept low.

3.1 System Development

The SUTACSICS is a client-server application. Both client and server side used a personal digital assistant (PDA) running Windows Mobile. Both client and side on the PDA were developed using Basic4PPC, a Visual Basic like programming language for Windows Mobile phone. Basic4PPC is based on the Microsoft .Net framework. The advantages of programming with Basic4PPC are its simplicity and the ease to integrate and control Window Mobile phone hardware component. The conceptual systems design is as shown earlier in Figure 4. All communications are provided using WIFI and portable battery-powered router. All the routers are running in bridge mode to provide redundant backup communication.

The Samsung Omnia smartphone was chosen as the development PDA because it has proven to be a capable and robust Wi-Fi and GPS enabled phone. In addition to that, it is also running on Windows Mobile 6.5. Each soldier will carry a PDA unit based on the Samsung Omnia as shown in Figure 5.

3.2 Section Leader

As the section leader is the one giving commands during a battle or combat, communication will be one way only. The section leader can select to give commands one to one, one to many or one to all. There is a drop-down list containing all common battlefield commands. In addition, the section leader can type in new commands on the fly.

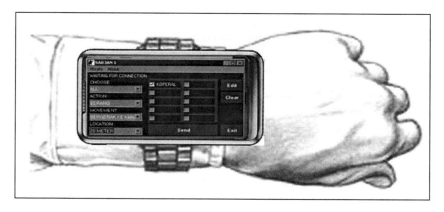

Fig. 5. SUTACSICS as a Section leader interface

3.2 Soldier

When a soldier receives a new command, the PDA vibrates. Even in the heat of a battle, the soldier can feel the vibration and see the command on the screen as indicated in Figure 6.

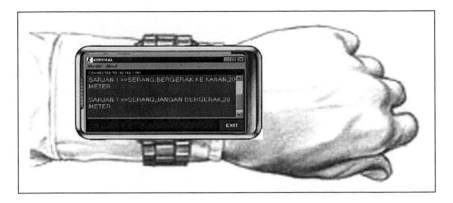

Fig. 6. SUTACSICS. Soldier interface

3.3 Security Features

Security features were also designed in the Small Unit Tactical Silent Communication System (SUTACSICS). At the start of any operation, the section leader will determine the login password. All the soldiers must know the password. The password will be a onetime use only. Password will not be transmitted in plaintext form over the network but in hash form. The password also acts as the encryption key to encrypt the commands sent from the section leader to the soldiers. All commands are encrypted using the RC2 algorithm. RC2 is a block cipher by Ron Rivest of Rivest, Shamir and Adleman (RSA). Even though RC2 is less secure as compared to RC4, it is faster to implement in a PDA device with limited computing power. Given enough time, the encrypted commands can be broken; the recovered commands are of no or little value as commands are used in real time.

3.4 Sample Basic4PPC Coding

This is a sample Basic4PPC coding for the server to send command to all clients. All the commands are encrypted before sending. If any of the clients are not connected, the server will remove the client from the system.

```
Sub SendToAll(data) 'Sent data to all clients. All data
are already encrypted.

ErrorLabel (errSendToAll)

    For i = 0 To alClients.Count - 1
      Control("stream" & alClients.Item(i),
      Binaryfile).WriteString (data) 'Send the data to
      each client
    Next

Return
```

```
errSendToAll:
      RemoveProblemClient  (i)  'Error  trapping  to  remove
      problematic clients.
End Sub

Sub RemoveProblemClient(i2) 'Remove problematic clients.

ErrorLabel (errRemoveClient)

  For x2 = 1 To 10

        If "CheckBox" & x2 = alClients.Item(i2) Then '
        Clear client listing from system

              Control("CheckBox" & x2).Checked = False
              Control("CheckBox" & x2).Enabled = False
              Control("CheckBox" & x2).Text = ""
              iparray(x2) = ""
              Control("CheckBox" & x2).Checked = False
              Control("client" & "CheckBox" & x2,
              Client).Dispose
              Control("stream" & "CheckBox" & x2,
              Binaryfile).Dispose
              AddObject("client" & "CheckBox" &
              x2,"Client")
              AddObject("stream" & "CheckBox" &
              x2,"BinaryFile")
              Control("client" & "CheckBox" & x2,
              Client).New1
              alClients.RemoveAt (i2)
              ccounter(x2 + 1) = ""

        End If

    Next

    cc = cc - 1

Return

errRemoveClient:

End Sub
```

4 Testing

The methodology used to test the use of SUTACSICS for command and control have not been conducted yet and will be done during the Malaysian Army small unit training exercises. The testing will be conducted in the Malaysian forest environment. Two small units with the same level of training and experience will be compared during simulated combat exercise. One unit will be fitted with SUTACSICS while the other will rely on the conventional method of command and control.

The opposing force will be located randomly in an area. The test units will have a general location of the opposing force. They will conduct an advance to contact maneuver to try to locate the opposing force. Upon contact, the unit will do fire and maneuver to close in and destroy the opposing force. The time to neutralize the opposing force and the number of simulated casualty of the test unit will be used to determine the effectiveness of the command and control method. The effectiveness of both units will be compared.

5 Conclusion

The Small Unit Tactical Silent Communication System (SUTACSICS) is a module that will be integrated into the Malaysian Army Small Unit Tactical Management System (SUTaMS), taking into considerations the holistic process in control and command of the army small units. It is anticipated that the system can increase the effectiveness of communication and survivability of the Malaysian Soldiers in small units operating in the Malaysian Dipterocarp forest environment. Every soldier's life is precious, and this will reduce the risk of harm coming upon our soldiers in combat.

6 Future Work

As indicated earlier, the Small Unit Tactical Silent Communication System (SUTACSICS) is one of the modules to be integrated into the Malaysian Army Small Unit Tactical Management System (SUTaMS). Future work will be done to add more modules into SUTaMS that will contribute to enhance the control and command method for the Malaysian Army Small Units. It will also be the starting point of the Malaysian Army Future Soldier Program. This study was funded by the Ministry of Higher Education, Malaysia (MOHE) based on the Exploratory Research Grant Scheme (ERGS).

References

[1] Headquarters, Department of The Army. US Army Field Manual 90-05 –Jungle Operation (August 16, 1982)
[2] Headquarters, Department of The Army. US Army Field Manual 7-8 – Infantry Rifle Platoon and Squad (March 1, 2001)
[3] WWF Malaysia The Malaysian Rainforest,
     http://www.wwf.org.my/about_wwf/what_we_do/forests_main/
     the_malaysian_rainforest/
[4] Headquarters, Department of The Army. US Army Field Manual 21-60 – Visual Signal (September 1987)
[5] Anderson, D.: American Cop - Silence is Golden (2011),
     http://www.americancopmagazine.com/articles/silenceIsGolden/
     index.html

Author Index